*Dedicated to Kelly and Stone, the two newest members
of the extended family of G. H. Sage*

Contents

Preface

Sport is sometimes trivialized as a playground separate from the real world. This is certainly not an accurate representation of sport's role in society. More accurately, sport is a microcosm of society as well as a site for culturally changing society. Indeed, as a microcosm and as a phenomenon for social change, sport has a profound influence on the social life of large numbers of people of all ages.

THE PURPOSE OF THIS TEXT

Three goals guide our efforts in writing this book. Our first goal is to sociologically analyze sport and, in so doing, to demythologize sport. This method promotes an understanding of how a sociological perspective contrasts from common-sense or taken-for-granted perceptions about sport and society. For most readers this will result in understanding sport in a new way. We identify various social theoretical perspectives and explore the ways in which they contribute to an understanding of contemporary sport. Our experience is that this approach helps readers to incorporate implicitly the sociological perspective in his or her repertoire for understanding other parts of the social world.

Our second goal is to impress on our readers in sociology—as well as in sports management, physical education, kinesiology, and related fields in social science, fitness, and health sciences—the importance of including the sociology of sport as a legitimate subfield in each of these disciplines. Our message to all of our readers is that sport is a social activity worthy of serious inquiry. It is a substantive topic as deserving of sociologists' attention as the standard specialties: family, religion, and politics. Not only is sport a microcosm of the larger society, but sports phenomena offer a fertile field in which to test sociological theories. Indeed, although the mechanical and physiological factors of sport are important, the social milieu in which participation is embedded is crucial with respect to who participates, when, where, and the consequences of such participation. Sport involvement is more than just making use of the levers of the body and using strength, endurance, and fitness to achieve objectives.

Our final goal is to make readers aware of the positive and negative consequences of the way sport is organized in North America. We are concerned about some of the trends in contemporary sport, especially the movement away from athlete-oriented activities and toward the impersonality of what we term "corporate sport." We are committed to advancing sport and society in a more humane and socially just direction, and this requires, as a first step, a thorough understanding of the principles that underlie the social structures and processes that create, sustain, and transform the social organizations within the institution of sport.

Our aim is to excite readers about current sociological issues, problems, and trends in sport. Accordingly, all of the chapters in the current edition have been thoroughly revised, and the content has been updated. We have tried to incorporate the salient research and relevant events that have occurred since the publication of the preceding edition of this book.

In contrast to the first two editions of this book, which focused on sport in the United States, the focus in all subsequent editions, including this one, has been broadened to include sport in Canadian society. There are many parallels between sport and society in the United States and Canada, as well as important differences. Finally, we have made a special effort in this edition to incorporate issues of social class, race/ethnicity, and gender throughout the text.

ORGANIZATION

In Chapter 1, we describe the unique focus of sociology as a discipline and identify the different analytic levels employed by sociologists. We identify the major sociological theories that provide different and important ways to understand sport. Next, we show how sport provides an ideal environment for utilizing certain sociological instruments and methodologies and affords a setting for the testing of sociological theories.

The phenomenon of sport represents one of the most pervasive social institutions in North America. In Chapter 2, we discuss the relationships between technological, industrial, and urban developments and the rise of organized sport.

The major theme of this book is that sport is a microcosm of society. Salient social values are identified in Chapter 3, and we discuss how sport reflects and reinforces the core values, beliefs, and ideologies of North American society.

For millions of people, involvement in sport begins in youth sports programs. In Chapter 4, we describe how children are socialized into sport, and we discuss some of the consequences of these sports experiences.

Sport and education are inexorably intertwined in North America. Chapter 5 examines interscholastic sport, focusing on the social sources responsible for the promotion of sports programs, the consequences of school sports programs, and the problems surrounding school sport.

Chapter 6 is devoted primarily to big-time intercollegiate sport. Although this level of sport is extremely popular, we focus here on the many problems that compromise the integrity of the educational mission of universities.

Chapter 7 analyzes four major social problems in sport: (1) violence, including participant and fan violence, athletes' abuse of women, and violence against athletes; (2) substance abuse by athletes; (3) athletes and eating disorders; and (4) sports gambling.

In Chapter 8, we explore the relationship between one of the oldest universal social institutions— religion—and one of the newest—sport. We trace the changing relations between the two institutions and show how contemporary sport has many of the characteristics of a religion. We also describe how religious agents and agencies use sport to promote religion and how athletes employ magico-religious rituals, taboos, and fetishes in the hope of enhancing their performances.

Although the sport establishment publicly disavows any relationship between politics and sport, they are closely related. In Chapter 9, we discuss the close ties between the two and show that there are several characteristics inherent in both institutions that serve to guarantee this strong relationship.

Economic factors play an overriding role in much of contemporary sport in the U.S. and Canada. The emergence of unprecedented affluence in certain sectors along with the enormous increase in interest in sport have had a dramatic economic impact. Chapter 10 describes the multi-dimensional aspects of economic considerations in sport, including the ongoing problems between owners and players.

There is a symbiotic relationship between sport and the mass media. In Chapter 11, we review the social purposes of the mass media and their relation to sport, the influence of the mass media on sport and the impact of sport on the mass media, and the role of the sports journalist.

Sport is typically assumed to be an egalitarian and meritocratic institution. In Chapter 12, we examine these two assumptions as they relate to social class and social mobility. The analysis shows that these beliefs are largely myths.

Systematic and pervasive discrimination against racial and ethnic minorities has been a historical feature of American society, but many Americans believe that sport has been and is free of racism. Chapter 13 documents the historical and contemporary facts illustrating that sport has had and still has many of the same racial problems as the larger society. Although the focus of this chapter is on African Americans and sport, Latinos, Asian Americans, and Native Americans and their connections to the sports world in the United States are also discussed.

The theme of Chapter 14 is that the world of sport has been the exclusive domain of males and that sociocultural forces have combined to virtually exclude female sport involvement. We discuss the problems of equity that persist despite changes in the opportunity structure. Also included in this chapter are issues of sexuality as they relate to women and men athletes.

The final chapter speculates on the future of sport in North America. The basic theme is that since sport reflects society, sport will undoubtedly undergo some transformation as society changes. We describe several current trends and possible future changes in society and discuss how each is likely to be manifested in sport changes.

Each chapter in this edition has a Notes section that provides readers with relevant references to the various topics found in the chapter. These, along with the websites listed at the end of each chapter, can be quite useful to students and researchers who seek additional information on a given topic.

NEW TO THIS EDITION

A lot has happened in the world of sport since the eighth edition of this text appeared. The revisions for the ninth edition have therefore been more extensive than usual, and we hope both students and professors will appreciate the additions and updates.

Expanded Explanation of Sociological Theories and Their Relevance to Sport

Sociological theories provide contrasting ways of understanding social life. In this edition we have written a more extensive explanation of sociological theories and their relevance to sports. After providing a detailed description of the various sociological theories in the first chapter of the book, we explain and elaborate on how those theories are relevant to understanding the sports topics that are the focus of the following chapters.

Updated Content and References

This edition focuses on current issues, such as sports academies, the changing role of parents and coaches in youth sports, and youth sports as "traveling leagues." Significant developments in high school and intercollegiate sports, making them more commercial and placing increasing pressure and stress on coaches and athletes, are explained. We have updated our suggestions for reform at both of these levels of sport. Recent trends in the social problems of sport—violence, substance abuse, eating disorders, and gambling— are highlighted. The socioeconomic topics of sport change quickly, so we have updated, described, and analyzed these transformations. Social media are playing an increasingly significant role in sport, so we identify the new social media forms and their relevance in contemporary sport. With each new trend and development in the sociology of sport we have provided the most up-to-date analysis, and the book has many references that support this new content.

Expanded Focus on Diversity

Although this text has always recognized the importance of diversity in sport and society, the current edition includes additional information on Native Americans, Latinos, Asians, and other minority groups in relation to sport. Recent opportunities for and achievements of minority and female athletes, coaches, and sports organizations, as well as the influence of globalization on promoting diversity, are identified and discussed.

New Tables and Figures

A variety of new tables and figures are found in each chapter. Some of them are updated to account for changes in the subject from previous editions. But there are also new tables and figures to illustrate subject matter that is new to this edition. The salaries of professional athletes and coaches, the wealth of the owners of professional sports team franchises, and the value of these franchises are a few of the examples of added tables and figures.

"Thinking About Sport" Boxes

There are more than twenty-five boxes in this edition, many of which are new. These boxes feature thought-provoking essays on sport topics that expand on and supplement the regular textual content in each of the chapters. For example, in Chapter 1 there is a new box entitled "Scholarly Organizations and Publications in the Sociology of Sport," whose purpose is to acquaint readers with various professional organizations and publications that publish sociology of sport research. Another example of a new box is found in Chapter 5, "Interscholastic Sport." The box is entitled "Cheerleading: Is It a Sport?" and the two sides of this controversial topic are discussed.

New Photos

Most of the photos in this edition are new, and they provide a pictorial supplement to the sports topics discussed. We have selected photos illustrating the diversity of participants in North American sports.

Web Resources

All of the entries in these end-of-chapter listings have been updated to highlight current sports organizations and resources. They also include annotated website information.

Reversed Order of Author Listing

This book began as a joint venture by Stanley Eitzen and two of his colleagues at the University of Kansas. Eitzen later moved to Colorado State University, and the project took off in a new direction when he met George Sage, a professor at the University of Northern Colorado. They agreed to coauthor the book, with Eitzen as senior author. Both authors contributed equally to each successive edition, but for this ninth edition Eitzen asked Sage to do the majority of the writing and thus recommended that the listing of authors be reversed, with Sage as senior author.

CHAPTER 1

The Sociological Analysis of Sport in North American Society

The study of sport can take us to the very heart of critical issues in the study of culture and society.
—Elliott J. Gorn and Michael Oriard*

College Bowl games and Super Bowls are part of North America's most popular sports events. They are part of the social institution that provides scientific observers with a convenient laboratory for examining values, socialization, stratification, and the economy, to name a few structures and processes that exist at the societal level. (AP Photo/ David Duprey)

*Elliott Gorn and Michael Oriard, "Taking Sports Seriously," *Chronicle of Higher Education* (1995): 52a.

A typical question people ask when they first hear there is a field of study called sociology of sport is "What has sociology got to do with sport?" The short answer to that question is that sociologists study social behavior of all kinds, from interpersonal social relations to group formations to formal social organizations. Sport is fundamentally a social phenomenon that encompasses all of these social forms of human activity. For this reason sport is viewed as an unusually appropriate and relevant topic for study by sociologists.

Sociologists also realize that sport is an extraordinarily popular and pervasive worldwide social endeavor, and therefore a suitable subject for study and analysis. Indeed, North Americans are inundated daily by sports, owing in part to the massive expansion of youth, high school, and intercollegiate sports, the enormous growth of professional sports, and the expanded mass media coverage of sports events, especially on television and the Internet, during the past twenty-five years.

It occurred to us that since so few people seem to realize that there is a field of academic inquiry called sociology of sport it would be appropriate to begin with a brief introduction to this field of study prior to launching our examination of the substantive topics that form the state of the art in sociology of sport at this time. That is what we do in the section that follows.

AN OVERVIEW OF SOCIOLOGY OF SPORT AS A FIELD OF STUDY

Sociology of sport as an organized field of study is less than fifty years old. It began at about the same time that sport psychology, sport history, and sport philosophy were emerging as systematic academic disciplines with a sport focus.

Most current sport sociologists have been involved in sport throughout their lives, first as youth sport athletes, then as high school athletes; a few were college athletes, and several were professional athletes. As college students, future sport sociologists—seeking to find a career to meet their needs and interests—took courses in the sport sciences. Many who ultimately became

sport sociologists were able to enroll in a sociology of sport course. In addition, while enrolled in college courses in traditional disciplines, such as psychology or sociology, they found ways to integrate those subjects into their interest in sports.

Although sociology of sport has not been a rapidly growing field of study, it has advanced to the point where it is taught in most colleges and universities, and it has attracted a group of dedicated scholars with interests in research and publication (see Box 1.1).

There are currently about 1,200 faculty members teaching courses in the sociology of sport in North American colleges and universities. This is not a large number, as academic and scholarly societies go, but the quantity of such courses has been increasing slowly throughout higher education and the future looks good for the development of the sociology of sport.

Sociology of sport scholars are often utilized as consultants and "experts" by newspaper sports reporters and sports television broadcasters, when they are doing a story having sociological relevance. Moreover, sport sociologists frequently publish their research in a variety of mainstream sociology journals beyond the three identified in Box 1.1.

Sport sociologists who teach, research, and publish were attracted to this discipline for many different reasons. Some were inclined toward a career involving sport because of their personal experiences in sport during their childhood and adolescence. Others were interested in pursuing an understanding of the connections between sports and the family, education, economy, politics, mass media, religion, and cultural identities such as race, gender, or disability. Like many other career-oriented people, sport sociologists aspire to learn about and understand the complex sociological meanings of and connections between general social practices and sport, in the hope that they can make positive contributions to both sport and society.

We hope this overview of sociology of sport was helpful in developing an understanding of what this field of study is about. The remaining sections in this chapter deal with general topics and issues that will form a foundation for the specific subjects that are described and analyzed in the chapters that follow.

Box 1.1   *Thinking About Sport:* Scholarly Organizations and Publications in the Sociology of Sport

Virtually every academic discipline (also called field of study) has formed associations or societies and created journals with the purpose of providing an outlet for advancing knowledge in the discipline through exchanging research findings and social networking as well as promoting its assets, visibility, and diversity.

In North America, the sociology of sport has a scholarly organization named the North American Society for the Sociology of Sport (NASSS). At present, there are about 400 NASSS members. The official scholarly publication of NASSS is the *Sociology of Sport Journal*, which is published quarterly by Human Kinetics Publishers. A second publication, the *Journal of Sport and Social Issues*, is published by Sage Publications (no relation to the co-author of this text). Annual conferences of NASSS are held in cities throughout the United States and Canada.

Internationally, the sociology of sport is represented by the International Sociology of Sport Association (ISSA), which was founded in 1965. ISSA sponsors a scholarly publication titled the *International Review for the Sociology of Sport*. ISSA is also a research committee of the International Sociological Association (ISA). At present, the ISSA has some 250 members from countries throughout the world. ISSA holds annual conferences, including congresses in conjunction with the World Congress of Sociology and the Pre-Olympic Scientific Congress.

We begin with a brief description of the importance of sport in society, followed by an introduction to the discipline of sociology and a discussion of how the sociological approach aids in our understanding of sport.

THE PERVASIVENESS OF SPORT

The subject of this book is *sport*, which we define as *any competitive physical activity that is guided by established rules*. Although seemingly a trivial facet of life, sport is important, particularly as our social lives become increasingly leisure-oriented. Sport constitutes much of our everyday conversation, reading material, recreational activities, and discretionary spending. More than one-tenth of the *World Almanac* is annually devoted to sports. In fact, sports receive more coverage in the almanac than politics, business, or science.

There is good reason for such coverage. According to the Sporting Goods Manufacturers Association (SGMA), nearly 79 percent of Americans are involved in some type of sport activity, recreational endeavor, team sport, or fitness program, with some 34 million active on a "regular basis" and another 42 million active on a "casual basis." One event, the annual New York Marathon, attracts more than 45,000 participants.

Newspapers devote more space to sports than to a variety of other topics, including business news, which would seem to be of more importance in a capitalist economy. *USA Today*, America's so-called Nation's Newspaper, devotes one of its four major news sections to sport. Indeed, for many readers, sports sections are the most closely examined part of the daily newspaper. Evidence of sportsmania is also seen in the amount of television time dedicated to sport: Almost one-fifth of major TV network time is devoted to sport, and some cable and satellite networks provide twenty-four-hour sports coverage. Many of the professional sport organizations now have their own subscriber TV networks—such as NFL Network, MLB Network, NHL Network, and NCAA Network.

Sport is also big business. According to the SGMA, manufacturers' sales of sporting goods in the U.S. in 2011 totaled $71.8 billion, up from $60.5 billion in 2004. Television networks bid billions of dollars for multiyear rights to televise college basketball tournaments, professional sports, and the Olympic Games. A thirty-second advertisement at the 2012 Super Bowl on CBS cost $3.5 million. Approximately $8 billion is annually bet illegally with bookies, off shore, and on the Internet on the Super Bowl outcome.

According to an estimate by *Forbes Magazine*, the New York Yankees were worth $1.1 billion in 2010. Soccer star David Beckham signed a five-year

Table 1.1 Number of Spectators at Major Sports Events in 2010

Sport	Number of Spectators
Major League Baseball	74,499,000
National Basketball Association	21,549,238
National Football League	21,907,000
National Hockey League	22,698,000
College Basketball	
Men's	32,821,000
Women's	11,135,000

Source: U.S. Census Bureau, Statistical Abstract of the United States: 2012, 131st ed. (Washington, DC: U.S. Government Printing Office, 2011).

contract in 2006 with the Los Angeles Galaxy that could be worth $50 million a year, and PGA golfer Phil Mickelson earns over $61 million from endorsements, exhibitions, and earnings from tournaments. Of the thirty-four games in the 2010 college football bowl series, twenty-two paid out over $1 million and five paid out $17 million. In 2011, the Ohio State University had an athletic budget of $126 million. Table 1.1 shows the very large scale of sports spectatorship in the United States. When these numbers are multiplied by the average cost of tickets, parking, and refreshments, the amount generated by sports attendance is huge. Similarly, with about half of the U.S. population regularly participating in sports, the amount spent on sports-related goods is enormous (about $60 billion in 2010 just for sports apparel).

THE DISCIPLINE OF SOCIOLOGY

As we noted above, sociology is the systematic study of social behavior interpersonally, in groups, and in organizations. Sociologists are especially interested in the social patterns that emerge whenever people interact over periods of time. They also study human groups and organizations, the size of which can range from a couple to a church, from a family business to a corporation, from a community to a nation. Regardless of size and purpose, similarities exist in group structures and in the processes that

create, sustain, and transform them. In other words, a group that forms to make quilts for charity will be similar in important ways to a group that forms with the goal of winning football games. We know, for example, that through recurrent interaction certain characteristics emerge: (1) a division of labor; (2) a hierarchical structure of ranks (i.e., differences in power, prestige, and rewards); (3) rules; (4) punishment for the violation of rules; (5) criteria for the evaluation of things, people, ideas, and behavior; (6) a shared understanding of symbols with special meanings (gestures, objects, or specialized language such as nicknames); and (7) member cooperation to achieve group goals.[1]

Sociologists are interested not only in the underlying order of social life but also in the principles that explain human social behavior. Sociology is joined in this quest by other social science disciplines—namely, psychology, political science, economics, history, and anthropology. Each of the social sciences has a unique orientation. Psychological explanations of human behavior focus on personality, mental processes, and human behavioral characteristics. Political scientists are concerned with governmental organization and the forms and uses of power and authority. Study of the production of goods and services is the domain of economists. Historians concentrate on individuals (mostly leaders), events, and trends of the past. Origins, development, and characteristic patterns of cultures, past and present, are the interests of anthropologists.

Each of the various social sciences is useful to sociologists because they all have humans as their central subject. Indeed, the literature of sociology is rich with information drawn from other social sciences in the pursuit of studying sociological questions. These might be the social conditions in the community or society such as varying degrees of unemployment, inflation, leisure time, urban blight, or restricted opportunities for minority groups. An extremely important external influence on human behavior has to do with the meanings that the members of a social organization share. These shared meanings constitute culture. Under the rubric of culture are the standards used to evaluate behavior, ideology, customs, and expectations for persons occupying various positions—all of which limit the choices of individuals, regardless of their biological heritage or their psychological proclivities.

Each individual in society is—because of his or her wealth, occupation, education, religion, racial and ethnic heritage, gender, and family background—ranked by others and by himself or herself. Placement in this complex hierarchy exerts pressures, subtle and blatant, on people to behave in prescribed ways. As sociologists have accumulated knowledge about all of these topics, they have integrated information from other social sciences to supplement their sociological findings.

The goal of this book is to provide a comprehensive sociological analysis and explanation of sport in North America. Such an inquiry, we hope, not only will be interesting and meaningful but also will introduce readers to a new way to understand the social world in general and the phenomenon of sport in particular.

Assumptions of the Sociological Perspective

We have seen that human behavior is examined through different disciplinary lenses and that each field of inquiry makes important contributions to knowledge. Of the disciplines focusing on human behavior, sociology is commonly the least understood, so we plan to introduce readers to the sociological ways of perceiving and interpreting the role of sport in society. We begin by enumerating the assumptions of the sociological approach that provide the foundation for this unique way of viewing the world.[2]

I. Individuals Are, by Their Nature, Social Beings

There are two fundamental reasons for the assumption that humans are naturally social beings. First, children enter the world totally dependent on others for their survival. This initial period of dependence means, in effect, that each individual is immersed in social groups from birth. Second, throughout history individuals have found it advantageous to cooperate with others for defense, for material comforts, to overcome the perils of nature, and to improve technology.

2. Individuals Are, for the Most Part, Socially Determined

The assumption that individuals are socially determined stems from the first assumption of the sociological approach, that people are social beings. Individuals are products of their social environments for several reasons. During infancy, children are at the mercy of others, especially parents. These persons can shape the potential behaviors of infants in an infinite variety of ways, depending on their proclivities and those of the society.

Parents have a profound impact on their children's ways of thinking about themselves and about others; they transmit religious views, attitudes, and prejudices about how other groups are to be rated. Children are punished for certain behaviors and rewarded for others. Whether children become bigots or integrationists, traditionalists or innovators, saints or sinners, athletes or nonathletes depends in large measure on parents, siblings, peers, and others with whom they interact.

Parents act as cultural agents, transferring the ways of the society to their children. As a consequence, a child is born not only into a family but also into a society, both of which shape the personality characteristics and perceptions of each individual. Society shapes our identity, our thoughts, and our emotions. Thus, the structures of society become the structures of our own consciousness; they do not stop at the surface of our skin but, rather, penetrate and envelop us. One's identity is socially bestowed and shaped by the way he or she is accepted, rejected, and defined by others. Whether an individual is attractive or plain, witty or dull, worthy or unworthy depends on the values of the society and the groups in which the individual is immersed. Although genes determine an individual's physical characteristics, the social environment, especially an individual's social class location, determines how those characteristics will be evaluated.

Suggesting that we are socially determined is another way of saying that we are, in many ways, dependent upon and manipulated by social forces. A major function of sociology is to identify the social forces that affect us so greatly. Accordingly, one task of sociology is to learn about issues such as racism, sexism, and homophobia in an effort to understand how they work. This is often difficult, though, because we typically do not recognize their existence. Social forces may have prompted us to believe and to behave in racist, sexist, and homophobic ways.

Saying that people are dependent on and manipulated by social forces does not imply a total social determinism. Such words are merely used to convey the idea that much of who we are and what we do is a product of our social environment. However, society is not a rigid, static entity composed of robots; there are nonconformists, deviants, and innovators as well. Although the members of society are shaped by their social environment, they also change that environment. Human beings are the shapers of society; in other words, they possess *human agency*, meaning that they have the capacity to make choices and to impose those choices on the world. This is the third assumption of the sociological approach.

3. Individuals Create, Sustain, and Change the Social Forms Within Which They Conduct Their Lives

An old but still popular saying—that "we are captains of our fate"—contains a core insight of sociology. In brief, the argument is that individual persons within social groups of all sizes and types (families, peer groups, work groups, athletic teams, corporations, communities, and societies) actually form, and are formed by, their members. The groups and organizations that interacting persons create become a source of control over them (i.e., they become puppets of their own creation), but the continuous interaction of individuals within groups and organizations also changes, influences, and helps construct and maintain these social entities.

Two important implications stem from this assumption that groups are created and sustained by persons through interaction. The first is that through collective action individuals are capable of changing the structure of society and even the course of history. Individuals are not passive. Rather, they actively shape social life by adapting to, negotiating with, and changing social structures. This process, too, illustrates *human agency*.

Second, these social forms that are created and changed by people have a certain momentum of their own that restricts change. Although human-made, the group's expectations and structures also take on a sacred quality—a sanctity of tradition—that constrains behavior in socially prescribed ways. By extension, we can infer that social arrangements, because they are a result of socially constructed activity, are imperfect. Slavery benefits some segments of society by taking advantage of others. A competitive free-enterprise system creates winners and losers. The wonders of technology make worldwide transportation and communication easy and relatively inexpensive, but they also create pollution and waste natural resources. These examples show that both positive and negative consequences emanate from human social actions and organizations.

Thinking as a Sociologist: Sociological Imagination

C. Wright Mills (1916–1962), in his classic *The Sociological Imagination* (1959), articulated an unusual form of creative thinking that has been a benchmark for sociologists for over half a century. He referred to this style of thinking as a sociological imagination, which requires an awareness of the relationships between the individual and the broader society inasmuch as individual circumstances are inextricably linked to the structure of society. A sociological imagination, according to Mills, enables sociologists (actually, all of us) to realize the connections between our immediate, personal lives and the detached, impersonal social world that surrounds and shapes us. The sociological imagination involves several related components:[3]

- The sociological imagination is stimulated by a willingness to view the social world from the perspective of others.
- It involves moving away from thinking in terms of the individual and her or his problem, focusing rather on the social, economic, and historical circumstances that produce the problem. Put another way, the sociological imagination is the ability to see the

societal patterns that influence individuals, families, groups, and organizations.

- Possessing a sociological imagination, one can shift from examining a single unemployed person to analyzing the societal change from manufacturing to a service/knowledge economy, from a homeless family to the lack of affordable housing, and from a racist coach to institutional racism.
- Development of a sociological imagination requires detachment from the taken-for-granted assumptions about social life and establishment of a critical distance. In other words, one must be willing to question the structural arrangements that shape social behavior.
- When we have this imagination, we begin to see the solutions to social problems not in terms of changing problem people but in terms of changing the structure of society.

Units of Sociological Analysis

We have seen that sociologists are interested in social organizations and in how social forces operate to channel human behavior. The scope of sociology ranges from individuals sharing common social characteristics to small groups to society.

The Micro Level

At the micro level, the emphasis is on the structure of relatively small groups, such as families, friendship groups, and such organizations as the Friday night poker club, the local Nazarene Church, the African Violet Society, and the Pretty Prairie High School football team. Some of the research questions of interest at this level are these: What are the principles underlying group formation, stability, and change? What are the most effective forms of organization to accomplish group goals? Under what conditions is member cooperation maximized? Under what conditions is member behavior least predictable?

Sports teams are especially useful research settings in which to test theories about social organization. Sociologists of sport have researched, for example, the organizational characteristics correlated with success (leadership style, leadership change,

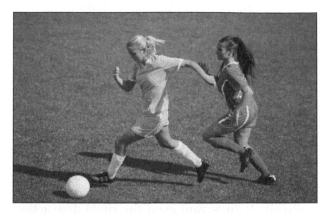

The pervasiveness of sport throughout North America is evident at the micro level with informal play. It exists also at the macro level, which is structured by teams, leagues, and large sport organizations. At both levels a great deal of social learning occurs that socializes participants into the larger culture. (istockphoto)

homogeneity of members). They have examined where in sports organizations racial discrimination is most likely to occur.

As a final example of the micro level, sport sociologists have researched sports teams to examine the important social processes of competition and cooperation. Sport provides innumerable instances in which competition and cooperation occur separately and simultaneously. On the one hand, sports contests are instances of institutionalized conflict. Therefore, they may serve to control undesirable aggression and violence in socially acceptable channels. On the other hand, sports teams require cooperation to be effective. An important question—some would say a central question—in sociology is this: What facilitates group cohesion? (Under what conditions do members pull together, and when do they pull apart?) The leaders of sports teams—coaches, managers, and athletic directors—spend a good deal of their time working to build group unity. Some are successful; others are not. Is it a matter of charisma, authoritarianism, homogeneity of personnel, winning, social control, or what?

The Macro Level

Social behavior exists in a larger social setting—a context that is also structured—with its own norms, values, statuses, roles, and social institutions. These components of social structure constrain social groups and the attitudes and behaviors of individuals, regardless of their group memberships.

Societal norms are societal prescriptions for how one should act and dress in given situations—for example, at a restaurant, church, school, concert, or football game. In other words, norms are situational. Why is the national anthem always played at sports events but not at concerts? Clearly, behavior considered appropriate for spectators at a football game (e.g., spontaneous screams of exuberance or despair, the open criticism of authority figures, and even the ritual destruction of goalposts) would be inexcusable behavior at a poetry reading. We know what is expected of us in these different situations. We also know how to act with members of the opposite sex, with elders, with social inferiors, and with equals. Thus, behavior in society is patterned and norm-structured. We know how to behave, and we can anticipate how others will behave. This allows social interaction to occur smoothly.

Values are also part of society's culture. They are the criteria we use in assessing the relative desirability, merit, or correctness of objects, ideas, acts, feelings, or events. This is the topic of Chapter 3, so we will only state here that the members of society are taught explicitly and implicitly how to judge whether someone or something is good or bad, moral or immoral, appropriate or inappropriate. North Americans, for example, believe that winning—in school, in sports, in business, and in life—is a major goal. They not only value success; they know precisely how to evaluate others and themselves by this critical dimension.

Statuses and roles are social positions (statuses) and behavioral expectations (roles) for individuals. There are family statuses (daughter, son, sibling, parent, husband, wife); age statuses (child, adolescent, adult, elder); gender statuses (male, female); racial statuses (African American, Hispanic, Native American, white); and socioeconomic statuses (poor, middle-class, wealthy). For each of these statuses, there are societal constraints on behavior. To be a male or a female in U.S. society, for example, is to be constrained in a relatively rigid set of expectations. Similarly, African Americans and others of minority status have been expected to "know their place." Historically, their "place" in sport was segregated as they were denied equal access to sports participation with whites. Even with civil rights laws requiring equality, the "place" of racial minorities often remains unequal—in sport at certain playing positions, head coaching, and administration.

Societal institutions are universally characteristic of societies, but popular usages of this term are imprecise, sometimes even incorrect. Sociologists use the term to mean social arrangements that channel behavior in prescribed ways in the important areas of social life. Social institutions are devised by the persons making up a society and passed on to succeeding generations to provide "permanent" solutions for crucial societal problems.

In sociology, a social institution is not merely something established and traditional (e.g., a janitor who has worked at the same school for forty-five years), nor is the term limited to a specific organization such as a school, a prison, or a hospital. An institution is much broader in scope and in importance than a person, a custom, or a single social organization.

Another way to characterize social institutions is to say they are cultural imperatives. They serve as regulatory agencies that channel behavior in culturally prescribed ways. All societies face problems in common, and their members are continually seeking solutions. Although the variety of solutions is almost infinite, there is a similarity in the outcomes sought—namely, stability and maintenance of the system.

Social institutions for family, education, polity, education, mass media, and religion thrive as part of all contemporary societies. For example, human societies instill in their members predetermined channels for marriage. Instead of being allowed a whole host of options (e.g., polygamy, polyandry, or group marriage), sexual partners in the United States and Canada are expected to marry and to set up a conjugal household. Although the actual options are many, the partners tend to choose what society deems appropriate. The result is a patterned arrangement that regulates sexual behavior and ensures a stable environment for the care of dependent children. See Table 1.2 for a list of common societal problems and the resulting institutions.

Table 1.2 Common Societal Problems and Resulting Institutions

Societal Problems	Institution
Sexual regulation, maintenance of stable units that ensure continued births and care of dependent children	Family
Socialization of newcomers to the society	Education
Maintenance of order; distribution of power	Polity
Production and distribution of goods and services; ownership of property	Economy
Understanding the transcendental; searching for the meaning of life, death, and humankind's place in the world	Religion
Understanding the physical and social realms of nature	Science
Providing for physical and emotional health care	Medicine

Unity and stability are crucial for the survival of society, and social institutions tend to provide these. By definition, then, social institutions are conservative. They provide the answers of custom and tradition to questions of societal survival. For this reason, any attack on a social institution is often met by aggressive, even violent, opposition.

Over the course of the past two centuries—with industrialization, modernization, globalization, and advanced technology—sport has become a social institution in nations throughout the world. Several societal needs are popularly believed to be served by sport:

- Sport serves as a safety valve for both spectators and participants, dissipating excess energies, tensions, and hostile feelings in a socially acceptable way.
- Athletes serve as role models, possessing the proper mental and physical traits to be emulated by other members of society.
- Sport is a secular, quasi-religious institution that uses ritual and ceremony to reinforce the values of society, thereby restricting behavior to the channels approved by custom.

Micro and Macro Levels and This Book

The primary focus of this book will be at the macro level. We will describe how sport reinforces societal values. We will analyze the reciprocal linkages of sport with other institutions—sport and education, sport and religion, sport and politics, sport and the economy, sport and the mass media—and we will ask: Who benefits, and who does not, from the way sport is organized? Although the level of analysis is macro, the research findings from social-psychological and micro studies will be included whenever appropriate.

SOCIOLOGICAL THEORIES: CONTRASTING WAYS TO SEE AND UNDERSTAND SOCIAL LIFE

Upon reading the word *theory*, many readers roll their eyes and say "Oh, no, not theory again." But because theory is so fundamentally a part of every knowledge domain, learning about it is essential if one hopes to become knowledgeable about a field of study. And in any case, theory is not all that complicated. It is merely an explanation or set of statements that attempt to explain observed phenomena and can be used to test predictions or hypotheses.

We all use theories, albeit informally, every day of our lives. We are constantly processing thoughts like "Given the experiences that I have had with _____, if I take this action, I believe that will happen." All of us undergo dozens of these mental machinations each day. We are using theory when we do so.

A fundamental feature of a scientific discipline—field of study—is that it is grounded in theoretical formulations; it is theory driven. A sociological theory offers an explanation of social life by making assumptions about the general patterns found. It is a way of making sense out of the complex social world, but as such it is always tentative, subject to new research findings and changing social conditions.

Those who prepare for a career in sociology must spend many hours of study learning about the theories of the leading social theorists of the past and present time. Such study serves as a foundation for teaching, research, and publication in sociology. As a result, most sociologists come to be guided by one particular theoretical perspective. They do not necessarily reject other theoretical formulations, but the focus of attention, the questions they ask, the relationships sought, the interpretations rendered, and the insights unraveled by one of the theoretical perspectives appear more persuasive than alternatives.

Several social theoretical perspectives provide vantage points from which to view social life. Each of these guides our thinking, narrows our perceptions to certain relevant phenomena, and, in doing so, helps us understand our social life. In the pages that follow, we discuss several major theoretical perspectives that are used to understand the social world and, for our purposes in this book, the world of sport. Each of these perspectives is useful because it focuses on a different feature of social life, giving us insights missing from the others.

Functionalism

The functionalist perspective views a society as analogous to a living organism, with each part—brain, heart, lungs—contributing functionally to the organism's survival. Thus, a human society is viewed as composed of various interdependent parts, primarily the social institutions—the economy, education, religion, government, and so forth—as the structured components that maintain the social system as a whole, contributing and promoting social value consensus and stability. The parts of the system are basically in harmony with each other, exhibiting the characteristics of cohesion, consensus, cooperation, reciprocity, stability, and persistence.[4] The high degree of social system cooperation—and societal integration—is accomplished because there is a high degree of consensus on societal goals and on cultural values.

Consensus in a social system, according to the functionalist perspective, is achieved through the interdependence of the different parts of the system. Even though there are obvious differences in resources among the various groups and organizations in society, countervailing pressures are expected to prevent abuse, exploitation, and domination by one group. It is expected that the poor and powerless will not revolt because they accept the values of the society and they believe the system is intrinsically just. All social change is

anticipated to be gradual, adjustive, and reforming because the primary social process is cooperation and the system is highly integrated. Societies, then, are basically stable units.

Functionalist advocates acknowledge that social change can lead to disruptions and that instability—dysfunctions—can lead to social system disorder, even volatility. However, self-correcting mechanisms of the social system are expected to reverse dysfunctions and restore the system's status quo.

North American Sport from a Functionalist Perspective

Functionalists examining any facet of society emphasize the contributions that various parts make to the stability of society. Sport, from this perspective, unifies and preserves the existing social order in several ways. For instance, sport is viewed as symbolizing the North American way of life—competition, individualism, achievement, and fair play. Not only is sport compatible with basic North American values, but it also is a powerful mechanism for socializing youth to adopt desirable character traits, such as accepting authority and striving for good health and physical fitness, both of which are useful for promoting and maintaining a nation's strength.

For functionalists, North American sport supports the status quo by promoting the unity of citizens through patriotism—national anthem, militaristic displays, and Christian religious rituals that accompany sports events. Can you imagine, for example, a team that espouses anti-establishment values in its name, logo, mascot, and pageantry? Would we tolerate a professional sport team called the Atlanta Atheists, the Boston Nazis, the Pasadena Pacifists, or the Sacramento Socialists? Finally, sport inspires us through the excellent and heroic achievements of athletes—the magical moments in sport when the seemingly impossible happens and the feelings of unity in purpose and loyalty of fans are displayed.

Functionalist theorists focus on the integrating benefits of youth, high school, and intercollegiate sport for students, faculty, alumni, and community members. They also look for positive consequences for participants such as grades, self-esteem, career aspirations, and the career mobility patterns of former athletes.

Clearly, then, sport from the functional perspective is seen as good: Sport socializes citizens into proper behavior, sport unites, and sport inspires. Conversely, questioning or criticizing sport in any way is viewed by functionalist theorists as challenging a foundation of North America's social order.[5]

Conflict Theory

The social theorist who articulated the fundamental tenets of this social theory, Karl Marx, never called his theoretical formulations "conflict theory," but his ideas about capitalist society have been historically adopted and modified and enunciated as conflict theory. The assumptions of conflict theorists are opposite from those of functionalist theorists. Instead of the social harmony that functionalism conceives, the conflict theory's perspective posits conflict as endemic to capitalist societies, especially because of the social class differences that emerge in capitalist society resulting from the ways people are organized for production, distribution, and consumption of material goods. The things that people desire, such as property, prestige, and power, are possessed by the socially elite, resulting in a fundamental cleavage between the wealthy and powerful and the disadvantaged—namely, the working class. Moreover, the wealthy and powerful class uses its resources to maintain its power and advantages.

The emphasis of the conflict perspective, then, is on the social, political, and material inequalities in society, and on the ways in which societal power and wealth are intertwined and dominate the rest of society, frequently leading to disharmony, disruption, instability, and conflict. Of course, conflict can take many forms, not necessarily outright violence; disagreement, tension, and hostility over needs, interests, values, and goals are likely to be more prevalent.

Functionalism's vision of social harmony, stability, and consensus is seen as unrealistic and illusionary by conflict theorists. They argue that what actually happens in society is that the wealthy and powerful, through their control of the decision-making apparatus, maintain their advantages by fostering ideological conformity—though it is sometimes achieved by coercion—through the government, economic system, schools, churches, and other social institutions. This is seen as an effective means of maintaining social order because it can be sustained through popular compliance, resulting in the underclass of individuals defining conditions that are actually hostile to their interests as being legitimate—a condition that Karl Marx called *false consciousness*.[6]

North American Sport from a Conflict Theory Perspective

The conflict perspective contends that the society reflects the interests of the powerful and advantaged, and that sport at every level—youth, high school, college, and professional—is organized to exploit athletes and achieve the goals of the elite (e.g., profits, recognition, public relations, prestige). Moreover, any critical questioning or instigation for reform in sports is repressed in several ways. First, the prevailing myths of capitalism, especially the notion that anyone can succeed if he or she works hard enough, are promoted and reinforced in sport. Popular locker-room slogans reinforce this: "Workers Are Winners," "Play as Hard as You Can for as Long as You Can." The highest praise a coach can give to an athlete is to say that she or he is "a hard worker."

Second, sport diverts attention of the large mass of people away from the harsh realities of poverty, job insecurity, rising debt, and dismal life chances that many of them experience. Third, sport gives false hope to African Americans, minorities, and other oppressed people. Many are led to believe that sport is a realistic avenue of upward social mobility; indeed, the high visibility of the few professional athletes seems to provide "proof" that sports ability readily translates into monetary success. The reality, of course, is that only an extremely small percentage of athletes ever achieves professional status.[7]

One sport sociology research tradition from a conflict perspective has focused on intercollegiate athletics. This research illuminates the power that the National Collegiate Athletic Association (NCAA) has over athletes, the cozy relationship between the NCAA and television networks, the resistance of the NCAA and university administrators to implementing Title IX (which requires equal treatment for women), the big-business aspect of big-time college sport, illegal tactics by coaches in recruiting athletes, and the exploitation of athletes.

Conflict/Cultural Social Theories

Several variants of the conflict perspective have gained popularity. We shall not attempt to identify or describe all of them, for that would take us far afield from our main interests in this book. However, we do think it is useful to briefly identify and discuss those variants that have had the most influence in sociology of sport: hegemony theory, feminist theory, and race theory. As a general category, they are often referred to as critical theories or cultural theories.

Hegemony theory, feminist theory, and race theory—like conflict theory—seek to understand the sources of power, how power works, and how individuals and groups exert human agency as they cope with, adapt to, and change existing power relationships. Instead of seeing society as dominating individuals completely, these theories view human agency as an omnipresent option.

Hegemony Theory

Hegemony theory stems from conflict theory, but it adds ideology and culture to the importance of the economy, politics, and the cultural patterns of dominance and influence in society. It highlights the role that dominant groups play in North American government, economic systems, mass media, education, and sport in maintaining and promoting their interests. By *dominant groups* we mean the powerful and wealthy who own most of the land, capital, and technology and who employ most of the workforce. Moreover, they translate their enormous economic resources into social and political power by occupying the top elective and appointed governmental positions, regardless of the political party to which they belong. Hegemony theorists give special attention to the social structure of dominance in North American society that privileges men over women, rich over poor, and whites over people of color.[8]

Applying hegemony theory to sport requires that we step back from thinking about sport merely as a place of personal achievement and entertainment and study sport as a cultural practice embedded in political, economic, and ideological formations. Of particular relevance is the question of how sport is related to social class, race, gender, and the control, production, and distribution of economic and cultural power in the commodified sport industry.[9]

Hegemony theorists agree with functionalists on many features of society but differ significantly in interpretation. Both sets of theorists agree that sport socializes youth, but hegemony theorists view this process critically because they see sport as a mechanism to socialize youth into obediently following orders, working hard, and fitting into a system that is not necessarily beneficial to them. Both agree that sport reinforces the status quo. Instead of interpreting this as good, as functionalists maintain, a hegemony theorist views this as bad because it reflects and strengthens the unequal distribution of power and resources in society.

While recognizing that sport is a microcosm of society, hegemony theorists go beyond that insight to emphasize that the conditions of sport can change from the top down (from power structures) or from the bottom up (from the interaction of the participants themselves). Whereas functionalism and conflict theories explain social life as deriving from a single source (value consensus for functionalists and the economy for conflict theorists), hegemony theorists emphasize the diversity of social life, stressing that understanding social phenomena requires looking at a number of forces (e.g., historical, cultural, economic, and political forces and the media).

Feminist Theory

Feminist struggles for political, social, economic, and educational equality of women have roots extending back in history for centuries. Feminist theories began as critiques of the dominant social theories that did not include women or did not take women's issues seriously. According to feminist theorists, inequalities faced by women are related to differential access, different treatment and exploitation, patriarchy, and male dominance. While critiquing these social and political relations, a great deal of feminist theory focuses on the promotion of women's rights and interests.

During the past hundred years, feminist issues have included social injustices as well as access to employment and equality in the workplace, equal political representation, equality of educational opportunity, redress for sexual harassment in all the social institutions, and legal access to contraception and abortion. Feminist theory rests on two fundamental assumptions: first, that human experiences are gendered and, second, that women are oppressed within patriarchy and have a commitment to change those conditions. Three of the most prominent themes addressed in feminist theory are patriarchy, stereotyping discrimination, and oppression.[10]

Sport from a feminist theoretical perspective is seen as a gendered activity in which males have the power. Some examples of feminist research topics focusing on sport are the ideological control of women through the underrepresentation of women athletes in media images, the trivialization of women athlete's accomplishments, the hidden discourse of homophobia, and "the construction of women as unnatural athletes and of female athletes as unnatural women."[11] Chapter 14 is devoted to a discussion of gender in North American sport. In that chapter we describe and analyze a variety of feminist theoretical topics as they play out in sport.

Race Theory

Race theory—often called critical race theory (CRT)—is "a framework from which to explore and examine the racism in society that privileges whiteness as it disadvantages others because of their 'blackness.'"[12] Its main concern is with the inescapable and inherent racism that is an everyday occurrence for people of color, a racism that is thoroughly rooted in the social fabric of North American society (and others as well), permeating its social structures and practices. Because racism is entrenched, it permeates all of the social institutions in which the white majority has profited, and continues to profit, from the persistence of such social practices; consequently, it tends to become a covert mechanism for maintaining racial prejudice and discrimination.

Race theory's primary mission is to analyze, deconstruct, and socially transform society to improve relationships among race, racism, and power. This theoretical perspective has been applied in a variety of contexts where institutionalized oppression

based on race occurs, especially in legal-judicial areas as well as in education, where educational opportunity and experiences form the basis for the future acquisition of income, wealth, health, and longevity.

According to sports studies scholar Kevin Hylton, for CRT analysts "the question is not *do* we live in a racist society? Rather it is a conclusion: *we do* live in a racist society and we need to do something about it. Therefore, anti-racism should be mainstreamed into the core business of sport."[13] Histories of North American sport reveal that sport has simultaneously been a powerful reinforcer of racist ideology and an instrument of opportunity for African Americans. With African Americans playing such a prominent historical role in both U.S. and Canadian sports, sports studies researchers have incorporated race theory into their research arsenal. The role of racial-ethnic minorities in sport is examined in more detail in Chapter 13.

Interactionist Theory

Interactionist theory is different from the preceding theories we have identified and described. All of those are in one way or another structural theories, so their scope of analysis is the macro level. That is, they concern the components of society: institutions (e.g., the economy), politics, religion, culture, the media, social classes, race, and gender. Our focus on topics in this book is at that level.

Although the structural theories pay some attention to how people give meaning to their lives, interactionist theory converges exclusively on this aspect of human activity, especially on how individuals and groups interpret and understand their social worlds by attaching meaning to symbols. This is an ongoing process, as the social world is continually constructed and reinvented by the participants.[14] The important sociological insight here is that meaning is not inherent in an object; instead, people learn how to define reality from other people in interaction and by learning the culture. This process is called the *social construction of reality*. Race and gender, for example, are socially constructed inasmuch as people attach social meanings to physical differences and females (see Chapters 13 and 14).

Sociologists of sport using interactionist perspectives have conducted various kinds of research by interviewing, watching, and listening to subjects. The goal is to determine how participants (players, coaches, officials, administrators, and spectators) understand their world. Other interaction-level research has centered on topics such as socialization into sport, the process of retirement from sport, male bonding in locker rooms, sport rituals, and the characteristics of sport subcultures (e.g., rock climbing, skateboarding, boxing, pool hustling, playground basketball, high school football, and professional golf played by women). We will describe and discuss these in more detail in various chapters.

Sociological Theories and Sociology of Sport: Our Position

Thus far we have identified and described several social theoretical perspectives, stressed that each has its unique view of the social world and how it works, and acknowledged that each provides valuable insights for understanding society—but also that none is complete. Each has its strengths and weaknesses, but none is endorsed by all sociologists. In the course of the following chapters, we will provide additional information about the relevance of these theories to the various chapter topics. As we do so, we will refer to the functionalist perspective by using that term. However, in the interest of brevity we shall conceptually collapse conflict, critical/cultural, hegemony, feminist, and race theories into a single concept, which we will call the conflict/cultural perspective because they are all underpinned by critiques of domination and oppression.

As for social theories and our positions regarding the social world of the U.S. and Canada, we draw certain insights from each of the social theories. However, our perspective assumes a basic critical stance about contemporary social practices and organizations, for three reasons.

First, we are skeptical about existing power arrangements because they are, by definition, oppressive toward the powerless segments of the population. We question dominant ideologies because they support the status quo. We measure myths against reality. This critical examination of social structure demystifies, demythologizes, and,

sometimes, emancipates. This, we feel, is the core of the sociological perspective.

In concordance with the general field of sociology, our underlying assumption is that things are not as they seem in sports. Do school sports serve educational goals? Are athletes in big-time college programs exploited? Does participation in sport build character? Are sports free of racism? Are school sports sexist? Is sport a realistic mechanism of upward mobility for lower-class youth? Is success, or failure, the most common experience of athletes? In making such queries we question existing myths, stereotypes, and official dogma. This type of critical examination of sport tends to demystify and to demythologize; it sensitizes us to the inconsistencies present in North American sport.

Second, our perspective directs attention toward social problems emanating from current structural arrangements. We ask: Under these social arrangements, who gets what and why? Who benefits from and bears the social costs of change and stability? Sport, much like the core institutions of the economy, religion, and family, is an area where these kinds of questions typically are not asked.

Third, our perspective seeks to determine how social arrangements might be changed to enhance the human condition. This leads us to the two goals we have had in writing this book: (1) to report what is known about sport and society from social science research[15] and (2) to make the case for reform. As social scientists, we are obliged to be as scientific as possible (using rigorous techniques and reporting all relevant findings whether they support our values or not). At the same time, however, we are committed to moving sport and society in a more humane direction.

To accomplish these goals, we combine a scientific stance with a muckraking role. The latter is important because it compels us to examine such social problems as drug usage in sports, the prevalence of racism and sexism in sports, illegal recruiting, the inhumane treatment of players by bureaucratic organizations and authoritarian coaches, and the perversion of the original goal of sport. Only by thoroughly examining such problems, along with the traditional areas of attention, will we realistically understand the world of sport and its reciprocal relationship with the larger society.

Sociology is not a comfortable discipline; looking behind the "closed doors" of social life can be unsettling, even troubling. The astute observer of society must ask such questions as these: How does society really work? Who really has the power? Who benefits under the existing social arrangements, and who does not? Asking such questions means that the inquirer is interested in looking beyond the commonly accepted explanations, in "seeing through" the façades of social structures. The sociological assumption providing the basis for this critical stance is that the social world is made by people and therefore is not sacred. A society's economic system, its law, its ideology, its distribution of power, and its sports institutions are all created and sustained by people. And, as a consequence, they can be changed by people. If we wish to correct imperfections in our society, then we must truly understand how social phenomena work and learn what changes will help achieve our goals.

The sociological perspective is discomforting to some people because understanding the constraints of society is liberating. (Traditional gender roles, for example, are no longer "sacred" for many persons.) However, liberation from the constraints of tradition also means freedom from the protection that custom provides. The robot-like acceptance of tradition is comfortable because it frees us from choice (and therefore blame) and from ambiguity. The understanding of society is a two-edged sword, freeing us but also increasing the probability of our frustration, anger, and alienation.

SPORT AS A MICROCOSM OF SOCIETY

The analyst of society is inundated with data. She or he is faced with the problems of sorting out the important from the less important and with discerning social patterns of behavior and their meanings. He or she needs shortcuts to ease the task. To focus on sport is just such a technique for understanding the complexities of the larger society.

Sport is an institution that provides scientific observers with a convenient laboratory within which to examine values, socialization, stratification, and bureaucracy, to name a few structures and processes that also exist at the societal level. The types of games people choose to play, the degree of competitiveness, the types of rules, the constraints on the participants, the groups that do and do not benefit under the existing arrangements, the rate and type of change, and the reward system in sport provide us with a microcosm of the society in which sport is embedded.

Common Characteristics of Sport and Society

Suppose an astute sociologist from another country were to visit the United States and Canada with the intent to understand North American values, the system of social control, the division of labor, and the system of stratification. Although she or he could find the answers by careful study and observation of any single institution, such as religion, education, polity, economy, or family, an attention to sport would also provide answers. It would not take that sociologist long to discern the following qualities in sport that are also present in the broader North American region.

The High Degree of Competitiveness

Competition is ubiquitous in North America. North Americans demand winners. In sports (for children and adults) winning—not pleasure in the activity—is the ultimate goal. The adulation given winners is prodigious whereas losers are maligned. Consider, for example, such popular locker-room slogans as "Show Me a Good Loser and I'll Show You a Loser" and "Lose Is a Four-Letter Word" or the different ways in which the winner and the loser of the Super Bowl game or Stanley Cup championship are evaluated. Clearly, to be second best is not good enough. "Nobody remembers who came in second" is the conventional wisdom. The goal of victory is so important for many that it is considered laudable even when attained by questionable methods. "Whatever you can get away with" is another conventional insight.

The Emphasis on Materialism

Examples of the value North Americans place on materialism are blatant in sport (e.g., players signing multimillion-dollar contracts, golfers playing weekly for first-place awards of more than a million dollars, professional teams being moved to more economically fertile climates, and stadiums being built at public expense for hundreds of millions of dollars).

The Pervasiveness of Racism

Although conditions have improved greatly over the past thirty years, racist attitudes and actions still affect who plays, the positions played, the numbers of starters, and the futures of minority group members in North American sport. Just as in the larger society, racial minorities in sport are rarely found in positions of authority.

The Pervasiveness of Male Dominance

Men control sport. Almost every major professional, amateur, and educational sport organization in North America is under the management and control of men. The proportion of women in leadership and decision-making positions in North American sport, those with power and influence, is quite small—far smaller, certainly, than would be expected based on the number of female sport participants. Significant shifts in the balance of gender dominance in sports are difficult to find.

Sport continues to contribute to the perpetuation of male dominance through four minimalizing processes: (1) defining—by defining sport as a male activity; (2) directly controlling—men control sport, even women's sport; (3) ignoring—by giving most attention to male sports in the media and through community and school budgets, facilities, and the like; and (4) trivializing—women's sports and women athletes continue to be belittled and diminished, especially in the mass media.[16]

The Domination of Individuals by Bureaucracies

Conservative bureaucratic organizations, through their desire to perpetuate themselves, curtail innovations and deflect activities away from the wishes of individuals and from the original intent of these organizations. Many sport organizations—the NCAA, intercollegiate athletic conferences, professional sport leagues—pride themselves on having adopted bureaucratic business practices.

The Unequal Distribution of Power in Organizations

The structure of sport in North America is such that power is in the hands of the wealthy (e.g., boards of regents, corporate boards of directors, the media, wealthy entrepreneurs, the Canadian and United States Olympic Committees [COC, USOC], the National Collegiate Athletic Association in the U.S., and Canadian Interuniversity Sport [CIS]). Evidence of the power of these individuals and organizations is seen in the exemptions allowed them by provincial and state governments, as well as by the Canadian and U.S. national governments, in dealing with athletes, in tax breaks, and in the concessions that communities make to entice professional sports franchises to relocate or to remain, and, incidentally, to benefit the wealthy of that community.

The Use of Conflict to Change Unequal Power Relationships

Conflict, in the form of lawsuits, strikes, boycotts, and demonstrations, historically and in more recent times has been used by labor groups, minorities, and the poor to rectify grievances. It is used by the less powerful (e.g., African Americans, women, and athletes) in sport and in society for similar reasons.

Sport Is Not a Sanctuary: Deviance Is Found Throughout Sport

Corruption, law-breaking, unethical behavior, delinquency, and so forth are endemic to human societies. Because sport reflects society, bad actors and bad actions will be found in sport as they are in society. Both fairness and unfairness are found. There are ethical and unethical athletes, coaches, and athletic administrators. It is impossible to imagine the worst about sports anymore. Cheating is accepted, drugs are common, rapists sneak into locker rooms, nothing is beyond belief.

LEVELS OF SPORT

One final task remains for this first chapter. We need to establish at the outset the subject matter of this book. As we noted near the beginning of the chapter, our object of study is *sport*, which we defined as any competitive physical activity that is guided by established rules. Competition, the first of the three characteristics of sport, involves the attempt to defeat an opponent. This opponent may be a mountain, a record, an individual, or a team. The second characteristic involves physical activity. One attempts to defeat an opponent through physical abilities such as strength, speed, stamina, and accuracy. Of course, the outcome is also determined by the employment of strategy and tactics, not to mention chance. Rules, the final characteristic of sport, distinguish it from more playful and spontaneous activities. The scope, rigidity, and enforcement of the rules, however, vary by type and level of sport, as we shall see.

We recognize that our definition of sport is too broad to be entirely adequate. A pickup game of basketball and a game in the National Basketball Association (NBA) are examples of two related but at the same time very different activities that fall under our definition.[17] In the same way, an improvised game of football is sport; so is professional football—although it has been argued that professional football is not sport because of its big-business aspects or because it is more like work than play for the participants. Clearly, there is a need to differentiate several levels. We do that by labeling them informal sport, organized sport, and corporate sport. These distinctions have been made by other sport analysts, and many of the ideas that follow stem from their insights.

Informal Sport

Informal sport involves playful physical activity engaged in primarily for the enjoyment of the participants. A touch football game, a neighborhood basketball game, and a playground game of baseball or softball are examples of this type of sport. In each of these examples, some rules guide the competition, but these rules are determined by the participants and not by a regulatory body. Furthermore, there are no formalized teams or leagues in informal sport.

Organized Sport

The presence of a rudimentary organization distinguishes *organized sport* from informal sport. There are formal teams, leagues, codified rules, and re-

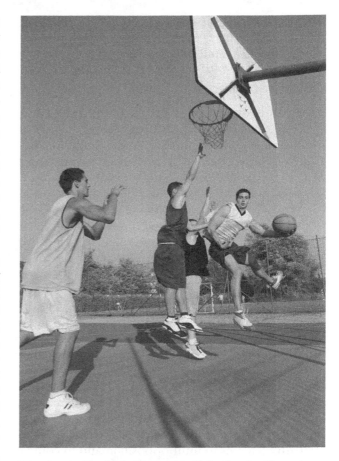

The sport of basketball crosses all the levels of sports participation, from the informal neighborhood pickup game to an organized high school game to the corporate level of the National Basketball Association. (istockphoto)

lated organizations. These exist primarily for the benefit of the players by working for fair competition, providing equipment and officials, scheduling, ruling in disputed cases, and offering opportunities for persons to participate. Public recreation department sport leagues, civic-sponsored sport leagues, Little League programs, interscholastic teams and leagues, and low-pressure college team leagues are examples of organized sport that have not lost the original purposes of the activity.[18]

A strong case can be made, however, that many youth sport programs have become too organized to maintain the goal of fun through the participation of young athletes. If so, they belong in the "corporate" category, as we shall see in Chapter 4. The same is true for high school sport in some situations, as illustrated in Chapter 5.

Corporate Sport

Corporate sport has elements of informal sport and organized sport, but it has been modified by economics, politics, and the mass media. According to observers of sports trends, corporate sport is a corrupted, institutionalized version of sport. It is sport as spectacle, sport as big business, sport as an extension of power politics. The pleasure in the activity for the participants has been lost in favor of extrinsic rewards for them, entertainment for fans and alumni, and potential profits for owners, alumni, and other business interests.

Whereas sports organizations at the organized sport level devote their energies to preserving the activities for the participants' interests, organizations at the corporate sport level have enormous power (often a monopoly). As their power increases, they devote less and less of their energy to satisfying the needs for which they were created. They become more interested in perpetuating the organization through public relations, making profits, monopolizing the media, crushing opposing organizations, or merging leagues to limit opposition and to control player salaries. They also reduce their own risk by being inflexible and noninnovative.

Professional sports leagues, big-time college athletics governed by the National Collegiate Athletic Association and Canadian Interuniversity Sport, and the Olympic Games governed by the International Olympic Committee (IOC) are examples of the bureaucracies that characterize corporate sport and subvert the pleasure of participating for the sake of the activity itself.

The three levels of sport can be placed on a continuum from play to work. As one moves from informal to corporate sport, the activities become more organized with a subsequent loss of autonomy and pleasure for athletes. Corporate sport dominates sport in North America; therefore, we will give considerable attention to corporate sport in this book. That level is but an extension of the organized sport level, however, so we will at times direct our attention toward noncorporate organized sport as well.

Pseudosport is another activity often included in the sports pages of newspapers, but one that we claim falls outside even our broad definition. The form of wrestling associated with the World Wrestling Federation (WWF)—now known as World Wrestling Entertainment—and activities involving teams such as the Harlem Globetrotters are examples of pseudosports. Although athletes are involved in these activities and the activities involve physical prowess, they are not sport because they are not competitive. They may be packaged as competition, but these activities exist solely for spectator amusement.

SUMMARY

Sociology of sport as an organized field of study is less than fifty years old. Though not a rapidly growing field of study, it has advanced to the point where it is taught in most colleges and universities, and it has attracted a group of dedicated scholars with interests in research and publication as well as in teaching this subject.

The perspective, concepts, and procedures of sociology are used in this book to describe and explain the institution of sport in North America. The subject matter of sociology is social behavior and social organization. Sport involves different types of social organizations, such as teams and leagues. These, in turn, are part of larger social organizations, such as schools, communities, international associations, and society. The task of this book is to understand the principles that underlie the structures and processes that create, sustain, and transform these social organizations. Most importantly, this undertaking requires that the observer examine the social arrangements of sport from a critical stance.

Some sample questions that must direct the serious investigator are these: How does the organization really work? Who really has the power? Who benefits, and who does not?

Several social theoretical perspectives provide vantage points from which to view social life. Each of these guides our thinking, narrows our perceptions to certain relevant phenomena, and, in doing so, helps us understand our social life. We present several major theoretical perspectives that are used to understand the social world and—for our purposes—the world of sport.

The two fundamental themes of this book have been introduced in this chapter. The first is that sport is a microcosm of society. Perceiving the way sport is organized, the types of games people play, the degree of emphasis on competition, the compensation of the participants, and the enforcement of the rules is a shorthand way of understanding the complexities of the larger society in which sport is embedded. The converse is true also. The understanding of the values of society, of its types of economy, and of its treatment of minority groups, to name a few elements, provides important bases for the perception or understanding of the organization of sport in society.

The second theme is that the prevailing form of sport—the corporate level—has corrupted the original intentions of sport. Instead of player-oriented physical competition, sport has become a spectacle, a big business, and an extension of power politics. Play has become work. Spontaneity has been superseded by bureaucracy. The goal of pleasure in the physical activity has been replaced by extrinsic rewards, especially money.

WEB RESOURCES

Sport

www.bus.ucf.edu/sportbusiness/
This is the website for the Institute for Diversity and Ethics in Sport, directed by Dr. Richard Lapchick at the University of Central Florida. It provides useful information, especially on race and gender.

www.sportinsociety.org
The site for Sport in Society at Northeastern University in Boston. Sport in Society educates and supports emerging leaders and organizations within sport with the awareness, knowledge, and skills to implement innovative and impactful solutions for social change.

www.nasss.org
This is the website for the North American Society for the Sociology of Sport and its members. It provides daily announcements about current issues, bibliographic information, job openings, and notices of upcoming conferences.

www.issa.otago.ac.nz/index.html
The official site of the International Sociology of Sport Association. The objectives of ISSA are to promote international cooperation in the field of sociology of sport; to exchange information among all countries concerning the results of research in the sociology of sport; to convene international seminars or symposia on aspects of the sociology of sport; and to prepare and circulate reports about the social background of sport and the status of the sociology of sport in different countries.

www.eass-sportsociology.eu/index.html
The European Association for Sociology of Sport (EASS) was established with the aim of promoting closer cooperation and networking among experts dealing with social issues related to physical activity and sport in Europe. Many of its scholars collaborate on research with North American sport sociology.

www.cnnsi.com
The website for CNN and *Sports Illustrated*, with data and features.

www.sportdiscus.com
The world's most comprehensive source of full text for sports and sports medicine journals, providing full text for 550 journals.

http://feminist.org/sports/index.asp
The website of the Feminist Majority Foundation (FMF). It reports on the issues that are important to feminists studying sport. FMF was created to promote leadership development, especially among young women, as well as empowerment of women on the Internet and in law, business, medicine, academia, and sports.

Social Theory

www.asatheory.org
News and resources for fans and practitioners of sociological theory of all kinds. There are several links for announcements, conferences, student pages, and other resources.

General Sources

www.asanet.org
Home page of the American Sociological Association, which is dedicated to advancing sociology as

a scientific discipline and profession serving the public good. With over 14,000 members, ASA encompasses sociologists who are faculty members at colleges and universities, researchers, practitioners, and students.

www.census.gov/compendia/statab/
Summary information on economic, demographic, social, and other characteristics of the U.S. population as found in the latest edition of the *Statistical Abstract of the United States.*

www.infoplease.com
All the data that make almanacs useful, retrievable by key word or category.

NOTES

1. See John G. Bruhn, *The Sociology of Community Connections* (New York: Springer, 2005); Joseph Healey, *Race, Ethnicity, Gender, and Class: The Sociology of Group Conflict and Change,* updated 5th ed. (Newbury Park, CA: Pine Forge Press, 2009); and Charles Tilly, *Identities, Boundaries & Ties* (Boulder, CO: Paradigm Publishers, 2005).

2. For an elaboration of the discipline of sociology and the sociological perspective, see D. Stanley Eitzen, Maxine Baca Zinn, and Kelly Eitzen Smith, *In Conflict and Order: Understanding Society,* 12th ed. (Boston: Allyn & Bacon, 2010), chs. 1–2; Richard T. Schaefer, *Sociology,* 12th ed. (New York: McGraw-Hill, 2009), chs. 1–2; and Kerry Ferris and Jill Stein, *The Real World: An Introduction to Sociology,* 2nd ed. (New York: W. W. Norton, 2009).

3. This is the original publication in which "the sociological imagination" was articulated. See C. Wright Mills, *The Sociological Imagination* (New York: Oxford University Press, 1959); see also D. Stanley Eitzen and Kelly Eitzen Smith, *Experiencing Poverty: Voices from the Bottom,* 2nd ed. (Boston: Allyn & Bacon, 2008).

4. George Ritzer, *Classical Sociological Theory,* 6th ed. (New York: McGraw-Hill, 2010); Charles H. Powers, *Making Sense of Social Theory* (Lanham, MD: Rowman & Littlefield, 2010).

5. For a full description of functionalism and its relationship to sport, see John W. Loy and Douglas Booth, "Functionalism, Sport and Society," in *Handbook of Sport Studies,* ed. Jay Coakley and Eric Dunning (London: Sage, 2000), 8–27.

6. Ritzer, *Classical Sociological Theory,* pp. 128–156; see also Ben Agger, *Critical Social Theories,* 2nd ed. (Boulder, CO: Paradigm Publishers, 2006).

7. For a discussion of the conflict perspective and its relationship to sport, see Bero Rigauer, "Marxist Theories," in *Handbook of Sport Studies,* ed. Coakley and Dunning, 34–47.

8. The theory of hegemony in class societies is fully presented in Antonio Gramsci and Quintin Hoare, *Selections from the Prison Notebooks,* ed. Geoffrey Nowell Smith (New York: International Publishers, 1971); see also Simon During, *Cultural Studies: A Critical Introduction* (New York: Routledge, 2005).

9. George H. Sage, *Power and Ideology in American Sport: A Critical Perspective,* 2nd ed. (Champaign, IL: Human Kinetics, 1998).

10. The author of this book is considered one of the icons of the feminist movement. See bell hooks, *Feminist Theory: From Margin to Center* (Boston: South End Press, 2000); see also Carole McCann and Seung-kyung Kim, eds., *Feminist Theory Reader: Local and Global Perspectives,* 2nd ed. (New York: Routledge, 2009).

11. Susan Birrell, "Feminist Theories for Sport," in *Handbook of Sport Studies,* ed. Coakley and Dunning, 68.

12. Kevin Hylton, *"Race" and Sport: Critical Race Theory* (New York: Routledge, 2009), 22; see also Joshua Glasgow, *A Theory of Race* (New York: Routledge, 2009).

13. Kevin Hylton, "How a Turn to Critical Race Theory Can Contribute to Our Understanding of 'Race': Racism and Anti-Racism in Sport," *International Review for the Sociology of Sport* 45, no. 3 (2010): 338.

14. Peter Donnelly, "Interpretive Approaches to the Sociology of Sport," in *Handbook of Sport Studies,* ed. Coakley and Dunning, 77–92. For an insightful example of interpretative sociology, see Joseph R. Gusfield, "Sport as Story: Form and Content in Athletics," *Society* 37 (May/June 2000): 63–70.

15. For an excellent anthology of sociology of sport research and essay literature, see D. Stanley Eitzen, *Sport in Contemporary Society: An Anthology,* 8th ed. (Boulder, CO: Paradigm Publishers, 2009); see also D. Stanley Eitzen, *Fair and Foul: Beyond the Myths and Paradoxes of Sport,* 4th ed. (Lanham, MD: Rowman & Littlefield, 2009).

16. Eileen McDonagh and Laura Pappano, *Playing with the Boys: Why Separate Is Not Equal in Sports* (New York: Oxford University Press, 2009).

17. For a thorough discussion on the differences between play, game, and sport, see John W. Loy and Jay Coakley, "Sport," in *The Blackwell Encyclopedia of Sociology,* Vol. 9, ed. George Ritzer (Oxford: Blackwell Publishing, 2007), 4643–4653.

18. For examples of people who compete for the sheer joy of the competition, see Robin Chotzinoff, *People Who Sweat: Ordinary People, Extraordinary Pursuits* (New York: Harcourt Brace, 1999).

Social and Cultural Transformations and the Rise of Sport in North America

[T]hroughout [North] American history the form and purpose of sporting events have been closely connected to the larger society from which they arose.
—Richard O. Davies*

A college football team during the mid-1920s. Football was the most popular college sport by the 1920s. At that time, helmets had no face masks, and uniforms were plain and made from cotton and wool, not the high-tech fabrics of today. (Photo courtesy of the University of Northern Colorado Archives)

*Richard O. Davies, *Sports in American Life: A History* (Malden, MA: Blackwell, 2007), xvi.

The forms, functions, and practices of sport in any given society are rooted in historical, social, and cultural traditions, and it is our contention that a study of sport based solely on the present will result in an incomplete picture of sport as a social and cultural practice. Thus, one who studies the sociology of sport in North America without learning about sport's history on this continent will never truly understand the social and cultural forces that underpin contemporary sport. In this chapter we examine the changing sociocultural conditions of Canadian and American societies over the past four hundred years and attempt to demonstrate how these conditions have affected and influenced the rise and current state of North American sport.

The United States and Canada have experienced similar stages of historical development. Each went through a period of British control; each had a period of westward expansion; each experienced a massive influx of immigrants from Europe; and each underwent urbanization and industrialization during the late nineteenth century. The two countries share a common language, they share a border for more than 3,000 miles, and about 85 percent of the Canadian population lives within one hundred miles of the American-Canadian border. It is hard to imagine any two countries in the world having closer social and cultural ties than Canada and the U.S.[1]

Over the past four centuries, the United States and Canada have grown from a few widely scattered and disunited settlements located along the eastern seaboard of part of North America into two of the most modern and industrially advanced nations in the world. They have also become two of the leading nations in sports. Fostered by a variety of historical, political, social, and economic conditions, sports have become a major national pastime for the people of both countries. From agrarian societies whose inhabitants had little time for games and sports except on special occasions, North Americans have become two nations of citizens who watch ten to twenty hours of sports on television each weekend and consider it almost a duty to participate in some form of exercise or sport for recreation.

PRE-COLUMBIAN AND COLONIAL TRADITIONS IN NORTH AMERICA

For many centuries before European colonization began in what is now Canada and the United States, Native American settlements were scattered throughout North America. It is estimated that some 6–8 million native peoples were dispersed across the continent at the time of Columbus's voyages. What is quite clear is that although there was great diversity among the cultures of Native Americans, they all enjoyed a variety of physical play and game activities. In his book *American Indian Sports Heritage*, Joseph Oxendine—himself a member of the Lumbee tribe who grew up in a segregated Native American community in North Carolina—asserts that "games among traditional American Indians ranged from the seemingly trivial activities primarily for the amusement of children to major sporting events of significance for persons of all ages."[2] Typically, there was a close linkage between the games and sports and the world of spiritual belief and magic.

Among the various sports that were popular with Native Americans long before European settlement in North America, lacrosse seems to have been one of the most popular; thus lacrosse is often recognized as the oldest North American sport, with roots running deep into Native American history. It is perhaps the best-known Native American game because it is currently played in clubs, secondary schools, and universities throughout North America. In 1994 the Canadian Parliament recognized lacrosse as Canada's "national summer sport."[3]

The Colonists Restrict Physical Activities

During the two centuries following Columbus—the sixteenth and seventeenth centuries—Spain, France, and England explored and colonized most of North America. But by the late eighteenth century, Great Britain had triumphed over the other two countries and controlled the entire eastern half of what is now the United States and the eastern two-thirds of what is now Canada (except for two small fishing islands off the coast of Newfoundland, which remained under the control of France).

We are accustomed to thinking that the wide array of formalized participant and spectator sport that we currently enjoy has always existed. But, unimaginable as it seems, there were no formally organized participant or spectator sports during the colonial period in North America. In the first place, people had very little leisure time or opportunity to engage in games and sports. The harsh circumstances of wresting a living from the environment necessitated arduous daily work. Colonists had to devote most of their efforts to basic survival tasks.

A second factor restricting sports involvement was the church. Religion was the most powerful social institution in the North American colonies. Puritanism was prominent in the New England colonies, and other Christian religions dominated social life in the middle and southern colonies. (The subject of sport and religion is examined more fully in Chapter 8.)

All of these religious groups placed severe restrictions on play and games, with the Puritans being the most extreme. They directed attacks at almost every form of amusement: dancing for its carnality, boxing for its violence, maypoles for their paganism, and play and games in general because they were often performed on the Sabbath. Moreover, religious sanctions were closely bound to the dislike for playful activities of any kind. Honest labor was the greatest service to God, and a moral duty. Any form of play or amusement signaled time-wasting and idleness and was therefore defined as wicked. That everyone has a calling to work hard was a first premise of Puritanism. Followers believed that it was not leisure and amusement but diligent work that symbolized the glorification of God.[4]

Laws prohibiting a form of social behavior and the actual social customs and actions of a people rarely coincide. In the case of the colonies, religious and legal strictures failed to eliminate the urge to play among the early North Americans. Although frequently done in defiance of local laws, sports such as horse racing, shooting matches, cockfights, footraces, and wrestling matches were engaged in

throughout the colonies to break the monotony of life.

The most popular sports of the gentry were cockfighting, hunting, dancing, and—most popular of all—horse racing. Other recreational activities were popular among those who frequented the taverns. The tavern was a social center, primarily for drinking but also for all manner of popular pastimes, such as cards, billiards, bowling, and rifle and pistol target shooting.[5]

As colonial settlement moved west into the hinterland in the eighteenth century, religious restrictions against sport became less and less effective. Men and women in the backcountry enjoyed a variety of competitive events when they met at barbecues and camp meetings. They gambled on these contests, especially horse races, cockfights, and bearbaiting.

The physical activities that marked these infrequent social gatherings were typically rough and brutal. Two popular activities were fistfights, which ended when one man could not continue, and wrestling, in which eye gouging and bone-breaking holds were permitted.[6] Horse racing was the universal sport on the frontier, for every owner of a horse was confident of its prowess and eager to match it against others. Both men and women were skillful riders. The other constant companion of the frontiersman—the rifle—engendered a pride in marksmanship, and shooting matches were a common form of competition.[7]

Life in the colonies was quite different for African slaves, who numbered approximately 200,000 in the mid-eighteenth century, just before the American Revolution. The majority lived in what is now the southeastern United States, where plantations had developed. Most plantation slaves worked in the fields, but some were craft-workers, messengers, and servants.

Slaves were often given the responsibility for the care and maintenance of the horses owned by plantation owners for the purpose of entering them in the popular horse racing events throughout the South. Because black slaves were often adept at handling horses, many plantation owners used them as jockeys for the horses they entered in races. Boxing was also popular; some plantation owners pitted their slaves against slaves of other plantation owners, with owners gambling on the outcome an integral part of the bouts.[8]

When not working at their assigned jobs, games and sporting activities were commonly played in slave quarters by children and adults. Most plantation owners actively promoted these physical activities as a way to foster social harmony, relaxation, and fun. We will have more to say about African Americans in sport in Chapter 13.

EARLY NINETEENTH CENTURY: TAKEOFF OF INDUSTRIALIZATION, TECHNOLOGY, AND ORGANIZED SPORT

Play, games, and sports in every society are always closely tied to the political, economic, religious, and social institutions as well as the cultural traditions and customs. The major catalyst for the transformation of North American sport was a series of inventions in England in the late eighteenth century that completely changed the means by which goods were produced. These inventions made possible technological advances that ushered in two of the most important developments in human history—the industrial revolution and the technological revolution.

The major characteristic and social consequence of the industrial revolution was the factory system. The initial impact was seen in the textile industry. The spinning of thread and the weaving of cloth had traditionally been done at home on spinning wheels and handlooms, but new methods for performing these tasks enabled them to be done in factories by power-driven machinery.

Other industries emerged. The successful smelting of iron with the aid of anthracite coal was perfected around 1830. By 1850 improved methods of making steel had been developed. Steel production was the backbone of industrial development because the machinery for factories was primarily made from steel. Artisans and craftspersons were transformed into an industrial workforce.

As Figure 2.1 shows, the proportion of workers engaged in agriculture has steadily decreased—from

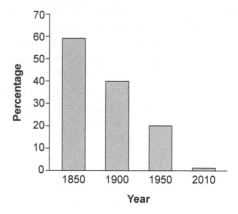

Figure 2.1   Percentage of Labor Force in Agriculture

Source: U.S. Census Bureau, *Statistical Abstracts of the United States: 2011* (Washington, DC, 2011).

approximately 60 percent in 1850, to 40 percent in 1900, to less than 10 percent in 2010. Industry needed a plentiful supply of labor located near plants and factories, so population shifts from rural to urban areas began to change population characteristics and needs. Urbanization created a need for new forms of recreational activities, and industrialization gradually supplied the standard of living and the leisure time necessary to support broad-based forms of recreation and organized sport.[9]

Building a Framework for Organized Sport

In the first few decades of the nineteenth century, North Americans enjoyed essentially the same recreation and sports as they had during the colonial period. As conditions gradually changed from a rural to an increasingly urban population and from home trades and individualized occupations to large-scale industrial production, a growing interest emerged in spectator sports. Rowing, prizefighting, footracing (the runners were called pedestrians), and similar activities were especially popular, but the sport that excited the most interest was horse racing, with its traditions going back to early colonial days.

In May of 1823 a horse race between Eclipse and Sir Henry—the superstar horses of that era—

attracted one of the largest crowds ever to witness a nineteenth-century sporting event in North America. A crowd estimated at 75,000 overwhelmed the racecourse. But thoroughbred racing was not the only popular form of horse racing. Harness racing had an enthusiastic following, and it has even been claimed that harness racing was the first modern sport in North America.[10]

Horse racing was also much in demand in Canada. In *Canada's Sporting Heroes*, S. F. Wise and Douglas Fisher described its popularity in Quebec: "Almost from the outset of British rule in 1763 French Canadians took readily to . . . horse racing. . . . By 1829, interest was so great that special boat trips were laid on to bring Montrealers to Quebec for the races, and the Montreal newspaper *La Minerve* held its presses in order to bring its readers the latest results. . . . By the 1850s . . . regular race meetings were held in forty towns and villages throughout the province."[11]

Native American, French, and British traditions contributed to Canada's other sporting interests in the early nineteenth century. Native American games of lacrosse, snowshoeing, and canoe activities were adopted by the settlers. British and French settlers also took enthusiastically to physical activities that could be played in the cold northern climate, so sleighing, ice-skating, and curling were popular in the winter, while hunting, fishing, fox hunting, and horse racing were popular in the short Canadian summers.[12]

The transformation from occasional and informal sport to highly organized commercial spectator sport began for both the United States and Canada during the period before the American Civil War. Thus, the framework of modern sport was established during the first half of the nineteenth century, setting the stage for the remarkable expansion of mass popular sport and professional sport that followed in the second half of the nineteenth century.

The Technological Revolution and Sport

Technological advances have been a dominant force for social change, for adaptations in social relationships, and for the transformation of business and governmental organizations over the past two hundred years. Beginning in the early nineteenth century, technological advances made possible the large-scale manufacturing that is characteristic of industrialization. Through technology, which is the practical application of science to industry, many kinds of machines, labor-saving devices, and scientific processes were invented or perfected. Technological development was one of the most significant forces transforming sport from informal village festivals to highly organized sports. Of course, the technological revolution was only one of the factors contributing to the rise of modern sport, but ignoring its influence would result in an incomplete understanding of contemporary sport forms.

New Forms of Transportation Broaden Sport Opportunities

One area of technological innovation that had an enormous impact on the rise of sport was transportation. Travel of any kind was difficult and slow in the pre-1800 period. A distance that today takes hours to travel took more than the same number of days in those times. Modes of transportation were limited to foot, horse, and boat. Roads, when they existed, were primitive, dangerous, and often blocked by almost impassable rivers.

The first notable technological breakthrough in transportation came in the early nineteenth century with the development of the steam engine. This invention and its use on boats made it possible to fully develop river traffic. The first successful steamboat in North America, the *Clermont*, was built by Robert Fulton, and in 1807 it chugged 150 miles up the Hudson River from New York to Albany in about thirty hours. In time, steamboats stimulated the building of canals and the enlarging of rivers, thus opening new areas that had previously been isolated and cut off from commerce and trade.[13]

The steamboat did not solve all the transportation problems; river travel was of no help to people who did not happen to live near large rivers. Furthermore, it was not a particularly fast mode of transportation because the large steamers sometimes had to thread their way carefully through very narrow or shallow water.

A new form of transportation began to compete with river transportation around the time that canal building reached its peak. This was the railroad. A fourteen-mile stretch of the Baltimore and Ohio Railroad was opened in 1830. Railroad construction expanded rapidly—mostly short lines connecting principal cities—and by 1840 nearly 3,000 miles of track were in use in the United States.

It was the steamboats and railroads of the first half of the nineteenth century that had the first significant impact on sport. As one of the first products of the age of steam, steamboats served as carriers of thoroughbred horses to such horse racing centers as Vicksburg, Natchez, and New Orleans, all located along the Mississippi River. Crowds attending horse races or prizefights were frequently conveyed to the site of the event via steamboats. The riverboats on the Mississippi and the St. Lawrence also served as carriers of racing or prizefight news up and down the river valleys.

More important to the development of organized sport was the railroad. In the years preceding the American Civil War, the widespread interest in thoroughbred and harness races was in great part nurtured by railroad expansion, as horses and crowds were transported from one locality to another. Similarly, participants and spectators for prizefights and footraces were commonly carried to the sites of competition by rail. Scheduling the fights where they would not be disrupted by the authorities frequently became necessary because prizefighting was outlawed in many cities. This meant that spectators often had to use the railroad to get to the site of the bout.

New Forms of Communication Enable Dissemination of Sport Information

As important as transportation was to the rise of North American sport, the new forms of communication over the past century and a half have been equally significant. The invention and development of the telegraph was the most important advance in communication during the first half of the nineteenth century. Samuel F. B. Morse perfected an electrical instrument by which combinations of dots and dashes could be transmitted along a wire, and the first telegraph line was built between Baltimore and Washington, DC, in 1844. Soon telegraph lines stretched between all the principal cities, and by 1860 some 50,000 miles of line existed

east of the Rockies. Meanwhile, Western Union was extending its lines to the Pacific coast, putting the Pony Express out of business a little more than a year after it was founded.

From its invention in 1844, the telegraph rapidly assumed a significant role in the dissemination of sport news because newspapers and periodicals installed telegraphic apparatuses in their offices. Only two years after its invention, the *New York Herald* and the *New York Tribune* had telegraphic equipment. By 1850, horse races, prizefights, and yachting events were regularly reported over the wires.

Simultaneously with the development of the telegraph, a revolution in the dissemination of news occurred with improvements in printing presses and in other processes of newspaper and journal production. The telegraph and the improved press opened the gates to a rising tide of sports journalism, but the journalistic exploitation of sports did not actually take off until the last two decades of the nineteenth century.

While advances in electrical forms of communication were instrumental in the rise of sport, other communications media supplemented and extended sport publicity. In the early years of the nineteenth century, sports were more directly aided by magazine and book publishers than they were by newspapers. However, the rise of sports journalism was closely tied to new inventions in printing processes as well as to the telegraph network that spanned the continent in the mid-1800s.

As early as the 1830s, several of the largest newspapers were giving extensive coverage to prizefights, footraces, horse races, and other sports. What was perhaps the most notable newspaper concerned with sports in the United States—*The Spirit of the Times*—appeared in 1831 and survived until 1901.[14]

LATTER NINETEENTH CENTURY: THE BEGINNINGS OF MODERN SPORT

Entering the second half of the nineteenth century, North America was predominantly a land of small farms, small towns, and small business enterprises. But over the next fifty years economic, technological, and social changes transformed the lives of Americans and Canadians. Both countries evolved from rural and traditional societies into modern, industrialized nations. By the beginning of the twentieth century, citizens and immigrants in both nations were laboring in factories owned by large corporations.

Before 1850, U.S. industry had been largely concentrated in New England and the mid-Atlantic states, but by 1900 industrialization and manufacturing spread out to all parts of the country. As the factory system took root, however, a capitalistic class began to emerge, and a new form of business ownership, the corporation, became the dominant form of organization.

By the 1890s, corporations produced nearly three-fourths of the total value of manufactured products in the United States. The large corporations developed mass-production methods and mass sales, the bases of big business, because of the huge amounts of money they controlled.

Meanwhile, the conflict over control of the vast Canadian expanse of the continent, which had remained unresolved throughout the sixteenth, seventeenth, and eighteenth centuries, was finally settled with the Confederation of Canadian Provinces in 1867. Canada became the first federal union in the British Empire, and the second half of the nineteenth century was a period of consolidation of provinces within the union.

Canadian industrialization was proceeding along a trajectory similar to that in the northeastern United States, and by the middle of the nineteenth century Canadian industry was well under way in Montreal and Quebec City. Little by little, factories appeared in those cities and provided jobs for thousands of workers. At the time of confederation, manufacturing in Canada was still primarily of a local handicraft nature requiring very little capital, and much of the trade was based on farming, fishing, and timber products. However, beginning in the 1870s, Canadian manufacturing received an impetus from the new industrial revolution of steel and railroads, and advanced technology and corporate organization fostered a unified market and a factory system of specialized mass production to serve it.

As technology increased the means of industrial production in both Canada and the United States, more and more people gave up farming and came to the cities to work in factories and offices. They were joined by a seemingly endless stream of immigrants who sought a better life in North America. Factories multiplied, and towns and cities grew rapidly. The first U.S. census, completed in 1790, recorded a population of nearly 4 million, about 6 percent of whom were classified as urban; by 1900 the population had risen to 76 million, with some 40 percent living in urban areas.

Figure 2.2 shows the general pattern of growth in urban population. From 1860 to 1910 the number of U.S. cities with populations over 100,000 increased from 9 to 50. The 1871 census of Canada reported that there were only 20 communities with more than 5,000 residents; by 1901 there were 62, and 24 of those had a population of more than 10,000.

Urbanization and the Rise of Modern Sport Forms

Urban influences in both the United States and Canada had made their marks by the mid-nineteenth century, and the increasing concentration of city

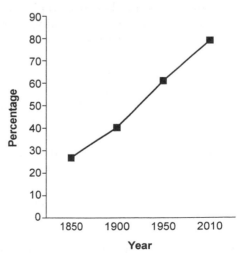

Figure 2.2 Percentage of U.S. Population in Urban Areas

populations and the monotonous and wearisome repetition of industrial work created a demand for more recreational outlets. Urbanization created favorable conditions for commercialized spectator sports, while industrialization gradually provided the leisure time and standard of living so crucial to the growth and development of all forms of recreation and sport.

Towns and cities were natural centers for organizing sports. The popular sport of horse racing centered in New York, Boston, Charleston, Louisville, and New Orleans, and the first organized baseball clubs were founded in such communities as New York, Boston, Chicago, St. Louis, and Toronto. Yachting and rowing regattas, footraces, boxing events, billiard matches, and even the main agricultural fairs were held in or near the larger cities.

Diffusion of Sport from the Upper to the Lower Classes

Nothing in the recreational and sport scene was more startling than the sudden spread of sporting activities from the wealthy class into the upper-middle, the middle, and even the working class. Millionaires pursued horse racing, yachting, lawn tennis, and golf. Working women and young ladies of the middle class turned to rowing and cycling, and working-class men played pool, fished, hunted, backed their favorite boxers, and gradually tried their hands at the sports of the affluent classes. The long winters in Canada provided plenty of opportunity for both affluent and working people to participate in skiing, ice-skating, curling, and other cold weather sports.

During the second half of the nineteenth century, people tried to adapt to the new urban-industrial society by forming subcommunities based on status. One type of status community was the athletic club, formed by younger, wealthy men who shared a common interest in sports. The private clubs were a major stimulus to the growth of yachting, baseball, lawn tennis, golf, track and field, and country clubs. Essentially the same pattern of upper-class promotion of organized sport through social elite sports clubs existed in Canada. Thus, members of the social elite in both the United States and Canada deserve much credit for early sporting promotion and patronage.[15]

New sports introduced by the wealthy were often adopted by the working class. Baseball is a classic example of this pattern. From an informal children's game played throughout the eighteenth century, baseball developed codified rules in the 1840s, and groups of upper-social-class men organized clubs, taking care to keep out lower-social-class persons. The first of these baseball clubs, the Knickerbockers of New York, was primarily a social club with a distinctly upper-class flavor; it was similar to the country clubs of the 1920s and 1930s before they became popular with the middle class. A baseball game for members of the Knickerbockers was a genteel amateur recreational pursuit, with an emphasis on polite social interactions rather than an all-out quest for victory.[16]

In the United States the Civil War wiped out this upper-class patronage of the game, and a broad base of popularity existed in 1869 when the first professional baseball team, the Cincinnati Red Stockings, was formed. This was followed in 1876 by the organization of the first major league, and baseball became firmly entrenched as the American national pastime by the end of the century.

Baseball attracted the interest of Canadians as well, and by 1859, Torontonians had begun playing the game, spurring an expansion of play to other cities. In the mid-1880s, clubs from Toronto, Hamilton, London, and Guelph had formed Canada's first professional baseball league. By the end of the nineteenth century, baseball was solidly embedded in Canada's sporting culture.[17]

At about the same time, ice hockey, which was to become Canada's national pastime, was making its own early history. It seems to have been played in its earliest unorganized form in the mid-1850s, but the first public showing of the game took place in 1875. Ice hockey quickly became a favorite sport of Canadians.

As cities grew, an element of the population that journalists referred to as "rabble" and "rowdies" stimulated interest in organized sports. Wherever sports events were held, members of this group could be found gambling on the outcome and generally raising the emotional atmosphere of the event by wildly cheering their favorites and booing or attempting to disconcert those whom they had bet against. Although sports organizers publicly

Portraits of the original Cincinnati Red Stockings team members, ca. 1869. This was the first professional baseball team in the United States. The Red Stockings played games from coast to coast and chalked up a fabulous winning streak of sixty-five games without a defeat. (Library of Congress)

condemned the actions of this unruly element, they secretly spurred them on because this group often helped ensure the financial success of sporting events.

The Role of African Americans in Sports

Despite living under conditions of slavery in the southern colonies, African Americans engaged in a wide variety of games and sport. Some were even trained by their plantation owners as boxers and jockeys. Emancipation in the mid-1860s gave African Americans hopes of participating in sports along with whites, but the post–Civil War years saw a mass social disenfranchisement of African Americans (see Box 2.1). Although a few African Americans played on professional baseball teams in the second half of the nineteenth century, many white players refused to play with the black players,

so team owners stopped hiring blacks. As other professional and amateur sports developed during the latter nineteenth century, African Americans were barred from participation in most of them. This issue is discussed in more detail in Chapter 13.

The Role of Immigrants in Sports

Between 1870 and 1900, some 12 million persons immigrated to the United States. At the beginning of this period, one-third of all U.S. industrial workers were immigrants; by 1900, more than half were foreign-born. During the same period approximately 1.2 million immigrants entered the Canadian provinces.

Immigrants in both countries contributed to the rise of sport in a variety of ways. First, many immigrants settled in the cities and became a part of that urban population that sought excitement through sport and recreation as an antidote to the typically dull and monotonous jobs they held. Second, because a great many of these nineteenth-century immigrants did not possess the strict religious attitudes toward play and sport of the fundamental Protestant sects, they freely enjoyed and participated in sports of all kinds. Third, the immigrants brought their games and sports with them to North America. Cricket, horse racing, and rowing were widely popular with the British immigrants. The Germans brought their love for lawn bowling and gymnastics. German *turnverein* (gymnastic clubs) were opened wherever Germans settled; by the time of the Civil War, there were approximately 150 American *turnverein* with some 10,000 members.[18]

In Canada in 1859, German migrants had organized a *turnverein* in what is now Kitchener, and a Turner Association with forty members was active in Toronto in 1861. The Scots pioneered in introducing track-and-field sports to North America with their annual Caledonian games. In a definitive study, sport historian Gerald Redmond quite convincingly showed that the "emigrant Scots" were a dominant force in the development of Canadian sport in the nineteenth century.[19]

The Irish seemed to have a particular affinity for the prize ring, and some of the most famous nineteenth-century boxers in North America were immigrants from Ireland. Two Irish American

Box 2.1   *Thinking About Sport:* Horse Racing and the Great African American Jockeys

Baseball was not America's first "national pastime." Before the Civil War it was horse racing that captured the sporting interest and enthusiasm of Americans, and 150 years before Jackie Robinson, African American jockeys competed alongside whites in horse races throughout the country. In spite of the slavery system, racehorse owners and trainers recognized the skill, courage, and determination of African American jockeys and didn't hesitate to use them to win horse races. But most people are unaware of the excellence of the African American jockeys during this period because, as one historian put it, "The black jockeys were ridden out of history."

The status of black jockeys remained high in the years immediately following the Civil War. Indeed, in the first Kentucky Derby, held in 1875, the jockey on the winning horse was an African American, Oliver Lewis. More impressive, of the fifteen jockeys in that race, thirteen were African Americans. This was not unusual: Until Jim Crow laws set in, segregating blacks and whites near the end of the nineteenth century, African Americans dominated the sport of horse racing—much as they do in NBA basketball today. Most horse racing

historians regard Isaac Murphy as the greatest jockey in the country in the decade and a half between 1884 and 1900. Murphy won his first Kentucky Derby in 1884. He became the first jockey to win two consecutive Kentucky Derbys, and his record of riding three Kentucky Derby winners was not equaled until 1930.

By the end of the 1890s, African American jockeys were the subjects of virulent racism sweeping the country in the form of a landmark U.S. Supreme Court decision, *Plessy v. Ferguson,* which upheld the constitutionality of racial segregation in public venues under the doctrine of "separate but equal." In his book *The Great Black Jockeys,* historian Edward Hotaling laments: "By the early 1900s, the great black jockeys had gone from winning the Kentucky Derby to not being able to get a mount. . . . For all intents and purposes they had vanished from the American racetrack." And their records of excellence, courage, and achievements have all but vanished from sports history, along with the admiration that should be theirs.

Source: Edward Hotaling, *The Great Black Jockeys* (Rocklin, CA: Forum, 1999).

boxing champions, John L. Sullivan and James J. Corbett, were among the most popular sports heroes of the century.

The Beginnings of Intercollegiate Athletics

The first North American colleges were established during the colonial period. They were small, widely scattered, and religiously oriented, and in what became the United States, most were less than thirty years old when the colonial period ended. During the latter half of the nineteenth century, colleges became the source for one of the most popular forms of sport: intercollegiate athletics.

Intercollegiate athletics began in the United States in 1852 with a rowing match between Harvard and Yale. But it was not until the 1870s and 1880s that intercollegiate sports became an established part of higher education and contributed to the enthusiasm for athletic and sporting diversions. Football became an extremely popular spectator sport during this era. It was a sport for the affluent classes rather than for the masses because it largely

reflected the interests of the college students and alumni; the pigskin game (an early nickname for the sport) nevertheless did develop into a national sport by 1900.

After students organized teams, collegiate sports revolutionized campus life, serving as a major source of physical activity for many students and a significant source of entertainment for other students, alumni, and the general public. In the United States, intercollegiate athletics gradually became more than merely a demonstration of physical skills between rival institutions. Students, alumni, and the public began to regard victory as the measure of a college's prestige. Campus and commercial editors increased their coverage, and sports events became featured items in newspapers and magazines. As a result, this increased coverage focused attention on winning and made contest results appear to be an index of an institution's merit.[20]

Thus, a belief emerged throughout American colleges that winning teams favorably advertised the school, attracted prospective students, enhanced alumni contributions, and—in the case of state-supported universities—increased appropriations from the state legislature. The notion that successful teams brought renown to the college (and to its president) must surely have been in the mind of University of Chicago president William Rainey Harper when he hired Yale All-American Amos Alonzo Stagg in 1890. He asked Stagg to "develop teams which we can send around the country and knock out all the colleges. We will give them a palace car and a vacation too."[21]

Technological Innovation and Sport: Transportation

Technological innovation continued to serve as a dominant force for shaping social change through-out the second half of the nineteenth century. Transportation was one of the most prominent areas of its influence, as the growth of the railroad industry continued throughout the latter nineteenth century. Shortly after the Civil War, the Central Pacific and Union Pacific workers laid the final rail to complete the first transcontinental line in North America. Other lines followed in the last three decades of the 1800s. Similar events were occurring in Canada. In November 1885 the transcontinental Canadian Pacific Railway was completed.[22]

The railroad played an instrumental role in staging the first intercollegiate athletic event, a rowing race between Harvard and Yale. According to sport historian Ronald A. Smith, "the offer by a railroad superintendent to transport and house the crews of the two most prestigious

The start of the race, Kelowna, British Columbia, 1909. Thoroughbred and trotting racing were among the sporting pursuits fostered by railroad development. (G. H. Hudson/Library and Archives Canada)

colleges [Harvard and Yale] at a vacation spot over a hundred miles from the Cambridge campus and nearly twice that distance from New Haven was the beginning of . . . college sport in America."[23] The offer was accepted, and the Boston, Concord, and Montreal Railroad transported the participants and fans to New Hampshire's Lake Winnipesaukee for the event.

In 1869 the first intercollegiate football game, between Rutgers and Princeton, was attended by students riding a train pulled by a jerky little locomotive engine that chugged out of Princeton, New Jersey, on the morning of November 6, 1869. The historic McGill-Harvard football match of 1870, which pitted a Canadian university against an American university, would not have been played without the convenience of railway transportation. Throughout the final decades of the nineteenth century, intercollegiate athletic teams depended upon the railroad to transport teams and supporters to football, baseball, and rowing events as well as to other collegiate athletic contests.

Fledgling professional baseball clubs made use of the rapidly expanding railroad network in the 1870s, and the organization of the National League in 1876 became possible primarily because of the continued development of connecting lines. As Major League Baseball developed, the formation of teams followed the network of rail lines, a pattern that remained basically undisturbed until the late 1950s, when teams began to travel by air.

Many other sporting pursuits were fostered by railroad development after 1865. Widespread interest in thoroughbred and trotting racing was in large part sustained by the expansion of the railway system. Interregional races became possible, and horses and spectators were carried from all over the country to track races. The rail lines capitalized on public interest in prizefighting, too, despite its illegality, and frequently scheduled excursion trains for important bouts. America's first heavyweight champion, John L. Sullivan, acquired his popularity largely through his train tours to various parts of the country.

The role played by the railroads in the promotion of sport in the United States was being dupli-

cated in Canada. The Canadian Pacific Railway Company had a special interest in the Montreal Baseball Club and offered full exemption for team managers, and special half-fare rates to teams willing to play the club. Rowing was also popularized by the railroads as there were many generous concessions granted to rowing enthusiasts.

Technological Innovation and Sport: Communication

The Atlantic cable, successfully laid in 1866 by Cyrus Field, did for intercontinental news what the telegraph had done for national communication. The cable reduced the time necessary to send a message between Europe and North America from ten days (by steamship) to a moment or so. This advance in communication was a boon to sports enthusiasts, for it overcame the frustration of having to wait two or three weeks to get sports results from England and the rest of Europe.

In 1869, when the Harvard crew traveled to England to row against Oxford on the Thames River, enormous national interest centered on the match. Along the sidewalks in New York, the Harvard-Oxford race was the main topic of conversation. According to a New York newspaper reporting on the event, the results of the race were "flashed through the Atlantic cable as to reach New York about a quarter past one, while the news reached the Pacific Coast about nine o'clock, enabling many of the San Franciscans to discuss the subject at their breakfast tables, and swallow the defeat with their coffee."[24] All this was the culmination of a campaign in transatlantic news coverage that had begun months earlier and served as the first real test of the Atlantic cable. The combination of telegraph and Atlantic cable aroused great interest in international sport.

The major communications breakthrough in the latter part of the nineteenth century was the telephone, which was first exhibited at the Centennial Exposition in Philadelphia in 1876. There, Alexander Graham Bell demonstrated that an electrical instrument could transmit the human voice. Although at first most people thought of the telephone as a plaything, business and industrial leaders saw its possibilities for maintaining communication with their far-flung interests.

Newspapers were one of the first businesses to make extensive use of telephone service, and the sports departments founded by many of the newspapers in the last two decades of the nineteenth century depended on the telephone to obtain the results of sports events. By the end of the century, the telephone was an indispensable part of sports journalism.

The expansion of sports journalism in the latter three decades of the nineteenth century related not only to the universal use of telegraphy by publishers, which made possible instantaneous reporting of sports events, but also to the realization by editors of the popular interest in sports. Indeed, sport emerged as such a standard topic of conversation that newspapers and magazines extended their coverage of it in the 1880s and 1890s.

At the same time, the number of newspapers in the United States increased sixfold between 1870 and 1900 (from 387 to 2,326), and their combined circulation rose from 3.5 million to 15 million. Publishers and editors recognized the growing interest in sport and began to cater to it to win large circulations. New York papers such as the *Herald*, the *Sun*, and the *World* devoted enough attention to sports that a new form of reporter, the sports journalist, emerged. It remained, however, for William Randolph Hearst to develop the first sports section for his paper, the *New York Journal*.[25]

The publication of various kinds of books about sports increased in the mid-nineteenth century, too. Athletic almanacs and dime novels extolling the exploits of athletes and sportsmen grew in popularity. Two books by Thomas Hughes, *Tom Brown at Rugby* and *Tom Brown at Oxford*, were responsible for a rising desire for sports fiction. In 1896 Gilbert Patten began pouring out a story a week of the heroic achievements of a fictional athlete by the name of Frank Merriwell to meet the demand for boys' sports stories. At the height of Frank Merriwell's popularity, circulation reached an estimated 200,000 copies per week. Before he was through, Patten had produced 208 titles, which sold an estimated 25 million copies.[26]

Technological Innovation and Equipment to Play Modern Sports

Modern sports are dependent upon inexpensive and dependable equipment for their popularity. Corporate organization and basic production of goods developed in sport just as they did in other industries. Although the manufacturing and merchandising of sporting goods were still in the pioneer stage of development in the late nineteenth century, much of the growing popularity of sport and outdoor recreation was due to technological advances that made possible the standardized manufacture of bicycles, billiard tables, baseball equipment, sporting rifles, fishing rods, and numerous other items.

The first major sporting goods corporation was formed in 1876 by Albert G. Spalding, a former pitcher for the Boston and Chicago baseball clubs. Beginning with baseball equipment, he branched out into various other sports. By the end of the century, A. G. Spalding and Brothers Company had a virtual monopoly in athletic goods. Department stores, led by Macy's of New York City, began carrying sporting goods on a large scale around the early 1880s. Sears, Roebuck devoted eighty pages of its 1895 catalog to sporting equipment.[27]

With the rising popularity of numerous sports in the twentieth century, advances in technology that have made possible the introduction of newer and better equipment, and improved manufacturing and distribution methods, the sporting goods industry has become a multimillion-dollar-a-year industry. Several large corporations control a major portion of the business, but with the proliferation of sports, many small companies also produce a variety of sports equipment.

Other Technological Breakthroughs and Sport

Other technological advances had a marked, though perhaps less obvious, influence on the transformation of sport. Improvements in photography developed rapidly in the years following the Civil War, as cumbersome equipment was replaced by the more mobile Eastman Kodak, which also produced clearer pictures. Indeed, sport played an important role in the early development and popularization of the camera. In 1872 Eadweard Muybridge, with the prodding of Leland Stanford, made the first successful attempt to record the illusion of motion by photography. He was interested in discovering whether a trotting horse leaves the ground entirely at some point in its gait (it does). By setting up a battery of cameras that went off sequentially, he successfully photographed the movements of the horse. The clarity of these pictures led Muybridge to realize that his technique could be extended to analyze the movements of all kinds of species. He subsequently photographed a host of walking and running animals. His monumental eleven-volume study, titled *Animal Locomotion* (1887), included thousands of pictures of horses, birds, and even human athletes. Other experimenters gradually perfected the techniques that gave birth to the true motion picture.

We have already described how advances in the use of electricity led to important developments in communication, but the use of electricity to produce light had an equally significant impact on sport. When Thomas A. Edison invented the incandescent bulb in 1879, he inaugurated a new era in the social life of North Americans. With the invention of the lightbulb, sports events for the first time could be held at night. Within a few years, electric lighting and more comfortable accommodations helped lure athletes and spectators into school and college gymnasiums and into public arenas and stadiums.

Prizefights, walking contests, horse shows, wrestling matches, basketball games, ice hockey games, curling matches, and other sports began to be held indoors in lighted facilities. Madison Square Garden in New York City had electric lights by the mid-1880s (the current Madison Square Garden is its fourth incarnation), where they were used for a variety of sports events. Much of the appeal of indoor sporting events was directly attributed to the transformation that electric lighting made in the nightlife of the cities.

One final example of the part an invention has played in sport is the vulcanization of rubber by Charles Goodyear in the 1830s. It eventually influenced equipment and apparel in every sport. Elastic and resilient rubber balls changed the nature of every sport in which they were used; equipment made with rubber altered many tactics and techniques. The pneumatic tire developed in the 1880s revolutionized cycling and harness racing in the following decade, and it played a vital role in the rise and spectacular appeal of auto racing.

The Cult of Manliness and Sport

The technological, social, and occupational changes of the nineteenth century prompted concern about the impact of modernization on traditional cultural male roles and behavior. There was mounting evidence that modernization was indeed altering institutions of socialization and drastically changing traditional male roles and responsibilities. Writers, educators, and influential national leaders expressed fear that men were losing "masculine" traits—such as toughness, courage, ruggedness, and hardiness—to effeminacy. There were even worries about the future of the U.S. and Canada as nations, if men lost their masculine traits. Various organizations—the Boy Scouts, the YMCA, and athletic clubs—arose to promote a broadly based devotion to manly ideals to toughen up boys for life's challenges.

Within this perceived threat to masculinity, sport, with its demands for individual competition and physical challenge, was advocated as an important preparation for manhood. In towns and cities throughout the United States and Canada, sport rose as a counterforce to what many men saw as the "feminization" of North American civilization. Sport was seen as a sanctuary from the world of female gentility; it catered to men who felt a need to demonstrate their manhood. Organized sport participation had become a prominent source for male identity and a primary basis for gender division.

The cult of manliness became pervasive in the upper and middle classes and rapidly trickled down to working-class social life. One sport historian declared: "The frequency with which writers began to assert that sport could serve as a means of promoting manliness was in direct response to both the impact of modernization on urban society and the role of modernization in redefining the masculine role and creating a new middle-class view of proper sexual behavior."[28]

Defining sport as an inculcator of manliness had the obvious effect of discouraging women from all but a few sports—and women could participate in those only in moderation. Indeed, women who wished to participate in competitive sports and remain "feminine" faced almost certain social isolation and censure.

Of course, it was not just the cult of manliness that discouraged female involvement in sport. Responsibility for domestic labor and child-rearing weighed heavily against women's engagement in sport as either participants or spectators. Victorian attitudes and religious moral codes also militated against sport for women. In spite of these obstacles, many upper-class and college women were ardent participants in croquet, archery, lawn tennis, rowing, and bicycling (see Box 2.2).

Muscular Christianity and Intellectuals

In parallel with the cult of manliness another cultural trend was gaining attention. The grasp of religion on the early-nineteenth-century mind was so strong and conservative that sport could penetrate only the periphery of social life. But reaction to the

---

Box 2.2   Thinking About Sport: Women on Bicycles

For women of the latter nineteenth century the first struggle was for the right to ride a bicycle, because there was a segment of society that staunchly believed that physical activity should remain a man's world and that women should refrain from active pursuits. Susan B. Anthony, a prominent American civil rights activist who played a pivotal role in the nineteenth-century women's rights movement, described the socially significant role the bicycle had in advancing women's status:

> Let me tell you what I think of bicycling. I think it has done more to emancipate women than anything else in the world. It gives women a feeling of freedom and self-reliance. I stand and rejoice every time I see a woman ride by on a wheel . . . the picture of free, untrammeled womanhood.

Source: Quoted in Sue Macy, "The Devil's Advance Agent," American History 46, no. 4 (October 2011), p. 45.

Puritan belief that pleasure was the companion of sin emerged when liberal and humanitarian reform became a major concern. One aspect of the social reform that became known as the "Muscular Christianity Movement" was the effort to improve the physical health of the population. The crusaders noted that a great deal of human misery was the result of poor health, and they believed that people would be happier and more productive if they engaged in sport to promote physical fitness and enhance leisure.

Muscular spirituality leaders were highly respected persons, willing to risk their positions and reputations on behalf of exercise and sport. The Beecher families, famous for their Christian reform positions, were among the first active crusaders for exercise and sport. Catharine Beecher wrote a book in 1832 entitled *Course of Calisthenics for Young Ladies*, but her most influential book was *A Manual of Physiology and Calisthenics for Schools and Families*, published in 1856. This book not only advocated physical exercise for girls as well as for boys but also promoted the introduction of physical education into American schools.

Throughout the second half of the nineteenth century, physical activity continued to be supported by many respected persons. Noted author Oliver Wendell Holmes claimed that more participation in sport would improve everything in American life from sermons of the clergy to the physical well-being of individuals. Equally vigorous in his advocacy of sport was the renowned Ralph Waldo Emerson, whose status in the intellectual community served to increase the impact of his support. The combined attention of the clergy, social reformers, and intellectuals to the need for physical fitness and wholesome leisure had a favorable effect upon public attitudes because sport suddenly became important to many people, especially the young, who had previously shunned it.[29]

Social Philosophy and Organized Sport

The profound changes in interpersonal relations created by the technological and industrial revolutions required that moral and social justifications be sought for the role of capitalism, the economic system in which trade and industry are controlled by private owners for profit. Leading capitalists found their chief justification in two related ideas, the gospel of wealth and social Darwinism. According to the gospel of wealth, great rewards awaited those who applied themselves and followed the rules. Money and success are the just rewards for hard work, thrift, and sobriety; the mass of humanity remains poor because of their own laziness and natural inferiority. Government, according to this notion, should merely preserve order and protect property; it should leave control over the economy to the natural aristocracy, who have won and hold their leadership in the competitive struggle of the marketplace.

Social Darwinism, probably the most important social philosophy in the latter third of the nineteenth century, supplied a biological explanation for the gospel of wealth. As an integrated philosophy, it was largely the product of the fertile mind of the British political theorist and sociologist Herbert Spencer. Spencer was profoundly impressed by Charles Darwin's findings in the field of biology, and he constructed his system on Darwin's principles of the survival of the fittest. Darwin had reported that in the animal world an ongoing, fierce struggle for survival destroys the weak, rewards the strong, and produces evolutionary change. Struggle, destruction, and the survival of the fit, Spencer argued, are essential to progress in human societies as well. The weak threaten the road to progress and deserve to perish. The strong survive because they are superior.

Spencer's theories had great popularity and markedly penetrated North American thought. American historian Richard Hofstadter claimed that "American society saw its own image in the tooth-and-claw version of natural selection and . . . its dominant groups were therefore able to dramatize this vision of competition as a thing good in itself."[30] This was the case for several reasons but perhaps chiefly because social Darwinism was made to order to suit the needs of the ruling business interests. It justified the "success ethic" in the name of progress; it justified economic warfare, poverty, exploitation, and suffering as the survival of the fittest.

The chief North American expositor of social Darwinism was William Graham Sumner, who in 1875 at Yale taught one of the first sociology courses in North America. Sumner based his sociology on the notion that human life encounters formidable obstacles and threats to its survival. There is a fundamental struggle to "win" (a favorite word of Sumner's) under the conditions imposed by nature. In this process humans always compete with others. Sumner argued, "Every man who stands on the earth's surface excludes every one else from so much of it as he covers; everyone who eats a loaf of bread appropriates to himself for the time being the exclusive use and enjoyment of so many square feet of the earth's surface as were required to raise the wheat."[31]

Sumner linked competition to the emergence of virtues, such as those of perseverance and hard work, which were presumed to be answers to the struggle against nature. Winning was seen as the just reward of the superior individual; losing was viewed as the overt manifestation of inferiority.

A number of observers have noted that the rise of highly organized sport coincided with the emergent popularity of social Darwinism and that the high degree of emphasis on winning games demonstrated in North American sport is an orientation congruent with this social philosophy. American football players often remark that success in their sport is like "the law of the jungle" or "the survival of the fittest." Similar opinions about ice hockey are sometimes expressed by Canadian ice hockey players.

TWENTIETH AND TWENTY-FIRST CENTURIES: THE MODERN WORLD AND SPORT

The United States witnessed a population explosion in the twentieth century; it began the century with 76 million and ended it with a population in excess of 281 million and an urban population of around 85 percent of the total. Canada experienced a similar trend. In 1900 its population was approximately 4 million, with less than 20 percent living in towns and cities; in 2000 Canada had a population of more than 30 million, more than 77 percent of whom were urbanites.

The concentration of large groups of people in towns that soon would become thriving cities made it possible for sport to be transformed from informal and spontaneous events to organized, highly competitive activities. In other words, industrialization and urbanization were major contributors to the rise of sport, greatly enhanced, of course, by the revolutionary transformations in communication, transportation, and other technological advances.

The Maturing of Modern Sport

The final three decades of the nineteenth century saw the rising tide of sports begin to take a place in the lives of North Americans, but it was in the first half of the twentieth century that the sporting spirit became a prominent part of the social life of large numbers of people. Between 1900 and World War II, sport became the most pervasive popular cultural practice in North America.

Urban areas fostered sport through better transportation facilities, a growing affluent class, a higher standard of living, more discretionary funds for purchasing sporting equipment, and the ease with which leagues and teams could be organized. The wealthy were no longer the only people with the leisure and the means to enjoy recreational pursuits. Working-class persons

Women's college basketball team, 1901. In the first thirty years of the twentieth century, the athletic spirit became a prominent part of the social life of large numbers of people. Between 1900 and World War II, sport became the most pervasive popular cultural practice in North America. (Photo courtesy of the University of Northern Colorado Archives)

gradually won shorter working hours and higher wages, enabling them to spend larger sums of discretionary money on entertainment, one form of which was sport.

Thus, sport discarded its aristocratic trappings and rapidly emerged as a popular form of entertainment and recreation. James Bryce, a British observer of American life in 1905, wrote, "[Sport] occupies the minds not only of the youth at the universities, but also of their parents and of the general public. Baseball matches and football matches excite an interest greater than any other public events except the Presidential election, and that comes only once in four years. . . . The American love of excitement and love of competition has seized upon these games."[32]

No single event heralded the beginning of what has been designated as the era of modern sports, but the Roaring Twenties acted as a bridge connecting the old pastimes to twentieth-century sport. Sport seemed to be the most engrossing of all social interests in the 1920s; it became a bandwagon around which students and alumni, business and transportation interests, advertising and amusement industries, cartoonists and artists, novelists and sports columnists rallied. Indeed, the 1920s are still looked upon by some sport historians as sport's golden age. Some of America's most famous athletes rose to prominence during those years: Babe Ruth, the "Sultan of Swat"; Knute Rockne and the "Four Horsemen of Notre Dame"; Jack Dempsey, heavyweight boxing champion; Bill Tilden and Helen Willis Moody in tennis; and Bobby Jones and Glenna Collett in golf. In Canada, Howie Morenz, James Ball, Ethel Catherwood, Bobbie Rosenfeld, and Myrtle Cook thrilled the masses with their sports achievements. These are only a few of the coaches and athletes who contributed to the growing popularity of sports.[33] See Box 2.3 for the story of Jim Thorpe, perhaps the greatest athlete of that era.

From the 1920s onward, sport increasingly became a pervasive part of North American life, penetrating into every level of the educational systems and into the programs of social agencies and private clubs. This became especially true of the business world; sport affected such areas of the economic system as finance, fashion, mass media, transportation, communication, advertising, the sporting goods industry, and a variety of marginal enterprises that profit from sport.

North American business and labor organizations contributed to the rise of sport through organized industrial recreation programs for millions of workers. During the nineteenth century most industrial leaders showed little interest in the health and welfare of their employees; by the beginning of the twentieth century, however, voices inside and outside industry were pleading for consideration of the worker as a human being, with special focus on the worker's physical and mental health. Business and labor leaders began to realize that perhaps opportunities for diversion, whether in intellectual or recreational directions, might enhance employee health and morale and increase productivity.

The idea of providing company-sponsored recreation as a phase of business management caught on, and programs of all sorts came into existence. By the 1950s thousands of companies were sponsoring various forms of industrial recreation with more than 20 million employees participating. From the 1930s to the 1950s, the best amateur teams in basketball, baseball, and softball were company-sponsored teams. The National Industrial Basketball League included the Phillips 66ers, the Goodyear Wingfoots, and the Peoria Caterpillars. Championships in the National Baseball Congress and Amateur Softball Association were dominated by company-sponsored teams.

Industrial employee recreation programs have grown enormously over the past fifty years, and today industry spends more on sports equipment than all schools and colleges combined. Three-fourths of all firms employing more than a thousand people have some form of exercise and sports program, and more than 10,000 companies now have full- or part-time recreation managers.

Labor unions, originally formed to acquire better pay and working conditions for industrial employees, gradually broadened their interests to include the health and mental welfare of their members. The United Automobile Workers (UAW) established a recreation department in 1937 based on a strong policy of organized recreation for all ages. Other unions have programs that include

---

Box 2.3   *Thinking About Sport:* Jim Thorpe, the *Original* All-American

When people are asked to name the greatest athletes of the first half of the twentieth century, Babe Ruth, Jesse Owens, Ty Cobb, Red Grange, Joe Louis, and Mildred "Babe" Didrikson-Zaharius are the athletes who are most often identified. Except for Babe Didrikson-Zaharius, all made their athletic reputations in a single sport.

Despite the sports achievements of the athletes who are most frequently identified as the greatest of their era, a persuasive case can be made that Jim Thorpe's achievements surpassed all the others of the twentieth century. Thorpe excelled in not one but several sports at the highest level. Accordingly, in 1950 the Associated Press (AP) named Thorpe the greatest athlete of the first half of the twentieth century. In 1999, he was ranked third on the AP list of top athletes of the twentieth century. And from 1996 to 2001, he was repeatedly awarded ABC's Wide World of Sports Athlete of the Century award.

Jim Thorpe was a Native American born and raised on the Sauk and Fox Nation reservation in Oklahoma. In 1904, as a teenager Thorpe enrolled at the Carlisle Indian School in Carlisle, Pennsylvania. Following a hiatus of several years, he returned to Carlisle, and his athletic career took off under the coaching of "Pop" Warner, one of the most renowned American college football coaches at that time. The little known and little respected Carlisle football team nevertheless played against the best college teams in the country. In 1911 and 1912, Jim Thorpe played on both offense and defense and was also the team's kicker and leading tackler. In 1911, he scored all of Carlisle's points in an 18–15 upset of Harvard while leading Carlisle to a 11–1 season. In 1912, he made twenty-five touchdowns and 198 total points and led Carlisle to the national collegiate championship. Thorpe was chosen as an All-American in both 1911 and 1912.

Thorpe's sports achievements were not limited to football. He was one of the most versatile athletes in modern sports. In 1912 he won a place on the U.S. Olympic track and field team, and at the Olympic Games in Stockholm, Sweden, he won Olympic gold medals in the pentathlon and decathlon. However, when it was discovered that he had played two seasons of semi-professional baseball before competing in the Olympics, thus violating the Olympic amateur rules, his Olympic titles and medals were revoked. In 1983, thirty years after Thorpe's death, the International Olympic Committee (IOC) restored Thorpe's status as an amateur, and duplicate Olympic medals in his name were given to the Thorpe family.

Between 1913 and 1919 Thorpe played Major League Baseball for the New York Giants, the Cincinnati Reds, and the Boston Braves. While playing major league baseball, Thorpe continued to play football. In 1915 he signed a professional football contract with the Canton Bulldogs, a member of the Ohio League. The team won league championships in 1916, 1917, and 1919. In all, Thorpe played with six different teams during his career as a professional football player, ending with a stint with the Chicago Cardinals in 1929, when he retired at the age of 41.

Perhaps the most impressive manifestation of Jim Thorpe's athletic stature is that he was inducted into the College Football Hall of Fame, the Pro Football Hall of Fame, and the Track & Field Hall of Fame. No other athlete of the twentieth century comes near that accomplishment.

---

almost everything in the way of leisure-time activities: Among these are team and individual sports, social functions, dancing instruction, handicrafts, orchestras, and hobby clubs.

Two major developments in sport characterize the past thirty years: the colossal expansion of amateur and professional sports and the boom in participant sports. Amateur sports, from youth to intercollegiate athletic programs, have multiplied at a bewildering pace. Baseball and football in the United States and ice hockey in Canada were once about the only sports sponsored for youth, but now there are organized youth programs in more than twenty-five sports—from swimming to motor bicycling—and it is possible for children as young as six years of age to win a national championship. High school and collegiate programs, which used to be limited to three or four sports for males, have now been expanded to include fifteen to twenty sports for both males and females.

Professional sports teams are corporate organizations that function similarly in many respects to corporations of any other kind, albeit with certain tax and monopolistic advantages not given to other businesses. In 1922 the U.S. Supreme Court exempted baseball from antitrust legislation. Since that time owners of baseball and other professional sports teams have used that decision, and more recent ones, to define their special legal and economic position. (The legal and economic position of corporate sport is more fully discussed in Chapter 10.)

The first professional baseball team was player-owned and player-controlled, but major league teams were organized into business corporations in the latter part of the nineteenth century and continue as business enterprises made up of separate corporations under a cartel form of organization. The National Football League (NFL) began in 1920, and industry had a hand in its development. The Acme Packing Company in Green Bay, Wisconsin, sponsored a local team, which was fittingly called the Packers; and in Decatur, Illinois, the A. E. Staley Manufacturing Company started the team that became known as the Chicago Bears. From these humble beginnings, professional football is now a multibillion-dollar-a-year business, and most of the franchises in the NFL are worth more than $1 billion each.[34]

Ice hockey is another team sport that first became popular in the late 1800s, but its early development took place in Canada rather than the United States. The first professional hockey team was formed in 1903, and the first professional league was established a year later. In 1917 the National Hockey League (NHL) was organized.

The first rules for basketball were composed in 1891 by James Naismith, a physical training instructor at what is now Springfield College. Basketball quickly became popular in secondary schools and colleges, especially women's colleges; by the 1920s, teams of paid players were touring North America. But it was not until after World War II that a stable professional league was established: in 1949 the National Basketball Association (NBA) was organized.

Over the course of the twentieth century more than a dozen professional team sport leagues were formed, but the Big Four—consisting of baseball, ice hockey, football, and basketball—retained an enduring dominance in spectator attendance and general popularity. Table 2.1 outlines the origins of the Big Four.

Table 2.1 Origins of the Four Major Professional Team Sport Leagues

League	Founding Year
Baseball	
National League	1876
American League	1901
Hockey	
National Hockey League	1917
Football	
National Football League	1920
Basketball	
National Basketball Association	1949

On-site spectator sports in the United States have gross paid admissions of an estimated $1 billion per year. Some 45 million admissions are paid to horse racing, 75 million to professional baseball, 22 million to professional basketball, 22 million to the NHL, 49 million to college football, 44 million to college basketball (men's and women's), and about 22 million to professional football.[35] These figures are, of course, dwarfed by the number of people who watch televised sports events.

Participant sports, the second main development of the past generation, have been products of increased leisure and income. The construction of facilities and the manufacture of equipment inexpensive enough for the large mass of working-class people have had an important impact on participant sports. Moreover, a concerned awareness of the increasingly sedentary lifestyle of persons in all socioeconomic strata and of the rise in diseases related to this lifestyle has stimulated mass participation in sport and exercise.

Perhaps most remarkable is the running boom that has swept North America, where there are more than 25 million runners/joggers. Virtually every major city has a marathon that draws thousands of runners (e.g., Boston, New York, Toronto, Atlanta, Montreal). Even allowing for a considerable margin of error in the participation reports, sport involves an enormous number of people. Increased leisure and income are undoubtedly the main causes for the extraordinary development of participant sport in the current generation. See Table 2.2 for an example of Canadian sport participation.

Table 2.2 Profile of Canadians Who Regularly Participate in Sport, 2005

	Total			Male			Female		
	Population (thousands)	Participants (thousands)	%	Population (thousands)	Participants (thousands)	%	Population (thousands)	Participants (thousands)	%
Total	26,106	7,314	28.0	12,867	4,568	35.5	13,239	2,745	20.7
Age group									
15–18	1,796	1,061	59.1	919	608	66.1	877	454	51.7
19–24	2,567	1,099	42.8	1,314	678	51.6	1,253	421	33.6
25–34	4,365	1,348	30.9	2,198	899	40.9	2,167	449	20.7
35–54	9,942	2,509	25.2	4,965	1,545	31.1	4,977	965	19.4
55+	7,436	1,296	17.4	3,472	839	24.2	3,964	457	11.5

Source: Fidelis Ifedi, *Sport Participation in Canada, 2005,* Statistics Canada (Minister of Industry, 2008), p. 27, http://www.statcan.gc.ca/pub/81-595-m/81-595-m2008060-eng.pdf.

Twentieth-Century Technology and Sport: Transportation

By the beginning of the twentieth century, almost every realm of American and Canadian social life, including sport, shared in the powerful impact of the railroad, and in the years up to World War II this influence continued unabated. Perhaps one of the most significant contributions of the railroad to sport in the twentieth century was the opening of new areas for recreation. For example, the initial stimulus for the popularization of skiing was the "snow train."

The first snow train left Boston's North Station in 1931. Four years later such trains were leaving New York's Grand Central Station; on board were thousands of ski enthusiasts intent on spending a weekend on the slopes of New England. Railroads were responsible for the development and promotion of a number of North America's most popular winter sports resorts in the western states and provinces.

As important as the railroads were to improving transportation and stimulating industrialization, their impact on the social life and transportation habits of North Americans was minuscule in comparison to that of the development of the automobile. This invention and subsequently that of the airplane were two modes of transportation that completely revolutionized travel and numerous other aspects of life.

In addition to their contributions to transportation, the automobile and airplane created new industries involving billions of dollars in capital and employing millions of workers. They stimulated the construction of millions of miles of highways, and they spawned many industries and occupations related to auto and aircraft production and use. The growth of metropolitan areas, especially suburban and satellite towns outside large cities, was also stimulated by the automobile.

Inventors in Europe and the United States had successfully developed an internal combustion engine powered by gasoline by the last decade of the nineteenth century. Initially, however, there was little general interest in the converted bicycles that were the first automobiles because they were used either for racing or as a toy for the rich. Then a young man by the name of Henry Ford saw the potential of the automobile as a means of popular transportation. Realizing that he would have to gain financial backing for the auto through racing, he built a huge-engined racing car, the "999," and hired a professional bicycle rider by the name of Barney Oldfield to race it. After the 999 easily won against its challengers, the 999 did what it was intended to do: It advertised the fact that Henry Ford could build a fast motorcar. A week after the race he formed the Ford Motor Company.[36]

Racing was the first and foremost attraction of the automobile in the days when its usefulness for any other purpose was questioned. In 1895 H. H. Kohlsaat, publisher of the *Chicago Times-Herald,* sponsored the first automobile race in America; automobile races had already become a fad in Europe. Early automobile manufacturers recognized the commercial value of races and used them as a major marketing technique to win public interest. This particular aspect of automobile racing continues. Throughout the twentieth century, automobile racing grew in popularity and included a bewildering array of forms—midget autos, stock cars, hot rods, drag racing, NASCAR, and so forth.

The automobile contributed to the rise of sport in many ways beyond racing. It was a significant instrument for cultural change to the modern lifestyle. For countless millions, it progressively opened up broader horizons of spectator and participant sport. It provided an easy means of transportation from city to city and from the country to the town or city. Thus, large stadiums and other sports facilities could be conveniently reached by large groups of people. Also, for the first time, golf courses, ski resorts, tennis courts, bathing beaches, and areas for such field sports as fishing, camping, and hunting were within practical reach of large masses of the population. All this would have been impossible without the transportation provided by the automobile.

In 1903 Orville and Wilbur Wright successfully flew an airplane, but it was not until World War I that airplanes were used on a large scale, first for scouting enemy movements and later in actual combat. During the 1920–1940 era, aircraft design was improved, airports were constructed, and regular passenger, mail, and express lines were established. World War II provided for further development, and soon airplanes became the prominent mode of long-distance public transportation. Airplanes have in effect shrunk the continent—actually, the world—by reducing traveling time.

Until about the mid-1950s, most professional and collegiate athletic teams traveled by rail. With improvements in all phases of air transportation, the airplane became the common carrier of teams. The expansion of professional sports franchises from the East and Midwest into the West and the South and the increased number of pro sports teams could only have been achieved with air travel. Interregional collegiate football and basketball games were rare until air travel made it possible to take long trips in a short period of time. Inter-regional contests then became a part of the weekly schedule of collegiate sports.

The Technological Revolution and Sport: Communication

Mass communication is the glue that serves to integrate people into their society, and it has helped shape and mold the development and popularity of the sport culture. In 1896 an Italian scientist, Marchese Guglielmo Marconi, patented the wireless technology and showed the possibility of telegraphy without the use of wires. Within a few years, wireless telegraphy was carrying messages to all parts of the world.

One of the first stories to be covered by wireless was a sports event. Marconi was hired by the Associated Press in 1899 to report on the international yacht race involving Scotland's Sir Thomas Lipton's *Shamrock* and America's *Columbia*. Thus, wireless communication took its place along with the telegraph and the telephone in intensifying public interest in sport and stimulating the rise of sport.

The next important step in electrical communication was the radio, which until 1920 was mainly a toy for amateur scientists. However, in 1920 a radio station in Pittsburgh began broadcasting, and a new communication medium and industry was under way. Radio broadcasting of sports events actually preceded the beginning of public broadcasting. On August 20, 1920, the radio station of the *Detroit News* went on the air to announce the results of the World Series baseball games. This was before the first public radio station in Pittsburgh made its initial broadcast in November of that year. Also in 1920, the first college football game was broadcast from a station in Texas.[37]

Radio came of age in the hectic 1920s, and while music and news broadcasts were the standard programs, sports events were rapidly absorbed into the entertainment schedule. One sports history analyst declared: "Broadcast radio . . . joined the roiling swirl of sports ballyhoo. . . . Radio not only gave distant fans their first real-time play-by-play accounts, the medium also created the first true national audience. Radio was one of the last components in creating the period's mass culture."[38] Radio and sports were indeed natural partners.

Radio dominated broadcasting during the 1930s and 1940s; it was not until the early 1950s that television began to overshadow radio in providing information and home entertainment. Persons under the age of forty have grown up watching television; it is just taken for granted. Indeed, TV sets are on for an average of eight hours per day in U.S. and Canadian homes. Some media experts claim that college students today spend more waking hours watching television than doing any other single thing.

Although television had been experimentally developed prior to World War II, it was not until the late 1940s that technology and marketing combined to produce models for home use. The major television boom occurred in the early 1950s; by 1957 television was a fixture in most households and no longer a novelty. As television sets became available to the public and the broadcasting of programs expanded, it quickly became evident that televised sports events would be immensely popular, and television continually expanded its coverage of sports. More will be said about the television-sport nexus in Chapter 11.

During the twentieth century the sports page became an indispensable part of every newspaper. The same sport history analyst we quoted above noted: "Better information distribution helped foster increased sports coverage. News syndicates, newspaper chains, and wire services facilitated widespread dissemination of event reporting. Individual papers didn't have to send a reporter to the game any longer, because they could just buy the Associated Press (AP) write-up."[39] From a concentration on a few sports, such as baseball, college football, horse racing, and boxing, attention was gradually given to an enormously wide range of sports. Currently, many newspaper publishers believe that the sports section is the most important factor in a newspaper's circulation.

Along with the newspaper, magazines and books have done much to attract attention to sports in the past century and a half. Even before the American Civil War, a host of turf journals appeared; many periodicals were also devoted to field sports and outdoor life. Sports journals proliferated in the late nineteenth century, so that almost every sport had at least one periodical devoted

to it. This trend has continued, and a substantial portion of shelf space in newsstands is occupied by magazines about sports. (More will be said about this in Chapter 11.)

In its early years the motion picture industry concentrated primarily on boxing. The first commercial motion picture was a six-round bout between Young Griffo and Battling Barnett in 1895. Motion pictures of boxing championships were one of the most popular forms of spectator sport in the first three decades of the twentieth century and served to stimulate the public appetite for organized sports. In recent years videotapes, computers, high-speed cameras, and an array of photo-communication instruments have become indispensable to coaches for scouting opponents and for reviewing the performances of their own athletes. Collegiate and professional coaches of some sports spend as much time electronically viewing as they spend on almost any other coaching task.

The impact of the still camera cannot be overlooked either. Beginning in the early years of the twentieth century, newspapers and magazines made extensive use of pictures to show the performance of athletes in the heat of competition or to illustrate the correct (or incorrect) method of performing a skill. The popularity of sports magazines, especially *Sports Illustrated*, is largely due to the superb photographs that are part of each issue. This has had the effect of further nurturing sports by keeping them in the public eye.

Other Technological Innovations and Sport

Although indoor sports were greatly stimulated by electric lighting, baseball, America's national pastime, did not discover the value of this invention until the 1930s. Social historians record 1930 as the year of the emergence of night baseball. The first such ventures took place in Des Moines and Wichita in the summer of 1930. Several minor leagues quickly adopted night baseball, but it was not until 1935 that Cincinnati played the first night major league game. Only in the 1940s did night baseball gain general acceptance in the major leagues; the first World Series night game was not played until 1975. The owner of the Chicago Cubs for many years, Phillip K. Wrigley, never accepted night baseball, and lights were not installed at Wrigley Field until the summer of 1988.

Sport in Education

As stated previously, intercollegiate sport began as a form of student recreation but rapidly grew in popularity among the general public. Indeed, during the past fifty years it has become a form of big business. The practice of using sport as the right arm of the public relations department of a college, which began in the late nineteenth century, continues to the present.

This system of intercollegiate sport is unique to the United States, and it has been one of the most significant forces in the development of American organized sports. High school sports are modeled on this system, and many nonschool youth sports programs have been organized as feeder systems to the high school and college programs. Finally, the intercollegiate programs serve as a farm system for many of the professional sports. (In Chapters 5 and 6 we discuss the topic of sport in education in depth.)

Until the 1970s, Canadian universities tended to model athletic programs after the British tradition, meaning that programs were primarily sponsored and administered by students, and little emphasis was given to their commercial exploitation. In recent years an "American model" in intercollegiate sports has been increasingly adopted, causing some observers to claim that this is another example of the homogenization of American and Canadian cultures.

SUMMARY

In this chapter we have reviewed the rise of sport in North America. Contemporary sports are grounded in political, economic, technological, and social conditions and events of the past. Sports today are possible only because of what has happened in the past, and sports of the future will depend on what happens in today's societies.

Despite overwhelming natural and social barriers that made involvement in games and sporting activities difficult for European colonists in North America, colonists still engaged in a wide variety of playful physical activities. But it was not until the beginning of the nineteenth century that conditions became favorable for organized sports to become a popular cultural practice for large numbers of citizens. Technological innovations and the accompanying industrial revolution were instrumental in stimulating a transformation in social conditions that gave rise to modern sport. Urbanization was also a significant factor, because the evolution of modern sports in North America became possible only with large urban populations scattered across the continent. During the nineteenth century, influential persons among the clergy and the intelligentsia, as well as social reformers, helped develop the attitudes, values, and beliefs that are the foundation of modern sport.

During the first half of the twentieth century, sport became a pervasive part of North American life, penetrating into every level of the educational systems and into the economic and cultural systems in the form of professional sports. The two major trends in sport that characterize the past thirty years are the enormous expansion of amateur and professional sports and the burst of growth in participant sports.

WEB RESOURCES

www.nassh.org
The official website of the North American Society for Sport History. The purpose of NASSH is to promote, stimulate, and encourage study, research, and writing of the history of sport. This site lists sport history publications and sport history scholars. One of its links is to the *Journal of Sport History*.

www.northnet.org/stlawrenceaauw/sports.htm
The website of Women's Sports History Resources. It is a clearinghouse for many women's sports websites that focus on the history of women in sport.

www.kansasheritage.org/people/naismith.html
A brief history of Dr. James Naismith, the inventor of basketball, and how he developed the rules and actions for playing the game.

www.baseball-almanac.com
The online baseball almanac. A reference source for individual and team records and statistics.

NOTES

1. David M. Thomas and Barbara B. Torrey, eds., *Canada and the United States: Differences That Count*, 3rd ed. (Aurora, Ontario, Canada: Garamond Press, 2007); see also John H. Thompson and Stephen J. Randall, *Canada and the United States: Ambivalent Allies*, 4th ed. (Athens: University of Georgia Press, 2008).

2. Joseph B. Oxendine, *American Indian Sports Heritage* (Lincoln: University of Nebraska Press, 1995), 3; see also C. Richard King, ed., *Native Athletes in Sport and Society: A Reader* (Lincoln, NE: Bison Books, 2006).

3. Thomas Vennum, Jr., *American Indian Lacrosse: Little Brother of War*, reprint edition (Baltimore: Johns Hopkins University Press, 2007); see also Donald M. Fisher, *Lacrosse: A History of the Game*, reprint edition (Baltimore: Johns Hopkins University Press, 2011).

4. Bruce C. Daniels, "Sober Mirth and Pleasant Poisons: Puritan Ambivalence Toward Leisure and Recreation in Colonial New England," in *Sport in America: From Colonial Leisure to Celebrity Figures and Globalization*, Vol. 2, ed. David K. Wiggins (Champaign, IL: Human Kinetics, 2010), 5–21.

5. Herbert Manchester and Paula Welch, *Four Centuries of Sport in America, 1490–1890* (Lanham, MD: Derrydale Press, 2001); see also Elliott J. Gorn, *A Brief History of American Sport* (Urbana: University of Illinois Press, 2004).

6. Elliott J. Gorn, "'Gouge and Bite, Pull Hair and Scratch': The Social Significance of Fighting in the Southern Backcountry," in *Sport in America*, Vol. 2, ed. David K. Wiggins (Champaign, IL: Human Kinetics, 1995), 35–50.

7. Nancy L. Struna, *People of Prowess: Sport, Leisure, and Labor in Early Anglo-America* (Urbana: University of Illinois Press, 1996). For an excellent discussion of Canadian sports and other physical activity during this period, see Don Morrow and Kevin B. Wamsley, *Sport in Canada: A History*, 2nd ed. (New York: Oxford University Press, 2009).

8. T. H. Breen, "Horses and Gentlemen: The Cultural Significance of Gambling Among the Gentry of Virginia," in *Sport in America*, Vol. 2, ed. Wiggins, 23–39. For a good discussion of the swimming feats of slaves during the colonial period, see Kevin Dawson, "Enslaved Swimmers and Divers in the Atlantic World," *Journal of American History* 92 (March 2006): 1327–1355.

9. Paul Le Blanc, *A Short History of the U.S. Working Class: From Colonial Times to the Twenty-first Century* (Amherst, NY: Humanity Books, 1999).

10. Nancy L. Struna, "The North-South Races: American Thoroughbred Racing in Transition, 1823–1850," *Journal of Sport History* (Summer 1981): 28–57; and Melvin L. Adelman, "The First Modern Sport in America: Harness Racing in New York City, 1825–1870," in *Sport in America*, Vol. 2, ed. Wiggins, 5–32.

11. S. F. Wise and Douglas Fisher, *Canada's Sporting Heroes* (Don Mills, Ontario: General Publishing, 1974), 7.

12. For an extended discussion of this topic, see Morrow and Wamsley, *Sport in Canada: A History*.

13. For an excellent discussion of the *Clermont* steamboat on the Hudson River, see John H. Hamilton, *Hudson River Pilot: From Steamboats to Super Tankers* (Hensonville, NY: Black Dome Press, 2001), ch. 2.

14. William David Sloan, *The Media in America: A History*, 7th ed. (San Ramon, CA: Vision Press, 2008).

15. Benjamin G. Rader, *American Sports: From the Age of Folk Games to the Age of Televised Sports*, 6th ed. (Upper Saddle River, NJ: Prentice Hall, 2008), 65–79. In 1897 one of these clubs, the Boston Athletic Association, sponsored the first Boston Marathon, now one of the world's premier sports events.

16. There are many histories of baseball, but two of the best are George Vecsey, *Baseball: A History of America's Favorite Game* (New York: Modern Library, 2008) and Benjamin G. Rader, *Baseball: A History of America's Game*, 3rd ed. (Champaign: University of Illinois Press, 2008).

17. William Humber, *Diamonds of the North: A Concise History of Baseball in Canada* (New York: Oxford University Press, 1995); see also Bob Elliott, *The Northern Game: Baseball the Canadian Way* (Toronto: SportClassic Books, 2005).

18. Robert K. Barney, "Forty-Eighters and the Rise of the Turnverein Movement in America," in *Ethnicity and Sport in North American History and Culture*, ed. George Eisen and David K. Wiggins (New York: Praeger, 1995), 19–42; see also Annette R. Hofmann, "Lady *Turners* in the United States: German American Identity, Gender Concerns, and *Turnerism*," *Journal of Sport History* 27 (Fall 2000): 383–404.

19. Gerald Redmond, *The Sporting Scots of Nineteenth-Century Canada* (East Brunswick, NJ: Fairleigh Dickinson University Press, 1982); see also Emily Ann Donaldson, *The Scottish Highland Games in the United States* (Apollo Bay, Victoria, Australia: Firebird Press, 1999).

20. John S. Watterson, *College Football: History, Spectacle, Controversy* (Baltimore: Johns Hopkins University Press, 2000).

21. Amos Alonzo Stagg, quoting William Rainey Harper, in a letter to his family dated 20 January 1891, quoted in Richard J. Storr, *Harper's University: The Beginnings* (Chicago: University of Chicago Press, 1966), 179.

22. There is a large literature on the history of railroading in North America, but these two books stand out: Claude Wiatrowski, *Railroads Across North America: An Illustrated History* (Minneapolis: Voyageur Press, 2007), and Kevin EuDaly, Mike Schafer, Steve Jessup, Jim Boyd, Steve Glischinski, and Andrew McBride, *The Complete Book of North American Railroading* (Minneapolis: Voyageur Press, 2009).

23. Ronald A. Smith, *Sports and Freedom: The Rise of Big-Time College Athletics* (New York: Oxford University Press, 1990), 27–28.

24. *Frank Leslie's Illustrated Newspaper*, Vol. 29 (New York), 28 September 1869, p. 2.

25. Sloan, *The Media in America: A History*.

26. Rader, *American Sports*, 100–101.

27. George H. Sage, "The Sporting Goods Industry: From Struggling Entrepreneurs to National Businesses to Transnational Corporations," in *The Commercialization of Sport*, ed. Trevor Slack (New York: Routledge, 2004), 29–51.

28. Michael Kimmel, *Manhood in America: A Cultural History*, 2nd ed. (New York: Oxford University Press, 2005).

29. Susan L. Roberson, "'Degenerate Effeminacy' and the Making of a Masculine Spirituality in the Sermons of Ralph Waldo Emerson," in *Muscular Christianity: Embodying the Victorian Age*, ed. Donald E. Hall (Cambridge: Cambridge University Press, 2008), 150–173; and Tony Ladd and James A. Mathisen, *Muscular Christianity: Evangelical Protestants and the Development of American Sport* (Grand Rapids, MI: Baker Books, 1999).

30. Richard Hofstadter was a professor of American History at Columbia University. He became an iconic historian whom twenty-first-century scholars continue to cite because his publications remain relevant in illuminating Herbert Spencer's social Darwinism. See Richard Hofstadter, *Social Darwinism in American Thought* (New York: G. Braziller Publisher, 1959), 201; see also Alexander Rosenberg, *Darwinism in Philosophy, Social Science, and Policy* (New York: Cambridge University Press, 2000).

31. Although this reference is quite dated, the quote we have used provides the best articulation we have seen of Sumner's position on social Darwinism. See Albert Galloway Keller, ed., *Essays of William Graham Sumner*, Vol. 1 (New Haven, CT: Yale University Press, 1934), 386.

32. James Bryce, "America Revisited: The Changes of a Quarter-Century," *Outlook* 25 (March 1905): 738–739.

33. For interesting biographical accounts of some of the luminaries of sports in the 1920s, see Michael K. Bohn, *Heroes & Ballyhoo: How the Golden Age of the 1920s Transformed American Sports* (Dulles, VA: Potomac Books, 2009).

34. Benjamin G. Rader, *Baseball: A History of America's Game*, 3rd ed. (Champaign: University of Illinois Press, 2008); Frank P. Jozsa, Jr., *Football Fortunes: The Business, Organization and Strategy of the NFL* (Jefferson, NC: McFarland, 2010).

35. U.S. Census Bureau, *Statistical Abstract of the United States: 2011*, 130th ed. (Washington, DC: U.S. Government Printing Office, 2011), tables 1243 and 1244.

36. Russ Banham, *The Ford Century: Ford Motor Company and the Innovations That Shaped the World* (Sioux City, IA: Artisan, 2002).

37. Sloan, *The Media in America: A History*.

38. Bohn, *Heroes & Ballyhoo*, 7.

39. Ibid., 5.

CHAPTER 3

Sport and North American Culture and Values

Some . . . have argued vehemently that spectator sports represent all that is bad in American culture, that classism, racism, sexism, substance abuse, and violence in society are reinforced by the sports that fans love. Others point to the good in sports—how they exemplify concepts of community, teamwork, and striving for excellence. Both points of view are valid.
—Kevin G. Quinn*

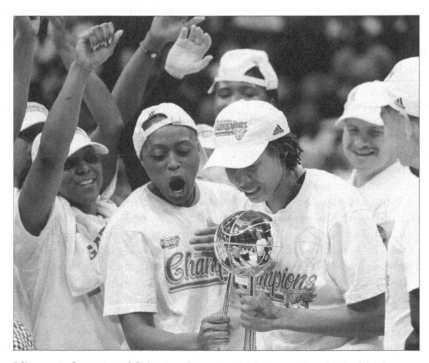

Minnesota Lynx guard Seimone Augustus, right, weeps as she holds the WNBA championship trophy with teammate Charde Houston, left, after the Lynx defeated the Atlanta Dream to complete a three-game sweep of the WNBA championship series, 2011. (AP Photo/David Goldman)

*Kevin G. Quinn, *Sports and Their Fans* (Jefferson, NC: McFarland Publishers, 2009), 123.

Many concepts and terms that sociologists use are mystifying to the average person. *Social organization* is one such term. Yet its meaning is quite straightforward: Social organization is the process by which human behavior becomes organized to deal with the social situations in which people find themselves. One facet of social organization is *culture*, which refers to the knowledge that members of a social organization share and that unites them and guides their behavior; it consists of the language, religious beliefs, food, clothing, material objects, and other common artifacts and characteristics of members of that particular social organization. It is through culture that people and groups define themselves, adapt to shared expectations, and become part of a community, or society. One element of a culture is social values (also called cultural values), which are collective conceptions for evaluating and judging what behavior is considered appropriate, desirable, moral, proper, and important. We discuss the meaning of values in more detail below.

CULTURE, VALUES, AND SOCIAL THEORIES

Culture and values are typically enduring and are sustained and reproduced from one generation to the next. Without the social transmission of culture and values, each generation would have to re-create their own customs, beliefs, language, rituals, and so forth. Nevertheless, culture and values are not fixed and unchanging. Change is ongoing—sometimes very slowly, other times quickly—depending on particular conditions. Every social grouping has members who do not internalize and adopt the cultural values. There is even a derogatory word for such individuals—deviant. See Figure 3.1 for examples of how some values change and others endure.

All of the social theories that we identified and summarized in Chapter 1 concur that culture and values are essential to social organization, even though their perspectives on this issue vary. For adherents to functionalist theory, collective values solve the fundamental problem of social integration. They are symbolic representations of existing society and therefore promote unity and consensus in a society, and they must be preserved because social stability requires a consensus and the support of group members. Social cultural customs, rituals, traditions, and myths build strong common values that provide support, consensus, and stability while strengthening the social order.

Conflict/cultural theorists acknowledge the crucial role of culture and values in creating and maintaining stability and consensus in society, but in capitalist society—the main focus of conflict/cultural theorizing—the most powerful members of a society are a dominant capitalist class who form and shape cultural values that preserve their powerful economic, political, and social interests. This ruling capitalist class constructs and controls not only the means of economic production but also the apparatus for shaping beliefs about the existing cultural values through the social institutions of education, economy, religion, politics, and media in ways that benefit capitalist interests within that society.

In Chapter 1 we identified various social theoretical variants that are classified as conflict/cultural theories. Although they have compelling differences, all of these theories consider culture and values to be central concepts in social analyses—indeed, so central that one of the theoretical perspectives is called "cultural studies." Yet each has its own unique point of view with regard to the role of these concepts. Because conflict/cultural scholarship is interdisciplinary in scope, theorists in this field draw on a broad range of theories and practices. We shall only briefly examine culture and values as they relate to hegemony, feminist, and race theories.

As we also noted in Chapter 1, one of the features of hegemony theory is its focus on cultural patterns of dominance and the role that dominant, powerful groups play in shaping culture and values. These dominant groups translate their enormous economic resources into social and political ideologies about cultural values that are disseminated through all of the social institutions. Such ideologies thus come to be seen as norms that legitimate social beliefs and practices; they seem right and natural—a simple matter of common sense, or of human nature. But the reality is that these ideologies overwhelmingly benefit the ruling class. In this way, according to the hegemonic perspective, a

Figure 3.1   Freshman Trends in Students' Values

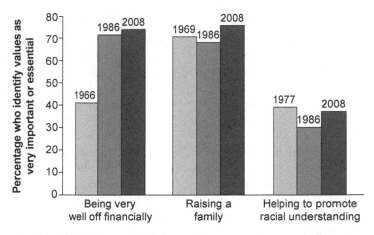

Note: Beginning dates for some questions have varied.

Sources: Adapted from John H. Pryor, Sylvia Hurtado, Victor B. Saenz, and William S. Korn, *The American Freshman: Forty Year Trends, 1966–2006*, Higher Education Research Institute (Los Angeles: UCLA Graduate School of Education & Information Studies, April 2007); and John H. Pryor et al., *The American Freshman: National Norms for Fall 2008*, Higher Education Research Institute (Los Angeles: UCLA Graduate School of Education & Information Studies, December 2008).

dominant class penetrates all levels of the society with its version of cultural reality. Domination is contoured primarily through an "active consent" of the mass of members, but it is a consent that has been molded by a narrow leadership.

Both feminist and racial theorists share hegemony theorists' interpretation of the social production of cultural values. They maintain that dominant groups form and shape culture and values through the various social institutions that keep women and minority racial groups subordinate and subservient to the ruling class.

One of the most often-heard statements about sport is that it is "a microcosm of society." If indeed sport is a microcosm of society, then the types of sports, the way in which sport is organized, and who participates and who does not all offer clues about the nature of a society. The study of sport, like the study of any institution, should provide important indicators about (1) a society's culture, (2) a society's values, (3) a society's social structure (social stratification and social organization), and (4) a society's problems.

In this chapter we examine the reciprocal relationship between sport, on the one hand, and

society, culture, and values on the other. The relationship is interdependent because cultural values affect the kinds of sports that are played, the way they are organized, the way they are played, and the motivations for participation in them. However, the converse is also true in that sport affects the culture and values in a society. To briefly illustrate, sport, like all social institutions, is conservative primarily because it reinforces cultural values, thus fulfilling a social function that functional theorists view as essential for social order, while conflict theorists would view sport as reinforcing the status quo, with all of its problems and social injustices.

In keeping with the theme of this book, we use the term *North American* in our description of culture and values, but we recognize these are not identical in the two countries that comprise North America. However, as we noted in Chapter 2, Canada and the United States do have close social and cultural ties, and there are many similarities—albeit dissimilarities as well—between the predominant values of the two nations.

The factors that work to differentiate Canadian values from American values are, first, that Canada has a long history of having accepted English rule after the Americans rebelled against it; second, that Canadians have two dominant religions, the Anglican religious heritage from the British and the Catholic heritage from the French, while Americans are more religiously pluralistic; and third, that Canada wants to nurture its own culture and values separately from the overwhelming influence of the United States.

Strong factors also work toward a congruence of values: (1) Many Canadians have received their higher education in the United States, (2) Canadian and American immigration laws are similar and have been largely responsible for creating cosmopolitan similarities between the two countries, (3) Canadians typically watch U.S.-made television and movies and read American newspapers and magazines, and (4) American corporations have a strong presence in Canada.[1]

In the following sections of this chapter, when we describe cultural values that we believe overwhelmingly apply only to the United States or to Canada, we will specifically use the name of that country. In all other instances we will use the term *North American,* and readers can use their own judgment as to how similar or dissimilar the two countries are with respect to the values in question.

THE NORTH AMERICAN VALUE SYSTEM

Humans are a valuing species.[2] That is, human beings live in an affectively charged world where some things are preferred over others. Some objects, people, or ideas are considered wrong, bad, or immoral; others are believed correct, good, or moral. Some goals are deemed worthy; others are not.

Values are the culturally prescribed criteria by which individuals evaluate persons, behaviors, objects, and ideas as to their relative morality, desirability, merit, or correctness. Thus, values are the basis for making decisions. The phrase *culturally prescribed* is an important qualifier in this definition because it implies that human beings are *socialized*—that is, taught the criteria by which to make such judgments. Children learn from their parents, peers, churches, schools, and the media

what is right or wrong, moral or immoral, correct or incorrect.[3]

Before we begin an examination of values widely held in North America, several caveats should be mentioned. First, diversity in North American societies precludes any universal holding of values. Some individuals and groups reject the dominant values, and members of certain ethnic and religious groups have very different values. Moreover, differences in emphasis of the dominant values exist because of region, social class, age, and size of community.

Second, the system of North American values is not always consistent with behavior. For example, North Americans have always valued hard work as the means to success, yet rich persons who may have inherited their wealth are highly esteemed. Moreover, the value of equality of opportunity that North Americans verbally embrace is inconsistent with the injustices suffered by people on the margins, most notably the poor and minority groups.

Third, the values themselves are not always consistent. How does one reconcile the coexistence of individualism with conformity or of competition with cooperation? To minimize the problem of inconsistencies, we will present only the most dominant of North American values.[4]

Individual Striving for Success

The highly valued individual in both North American societies is the self-made person—the person who has achieved money and status through his or her own efforts in a highly competitive system. Cultural heroes are persons like Warren Buffett, Bill Gates, Oprah Winfrey, Samuel Walton, and Frank Stronach (a Canadian), each of whom rose from humble origins to the top of her or his profession.

Success is typically narrowly defined as individual achievement—winning first place, winning a championship, outdoing all others. In the occupational world economic success (income, personal wealth, and possessions) is the most commonly used measurement of success. Economic success, moreover, is often used to measure personal worth. Indeed, it has often been observed that the striking feature of North American culture is its tendency to identify standards of personal excellence with occupational achievement.

Competition: The Fundamental Social Process

Competition is highly valued in North American societies. In fact, in the case of the U.S., it is often contended that competition has made it the dominant nation in the world. It is not just competition, though, but winning in competitive situations that is so highly valued. Permeating North American life is an almost religious belief in the power of competition to bring success. Being victorious in competition is so highly valued that extraordinary rewards are heaped on victors. Thus, the U.S. has been characterized as a "winner-take-all" society by some social analysts.[5]

Motivated by the hope of being victorious in competition or by fear of failure, many citizens believe that the United States must be first in war, the arms race, the Olympics, or the race to place humans on Mars. This competitive zeal was behind the United States' race to be the first nation to land its citizens on the moon.

Competition pervades all of the social institutions of North American societies. The prominence of competition in schools is seen in the selection process for athletic teams, cheerleading squads, debate teams, choruses, bands, and play casts. In each case, competition among classmates is the criterion for selection. Even the grading system is often based on comparisons of classmates with one another.

The foundation of the capitalist economic system is competition: Businesses compete against each other for customers for their products and services, and workers compete against each other

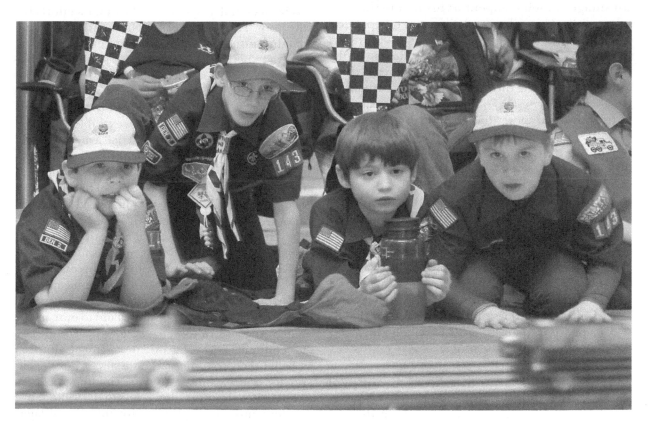

Cub Scouts from Pack 143 watch model cars race in the Pinewood Derby in Great Falls, Montana. In a pinewood derby, wooden model cars made by the scouts are raced down an inclined track. (AP Photo/ *Great Falls Tribune*, Robin Loznak)

for the best-paying and highest-status jobs. North American governments are composed of officials who have competed against others in elections to secure the positions they have.

Even youth social-recreational programs are based on competition. The Cub Scouts program, because of its reliance on competition, is considered an all-American organization. In the first place, individual status in the den or pack is determined by the level one has achieved through the attainment of merit badges. Although all boys can theoretically attain all merit badges, the boys are pitted against one another to see who can obtain the most. Why is such a practice accepted, indeed publicized? The answer, simply, is that it is symbolic of the way things are done in virtually all aspects of North American life.

An important consequence of this extreme emphasis on competition is that some people take advantage of their competitors in order to compete successfully. This is done rather routinely in political campaigns with "dirty tricks," misleading advertising, and illegal contributions to win elections. In the business world, we find some people who use theft, fraud, interlocking directorates, and price fixing to get ahead dishonestly. Following are some examples of how this zeal to win has caused people to cheat:

- About sixty major corporations have had to restate their earnings after overstating them to boost their stock value.
- The Internal Revenue Service has found consistently that three out of ten people cheat on their income taxes.
- Employees embezzle or pilfer an estimated $10 billion from their employers annually.
- The Center for Academic Integrity has found that the percentage of students who approve of plagiarism is rising, and it estimates that 75 percent of all students have been involved in some form of cheating.[6]

A related problem, the abuse of nature for profit (although not a form of cheating), deprives others of limited resources and degrades the general quality of life so that the profiteer can pursue economic success. The environmental crisis is caused by individuals, corporations, and communities who find pollution solutions too expensive. Thus, in looking out for themselves, they ignore the short- and long-range effects on social and biological life. In other words, competition, although a constant spur for individuals and groups to succeed, is also the source of some illegal activities and social problems in the United States.

The Socially Valued Means to Achieve

There are three related, highly valued ways to succeed in North American societies. The first is through *hard work*. North Americans, from the early Puritans to the present day, have elevated persons who are industrious and denigrated those who are not. Most North Americans, therefore, assume that poor people deserve to be poor because they are allegedly unwilling to work as hard as persons in the middle and upper classes. This explanation places the blame on the victim rather than on a social system that systematically thwarts efforts by the poor. Their hopelessness, brought on by a lack of education, by their skin color or gender, or by a lack of experience, is interpreted as their fault and not as a function of the economic system.[7]

This typical interpretation, moreover, is buttressed by the success of some individuals who grew up in poverty—the rags to riches example. They are presented as dramatic evidence that a meteoric rise in fame and fortune is possible through the blending of hard work and talent. Some will contend that these persons succeed not because of the openness of the system but because they managed somehow to overcome its roadblocks.

The two remaining valued means to success are *continual striving* and *deferred gratification*. Continual striving has meaning for both the successful and the not-so-successful. For the former, it means that a person should never be content with what she or he has; there will always be more land to own, more money to make, or more books to write. For the latter, continual striving means a never-give-up attitude, a belief that economic success is always possible, if not for oneself, at least for one's children.

Deferred gratification refers to the willingness to deny immediate pleasure for the sake of later rewards. The hallmark of the successful person in North America is such a willingness, whether to stay in school or to work at two jobs or to go to night school. One observer has asserted, for example, that the difference between the poor and the nonpoor is whether they are future- or present-time oriented.

Superficially, this assessment appears accurate, but we argue that the lack of a future-time orientation among the poor is not a subcultural trait but basically a consequence of their hopeless situation due to structural constraints. Moreover, there is a question of whether this value still prevails among the children of the nonpoor.

Progress Overcomes the Status Quo

Societies differ in their emphasis on the past, on the present, and on the future. North Americans, while giving some attention to each time dimension, stress the future. They neither make the past sacred nor remain content with the present. They place a central value on progress—on a brighter tomorrow, a better job, a bigger home, a move to the suburbs, a college education for their children, and self-improvement.

North Americans are not satisfied with the status quo; they want growth (bigger buildings, faster planes, bigger airports, more business moving into the community, bigger profits, and new world records). Many want to change and conquer nature (dam rivers, clear forests, rechannel rivers, seed clouds, spray parks and residential areas with insecticides, and replace grass with artificial turf), although the ecological crises are leading more and more people to question this value.

Although the belief in progress implies that change is good, some things are not easily changed because they are considered to have a sacred quality: social institutions, cultural values, and the nation-state. Thus, even while valuing technological change, North Americans resist fundamental changes in their society.

Materialism: Acquisitions and Consumption

"Hard work pays off" is a basic belief in North American culture. The payoff is success not only in one's profession but also in economic standing, in income, and in the acquisition and consumption of goods and services that go beyond adequate nutrition, medical care, shelter, and transportation. The

superfluous things that we accumulate or strive to accumulate, such as country club memberships, jewelry, stylish clothes, lavish houses in prestigious neighborhoods, boats, second homes, swimming pools, and season tickets to the games of our favorite teams, are symbols of success in the competitive struggle. However, these have more than symbolic value; they are also elements of what North Americans consider the "good life."

The North American emphasis on materialism is reflected in the motives of college students. As Figure 3.1 illustrates, surveys of first-year college students find that "being very well-off financially" has become of much greater value to college students over the past forty years. This materialism is also seen indirectly in the most commonly chosen major—business.

The emphasis on having things has long been a facet of North American nations. These countries have always been lands of opportunity and abundance. Although many persons are unable to fully participate in this abundance, the goal for most persons is to accumulate those things that bring status and that provide for a better way of life by saving labor or enhancing pleasure in their leisure time.

Social Conformity

Social organizations do not tolerate total freedom by individual members. Without a minimum of cooperation and of conformity to laws and customs, there is anarchy. To avoid disorder and lawlessness, societies socialize individuals into acceptable beliefs and practices. For their part, individuals actually seek to be socialized. We seek the approval of our family, peers, and colleagues and therefore try to be successful by some shared standards of achievement or of conformity. Conformity, then, is a characteristic of all social organizations. The degree of conformity required, however, varies greatly from one social organization to another.

Analytically, we can separate conformity in North American societies into two levels. At one level are the official expectations of behavior by the community, the state or province, and the nation: the customs and the laws individuals are expected to obey. Deviations from these expectations are punished by fines, imprisonment, gossip, or other negative *sanctions*. The threat of these sanctions is usually enough to ensure conformity. More than this, however, we are socialized to desire a great deal of conformity.

At another more personal level, individuals tend to conform to the expectations of groups with which they closely identify: families, peers, ethnic groups, religious groups, and work groups. Within the context of society-wide expectations for behavior, there is greater diversity: Suburbanites conform to other suburbanites, as do ghetto residents, teenagers, the jet set, union members, and businesspersons with their peers. Some social analysts have characterized U.S. citizens as being *other-directed*. By this they mean that Americans are oversensitive to the opinions of others. They continually have their antennas out, picking up signals from those important to them. Other analysts point to the same phenomenon in the organizational context of social life. They argue that the bureaucratic trend in the U.S. forces many persons to conform. Rules must be followed, boats must not be rocked, if individuals are to get ahead in bureaucracies.

Bureaucratic organization is authoritarian and hierarchical in both the U.S. and Canada. It is also rational. That is, it is based entirely on certain understood and accepted rules designed to efficiently serve the organization's goals. The interests of the organization are paramount in the development of these rules, and the formal aspects of a bureaucracy manifest these interests and rules.

The influence of bureaucracy is a source of norms regulating a large number of activities both within and beyond large-scale organization boundaries. So powerful and so pervasive are the organizations that employ bureaucratic methods that the value orientations engendered by this form of organization have attained the status of core values for North America's nations. They so permeate the fabric of every social institution that the socialization process is largely devoted to conditioning youth to this orientation.

NORTH AMERICAN SOCIAL VALUES AND SPORT

Now that we have outlined the general social value system of North Americans, we will examine their relationship with North American sports. We have repeatedly pointed out that sport mirrors a society's basic structure and values. Many reasons exist for the tremendous popularity of sport in Canada and the United States. The conditions of modern mass society constitute an important set of factors. Individuals living in an urban and bureaucratic society tend to feel alienated; in effect, they have feelings of isolation, powerlessness, self-estrangement, and meaninglessness. A little over a decade ago Robert Putnam, professor of public policy at Harvard, showed in his research that people have become increasingly disconnected from one another as community structures have disintegrated—a trend that seems to have continued. And that is cause for concern. According to Putnam, people need to identify with others in a cause that will give meaning to their existence and an escape from an otherwise humdrum world.[8]

Public policy experts frequently claim that although sport tends to mirror the larger society, it has a tendency to counteract the community isolation noted by Putnam. Sports teams, each pursuing victories, representing factories, schools, neighborhoods, cities, or nations, provide an important source of identification for U.S. and Canadian citizens who otherwise do not feel connected with others. They provide entertainment, diversion, and great expectations. The popularity of sports, influenced by television, newspapers, and magazines, has generated interest in sports by creating heroes and by continually bombarding the public with statistics, human-interest stories, and coverage of the sporting events themselves. Furthermore, the increased leisure time available to most North Americans, coupled with the relatively high standard of living that many people enjoy, provides much of the basis for the rise in attendance figures at sports events and the rise in sport activity itself.

In learning the culture (through the socialization process), most North Americans have internalized values that predispose them to be interested in the outcome of competitive situations, and competition is the sine qua non of sport. We focus on several of the most important values below.

Competition and Success in Sport

Functionalism views sports as an almost sacred activity that socializes participants about competition values. As in the larger society, there is a tremendous emphasis in North American sport on competitive success. Winning is glorified by all who participate. The following epigrams by various coaches exemplify this emphasis on winning:

In our society, in my profession, there is only one measure of success, and that is winning. Not just any game, not just the big game, but the last one.
(head coach of the Oakland Raiders)

Defeat is worse than death because you have to live with defeat.
(head basketball coach at the University of Minnesota)

There are only two things in this league, winning and misery.
(coach of the Miami Heat)

Our expectations are to play for and win the national championship every year. . . . Second, third, fourth, and fifth don't do you any good in this business.
(head football coach at the University of Miami)

Whether in school or in business or in politics, or in sports, North Americans demand winners. Coaches are fired if they are not successful; teams are booed if they play for ties. Inevitably, coaches faced with the option of taking a tie or gambling on winning (with a high probability of losing) will go for the win with the comment, "We're not here to play for a tie." The thirty-two teams in the National Football League who do not win the Super Bowl in a given year are considered losers. Not even the members of the runner-up team consider themselves successful: For them, they did not win the only game that really counts.

Coaches do all they can to socialize their athletes with the value orientation that winning is the most admired achievement in sport. They reinforce winners with praise, honor, and status. Numerous reinforcers are used to illustrate that the primary goal of sports competition is to succeed (to win). Coaches also do all they can to instill in their athletes the character traits that they believe will produce winning teams (e.g., loyalty, enthusiasm, initiative, self-control, confidence, poise, hard work, and ambition).

Conversely, they ridicule losing athletes and teams. As an example of a technique used to instill

in athletes the desire to excel, one coach of a youth league football team (fourth, fifth, and sixth graders) in Lawrence, Kansas, had his young boys yell "I'm a girl!" before they could let their legs touch the ground during a leg-lift exercise. This fear of humiliation kept many boys doing the exercise beyond their normal endurance and, the coach probably assumed, increased their potential for winning.

Another coaching technique to instill in athletes the goal of winning has been to place slogans on the locker room walls to exhort players to value certain behaviors. Commonly, such slogans espouse the competitive spirit:

"Lose" is a four-letter word.
Second place is for the first loser.
A quitter never wins, a winner never quits.
When the going gets tough, the tough get going.
Never be willing to be second best.
Win by as many points as possible.

The demand for winners is found at all levels of sport. Beginning with many youth sports, winning is everything, as evidenced by the pressures commonly found in adult-sponsored children's sports programs. An example of the emphasis on winning among youngsters can be seen in the contests sponsored by some business corporations. NFL Pepsi sponsors a Punt, Pass, and Kick contest for youngsters six through fifteen and Aquafina and Major League Baseball sponsor a Pitch, Hit, and Run contest for baseball skills. In each case, winners are selected at the local level and proceed through the various state and regional tournaments until a national winner is found for each age category. In one year, there were 1,112,702 entrants in the Punt, Pass, and Kick contest and only 6 winners. Why would an organization sponsor an event that produced 6 winners and 1,112,696 losers? Perhaps the reason is that this, too, is a microcosm of the larger society.

The obsession with winning has led to scandals throughout the sports world, as we shall note throughout this book. Most visible is the illegal recruiting of athletes by colleges and universities. In the quest to succeed (i.e., win), some coaches have violated NCAA regulations by arranging to have transcripts altered to ensure athletes' eligibility; by enrolling athletes in classes and obtaining for them academic credits for course work never taken; by allowing substitutes to take admissions tests for athletes of marginal educational ability; by paying athletes for nonexistent jobs; by illegally using government work-study funds for athletes; and by offering money, cars, and clothing to entice athletes to their universities.[9]

When "winning is everything," players and coaches may turn to other forms of cheating. Many athletes take drugs to enhance their performance artificially. This practice is so commonplace, even expected, in some sports that we might call steroids that increase bulk and strength "vocational drugs." Players may try to gain an unfair advantage also by such practices as "doctoring" a pitch or "corking" a bat in baseball, curving the blades of the stick beyond the legal limits in hockey, pretending to be fouled in basketball, or "boosting" the manifold pressure to gain a horsepower advantage in automobile racing.[10]

One of the problems with the hyperemphasis on winning is that it tends to warp sport. Sport, in its pristine form, emphasizes the playing of the contest with thrills achieved from strategy, luck, finesse, cunning, practice, and skill. When winning is everything, however, the playing of the game becomes secondary. In effect, the destination becomes more important than the journey. When this occurs, sport is diminished. Today, on all levels of sports, the most important thing is not merely to take part but to win; the most important thing is not the struggle but the triumph; the essential thing is not to have played well but to have won. But remarkable exceptions to the traditional norms occasionally occur (see Box 3.1).

Such a heavy emphasis on winning is not a natural phenomenon but rather a cultural one. Games in many societies have no competitive element but reflect a different emphasis because of their cultural values. For contrast, let us examine a game

---

Box 3.1   *Thinking About Sport:* Western Oregon Softball

Athletes sometimes make up their own rules. A home run in a college women's softball game may go down as one of the greatest home runs of all time, but not for the reasons you would ordinarily imagine. On April 26, 2008, during a softball game between Western Oregon University and Central Washington University at Central Washington's 300-seat stadium, the score was 0–0 when a Western Oregon senior, Sara Tucholsky—a part-time starter in the outfield throughout her four years, who had never hit a home run in her career—hit a three-run homer over the fence, giving her team the lead.

Tucholsky missed first base on her home-run trot, and while doubling back to tag first base she tore a ligament in her right knee and fell a few feet from first base. The umpires ruled that any assistance from coaches or trainers while Tucholsky was an active runner would result in an out, so the only option was to substitute a pinch runner for her at first base and record her hit as a two-run single instead of a three-run home run.

At that point, in stepped CWU's Mallory Holtman, a four-year starter who held just about every softball offensive record at Central Washington. "Excuse me," she said. "Would it be OK if we carried her around and

she touched each bag?" The umpires knew of no rule against doing so and the coaches for both teams were not opposed, so Holtman and shortstop Liz Wallace lifted Tucholsky and, supporting her weight between them, slowly walked around the bases, stopping at each one so that Tucholsky's left foot could touch it.

Reflecting upon what she did, Holtman said, "Honestly, it's one of those things that I hope anyone would do it for me." She seemed to honestly believe that any player on any field would have acted as she had done. "In the end, it is not about winning and losing so much," Holtman said. "It was about this girl. She hit it over the fence and was in pain, and she deserved a home run."

Tucholsky's home run sent Western Oregon to a 4–2 victory, ending Central Washington's chances of winning the conference and advancing to the playoffs.

Sources: Andy Gardiner, "Sporting Act Draws National Notice," *USA Today,* 2 May 2008, p. 10C; Graham Hays, "Central Washington Offers the Ultimate Act of Sportsmanship," *ESPN. com,* 28 April 2008, http://sports.espn.go.com/ncaa/columns/story?columnist=hays_graham&id=3372631; Associated Press, "'Unbelievable' Sportsmanship in Softball Game," 30 April 2008, http://nbcsports.msnbc.com/id/24392612/.

from another society that would never capture the enthusiasm of North Americans.

The Tangu people of New Guinea play a popular game known as *taketak*, which involves throwing a spinning top into massed lots of stakes driven into the ground. There are two teams. Players of each team try to touch as many stakes with their tops as possible. In the end, however, the participants play not to win but to draw. The game must go on until an exact draw is reached. This requires great skill, since players sometimes must throw their tops into the massed stakes without touching a single one. *Taketak* expresses a prime value in Tangu culture, that is, the concept of moral equivalence, which is reflected in the precise sharing of foodstuffs among the people.

This example underscores our contention that a society's sports mirror its basic values. Cooperative societies have sports that minimize competition, and aggressive societies have highly competitive games.

The Valued Means to Achievement in Sport

In organized and corporate sport, as in society overall, the goal of individual achievement must be accomplished through continuous hard work and sacrifice. The work ethic is also the sports ethic. Someone wins with enough work and sacrifice or, conversely, someone loses without enough work. This is institutionalized by the slogans that coaches use to inspire hard work in their athletes:

> *The will to win is the will to work.*
> *Practice makes perfect.*
> *Success is 99 percent perspiration and 1 percent inspiration.*
> *No one ever drowned in sweat.*
> *By failing to prepare yourself you are preparing to fail.*
> *There is no substitute for hard work.*
> *It's better to wear out than to rust out.*

Soccer players carrying out the traditional post-game hand-slap with opponents. A great deal of social learning of cultural values occurs in youth sports: sportsmanship, competition, self-discipline, sacrifice, authority. (istockphoto)

There is a distinctive loathing in North American sports for athletes and teams who lose more often than they win in spite of their dedication and sustained best efforts to achieve victories. Athletes and coaches who lose are variously accused of not trying hard enough, not sacrificing enough, and not wanting to win badly enough; some are even called quitters. Conflict/cultural theorists regard this as sport's adaptation of a common belief found in the general society: that "poor people are poor because they are lazy and unwilling to work hard." When this view is applied to sport it becomes the false idea that winning can be achieved simply by hard work and that losing can be blamed on individual lack of effort.

Progress in Sport

Coaches, athletes, and fans place a central value on progress. Continued improvement (in mastering new techniques, in winning more games, or in setting new records) is the aim of all athletes and teams. For example, track-and-field stars, swimmers, and athletes in other sports where performances can be precisely quantified undergo great pressures to set new records each time they compete. Indeed, athletes in team sports are always under pressure to achieve outstanding win-loss records. These demands come from the fans, from the press, from promoters, from parents, and often from the athletes themselves.

Materialism in Sport

Although the value that North Americans place on success in competitive situations has the most important impact on the way sport is organized, materialism also has an important value consideration. Big-time college and professional teams in particular are driven by money concerns. Schools, the NCAA, Canadian Interuniversity Sport, professional team owners, and leagues make lucrative arrangements with television networks that have a dramatic effect on sports (e.g., scheduling, timing, and number of time-outs). Professional teams that do not show a high enough profit may be moved to another city in the search for more money because team owners typically have no loyalty to the cities that subsidize them. They move their teams to

places where more money can be made or threaten to move in order to receive greater benefits from their host cities.

Athletes, too, are plainly motivated by material concerns. PGA golfers Tiger Woods and Phil Mickelson have both earned over $60 million in annual winnings and endorsements in recent years. With free agency, team sport athletes move from team to team, securing ever larger contracts. LeBron James of the Miami Heat and Alex Rodriguez of the New York Yankees, for example, have made more than $40 million annually in the past few years.[11] Accumulating obscene amounts of money appears to be the goal of many athletes, rather than love of the game and loyalty to teammates and fans. Olympic athletes parlay their sports accomplishments into millions for endorsements, personal appearances, and the like. College football and basketball coaches sometimes break their contracts to coach at another school. Free agents in professional sports commonly sign with the highest bidder and often try to renegotiate contracts before they expire. In such instances, team and fan loyalty is all but forgotten.

Athletes hire lawyers to negotiate for the highest possible bonuses and salary arrangements. They hold out individually and even strike collectively, on occasion, for better material comforts (see Chapter 10). Furthermore, athletes often engage in activities calculated to increase attendance at contests. Boxers and their promoters are well known for this. Star athletes also devote much of their energy to making money by endorsing products and projects, making personal appearances, and giving inspirational talks. In 2009, golf megastar Tiger Woods became the first athlete to have earned $1 *billion* from his winnings, personal appearances, and endorsements.

Sports fans, too, are influenced by material considerations. They like plush stadiums with expensive scoreboards and other amenities. They are excited by athletes playing for large stakes (e.g., the difference between first and second place in a golf tournament may be as much as a million dollars).

Conflict/cultural theorists have been critical of the "big business" that permeates all levels of contemporary sport, where profitability has become more important than the health and safety of athletes. They're also critical of the coercion and exploitation that are employed to push athletes to harmful physical and psychological extremes.

External Conformity in Sport

Conformity is highly valued in North American sport. Coaches generally demand that their athletes conform to the societal behavior norms in hairstyles, manner of dress, and speech patterns. This is probably the result of two factors: First, coaches feel that their precarious jobs may be in further jeopardy if they permit athletes to act outside societal standards; second, coaches tend to be conservative themselves and believe it is important to reproduce conservative values in the athletes they coach.

Coaches of team sports place a high value on team unity, emphasizing subordination of self to team success. Athletes are expected to subordinate their wills to achieve team success, as the following coaching clichés indicate:

> There is no "I" in team.
> There is no "U" in team.
> A player doesn't make the team, the team makes the player.
> United we stand, divided we fall.
> Cooperate—remember the banana; every time it leaves the bunch, it gets skinned.

Another aspect of external conformity, found both in sport and in the larger society, is the acceptance of authority. Coaches typically structure coach-athlete relationships along authoritarian lines, and their system, the rules, and the structure of power are not challenged. They analyze and structure team positions for the precise specialization of the athletes, and they endeavor to control player behavior not only throughout practice and contest periods but also on an around-the-clock basis.

Under this form of management, the athletes are the instruments for achieving organizational goals. In most cases they are not consulted about team membership, practice methods, strategy, team rules, or any of the other dynamic functions of a team. Thus, athletes learn the structure of contemporary corporate society by comprehending the hierarchy of power within modern sport. Under the pretext of a game that is supposed to develop the character of the participants, sport in fact reproduces the world of work. Thus, play is transformed into work. The playfulness, fun, and creativity of sport are muted by the absolute control of coaches over their teams and players; if players wish to participate, they must conform to the coach's system. Indeed, many coaches actually tell their athletes, "It's my way or the highway."

SUMMARY

North American values are clearly reinforced and reproduced in sports. Just as important is the insight that sport in society, through its organization and the demands and the emphases of those in power, reinforces societal values. This reciprocity places sport squarely in the middle of society's "way of life." It is precisely because sport is so intertwined with the fundamental values of society that any attack on sport is usually interpreted as unpatriotic. Hence, criticism of sport is rarely taken seriously. We should keep this in mind in subsequent chapters as we examine the positive and negative consequences of sport in society. Any proposed changes in sport must be related to the values of society.

WEB RESOURCES

www.icice.org/resources/repository/
b630a082cebdb5ab3e9e7c94f9ea8cbf.pdf
An instructional PDF file whose topic is "Why Do Americans Act Like That? A Guide to Understanding the U.S. Culture and Its Values."

www.americanpopularculture.com
Americana is dedicated to the study of American popular culture. *Americana: The Journal of American Popular Culture* is published by this organization. *Americana* examines such issues as social justice, human rights, environmental awareness, the human condition, and diversity and often publishes articles about sports.

www.asanet.org/sections/culture.cfm
The purpose of the American Sociological Association's Section on Culture is to encourage development of the sociology of culture through the organized interchange of ideas and research. The Section on Culture considers material products, ideas, and symbolic means and their relation to social behavior.

http://charactercounts.org/sports/sportslinks.htm
This website provides numerous links for sport organizations and sportsmanship.

NOTES

1. David M. Thomas and Barbara B. Torrey, eds., *Canada and the United States: Differences That Count*, 3rd ed. (Aurora, Ontario, Canada: Garamond Press, 2007); see also John H. Thompson and Stephen J. Randall, *Canada and the United States: Ambivalent Allies*, 4th ed. (Athens: University of Georgia Press, 2008).

2. Much of this discussion on values can be found in D. Stanley Eitzen and Maxine Baca Zinn, *In Conflict and Order: Understanding Society*, 12th ed. (Boston: Allyn and Bacon, 2010), 92–103.

3. Roy D'Andrade, *A Study of Personal and Cultural Values: American, Japanese, and Vietnamese* (New York: Palgrave Macmillan, 2008).

4. There is a substantial literature on U.S. values, much of it having a particular political viewpoint. The following publications focus more on the topic of values than on that of politics: Charles Churchyard, *National Lies: The Truth About American Values* (Cambridge, MA: Axroide Publishing, 2009); Kurt Anderson, *Reset: How This Crisis Can Restore Our Values and Renew America* (New York: Random House, 2009); and Jon P. Alston, Theresa M. Morris, and Arnold Vedlitz, "Comparing Canadian and American Values: New Evidence from National Surveys," *American Review of Canadian Studies* 26, no. 3 (Autumn 1996): 301–314.

5. For a well-documented and devastating critique of competition in American culture, see Pauline Vaillancourt Rosenau, *The Competition Paradigm: America's Romance with Conflict, Contest, and Commerce* (Lanham, MD: Rowman & Littlefield, 2003).

6. Slosar, *The Culture of Excess: How America Lost Self-Control and Why We Need to Redefine Success* (New York: Praeger, 2009); see also Mortimer B. Zuckerman, "Our Cheating Hearts," *U.S. News & World Report*, 6 November 2006, p. 88; and Susan D. Blum, *My Word! Plagiarism and College Culture* (Ithaca, NY: Cornell University Press, 2009). The Center for Academic Integrity is affiliated with the Robert J. Rutland Institute for Ethics at Clemson University in Clemson, South Carolina; its web address is www.academicintegrity.org.

7. Joel F. Handler and Yeheskel Hasenfeld, *Blame Welfare, Ignore Poverty and Inequality* (New York: Cambridge University Press, 2006). The classic book on this topic, and the one most cited, is William Ryan, *Blaming the Victim*, rev. ed. (New York: Pantheon Books, 1976).

8. Robert D. Putnam, *Bowling Alone: The Collapse and Revival of American Community* (New York: Simon & Schuster, 2000). Sociologists have recently found that the average American has only two close friends, and a quarter don't have any; see Miller McPherson, Lynn Smith-Lovin, and Matthew E. Brashears, "Social Isolation in America: Changes in Core Discussion Networks over Two Decades," *American Sociological Review* 71 (June 2006): 353–375.

9. Jack Carey, "NCAA Slams USC with Sanctions," *USA Today*, 11 June 2010, pp. 1C–2C. For an excellent account of the athletic problems at one university, see William C. Dowling, *Confessions of a Spoilsport: My Life and Hard Times Fighting Sports Corruption at an Old Eastern University* (University Park: Pennsylvania State University Press, 2007).

10. For many other examples, see D. Stanley Eitzen, *Fair and Foul: Beyond the Myths and Paradoxes of Sport*, 4th ed. (Lanham, MD: Rowman & Littlefield, 2009), ch. 4.

11. Jonah Freedman, "The 50 Highest-Earning American Athletes," *SI.com* (2011), http://sportsillustrated.cnn.com/specials/fortunate50-2011/index.html.

CHAPTER 4
Youth and Sport

If I can't win I don't want to play.
—Slogan on the T-shirt of a fourteen-year-old girl training at the
International Performance Institute at IMG Academies in Bradenton, Florida

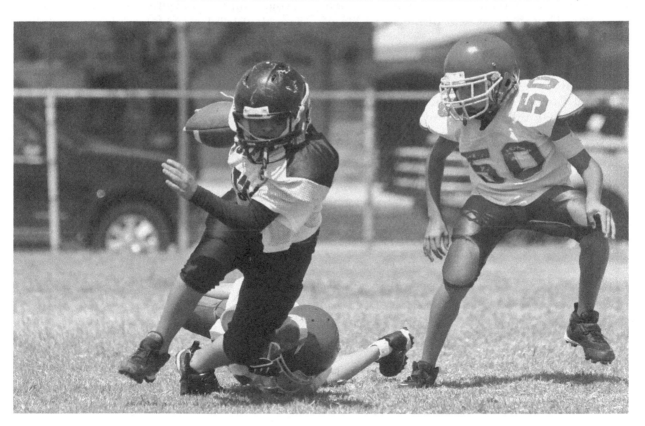

It is often claimed that there is a youth sport for every boy and girl in North America. Youth sports programs are organized by thousands of local and regional sport organizations and more than twenty-five national agencies. (istockphoto)

More people participate in sport during their youth than at any other time in their lives. Although for many young boys and girls sports involvement is limited to informal neighborhood play, an increasing number of North American youth participate in highly organized athletic competition. Indeed, youth sports are now a $5 billion industry.

YOUTH SPORTS PROGRAMS: SOMETHING FOR EVERYONE

Youth sports programs have grown to include greater numbers of participants, and new programs have been created to include a bewildering variety of sports. Thus, a great deal of the social life of youngsters is spent playing sports. Nonschool youth sports programs in North America are organized by more than twenty-five agencies and by thousands of local and regional sports organizations. The National Council of Youth Sports estimates that more than 60 million boys and girls participate in organized youth sports throughout the United States, while some 5 million Canadian youth participate. The results of a comprehensive study of nationwide surveys initiated by the Women's Sports Foundation and conducted by the Center for Research on Physical Activity, Sport, and Health at D'Youville College are shown in Figure 4.1. Surveys of Canadian youth report similar findings. Thus, between 70 and 72 percent of all American and Canadian youth under the age of seventeen participate in organized and team sports as they pass through childhood and adolescence.

Little League baseball is the largest of the youth sports organizations, with leagues in every U.S. state and in eighty countries (200,000 leagues at present) and with more than 2.5 million youngsters engaged in Little League annually. There are several baseball divisions for boys and girls based on age as well as several softball divisions for girls based on age. Pop Warner football celebrated its eightieth year in 2009 and has 400,000 kids in its program.

In terms of participants, soccer has been growing faster than any other youth team sport during the past decade and now has some 10,000 teams and about 5 million young boys and girls playing the sport. With such growth involving youth in

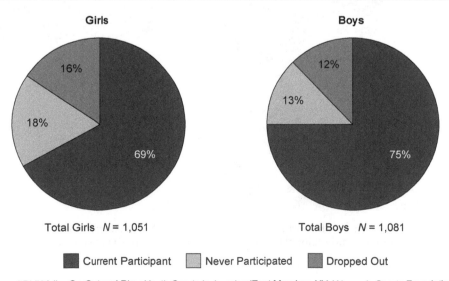

Figure 4.1   Participation in Organized and Team Sports

Girls — Total Girls N = 1,051 — 69%, 18%, 16%

Boys — Total Boys N = 1,081 — 75%, 13%, 12%

■ Current Participant   ■ Never Participated   ■ Dropped Out

Source: Don Sabo and Phil Veliz, *Go Out and Play: Youth Sports in America* (East Meadow, NY: Women's Sports Foundation, 2008).

Little League baseball is the largest youth sport organization in North America, with leagues throughout the U.S. and Canada and in over eighty countries. Initially, Little League baseball was for boys only, but after several lawsuits challenging the ban on girls, the "boys only" rule was dropped and girls legally won the right to participate in Little League. (istockphoto)

North America, soccer enthusiasts claim that the national pastimes in the U.S. and Canada—baseball and hockey—will be displaced by this more global pastime.

More than 3,000 YMCAs in the United States and Canada provide some 8 million boys and girls the opportunity to participate in organized sports. The Junior Olympics Sports Program sponsors more than 2,000 local, state, regional, and national events in twenty-one different sports.

The popularity of ESPN's X Games has stimulated the rise of several new youth-oriented extreme sports, such as in-line skating, freestyle bicycling, BMX racing, snowboarding, and skateboarding, all having had explosive growth. There is even a National Hot Rod Association Jr. Drag Racing League and go-kart racing with more than 55,000 youngsters ages eight to seventeen competing at more than 140 racetracks. Girls' participation in organized sports in the United States and Canada has experienced dramatic increases over the past twenty years, and girls represent about 35 percent of the participants.[1]

There is a well-organized outlet for almost every child who has an interest in being involved in sports. Parents can enroll their children in age-group

gymnastics and swimming programs at three years of age; ice hockey, soccer, football, T-ball, and a half-dozen other sports begin at age four. Indeed, an early start is considered essential when parents or children have professional or Olympic-level aspirations.

The major promotional forces behind these youth sports programs have been parents and interested laypersons, while educators, physicians, and psychologists have tended to be less enthusiastic. Indeed, educators have rather effectively prohibited interscholastic sports in the elementary schools and have severely restricted school sports in the middle and junior high schools. They have, however, been ineffectual in controlling nonschool programs.

As sports for children and adolescents have expanded and diversified, a wide variety of sponsors have emerged. The types of agencies that sponsor youth sport in the United States are quite varied, and an example of each is shown in Table 4.1. Canadian youth sport funding comes from various sources. The major sources are the government, community fund-raising, private sponsorships, and registration fees. Virtually all of the national associations receive over half of their money from the federal government. At the local level, fund-raising and registration fees account for more than half of the total money.

Such a bewildering number of youth sports programs with varying structural arrangements exist that it is somewhat foolish to talk about them as though they were all alike. There are programs that emphasize participation and carefully regulate the type and extent of stress placed on the players. On the other hand, there are programs in which adults intrude enormously on the play of the youngsters; in many of these the purpose is simply to train children to become champions. An example of the former is the IMS Sports Academies in Florida, which are quite clearly devoted to producing champions in several sports.

There are many academies and clubs devoted to a variety of sports scattered across North America training athletes to become pros or Olympic-level competitors. Indeed, the U.S. Soccer Federation established Project 2010, a program to recruit and

Table 4.1   Categories of Agencies That Organize Youth Sports

Type of Agency	Example of Type
National youth sport organization	Little League Baseball
National youth agency	Boys and Girls Clubs of America
National governing body	U.S. Wrestling
National service organization	American Legion Baseball
National religious organization	Catholic Youth Organization
Regional youth sport organization	Soccer Association for Youth
State school activity association	Ohio High School Activities Association
Local school district	Norton, Kansas, Public School
Local service club	Greeley Lions Club
Municipal recreation department	Fort Collins Recreation Department
Private sports club	Front Range Volleyball Club

train young soccer players with the aim of winning the World Cup by 2010. Although the U.S. Men's National Team did not win the World Cup, it did qualify for the 2010 FIFA World Cup in South Africa.

Despite variations in youth sports forms and functions, advocates of youth sports programs claim that they provide a means for the development of such personal-social attributes as self-discipline, cooperativeness, achievement motivation, courage, persistence, and so forth. Proponents of organized youth sports typically view them as good preparation for the realities of adult life. Additionally, advocates contend that the physical activity involved in playing sports promotes health and fitness. These are all attributes, attitudes, and values that functional theorists view as socially efficient and useful for socializing youth to perform cooperatively and consensually with others, thus promoting social stability.

On the other hand, critics of highly organized youth sports claim that excessive psychological and physical demands are frequently placed on participants. A conflict/cultural perspective contends that the encroachment of adults into the world of young persons reduces the value of play as a spontaneous, expressive experience. Advocates of this social theoretical perspective make a case that youth sports frequently seem to be conducted for the self-serving needs of parents and youth sports leaders. Pressure from parents and coaches forces many elite child athletes to strive for perfection, and that pressure is responsible for dropping out, burnout, overuse injuries, and a host of other physical and psychological ailments.[2]

THE RISE OF YOUTH SPORTS PROGRAMS: THE TAKEOFF AND EXPANSION OF A NEW FORM OF SPORT

Two independent but interrelated developments in the sociocultural milieu of North American society during the past two generations were primarily responsible for the rise and expansion of youth sports programs. The first was the rise of organized and corporate sport in all parts of both the U.S. and Canada. The first half of the twentieth century witnessed an enormous growth in popular spectator sports, such as Major League Baseball, collegiate football, professional ice hockey, boxing, and others. High school athletics became an integral part of North American education, and the overall obsession with these forms of organized sport eventually trickled down to preadolescent youth.

The second development promoting the growth of youth sports programs was that childhood was seen as a particularly opportune time for nurturing attitudes and habits that would prepare youth for adulthood. Youth leaders urged the use of sports for the development of desirable personal-social skills. When the schools refused to sponsor sports for preadolescent youth, the task was left to voluntary agencies, and responsibility for sport competition for preadolescents was assumed by child-oriented organizations outside of the educational framework.[3]

Until the 1970s most organized youth sports programs were for boys only, but growing out of the attack on gender discrimination in all aspects of social life by the women's movement, exclusion of girls from organized sport became unacceptable. The Little League's ban against participation by girls was challenged in 1973, and after several lawsuits girls legally won the right to participate in Little League baseball.

Over the past twenty years organized youth sport has become available in almost every sport in which girls have wished to participate. The initial reservations, and even objections, to girls' sports participation gradually declined and have been replaced by enthusiastic endorsement by almost everyone. However, there are those who question the wisdom of merely incorporating girls into the prevailing youth sport system. They argue that the structure of traditional youth sports programs allows little creative development and little chance to invent new ways of organizing sporting activities.

OBJECTIVES OF YOUTH SPORTS PROGRAMS

Regardless of the sponsoring organization, the objectives of most youth sports programs are quite similar. They are intended to provide young boys and girls with opportunities to learn culturally relevant sports skills. Inasmuch as sport is such a pervasive activity in North American culture, developing sports skills becomes almost a public duty. Equally important in the objectives of these programs, however, is the transmission of attitudes and values through interpersonal associations with teammates and opponents and through deliberate actions on the part of coaches, officials, and parents.

Thus, youth sports are viewed as an environment for promoting attitudes and values about such things as competition, sportsmanship, discipline, authority, and social relationships. The original certificate of the federal charter granted to Little League baseball illustrates the objectives of most youth sports programs: "To help and voluntarily assist boys in developing qualities of citizenship, sportsmanship, and manhood. Using the disciplines of the native American game of baseball, to teach spirit and competitive will to win, physical fitness through individual sacrifice, the values of team play, and wholesome well-being through healthful and social association with other youngsters under proper leadership." Girls are now participants in Little League baseball, but otherwise its objectives are still the same. A girls' softball program was introduced in 1974. Today more than 5,200 charters and more than 350,000 youngsters participate in this phase of the Little League program.

What Do Young Athletes, Their Parents, and Coaches Want from Sports?

Many books and articles for parents, coaches, and athletes about youth sports have enumerated the benefits of sports for young athletes. The most commonly listed benefits are:

1. Helps a child's overall physical development.
2. Gives the child the opportunity to become familiar with his/her body and to learn the body's needs and limitations.
3. Is social as well as physical and thus teaches young athletes how to interact with his/her peers.
4. Teaches cooperation, teamwork, and how to follow rules.
5. Helps the child learn for him/herself if winning or losing is important.
6. Gives parents the opportunity of offering the child unqualified support.
7. Helps the child gain acceptance and credibility among his/her peers.

Beyond the benefits that youth sports are believed to provide for participants, a functionalist perspective views community-based youth sports programs as bringing together members of a community, thus functioning to satisfy a need by contributing a link with symbols of stability, order, tradition, and a communal focus.

The extent to which youth sports actually serve these functions is hard to quantify, but there is little doubt that substantial community financial and human resources are poured into the programs. Local merchants sponsor teams; coaches volunteer their time; groundskeepers, concession-stand operators, scorekeepers, and so forth facilitate the ongoing operations of the programs; and parents turn out in large numbers to cheer their children. In addition, playing fields are built and maintained, and equipment is largely furnished, with taxpayers' money. Youth sports are indeed a significant community activity in towns and cities throughout Canada and the United States.

Conflict/cultural theorists agree with some of these communal outcomes of youth sport, but they contend that youth sports also serve to divert attention away from many community problems and social issues that are prevalent in communities throughout North America.

SOCIALIZATION AND SPORT: INVOLVEMENT IN SPORT AND ITS CONSEQUENCES

With youth sports as pervasive as they are in North America, issues about the social forces promoting youth sports involvement are important for understanding how youngsters get into organized sports and what the consequences of these experiences are. In the broadest sense the process of becoming a young athlete is part of a socialization process.

Socialization is the process of learning and adapting to a given social system. In the context of society, the activity of socialization is called cultural transmission and is the means by which a society preserves its norms and perpetuates itself. At birth, infants are certainly living organisms, but they are not social beings. Humans raised under daily social interaction demonstrate the impact of their culture upon them, and this is called socialization.

Socialization continues throughout an individual's life cycle, but the years from birth to adolescence are considered critical, for in these years the basic cultural transmission takes place. Numerous people are involved in the socialization of an individual, but because of their frequency of contact, their primacy, and their control over rewards and punishments, the primary agents and agencies for socialization are families, peer groups, schools, churches, and mass media.

The outcomes of the socialization process are attitudes, values, knowledge, and behaviors that are related to the culture of which individuals are a part and to the roles that they will play in it. Thus, as children in a society interact with others through language, gestures, rewards, and punishments, they learn the attitudes, the values, and the expectations of various individuals in that society as well as the behaviors considered appropriate to the various situations of their social life.

As we noted in Chapter 1 and in an earlier section of this chapter, social theorists view the process and outcomes of socialization quite differently. The functionalists emphasize the importance of socializing each new generation toward maintaining the existing social order. Conflict/culturalists tend to problematize the existing social order, especially the inequalities, injustices, and various forms of discrimination present within the existing social organization.

Socialization is not merely a one-way process from socializers (parents, peers, and so forth) to the children; instead a reciprocal interaction process is also at work, and youngsters actually influence the attitudes, values, and behaviors of adults. Often-heard comments among parents include "I've certainly learned some things from my kids" and "My kids have made me change my mind about _____." There is little doubt that young athletes continually influence the attitudes and behaviors toward sport of various socializing agents, including parents, coaches, teachers, and peers.

The topic of socialization and sport may be divided into two subtopics for analysis: (1) socialization into sport and (2) socialization via sport. In the first the focus is on the agents and agencies that attract, or draw, children into sports; that is, an analysis of the ways in which children become involved in sports. An analysis of socialization via sport concentrates on the consequences, or outcomes, of sports involvement. First we direct our attention to socialization into sport; socialization via sport is addressed later in this chapter.

SOCIALIZATION INTO SPORT: WHY DO CHILDREN BECOME INVOLVED IN ORGANIZED SPORTS?

An analysis of socialization into sports is concerned with who becomes involved in sport, which social agents and agencies are responsible for guiding young people into such involvement, how persons learn sports roles, and what the social processes for becoming involved are. One thing is quite clear: There is an enormous variety in the process of becoming involved in sport. Canadian sport sociologist Chris Stevenson has conducted several research projects on the life histories of athletes in an attempt to discover how they became involved in sport. He found that "here were fathers involved, mothers involved, friends, teachers, sisters and brothers, coaches, and friends of the family."[4]

Families

The family is the first and perhaps the most important social environment in a young person's life, and there is overwhelming evidence that the family—its social status, its structure, and its patterning of activities—is a significant influence in socializing boys and girls into sport.

One important factor in the sport involvement of youngsters is the structure of the family. Families vary in size from a single child to sometimes more than a dozen offspring; following divorce or the death of one parent, some families become single-parent families. According to the U.S. Census Bureau, the proportion of traditional families, meaning married couples with or without children, is at its lowest, 50 percent, in at least 200 years. Almost half of all U.S. children are growing up without both natural parents in the household.[5]

Participation in youth sports programs cuts across all socioeconomic strata; however, children from working-class families are overrepresented in some youth sports, and children from upper-middle-class families in others. Parents socialize their children into sports that are deemed most appropriate for their socioeconomic status. For example, age-group tennis players, skiers, gymnasts, golfers, and swimmers tend to come from upper-middle-class families. On the other hand, youth baseball, boxing, wrestling, and football programs tend to attract youngsters from middle- and working-class families. (Chapter 12 deals with the social stratification aspects of sports in more detail.)

Parents

Children tend to adopt the attitudes and values of their parents. Parents who reward the acquisition of motor skills and who themselves engage in sporting activities tend to socialize their children to an interest in physical activity. Indeed, several investigators have found that parents are important agents of sport socialization for both their sons and their daughters.

Parental influence appears to occur through their own participation (the modeling influence) and through their interest in and encouragement of their offspring's involvement in sport. Surveys of North American families have found that around 75 percent of parents engage in some kind of sports activity with their children. Thus, research suggests that parental encouragement and actual participation are primary sources of sport socialization. A high percentage of fathers and mothers of young female athletes actually engage in sport themselves, and overall, parents are the most salient social agents in encouraging female athletes to participate.[6]

Although parents have received considerable attention as a factor in influencing the sport involvement of their offspring, very little is known about the specific contributions that each parent makes. Some investigators have reported that the father is frequently the most significant socializing agent in the family and the most important predictor of sport participation for both boys and girls. Others have reported a tendency for the same-sex parent to have greater influence on sport involvement than the opposite-sex parent. More specifically, they have found that fathers' sports interests are more strongly related than mothers' interests to direct primary participation for both males and females. Christine Brennan, sports columnist for *USA Today*, recounts how her father nurtured her interest in sports: "I got my first inkling something was up with this man [her father] when his 5-year-old daughter [Christine] told him what she wanted for her birthday and he went right out and bought it for her. It was a baseball mitt." She continues: "In the years that followed, this man would attend almost every high school game his children ever played."[7]

Mothers have recently become more involved in their children's sports, and this phenomenon has been popularized with the label "soccer mom." In a study of the experiences of a group of upper-middle-class mothers whose sons played soccer, sport sociologist Lisa Swanson found that these women were using their economic capital "to produce, in their words, 'good boys.'" Swanson notes that the mothers' efforts resulted in the reproduction of their social class perceptions and lifestyle patterns in their sons.[8]

Parents who have been asked about their children's involvement in organized sports programs usually expressed rather strong support, and parents of youth sport athletes have rated the coaches as excellent or good. They generally view sports as having had a positive effect on family life and as helping parents in socializing their children, in that they teach youngsters useful personal and social skills. In the case of the "soccer moms" whom Lisa Swanson studied, the mothers were enthusiastic about their sons' soccer experiences because, "ultimately, the soccer field provided a space in which upper-middle-class mothers could perform a class-appropriate use of the sons' bodies and, in so doing, reproduce the upper-middle-class" perceptions and lifestyle.[9]

For those parents whose children are training for elite status, for instance to be an Olympic-level athlete or a professional athlete, there are fears, sacrifices, and constant pressures. Is the child being robbed of his or her childhood in the tightly structured training environment? Are the sacrifices of the child living away from home year-round worth it? Are the costs for coaching worth it? There is also the constant realization that unless the child continues to improve against the competition, he or she will be dropped by the coach or the program or both. When parents set for their child the goal of achieving professional standing, pressures are inevitably applied to the child's performance.[10]

In the literature on socialization into sport, little attention has been given to the ways in which youths influence their parents to become involved. Instead, most research has presented a one-dimensional socialization process in which the offspring are the learners and the parents are the socializers. Some sociologists have called for greater attention to the symbolic interactionist perspective, which sees social interacting as reciprocal and negotiable. In this view, analysis of parent effects needs to be balanced by analysis of child effects and of the two-way "reciprocal-effects synthesis." With respect to sport, in addition to parental encouragement of offspring, some family adjustments may produce reverse socialization, with parents being socialized into sport through their children's participation. Indeed, many parents learn about sport and become involved in sport from their children. Therefore, the socialization between parents and their children is frequently bidirectional. Thus, although parents may initially steer their children into sport, the child's involvement often has behavioral and attitudinal consequences for the parents.

Siblings

A rather consistent association has been shown between parents' sports involvement, their support, and their encouragement and the involvement of their children in sport, but the influence of siblings is not so clear. Still, a number of studies examining factors that affect the sport and physical activity participation of youngsters have identified siblings as a positive social influence. It is probable that the example of an older brother or sister participating in organized sport spurs younger children to become involved. One of the athletes Chris Stevenson interviewed about becoming involved in sport said, "I have two brothers and we used to play hockey and we used to play football. . . . When I was little I used to do everything they would do."[11] Siblings certainly play a positive role in influencing the social environment apart from parents.

Peers

As important as the family is, the neighborhood and the peer group also serve as powerful socializing agents for sport involvement, especially as youngsters move into adolescence. Typically, during adolescence less time is spent with the family, and more time is spent with peers. Interactions with peers in the neighborhood and at school almost force compliance with their interests and activities. When peers are involved in sports, young people frequently experience a great deal of pressure to become involved also or else give up cherished social relationships. Very few studies have examined the influence of socializing agents on the process of socialization of boys and girls into sports, but research in other physical-activity contexts has found that peers are a major influence throughout childhood and adolescence.[12]

Coaches

Coaches are not often the persons responsible for initiating young boys and girls into sports, but for many youngsters an extremely close, emotional bond develops between athlete and coach, a bond that frequently becomes the main reason for continuing involvement. From the huge number of volunteer coaches to those who make their living coaching, coaches exert a tremendous influence on young athletes. Most young athletes perceive the role of "coach" in terms of someone to be socially admired. Also, for many young athletes the sports skills they have acquired, an important source of self-esteem, have been learned and developed under the leadership of their coaches. Their coaches are therefore seen as people who have helped young athletes acquire some of their most important possessions. Many ex–youth athletes, years after they have stopped competing, still consider their former coaches to be the most significant adults in their lives.

Schools

Of course, the school, with its physical education classes, is a significant socializing agent for North American children. Thanks to universal education and a physical education curriculum that typically puts a great deal of emphasis on learning sports skills, most children are taught the rudiments of a variety of sports in school. (Chapter 5 deals further with sport in high school.)

Mass Media

The mass media are a powerful force for the sport role socialization of young boys and girls. Youngsters are virtually inundated with sports via newspapers, magazines, the Internet, and especially television. It is obvious that the mass media bring sports to the attention of the young. Few youngsters do not know the names of the NFL, NHL, NBA, and MLB teams. A great many boys and girls have heroes among professional and Olympic athletes, and many of them have plastered their bedroom walls with sports posters.

Sports video games emerged early in the history of television, and their popularity continues to grow as new sports games and new platforms come into the market. They now emulate more than two dozen traditional sports. Although sports video games are played by people of all ages, the most frequent players are children and adolescents. In the process of playing these games, young boys and girls are socialized into the skills, strategies, and tactics of sports, and many are motivated to try those same sports in their social environments. One study found that children who play sports-themed video games were likely to participate in real sporting activities as well.[13]

During the past decade, television programming has expanded to include a number of youth sports events. Perhaps the most prominent of these is the Little League World Series. Several days of the series are shown on TV. Several other youth championship events also are now televised. *USA Today*, which is sold worldwide, has a prominent place in its sports section for high school sports—including state-by-state results of high school championship events and a national ranking of the top twenty high school teams in several sports. Many young readers of *Sports Illustrated Kids*, *USA Today*, and SIKIDS.com are undoubtedly influenced to become involved in sports because of the media coverage. After all, the most immediate role models and heroes of younger athletes are the athletes featured on TV, on the Internet, and in magazines and newspapers.

Parents, siblings, peers, coaches, schools, and the media, then, are the main sport socializing agents and agencies that act on youth. They are so influential that it is a rare youngster who is not affected in some way by sport as he or she passes through childhood and adolescence.

Participants: Youth Athletes

Studies of participants in youth sports programs usually find that they have positive attitudes toward their experiences. When asked what they like most about their sports experiences, young athletes typically list the fun of being on an organized team, the chance to meet others and make friends, and the opportunity to improve their skills. Comprehensive analyses of youth sports have found there is a common cluster of the most important reasons kids play organized sport (see Table 4.2). According to sport psychologists at the Massachusetts General Hospital Sport Psychology Program, young athletes report that their motivation to play sports is based primarily on competition—with social, fitness/fun, and teamwork reasons also contributing. However, the researchers also found gender differences in the motivations to play sports.[14]

Although millions of youngsters enthusiastically participate in organized youth sports each year and many continue for as long as they are eligible, a surprisingly large number do not continue to take part in sport; they become dropouts. Indeed, as many as one-third of youth sports participants voluntarily drop out of sport each year. Seventy percent of kids by the age of thirteen drop out of youth sports programs. Researchers have tried to ascertain the motives for sports withdrawal. They have found that the disappointment of not getting to play, poor umpiring, and being scolded for mistakes by coaches, parents, or both are the things that young participants dislike most.[15] In studies that asked participants why they discontinued youth sports involvement, the ten most often cited reasons for both boys and girls were these:

1. I lost interest.
2. I was not having fun.
3. It took too much time.
4. Coach played favorites.
5. Coach was a poor teacher.
6. I was tired of playing.
7. Too much emphasis on winning.
8. Wanted a nonsport activity.
9. I needed more time to study.
10. Too much pressure.

The picture that emerges from studying young athletes and their views of participation in youth sports is that they want to have fun and learn skills, but since many of them encounter pressures to train and win, some simply drop out of organized sport programs. For them, the promise of fun, sociability, and skill acquisition through sports is lost.

SOCIALIZATION VIA SPORT: PROCESS AND OUTCOMES

The extent to which the attitudes, values, beliefs, and behaviors of North American young people are actually influenced by participation in organized youth sports programs is largely unknown because

Table 4.2   The Ten Most Important Reasons Why Youth Play Sports

Boys	Girls
1. To have fun	1. To have fun
2. To improve skills	2. To stay in shape
3. For the excitement of competition	3. To get exercise
4. To do something I'm good at	4. To improve skills
5. To stay in shape	5. To do something I'm good at
6. For the challenge of competition	6. To be part of a team
7. To be part of a team	7. For the excitement of competition
8. To win	8. To learn new skills
9. To go to a higher level of competition	9. For the team spirit
10. To get exercise	10. For the challenge of competition

Source: Compilation from various youth sport publications.

few investigations have been undertaken on this topic. Thus, little empirical evidence exists to substantiate the many claims that have been made about the contributions of sport to psychological and social attributes of participants. The major reason is that sport constitutes only one of many forces operating on young people. Every child is subjected to a multitude of social experiences that are not sport-related. Thus, much of what we think we know about the effects, or consequences, of sport participation is impressionistic, and this fact needs to be remembered in any discussion of the topic.

There are several principles of socialization theory, however, that likely hold true with regard to youth sports. In general, the influence of sports experiences will be stronger

1. when the degree of involvement is frequent, intense, and prolonged
2. when the participation is voluntary rather than involuntary
3. when the socializer (e.g., the coach) is perceived as powerful and prestigious
4. when the quality of relationships is high in expressiveness

Two Forms of Play: Peer Group and Adult-Organized

Several social scientists have suggested that the social context in which a sport activity takes place determines its social outcomes. The observational studies of several sport sociologists who have studied children and adolescents and their sports involvement indicate that there are two distinct social contexts in which sports activities take place: "peer-group" and "adult-organized." They have characterized and contrasted the potential socialization outcomes for these two forms of play in terms of their organization, process, impetus, and social implications.

Organizational Differences

In organized team sports the most salient characteristics are that both action and involvement are under adult control and that the actions of the players are strictly regulated by specialized rules and roles. For example, Little League games are organized as performances rather than play. They are modeled after professional sports. Young athletes on organized sports teams learn to stand still—with mouth closed—and listen to the coach's instructions or weather the coach's sometimes blistering criticism.

Youth sport coaches are remarkably similar in the way they organize practice sessions. Activities during practice tend to be very rule-bound. Coaches allow little flexibility in the executing of skills or in the performing of other tasks associated with practice. The youngsters tend to wait to be told what to do, often waiting for directions on how to do things that are routine. Spontaneous behavior, when it occurs, consists of "horsing around" while waiting to practice some given task.

Very few decisions on any aspect of the practice are made by the youngsters. Most decisions are made by the coaches, and the participants are expected to carry them out obediently. The emphasis in the organized setting tends to be on the development of sport skills, not on the development of interpersonal skills.

With respect to play, before the age of seven children rarely play games spontaneously; if they play them at all, it is usually on the initiative of adults or older children. Thus, organized sports programs for youngsters under the age of seven are not organized extensions of what children of that age would be doing anyway; they are simply testaments to the power and influence adults have on young children. For example, out of a desire to make sure their children do not get behind, many parents are enrolling offspring as young as four years of age in organized sports.

When peer play is found, usually among youngsters over the age of seven, it is player-controlled. In one study, researchers observing children's play on a public school playground found that "[c]hildren's choices of what to play, which games or sports, were influenced by a number of considerations: what was 'going on,' the equipment available, novelty, the weather, friendship groups . . . and, finally, those mysterious fads and fashions that cause a game to be hugely popular for a period until it loses appeal and another takes its place."[16]

Players rely on informal norms of conduct and informal rules to regulate the game. The youngsters make consensual decisions on groupings and game rules. Teams are usually organized informally; this is done quickly and typically with little friction. The games children choose in free play generally have fewer rules and fewer specialized roles than the games organized by adults, and children vary the rules in the process of play to suit the situation. In informal peer "sandlot" games the authority structure operates uniquely. There is an authority structure, but the structure works through moral suasion rather than through role occupancy.

Process Differences

The process of play in peer-group sport and adult-organized sport is also quite different. In the former, teams are chosen, and the game usually begins quickly. Field researchers of children's informal sports frequently note the efficiency with which the youngsters go about getting the teams chosen and the game under way. Arguments about rule interpretations or a "call," such as whether a player is "safe" or "out," when they do occur, usually cause only minimal delays. Shouts of "Let him have it" or "Play it over" usually settle the debate, and play is resumed.

In the informal peer-group games the primary focus tends to be on a combination of action, personal involvement, keeping the game close, and the reaffirming of friendships. The quest for victory, or a "win," is not one of the salient outcomes; instead of a narrow focus on winning there is often a search for self-mastery—that is, attempting to create situations that require performing up to a personal standard of satisfaction. The public-school-playground researchers quoted above stressed that "in the end, what the players most enjoyed, beyond winning, was the exhilaration of exercising skill, strength, speed, and coordination along with teammates."[17]

By contrast, in the play process of organized youth sports, there tends to be an emphasis on order, punctuality, respect for authority, obedience to adult directions, and a strict division of labor. Coaches typically insist on order, sometimes prohibiting participants from talking unless the coach speaks to them. The coach's concern for order and discipline often reduces the amount of playing time. Organizing the practice session or stopping practice to discuss mistakes or to punish

misbehavior sometimes takes up significant portions of the practice session. The participants become so accustomed to following orders in an organized sport setting that they frequently will cease to play altogether if the coach is absent or not directly supervising. Close observation by the coach is required to keep them playing.

In organized youth sports the participants have no say in the rules; adults make the rules. In the programs of national sports agencies (such as Little League baseball), a national rulebook is published to which all participants must conform. Thus, in this form of sport, participants are merely followers, not makers or interpreters, of the rules.

Winning is frequently the overriding goal in formal youth sports programs. By striving for league standings, by awarding championships, by choosing all-star teams, such programs send the not-so-subtle message to youngsters that the most important goal of sports is winning.[18]

Impetus Differences

The impetus of peer play comes entirely from the youngsters; they play because they enjoy it. They are free to commence and terminate a game based on player interest. Conversely, the impetus of play in organized sports programs comes from the coaches; they schedule the practices for a given time and end practices when they see fit. Games are scheduled by a league authority and are played in a very rigid time frame. The youngsters have no choice but to play in the way the adults wish them to play. Their own enjoyment appears to be of little concern to the adults. Coaches and many players expect participants to adhere to a Puritan work ethic, and the word *work* is ever-present in practices and games. "Come on, work hard" and "Take pride in your work!" are proddings frequently used by coaches and parents.

Social Implications of the Two Forms of Play

Adult-sponsored youth sport is basically an organized structuring of groupings, activities, and rules that are imposed upon the participants. Peer play, on the other hand, is a voluntary activity with a flexible process of social exchange based on consensus. Youngsters are therefore exposed to quite different experiences in what appear to be similar sport activities.

What are the social implications of these two different forms of organization of play activities for the socialization of youngsters? The application of arbitrary, adult-imposed rules in organized youth sport markedly contrasts with the spontaneous group-derived rules in peer-group play. This contrast is a function of the different roles of the peer group and of adults in the socialization process. The role of the peer group serves to bridge the gap between the individualistic world of children and the orientations of the wider society. The role of the organized team serves to emphasize the adult, universalistic-achievement orientations deemed appropriate by the society.

The differences between the goals of peer-group play and organized team effort become apparent in their emphasis on means and ends. In the peer context, play is not overly concerned with ends; the essence of the play is the play—its fun, decisions, ritual, and personal interactions. In contrast, in organized sports, play tends to be incidental.

For the adults who organize sport programs, play is identified with ends. That is, to win, to teach youngsters to play soccer, baseball, and so forth in the short run, and to develop certain attitudes and values toward social relationships and activities that in the long run tend to reproduce the requirements of occupational life by emphasizing punctuality, periodicity, and performance. Indeed, it has been argued that organized sport socializes young athletes to accept authoritarian leadership and carry out coaches' directions without question, thus suppressing their own creative initiatives and personal growth.[19]

In peer play, there tends to be an elaboration of means either through varying the rules, particularizing relationships, or encouraging novelty. The games chosen in free play (in which less specialization of roles tends to occur) permit more elaboration of means. For example, the youngsters find many ways to use the same ball in their games. In organized sports the codified rules (enforced by coaches and officials) permit only one way to use a ball, a one-size field, a certain number of players to a side, and so forth. In organized sports programs, disputes about "calls" or about rules do not occur between players because they are made

and applied by referees and coaches. Therefore, the experience in peer play emphasizes interpersonal skills (negotiations and compromise), while the experience in organized sport is dominated by a knowledge of and dependence on strict rules and with the acceptance of the decisions of adults, who are in positions of legitimate authority.

Applying a model of enjoyment of social experience, the Flow Model, to formal and informal sport settings, two noted researchers and authors of *Flow in Sports* report a high positive correlation between challenges and skills in informal sports settings but not in adult-supervised settings. They suggest that the flow experience is easier to achieve when adolescents are in control of the activity, probably because they can manipulate the balance between challenges and skills more easily in an informal setting.[20] Unfortunately, as the 2010 Sporting Goods Manufacturing Association's report on active segments of the U.S. population noted, "casual/pick-up" play in youth continues to decline, primarily because more young athletes are specializing in one sport at an earlier age.[21]

To summarize, what is implied by an analysis of these two play forms is that play behavior in the peer group is quite different from play behavior in the youth sports program. We are not arguing that one of these forms of play is good and the other bad. What we are emphasizing is that the variations in the social organization of children's play undoubtedly have different social consequences for them.

DEVELOPMENT OF PERSONAL-SOCIAL ATTRIBUTES THROUGH SPORT

As noted earlier in this chapter, the primary justifications of youth sports programs are the opportunities they provide for young boys and girls to learn culturally relevant sport skills and to develop desirable personal-social characteristics. "Sport builds character" is one of the most frequently recited slogans for the supposed outcomes of sport for youth. It inevitably is used by community leaders, school officials, parents, coaches—virtually everyone—when a discussion turns to the purpose of organized sports for children and adolescents. Although the learning of attitudes, values, and moral behavior is a core aim of youth sports, there is very little definitive research on the outcomes of sports participation—that is, the effects of sport involvement on the personal and social development of children.

Youth Orientation Toward Sport

There has been a sustained interest in the effects of sports experiences on the orientations youth have toward sport. One of the orientations sport sociologists have focused on is whether participation in organized sport influences what participants think is most important about playing. Specifically, they have studied orientations that emphasize the process (playing fair, playing for fun) and orientations that emphasize the product (playing to win); the latter is called a "professional" attitude.

Researchers have found, overall, that there is a strong tendency for both males and females who have been involved in organized sports to have more professionalized orientations than peers who have not been involved in organized sports. Elite athletes, both males and females, display a strong professional orientation toward sport. These findings are probably not surprising, given the structural conditions of organized sport, which socializes youngsters into accepting and internalizing values of success-striving, of competitive achievement, of personal worth based upon sports outcomes, and of subjection of self to external control. Although it is difficult to credit (or discredit) sports participation entirely for greater professionalized attitudes toward sport, it does seem that sport for fun, enjoyment, fairness, and equity is often sacrificed at the altar of skill and victory as children continue their involvement in organized sports.[22]

Sportsmanship in Youth Sports

Sportsmanlike behavior—striving to succeed but committed to playing by the rules and observing ethical standards that take precedence over strategic gain when the two conflict—is universally admired, but it sometimes conflicts with the quest for victory. In the sport culture at all levels, good sportsmanship and fair play are the accepted standards and are overwhelmingly practiced by those involved in organized sports. But the prevalence of good sportsmanship throughout sports is rarely noted in the public discourse or in the media. This is true because it is the expected, the normative, behavior. On the other hand, poor sportsmanship, like deviant behavior in most social settings, gets noted, gets attention, gets reactions, and therefore often seems to overshadow good sportsmanship in personal conversations and in media stories. In the following paragraphs on this topic, we will describe some findings about poor sportsmanship, but the reader should keep in mind what we have said here about good sportsmanship.

Sportsmanship and fairness underlie the social convention of virtually all youth sports programs, but on the other hand, victory in organized sports competition often carries more salient rewards. The slogan "It's not whether you win or lose but how you play the game," while never universally embraced in the culture of organized sport, is acknowledged by many coaches, athletes, and parents as an appropriate attitude for playing well, playing within the rules, and playing in a sportsmanlike manner rather than for the mere winning of a sporting event.

That standard is challenged by the slogan "Winning isn't everything, it's the only thing." When taken seriously, this latter slogan suggests that any means or methods are legitimate in the pursuit of victory. It has been accompanied with practices like trash talking, intimidating opponents, taunting and ridiculing opponents, and deliberately violating the rules of the sport—all in the interest of "getting the edge" and winning the sporting event. For example, a study of youth sports conducted by researchers at the University of Missouri–St. Louis, the University of Minnesota, and Notre Dame involving 803 young athletes ages nine to fifteen, along with 189 parents and 61 coaches, found, according to the athletes:

- two in ten admitted to cheating often.
- nineteen percent had tried to hurt an opponent often.
- twenty-seven percent had acted like "bad sports" after a loss.
- seven percent of their coaches had encouraged the athletes to cheat.
- eight percent of their coaches had encouraged the athletes to hurt an opponent.[23]

These percentages may seem low, but they are made up of hundreds of individual respondents, so the sum of the incidents is actually quite large, and thus disturbing. See Box 4.1 for further discussion on this topic.

There are a number of sources of a trend toward increasingly unsportsmanlike attitudes and behaviors in youth sports. Professional and college athletes have always profoundly influenced young athletes, because they are the role models and heroes of youth sport athletes. Young athletes adopt the attitudes, manner, and behavior of their heroes. Unfortunately, those heroes often display the trash talking, intimidating, ridiculing, and rule breaking that have sifted down to youth athletes.

Coaches and parents are other powerful sources for socializing young athletes about sportsmanship attitudes and behaviors. Many coaches and parents are aware of their influence and make a valiant effort to make sport a positive experience, emphasizing fun, fair play, and good sportsmanship. Regrettably, a growing number of other coaches and parents are out of control. Many have become models of bad sportsmanship for young athletes. More about this can be found in the "Adult Intrusion in Youth Sports" section of this chapter.

An ominous societal trend might be contributing to the growing unsportsmanlike behavior of young athletes. There is widespread acknowledgment that acts of "incivility" between people have become more common in North American culture (more about this in Chapter 15). Such actions undoubtedly influence the culture of sport and become translated into poor sportsmanship at all levels.

Efforts are being made to counteract the trend toward unsportsmanlike conduct. The Institute for International Sport at the University of Rhode Island has been sponsoring an annual National Sportsmanship Day for more than fifteen years. The Positive Coaching Alliance at Stanford University, through partnership with more than 1,100 youth sports organizations, leagues, schools, and cities nationwide, has conducted 6,000-plus workshops for youth sports coaches, parents, organizational leaders, and athletes. Also, the National Alliance for Youth Sports has publicly affirmed good sportsmanship and committed to developing policies to reward sportsmanlike behaviors and punish unsportsmanlike actions in events under their jurisdiction. Even though these efforts are against the prevailing trend, there are encouraging signs that they are having some positive effects on sports at all levels.[24]

Character Development in Youth Sports

From the beginning of organized youth sports forms there has been a prevailing impression that the sporting environment is particularly useful for young athletes to learn moral values and principles. The slogan often used to affirm this is "sport builds character." Like most slogans, this one is not grounded in empirical findings, and when research has been conducted to ascertain the effects of sport involvement on character development, the

---

Box 4.1 *Thinking About Sport:* Which Is It, Poor Sportsmanship or Just Being a Great Competitor?

As the emphasis on winning and "doing whatever it takes" to win has become more prevalent in youth sports, the line between good and poor sportsmanship has become blurred for many youth sport coaches, athletes, and parents. Here is an example: Referring to one of his young pitchers, a coach explained, "He's just a fierce competitor. Nobody competes better." The coach went on to recount how once when this pitcher lost his bid for a perfect game in the sixth inning, "he didn't get upset. He didn't say anything. You couldn't tell by his demeanor, but he wound up and hit the next batter right between the shoulder blades." The coach proudly exclaimed: "I love to have pitchers who are great competitors like that." The young pitcher was praised for deliberately hitting a batsman for something he had nothing to do with—spoiling the pitcher's perfect game. What did the young pitcher learn from his coach about sportsmanship in this episode?

findings have provided little in the way of specific or consistent answers.

Because the word *character* is so ambiguous and therefore has so many meanings to people, researchers have turned to assessing moral development and moral reasoning as a means of measuring the "character" outcomes of sports involvement. At the Center for Ethics at the University of Idaho, Sharon Kay Stoll and her colleagues Angela Lumpkin and Jennifer M. Beller conduct research about competitive ethics, moral development, and moral reasoning.

At the Center for Ethics, moral development refers to "the evolving growth process by which one learns to take the welfare of others into consideration when making moral decisions," and moral reasoning is "the ability to systematically think through a moral problem, taking into consideration one's own values and beliefs while weighing them against what others value and believe."[25]

Moral development and moral reasoning are primarily acquired through an individual's social learning experiences. Political leaders, business leaders, sport administrators, coaches, parents, and virtually all sectors of public life see organized youth sports as a perfect classroom for improving moral development and moral reasoning.

The substantial body of research findings on moral development and reasoning among athletes and their nonathlete peers suggests that young athletes who have been involved in organized sports programs have significantly less mature levels of moral development and reasoning than nonathletes. Some research, however, has found no significant differences between athletes and nonathletes on these variables.[26]

Critics of the findings of differences between athletes and nonathletes point to both theoretical and methodological limitations of this research. Others argue that the reasons for such differences may or may not be related to sports experiences of the athletes—that is, the differences may have existed prior to the sports involvement of the athletes. Unfortunately, the research design of these studies makes it impossible to determine whether the differences found between sports participants and nonparticipants are the result of participation or whether persons with certain personal-social characteristics are initially attracted to and remain involved in sports. Therefore, differences that exist between young athletes and nonathletes are not necessarily a consequence of sport involvement.

The effects of sports involvement on young athletes' moral development are still a topic for future researchers to unravel. However, the findings of the empirical research at this time do suggest that slogans implying that youth sporting experiences universally develop positive personal-social characteristics—and thus "build character"—are too simplistic.

A question often asked about the sport and character development issue is: "Are there experiences during sports participation that *might* hamper moral development?" If we accept the notion that children learn normative behavior from sports and if we agree that social-norm deviance is present in sport, clearly youth sports programs may be providing patterned reinforcement of attitudes, values, and behaviors that are at variance with the development of moral reasoning. Deviation from the ideal norms occurs frequently in sports (e.g., incidents of athletes physically attacking one another during games, the booing of officials, and even the incorporation of deviance as part of the strategy of the game, such as spearing in football, illegal body checking in hockey, and so forth). There are well-planned, deliberate violations of the rules to make winning difficult for the opponent in most sports. Acceptance of such behavior is likely associated with internalization of lower levels of reasoning.

Although one may question the extent to which moral learning in sports generalizes to larger social relations, one certainly must consider the possible social effects on athletes who play under coaches who encourage unethical behavior. Convincing evidence from social learning experiments demonstrates that youngsters do model the attitudes and behaviors of people they respect and admire, and young athletes almost universally have high regard for their coaches.

Besides moral development, there are other social outcomes to which sports involvement during youth may contribute. Competence in sports skills apparently does influence self-evaluation and social esteem with peers. Sports provide innumerable opportunities for the individual to perceive the feelings of others and their judgments. Thus, experiences in sports may be instrumental in development of a self-image or self-concept. Several investigations have shown that sports abilities and interests are related to a positive self-concept, and research has consistently shown that young sports participants score higher on a variety of tests that measure mental health. Finally, but no less important, research suggests that encouraging sport participation during childhood and adolescence may result in an increase in the likelihood of participation later in life. We want to emphasize that most of the research on these topics is designed to measure relationships between the variables, not causal outcomes.

POTENTIAL PSYCHOSOCIAL PROBLEMS IN YOUTH SPORTS

A variety of social problems have arisen with the growth and expansion of organized youth sports, and there is increasing apprehension about potential harm to youngsters in these sports programs. Although youth sport literature is rife with critics who have axes to grind or converts to proselytize, the fact is they often make some very telling points. There is little doubt that some very abusive practices are taking place in the world of youth sports. Having said this, we wish to reemphasize the point we made in the previous section, namely that many young people experience positive personal-social growth experiences through youth sports. The kinds of outcomes experienced by youngsters are primarily contingent upon parents and coaches, for they are the most powerful "significant others" in the lives of young boys and girls.

In this section we discuss some of the most common problems of youth sports. It is not our intent to make specific accusations or to condemn all youth sports. We merely suggest that the social experiences of some youth sports athletes may have social consequences that are perhaps unintended and unwanted.

Adult Intrusion in Youth Sports

The rationale behind the organization of youth sports programs is admirable: to provide young boys and girls with structure for their sports, opportunities for wide participation, proper equipment for their safety, and adult coaching to help them learn the fundamental skills and strategies. But there is overwhelming agreement that one of the major problems of youth sports is the intrusion of adults into the sports life of youngsters. According to the National Alliance for Youth Sports (NAYS), "twenty-eight percent of adults say they've witnessed a physical confrontation involving coaches, officials or parents during a youth sporting event, and . . . say [there] is a 'growing epidemic' of bad behavior in youth sports."[27]

Parents and Coaches: Expectations and Pressures

John Engh, the chief operating officer of NAYS, affirms that "[f]rom an anecdotal perspective we know that there are way too many adults that are living out their sports dreams through their children's experiences. . . . We hear from hundreds of communities about the trouble they are having managing their volunteers and the parents involved with their leagues."[28] It appears that these adults expect a payoff and that payoff is athletic achievement by way of victories and championships. When a youngster achieves, parents and coaches see that success as, in a way, their own personal achievement. If the young athlete fails to live up to performance expectations, he or she may feel like a personal failure, as well as feeling he or she didn't fulfill the expectations of others. These pressures on a young athlete are exemplified by the practice of parents employing personal trainers for their offspring. One journalist notes, "In the past decade, the number of parents hiring professional trainers for their grade-school athletes has exploded. . . . Parents shell out $50 to $100 an hour for individual coaching."[29]

For parents and coaches whose aspirations are national rankings and a professional sports career for the youngsters involved, youth sports are not play and games; as one sports writer claimed about youth soccer, "Youth soccer is big business now."[30]

The parents of Venus and Serena Williams have become the role models for thousands of parents throughout North America. They have devoted most of their adult lives, and the childhood lives of these athletes, to the pursuit of their daughters' professional sports careers. Their success in achieving professional sports careers for their offspring, and the celebratory status accompanying it, have set a course that countless parents now follow for their children. "If the Williamses can do it, we can too" seems to be the attitude of parents who adopt this course. In addition to professional careers, some parents aspire for their child to receive a college athletic scholarship, while others aspire to their child winning an Olympic berth.

Because such aspirations have become so commonplace, they have changed the structure of youth sports and some families' lives. In previous generations children and youth played year-round, alternating the sport with the season. That's not the case anymore as parents let unrealistic dreams shoehorn their children into one-sport specialization. The day of the three-sport high school athlete is disappearing as even ten-year-olds who show some promise in a particular sport are told to stick to that sport year-round. Gregg Heinzmann, director of the Youth Sports Research Council at Rutgers University, finds the trend troubling: "We see it exploding in recent years from the standpoint of not only parents hiring privatized instruction, but children focusing on one sport to the exclusion of all others and at younger and younger ages."[31]

Among the reasons for such early specialization: College coaches now recruit middle school athletes as young as thirteen and fourteen years old. As pressures to win increase and competition for the top prospects grows fiercer, college coaches justify recruiting pre–high school athletes by arguing "You've just got to be first" to go after them.[32]

Traveling Teams and Club Teams

Now it is "traveling teams" or "club teams" that have become a popular form of youth sport organization. Sport psychologists at the Massachusetts General Hospital characterize traveling teams as fostering "a hypercompetitive 'every kid for himself or herself' mentality, with little regard for anything but winning and the development of individual talent in one sport. . . . [They] paint a rosy picture of their character-building goals in their mission statement. . . . But all too often these are empty promises."[33]

Traveling teams are composed of kids who have risen through local teams to be selected for the more competitive travel teams. These young athletes are drawn from mostly suburban neighborhoods and towns in a given region. They have two- to three-hour practices three or four times per week, and they make single-day or weekend-long pilgrimages to play other similarly skilled teams in distant towns—often in other states or provinces.

The extremes to which this goes are illustrated in the saga of a boy who played 127 baseball games in one year in the ten-and-under leagues. The founder of the National Alliance for Youth Sports feels that the point of saturation has been reached—a revolving door of never-ending seasons.

For both the young athletes and their families the commitment to traveling teams is almost total. The young athletes must abandon other organized sports to concentrate on the travel team. They must commit to specializing in one sport, and often must compete with their team year-round. Family lives must be recentered around the sports world of the traveling teams. The new breed of sports parents are road warriors who drive thousands of miles every season and spend weekends and evenings watching their kids practice and play. And they write many checks because it is very expensive to support a traveling or club team athlete.

Sports Academies and Youth Olympic Games

The trends of parental intrusion into youth sports, traveling teams, hyperorganization, and hypercompetitive youth sports have spawned a commercial industry devoted to coaching and training young athletes for the lofty sports goals they and their parents often have. This new industry goes way beyond the traditional sports camps that have been held by college coaches and professional athletes for the past twenty-five years. Although the daily or weekly sports camps are still popular throughout North America, sports academies have become the ultimate in coaching and preparing young athletes whose parents strive for NCAA Division I college scholarships, professional careers, and Olympic berths for their children.

IMG Academies, headquartered on a sprawling 400-acre campus in Bradenton, Florida, is the elite model of the academies. According to its website, "IMG Academies is the largest, most successful multi-sport training and education institution in the world. More than 12,000 junior, collegiate, adult and professional athletes from over 75 countries attend each year." IMG Academies offers programs throughout the year for the IMG Bollettieri Tennis, IMG Leadbetter Golf, IMG Baseball, IMG Basketball, IMG Soccer, IMG Madden Football, and IMG Lacrosse academies as well as the IMG Performance Institute. A one-year, full-time boarding plan costs over $45,000. With the addition of special private lessons, some parents pay up to $100,000 per year. Some children remain at IMG Academies for several years.[34]

Similar high-tech sports performance training centers are popping up, mostly in suburbs, across the country. Some cater to young athletes who want to become "the best" in specific sports; others focus on arcane skills designed to improve agility, strength, speed, and power—the fundamentals of all sports. Overwhelmingly the athletes come from affluent families. Sports academy and sports performance training center athletes tend to be members of middle- and upper-middle-class families. Parents of these athletes report annual expenses for their athlete son or daughter ranging from $12,000 to over $100,000.

IMG Academies officials admit that the real basis for admission is parents' ability to pay, not physical prowess. Golf's renowned teaching pro, David Leadbetter, says of his IMG Leadbetter Golf Academy, "We don't want only rich kids to come here." But, he acknowledges, "there's certainly a class factor. It's expensive to play golf." Obviously, poor families cannot afford such expenses for their children's sports programs. In recent years public money for recreation centers and after-school sports programs has declined, and for children growing up in poor families in poor communities, youth sports opportunities are severely limited.

Commenting on how the academy system training centers put youth from poor families and the school sports teams they belong to at a disadvantage, the former commissioner of the Colorado High School Activities Association said: "They bust their butt at [inner-city schools] and once in a while put together good teams. But mostly, they get kicked; they have no chance. It's totally a case of haves and have-nots. You can almost name the sport. Even volleyball and basketball. These are inner-city games, but it's the well-heeled suburban schools that have the best teams."[35]

One infamous exception to this system of social class privilege is youth basketball. Basketball shoe corporations Nike and Adidas, working with the Amateur Athletic Union (AAU) and sport-shoe-sponsored coaches, seduce young, mostly poor inner-city kids to play in tournaments all over North America. According to USA Today sports writer Jim Halley, the young players play more than eighty games in a summer. One AAU basketball official admitted, "Teams are probably playing too many events." But he rationalizes, "There's so much pressure from parents and players to play more events for exposure that it takes away from what we're about—and that's developing players."[36]

The young athletes and their parents are showered with merchandise, flown to tournaments, fawned over, and then subtly steered toward high schools whose teams happen to have lucrative shoe deals with the companies. Even some of the driving forces behind this system are calling it the "cesspool of amateur basketball."

In a seemingly never-ending search for higher and higher levels of competitive sports for youth, adult intrusion into youth sports has gone global with the creation of the Youth Olympic Games (YOG), an international multi-sport event first held in Singapore in 2010. These games are planned to be held every four years in staggered summer and winter events, similar to the current Olympic Games format. They are designed to be a media-driven extravaganza that will boost Olympic enthusiasm and participation among younger fans and athletes worldwide.

Like Mount Everest climbers, a few youth sport athletes do make it to the top and become professional athletes or Olympians. They become celebrities, and newspaper and magazine stories about them frequently report their odyssey through youth sports programs. But they are the very few out of millions of youth who play sports each year, and whose parents fantasize that their son or daughter will become the next LeBron James, Serena Williams, Derek Jeter, or Michelle Wie.

Unfortunately, despite thousands of dollars spent by parents and untold hours of practicing and playing games by young athletes, fewer than

1 percent of them will even receive a college athletic scholarship. And less than 1 percent of those who play college sports will become professional or Olympic athletes. Occasionally the stories of athletes who did not fulfill their, or their parents', dreams of sporting fame come to light. There are even the sad stories of successful professionals and Olympians who publicly share their experiences of pressure, abuse, depression, and the loss of childhood through the years of struggling to achieve sporting prominence.

Certainly, children who are sent to train in sports academies in another part of the country and who are coached by well-known coaches, compete in national and international sports events, or turn professional during their adolescence are under immense pressures, for they are competing to live up to the expectations of their parents, their coaches, the media, and themselves, and it is a heavy burden. Perhaps the poster-parents for putting burdens on offspring are Scott and Mari Maattanen-Silva, the father and mother of a five-year-old boy, Jan, who shows promise as a future tennis champion. They sold their house and two cars in Rancho Cordova, California, and moved to France so that Jan could train in tennis full time. "I think there's a pretty good chance of him going all the way," his father told *Today Show* co-host Meredith Vieira.[37]

Many former youth sports athletes remember their years in youth sports programs as being fun, exciting, and even, for some, the best years of their lives with their family. However, several writers have documented these years as being filled with stress, fear, abuse, and torment for some young athletes. Tom Farrey's book *Game On: The All-American Race to Make Champions of Our Children* details the impact of parents who lose perspective and, driven by their own aspirations and goals for their children, subject their kids to unrelenting pressure and anxiety. Farrey offers many excellent suggestions that will lead to better sports for youth.[38]

Adult intrusion into the world of youth sports can rob the young participants of some of the greatest potential of sports, and that is the opportunity to have fun and to develop self-discipline and responsibility for one's own actions. Many youth sports programs are dominated by the coaches, who make all the decisions; they decide who plays, where they play, what tactics to employ, and what plays to run. In effect, the youngsters are the "hired help" who carry out the orders and do not ask questions if they do not want to be labeled "problem athletes." Thus, the imposition of adult dominance and decision making in youth programs appears to do little to develop self-discipline and self-responsibility in children.

We want to make clear that we do not condemn all youth sports programs, but dominance by some parents and coaches tends to conflict with the true spirit of play by exaggerating the importance of technique, efficiency, and winning—such programs can deprive youngsters of the fun and play elements of sport (see Box 4.2).

Violent Behavior and Sexual Abuse Toward Youth Athletes

Perhaps the most objectionable forms of adult intrusion into children's sports involve violent behavior: physical assaults by parents and coaches, and sexual abuse of young athletes by youth sport coaches. With regard to physical assaults, youth sport administrators admit they are dealing with what many call "sideline rage" and they say it is at epidemic levels. Recent reports from over 2,000 chapters of the National Alliance for Youth Sports have indicated that about 15 percent of youth games involve some sort of verbal or physical abuse from parents or coaches. The specific incidents vary, but they are widespread throughout North America and they all involve assaultive actions.

A reader survey by *Sports Illustrated for Kids* reported that 74 percent of more than 3,000 respondents said they had witnessed out-of-control adults at their games. A similar survey by *Sporting Kids Magazine*, with 3,300 coaches, parents, youth sports administrators, and youth athletes responding, found that 84 percent said they had seen parents acting violently, such as shouting, berating, and using abusive language. Here are accounts of a few recent incidents:

- After a basketball game between ten- and eleven-year-olds in Iowa, the mother of one of the players attacked a pregnant referee. According to police reports, the attacker grabbed the referee by the hair, threw her to the ground, and kicked her.

Box 4.2 *Thinking About Sport: A Teachable Moment or a Reaction by the Coach?*

Behind by one run in the fifth inning of the Colorado state-qualifying American Legion B District Tournament baseball game against an archrival, the coach yanked his centerfielder from the game after the player threw his glove twice in a fit of anger when he failed to make a play and allowed a run to score.

The coach's action may not seem unusual, but in this case the coach showed the extent of his priorities inasmuch as he did not have another player to replace the one that was yanked. The team had no substitutes on the bench.

With only eight players to finish the game, the disciplinary action put the coach's team at a huge disadvantage because the team had to finish the game with only two outfielders and accept an automatic out every time the yanked player's place in the lineup came up.

The coach said he did what he did because he thought it was important to show [the disciplined player] the value of "trusting your teammates and not being an individual. If we didn't care about him or we didn't think he was a player then you just let that kind of stuff go. When you know he's a player and he's a good kid you can't let it go."

Postscript: After prolonged discussion by the umpires, and over the vigorous objection of the coach, the umpires ruled—incorrectly, it turns out—that a coach cannot remove a player from a game if the team does not have another player to replace the removed one.

Source: Coach quoted in Tom Wright, "Coach Calls It Right in Defeat," *Greeley Tribune*, 21 July 2007, p. B5.

- At a girls' rugby tournament game in California, a coach and several parents beat the opposing coach unconscious with kicks to the head and face, according to witnesses.
- Coaches of the Tri-Community YMCA basketball program in Southbridge, Massachusetts, sent letters to parents telling them that they were barred from attending the final game of the season due to continued unruly behavior.

Social scientists who have tried to explain these violent incidents point to the culture of violence in the wider society. Richard Lapchick's Institute for Diversity and Ethics in Sport at the University of Central Florida studies the interrelationships between society and sport. Lapchick blames the increase in parental violence on the rise of violence in other sectors of society. Indeed, one of the most hotly discussed current social issues is the rise in interpersonal incivility today. Other social analysts suggest that the excesses, aggression, and "in your face" actions that characterize contemporary cultural behavior are at work in professional sports for all to see: NFL players spitting in the face of opponents; NBA players charging into the stands to punch fans; NHL players sucker-punching opponents, and, in one case, knocking an opponent unconscious and then driving him headfirst into the ice.

Parents and coaches are part of a social system that is larger than just sport; they are not immune to happenings in the broader society and in professional sports. There is also an additional factor for them. Many parents and coaches have become so ego- and emotionally involved with their children's sports or with the kids they are coaching that they have lost control over their own behavior. After spending a year examining the landscape of youth sports, the *Columbus* (Ohio) *Dispatch* reported that more than 40 percent of the youth sports athletes they interviewed said their parents pressured them to play, and 10 percent said their parents' behavior during games embarrassed them.

Social problems typically produce collective actions aimed at remedying them. Various efforts are being made to stem the tide of escalating parent and coach "sideline rage." The goal is to educate parents and coaches and hold them accountable for their actions. For the past decade the Positive Coaching Alliance (PCA) has been holding workshops for youth sport coaches. According to its website, the PCA is a nonprofit organization based at Stanford University with the mission to transform youth sports so sports can transform youth. PCA was created to transform the culture of youth sports to give all young athletes the opportunity for a positive, character-building experience. It has three national goals:

1. To replace the "win-at-all-costs" model of coaching with the "double-goal coach" who wants to win but has a second, more important, goal of using sports to teach life lessons;
2. To teach youth sports organization leaders how to create an organizational culture in which honoring the game is the norm; and
3. To spark and fuel a "social epidemic" of positive coaching that will sweep this country.

Since 1998, PCA has conducted thousands of workshops nationwide for roughly 200,000 youth sports leaders, coaches, parents, and athletes that have helped create a positive sports environment for more than 1 million youth athletes.[39]

The National Alliance for Youth Sports is another organization that advocates for positive and safe youth sports. It created the Parents Association for Youth Sports (PAYS) to give parents a clear understanding of their roles and responsibilities in youth sport. It does that through a thirty-minute program that teaches parents sportsmanlike behaviors they can then pass on to their children. Parents access the program through a participating sports organization or online. Over five hundred organizations are currently using PAYS in an effort to prevent parent behavior problems in their programs.[40]

Some communities have begun hiring paid, trained supervisors to oversee all youth sports in the community. Other communities now require parents and coaches to sign an agreement spelling out a code of conduct. Without the signatures, parents' children cannot play in the programs and coaches cannot coach.

As serious as the physical assaultive behavior of some parents and coaches is, surely the most distressing and odiously violent adult in youth sports is the child molester, the pedophile (a Greek word literally meaning "lover of children"). Until a few years ago, molestation was a nonissue in youth sports. The few scattered reports of sexual abuse of young athletes had been so rare that the media had largely ignored them.

However, in the fall of 1999, a *Sports Illustrated* special report entitled "Every Parent's Nightmare" shocked people in both the United States and Canada. The report began: "The child molester has found a home in the world of youth sports, where as a coach he can gain the trust and loyalty of kids—and then prey on them." The report identified a half-dozen or so youth sport child molesters. One of them confessed that he had molested "a couple of hundred children over three decades." A decade later, in 2010, an article in *USA Today* titled "Abuse Allegations Rock the Swim World" reported on five lawsuits claiming sexual abuse of youth swimmers. Thus, coaching behavior of this kind continues in youth sports.[41]

The fact that sexual molesters are found in youth sport is just another example of the linkages between the sports world and the broader society. But these recent revelations and frightening truths about child molestation in youth sports have made everyone connected to youth sports more vigilant in the selection and monitoring of coaches.

Disruption of Education

Another major social problem for young boys and girls who are being groomed for professional careers and Olympic status is that normal school attendance becomes impossible. At first the sports career and school may coexist peacefully, but when young athletes must practice six to eight hours per day, travel to distant cities and even foreign countries to participate in competition, and perhaps move from one region of the country to another to receive the desired coaching, normal educational routines must be disrupted. One example of this situation is sports academies, where more and more of the young athletes are being groomed for pro sport careers, Olympic berths, and a shot at fame and fortune.

Tennis, golf, swimming, figure skating, speed skating, skiing, soccer, and gymnastics require most of those who hope to become national- and international-level performers to train with the best coaches. There are so few of them in each sport that most athletes have to leave their home and take up residence sometimes thousands of miles away to be near the best coaches and facilities.

Several solutions have emerged to meet the needs of young athletes who are in full-time training. One solution is the employment of tutors for the youngsters. Increasingly, however, such informal arrangements are giving way to more formal academies where children live, train, and go to school in one complex.

Most of the sports academies point with some pride to the academic records of their students. Of course, these students are almost uniformly from upper-middle-class families, and they receive tutorial instruction or are in classes with a low student-to-teacher ratio. While these alternatives may result in a good education for such youngsters, a question can be raised about the disruptive effects of going to school in an environment dominated by sport practices and competition, and about the restricted interpersonal relationships present in such an environment.

This leads to a fundamental question: Is sport involvement so important during the growing-up years that children must be robbed of the normal experiences of childhood? Undoubtedly, some parents and coaches answer yes, and for those very, very few who become Olympic champions or successful professionals, this assessment may be justified. For the vast majority of young athletes who endure this lifestyle and do not achieve the desired goal, however, a childhood may be lost. Examples of this abound in the stories of former athletes who spent their youth in sports academies and never became college, professional, or Olympic athletes.

Risk of Injury

Daily living has risks and the potential for injury. Going through childhood and adolescence without risk and injury would be like missing a part of one's life. Given this, there are nevertheless some activities in which the chance of injury is greater than normal, and when these activities are forced on youngsters by adults, the issue of abuse is present. Medical concern for the young athlete has a long history, and most persons associated with youth sports have heard the arguments about "Little League elbow" and about the dangers of tackle football and ice hockey for preadolescent youngsters.

There is, however, a growing concern that goes beyond Little League elbow and broken bones and concussions in football or hockey to "swimmer's shoulder" and "gymnast's back." Dr. James R. Andrews, president of the American Orthopaedic Society for Sports Medicine, says that 60 percent of the athletes he operates on these days are high school athletes or younger. He argues, "I don't think epidemic is too strong a word. . . . We're seeing kids hurt before they even have a chance to become athletes." That organization has launched a campaign to curb sports injuries in children called STOP (Sports Trauma and Overuse Prevention). According to Andrews, the main culprit is sport specialization: "You just have this enormous pressure nowadays on kids to play one sport year-round."[42]

The accelerated training regimens of many current youth athletes that extend up to eight hours per day, six—even seven, in some cases—days a week, throughout the year, raise serious questions about physical injury. Physicians are seeing a dramatic increase in overuse injuries among children in organized sports. Dr. Andrews alone is "seeing four times as many overuse injuries in youth sports than five years ago and more kids are having surgery for chronic sports injuries." As noted above, Andrews and other "experts attribute this increase to the fact that more youth today are specializing in one sport at an early age and training year-round. All these injuries can be linked to overuse; doing too much, too often . . . as the competition, access and seasons expand to year-round."[43]

The "Winning Is the Only Thing" Ethic and Youth Sports

The final topic we discuss in this section on potential psychosocial problems of youth sports is one that lurks throughout youth sports. We call it the "winning is the only thing" ethic. To understand this ethic in youth sports, it is helpful to understand its linkages to the broader culture of the United States. Social analysts of U.S. culture have noted what many have referred to as a hypercompetitive feature, a trait that is not as prominent in the culture of other modern societies.[44]

The United States' form of capitalist economy came into prominence with the robber barons of the latter nineteenth century and continues today with most industries dominated by huge corporations that have driven other enterprises out of business. The major form of testing in America's educational system is based on competition against other students or against standardized norms for good grades and educational advancement. America's media compete vigorously against each other for readers, listeners, and viewers. The political system is democratic and citizens have an opportunity to vote for the candidates of their choice, but the candidates compete fiercely to win the election. These features exist to a lesser extent in Canada.

It is perhaps not surprising, then, that hyper-competitiveness has permeated U.S. sports since the rise of organized sports forms. At every level of organized sports, winning has been richly rewarded, either in monetary form or in social status. Some of the most admired sports celebrities have exuded a win-at-all-costs attitude. The slogans of sports culture have emphasized an uncompromising attitude about winning: "Winning isn't everything, it's the only thing"; "Show me a good loser, and I'll show you a loser"; "*Lose* is a four-letter word"; "Feel no sympathy for the loser."

As we have previously noted, coaches and athletes at the professional, college, and high school levels are the role models and heroes of youth sport athletes, who tend to internalize the attitudes, values, and behaviors of older athletes. Their other role models and heroes are parents and coaches who are in daily contact with them and are powerful and direct in their socializing influence. Young athletes form fundamental attitudes, values, and beliefs from these interactions.

Although "winning is the only thing" is widely accepted for child athletes thrown into the big business of elite sports, such an ethic can become a terrible burden for young athletes. Win-loss records define them. Winners are accorded prestige and honor; losers suffer disdain and ridicule. Because being labeled a loser is the epitome of criticism in our society, many young athletes experience stress and develop anxiety and other forms of psychosocial trauma.

With more and more professional athletes making huge salaries, and with top amateur athletes earning money and getting considerable media attention, more and more junior and age-group athletes are in training to become professional or Olympic-level athletes, and the pressures have become even more intense on these youngsters. What for most boys and girls is play becomes a job for some young athletes. In spite of the hours, even years, of hard work put in by these ambitious young athletes (and their parents), the issue of child labor has rarely come up, and the laws prohibiting child labor have never been applied to elite youth athletes.

There is no safety net protecting youth athletes—not the parents, not the coaches, not the sport organizations where they play. Child labor laws prohibit a twelve-year-old from working forty hours a week at a McDonald's restaurant, but that same boy or girl can labor for forty hours or more at a gym or a tennis court or an ice skating rink without drawing any attention from the government.

The extent parents, coaches, and young athletes will go to, when winning becomes the only thing, has been well documented. The types of behaviors, with the attitudes toward sports to which they have been conditioned, do little to promote personal-social growth and the "character traits" that are universally endorsed as outcomes of sports involvement.

We wish to reemphasize that we are not denying the quest for victory has its place in youth sports. Striving for victory in a competitive situation is a perfectly legitimate goal. We do think, however, given the organizational nature of many youth sports programs and the emphasis on winning for elite-level young athletes, that there is a tendency to allow winning to become the only goal. When this happens in youth sports, the enormous potential benefit of sport involvement for a healthy self-concept development is jeopardized.

SPORTS ALTERNATIVES FOR THE YOUNG ATHLETE

Although youth sports programs have many problems, the alternatives that many children and adolescents have adopted have more undesirable consequences for their physical, mental, and social development. According to the Centers for Disease Control and Prevention (CDC), the nature of American childhood has changed: Children and adolescents are spending their time mostly indoors, watching television, playing video games, and surfing the Internet. Studies by the National Sporting Goods Association found that an indoor childhood has become more typical in the past decade, while there have been huge declines in spontaneous outdoor activities such as bike riding, swimming, and touch football. Richard Louv, author of *Last Child in the Woods*, a book about how children have lost touch with nature, claims that parents think their kids are safer in front of the Xbox in the next room. The enticement of video games and television is not the only thing keeping young boys and girls indoors. Frequent news reports of pedophiles and missing children have made parents fearful of allowing their kids to play on their own in the neighborhood and parks.[45]

One of the major consequences of childhoods spent mostly indoors playing video games and watching television is the increase in obesity among the young population. Surveys by the CDC have found that childhood obesity has more than tripled in the past thirty years. The rate of obesity among children aged six to eleven years increased from 6.5 percent in 1980 to 19.6 percent in 2008. The rate of obesity among adolescents aged twelve to nineteen years increased from 5.0 percent to 18.1 percent. The CDC defines *overweight* as being at or above the 95th percentile of the CDC body mass index. Overweight and obesity are major risk factors for chronic diseases, including type 2 diabetes, hypertension, osteoporosis, and some cancers. Obese youth are more likely to have risk factors for cardiovascular disease, such as high cholesterol or high blood pressure. In a population-based sample of five- to seventeen-year-olds, 70 percent of obese youth had at least one risk factor for cardiovascular disease.[46]

Emphasizing Personal Growth and Self-Actualization

Our major contention in this book is that sports for youth have virtually unlimited potential for promoting personal growth, self-actualization, and social competency. Therefore the goal of youth sports should be nothing less than self-fulfillment of the individuals engaged in and influenced by them. The emphasis of such programs should be upon personal expression and the value of participation, upon offering everyone the opportunity to engage in sports in a way that youngsters experience no feeling of humiliation if a contest is lost. Why must sport be justified on the basis that it does things other than providing a lot of joy and self-fulfillment for the participants?

An increasing number of attempts have been made to improve youth sports by designing programs based on principles that place the personal- social needs of the participants first and the ambitions of adults far behind. There is a growing literature describing these programs and discussing ways and means by which parents and coaches can improve the quality of the sporting experience for young boys and girls. (See Box 4.3.) Three of the best books on this subject are *Whose Game Is It, Anyway? A Guide to Helping Your Child Get the Most from Sports, Organized by Age and Stage*; *Home Team Advantage: The Critical Role of Mothers in Youth Sports*; and *Surviving Youth Sports: A Manual for Parents*.[47]

Box 4.3 *Thinking About Sport*: Top Five Steps to Being a Good Sports Parent

1. Do not pressure your child into participating in sport; ask if she or he is interested.
2. If your child plays youth sports, continue to inquire whether he or she is enjoying it.
3. Don't criticize your child's coaches or referees on the field or in front of your child.

4. Make fun and skill development top priorities in your child athlete's participation—not just winning and losing.
5. Be supportive of your child's sport participation. Frequently tell your child how much you enjoy watching her or him play.

Alternative Sports

Baseball, football, basketball, and ice hockey were the dominant sports when organized youth sports programs were first getting started in North America. Although these are still quite popular youth sports, there is now much more variety in the sports available for kids. The newest trends in youth sports are coming from what are called "alternative sports" and "extreme sports"—sports that youngsters are developing largely themselves. The term *alternative sports* is used because many youngsters have become involved in them as a rejection of the norms and values of traditional youth sports.

One of the problems alternative sports have all experienced is corporate takeover: Advertisers and television executives discovered they could package these sports to make them attractive to young television audiences, and that they could sell TV commercial time to advertisers with products appealing to teenage and young adult male audiences. The X Games were created by ESPN to capture the growing popularity of alternative and extreme sports among the young for the purpose of generating profits for ESPN and the advertising corporations. ESPN's X Games will be discussed in more detail in Chapter 11.

Cooperative Games

Cooperative games have been advocated by many youth sports leaders who believe that one of the objectives of sports and physical activity programs for youth should emphasize the learning of cooperative behavior. A number of educators and coaches have experimented with play and games as a means of developing positive cooperative behavior among children. They have found that cooperatively structured games are effective in producing cooperative social interaction among children.[48]

Youth Sports Coaches

It is estimated that there are some 7.5 million volunteer youth sports coaches in North America, most of whom have had no formal instruction in the developmental or educational aspects of teaching/coaching. Thus, there is agreement by almost everyone associated with youth sports that the vast majority of youth sports coaches are ill equipped for their role. Without them, though, millions of boys and girls would not have the opportunity to participate in organized sports.

In an effort to help volunteer coaches become more knowledgeable, some youth sports programs have instituted mandatory clinics, workshops, and certification programs for all of their coaches. The American Sport Education Program (ASEP) is a complete education package that has been adopted by many youth sports organizations throughout the United States and Canada. Since its founding in 1976, ASEP has been a valuable education training tool for youth sports coaches. ASEP coaches learn to teach skills and strategies, plan effectively for their season, prepare athletes for competition, and understand the developmental needs of young athletes. Its curriculum is built on the philosophical foundation of "Athletes First, Winning Second."[49]

The National Youth Sport Coaches Association (NYSCA) has been a pioneer in the development of a national training system for volunteer coaches. More than 3 million coaches have attended NYSCA clinics since the program began in 1981. At the end of each NYSCA clinic, coaches must (1) pass an exam that tests their understanding of the information conveyed in the clinic and (2) sign a pledge committing them to uphold the association's code of ethics. The NYSCA Coaches' Code of Ethics is shown in Box 4.4.

The Coaching Association of Canada (CAC) sponsors the National Coaching Certification

A coach reviewing strategies with his team. There are an estimated 7.5 million volunteer youth sports coaches in North America. (istockphoto)

Box 4.4 *Thinking About Sport:* **NYSCA Coaches' Code of Ethics**

I hereby pledge to live up to my certification as a NYSCA Coach by following the NYSCA Coaches' Code of Ethics.

- I will place the emotional and physical well-being of my players ahead of a personal desire to win.
- I will treat each player as an individual, remembering the large range of emotional and physical development for the same age group.
- I will do my best to provide a safe playing situation for my players.
- I will promise to review and practice the basic first aid principles needed to treat injuries of my players.
- I will do my best to organize practices that are fun and challenging for all my players.

- I will lead by example in demonstrating fair play and sportsmanship to all my players.
- I will provide a sports environment for my team that is free of drugs, tobacco, and alcohol, and I will refrain from their use at all youth sports events.
- I will be knowledgeable in the rules of each sport that I coach, and I will teach these rules to my players.
- I will use those coaching techniques appropriate for each of the skills that I teach.
- I will remember that I am a youth sports coach, and that the game is for children and not adults.

Source: National Alliance for Youth Sports, http://www.nays.org/.

Program (NCCP), which is a collaborative program of the government of Canada, the provincial/territorial governments, the national and provincial/territorial sport organizations, and the CAC. Many youth sports organizations encourage, and some even require, formal training for their coaches. The NCCP attempts to ensure that youth coaches have the necessary knowledge, skill, and values that are prerequisite to effective youth sport coaching.[50]

Bill of Rights for Young Athletes

Guarantees of personal liberty for all U.S. citizens are found in the Bill of Rights, which are the first ten amendments to the Constitution of the United States. Similar safeguards have also been written into most state constitutions. In Canada the Charter of Rights and Freedoms guarantees Canadians a broad range of personal liberties. Many business organizations have also developed a bill of rights for their employees as a commitment to employees that they will be treated with dignity and respect, and that their needs and interests will be protected.

In an attempt to protect youth from adult exploitation in sports, a group of medical, physical education, and recreation leaders formulated a Bill of Rights for Young Athletes several years ago. The ten rights are targeted to coaches, leaders of recreation programs, officials, and parents in the

hope that their implementation will promote the beneficial effects of athletic participation for all who are involved. These rights are:

1. The right to participate in sports.
2. The right to participate at a level commensurate with each child's maturity and ability.
3. The right to have qualified adult leadership.
4. The right to play as a child and not as an adult.
5. The right to share in the leadership and decision making of their sport participation.
6. The right to participate in safe and healthy environments.
7. The right to proper preparation in sports.
8. The right to an equal opportunity to strive for success.
9. The right to be treated with dignity.
10. The right to have fun in sports.

Many youth sport organizations have adopted the Bill of Rights for Young Athletes as a guarantee to the young athletes and their parents that the athletes' development and welfare will be protected. Typically, the bill of rights is included in materials given to the athletes and their parents when they sign up to play in a particular sports program.[51]

In Canada, a National Task Force on Children's Play, created by the Canadian Council on

Children and Youth, has formulated Fair Play Codes that emphasize sport's potential for promoting desirable values among youthful participants.

SUMMARY

There has been an enormous increase in community-sponsored youth sports programs. There has also been a growth in elite youth sport in which the youngsters train and compete with aspirations of becoming professional or Olympic-caliber athletes. An estimated 60 million North American and some 5 million Canadian boys and girls participate in these programs each year. Two of the most salient factors contributing to the growth of these programs are (1) the rise of organized and corporate sport, followed by the desire to participate and to spectate on the part of large numbers of people, and (2) the realization by Canadians and Americans of the importance of providing varied opportunities for their children.

The objectives of most youth sports programs are to provide participants with an opportunity to learn culturally relevant sport skills and to develop attitudes and values about such things as competition, cooperation, sportsmanship, discipline, authority, and social relationships. There are, however, programs that are blatant career-training programs.

The extent to which the attitudes, values, beliefs, and behaviors of participants are actually influenced by organized youth programs is largely unknown. Most studies of attitudes toward youth sports suggest that parents and participants believe that they are more beneficial than detrimental to the development of young boys and girls. Participants in these programs are socialized into them by a variety of social agents and agencies, parents, siblings, peers, coaches, the mass media, and so forth.

The social context of the informal, peer-organized sports activities is vastly different from that of the adult-organized youth sports programs. Thus, the play behavior in the two social contexts is likely to lead to quite different learning.

There are a number of problems in organized youth sports. One is that the intrusion of adults into the play of youngsters may rob the young participants of many of the values of play. A second is that the norm learning involved may actually be at variance with North American social norms. A third is that normal educational experiences may become impossible. A fourth is that intense training and competition for prolonged periods of time may cause both acute and chronic injury. Finally, the overemphasis on winning in some youth programs threatens to overshadow the expressive, self-fulfilling potential of sports participation.

A number of interesting efforts have been made to develop alternative youth sports programs; in most cases the emphasis of these programs is on fun, participation, and skill learning. One group of researchers has developed a system for helping coaches improve their coaching behavior, and in both the United States and Canada, courses have been developed to help coaches become more effective. In an attempt to protect young athletes from adult exploitation in sports, a Bill of Rights for Young Athletes and Fair Play Codes have been formulated.

WEB RESOURCES

www.livestrong.com/article/348964-national-youth-sports-safety/
The National Youth Sports Safety Foundation (NYSSF) does not have its own home page, but information about the NYSSF can be found at this URL. The NYSSF is a national nonprofit, educational organization dedicated to reducing the number and severity of injuries youth sustain in sports and fitness activities.

www.asep.com
The website for the American Sport Education Program. When it was founded, ASEP was called the American Coaching Effectiveness Program (ACEP). ASEP's goal is to provide quality education for coaches, officials, administrators, parents, and athletes in order to make the sport experience the best it can be for all involved.

www.nays.org/coaches
As part of the National Alliance for Youth Sports (NAYS), the National Youth Sports Coaches

Association (NYSCA) provides training, support, and continuing education to adults who volunteer to coach out-of-school youth sports teams. The NYSCA program works to "sensitize" coaches to their responsibilities when working with children in sports.

www.coach.ca
The Coaching Association of Canada unites stakeholders and partners in its commitment to improving the skills and stature of coaches and, ultimately, expanding their reach and influence. Its programs empower coaches with knowledge and skills, promote ethics, foster positive attitudes, build competence, and increase the credibility and recognition of coaches.

www.littleleague.org
The official site of Little League baseball.

www.youthsportsusa.com
A good overall site for a broad range of information about youth sports.

www.safekids.org
This site is dedicated to providing information and educational resources to protect kids from their number-one killer—unintentional injury.

www.popwarner.com
Pop Warner Little Scholars (PWLS) is a nonprofit organization that provides youth football as well as cheer and dance programs for participants in forty-two states and several countries around the world.

http://jrdragster.nhra.com
The NHRA Jr. Drag Racing League is for boys and girls of all ages.

NOTES

1. Several of the websites listed at the end of the chapter are excellent resources for learning more about the variety of programs and tournaments that sponsor youth sports.

2. Mark Hyman, *Until It Hurts: America's Obsession with Youth Sports and How It Harms Our Kids* (Boston: Beacon Press, 2010); Tom Farrey, *Game On: The All-American Race to Make Champions of Our Children* (New York: ESPN, 2008); and Michael Sokolove, *Warrior Girls: Protecting Our Daughters Against the Injury Epidemic in Women's Sports* (New York: Simon & Schuster, 2008).

3. Jack W. Berryman, "The Rise of Boys' Sports in the United States, 1900–1970," in *Children and Youth in Sport: A Biopsychosocial Perspective*, ed. Frank L. Smoll and Ronald E. Smith (Madison, WI: Brown & Benchmark, 1996), 4–14; see also Lance Van Auken and Robin Van Auken, *Play Ball!: The Story of Little League Baseball* (University Park: Pennsylvania State University Press, 2001).

4. Christopher Stevenson, "Becoming an International Athlete: Making Decisions About Identity," in *Inside Sports*, ed. Jay Coakley and Peter Donnelly (New York: Routledge, 1999), 89.

5. U.S. Census Bureau, *Statistical Abstracts of the United States: 2010*, 129th ed. (Washington, DC: U.S. Government Printing Office, 2010), 54–55.

6. Brooke de Lench, *Home Team Advantage: The Critical Role of Mothers in Youth Sport* (New York: Collins, 2006); and Marlene A. Dixon, Stacy M. Warner, and Jennifer E. Bruening, "More Than Just Letting Them Play: Parental Influence on Women's Lifetime Sport Involvement," *Sociology of Sport Journal* 25, no. 4 (2008): 538–559.

7. Christine Brennan, "Old Sportsman Saw Way Before Title IX," *USA Today*, 17 May 2001, p. 3C; see also Michael A. Messner, *It's All for the Kids: Gender, Families, and Youth Sports* (Berkeley: University of California Press, 2009). For an excellent review on this topic, see Thelma S. Horn and Jocelyn L. Horn, "Family Influences of Children's Sport and Physical Activity Participation, Behavior, and Psychosocial Responses," in *Handbook of Sport Psychology*, 3rd ed., ed. Gershon Tennenbaum and Robert C. Eklund (New York: John Wiley, 2007), 685–711.

8. Lisa Swanson, "Soccer Fields of Cultural [Re] Production: Creating 'Good Boys' in Suburban America," *Sociology of Sport Journal* 26, no. 3 (2009): 421.

9. Ibid., 422.

10. For a penetrating and sobering series of stories about youth in sport at various ages, see Farrey, *Game On*; see also Donald W. Albertson, *Catch a Rising Star: The Adult Game of Youth Sports* (Austin, TX: Turnkey Press, 2006).

11. Stevenson, "Becoming an International Athlete," 89; see also Horn and Horn, "Family Influences of Children's Sport and Physical Activity Participation, Behavior, and Psychosocial Responses," 702–706.

12. Alan L. Smith, "Peer Relationships in Physical Activity Contexts: A Road Less Traveled in Youth Sport and Exercise Psychology Research," *Psychology of Sport and Exercise* 4, no. 1 (2003): 25–39.

13. "Kids Who Play Sports Games Likely to Play Sports in Real Life," *GamePolitics*, 8 July 2010, http://www.gamepolitics.com/2010/07/08/kids-who-play-sports-games-likely-play-sports-real-life.

14. Richard D. Ginsburg, Stephen Durant, and Amy Baltzell, *Whose Game Is It, Anyway?* (Boston: Houghton Mifflin, 2006), ch. 8.

15. Ibid., ch. 10; see also Robert S. Weinberg and Daniel Gould, *Foundations of Sport Psychology and Exercise Psychology,* 5th ed. (Champaign, IL: Human Kinetics, 2010).

16. Deborah Meier, Brenda S. Engel, and Beth Taylor, *Playing for Keeps: Life and Learning on a Public School Playground* (New York: Teachers College Press, Columbia University, 2010), 83.

17. Ibid., 88.

18. For a persuasive account of how adults are turning youth sports into a high-pressure, big-money enterprise, see Hyman, *Until It Hurts.*

19. Albertson, *Catch a Rising Star.*

20. Susan A. Jackson and Mihaly Csikszentmihalyi, *Flow in Sports: The Keys to Optimal Experiences and Performances* (Champaign, IL: Human Kinetics, 1999); see also Bob Bigelow and Tom Moroney, *Just Let the Kids Play: How to Stop Other Adults from Ruining Your Child's Fun and Success in Sports* (Deerfield Beach, FL: HCI, 2001); and Kenneth R. Ginsburg, "The Importance of Play in Promoting Healthy Child Development and Maintaining Strong Parent-Child Bonds," *American Academy of Pediatrics* 119, no. 1 (2007): 182–191.

21. Sporting Goods Manufacturing Association, "SGMA Study Identifies Active Segments of U.S. Population," 20 July 2010, https://www.sgma.com/press/view.php?id=237.

22. For a review of the professionalization research, see David Light Shields and Brenda Light Bredemeier, "Advances in Sport Morality Research," in *Handbook of Sport Psychology,* 3rd ed., ed. Gershon Tennenbaum and Robert C. Eklund (New York: John Wiley, 2007): 663–664.

23. David Light Shields, Brenda Light Bredemeier, Nicole M. LaVoi, and F. Clark Power, "The Sport Behavior of Youth, Parents, and Coaches: The Good, the Bad, and the Ugly," *Journal of Research in Character Education* 3, no. 1 (2005), 43–59; see also "Lack of Sportsmanship Exposed in New Athletic Survey Points to Changing Attitudes Among Today's Young Athletes," *American Chronicle,* 9 August 2010, http://www.americanchronicle.com/articles/yb/147394879.

24. See, for example, National Alliance for Youth Sports, http://www.nays.org, and the Positive Coaching Alliance, http://www.positivecoach.org; see also David Light Shields and Brenda Light Bredemeier, "Why Sportsmanship Programs Fail, and What We Can Do About It," *Journal of Physical Education, Recreation and Dance* 82, no. 7 (2011): 24–29.

25. Angela Lumpkin, Sharon K. Stoll, and Jennifer M. Beller, *Sport Ethics: Applications for Fair Play,* 3rd ed.

(New York: McGraw-Hill, 2003), 267–268; see also Angela Lumpkin, *Modern Sports Ethics: A Reference Handbook* (Santa Barbara, CA: ABC-CLIO, 2009).

26. For a recent thorough review of this topic, see Shields and Bredemeier, "Advances in Sport Morality Research," 662–684; see also President's Council on Physical Fitness and Sports, "Sports and Character Development," *Research Digest,* March 2006.

27. Reported in D. S. Woodfill, "Queen Creek Puts Youth Coaches Through Sportsmanship Training," *The Arizona Republic,* 15 July 2010, http://www.azcentral.com/news/articles/2010/07/15/20100715queen-creek-coach-sportsmanship-training.html.

28. Ibid.

29. Karina Bland, "Expert Coaching," *The Arizona Republic,* 31 March 2008, p. D1.

30. Chris Dempsey, "Demand Grows for Accountability," *Denver Post,* 11 May 2008, p. 18C.

31. Quoted in Bland, "Expert Coaching," p. D2.

32. Andy Staples, "Too Young to Go Steady?" *Sports Illustrated,* 19 May 2008, pp. 14–15; see also George Dohrmann, *Play Their Hearts Out: A Coach, His Star Recruit, and the Youth Basketball Machine* (New York: Ballantine Books, 2010).

33. Ginsburg, Durant, and Baltzell, *Whose Game Is It, Anyway?,* 61; see also the series of articles cited in Rian Q. Landers, Russell L. Carson, and Bonnie Tjeerdsma Blankenship, "The Promises and Pitfalls of Sport Specialization in Youth Sports," *Journal of Physical Education, Recreation and Dance* 81, no. 8 (2010): 14–39.

34. For a comprehensive description of these IMG academies, see IMG Academies, http://www.imgacademies.com.

35. Quoted in Clay Latimer, "Under a Nonstop Watch," *Rocky Mountain News,* 19 December 2005, p. 8C.

36. Jim Halley, "New Rules Create Hoops Overload," *USA Today,* 2 August 2010, p. 8C.

37. Quoted in Mike Celizic, "Nice Serve! Five-Year-Old Tennis Prodigy," *TODAY.com,* 3 August 2007, http://today.msnbc.msn.com/id/20107032/ns/today-today_people; see also Ken Paul Mink, *So, You Want Your Kid to Be a Sports Superstar* (Victoria, BC: Trafford Press, 2006).

38. Farrey, *Game On.*

39. Positive Coaching Alliance, http://www.positivecoach.org.

40. National Alliance for Youth Sports, http://www.nays.org; see also Parents Association for Youth Sports, http://paysonline.nays.org.

41. William Nack and Don Yaeger, "Every Parent's Nightmare," *Sports Illustrated,* 13 September 1999, pp. 40, 42; and Vicki Michaelis, "Abuse Allegations Rock the Swim World," *USA Today,* 12 August, 2010, pp. 1A–2A;

see also Gretchen A. Kerr and Ashley E. Stirling, "Child Protection in Sport: Implications of an Athlete-Centered Philosophy," *Quest* 60 (2008), 307–323.

42. Quoted in Mark Hyman, "A Children's Crusade," *Sports Illustrated*, 7 June 2010, p. 18; see also the STOP website at http://www.stopsportsinjuries.org and Glenn S. Flesig, et al., "Risk of Serious Injury for Young Baseball Pitchers," *The American Journal of Sports Medicine* 39, no. 2 (2011): 253–257.

43. Quoted in Elizabeth Quinn, "Youth Sports and Overuse Injuries," *About.com* Sports Medicine, 8 September 2009, http://sportsmedicine.about.com/od/children/a/overusekids.htm.

44. Pauline Vaillancourt Rosenau, *The Competition Paradigm: America's Romance with Conflict, Contest, and Commerce* (Lanham, MD: Rowman & Littlefield, 2003).

45. Richard Louv, *Last Child in the Woods: Saving Our Children from Nature-Deficit Disorder* (Chapel Hill, NC: Algonquin Books, 2008). For an excellent discussion on promoting physical activity for youth, see President's Council on Physical Fitness and Sports, "Promoting Positive Youth Development Through Physical Activity," *Research Digest*, September 2009.

46. See Centers for Disease Control and Prevention, "Childhood Obesity," 3 June 2010, http://www.cdc.gov/HealthyYouth/Obesity.

47. Amy Ginsburg, Richard Durant, and Stephen Baltzell, *Whose Game Is It, Anyway?* (Boston: Houghton Mifflin, 2006); Brooke de Lench, *Home Team Advantage* (New York: Harper, 2006); and C. John McCoglin, *Surviving Youth Sports: A Manual for Parents* (Bloomington, IN: Trafford Publishing, 2006).

48. Terry Orlick, *Cooperative Games and Sports: Joyful Activities for Everyone* (Champaign, IL: Human Kinetics, 2006); Josette Luvmour and Sambhava Luvmour, *Everyone Wins: Cooperative Games and Activities* (Stony Creek, CT: New Society Publishers, 2007); Bobbi Conner, *Unplugged Play: No Batteries. No Plugs. Pure Fun* (New York: Workman Publishing, 2007); and Daniel Gould and Sarah Carson, "Life Skills Development Through Sport: Current Status and Future Directions," *International Review of Sport and Exercise Psychology* 1, no. 1 (2008): 58–78.

49. American Sport Education Program, http://www.asep.com.

50. Coaching Association of Canada, National Coaching Certification Program, http://www.coach.ca/eng.

51. David Paulo, *Human Rights in Youth Sports: A Critical Review of Children's Rights in Competitive Sport* (New York: Routledge, 2005).

CHAPTER 5

Interscholastic Sport

While there will be a precious few who turn sports into a career, the vast majority of high school student-athletes have a different focus. Studies suggest that the No. 1 reason is simply to have fun and to be part of a team. Many students who join a high school team and become successful in a sport gain a new sense of confidence that changes their lives.
—Robert B. Gardner and Nina van Erk*

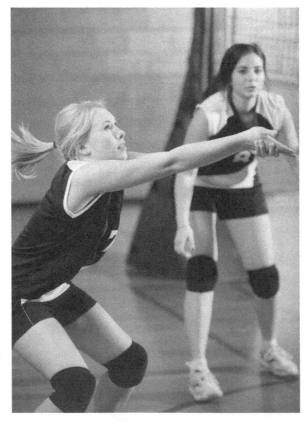

Interschool high school sports in North America have become vitally important as a means of unifying the entire school in a common cause—supporting the local teams. While historically high school sports were exclusively a male preserve, Title IX of the Educational Amendments Act of 1972 and similar legislation in Canada have moved high school sports toward gender equity. (istockphoto)

*Robert B. Gardner, NFGS Executive Director, and Nina van Erk, NFHS president, "High School Sports Participation Continues to Rise," *High School Today*, October 2010, p. 1.

The formal systems of education in the United States and Canada are the foundational social institution for preparing each generation to take its place in preserving and advancing its nation. It is here that the young learn cultural values and roles and acquire the skills that will be necessary throughout their adult lives. In North America over 90 percent of adolescents between the ages of fifteen and eighteen are enrolled in high schools. (The term *secondary school* is also used in Canada.)

THE ROLE OF HIGH SCHOOLS: DIFFERING INTERPRETATIONS

Social theorists have differing interpretations about the role of high schools. A functionalist perspective of the high school views it as the primary social institution for performing a number of social reproduction functions: transmitting knowledge and conveying the dominant culture, promoting social and political integration, providing a common moral code for social cohesion, maintaining social control, and sorting and selecting students for their adult roles in society. This last function typically plays out through competition for grades, with intellectually brighter and more socially competent students earning higher grades and thus having better potential for high-status occupations as adults. Beyond that, for functionalists the tasks performed by the schools are seen as important training for teaching and learning social skills and the "rules" of the larger society, and are thus beneficial to individuals and to society as a whole.[1]

While recognizing the importance of a high school education in both North American countries, conflict/culturalists view high schools as organizations with a distinctive elite orientation, with sharp inequalities in the educational opportunities available for students from different minority racial and ethnic groups and for female students. They stress that the sorting and selecting of pupils are highly biased according to students' socioeconomic backgrounds, giving students from affluent and wealthy families a

variety of advantages on achievement tests; these enable such students to qualify for the best universities, which, in turn, increase the likelihood of their economic and social success in adulthood. Although some children from poor families do well in school, most economically disadvantaged students are denied the same educational opportunities afforded to children of affluent parents. The consequence is that schools tend to serve a social reproductive role that preserves a variety of social and economic inequalities from one generation to the next.[2]

The social theoretical positions we have identified thus far can be directly or indirectly applied to the topics we examine in this chapter. First, we

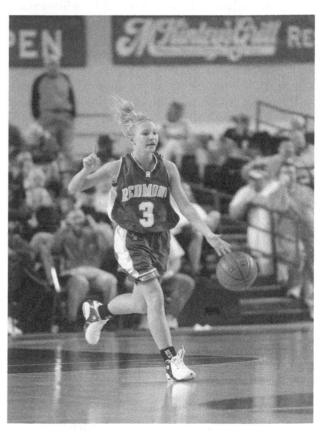

A high school varsity basketball point guard playing in the state tournament at the Tacoma Dome in Tacoma, Washington. Participation by girls in high school sports has increased dramatically in the past two decades. (Big Stock Photo)

describe the status of sport in North American education; next, we explore the positive and negative consequences of secondary school sport for the school, the community, the individual, and the society; finally, we assess the relationship between sport and education by examining inherent problems and dilemmas.

THE STATUS OF SPORT IN SECONDARY SCHOOLS

Interschool sports are an extracurricular program that is inexorably intertwined in high schools of the United States, and increasingly in Canadian secondary schools. In the 2010–2011 school year, about 7.6 million boys and girls in the United States were involved in over thirty-five different sports at the high school level. Of this total, 41.4 percent were girls and 58.6 percent were boys (see Table 5.1). This high level of involvement, however, is not the case elsewhere in the world. In most countries, sports programs for high-school-age youth are organized through community-based athletic clubs, *not through the schools.*

Canada is somewhat unusual in that it has both high school sports and community sports clubs for adolescents. Hockey, the most popular sport for male participation in Canada, is organized only as a community sport in most areas. The less popular male sports and all of the female sports are organized primarily through the high schools.

Ascertaining the degree to which interschool sports contributes to the educational mission of schools is difficult. The conventional view is that participation in sport has educational benefits. High school athletes benefit, it is commonly argued, by learning about dedication and sacrifice, by learning to play by the rules, by working together with teammates toward a common goal, by learning achievement orientation, and by meeting school academic requirements to stay eligible.

A less popularly held view is critical of high school sports programs as they are now conducted. From this perspective, school sports are believed to actually be detrimental to core educational goals. Moreover, spokespersons of this view assert that although sport participation may lead to positive behaviors, it is also an environment where some individuals learn bad behaviors. For example, although some athletes and coaches play by the rules, others circumvent them; sports experiences can teach good sportsmanship, but they can also teach poor sportsmanship; and while there is integrity in some high school sports programs, there is hypocrisy in others. For those who have witnessed a growing trend in the negative outcomes in high school sports programs, they often believe that sport and education have become incompatible, and some have even advocated abolishing high school sports programs.

Table 5.1   National Federation of State High School Associations Athletics Participation Summary

Year	Participants		
	Boys	Girls	Total
1990–1991	3,406,355	1,892,316	5,298,671
1995–1996	3,634,052	2,367,936	6,001,988
2000–2001	3,921,069	2,784,154	6,705,223
2005–2006	4,206,549	2,953,355	7,159,904
2009–2010	4,455,740	3,172,637	7,628,377
2010–2011	4,494,406	3,173,549	7,667,955

Source: National Federation of State High School Associations athletics participation data (2011), http://www.nfhs.org/Participation/SportSearch.aspx.

THE CONSEQUENCES OF SPORT FOR SCHOOLS, COMMUNITIES, AND INDIVIDUALS

Interschool high school sports in the United States have become so vitally important that high schools might appear to an outsider to be more concerned with sports than with scholarly endeavors. Social analysts who have studied the social climate of high schools have remarked about the prominent role of sports. They invariably comment about the presence of trophy cases near the main entrance to the high school buildings. The gold and silver trophies, as well as the footballs, basketballs, baseballs, and track batons are, with rare exceptions, the hardware symbolizing sports victories and championships. The overall display suggests that one is entering a sports club, not an educational institution.

In the hallways, student conversations and activities are dominated by talk about the outcomes of the school's sports teams during the previous week or about the upcoming Friday football or basketball games. All-school pep rallies are regularly held to allow students and cheerleaders to practice school cheers for the upcoming sporting events. The persistent social ambiance of the typical high school is about sports. Academic matters seem to be of secondary importance to students, teachers, and administrators. Indeed, school administrations and communities are usually much more willing to spend large sums of money for sports teams and sports facilities than they are for academic equipment and buildings. They are also willing to allow a disproportionate amount of time to be spent on sports and related activities. Why are athletes and sports teams given such extraordinary importance? The reason is that they are believed to have positive consequences for the high schools, the communities, and the participants.

The Consequences of Sport for the High School

All organizations require a minimum amount of unity; members must give an organization some allegiance for it to survive. Allegiance can stem from pay, ideology, chances for promotion, or the cooperative need to accomplish a collective goal. High schools, however, do not have the usual means to promote unity among their members. Grades, the equivalent of pay, do not always work because part of the school population is indifferent to them, and because they are so often dependent on defeating one's peers. Moreover, students are forced by custom and by law to attend school; this ensures their physical presence but not their involvement in the school's academic objectives.

Aside from sports contests, schools do not have collective goals, only individual ones. Therefore, any activity that promotes loyalty to the school serves a useful and necessary purpose. Interschool sports provide a unique means of unifying the entire school. Different races, social classes, teachers, school staff, and students unite in a common cause—the defeat of a common opponent, sports teams from other high schools. The collective following of a sports team can also lift morale, thereby unifying the school (although we should remember that unity is usually accomplished when teams win; losing teams may actually increase the possibility of division).

Athletics serves not only to unify student bodies but also to minimize conflict between students and teachers. High school population segments often become fragmented into cliques, thus preventing a collective morale from arising and sometimes becoming conflict groups. Interschool sports programs can sometimes alleviate problems of this sort and become a powerful factor in building up school spirit, unifying various student groups as well as teachers and students.

In addition to the unifying function of high school sports, they serve a social control function, which has several facets. First, sports activity may make students more mannerly, inasmuch as it drains athletes' surplus energies. For athletes and nonathletes alike, sport may serve as a diversion from undesirable activities. Likewise, it gives students something to converse about and something to do with their time, thereby keeping them from mischief and from questioning school rules and policies. Second, athletes, because they must obey training rules if they want to compete, serve as examples of good behavior. Within the high school student culture, athletes have high status, and by virtue of their favored position, they may tend to have a modeling role favored by school administrators and teachers. If this assumption is correct and nonathletes tend to admire them, then athletes may preserve harmony in the school.

School boards and school administrators support high school sports programs for self-serving reasons—school and community cohesion, financial support, and social control. They encourage sports participation not only because they want to encourage physical fitness but, more importantly, because they believe that sports involvement socializes students into the values of the nation. Schools want students to follow rules, to be disciplined, to work hard, to fit in—all of which are virtues in terms of learning their place in the hierarchical society where they will live as adults. Sports, it is believed by those who organize and manage high schools, accomplishes these aims. Functional social theorists approvingly point to interschool sports as a perfect venue for reproducing the cultural values and promoting social consensus and stability.

A final social control function of high school sports is their use by the school administrators and teachers to encourage intellectual activities among the students. A contingency for participation in sports is the maintenance of a certain grade point average (GPA), so athletes must at least meet this minimum. Consequently, the high school sports programs may have the concomitant effect of keeping some youngsters from dropping out of school because of their desire to participate.

The Consequences of Sport for the Community

We have already noted that school athletics appears to be an effective means for channeling the interest and loyalty of the community. Clearly, this enthusiasm generated by sports is a unifying agent for the community. Regardless of occupation, education, race, or religion, residents can and do unite in backing a school's teams. In addition, high school sports are very entertaining. They provide action, excitement, fantasy, and escape in the otherwise humdrum world of many rural small towns and even urban communities.

Of course, communities vary in their attachment to high school athletic teams. Typically, the community members concentrate their interests around boys' football and basketball. Most often, individual sports are ignored by communities, and girls' games are often minimized, too. Small communities are generally more involved in high school sports than are large urban communities.

The focus on a sport may also vary by geographical location, with high school basketball the rage in Indiana, hockey in Minnesota, and football in Texas. H. G. Bissinger, for example, has written of the importance of high school football in Odessa, Texas. Bissinger, a Philadelphia reporter, lived in Odessa for a year chronicling life in that town as it centered on high school football. One excerpt from Bissinger's book *Friday Night Lights* (after which the TV series was patterned) illustrates the importance of football to the town and its inhabitants: "Bob Rutherford, an affable realtor in town, might as well have been speaking for thousands when he casually said one day as if talking about the need for a rainstorm to settle the dust, 'Life really wouldn't be worth livin' if you didn't have a high school football team to support.'"[3]

The Consequences of Sport for Participants

High school students participate in sports for a variety of reasons. One important reason is the extraordinary popularity of high school sports and its ability to generate high social status for males and, increasingly, for females. H. G. Bissinger has described just how important it was to be a football player at Permian High School in Odessa, Texas, in the 1990s: "[They were] gladiators, the ones who were envied by everyone else, the ones who knew about the best parties and got the best girls and laughed the loudest and strutted so proudly through the halls of school as if it was their own wonderful, private kingdom."[4]

This description of the high school student culture rings true two decades after Bissinger wrote it. Clearly, high school athletes continue to reap substantial rewards for their sports participation. They receive fame and acclaim from peers, neighbors, teachers, and even strangers. A high school star (especially a male) can become a legend, a deity canonized in newspapers and immortalized through countless retold exploits. Even nonstar athletes have celebrity status. They enjoy praise and honor, special favors from businesses and the community, and popularity with the opposite sex.

A socially defined position within a large group or society is called a *status*, and statuses are hierarchically ranked from low to high. Achievement in high school sports is for the most part the basis for high status among male peers. The athlete, regardless of other attributes, is favored over the nonathlete, with the highest preference being "scholar-athlete." For young females, popularity is judged more by their being in the "in-group" than by their scholarship. Membership in the "in-group" is crucial, and being an athlete is not sufficient for inclusion. For females, social background and physical appearance are more important for social status than sports achievement. Social scientists have suggested that this may be changing for high school girls, as their participation in sports has increased rapidly during the past two decades and is becoming more and more acceptable.

But popularity and social status are not the only reasons high school boys and girls play sports. Many participate because they enjoy the physical activity and because they derive great pleasure from being part of a cohesive unit striving for a common goal. Sometimes forgotten, however, is that many students participate because all of the normative influences pull them in that direction. There are many pressures to participate in high school sports. Of course, if students are socialized to desire participation, they may not feel the demands.

Regardless of the motivation for participation in sport, there are other potential consequences of participation. Several are considered here: academic benefits, character development, and adjustment to failure and life after sport.

Academic Benefits

Does participation in high school sports help or hinder the academic achievement of athletes? Arguably no topic in sociology of sport has generated more discussion and debate than the relationship between high school athletic participation and educational achievement. For almost half a century

researchers in sociology of sport, secondary education, sociology of education, psychology, and sport management have studied this topic. A report by sociologist Douglas Hartman that was funded by the LA84 Foundation is the most recent summary and overview about the relationship between interscholastic high school sports participation and education achievement. According to the report, research "has time and again demonstrated a strong and positive correlation between high school sports participation and academic achievement. . . . Students who participate in high school sports tend, on average or in general, to perform better academically than their non-athletic peers . . . [and] the positive academic effects of sports appear . . . to be stronger for girls."[5]

This finding could be interpreted as validating the conventional wisdom that athletic participation builds discipline, a work ethic, and other achievement-oriented qualities that translate into better students. But Hartman cautions that "empirical evidence that demonstrates a strong statistical correlation between sports participation and educational attainment does not mean that sports automatically and inevitably contributes to academic achievement at either an individual or institutional (i.e., school) level. Correlation, in short, does not necessarily indicate causation. In fact . . . the relationship between sports participation and academic achievement . . . is far more complicated, multifaceted, and contingent *and* less direct than this."[6]

The relationship is contingent upon a variety of social factors, such as socioeconomic background, type and intensity of sports participation, and the ways in which sports are contextualized and connected to academic attitudes and activities. Furthermore, other issues exist whenever athletes are compared with nonathletes. The two categories differ not only in terms of sports involvement but with respect to academic achievement as well. First, athletes may have a higher grade point average because they are required to meet a minimum grade level to be eligible for sports. This grade barrier can prevent students with low academic performance from attempting to participate in athletics, thus increasing the likelihood that the athlete group will have higher average grades than the nonathlete group.

Second, either rebellious students may choose not to participate in sport or coaches may dismiss them from teams because they do not fit in. Under these circumstances, too, the athlete group will likely have better grades.

Third, athletes may get extra help from tutors and teachers, take easier courses in order to handle the rigors of being athletes, or receive outright gifts of good grades from sympathetic teachers. Where such conditions exist, the result may be better grades for an athlete group but not because being an athlete makes one a good student.

Finally, there is the question of whether athletes may differ from nonathletes in ways unrelated to sport. For example, there is a retention process that takes into account who enters and who drops out of high school athletics between the sophomore and senior years. Research findings across several social science disciplines clearly show that those who begin and remain in high school sports tend to be economically privileged in terms of family social class, cognitive ability, academic achievement, and self-esteem. In short, high school athletes possess a number of personal, social, and academic advantages over their nonathlete peers even before they participate in high school sports.

Because there are significant differences between athletes and nonathletes that could affect their academic performance, without statistically taking those variables into account we cannot determine whether the differences found in much of the research on athletes versus nonathletes result from playing sports or are merely correlational. Thus, we should not infer that sports participation makes athletes perform better in the classroom.[7]

Character Development

We noted in Chapter 4 that there are a number of questionable assumptions about the claim that "sport builds character." Although many people take this slogan for granted, there have been few well-conceived and implemented empirical research studies on the effects of high school sport involvement on the social development of athletes. We can suggest several reasons for this. First, the word *character* is vague; character is a socially constructed concept amenable to a variety of meanings and interpretations. When left unspecified there is

no way of knowing which meaning or interpretation is intended. To be amenable to verification, the definition of character needs to be anchored to a set of specific attitudes, values, and behaviors. Second, there are differing cultural ideas about which character traits are considered "good." After all, the exhibition of a particular behavior or trait in a specific situation might be considered a demonstration of good character in one culture but bad character in another.

Third, even if one clearly defines what one means by character in a given setting, it is extremely difficult to empirically verify the character-building effects of sport involvement. Traditional experimental designs are impractical because it is almost impossible to arrange the necessary controlled conditions for relevant data collecting. Cross-sectional research designs, which provide data about relationships between variables, are worthless in the context of substantiating causal effects. Some studies have attempted to analyze the effects of sport involvement on a single discrete variable such as courage or self-discipline, but at the expense of almost trivializing the symbolic interactions that occur in a complex social setting like sport. So such an approach is too simple to yield any meaningful information.

Because statistically verifying that sport builds character is so difficult, those who advocate this approach are reduced to relating anecdotes such as how particular athletes displayed courage, perseverance, or self-discipline in the course of a game or how a team showed dedication and teamwork. But a perusal of the nation's newspapers on any given day will reveal stories of courage, loyalty, perseverance, and so on, by people who have never participated in sport. So character qualities often attributed to athletes are neither confined to nor peculiar to them.

Another common form of anecdotal evidence is the personal account of "what sport did for me." Such testimonials are often given by former athletes who attribute their post-playing achievements to their sport experiences. Regardless of the form, of course, anecdotal evidence is unacceptable as scientific proof.

To these problems we can add the question of whether the "character" displayed by athletes or former athletes was present before they played organized sport or whether their particular preexisting character dispositions may actually have predisposed them to take up sport in the first place. Several sport studies researchers have suggested such possibilities.[8]

Our comments about the problems of empirically supporting claims that sport builds character should not be misunderstood. We are not asserting that high school sports participation has no effect on the personal-social development of athletes. Indeed, there is convincing, empirically grounded evidence that salient social experiences are powerful socializers. Sport involvement is an exciting form of human expression; many people find sports a source of great fun, joy, and self-satisfaction, and young athletes' values and beliefs are undoubtedly shaped by their experiences. But the exact effects of high school sports on attitudes, values, and behaviors (character) depend greatly on the social contextual conditions of the sporting experience, and the social contexts in which sports take place vary widely. Moreover, perhaps the sport setting is merely a particularly good setting for enabling persons to exhibit preexisting character traits; the fact that some athletes or former athletes display culturally valued personal and social characteristics cannot be wholly attributed to their sport experiences without an enormous leap of faith.

The overarching question is this: Does sports participation make a difference in "character"? As we have said, the data are contradictory. It is difficult to make the causal link. We believe that sports participation does not *build* character, discipline, and other achievement-related qualities in young men and women. Instead, there is a social dynamic that we feel may be working whereby, on the one hand, high school boys and girls are weeded out by coaches or drop out voluntarily because they do not possess the personal-social traits needed while, on the other hand, those who are imbued with the positive traits of hard work, discipline, goal orientation, and willingness to obey orders remain on high school sports teams.

Adjustment to Failure and Life After School Sport

Two problems for individual high school athletes are often overlooked. First, for many, sport leads to a series of failures. Either they fail to make the team, or if they make the team they sit on the bench, or their team loses many more times than it wins. In a success-oriented society, what are the effects of all the failures that sport often generates? At the individual level, failure can be devastating for some. They may be defined by others and by themselves as losers, which is a strong negative label in a society that places such high value on winning. This may negatively impact their self-esteem, confidence, and assertiveness. It may lead to mental health problems.

Another problem is one of adjustment after a career in sport is finished. The odds of making a team at the next level are remote: Only 5 percent of high school football players, 2 percent of male high school basketball players, and 3 percent of female high school basketball players will participate in college; the odds of making it from college into the pros in these sports are even lower (see Table 5.2). Clearly, these long odds mean that most

Table 5.2 Long Shots: Odds of High School Athletes Playing in College and Professionally

	Odds of Playing in College	Odds of Playing Professionally
Football	1 in 17	8 in 10,000
Men's Basketball	1 in 35	3 in 10,000
Women's Basketball	3 in 100	1 in 5,000
Men's Ice Hockey	11 in 100	1 in 300
Baseball	3 in 50	1 in 200
Men's Soccer	3 in 50	1 in 1,250

Source: Todd Jones, Mike Wagner, and Jill Riepenhoff, "Chasing the Myth," *Columbus Dispatch,* September 1, 2010, http://www.dispatch.com/live/content/special_reports/stories/2010/youth_sports/day4-chasing-a-myth.html.

high school athletes will end their sports careers at the conclusion of high school.

After the glory years, what happens to former athletes when they are considered has-beens? Does participation in sport have carryover value to other endeavors where there is no hero worship, no excitement, and no fame? What happens to the athlete who finds himself or herself suddenly outside the world that has until now been at the center of his or her life and the principal source of identity and social status? Do former athletes become embittered and turn away from sport, or do they fill their time reliving the past, attending games, Monday-morning quarterbacking, and watching sports on television? How does the athlete, when compared to the nonathlete, adjust to job, marriage, and upward or downward mobility? Unfortunately, little research has been done on the effects of this shift away from the limelight when high school sports participation has ended.[9]

PROBLEMS, DILEMMAS, AND CONTROVERSIES

We have noted that sport in secondary schools has a variety of consequences for the schools, the community, and the participants, but many people wonder about the educational benefits of these sports programs. In this section we focus on some of the problems, dilemmas, and controversies of interscholastic sport as it is presently organized.

The Subversion of Educational Goals

It is often argued that time-consuming, commercially oriented, expensive high school sports programs consume an inordinate amount of time in the school day and that the large amounts of money devoted to sports could be better spent on academic matters. There is also objection to the tendency to give star athletes preferential treatment in their schooling. Athletes may be passed even though they have not mastered the subject matter. The qualifications of coaches are also often questioned. It is estimated that only about 50 percent of high school coaches are high school teachers;

indeed, many have never taught in the classroom and have little training or legitimate certification in coaching. In short, the coach in many high schools has no connection with the academic institution.

Increasingly, high school sports have come under criticism for becoming less about education and more about entertainment. This is coupled with the charge that high school sports now have no connection with lifelong health and fitness-for-life concepts. The argument is that skills emphasized in football and basketball, the objects of most public attention, are irrelevant beyond the school years. Moreover, at a time when obesity is becoming more and more of a problem, athletes in some sports are encouraged to gain weight. For example, five of the offensive linemen on the Santa Ana Mater Dei High School (California) in 2009 averaged 285 pounds. (That's 27 pounds more *per man* than the five linemen who started for the 1972 Miami Dolphins, who went undefeated and won the Super Bowl.)

The Reinforcement of Gender Roles

In Chapter 2 we described how sport in North American schools has historically been almost exclusively a male preserve. This is clearly evident as one compares by gender the number of participants and facilities. We will examine sexism in sport in greater detail in Chapter 14; therefore, the discussion here is limited to only several unintended ways in which school sport works to maintain the conventional expectations for masculine and feminine roles (see Box 5.1).

With the implementation of Title IX (see Chapter 14) and the efforts to bring gender equity to school athletic programs, the number of female sport participants increased dramatically—from 300,000 girls involved in high school sports in 1971 to more than 3.17 million in 2011. Put another way, the growth in girls playing high school sports rose from 1 in 27 in 1971 to 1 in 2.5 in 2011. Also, about 1 in 45 high school wrestlers in 2011 were girls, a sport that is traditionally male.[10]

Although attempts have been made to equalize female and male programs in facilities, equipment, coaching, and transportation, inequities remain. Football, with its high cost and large number of

Box 5.1 _Thinking About Sport:_ Cheerleading: Is It a Sport?

Two-Four-Six-Eight, Who Do We Appreciate? This familiar cheerleader yell is usually directed to a particular athlete, but cheerleaders also need appreciation. They are the "spirit-makers" of the high school and the spectator entertainers at sporting events. What would high school football and basketball games be without cheerleaders to provide support for the players and enthusiasm to the fans watching the contest? Cheerleaders are as indispensible as the athletes who play in the various high school sports teams throughout North America. In the U.S., cheerleading ranks as one of the most popular extracurricular actives for girls: An estimated 3.5 million cheerleaders over the age of fourteen—95 percent are females—participate in year-round programs paralleling the fall, winter, and spring sports. Originally, cheerleading was merely a matter of leading the crowd in supportive cheers, but it currently entails complex, orchestrated performances involving advanced tumbling and acrobatic stunts. Many cheerleaders also attend summer training camps and state/province and national competitions.

The popularity of cheerleading, the practice and training needed to acquire advanced skills, and the widespread competitions in cheerleading have led to the demand that cheerleading be granted the status of a sport. A fundamental issue here is whether cheerleading is _really a sport_. Advocates for granting cheerleading the status of a sport argue that the activity requires the acquisition of complex physical skills, and that there are many cheerleading competitive events now available for cheerleading squads. Opponents of designating cheerleading a sport argue that the status of _sport_ implies a competition among teams and not all cheerleading squads actually compete against other teams. They also claim that scoring in cheerleader competitions is too subjective—in other words, that it is based on human judgment rather than on an objective goal or measurement of time.

The issue of whether cheerleading is a sport has been litigated. In 2009, the Wisconsin supreme court heard a case involving an accidental injury sustained during a cheerleading practice. The court ruled that cheerleading is a full-contact sport in high schools in that state. But the issue is not settled for all jurisdictions and at all competitive sports levels. At the college level, a 2010 lawsuit involved the question of whether college cheerleading qualified as a sport for purposes of Title IX. The federal judge, citing a current lack of program development and organization, ruled that it does not but may in the future.

Two organizations—USA Gymnastics and USA Cheer—have announced plans to create a new sport out of competitive cheerleading in an effort to get cheerleading competitions recognized by the NCAA.

Sources: Associated Press, "Wisconsin Court: Cheerleading a Contact Sport, Participants Can't Be Sued for Accidental Injury," _FoxNews.com_, 27 January 2009, http://www.foxnews.com/story/0,2933,483704,00.html; Pat Eaton-Robb, "U.S. Judge in Conn.: Cheerleading Not a Sport," _msnbc.com_, 21 July 2010, http://www.msnbc.msn.com/id/38347400/?GT1=43001.

participants, continues to skew budgets in favor of males. The scheduling of games and media attention also stress male sports.

Finally, a major trend in high school sports is that as women's sports have gained in popularity, money, and respect, men have gained more and more control over them. Men are more likely than women to be athletic directors and coaches of women's sports at the high school and college levels. Male athletes see male role models exclusively as coaches and administrators, but female athletes are usually denied female role models in positions requiring decisiveness, confidence, and self-assurance. Thus, females once again receive the unambiguous message that the more responsible a position is in an organization, the more likely men are to occupy it. Occasionally, however, breakthroughs occur and challenge old gender traditions. There are now a handful of women coaching boys on varsity high school basketball and football teams.[11]

Cheating

Cheating involves a violation of the rules to gain an unfair advantage over an opponent. It occurs at all levels of sport and may be done by individual players, teams, or coaches. Baseball historian John Thorn claims that "cheating is not merely countenanced in baseball, it is loved."[12] The types of cheating depend on the sport and the ingenuity of the participants.

Clearly, cheating is antithetical to educational values and should have no place in educational programs. However, as high school sports victories have become increasingly important to the school and community, as well as to the job security of high school coaches, cheating has become inevitable. Some high school players are coached to use illegal but difficult-to-detect techniques. One example is holding or tripping by offensive linemen in football. In basketball it is often advantageous to touch the lower half of the shooter's body because the referee usually watches the action around the ball. A form of cheating often taught basketball players is to fake being fouled. The intent is to fool an official who is out of position and to receive an undeserved free throw. Similar faking of an injury to get an advantage occurs commonly in soccer when a player is bumped during play and then acts as if he or she has been fouled, writhing in pseudopain in the hope that the referee will award him or her a penalty kick for the phony injury. So, too, in football when punters act as if they had been hit by an onrushing lineman.

Coaches sometimes break the spirit of a rule if not the rule itself. For example, some high school governing organizations prohibit teams from having organized practices before a certain date, yet coaches insist on players practicing, with captains in charge or coaches at a distance yelling orders. Most secondary school governing organizations prohibit the inducement of athletes to transfer from one high school to another. But stories abound throughout secondary education about coaches who have recruited athletes, or lost athletes to coaches who recruited them away. Coaches typically claim it was the athletes who initiated the transfer, while athletes say they were recruited, so it is always difficult to know what the truth is. Either way, however, this form of cheating has been widespread.

An extreme example of high school transferring occurred recently in the Phoenix, Arizona, area. A basketball player, who was still only a junior, had already played at five high schools: Phoenix Desert Vista, Phoenix Sunnyslope, Gilbert Highland, Chandler Basha, and Mesa Desert Ridge. The coach at one of the high schools said: "I don't think it's any program or coach. It's how the world runs in high school basketball."[13] The Colorado High School Activities Association has reduced the likelihood of this kind of thing by allowing students to transfer before the start of the school year even if their only reason for transferring is sports. But such a rule invites recruiting and various inducements to athletes and their parents to change schools.

At Brentwood Academy, a private school located in a suburb of Nashville, Tennessee, the football coach sent a letter to eighth-grade boys admitted to the school, inviting them to spring football practice (i.e., to practice with the high school players while they were still eighth graders). The Tennessee Secondary School Athletic Association (TSSAA) ruled that this was a violation of its recruiting policy, and imposed sanctions against Brentwood Academy. Brentwood filed a suit against TSSAA, claiming TSSAA had violated Brentwood's First Amendment free speech guarantees, thus denying the coach and his school freedom of expression. For the next ten years the case went back and forth through federal courts. Finally, in 2007 the U.S. Supreme Court heard arguments in the case and ruled unanimously in favor of TSSAA, saying that "the coach's pre-enrollment solicitation violated the TSSAA'a anti-recruiting rule and that he had ample notice that his conduct was prohibited." The Supreme Court went on to say that the "First Amendment does not excuse Brentwood from abiding by the same anti-recruiting rule that governs the conduct of its sister schools."[14]

A different form of cheating involves the use of drugs so that an athlete may compete at a higher-than-normal level of ability (see Chapter 7). This is sometimes done at the insistence of trainers and coaches, sometimes by an athlete's own decision. A 2009 national survey found that for high school seniors, fewer than 2 percent of boys and girls had taken anabolic steroids in the previous twelve months.[15] Thus, it appears that, at least in the case of steroids, use of this substance among high schoolers is not widespread.

Unsportsmanlike Behavior of Fans

The intensity of sports competition sometimes leads some fans to cross the line. This may involve fighting, insulting opposing teams' players and fans, yelling obscenities, and other obnoxious behaviors. Several unhealthy examples illustrate this point.[16]

- In Phoenix, Arizona, when a football player was injured, fans from the opposing team shouted "broken neck, broken neck."
- Also in Phoenix, students wore green T-shirts implying that the players on the largely Latino team they were playing against had green cards, and thus were foreigners.
- In Thomasville, Georgia, the police department issued a "brawl warning" after two incidents at high school basketball games where parents and grandparents went onto the court to enter into fights that broke out between opposing teams.

As a journalist has noted more generally, "Personal attacks, jeers and politically incorrect clothing can detract from the sportsmanship and camaraderie that high school athletics are supposed to promote. They can also lead to violence, stereotyping, loss of self-esteem and distractions for players trying to focus on the game."[17]

Autocratic Coaches

The authoritarian control by coaches that athletes experience in youth sports is employed by most high school coaches as well. So another criticism of high school sports is the almost total control that coaches exercise over their players' lives. Many coaches, for example, dictate hairstyles, clothing, dating, whom the players associate with, church attendance, and the like. Many also monitor their players' behavior off the field (bed checks) and restrict freedom of choice (what position to play, mandatory off-season weight lifting). Most coaches impose their will on their teams concerning team rules, discipline, play calling, and personnel decisions.

This model of leadership is a source of criticism from a conflict/cultural theoretical perspective because such behavior often becomes coercive and exploitive and is counterproductive for learning democratic actions and values by athletes. Two sport studies scholars who have exhaustively studied high school sports contend that high school athletes "exercise no control over organized school athletics."

Instead, administrators, teachers, and coaches "determine every aspect of school sports: the rules of the games, who is eligible, who may coach, what may constitute practices, how many games may be played, and when and where those games may occur."[18] However, a functionalist perspective would view this model as appropriate for instilling habits and values for coping with the hierarchically structured organizations of contemporary life in North America.

Whether coaches have the right to infringe upon the civil liberties of their charges is certainly a legal question. Beyond that, there is the question of the educational value of controlling these teenagers on and off the field. A system that impedes personal autonomy fosters dependence and immaturity rather than the presumed virtues of participation, which are leadership, independence, and self-motivation. Moreover, a relevant question here is whether subservience to an autocrat prepares one for life in a democracy.[19]

Excessive Pressures to Win

Many of the problems found in high school sports result from the excessive emphasis on winning. The sociological explanation for the tendency of coaches to be authoritarian, or to cheat, or to be hypocritical, lies not in their individual psyches but in the intensely competitive system in which they operate.

In the U.S., the success or failure of a team is believed by most persons to rest with the coach. This pressure to win brings some coaches to use illegal inducements to attract athletes to their schools, or to teach their linemen to hold without getting caught, or to look the other way when athletes (who face the same pressures to succeed) use drugs to enhance performance. The absolute necessity to win also explains why some coaches drive their players too hard. Thus, what some persons might label brutality has been explained by some coaches as a necessity to get the maximum effort from players.

Finally, authoritarianism can be explained by the constraints on the coaching role. Democracy is unthinkable to most in the coaching profession because coaches are liable for the outcome in an extremely uncertain situation. They cannot control injuries, officiating, mental lapses by athletes, or the bounce of the ball, so most coaches are convinced that they must seek to control as much else as possible.

Another consequence of the excessive stress on winning is that sports participation becomes work rather than play. The emphasis is on the outcome rather than on enjoyment of the process. Fun has become equated with winning rather than with pleasure in participating.

Elitism

Interscholastic sport programs are elitist. That is, they are for the few, not the many. It is the experienced, the highly trained, and the physically gifted who make up high school sports teams. If sports participation is believed to have educational benefits, how can schools justify limiting teams to the most gifted athletes? Why should participation be restricted almost exclusively to the fast, the strong, or the tall? As a *Los Angeles Times* article said: "High school athletes are fitter, more skilled and better trained than ever before. But these top-notch athletes, say many health and fitness experts, have become the singular focus of the youth sports system—while teenagers of average or low ability no longer warrant attention."[20]

There are two reasons for limiting sports opportunities for high school students. One is that school boards and administrators funnel most of their limited funds toward those sports that entertain the public (football and basketball). In effect, then, the goal of high school sports has shifted from an educational endeavor to public entertainment. Second, because of limited financial resources, many schools have eliminated freshman/sophomore teams, some sports programs such as golf and tennis, and intramural sports programs. Even physical education classes have been cut from many schools.

The result is that sports and the use of sports facilities are increasingly being turned over to the physically gifted for the purpose of exhibiting their prowess publicly. Consequently, high schools have largely ignored sports programs for students with disabilities. In the 2010–2011 school year, only about 300 U.S. high schools out of more than 17,000 provided sports for students with disabilities, with 3,066 participating. The most popular "adapted sport" was soccer.[21]

Sport Specialization

Not surprisingly, the growing trend in youth sport for one-sport specialization manifests itself in one-sport high school athletes who limit their participation and year-round training to that sport. This was first the case in individual sports (running, swimming, gymnastics, tennis), but it is now increasingly found in team sports as well, especially in large high schools. As the director of educational services for the National Federation of State High School Associations recently noted: "While we are aware that a growing number of athletes are focusing on a single sport, we strongly feel it's important to promote athletes playing multiple sports. It is our wish that more schools and coaches should encourage their student-athletes to play more than one sport."[22]

The arguments for this practice are that refined skill levels lead to optimal individual and team performance, it encourages excellence, and it increases the chances for obtaining a college athletic scholarship. The possible negative consequences of this practice include physical and psychological burnout, injuries from overuse, creation of a professional atmosphere for athletes that is inappropriate for adolescents, friction among coaches who compete for athletes, and the use of athletic facilities limited to the few.

Budget Shortfalls

School districts fund sports in their districts, supplemented by ticket sales. Many districts have experienced a fiscal crisis with declining appropriations from the federal and state governments. This has especially affected urban school districts, as wealth has left the city for the suburbs. The trend appears to be for more budget tightening as the federal government shifts more programs to the states and the mode of the electorate is to reduce taxes.[23]

Three strategies to overcome these declining revenues have been employed to continue the financing of sports (and other extracurricular activities), each having negative consequences for high school sports programs. First, schools have reacted to budget shortfalls by reducing or eliminating some sports (almost always individual sports with no potential for producing revenue) or the number of teams (eliminating sophomore or junior varsity teams). This solution, of course, reduces the number of participants and makes the sports all the more elitist.

Football teams are typically not subject to elimination (although the number of players might be reduced). This is ironic because it is the most expensive sport in the number of coaches required, the cost of equipment (about $5,000 per player), and the cost of insurance. The sacredness of football poses another problem: Because it is almost exclusively for males—although in 2011 there were 1,556 females playing on high school football teams out of the slightly more than 1 million football players—and as other sports are reduced or eliminated, the proportion of the athletic budget going for males becomes all the more unbalanced.[24]

A second solution to meager budgets is to charge a fee for all participants. Pay-for-play has become increasingly popular throughout North America, with the fees varying from $50 per sport to as much as $600. This practice has usually resulted in a reduction in numbers of participants. Most important, it has created difficulty for students from lower-income families, especially reducing their participation. Thus, sport becomes not only elitist in skill level but also elitist in terms of socio-economic class.[25]

The third strategy employed by some districts has been to seek corporate sponsorship. Corporations have been solicited to promote certain events, purchase advertising, and buy scoreboards, artificial turf, a track, or a team bus (a few schools in Texas have sold the naming rights of their stadiums for more than $1 million). Several questions arise when this practice occurs. Is the commercialization of high school sport compatible with educational goals? Will those who control the resources of a program ultimately control it? In other words, will companies that donate thousands of dollars to a high school program have an influence on schedules, coach selection, and use of the facilities? Will they encourage a win-at-any-cost philosophy, since they do not want to have their products associated with a loser?

Corporate High School Sport Programs

There are five indicators that sport is already at the corporate level in some schools and moving

generally in that direction across the United States.

First, some schools are closely resembling sports programs in big-time universities (see Chapter 6) by selling naming rights to stadiums and arenas, trademarking their names and logos, hiring coaches for salaries far exceeding those of teachers, selling personal seat licenses (e.g., reserving seats for as much as $1,000 a season), and spending vast sums on football and basketball budgets. In 2010 the school district of Allen, Texas, began work on a new football stadium that is set to open in 2012 and will cost $59.6 million. The stadium will seat 18,000 fans, and that will merely tie Allen for the fifth-largest high school stadium in Texas. "That's Texas for you," said the president of the Thomas B. Fordham Institute, an education think tank in Washington, DC; "this is, of course, ridiculous in a period of tight money."[26] Although this is an extreme example, there are other high schools in Texas, Ohio, Pennsylvania, Louisiana, Georgia, Florida, and elsewhere with similar outlays for their sports programs, revealing the priority of sport in these schools and making it clear that sport has taken on the characteristics of corporate sport.

A second indicator of the trend toward corporate sport at the high school level is the existence of fraudulent "prep schools" (mass media stories refer to them as "fake prep schools") that exist basically to inflate transcripts of those who are marginal students but excellent athletes. These high schools play the best schools around the country, providing their athletes exposure but also making their transcripts acceptable to big-time college sports programs. Red Lion Academy in Delaware, with fewer than 300 students, is attempting to build a national high school sports power loaded with college prospects. Through an arrangement with the Delaware Interscholastic Athletic Association, Red Lion can offer financial aid to football and boys' basketball athletes, conduct spring football practices, and begin fall football practice earlier than other state high schools. In exchange for these privileges, Red Lion cannot play other Delaware high schools or compete for a state championship. Instead, it will play a national schedule of games.[27]

The NCAA in 2007 beefed up its transcript screening and inspection operation against these schools, disqualifying some, and announced that it would no longer accept transcripts from several nontraditional high schools that had failed to pass muster under a new academic review program. The *New York Times* editorialized that the problems may go deeper: "The storefront prep schools have been easy enough to identify. But the NCAA must now take a closer look at schools one level down that look legitimate but that may be just as willing to shortchange athletes' education as their fly-by-night counterparts. State departments of education also have a major role to play in curbing these abuses."[28]

A third indicator that sport in high school is becoming corporate is the combined effect of increased exposure and commercialization, which is moving high school sport to more closely resemble big-time college programs. High schools used to play games against league rivals and participate in tournaments at the state level. For many schools this continues to be the case, but some now participate in national tournaments in Hawaii, Florida, Las Vegas, and elsewhere.

These events are sponsored by various corporations. For example, the McDonald's Classic is a high school boys' basketball tournament held every year in Erie, Pennsylvania. Nationally ranked teams with NCAA Division I and NBA-bound players travel to Erie for the opportunity to play against other top teams for the championship and bragging rights. The annual ESPN RISE National High School Invitational is composed of eight of the nation's top boys' basketball teams and four of the top girls' teams. It is considered one of the leading high school basketball tournaments in the country. Each game is broadcast on the ESPN network. In 2001 there were no national high school football all-star games. In 2012 there were five.[29]

Prior to national media coverage of high school sports, media attention tended to be local. Today, *USA Today* lists the twenty-five top-ranked high schools for the sport in season (separate lists for boys' and girls' teams) in the nation. *USA Today*, *Parade*, and other national publications select high school All-American teams and coaches of the year. SportsChannel, Madison Square Garden, Fox Sports Net, and ESPN now produce weekly "magazine" shows on high school sports.

Perhaps most surprising, in 2010 the National Federation of State High School Associations (NFHS), the umbrella organization for governing high school sports in the U.S., published this statement on its website: "The National Federation of State High School Associations has led the development of education-based interscholastic sports [and] has joined with the sports and entertainment marketing giant IMG to establish and sanction national high school championships. Plans are underway to hold national championship events in boys' and girls' tennis, golf, lacrosse, and 7-on-7 football, and to ultimately stage championships in 20 sports."[30] This shocked high school administrators and coaches throughout the country. Objections quickly piled up, and one year later, in February 2011, the following statement was made by the NFHS executive director and NFHS president: "After much debate and discussion during the past few years, the NFHS membership has re-affirmed the organization's longstanding stance against national championships in high school sports."[31]

As corporate ventures continue establishing national high school championships, Nike, Reebok, and Adidas are paying some coaches of the nationally ranked teams to outfit their teams with their products and to help steer their athletes to play in colleges that are "Nike schools" or "Reebok schools" or "Adidas schools."

The fourth indicator of high school sports becoming corporate is the turning of young elite athletes into "professionals." It starts with some promising elementary and junior high school athletes being "grade retained" (held back a year) to give them an extra year before college to increase their skills, size, speed, strength, coordination, and maturity. Many young athletes are recruited to attend certain high schools. While in high school, some accept gratuities that technically make them professionals. Several educational administrators have asserted that elite high school athletes, by any honest measure, are professionals. They are routinely paid by coaches or agents and provided with cash, cars, and other gifts. Many are recruited to attend certain high schools.

Top high school athletes play and train at their sport year-round. During the summers they play in high-level leagues and attend camps run by college coaches or shoe companies to hone skills and become recognized by agents, scouts, and coaches. This continues throughout the high school years, with increased pressure to succeed. What was once play has become work.

Finally, the fifth indicator of the corporatization of high school sports is that the elite high school athletes are the objects of intense recruitment by colleges throughout their high school career. The experience is flattering to the athletes, but it has a tendency to inflate their egos and get in the way of their education. It also tends to make them cynical about education because of the often sleazy aspects of recruiting. A more important consequence is that these athletes are on the market. As such, they ultimately will be purchased by a university athletic department. For high school athletes to be treated as commodities is the essence of corporate sport.

EFFORTS TO REFORM HIGH SCHOOL SPORTS

Many educators and others are concerned about the path that high school sports are taking. As we have seen, there are school districts with 20,000-seat stadiums, there are high school coaches who do not teach in the classroom, some high school coaches make thousands of dollars from shoe companies, and there are nationally televised games. Under these conditions, the pressure on coaches and athletes has become intense.

The potential for abuse and exploitation of athletes has increased. We see more and more scandals involving payments and other gifts to high school players, recruiting, altered transcripts, and pressures on teachers to "give" athletes grades. Clearly, the education of the athletes tends to become secondary. In short, high school sport is moving in the same direction as sport at the college level, that is, toward commercialization, overemphasis, exploitation, and elitism, and away from the educational mission of schools.

What follows are suggestions for reforming high school sports. We are not public policy experts, but we think that we have some ideas that can promote discussion about changes in high school

sports that, in turn, might lead to some reforms. The principle guiding our suggestions is that high school sports should be organized to maximize educational goals.

1. *Resist all efforts to "corporatize" high school sports.* High school sports should not be in the entertainment business. Nor should they allow the encroachment of corporations into their world. Moreover, high school sports should be kept in perspective; that is, they should not put undue pressure on coaches and players. In effect, to counter high school sport becoming corporate, several reforms must be instituted:

- Ban national televising of high school sports. High school should be a time for students to establish a sound academic foundation. High school sports should be seriously conducted as an extracurricular activity, not as a televised, overemphasized spectacle. The lure of national newspaper and television coverage is certainly distracting to the parents of athletes, the community, and the athletes themselves.
- Return to the practice of scheduling only teams within the high school's state or adjoining state (or province in Canada). It has been suggested that high school sports introduce a "bus rule": If a team is able to travel comfortably in a bus to play another school, a game can be scheduled. Sending high school teams throughout the country to play is unnecessary, and merely commercially exploits the athletes.
- Eliminate postseason all-star games. Their only intent is promotional and commercial.
- Do not permit athletic shoe companies and other corporations to intrude in high school sports. This means that corporations must not be allowed to have high school coaches on their payrolls or to sponsor summer camps.

2. *Enforce an educationally defensible standard of school academic performance for athletes to be eligible to participate in sports.* Many school jurisdictions have low academic requirements for athletes. Many actually accept a D average for sport eligibility. Low eligibility standards do not prepare athletes for college, and they convey the message that academics are not important. Some school districts and states

(and provinces) have instituted a "No Pass No Play" rule, requiring at least a C in all subjects to be eligible to participate in extracurricular activities.

An effort intended to help reform school athletics through academic standards was instituted by the NCAA at the behest of the American Council on Education. The rules they first imposed have changed since their beginning some twenty-five years ago, but essentially they require a minimum GPA in core high school courses and a minimum Scholastic Achievement Test (SAT) score.

These NCAA eligibility rules seem to be working; that is, high school athletes are apparently better academically prepared for college than they were a generation ago. The number of new college recruits who are ineligible is diminishing. Again, caution should guide the interpretation of this apparent good news. This lower rate may not be a consequence of better preparation for students. The colleges may be less willing than in earlier years to offer scholarships to marginal students because their scholastic failures are embarrassing to the academic community. Another possibility is that marginal students opted to play in community colleges where the rules do not apply. Despite these cautions, it appears that the new academic demands are helping. High school athletes and their coaches are taking academics more seriously.

3. *Bring coaches back into the teaching profession.* High school coaches should be part of the faculty, teaching courses and being responsible for nonsport duties just as are other faculty members. Coaches should be certified coaches, trained in first aid, the technical aspects of their sport, and the physiological and psychological aspects of adolescence. Coaches must be certified teachers, subject to the same rights and responsibilities as other teachers, including tenure. This will enhance the job security of coaches, thereby lessening somewhat the fanatical "win-at-all-costs" attitude.

4. *Minimize the elitism of sports: Find ways to encourage more students to play on high school sports teams.* Schools should provide more school teams in more sports. Why not have two football teams, one for those weighing more than 150 pounds and one for those under that weight? Basketball could be divided into teams over and under a certain height. Consider this: Parents, teachers, administrators,

and even the general sports fan uniformly claim that participation in sports promotes the physical and social development of athletes. Assuming there is some validity to that claim, isn't the logical conclusion that playing sports would be more valuable than merely watching them? If it is, high schools should provide sports opportunities for every student who wishes to participate.

5. *Increase student decision making in sports programs.* One of the great ironies of school sports programs is that they are thought to enhance responsibility, autonomy, and leadership qualities in participants. However, as presently organized with autocratic coaches, imposed rules, and all decisions made by adults, these goals are not being achieved.

Could sports be organized so that the athletes are involved in the rule-making? Could they be organized so that elected player representatives could

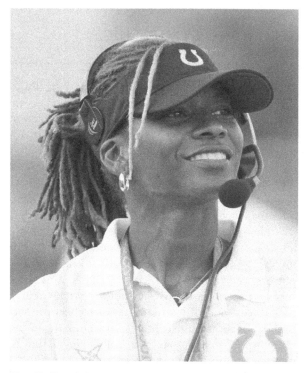

Natalie Randolph is the head coach of the football team at Coolidge High School in Washington, DC. She is believed to be the only female head coach in the country. In 2011 Randolph led the Colts to an 8–2 record and a berth in the most popular game of them all in the nation's capital—the Turkey Bowl city championship. (AP Photo/Jacquelyn Martin)

apply punishments for rule violations? Could team captains work with coaches on game strategies and make decisions during games?

Although rare, there have been some coaches who have experimented with promoting athlete involvement in decision making. To provide the most detailed example of an experiment with democracy in high school football coaching, we have to go back forty years to describe a program used by a California high school football coach at several schools in the state. At one high school his teams won forty-five consecutive games. His system of coaching was unique. The players voted on who should be in the starting lineup, they decided what positions they wanted to play, and they established the guidelines for discipline. In other words, this system was democratic. Some critics accused the coach of shirking responsibility, promoting disunity, and aiding agitators. The irony is that these evils were the presumed consequences of a democratic system, but the coach believed that his system would:

1. increase confidence between players and coaches.
2. promote team cohesion.
3. teach responsibility, leadership, and decision making, thereby fostering maturity rather than immaturity and independence rather than dependence.
4. increase player motivation—instead of being driven by fear, harassment, and physical abuse by the coach, the players would have to impress their peers.
5. free the coach to teach skills, techniques, and strategies.
6. allow the players to experience the benefits of democracy.

The coach summed up his system this way: Most coaches insist football isn't the place for social experimentation. But athletes don't get practice in making decisions. The vote takes the problems of accountability and responsibility and puts them where they belong, with the athletes. Coaches become teachers, which is what they're being paid to do. Their job is to teach, to help athletes reach a level of independence. At any level this is how democracy works and why it succeeds.

SUMMARY

The theme of this chapter has been the relationship between school sport and educational goals. Our conclusion is that for sport to be compatible with educational goals, it should be structured as organized sport, not corporate sport. The data presented in this chapter, however, suggest that school sport is moving in the direction of corporate sport.

Sport at the elementary school level tends to accomplish educational goals (e.g., fostering good health practices, teaching skills, demonstrating the value of teamwork, and providing the experience of striving for a goal) in a playful, enjoyable atmosphere. At each successive educational level, however, the nature of sport changes; it becomes more serious, bureaucratized, and elitist, and its outcome becomes more crucial.

The serious question for educators is whether there is a place for corporate sport in education. This does reflect the corporate domination of American institutions, but is it appropriate for sport in high schools? To resist this trend is a form of emancipation with sport as the tool.

WEB RESOURCES

www.nfhs.org
The website for the National Federation of State High School Associations, which supplies data on a variety of topics, including participation by gender.

www.aahperd.org/naspe/
The website of the National Association for Sport and Physical Education (NASPE). Its mission is to enhance knowledge, improve professional practice, and increase support for high-quality physical education, sport, and physical activity programs.

www.ncwge.org/PDF/TitleIXat35.pdf
The National Coalition for Women and Girls in Education's assessment of progress toward gender equity in the thirty-five years since Title IX was instituted.

www.highschoolsports.net
Widely considered to be the nation's number-one Internet site devoted to high school sports.

NOTES

1. David B. Bills, *The Sociology of Education and Work* (Malden, MA: Blackwell, 2004).

2. Sara McLanahan and Christine Percheski, "Family Structure and the Reproduction of Inequalities," *Annual Review of Sociology* 34 (2008): 257–276.

3. Bissinger, *Friday Night Lights: A Town, a Team, and a Dream* (Reading, MA: Addison-Wesley, 1990), 20. For another, more scholarly ethnography of sport in a Texas community, see Douglas E. Foley, *Learning Capitalist Culture: Deep in the Heart of Tejas* (Philadelphia: University of Pennsylvania, 1990), especially 28–62.

4. Bissinger, *Friday Night Lights*, 127; see also Andrew W. Miracle, Jr., and C. Roger Rees, *Lessons of the Locker Room: The Myth of School Sports* (Amherst, NY: Prometheus Books, 1994), 69–74.

5. Douglas Hartman, *High School Sports Participation and Educational Attainment: Recognizing, Assessing, and Utilizing Relationship*, Report to the LA84 Foundation (Los Angeles: LA84 Foundation, 2008), 3, 5, 19.

6. Ibid., 9.

7. Kathleen E. Miller, Merrill J. Melnick, Grace Barnes, Michael P. Farrell, and Don Sabo, "Untangling the Links Among Athletic Involvement, Gender, Race, and Adolescent Academic Outcomes," *Sociology of Sport Journal* 22, no. 2 (2005): 178–193.

8. David Light Shields and Brenda Light Bredemeier, "Advances in Sport Morality Research," in *Handbook of Sport Psychology*, 3rd ed., ed. Gershon Tennenbaum and Robert C. Eklund (New York: John Wiley, 2007), 662–684; see also Angela Lumpkin, Sharon K. Stoll, and Jennifer M. Beller, *Sport Ethics: Applications for Fair Play*, 3rd ed. (New York: McGraw-Hill, 2003).

9. JoAnn T. Drahota and D. Stanley Eitzen, "The Role Exit of Professional Athletes," *Sociology of Sport Journal* 15, no. 3 (1998): 263–278.

10. National Federation of State High School Associations, "2010–11 High School Athletics Participation Survey" (2011), http://www.nfhs.org/Participation/SportSearch.aspx.

11. Jim Halley, "D.C. Coach Will Be in Spotlight," *USA Today*, 27 August 2010, p. 11C.

12. Quoted in D. Stanley Eitzen, *Fair and Foul: Beyond the Myths and Paradoxes of Sport*, 4th ed. (Lanham, MD: Rowman & Littlefield, 2009), 59; see also pp. 63–74.

13. Odeen Domingo, Jose E. Garcia, Richard Obert, and Jason P. Skoda, "Basha's Ellender Transfers to Desert Ridge," *The Ahwatukee Republic*, 10 January 2008, p. 13.

14. *Tennessee Secondary School Athletic Association v. Brentwood Academy*, U.S. Supreme Court, No. 06-427, pp. 2, 8.

15. Lloyd D. Johnston, Patrick M. O'Malley, Jerald G. Bachman, and John E. Schulenberg, *Monitoring the Future, National Results on Adolescent Drug Use: Overview of Key Findings, 2009*, U.S. Department of Health and Human Services (Bethesda, MD: National Institutes of Health, National Institute on Drug Abuse, 2009), http://www.monitoringthefuture.org/pubs/monographs/overview2009.pdf.

16. Colleen Sparks, "Intense Rivalries Pose Concerns," *Arizona Republic*, 9 February 2007, pp. A1, A16–A17; see also Ward Kanowsky, "Sports Should Teach Life Lessons," *The Greeley Tribune*, 17 April 2010, p. A6.

17. Sparks, "Intense Rivalries Pose Concerns," A16.

18. Miracle, Jr., and Rees, *Lessons of the Locker Room*, 62.

19. Eitzen, *Fair and Foul*, 134–140

20. Shari Roan, "Narrowing the Field," *Los Angeles Times*, 2 October 2006, http://articles.latimes.com/2006/oct/02/health/he-sports2.

21. National Federation of State High School Associations, "2010–11 High School Athletics Participation Survey."

22. Quoted in "Team Sports in America: What Sports Are Popular? Who Is Playing? *sgma.com*, 22 September 2010, http://www.sgma.com/press/view.php?id=253.

23. Kevin Simpson and Michael Booth, "A Sporting Chance," *Denver Post*, 24 April 2009, pp. 1A, 14A.

24. National Federation of State High School Associations, 2011, http://www.nfhs.org/content.aspx?id=3282.

25. Deven Carlson, Leslie Scott, Michael Planty, and Jennifer Thompson, *Statistics in Brief: What Is the Status of High School Athletes Eight Years After Their Senior Year?* NCES 2005-303 (Washington, DC: U.S. Department of Education, 2005).

26. Jim Halley, "High Schools Get in Logo Game," *USA Today*, 7 December 2010, pp. 1C–2C; Jim Halley, "$59.6M Stadium Price Not Too Big in Texas," *USA Today*, 26 August 2010, p. 1C.

27. Jeff Zillgritt, "Aspiring Power Has Doubters," *USA Today*, 18 August 2011, pp. 1C–2C.

28. "Shutting Down Fake 'Prep Schools,'" *New York Times*, 10 March 2007, p. A12; see also Bob Cook, "Findlay Prep, a Fake High School Basketball Team, Is Now More Fake Than Ever," *True/Slant*, 28 February 2010, http://trueslant.com/bobcook/2010/02/28/findlay-prep-a-fake-high-school-basketball-team-is-now-more-fake-than-ever.

29. "ESPN RISE National High School Invitational," http://rise.espn.go.com/boys-basketball/events/2011/04/NHSI.aspx; Jim Halley, "All-Star Games Waging Elite Competition," *USA Today*, 22 June 2011, pp. 1C–2C.

30. Steve Wieberg, "Prep National Title Events on the Horizon," *USA Today*, 25 January 2010, pp. 1C, 6C.

31. Robert B. Gardner and Nina van Erk, "State Associations Say 'No' to National Championships," *High School Today*, February 2011, p. 1.

CHAPTER 6

Intercollegiate Sport

The Department of Intercollegiate Athletics stands out as higher education's "Peculiar Institution." Yes, it is part of the campus. However . . . college sports as the Peculiar Institution asks for and receives entitlements and privileges seldom received by other units.

—John Thelin*

Indiana University guard drives to the basket against Evansville during an NCAA college basketball game in Bloomington, Indiana. (AP Photo/Darron Cummings, File)

*John R. Thelin, "Academics and Athletics: A Part and Apart in the American Campus," *Journal of Intercollegiate Sport* 1, no. 1 (2008): 72–81.

Sport is an enormously popular form of physical recreation on every college and university campus in North America. Campus recreation facilities overflow with students playing pickup games of basketball, ice hockey, racquetball, volleyball, and a half-dozen other sports. Over 60 percent of college students participate in campus intramural sports programs. Sport club teams—teams that athletic departments refuse to fund—are funded by college student governments and compete against other institutions. Finally, there is a formal intercollegiate sports program. More than 500,000 young men and women participate on more than 22,800 teams, according to the National Collegiate Athletic Association (NCAA) and the National Association of Intercollegiate Athletics (NAIA).

Canada and the United States have quite different systems of intercollegiate sports, although during the past two decades Canada's intercollegiate sports have begun to have many of the same features as the U.S. system. Actually, though, no other country in the world has a system of intercollegiate sports as elaborate and expensive as that in the United States.

The characteristics of intercollegiate sports programs vary widely. At one extreme, there are the programs where the student-athletes are an integral part of the student body, receiving no "athletic scholarships" for playing their sport. In these institutions, intercollegiate sports are primarily funded from general institutional accounts, games are played against colleges within the region, and spectator attendance at games is typically small, consisting mostly of students, parents of students, and alumni. Programs of this kind are classified as Division III by the NCAA, the major controlling body of intercollegiate sports. At the other extreme is Division I—so-called big-time intercollegiate sports. Sandwiched between those two is Division II. Here, member institutions are typically larger that Division III members and smaller than Division I institutions, and with less funding and fewer facilities than Division I institutions. See Table 6.1 for a more compete explanation of the differences between the NCAA Divisions.

Each of the NCAA Divisions has a variety of unique rules and policies to which institutions must adhere to retain their membership in the

Division of their choosing. These are complex and complicated and need not concern us in this chapter. Division I (henceforth D-I) is the Division of NCAA intercollegiate sports—especially the sports of football and basketball—that will be the main focus of this chapter.

BEGINNING AND DEVELOPMENT OF COLLEGE SPORTS

To recap what we said in Chapter 2, the first intercollegiate sports contest in the United States was a rowing race between Harvard and Yale in 1852. In 1869 the first intercollegiate football contest took place between Princeton and Rutgers. These early collegiate sports events were organized and managed by students. The faculties, administrators, and alumni were not involved. The original form of governance was modeled after the well-established sports in the private secondary schools of England. In the British model the sports were for the students, and as student recreations they were expected to be organized, administered, and coached through student initiative, not adult intervention.

However, in the United States students soon began losing control over their sports. The first college faculty athletic committee was formed by Princeton in 1881 and by Harvard a year later. In 1895 the first league (later known as the Big Ten) was formed. By 1905 there was a need for a national organization to standardize rules and address problems associated with college sport. The Intercollegiate Athletic Association was formed in that year. In 1910 it became the NCAA, and that organization has controlled college sport ever since, except for colleges controlled by the NAIA, which has nearly 300 member institutions located throughout the United States and Canada. Women's college sports were not a part of the NCAA until 1981.

Once intercollegiate sports was transformed so that students had virtually no voice in policy making, control became vested in coaches, school administrations, athletic corporations, booster organizations, leagues, and national organizations. Moreover, college sport was converted from an

Table 6.1   Differences Among the Three NCAA Divisions

Division I

Number of required sports: Division I programs must offer at least fourteen sports (at least seven for men and seven for women, or six for men and eight for women). The institution must sponsor at least two team sports (e.g., football, basketball, or volleyball) for each gender.

Scheduling: Each Division I program must play a minimum number of contests against Division I opponents.

Financial aid: Division I institutions must offer a minimum amount of financial aid but may not exceed established maximums. Football Bowl Subdivision football, men's and women's basketball, women's gymnastics, women's volleyball, and women's tennis are considered head-count sports for financial aid purposes in Division I. Financial aid equivalencies (one grant-in-aid package divided into smaller pieces) may be offered in all other sports.

Subdivisions: Division I allows for institutions to choose subdivisions based on the scope of their football programs. The three subdivisions are:

1. **Football Bowl Subdivision** (120 members): The Football Bowl Subdivision uses the postseason bowl system rather than a playoff to determine a national champion in football. FBS members must comply with higher standards for sports sponsorship (the overall program must offer sixteen teams rather than the fourteen required of other Division I members), football scheduling, and overall financial aid. In addition, FBS members must meet minimum attendance standards in football.

2. **Football Championship Subdivision** (118 members): FCS members determine their football champion through an NCAA playoff.

3. **Division I** (97 members): The remaining programs of Division I do not sponsor football.

Total Division I membership: 335 members.

Division II

Number of required sports: Division II programs must offer at least ten sports (at least five for men and five for women, or four for men and six for women). The institution must sponsor at least two team sports for each gender. The school also must have participating male and female teams or participants in the fall, winter, and spring seasons.

Scheduling: Each Division II program must play a minimum number of contests against Division II opponents. The minimums vary by sport.

Financial aid: Division II institutions must offer a minimum amount of financial aid but may not exceed established maximums. Financial aid equivalencies are common in all Division II sports.

Total Division II membership: 288 institutions.

Division III

Number of required sports: Division III programs must offer at least five sports for men and five for women.

Scheduling: Each Division III program must play a minimum number of contests against Division III opponents. The minimums vary by sport.

Financial aid: Division III student-athletes play for the love of the game, without an athletic scholarship.

Total Division III membership: 447 total members (432 active and 15 provisional/reclassifying).

Source: National Collegiate Athletic Association, http://www.ncaa.org/wps/wcm/connect/public/NCAA/About+the+NCAA/Who+We+Are/Differences+Among+the+Divisions/.

activity for the participants to a large-scale commercial entertainment industry, at least at the NCAA Division I level.[1]

Along with this transformation of intercollegiate sport have come many abuses—illegal recruiting practices, altered transcripts, phantom courses, the physical and psychological abuse of athletes, and the exploitation of athletes.[2] These abuses occur for two related reasons, which are pressure to win on the field and pressure to succeed financially. A persuasive case can be made that big-time intercollegiate athletics has severely corrupted the goals and ideals of higher education.

This chapter is divided into five parts: (1) student-centered college sport remains, (2) college sport as big business, (3) the NCAA and student-athletes, (4) educational performance and student-athletes, and (5) reform initiatives and intercollegiate sports.

STUDENT-CENTERED COLLEGE SPORT REMAINS

With all of the public and media attention on big-time intercollegiate sports (televised games, national rankings, All-American selections, bowl games, etc.), outside higher education there is little awareness of a form of college sports that has many of the features of the original motivation for college students to form sports teams. It is found in the NCAA Division III colleges. So as a contrast to the features of NCAA D-I sports, which will be the main focus of this chapter, we provide an outline of what Division III (D-III) sports programs are like. They are characterized by the following:

- They feature student-athletes who are subject to the same admission standards, academic standards, housing, and support services as the general student body.
- They provide a well-rounded collegiate experience that involves a balance of academics, competitive athletics, and the opportunity to pursue the multitude of other cocurricular and extracurricular opportunities offered the campus.
- Their playing seasons and eligibility standards minimize conflicts between athletics and academics, allowing student-athletes to focus on their academic programs and the achievement of a degree.
- They place primary emphasis on regional in-season and conference competition, while also offering thirty-six national championships annually.

- Athletic departments place special importance on the impact of athletics on the participants rather than on spectators. The student-athlete's experience is of paramount concern.
- The integration of athletics with the larger institution enables student-athletes to experience all aspects of campus life.
- They offer a competitive sports environment for student-athletes who play for the love of the game, without the obligation of an athletic scholarship.
- Perhaps the most surprising feature to those who are familiar only with "big-time" college sports, Division III has 447 institutional members—more than either of the other two NCAA Divisions.

Our main reason for describing the fundamental features of Division III sports is to show readers that there is more than one viable model of intercollegiate sports. Throughout the remainder of this chapter, as you read our description of D-I sports, we suggest you compare and contrast that form of college sports with D-III sports.

COLLEGE SPORT AS BIG BUSINESS

It is indisputable that big-time college sports are an extremely popular cultural practice in the United States. In addition to the exciting match-ups between teams representing highly esteemed universities, the sports events are accompanied by marching bands, cheerleaders, pom-pom groups, tailgate parties, and so forth. The enormously successful commercial entertainment business that has emerged from big-time college football and basketball is actually a popular cultural form of the same genre as theater, cinema, popular music, and, of course, professional sport. In each case, a group of talented persons, well trained in their specialty, provide amusement and entertainment for audiences who pay to watch the performances.

We recognize the enthusiasm and loyalty of devoted fans of big-time intercollegiate sports. A hard-fought, well-played game provides entertainment and excitement. But the pageantry and hoopla of big-time intercollegiate sports tend to mask its underlying profit-oriented structure—the explicit fact that it is a big commercial business. The overall annual revenue for college athletics programs is estimated at about $10.6 billion. It is an industry that is tightly integrated with three of the largest commercial industries: mass media, sporting goods and equipment, and entertainment. Other industries, such as transportation and hotels, have a significant footprint in the intercollegiate sports industry as well.

Big-time college sports are also about capital accumulation and the bottom line. All of the earmarks of capitalist enterprise have come to characterize the business of big-time collegiate athletics, and intercollegiate sport played for the personal, social, and emotional gratification of the participants has been jettisoned in the process. Many people view big-time intercollegiate sport as merely a form of fun and excitement, but people who work in that industry acknowledge its economic realities.

The following statements by various people associated with big-time college sports confirm that at least some of them are willing to describe big-time collegiate sport as it really is. The former athletic director at the University of Michigan said, "This is a business, a big business. Anyone who hasn't figured that out by now is a damned fool." The University of Arizona athletic director concurred, saying, "I think it's important for people to realize that [NCAA Division I] sports is . . . a big business." The University of Minnesota president told a special convention of the NCAA, "We in Division I are in an entertainment business and we can't fool ourselves." University of Houston executive vice president for administration and finance argued, "It's like any other entertainment business." One college sport analyst put it this way: "Big-time athletic departments [have become] franchises in College Sports Inc., a huge commercial entertainment enterprise with operating methods and objectives frequently opposed to the educational missions of the host universities. Feeding the growth [is] the increased revenue from the television networks for the rights to broadcast college sports events." He went on to explain how one college athletic director "defined the motivation of the men directing big-time intercollegiate athletics: 'There are three definitions. . . . Greed, greed, and greed.'"[3]

The intrusion of money into big-time college sport at that level is evident in the following representative examples:

- CBS and Turner Broadcasting will pay $10.8 billion from 2011 to 2024 to carry the NCAA men's basketball tournament. The broadcasting partners will show the fourteen versions of the tournament on four networks and carry each game nationally.[4]
- Coca-Cola Company has an eleven-year, $500 million contract with the NCAA, giving it the exclusive right to advertise and promote its beverages at the eighty-six championships in twenty-two sports sponsored by the NCAA.
- In 2011 the nation's largest athletic department, Ohio State University, had a total expenses budget of $126.3 million and employed more than 300 full-time workers and nearly 1,600 part-time employees. It oversees 377 acres, 16.9 million square feet of buildings, 926 varsity athletes, and 36 varsity sports.[5]
- The 2011 Bowl Championship Series (BCS) game between Auburn University and the University of Oregon in the University of Phoenix Stadium made a payout in excess of $21 million.
- The University of Alabama, one of the top collegiate teams in licensing revenue, has earned about $4.8 million in each of the last few fiscal years.
- T. Boone Pickens has donated $228 million to the Oklahoma State athletic department.

With a total fan base of more than 172 million, the college sports market is a prime target for corporate marketers. The president of IMG Sports and Entertainment said, "We know college sports can deliver one of the most desirable fan bases available for corporate marketers. When you combine the overall appeal of college sports with a top national brand like Rutgers, there is great potential for delivering a strong corporate partner to aid the university in growing its athletic programs."[6]

Notice that Rutgers University is merely a "brand" name to IMG Sports, not a university or an institution of higher education. It is just another brand—another commodity—to be marketed and sold like other commodities. Indeed, some universities have contracted with corporations to extend naming rights to their sports venues in exchange for various sums of money. See Table 6.2 for examples. Selling their stadium's naming rights is a way to increase revenue for athletics departments.

Paralleling the corporatization of big-time college sports, the salaries of the men and women who coach these teams have skyrocketed in a manner similar to those of CEOs and top executives in other industries of the corporate world. The examples in Table 6.3 show how well the highest-paid coaches of big-time programs are compensated.

The football coaches listed in Table 6.3 are only five of the approximately thirty head football coaches who made $2 million or more during the 2011 season. And lucrative college football salaries do not end there. At least sixty-six football assistants made $300,000 or more. A professor in the department of food and nutrition at Texas Tech said:

Table 6.2   Examples of Intercollegiate Sports Venues with Corporate Naming Rights

University	Name of Sports Venue
University of Maryland football/lacrosse stadium	Chevy Chase Bank Field at Byrd Stadium: Began a 26-year $20 million contract in 2006.
Texas Tech Red Raiders and Lady Raiders	United Spirit Arena: A 15,020-seat multi-purpose arena; home to the basketball and volleyball teams.
University of Minnesota football stadium	TCF Bank Football Stadium: Will pay $35 million over 25 years for the naming rights and other agreements.
Wake Forest University football stadium	BB&T Field: Began a 10-year arrangement—with unspecified financial considerations—in 2007.
College of Charleston men's and women's basketball and volleyball arena	Carolina First Arena: Opened in 2008 at a cost of approximately $45 million.
University of Louisville football stadium	Papa John's Cardinal Stadium: Papa John's Pizza founder John Schnatter has contributed more than $20 million to the University of Louisville over the past 10 years, and the naming rights have been extended until 2040.
Arizona State University basketball arena	Wells Fargo Arena: A 14,198-seat multi-purpose arena named after Wells Fargo & Co. in 1997.

Source: Wikipedia, "List of Sports Venues with Sole Naming Rights," http://en.wikipedia.org/wiki/List_of_sports_venues_with_sole_naming_rights.

Table 6.3   College Coaches' Compensation

Top Compensation for D-I Men's Basketball Teams in 2011 NCAA Tournament		Top Compensation for Football Bowl D-I Coaches in 2011	
Louisville	7.5 million	Texas	5.2 million
Duke	4.2 million	Alabama	5.1 million
Kentucky	3.9 million	Oklahoma	4.0 million
Kansas	3.6 million	LSU	3.9 million
Florida	3.6 million	Iowa	3.8 million

Sources: "An Analysis of Salaries for College Basketball Coaches," *USA Today*, 30 March 2011, http://www.usatoday.com/sports/college/mensbasketball/2011-coaches-salary-database.htm; "Major College Football Coaches' Pay," *USA Today*, 17 November 2011, p. 5C.

"Athletics has gotten so disproportionate to the rest of the economy and to the academic community, that it is unbelievable."[7]

But compensation to coaches in big-time collegiate sports programs does end with salaries. These coaches also receive gifts of housing, paid country-club memberships, use of private jets, travel allowances for family members, complimentary tickets in luxury boxes, use of vacation homes, free cars, and, in some cases, million-dollar annuities. In addition, rollover contracts give coaches "golden parachutes" if they are fired prematurely. For example, when Alabama fired Mike Shula in 2006, the university bought out Shula's contract for $4 million.

At the same time, and by comparison, the average compensation and benefits for presidents at public doctorate-granting (the most prestigious) universities was $427,400, with some 10 percent earning less than $300,000. Furthermore, the American Association of University Professors (AAUP) reported that the average salary for full professors at those same universities was $115,509.[8]

These examples demonstrate clearly that big-time college sport programs are not amateur sports. They are big business. The money generated comes from gate receipts, student athletic fees, the educational budget of the university, booster organizations, individual contributors, advertising income, contracts with shoe and apparel companies, television, and league reimbursements for the television and bowl or tournament appearances by league members.

Functionalism and Big-Time College Sports

Colleges and universities are part of the social institution of education, the institution that formally socializes members of society. A functionalist perspective views intercollegiate sport as an integral part of the process of cultural transmission, promoting social and political integration, maintaining social control, and contributing to social change. However, as we have shown, there are significant differences between the sports programs at D-III institutions and those at D-I institutions, so the functional consequences are quite different as well.

Although big-time college sports is part of the education institution, it has a huge footprint in the economic system and is clearly a commercial enterprise. In that role it functions to sponsor the production of an entertainment service. As we have noted, its revenues and expenses make it a multibillion-dollar industry.

Beyond its commercial role, big-time sports function in a variety of social, cultural, and public relations ways. For example:

- Administrators, faculty, and students at many universities believe sports teams are important parts of campus life and excellent vehicles for generating publicity and alumni support.
- These same groups believe that college sports add to campus spirit and unity, provide free advertising for the campus, help in name branding, and provide a link and outreach to alumni.
- As the student government president at Cincinnati put it, "There's a better feeling on campus, more pride for the university. It's something that connects students to the university other than going to class."[9]
- One athletic administrator said, "A strong successful athletic program is very important to the connection with alumni, donors and leaders in the state, and it magnifies the university . . . beyond the state. That's the visibility that the athletics program can have."[10]

Beliefs and Reality About Big-Time Sport Functions

Despite the commonly held belief that college athletic departments are doing well financially, the fact is that big-time intercollegiate sports are not profitable. Just the opposite. Only about 15 of the 120 NCAA Football Bowl Subdivision universities make more money than they spend each year. So at the same time that coaches' salaries are skyrocketing, many athletic departments have had to rely on general university and student fee subsidies.

According to *USA Today* analyses, about $1.8 *billion* in student fees and general university subsidies prop up athletic programs at the nation's top sports colleges, including hundreds of millions in the richest conferences. The amount of student fees going to intercollegiate sports programs account for as much as 23 percent of the required annual bill for in-state students. Perhaps just as troubling, *USA Today* investigators found that among the twenty universities nationally that had the highest estimated per-student athletics fees, fifteen do not disclose their per-student athletics fee charges on their billing statements, on their websites, or in other official school publications.[11]

Without millions in subsidies from general university and students fees, universities could not pay their bills, so subsidies are being directed toward revenue-pursuing athletic departments and away from core academic uses. In 2008–2009 the University of California at Berkeley subsidized athletics in the amount of $8.1 million from its general fund; in 2009–2010 the figure was $12.1 million. In 2007 Cal Berkeley forgave $31.4 million in athletics debts. *USA Today* reported that the average public-university subsidy for athletics was 8.8 million in 2009.[12] Over half of the athletic departments at public universities in the Football Bowl Subdivision are subsidized by at least 26 percent. At Rutgers University the percentage of total revenue coming from subsidies in 2010 was an astounding 42 percent, the highest among NCAA Division I public universities (see Box 6.1 for more about Rutgers).[13] A professor

---

Box 6.1   *Thinking About Sport:* The Contradictions of Big-Time College Sport

Big-time college sport is rife with contradictions that compromise the integrity of universities and their mission. In effect, these institutions of higher learning, organized for the best of reasons, allow blatant hypocrisy in their athletic programs. Consider the contradictions discussed below.

The overarching contradiction of big-time college sport is that as an organized commercial entertainment activity it compromises educational goals. The actions of big-time college sport are antithetical to educational goals in the following ways: (1) *Schools give disproportionately more per capita scholarship aid to athletes than to undergraduates with cognitive abilities and accomplishments.* (2) *Athletes are recruited as students, yet the demands of coaches and the athletic subculture are antithetical to the student role.* The time demands on athletes (practice, lifting weights, meetings, studying playbooks, and travel), the spotlight of publicity and resulting pressures, and the sense of entitlement that ensues from their adoring fans diminish the importance of academics for the athletes. (3) *In the search for success, big-time programs often enroll and subsidize ill-prepared and uninterested students solely for the purpose of winning games and producing revenue.* While some poorly prepared athletes find their intellectual footing in the academic environment, many do not. The "one-and-done" athletes who are recruited for just one year before they move on to the professional level, for example, are essentially poorly compensated migrant workers with no educational goals, making their year at school the height of educational hypocrisy.

Related to this is the practice where by some coaches at big-time programs recruit athletes with criminal backgrounds. While the redemption of wayward athletes is a worthy goal, the object is to win games at whatever the cost. (4) *Coaches, thought by many to be role models for building character, sometimes engage in breaking the rules in the process of recruiting athletes, keeping them eligible, or exceeding the rule limits for practice time.* (5) *Although big-time sports produce revenue for the athletic program, with few exceptions they lose money. To offset this, money is drained away from the educational functions of the university to subsidize athletic budgets.* According to a June 28, 2011, article in *USA Today*, subsidies from student fees and university funds account for $1 of every $3 spent on athletics at Division I schools. From 2006 to 2010, for example, Rutgers University received subsidies of $115 million. In effect, the athletic departments are diverting money away from the educational mission in order to prop up athletic department budgets. (6) *The final hypocrisy is that although big-time sport is a big business that benefits coaches, schools, television networks, advertisers, airlines, concessions, manufacturers of apparel and memorabilia, legitimate gambling sports books in Nevada, and local businesses, the actual producers of the many millions are not paid.* In short, the athletes are exploited.

The fundamental question for alumni, boards of regents, and university administrators is: How is big-time college sports justified when the system is rigged in opposition to the academic mission of universities?

at Wake Forest University said, "The word I would use is 'appalling.' It's appalling in the big picture and representative of what is going on in athletics with coaches' salaries and facilities."[14]

Big-time intercollegiate sports even receive subsidies from the federal government. As *USA Today* analysts have reported: "Athletic departments also derive hundreds of millions in public support through federal tax deductions donors can take for gifts to booster clubs. . . . The athletic programs surveyed received a combined $1.04 billion in donations in 2007–08, which likely translated into at least a $200 million federal tax subsidy of the programs." A sizable portion of the money donated to athletic programs gives the donors preferential seating at games and other benefits. John Colombo, a University of Illinois law professor who has written about tax exemption and college sports, has said that this is "essentially subsidizing seat licenses for wealthy football fans."[15]

The subsidies to intercollegiate sports programs are much greater if the venues in which the sports events occur are taken into account. That is, college football and basketball teams play in multimillion-dollar stadiums and arenas paid for by taxpayers, contributors, and, more typically, bonds that are paid off by students' fees at no expense to the athletic departments.

There are several reasons for the financial plight of big-time intercollegiate sports. First, the revenue-producing sports (football and men's basketball, and rarely women's basketball, with a few exceptions) are expected to fund the entire athletic program, which may include more than thirty sports.

Second, there is a constantly escalating arms race in big-time college sport. As we noted earlier, the pay for successful coaches rises rapidly in order to keep them. When a team succeeds, the coach's salary is raised by hundreds of thousands and the assistants by tens of thousands. Typically, successful programs constantly upgrade their facilities, including expanding the seating, adding luxury boxes, and improving weight rooms, locker rooms, and practice fields, which will either bring in more revenue or help in recruiting.

Third, the athletic departments spare no expense to fund the revenue-producing sports. A common practice, for example, is for the football team and for some basketball teams to stay in a local hotel the night before *home* games. Travel budgets for these teams and for their recruiters are generous. The conventional wisdom throughout the universe of big-time intercollegiate athletes has always been that extravagant expenditures for football and basketball programs were necessary because they led to winning teams, and winning teams in turn led to increased revenue to the university.

Unfortunately, and as with so many other "wisdoms" about intercollegiate sports, the facts don't support the claim. According to a report commissioned by the NCAA titled *The Empirical Effects of Collegiate Athletics*, for every $1 a university pays to build its athletic program, it gets $1 back in new revenue. In other words, the evidence supports a "one-for-one relationship between athletic expenditures and revenues, or equivalently, no effect of changes in athletic expenditures at a given school on net athletic revenues at that school."[16]

Further Consequences of the Commercial Orientation of Big-Time College Sports

The other social theoretical orientation we have described, the conflict/cultural perspective, argues that big-time college sports are like any other form of commercial business, where capital accumulation interests are an adjunct to exploitation and coercion, and that sports events encourage people to focus on wins and losses, on coaches and standings, and on cheering and temporary excitement, while deflecting attention away from pressing social issues—inequality, injustice, racism, sexism, violence.

Big-time college sports programs are a segment of the corporatized entertainment industry, and as with all the other enterprises in that industry, capital accumulation—making money—is paramount. There have been consequences: First, the lack of adequate revenue has led to budget cuts. Football and men's basketball produce revenue; therefore, they have been largely exempt from budget reduction. When the cuts are severe, some programs have been eliminated, and these casualties are in the so-called minor sports such as wrestling, lacrosse, gymnastics, swimming, water polo, tennis, and golf.

For example, during the past thirty years, over a hundred wrestling programs have been dropped by athletic departments.

Women's sports have been less vulnerable than the men's minor sports because of the protection of Title IX (see Chapter 14), but their programs have experienced cutbacks. The necessity of raising money through sports programs tends to make college sport more elitist (fewer and fewer participants) and limited to certain skills and physical types (the tall or the large or both). It ensures the dominance of male sports, at least football and basketball.

A second consequence: The commercial orientation of big-time college sport has prostituted the university and the purpose of sport. The necessity of making more and more money is a major source for the many abuses found in big-time college sport. Booster organizations that supply funds may influence which coaches are hired and when they will be fired. And corporate sponsors may intrude in various ways as they give or withhold their monies. In *Confessions of a Spoilsport: My Life and Hard Times Fighting Sports Corruption at an Old Eastern University*, William C. Dowling, a professor of English at Rutgers University, tells his story of mobilizing a group of students, faculty, and alumni who attempted to stop the move toward big-time sports at Rutgers, an institution with a distinguished Ivy League-type history. His explanation: Big-time college athletics is filled with "corruption and hypocrisy and self deception. [With] pious claims and brutally cynical behavior. [With] frightened faculty and powerful regents or trustees who see winning football and basketball teams as immeasurably more important than academic and intellectual values."[17]

A third consequence of an athletic department's search for money has meant that teams will reschedule games to fit the demands of television, even if it inconveniences their fans or interferes with athletes' studies. Football games are now played in the heat of August, on Tuesday, Thursday, and Friday nights, and anytime on Saturdays from 11 A.M. to 9 P.M.

Smaller D-I teams (those in the Football Championship Subdivision) now schedule one or two so-called guarantee games against major university (Football Bowl Subdivision) teams to receive up to a $1 million payment. These are also called "body bag games" because the players from the smaller schools often incur an unusually large number of injuries in the game. But playing the national powerhouse universities provides a huge and much-needed revenue stream for the smaller D-I schools.[18] The same pattern is carried out in D-I basketball, but for smaller guarantee amounts and, in most cases, without the increased injuries.

A fourth result of "going after the money" is that when the pressure to win becomes too great, the result can be a sub-rosa policy of cheating—that is, a policy of offering athletes more than the legal limit to lure them to a school and keep them there or using unethical means to keep them scholastically eligible. Over eighty years ago, a report by the Carnegie Foundation decried the widespread illegal recruiting practices of American colleges and universities. The problem has not only continued but mega-intensified. The scandals involve illegal and immoral behavior of overzealous coaches, school authorities, alumni, and boosters. Athlete recruits are not only suspect academically, but sometimes they also go over the line in antisocial behavior.

Finally, perhaps the most serious consequence of the "winning-at-all-costs to generate money" mentality pervading many athletic departments is that the education of the athletes is secondary to their sports performances. The pursuit of money has prostituted the university and the purpose of sport. Education is not the goal. Even sport as a pleasurable activity is an irrelevant consideration in the climate of big-time collegiate sport. Winning and money making are paramount.

Coaches proclaim that their athletes are students first and athletes only secondarily. This is the typical recruiting speech to prospects and their parents, but in practice the reverse is often true. The cynicism with which some coaches regard education is seen in the revelations concerning the enrollment of athletes in "phantom" courses (correspondence or residence courses that give credit for no work or attendance). Clearly, for a coach to permit this is to admit that the athlete's eligibility supersedes his or her learning. For the athlete, the message is equally clear. In this milieu the resulting evils are due not to the malevolent personalities of coaches and athletes but to a perverse system.

Because of the enormous demands on their time, athletes frequently must take a reduced course load and thus will not usually graduate in the normal number of years. Study halls and tutors are available, even required, for athletes; their primary function is to ensure athletic eligibility, not necessarily educational achievement. Athletes are often counseled to take easy courses, whether or not those courses fit their educational needs. Achieving an education is incidental to the overriding objective of big-time sports.

A Contradiction: Athletes as Amateurs in a Big-Business Environment

We have seen that large sums of money are generated by big-time college sports. The university athletic departments act like corporations (indeed, many are organized separately from their universities as corporations). Many individuals in the athletic departments (athletic directors, coaches, trainers, accountants, groundskeepers, equipment managers, academic advisors) make their living—some over $4 million annually—from their involvement in college sport.

The irony is that the athletes themselves—the major labor force in producing big-time college sport—are not paid for their labor. Young men (and more recently young women) on athletic scholarships are limited by NCAA rules to tuition, room, board, and books but expected to bring honor and lots of dollars to their universities. They are considered to be amateurs who participate for the love of sport untainted by money. Of course, by declaring that college sports are a form of amateur activity, the NCAA and its member universities are able to mystify the reality of big-time sports as professional and commercial enterprises.

The *2010–11 NCAA Division I Manual* declares that student-athletes must be amateurs and that they "should be protected from exploitation by professional and commercial enterprises."[19] Remarkably, although such a statement completely discounts, even denies, the blatantly commercialized nature of big-time intercollegiate athletics, it is able to manufacture support for the economic exploitation of student-athletes. The reality is that the athletic scholarship is merely a work contract. What colleges are really doing is hiring entertainers. The deceit of claiming that educational purposes preclude salaried compensation for the sport performances of athletes is testimony to the extensive attempts of the collegiate establishment to avoid its financial responsibilities.

Athletic scholarships are actually a wage below poverty level for student-athlete-entertainers who directly produce millions of dollars for athletic departments. As the director of the College Sport Research Center at the University of North Carolina, Richard Southall, put it: "College sports is a business and a free-market system for everyone except the athletes."[20]

Paying as little as possible to operate a business is called keeping overhead low; it's what every business owner strives to do. The NCAA and major universities have mastered this principle. No other American business operates so pretentiously, making huge sums of money while insisting the enterprise be viewed as an educational service. Tutored by the NCAA, the public accepts the premise that college athletes must remain amateurs, untainted by money.

Being a scholarship athlete in a big-time program has become a year-round commitment. Now that the football season has been extended to twelve games, some of the games are played in the last week of August, requiring that practices began three weeks earlier. If a football team is successful, the players continue into a December or January bowl game. That, in turn, is followed six weeks later by a month of spring practice. And when that ends, players are expected to lift weights and spend their summers on campus with "voluntary" workouts. But despite the increased workload and the great sums generated by big-time college sports programs, the athletes continue to be limited in remuneration to tuition, room, board, and books. Thus, the huge sums of money generated by athletes has not trickled down to them; their pay remains stagnant.

THE NCAA AND STUDENT-ATHLETES

The NCAA, or an organization like it, is necessary to provide a uniform set of rules for each sport, to adjudicate disputes among members, and to organize playoffs and tournaments. What has emerged, however, is a powerful monopoly, a monopoly that controls big-time college sport *for the interests of the universities, not the student-athletes*. This occurs in two ways: through the enforcement of "amateurism" and through rules that limit athletes' rights.

The Enforcement of "Amateurism"

First, as we have just discussed, the NCAA rules enforce a code of amateurism on student-athletes' labor, while the NCAA and its member institutions raise millions of dollars off the student-athletes. It is common for powerful organizations to interpret reality and create normative prescriptions so as to serve their interests, and the NCAA and its member universities have done this by means of the amateur ideology. They have made their case so persuasively that alternative images seem unthinkable.

By defining student-athletes as amateurs, schools keep the costs of operation low by *not* paying the athletes what they are worth. Consider this: In 2011 the expenses for student athletic scholarships for public D-I universities was between 8 and 13 percent of the operating revenue of the university athletic departments. If the distribution of

The goal of many young boys and girls is to become an intercollegiate athlete. It is a worthy goal, but there are unexpected challenges that college athletes face. Academic progress toward a degree must be pursued at the same time that demands to make the team and perform well enough to keep the athletic scholarship are ever-present. (istockphoto)

revenue of those athletic departments was similar to that of the main professional team sports, 50 to 60 percent of the revenue would go to the student athletes. By NCAA rules, however, the players were limited to their athletic scholarships. The universities obviously benefit from this arrangement.[21]

Universities benefit when intercollegiate athletes are defined as amateur because it enables the revenue generated from the sports programs to be free from taxation. Even though the scholarship appears to be a payment to employees (athletes) for services rendered, it is called a "grant-in-aid" for educational purposes. This avoids the rules of the IRS stipulating that revenue generated by employees is taxable income.

The NCAA has done all it can to retain the "amateur" status of college athletes. Specifically, it has argued strenuously that college athletes should not be paid a stipend in addition to tuition, room, board, and books because that would lessen its case that the athletes are amateurs. Consequently, the NCAA prohibits anything it considers "professional." Some examples:

- Athletes will lose their amateur status if they allow their pictures or names to be associated with commercial enterprise, whether they are paid for it or not.
- Athletes are not allowed to have a financial advisor (agent) until after their final college game.
- Athletes cannot receive payment for their athletic skills. Using this principle, the NCAA ruled that a New Mexico State University basketball player who had won a car by making a half-court shot at halftime in a professional basketball game (he was one of two spectators chosen at random for the shot) could keep either the car or his senior year of eligibility, but not both.
- Athletes cannot endorse products or otherwise use their name recognition for economic gain, but universities can use it in their publicity and can license and sell clothing, sports equipment, and souvenirs with the team logo.
- Athletes cannot sell their complimentary tickets (in fact, they cannot give their tickets

to anyone except family members, relatives, and students), yet coaches (some with hundreds of tickets) have no restrictions on their distribution.

- Coaches typically receive bonuses for taking their teams to a bowl or to the NCAA men's basketball tournament but their players do not.
- Athletes cannot be used to raise money for others, even charities. For example, the Lions Club of Alachua, Florida, was not allowed to raffle off a football signed by members of the University of Florida football team to raise money for its eye bank because, the NCAA ruled, the players were being exploited by selling their autographs.

These examples show the lengths to which the NCAA will go to enforce the "amateur" status of college athletes. They also demonstrate the hypocrisy of the NCAA. While keeping their athletes pure, the NCAA, the universities, and the individual coaches are engaged in a relentless pursuit of revenue estimated at well over $10 billion annually. We emphasize again that this revenue is generated by the athletes. Athletes literally can be walking billboards by wearing shoes, for which the coach receives thousands of dollars, but the athletes cannot receive anything other than the free shoes.

The NCAA will not even allow institutions to pay for travel expenses of players' family members to watch their sons play in a bowl or tournament for which their teams have qualified, yet the schools pay the expenses for an entourage of state legislators, members of the Board of Trustees, and the president and various vice-presidents from the university to attend.

The public has a perception of a benevolent NCAA that protects young student-athletes. The reality is that what the NCAA protects is its own self-interest. Its rules have been created to protect the profit structure of big-time college sports, and more than one sport economist has expressed the opinion that the big-time intercollegiate sport system is one of the most obvious forms of labor exploitation in the United States.

The Restriction of Athletes' Rights

The NCAA rules also work against athletes by restricting their rights as students. When young athletes sign letters-of-intent to play for a certain university, they make one-sided agreements. Foremost, these athletes have agreed to play for four years at a given institution. Should they change their minds and decide to attend a different college or university, they must wait a year to play at the new institution. If they select a university because of a particular coach, and the coach leaves before the athletes have enrolled in a school, under NCAA rules the athletes have signed with a university, not a coach, and they must stay or lose a year of eligibility. Even more one-sided in the universities' favor is the fact that, although athletes sign a four-year agreement to play for a university, the universities are required to make only a one-year commitment to the athletes. This one-year renewable commitment by universities gives coaches extraordinary power over athletes.

Each of these rules restrains the freedom of athletes but not that of the universities. The athletes are bound by a contract, but the institutions are not. Coaches may have contracts that allow them to leave at any time, or their university may not hold them to their contracts, but there are no exceptions for athletes. Coaches do not have to sit out a year if they move from one university to another, but players do if they leave for another university. The NCAA rules clearly protect the schools and coaches but not the players.

EDUCATIONAL PERFORMANCE AND STUDENT-ATHLETES

Research indicates that college athletes in big-time football and basketball programs do not perform at the same level academically as other athletes and the general student body. Their grades are lower, and they are much more likely to take easy courses in easy majors. Most significantly, they are much less likely to graduate. Before we examine the college performance of athletes, though, let's look at their preparation for college.

Academic Predictions for Student-Athletes at College

There are three standard measures of student preparedness for college—the combined score on the Scholastic Assessment Test (SAT), the American College Test (ACT) composite score, and the high school grade point average (GPA). Over the past twenty-five years the NCAA has enacted several policies designed to dictate minimum eligibility guidelines for freshmen in the association's Division I schools. These include minimum scores on the SAT or the ACT, a core group of high school courses, and a minimum grade point average within that core.

In spite of efforts to discourage coaches in D-I sports from recruiting unqualified students, marginal students who were good athletes continue to be recruited. Research at a number of universities shows that in most big-time programs, athletes in the so-called revenue sports (men's football and basketball) have received special treatment in the admissions process; that is, they've been admitted below the standard requirements for their universities. The *Atlanta Journal-Constitution* compared average SAT scores and GPAs of athletes with those of the nonathlete student body at fifty-four public universities, which included the members of the six major Bowl Championship Series conferences and other universities whose teams finished the 2007–2008 season ranked among the football or men's basketball top-25. Below are some of the findings:

- All fifty-four universities for which football SAT scores were available had at least an 88-point gap between team members' average score and the average for the student body.
- Football players averaged 220 points lower on the SAT than their classmates. Men's basketball was 227 points lower.
- Football players performed 115 points worse on the SAT than male athletes in other sports.
- The University of Florida had the biggest gap between football players and the student body, with players scoring 346 points lower than their peers.

- The differences between athletes' and nonathletes' SAT scores were less than half as big for women (73 points) as for men (170).
- Many universities routinely used a special admissions process to admit athletes who did not meet the normal entrance requirements. At the University of Georgia, for instance, 73.5 percent of athletes were special admits compared with 6.6 percent of the student body as a whole.[22]

Even in institutions with highly selective admission policies (e.g., Ivy League schools), athletes have a significantly better chance than nonathletes to be admitted even though their ACT/SAT scores are appreciably lower. Apparently institutions at all levels of intercollegiate sport are willing to take marginal students because of the athletic payoff.

Academic Achievement and College Athletes

Regardless of the fact that young athletes have always been recruited by coaches for their athletic ability, they have always been required to enroll in academic programs and take courses of study. And institutions have always required that athletes maintain a certain level of academic progress toward graduation in order to continue participating in the intercollegiate sport program. Of course, no rational person would quarrel with holding athletes to academic standards.

However, focusing on athletes' academic achievement, and seemingly demonstrating how athletes are being held to academic standards, while ignoring the time demands on athletes—practices, games, weight training, video viewing, travel to sites of games, and so on—suggests to the public that social pathology is the reason for the recurring scandals involving student-athletes, not the social structure of which they are a part. Such thinking deflects attention away from the more endemic social structural problems of big-time college sports—including the question of whether it is appropriate for a commercialized sport system that does not pay its main workforce a livable wage to be operating on college campuses.

Research data on class grades are somewhat difficult to interpret. The reason is that athletes in the revenue-producing sports are more likely than other athletes and other students to receive grades fraudulently (e.g., through "shady" correspondence courses, "friendly" professors, and surrogate test takers or term paper writers) or to take easy courses and cluster in easy majors—also known as "jock majors." Examples include:

- At Auburn the most popular football major is sociology, accounting for 17 percent of the team's declared majors. In a recent year football players were thirty-five times more likely to major in sociology than the student body. Fewer than 1 percent of the student body choose that major.
- At the University of Alabama, the most popular football major in recent years has been general studies in the College of Human Environmental Sciences (HES). Twenty-six percent of football players majored in general studies in HES compared with 2 percent of all Alabama students.
- At Virginia Tech, fewer than 1 percent of undergraduates majored in residential property management compared to 12 percent of the football players.
- At Wake Forest, there's been a football rush on the communications department, with thirty-four out of sixty (57 percent) players enrolled in that major.[23]

Nationwide clustering extends far beyond the universities identified above.

There are several possible reasons other than a genuine interest in the major for such clustering. The favored major may have fewer courses that conflict with practices and other sport-related demands, such as afternoon labs. The major may have less stringent admission requirements. And the major may be less demanding. For these reasons the players may choose the easy route, or sometimes they are guided by academic advisors in the athletic department to keep them eligible. A former president of the National Association of Academic Advisors who has directed student-athlete support programs at Michigan and Kansas State put it this way: "Athletes are not representative of the general student body. Our population is apples; their population is oranges."[24]

Graduation Rates and Student-Athletes

To its credit over the past decade, the NCAA—in conjunction with the Knight Commission on Intercollegiate Athletics—has made a significant effort to insist that universities hold their athletic departments responsible for the improvement of student-athletes' graduation rates. The NCAA Graduation Success Rate (GSR) and Academic Progress Rate (APR) were developed in response to college and university presidents who wanted graduation data that more accurately reflect the mobility among college students today. The GSR, similar to the Federal Graduation Success Rate (FGR), measures the proportion of a four-year institution's freshmen who earn a degree within six years at Division I institutions. The standard evaluations of NCAA student-athlete graduation rates involve comparisons with rates for the general student body.

Using the GSR measure, the NCAA reported that in 2011, the last year for which the NCAA has complete graduation records, Division I athletes had a GSR rate of 82 percent for freshmen student-athletes who entered college in 2004 and earned their four-year degrees. While this GSR is quite impressive, it masks some important information that puts quite a different light on the NCAA figures. For example:

- The NCAA's reported GSR includes student-athletes from thirty-six sports, including both men and women. When all GSRs are considered, for D-I women athletes the GSR rate was 88 percent and for men it was 73 percent.
- For D-I men's basketball the GSR was only 68 percent, while it was 86 percent for D-I women's basketball. The men's basketball team at the University of Southern California had a GSR of 38 percent, for the University of Connecticut's men's basketball it was 25 percent. Indeed, GSR rates below 50 percent were

common for men's basketball teams. Only 61 percent of African American male basketball players graduate compared to 84 percent of white male basketball players.

- For D-I football the GSR was 69 percent, but only 57 percent for the University of Texas, 54 percent for the University of Mississippi, and 46 percent for California State University at Fresno. Other universities had GSR rates for football that were below 55 percent.[25]

The NCAA's method of calculating graduation rates has been a source of controversy ever since it was formulated, primarily because critics believe it is biased to inflate actual student-athletes graduation rates. Most recently, a report by the University of North Carolina's Sport Research Institute calls the NCAA's GSRs misleading. Using adjusted statistics, the Chapel Hill–based institute claims that only 54.8 percent of Football Bowl Subdivision athletes at 117 schools graduated within six years, compared to 73.7 percent of other full-time students. According to the Sport Research Institute, the Division I basketball gap was even larger, with 44.6 percent of athletes earning degrees at 116 schools, compared to 75.7 percent of the general student body.[26]

The Impediments to Scholarly Achievement by College Athletes

Many college athletes are not only ill prepared for the intellectual demands of college, they also face a number of obstacles that impede their scholarly achievement. The pressures on athletes, especially those in big-time, revenue-producing sports, are well known, including physical exhaustion, mental fatigue, media attention, and demanding coaches. The time demands alone are onerous. During the season, the athletes spend fifty to sixty hours preparing for, participating in, recovering from, and traveling to games. As we described above, big-time college revenue sports have become a year-round occupation for the scholarship players. The NCAA permits only "voluntary" workouts in the summer, but that requirement is a sham—the athletes know

they must work out or risk losing favor with their coaches, at a minimum, or even risk losing their scholarships.[27]

The athletes in commercialized, professionalized college sports programs often have trouble reconciling the roles associated with their dual statuses of athlete and student. The pressures of big-time sport and the academic demands frequently result in the gradual disengagement of the athletes from their academic roles. Most athletes enter the university feeling idealistic about their impending academic performance; that is, they are optimistic about graduating, and many consider ambitious majors. For some, this idealism lasts until about the end of the first year and becomes replaced by disappointment and a growing cynicism, as student-athletes realize how difficult it is to keep up with their academic demands. The athletic role comes to dominate all facets of their existence.

Typically, student-athletes receive greater positive reinforcement from their athletic performance than from their academic performance, and they are increasingly isolated from the general student body. They become isolated culturally by their racial and socioeconomic differences from the rest of the students. They are even isolated from other students by their physical size, which others

College athletes in big-time, commercialized sports programs often have trouble reconciling the role of athlete with college student. Because of the pressures of maintaining their athletic scholarship, the athletic role often comes to dominate at the expense of the academic role. (istockphoto)

often find intimidating. They interact primarily with other athletes, who often demean academics.

As freshmen, athletes are frequently given courses with "sympathetic" professors, but this changes as the athletes move through the university curriculum. The academic expectations escalate, and the athletes are often unprepared. The resulting academic failure or, at best, mediocre academic performance leads to embarrassment and despair.[28]

The noneducation and miseducation of college athletes are especially acute for African Americans. Many come from economically disadvantaged backgrounds and from inadequate high schools. Every study that has compared African American athletes with their white counterparts has found them less prepared for college and more likely to fulfill this prophecy: African American athletes tend to enter college as marginal students and to leave the same way.

A social construction of the athlete as a "dumb jock" has been applied to all athletes, but it has had an accentuated application to African American athletes for several reasons. First, African American student-athletes must contend with two negative labels: the dumb athlete caricature and the dumb African American stereotype. This double negative tends to result in a self-fulfilling prophecy as teachers, fellow students, and the athletes themselves assume low academic performance by African American athletes. Moreover, as soon as an African American youngster is viewed as a potential athletic star, many teachers, administrators, and parents lower their academic demands because they assume that athletic stardom will be the athlete's ticket out of the ghetto.

In junior high school and high school, often little is demanded of African American athletes academically. These reduced academic expectations continue in college. The result? Many black scholarship student-athletes manage to go through four years of college enrollment virtually unscathed by education.[29] A major unintended consequence of this situation is that, unwittingly, the universities with big-time programs that recruit marginal students and do not educate them offer "proof" for the argument that African Americans are inferior to whites in intellectual potential.

REFORM INITIATIVES AND INTERCOLLEGIATE SPORTS

Everyone familiar with intercollegiate sports is aware of the numerous scandals that have beset major university football and basketball programs during the past few years. Despite a continuing parade of committees, commissions, and task forces whose purpose has been to reform big-time college sports, horror stories persist in the form of reports about violations of NCAA rules, low graduation rates among football and basketball athletes, and athletes receiving illegal money from boosters.

Scandals develop with a frequency that is astonishing even to the most cynical of observers. Hardly a week goes by without the disclosure of new violations of NCAA rules. Each revelation is followed by righteous promises from university authorities and the NCAA that change is on the way, that collegiate athletics are going to be cleaned up. But the NCAA has been unable to stop these violations or the conditions from which they breed.[30]

The most recent attempt to address the endemic problems of major college sports has been the Knight Commission on Intercollegiate Athletics. The trustees of the Knight Foundation created this commission in 1989 and directed it to propose a reform agenda for college sports. During more than twenty years of work, the Knight Commission has produced various reports as solutions for abuses in college sports, and some strides have been made to reconnect intercollegiate sports with the educational mission of colleges and universities. Still, in many ways little has changed.

For all of the chest pounding about reform, an analysis of changes that have been made or proposed over the years shows that reorganization of existing structural relations is conspicuously absent from reform efforts in intercollegiate athletics. According to the NCAA infractions database, over one-fourth of the major infractions cases in all of its divisions have involved football and basketball programs in universities from the six most prominent conferences.[31]

The *structure* of big-time, commercial college athletics—a structure that is largely responsible for the pervasive corruption and abuses—has been left intact, with no substantive changes. Hope for meaningful reform by the NCAA so that it would better serve the interests and needs of all college athletes is nowhere to be found. A statement made over a decade ago by Walter Byers, a former executive director of the NCAA, still applies: "College athletics reform movements spanning 90 years have been remarkably consistent. They never reformed much of anything."[32] Perhaps the following recent *USA Today* headlines illustrate this point:

> "NCAA Slams USC with Sanctions"
> "NCAA: Tressel Lacked Honesty, Integrity"
> "As Final Fours Begin, Scandals Dog NCAA"
> "It's NCAA's School for Scandal"
> "NCAA Suspends Eight Miami Players"[33]

On the positive side, big-time college sports provide entertainment, spectacle, excitement, and festival, along with excellence in sports. On the negative side, as we have seen, big-time athletics have severely compromised academe. Pursuit of educational goals has been superseded by the quest for big money. Winning big-time programs realize huge revenues from television, gate receipts, bowl and tournament appearances, and even state legislatures; therefore, many athletic departments and coaches are guided by a win-at-any-cost philosophy.

Can this fundamental dilemma be resolved? Can the corporate and corrupt sports programs at colleges and universities be changed to redress the wrongs that are making a mockery of their educational goals? Can the abuses be eliminated without sacrificing the high level of achievement by the athletes and the excitement of college sports?

We would like to think that having hope will bring about some necessary reforms in big-time college sports. After many years of studying college sports, we advance the following recommendations, which we hope will raise the consciousness of readers to begin thinking about how intercollegiate sports, especially at major universities, could be made more educationally focused, humane, and protective of the rights of student-athletes.

Specifically, reform must be directed at three crucial areas: the way sports are administered, the education of athletes, and the rights of athletes.

The Administration of Intercollegiate Sports

As a beginning, athletic departments must not be separated from their institutions as self-contained corporate entities. They must be under the direct control of university presidents and boards of regents. Presidents, as chief executive officers, must be accountable for the actions of their athletic departments. They must set up mechanisms to monitor sports programs to detect illegal and unethical acts. They must determine policies to maximize the educational experiences of student-athletes.

Coaches must be part of the academic community and the tenure system, to provide them with reasonable job security and to emphasize that they, too, are teachers. As educators with special responsibilities, they should earn salaries similar to those of academic administrators. They should not receive bonuses for winning championships. Such performance incentives overemphasize winning and increase the likelihood of cheating.

The outside incomes of coaches should be sharply curtailed. Money from shoe companies should go to the universities, not the coaches. If coaches fail to keep their programs ethical, they should lose their tenure and be suspended from coaching at any institution for a specified period, even, in special cases, forever. Among the important criteria for evaluating coaches' performance should be the proportion of athletes who graduate within six years. Actually, the conditions we recommend in these two paragraphs already exist in over four hundred institutions—those in D-III.

Athletic departments must be closely monitored and, when warranted, sanctioned externally. The NCAA is not, however, the proper external agent, since it has a fundamental conflict of interest. The NCAA is too dependent on sports-generated television money and bowl contracts to be an impartial investigator, judge, and jury.

Accrediting associations should oversee all aspects of educational institutions, including sports, to assess whether educational goals are being met. If an institution does not meet those goals because of inadequacies in the sports program, then it should lose accreditation, just as it would if its library was below standard or too few of its professors held doctorates.

Emphasizing the Education of Student-Athletes

Institutions of higher education worthy of the name must make a commitment to their athletes as students. This requires, first, that only athletes who have the potential to compete as students be admitted. A few, very few, may be admitted as exceptions, but they and other academically marginal students must receive the benefits of a concerted effort by the university to improve their skills through remedial classes and tutorials so that they can earn a degree.

Second, freshmen should be ineligible for varsity sports. Such a requirement has symbolic value, because it shows athletes and the whole community that academic performance is the highest priority of the institution. More important, it allows freshman athletes time to adjust to the demanding and competitive academic environment before they also take on the pressure that comes from participating in big-time sports.

Third, colleges must insist that athletes make satisfactory progress toward a degree. There should be internal academic audits to determine whether athletes are meeting the grade point and curriculum requirements for graduation. Currently, schools must provide the NCAA with graduation rates based on how many athletes graduate in six years. They must also be required to make these rates public, including giving them to each potential recruit.

Fourth, the time demands of sports must be reduced. Analyses of the time that the average major college football and basketball players spend on their sport have found that football players devote about 55 hours per week and basketball players 50 hours per week practicing, weight training, watching films, traveling to games, and being away from campus and missing classes during their respective seasons. These figures are excessive and should be reduced by at least one-third. Finally, mandatory off-season workouts should be abolished and spring football practice should be eliminated.

Commitment to Athletes' Rights

The asymmetrical situation whereby universities have the power and student-athletes do not must be modified. First, athletes should have the right to fair compensation for the work they do as public entertainers and for the revenues they generate. Athletic scholarships are often called "Free Rides" but they are far from that. A joint study by Ithaca College and the National College Players Association (NCPA) revealed that student-athletes in D-I universities receiving so-called full-ride scholarships were left with an average shortfall of $2,951 per year in education-related expenses that they had to personally pay for.[34] It appears that the leadership at the NCAA has finally begun to understand the injustice of the traditional athletic scholarship. In the fall of 2011 the NCAA Division I board of directors adopted a proposal that would allow athletes to be eligible for up to $2,000 annually to cover incidental expenses above the basic full-ride scholarship.[35] It is too soon to know whether that proposal will actually be adopted by the entire governing organization, but it is the first time it has even been seriously considered by the NCAA.

Second, the governing body of sports needs to establish a comprehensive athletes' bill of rights to ensure a nonexploitive context. At a minimum, it should include the following:

- The right to transfer to a different school after their sophomore year and be eligible to play immediately.
- The right to a four-year scholarship, not the one-year renewable scholarship at the option of the coach, as is the current NCAA policy. This too was a major breakthrough proposed by the NCAA Division I board of directors we identified above. They recommended that universities be permitted to offer multiyear scholarships in place of year-by-year renewals. Again, this awaits adoption by the NCAA governing body.
- The rights that other college students have, such as freedom of speech, protections from the physical and mental abuse of authorities, privacy rights, and the fair redress of grievances. There should be an impartial committee on each college campus, separate from the athletic department, that monitors the behavior of coaches and the rules imposed by them on athletes to ensure that individual rights are guaranteed.

- The right to make money from endorsements, speeches, and appearances.
- The right, as scholarship athletes and in effect employees of the institution, to be eligible for workers' compensation if injured. Most assuredly, they must be fully insured by their institutions for injuries.
- The right to consult with agents concerning sports career choices. With regard to agents, an executive with the NFL Players Association said: "The sordid reality of big-time college revenue sports isn't about corrupt agents; it's about a corrupt system that exploits and make billions off the performance of our country's finest athletes."[36]

SUMMARY

Without designating them all as such, we have examined and demythologized several myths in this chapter. The first myth is that college athletic programs are amateur athletics. Big-time college sport is big business. The second myth is that the athletic programs in the various schools make money. Relatively few do. The rest depend on various subsidies to keep afloat. A related myth is that these programs help the universities. Almost always the surplus monies are kept within the athletic departments. So, too, are the monies that sports attract from contributors. Also, when athletic departments are put on probation or otherwise punished for transgressions, the universities are hurt by the negative publicity.

Another myth is that the NCAA protects student-athletes. As we have seen, the NCAA rules are extremely one-sided in favor of the institutions over the athletes. Clearly, we have shown that the term *student-athlete* in big-time athletic programs is an oxymoron. Scholarship athletes in the revenue-producing sports are employees of their athletic departments. Their role of student is surely secondary to the role of athlete in most big-time programs. Similarly, athletes are not amateurs. They are just poorly compensated professionals.

Finally, the notion that sport builds character is a myth at the big-time, big-business level of intercollegiate sports. Cheating in recruiting is commonplace. Payments to athletes outside the rules are widely dispensed. Athletes are sometimes pampered. Rules for admittance to schools are bent for them. They are enrolled in courses with professors friendly to the athletic department. Athletes hear the rhetoric about sport building character and that education is first, but they see a different reality. In such a climate, cynicism abounds and the possibility of positive character development is diminished.

WEB RESOURCES

www.chronicle.com
The website for *The Chronicle of Higher Education*, which includes articles on college sport, including the latest data on graduation rates. On the home page, type "Intercollegiate Athletics" for articles on that topic.

www.bus.ucf.edu/sportbusiness/
This is the website for the Institute for Diversity and Ethics in Sport at the University of Central Florida. It provides the annual *Racial and Gender Report Card* with current data on race and gender in sport.

www.ncaa.org
The website of the National Collegiate Athletic Association.

www.thedrakegroup.org
The Drake Group seeks to reform intercollegiate athletics. This site provides position papers and data related to college sports.

http://english.cis-sic.ca/landing/index/
The official website of Canadian Interuniversity Sport. This site has many useful links.

www.unc.edu/depts/exercise/csri/
The College Sport Research Institute (CSRI), a nonprofit organization at the University of North Carolina, Chapel Hill, involving faculty from across the United States and around the world. CSRI is committed to supporting independent data collection and analysis related to college-sport issues.

NOTES

1. James J. Duderstadt, *Intercollegiate Athletics and the American University: A University President's Perspective* (Ann Arbor: University of Michigan Press, 2003); John Watterson, *College Football, History, Spectacle, Controversy* (Baltimore: Johns Hopkins University Press, 2000).

2. There is an enormous literature about the problems endemic to contemporary big-time college sports. We are listing some of the most notable books on this topic that have been published just in the past ten years. See Mark Yost, *Varsity Green: A Behind the Scenes Look at Culture and Corruption in College Athletics* (Stanford: Stanford University Press, 2010); William C. Dowling, *Confessions of a Spoilsport: My Life and Hard Times Fighting Sports Corruption at an Old Eastern University* (University Park: Pennsylvania State University Press, 2007); John R. Gerdy, *Air Ball: American Education's Failed Experiment with Elite Athletics* (Jackson: University Press of Mississippi, 2006); and James L. Shulman and William G. Bowen, *The Game of Life: College Sports and Educational Values* (Princeton: Princeton University Press, 2001).

3. All quoted in Murray Sperber, *Beer and Circus: How Big-Time College Sports Is Crippling Undergraduate Education* (New York: Henry Holt, 2000), 33; see also Charles T. Clotfelter, *Big-Time Sports in American Universities* (Cambridge: Cambridge University Press, 2011).

4. Richard Sandomir and Pete Thamel, "TV Deal Pushes N.C.A.A. Closer to 68 Team Tournament," *New York Times*, 23 April 2010, p. B9.

5. Kristi Dosh, "How Profitable is Ohio State University Athletics Department?" *The Business of College Sports*, 1 June 2011, http://businessofcollegesports.com/tag/ohio-state-university/.

6. Keith Sargeant, "Rutgers to Sell Naming Rights to Stadium, Arena," *My Centraljersey.com*, 30 June 2010.

7. Erik Brady, Jodi Upton, and Steve Berkowitz, "Coaches' Pay Soars Again," *USA Today*, 17 November 2011, pp. 1A–2A.

8. Steve Wieberg, Jodi Upton, A. J. Perez, and Steve Berkowitz, "College Football Coaches See Salaries Rise in Down Economy," *USA Today*, 10 November 2009, http://www.usatoday.com/sports/college/football/2009-11-09-coaches-salary-analysis_N.htm.

9. Quoted in Jodi Upton, Jack Gillum, and Steve Berkowitz, "Big-Time Sports: Worth the Big-Time Cost?" *USA Today*, 14 January 2010, p. 5C.

10. Quoted in Steve Berkowitz, Jodi Upton, Michael McCarthy, and Jack Gillum, "How Student Fees Quietly Boost College Sports," *USA Today*, 22 September 2010, p. 2A.

11. Berkowitz, Upton, McCarthy, and Gillum, "How Student Fees Quietly Boost College Sports," pp. 1A–2A; Michael McCarthy, "Students Are Unaware of Usage of Fees," *USA Today*, 22 September 2010, p. 6C; Jack Gillum, Jodi Upton, and Steve Berkowitz, "College Athletics Soaking Up Subsidies, Fees," *USA Today*, 14 January 2010, p. 1A; Upton, Gillum, and Berkowitz, "Big-Time Sports: Worth the Big-Time Cost?"

12. Steve Berkowitz, "Cal's Cuts Reveal Budget Pressures," *USA Today*, 29 September 2010, p. 10C; see also Wieberg, Upton, Perez, and Berkowitz, "College Football Coaches See Salaries Rise in Down Economy."

13. Upton, Gillum, and Berkowitz, "Big-Time Sports: Worth the Big-Time Cost?"; see also Steve Berkowitz and Jodi Upton, "Fees, Funds Help Foot Bill at Rutgers," *USA Today*, 28 June 2011, pp. 1C–2C.

14. Quoted in Gillum, Upton, and Berkowitz, "College Athletics Soaking Up Subsidies, Fees."

15. Upton, Gillum, and Berkowitz, "Big-Time Sports: Worth the Big-Time Cost?"

16. Jonathan Orszag and Mark Israel, *The Empirical Effects of Collegiate Athletics: An Update Based on 2004–2007 Data* (Indianapolis: National Collegiate Athletic Association, 2009), 7.

17. Dowling, *Confessions of a Spoilsport*, 1.

18. Jack Carey, "Small Football Schools Take Their Lumps for a Sum," *USA Today*, 3 September 2009, pp. 1A–2A.

19. National Collegiate Athletic Association, *2010–11 NCAA Division I Manual* (Indianapolis: National Collegiate Athletic Association, 2010), 4.

20. Quoted in Marlen Garcia, "O'Bannon Wants His Cut," *USA Today*, 22 July 2009, p. 7C; for a scornful account of college sports, see Taylor Branch, "The Shame of College Sports," *The Atlantic*, October 2011, pp. 80–110.

21. Jodi Upton and Jack Gillum, "What NCAA Schools Spend on Athletics," NCAA College Athletics Finance Database, *USA Today*, 2 April 2010, http://www.usatoday.com/sports/college/ncaa-finances.htm.

22. Reported in Alison Go, "Athletes Show Huge Gaps in SAT Scores," *U.S. News & World Report*, 30 December 2008.

23. Paul Newberry, "College Athletes Flock to Same Majors," *Greeley Tribune*, 6 September 2011, p. B2.

24. Quoted in Ken Booth, "Athletes Make Academic End Run," *al.com*, 30 March 2007, http://blog.al.com/bn/2007/03/athletes_make_academic_end_run.html.

25. National Collegiate Athletic Association, *Trends in Graduation: Success Rates and Federal Graduation Rates at NCAA Division I Institutions* (NCAA Research Staff, October 2011).

26. Richard Southall, E. Woodrow Eckard, Mark Nagel, Jenna Tomalski, and Greg Lewinter, "Adjusted Graduation Gap: NCAA Division-I Football," *The College Sport Research Institute* (Chapel Hill: University of North Carolina), 26 August 2010, http://www.unc.edu/depts/exercise/csri; see also Alan Scher Zagier, "Study: NCAA Graduation Rate Comparisons Flawed," *Huffington Post*, 2 April 2010, http://www.huffingtonpost.com/2010/04/20/study-ncaa-graduation-rat_n_544292.html.

27. George R. Mills, *A View from the Bench: The Story of an Ordinary Player on a Big-Time Football Team* (Champaign: University of Illinois Press, 2004); see also Yost, *Varsity Green*.

28. Krystal Beamon and Patricia A. Bell, "Academics Versus Athletics: An Examination of the Effects of Background and Socialization on African American Male Student Athletes," *Social Science Journal* 43, no. 3 (2006): 393–403; see also Yost, *Varsity Green*.

29. Audwin Anderson and Donald South, "The Academic Experiences of African American Collegiate Athletes: Implications for Policy and Practice," in *Diversity and Social Justice in College Sports: Sport Management and the Student Athlete*, ed. Dana D. Brooks and Ronald C. Althouse (Morgantown, WV: Fitness Information Technology, 2007), 77–94.

30. Ronald A. Smith, *Pay for Play: A History of Big-Time College Athletic Reform* (Champaign: University of Illinois Press, 2010).

31. Marlen Garcia, "Top Conferences Face Big-Time Scrutiny," *USA Today*, 3 June 2010, p. 2C.

32. Walter Byers, *Unsportsmanlike Conduct: Exploiting College Athletes* (Ann Arbor: University of Michigan Press, 1995), 337; see also Jack Carey, "Knight Commission: Athletics vs. Academic Spending Too Unbalanced," *USA Today*, 18 June 2010, p. 12C.

33. Jack Carey, "NCAA Slams USC With Sanctions," *USA Today*, 11 June 2010, pp. 1C–2C; Steve Wieberg, "NCAA: Tressel Lacked Honesty, Integrity," *USA Today*, 26 April 2011, p. 1C; Steve Wieberg, "As Final Fours Begin, Scandals Dog NCAA," *USA Today*, 1 April 2011, p. 8C; Christine Brennan, "It's NCAA's School Year for Scandal," *USA Today*, 31 March 2011, p. 3C; Jack Carey, "NCAA Suspends Eight Miami Players," *USA Today*, 31 August 2011, p. 1C.

34. NCPA Scholarship Shortfall Search, National College Payers Association, http://www.ncpanow.org/research?id=0018.

35. Andy Gardiner, "NCAA Enacts Rule Changes," *USA Today*, 28 October 2011, p. 7C.

36. Quoted in "When Student-Athletes Cheat, Corrupt Adults Escape Blame," Our View section of *USA Today*, 20 September 2010, p. 10A; see also Alexander Wolff and Dick Friedman, "The Athlete's Bill of Rights," *Sports Illustrated*, 5 March 2007, p. 69.

CHAPTER 7

Social Problems and North American Sport

Violence, Substance Abuse, Eating Disorders, and Gambling

Modern sports are undoubtedly in a mess. Corruption, exploitation, monopoly abuse, drug abuse, cheating, foul conduct on the field and criminal offenses off it— there is almost no form of human misconduct that cannot be found in abundance. . . . Yet sports have never been more popular than they are today.
—Stefan Szymanski*

New Jersey Devils' Eric Bolton (22) fights with Ottawa Senators' Chris Neil (25) an NHL hockey game (AP Photo/The Canadian Press, Fred Chartrand). The hockey fistfight is so common in the NHL that every team has one or two enforcers or designated hit men. Unfortunately, these violent tactics have resulted in career-ending injuries to several of the NHL's best players.

*Stefan Szymanski, *Playbooks and Checkbooks: An Introduction to the Economics of Modern Sports* (Princeton: Princeton University Press, 2009), 180.

Throughout this book we have emphasized the close relationship between sports and the broader North American society. It is not an exaggeration to say that the United States and Canada are plagued by a number of common major social problems—poverty, racism, sexism, healthcare, environmental destruction, and crime, to name just a few. Given the close connections between sport and society, it should come as no surprise that there are also pervasive social problems in North American sports.

OVERVIEW OF SOCIAL PROBLEMS IN SPORT

Social Theories and Social Problems

As a preliminary to focusing on the social problems in sport we briefly explain how the social theories we identified in Chapter 1 account for social problems. As we have noted before, functionalism views the social system as interdependent parts linked together into a stable, cohesive, cooperative entity. Social problems occur when members of society have not been adequately socialized toward adopting the prescribed norms and values that underlie the social cohesion and stability of that social system. Just as biological systems become ill when organs and cells do not function normally, society becomes "ill" when its parts—its citizens and culture—do not behave appropriately. Preventing or solving social problems requires strengthening social norms through proper socialization and moral education, much of which may be accomplished in the family, schools, churches, and workplace.

The conflict/cultural perspective views social problems as arising from competition among various groups and interests for power and resources, and it contends that particular components of society exercise power and control arising from particular unequal social arrangements. Social problems result when the mass of population is denied access to many of the political, economic, and social resources available to the powerful and wealthy. Solutions to social problems lie in eliminating inequality, injustice, and discrimination among social classes. Stronger controls are necessary to restrain the powerful and wealthy and to ensure that decisions and practices are based on promotion of the common good rather than on increased power and profit for the privileged.

Examples of Recent Social Problems in Sport

In the past decade, there have been a variety of social problems at every level of the sports world. On almost everyone's list, violence, substance abuse, eating disorders, and gambling have a prominent place. An outcry about the violence in sports has been triggered by the upsurge in the frequency of concussions among players in several sports—especially football and ice hockey. Numerous suggestions for changing the rules, modifying the equipment, and providing better medical attention at all events have been advanced. Literally hundreds of violent sports incidents occur each year involving groups of athletes, as in bench-clearing brawls; other incidents occur between spectators and athletes or just among spectators.

Substance abuse and eating disorders are also prevalent problems in sports. Steroids have been a staple among male athletes for decades, but researchers have recently found that steroid use has increased at an alarming rate among females. When the widespread use of Sudafed (a medication with pseudoephedrine) was revealed, it was referred to as the "NHL's dirty little secret" because of the on-ice "boost" it gave the players. Major League Baseball's Barry Bonds has been the subject of an ongoing federal investigation into his alleged use of steroids. Internationally, the Tour de France has been laced with positive drug tests and doping charges, and in a recent year the leader of the race in the final week was dismissed by his team for not complying with drug-testing rules prior to the race.

Eating disorders are common among females in so-called lean build sports and among male athletes in sports that use weight classifications, such as wrestling, weight lifting, and boxing. Deaths of both male and female athletes have been linked to eating disorders.

Gambling has been one of the most popular forms of excitement and entertainment in human history. It is common in all cultures, at all social strata, in most periods of the life cycle, and among both men and women. One by-product of gambling is addiction, and the behaviors of addicted gamblers often become social problems. Addicted gamblers have attempted to influence the outcome of sporting events. Gambling athletes have accepted money from gamblers to fix an event. Athletes themselves have bet on games in which they play.

These are the sports social problems that will be examined in the present chapter. They all are pervasive in North American sports, and they all have troubling consequences for the participants, fans, and others associated with sports.

VIOLENCE IN NORTH AMERICAN SOCIETY

Understanding the ways and means by which violence has come to play such a salient role in sports requires historically situating and culturally locating it within the larger culture in which sports are embedded.

Violence in Historical Context

Canada and the United States were literally born through violence. Early colonists in North America encountered a native population whom the colonists systematically imprisoned, killed, or placed on reserved lands. Thus it was mostly through violent means that European settlers acquired almost all of the land in the North American continent.

Both nations began in a climate of warfare. In the case of the American colonists, the Declaration of Independence literally furnished the rationale for the legitimate use of violence by the colonists. In Canada, settlers principally from France and England contended over the vast northern expanse of landmass for more than two hundred years, fighting many bloody battles until the Peace of Paris in 1763 finally ceded Canada to Great Britain.

Over the past two centuries, oppressed groups in North America have been subject to the violence of their oppressors and have used violence to struggle against their oppressors. Many Africans brought to North America throughout the colonial period

and up to the U.S. Civil War were victims of daily violence by slave owners. Concomitantly, African Americans have resorted to violence in every era of North American history to redress their grievances. As one African American civil rights activist said in justifying the use of violence: "Violence is as American as apple pie."

Actually, every ethnic minority group in North America has encountered hostility and violence and has also resorted to violent means to protect itself or to gain a measure of revenge. Asians, Chicanos, Hispanics, Irish, you name it: Every newly immigrated ethnic and racial group has been subject to violence in some form.

Throughout the nineteenth century, capitalism brought wage labor, horrible working conditions, and autocratic, sometimes brutal, bosses. By the later nineteenth century, workers had begun to organize into unions for collective action against the policies and practices of the industrialists. Such organizations were often met with force, which in many cases turned to violence by both capitalists and workers.

The expansion of the U.S. territories, which began in the early nineteenth century, has been mostly accomplished through violent military actions. Native Americans had most of their land taken away by violent means. Mexicans were driven out of what is now the southwest United States. Cuba and the Philippines were invaded and subjected to U.S. control.[1]

In summarizing the history of violence in American society, sociologists D. Stanley Eitzen, Maxine Baca Zinn, and Kelly Eitzen Smith wrote:

> Violence was necessary to give birth to the United States. Violence was used both to keep the blacks in servitude and to free them. Violence was used to defeat rebellious Indians and to keep them on reservations. Additionally, violence has been a necessary means for many groups in American society to achieve equality or something approaching parity in power and in the rights that all Americans are supposed to enjoy.[2]

This heritage of violence is learned in informal and formal ways by each new generation of young people, and it becomes embedded in their understandings about the culture of which they are a part. For the past century the United States has had the highest homicide rate of all the "developed" countries—from four to twenty times the rates in other industrial nations. Although the Canadian homicide rate is less than one-half the U.S. rate, it ranks fairly high among English-speaking developed countries. Americans living in cities report an alarmingly high rate of fear of being involved in a violent confrontation—that is, robbed, burglarized, or raped.[3]

Contemporary Violence in North America

It is not only the historical legacy that shapes the violent characteristics of North Americans. All anyone has to do is read each day's newspaper or watch the daily television news to get the latest stories of gruesome violence. The phrase "If it bleeds, it leads" captures television news directors' preference for opening newscasts with the most violent stories they can find.

Many popular films are violent. Examples include the movies *Ninja Assassin* and *Final Destination*. No other nation comes close to the United States with respect to TV violence: Children's daytime programs average 24 violent acts per hour, and evening prime-time programs average 7.5. The TV series *The Sopranos* and *CSI* are prime examples. Content analyses of widely popular video games—*Manhunt*, *Resident Evil*, and *Dead Rising*, for example—have found that as much as 89 percent of them contain content based on violent actions. In such games, the video player controls the weapons of murder and destruction, with bullets, missiles, and other lethal objects producing spectacular explosions and bloody images as they hit their targets. The overall ambiance is one of extreme, violent imagery. People do not have to leave their living rooms to witness massive doses of violence.

Several media studies over the past decade estimated that by the time the typical American reaches the age of eighteen, she or he has witnessed 200,000 dramatized acts of violence and 40,000 dramatized murders—not counting video games. A number of noted scholars from a variety of fields of study have reported a connection between movie-TV-video viewing and pro-violence attitudes and aggression in childhood and later aggressive behavior in adulthood among both males and females.[4]

More than any other Western nation, the culture of the United States promotes and glorifies violence; indeed, people in other countries are astounded by the salience of violent behavior and imagery in U.S. culture. Returning to the basic theme of this chapter—the connections between sport and North American society—we conclude that sporting practices would be an anomaly if violent behaviors did not play a prominent role.

VIOLENCE IN SPORT: TERMINOLOGY, THEORIES

Is It Violence or Aggression? Confusion in the Literature

Before focusing directly on violence in sport, it is necessary to begin with a brief excursion into the meaning of two key concepts that will be used in this section. The words *violence* and *aggression* are often found together, and some writers use them as synonyms. On the other hand, some behavioral and social scientists differentiate sharply between these two words. Still others believe that the concepts have come to have so many meanings that they do not have any meaning at all anymore.

Despite the variety of definitions and meanings assigned to the two concepts, we believe that a definition of aggression and violence in sport proposed by sport psychologist John Kerr is worth using as an operational framework for the purposes of this chapter. Kerr states:

> Aggression can be seen as unprovoked hostility or attacks on another person which are not sanctioned by society. However, in the sports context, the aggression is provoked in the sense that two opposing [athletes] or teams have willingly agreed to compete against each other. Aggression [and violence] in . . . [some] sports is intrinsic and sanctioned, provided the [behavior] remains permissible within the boundaries of certain rules, which act as a kind of contract in the pursuit of aggression (and violence) between consenting [athletes].[5]

We would add this qualifying statement: Illegal, unacceptable, and unsanctioned aggression or violence is any action in violation of the written and unwritten rules or norms of a sport.

In this chapter we shall use these two words in the way we just described, but when referring to other theorists' and researchers' works, it will be necessary to employ their terminology.

Theories About the Connection Between Violent Behavior and Sport

Two theories of human aggression dominated the scientific literature during the twentieth century: instinct theory and frustration-aggression theory. The first postulated that aggressive behavior is based in human instincts. This notion owed its popularity to two major proponents: Sigmund Freud, the founder of psychoanalysis, and Konrad Lorenz, a world-renowned ethologist. Both claimed that aggression is instinctive in humans and that humans can do very little to change or control this aggressive impulse. See Box 7.1 for additional descriptions of these theories.

Basing his theory of aggression on his studies of various animal species, Lorenz concurred with the outlines of Freud's notion that humans possess an aggressive impulse that requires periodic release and that by venting aggressive energy we become less aggressive, an effect known as *catharsis*. Aggressive releases of energy can take benign forms or destructive forms, and Lorenz believed that sports can help channel aggressive behavior into benign

forms. Although this model of aggression sounds plausible, it has been roundly attacked by both social and biological scientists.

A second theory of aggression that generated much interest and research is called frustration-aggression (F-A) theory. This theory proposed a specific process by which the underlying instinct to aggression is triggered: When an individual is frustrated by someone or something, he or she will aggress in order to purge the pent-up frustration. In other words, the existence of frustration leads to some form of aggression, although not necessarily an overt act of violence, which, as in the instinct theory, then produces a catharsis, a reduction in the instigation to further aggression.

When examined by the methods of empirical research, the Freud-Lorenz instinct theory, like the F-A hypothesis, has not stood up. Most studies show that aggression does not always occur when a person has been frustrated and that there is no cathartic effect after aggression is employed. One of the most telling arguments against the F-A hypothesis is research that has persuasively shown that not all aggressive behavior stems from prior frustrations and that the linkage between frustration and aggression is not as close as the theory claimed.[6]

The most recent theorizing about aggressive behavior has come from scholars who postulate that aggression is a learned social behavior (e.g., social learning theory, social cognitive theory, and social interaction theory). These theories emphasize the learning of aggression via vicarious or observational learning and reinforcement and through the

---

Box 7.1   *Thinking About Sport*: Theories About Aggression/Violence

INSTINCT AGGRESSION THEORY

Aggressive behavior is based in human instincts; humans cannot change or control this aggressive impulse. Aggressive impulse requires periodic release; sports can help channel aggressive behavior into benign forms.

FRUSTRATION-AGGRESSION THEORY

When an individual is frustrated, he or she will aggress in order to purge the pent-up frustration; the aggression

then produces a catharsis, which reduces the likelihood of further aggression.

AGGRESSION SOCIALLY LEARNED THEORY

Emphasis is on the learning of aggression via vicarious or observational learning and reinforcement through the interaction-socialization process, with a focus on learning, thinking, and interacting with peers, family, community, social institutions, and cultural practices in shaping aggressive behavior.

interaction-socialization process. A major assumption of these models is that individuals who observe esteemed others (parents, teachers, peers, coaches) exhibiting aggressive behavior and being rewarded for it will experience a vicarious reinforcement that has the same effect as personally receiving the positive reinforcement. Moreover, individuals who exhibit aggressive behavior and receive approval for it will tend to employ aggressive behavior in future situations that are similar.

In both cases, the prediction is that continued rewards for aggressive acts will eventually form a tendency to respond to various situations with aggressive actions. According to these socially grounded theories, the conditions most conducive to the learning of aggression seem to be those in which the individual is rewarded for his or her own aggression, has many opportunities to observe aggression, or is the object of aggression. Individuals who mature under such conditions learn to assume that violent behavior is natural and, thus, an appropriate interpersonal response in many situations. These individuals will continue to rehearse violent actions in both actual situations and in fantasy. They will dismiss alternative actions as inappropriate or inadequate. They will also come across situations in which such responses are readily elicited because of the similarity of cues to former situations in which a violent response was learned.

The converse is also true. That is, if an individual receives, or observes esteemed others receiving, some form of negative sanction or punishment, that aggressive behavior will be inhibited. Thus, negative reinforcement will eventually form a habit or tendency to respond to various situations nonaggressively.

It may be seen, then, that social learning, social cognition, and social interactionist theories depart drastically from the older models for explaining aggression. Whereas the instinct and F-A models ground aggression in biological explanations, the socially grounded theories focus on learning, thinking, and interacting with peers, family, community, social institutions, and cultural practices in the environment as shaping aggressive behavior.[7]

Socially based theories and cultural explanations have much more research support than the other aggression models, and we will describe some of that research in the next section. This is not to say, however, that the issue of the roots of aggression has been settled once and for all. Scientists of several disciplines continue to probe for answers to the mysteries surrounding the pervasiveness of human aggression.

Aggression Theories and Research on Sports

Advocates of the instinct and F-A theories have often claimed that participation in and observation of aggressive activities have a cathartic effect by allowing one to discharge pent-up aggressive energy, and sporting activities have often been suggested as a means of dispelling aggression in a socially healthy way. One disciple of Freud called sports "a salutary purgation of combative instincts," and he claimed that if those instincts are dammed up within, they will break out in disastrous ways. Konrad Lorenz wrote, "The most important function of sport lies in furnishing a healthy safety valve for that most indispensable and, at the same time, most dangerous form of aggression that I have described as collective militant enthusiasm."[8] He even suggested that if nation-states would devote more energy to sporting activities, the chances for war between countries would be reduced.

The basic problem with the notion that sports provide an outlet for the aggressive instinct is that it doesn't have a confirming empirical basis. Freud, Lorenz, and anyone else can make claims about the connections among instinct, aggression, and sport, but in order for the claims to be credible they need scientific confirmation. No empirical findings, from Freud, Lorenz, or any others, have provided compelling research evidence in support of their claims.

Applying the F-A theory to sport suggests that sports provide a setting for expressing aggression, thus producing a catharsis—a reduction in aggressive inclinations. On the other hand, it has been observed that frustrations that often accompany sporting contests can trigger aggressive and violent behaviors. In what has become a classic test of the prediction of theories about sport having cathartic effects, researchers assessed the hostility of male spectators before and after a football game and a gymnastics meet. They found that, contrary to the predictions of these theories, hostility actually increased significantly after observing the football game (a violent event), regardless of the preferred outcome of the game. However, there was no increase in hostility from spectators after observing the gymnastics meet (a nonviolent event).

In a follow-up to that study, the researchers studied men and women who were exposed to a professional wrestling match, an ice hockey game, or a swimming event. General support was found for the previous finding of increased spectator hostility as a result of observing violence. Hostility among subjects increased at the wrestling and hockey events, but such increases did not occur at the swimming competition.[9]

One researcher found that homicide rates in the United States increased immediately after televised broadcasts of highly publicized boxing matches; another found that domestic violence by men against women increases dramatically during the Super Bowl. These findings are exactly the opposite of what should happen according to the cathartic effect of aggression. Overwhelmingly, the findings suggest that, contrary to the predictions of instinct and F-A theories, aggression tends to produce more aggressive predispositions and actions rather than serving as a catharsis.

Several studies seem to support the view of socially oriented scientists that learned cultural behavior patterns explain aggressive behavior rather than aggressive behavior being the result of an innate drive in humans. A unique and interesting study by an anthropologist focused on the relationship between war and sport forms in different types of cultures. He assessed the correlation between types of societies, warlike and non-warlike, and the existence of combative sports. Using cross-cultural data on ten warlike and ten non-warlike cultures, the researcher found that warlike societies and combative sports were positively correlated—90 percent of warlike societies had combative sports, but only 20 percent of non-warlike societies had combative sports.

This same anthropologist did a time-series case study of the United States to see if the popularity of combative sports (e.g., boxing, hockey, and football) rose or fell during times of war. He found that during wartime, combative sports indeed rose in popularity and noncombative sports declined. Both investigations lead to the conclusion that war and combative sports are found together in societies. Combative sports are not channels for the discharge of aggressive tensions but rather seem to promote aggression.[10]

Directly and indirectly, sports research studies have found no support for the instinct and F-A theories of aggression. At the same time, support for the socially oriented theories has accumulated from a variety of sources.

VIOLENCE IN NORTH AMERICAN SPORT

Violent actions have been a part of sporting practices for as long as we have records of organized sports. In the ancient Olympic Games, the Greeks had boxing and pancration as a regular part of the program of events. In the former, there were no rounds and no weight classifications. The boxers continued to pummel each other until one boxer was hurt so badly that he could not continue or he acknowledged defeat. The pancration was a brutal all-out combination of wrestling and what we would call street fighting. The rules permitted almost anything, including kicking, choking, hitting, and twisting of limbs. Gouging of eyes and biting were illegal. The object was to maim the opponent so badly he could not continue or to force him to admit defeat, as in boxing.[11]

Physical tests of strength, endurance, and skill were popular in the Roman civilization and the Middle Ages, and many, such as gladiator spectacles, chariot races, jousts, and tournaments, were quite violent; indeed, deaths were common in these events. The irrepressible bare-knuckle boxing and the precursors to team sports, such as soccer and football, were popular in England and Europe during the eighteenth and nineteenth centuries; all were extremely violent.[12]

Violence as Part of North American Sports

Just bring along the ambulance
And call the Red Cross nurse,
Then ring the undertaker up,
And make him bring a hearse;
Have all the surgeons ready there,
For they'll have work today,
Oh, can't you see the football teams
Are lining up to play.

—A popular jingle in the 1890s

Violent actions in sports have always had a special meaning separate from violence in the wider social context. Violent behavior in the larger society, except for a few situations such as war, typically carries with it negative sanctions in the form of norms or laws; violent behavior is punished. On the other hand, violent actions are actually encoded into the rules of some sports, and there are sport-specific techniques, tactics, and strategies that are quite violent but considered perfectly appropriate in playing the sport. Violent actions have consequences, and regardless of where they occur, they frequently lead to injuries to those subjected to the violence. Following are some of the consequences associated with North American sport:

- Concussions are currently considered the most serious sports injury issue in North American sports. This is reflected in the titles of newspaper and magazine articles within a three-month period in 2011: "Concussions: The Hits That Are Changing Football," "NHL Concussions Touch Off Debate," "Concussions to Be Hot Topic," "NBA Mulling Formal Concussion Policy," and "High School Athletes Face Serious Concussion Risks." Compiling statistics from various sources, *Time Magazine* reported that 6.3 percent of college football players suffered concussions, and 70 percent of college football players reported having concussion-like symptoms.[13]
- In 2010 352 NFL players—21 percent—were placed on the season-ending injured reserve list. Each week NFL teams sustain an average of 3.7 injuries to their 50-man rosters.

- The Center for Injury Research and Policy reported that in 2009 there were 55,000 concussions in high school football, 29,167 in high school girls' soccer, and 20,929 in high school boys' soccer. Moreover, high school athletes who sustain a concussion are three times more likely to sustain a second concussion.

The social consequences of these sports injuries are sometimes devastating. Some athletes sustain injuries that are chronic and cause pain throughout the individuals' lives. In other cases injured athletes have become quadriplegic and are confined to a lifetime in a wheelchair. At the most extreme are the athletes who die from their injuries.

One major justification for the legitimate use of violence in sport is that participants play knowing the rules and therefore understanding that they will be subject to violent actions against them. Just the opposite is typically true in the larger society: People expect they will not be subject to violence and that there are laws that protect them from violent actions. Of course, as we have previously described, this has not always been the case. If, as some analysts have suggested, violence is as American as apple pie, violence in North American sport is as natural as the knockout punch, the "bell-ringing" tackle, and the body check.

Sports and violence are almost inseparable. One example can suffice to illustrate this point. In a *Sports Illustrated* article titled "The Big Hit," the writer states:

Everything in [NFL] football begins with the big hit and flows from there, like blood pumping from a beating heart, feeding limbs and organs. . . . And big hits are big business. They not only fuel the core audience but also spawn cottage industries such as ESPN's Monday-night "Jacked Up" segment highlighting the weekends' five biggest legal, noninjury hits, and EA Sports's fabulously popular *Madden NFL* video games, in which crushing hits are enabled by movements on the controllers.[14]

A Philadelphia Eagles player claimed "people want to see violence, and every collision in the NFL is violent." An NFL Players Association executive asserted, "Typically the greater physical domination and degree of violence a team does to its opponent, the more likely that team will win the game." A *USA Today* editorial explained that "the fans have never complained about a little violence. They even enjoy it." Not long ago, the sports network ESPN had entire segments of their shows glorifying bone-crunching hits.[15]

The inherent features of some sports—the skills required to achieve victory, the strategy and tactics, and the rules—literally demand violent actions. Several "body contact" sports include tackling, body checking, collisions, and legal "hits" of various kinds, so violence is intrinsic to their actions. Indeed, it is taken for granted that when athletes engage in these activities they automatically accept the inevitability of contact, the probability of some bodily injury, and even the prospect of serious injury.

Boxing is perhaps the most obvious example a violent sport. The entire objective of a boxing match is for the two contestants to try to injure the other so severely that one cannot continue. A knockout, in which one's opponent is rendered unconscious (or at least semiconscious), is what every fighter strives for. In the past fifty years over 500 boxers have died from injuries sustained in the ring, mostly from cerebral blood clots.

Ultimate Fighting Championship (UFC)—which combines the striking techniques of boxing and kickboxing with the ground techniques of jujitsu and wrestling—has recently become the most popular hand-to-hand combat sport. In 2007, UFC broke the pay-per-view industry's records for a single year, surpassing World Wrestling Entertainment (WWE) and boxing. As of 2011, viewers can access UFC programming on pay-per-view television in the U.S. as well as in over 130 countries and 20 different languages worldwide.

Still, few people understand the relationship between the violence of a sport and the frequency of injuries, and how serious some of them are. But they are the markers of the violence in a sport. Injuries are so common in the NFL that during the season, newspapers publish a weekly "casualty" list of each team in the league. In a survey of 870 former NFL players, 65 percent reported they had suffered a "major injury," one that forced them to miss at least eight games. Seventy-eight percent reported

some kind of physical disability from their pro football injuries. One retired player has had 30 knee surgeries, dating back to his college days. Another retired player suffered at least 15 concussions while playing in the NFL. One Denver Broncos guard had 28 surgeries and was still an active player. After 13 surgeries on the ankle of another former NFL player, the physicians cut off the leg eight inches below the knee.[16]

College and high school football violence takes its toll too. According to the National Athletic Trainers' Association, about 37 percent of U.S. high school football players are injured badly enough each year to be sidelined for at least the remainder of the day. About eight high school football players die each year from football-related injuries.

Casualty rates in the Canadian Football League are comparable. But in Canada it is ice hockey where playing with pain and injuries has always been an essential part of the sport culture. There is a clear understanding that hockey is a physical and sometimes violent game. Players are going to be injured, either as part of the regular physical nature of the game or in the fights that are strategically employed.[17]

A number of sports, such as baseball, basketball, soccer, National Association for Stock Car Auto Racing (NASCAR), water polo, and so forth do not have the inherent violence found in others, but the methods employed and the way the rules are being interpreted are increasingly encouraging strategy and tactics resulting in violent actions.

Borderline Violence

What in the sports culture is called "borderline violence" is a category of violent actions that are prohibited by the official rules of a given sport but routinely occur and are more or less accepted by everyone; they have become the unofficial norms. Included here are the late hit in football, hockey fist-fighting, the knockdown pitch in baseball, the high tackle in soccer, and the deliberate foul in basketball. All such actions occasionally produce serious injuries; they also occasionally trigger bench-clearing brawls among the athletes. Although penalties are often meted out for these actions, the punishments are typically not severe enough to deter their future occurrence.

Often the intent behind much of this type of violence in sport is to "get the edge" over an opponent through "intimidation." The fistfight in ice hockey, the "brushback" pitch and the "break-up-the-double-play slide" in baseball, "clotheslining" and hitting wide receivers even when they are not directly involved in the play in football—all are done with the intent of breaking opponents' attention and concentration on the tasks they are trying to perform. Indeed, in NHL hockey and NBA basketball it has been a common practice of teams to carry an "enforcer" or "intimidator" on the roster. One general manager of an NHL team acknowledged that every team likes to have one or two enforcers or designated hit men so that the rest of the team feels comfortable.[18]

Although the objects of these tactics may not be physically harmed, there are cases in most sports where these "enforcer" tactics have extended beyond borderline violence and resulted in career-ending injuries: While Rudy Tomjanovich, who later coached the Houston Rockets to two consecutive NBA championships, was an NBA player, he was slugged in the face by another player, ending his playing career in basketball. In March 2004, the NHL's Vancouver Canuck Todd Bertuzzi punched the Colorado Avalanche's Steve Moore from behind and drove his face into the ice, causing three fractured neck vertebrae. Moore was wheeled off the ice on a gurney, and he never played another game in the NHL.

These are, of course, some of the most well-known examples of violent actions that have led to major injuries. There are literally hundreds of other incidents where the quasi-criminal violence shortened the victim's sports career or rendered him permanently impaired for the remainder of his

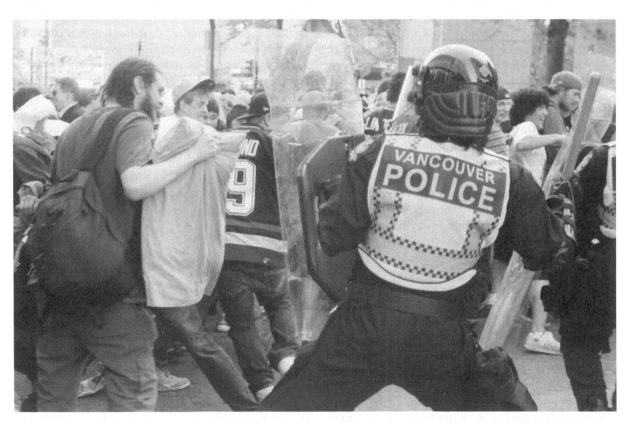

Police stand in front of people on the street following Game 7 of the NHL hockey Stanley Cup Finals between the Vancouver Canucks and the Boston Bruins on June 15, 2011, in Vancouver, British Columbia. (AP Photo/The Canadian Press, Geoff Howe)

career. Whenever current and former pro athletes get together to talk about their playing experiences, they recount stories about the "dirty play" or the "cheap shot" that had long-term consequences for the victim.

Although comparative figures are hard to come by, there is a widely held perception that all of the types of sports violence previously described are increasing in North America. Articles deploring this trend regularly detail the latest incidents of sports violence, with pleas to everyone, from the athletes to the highest officials in government, to end the growing menace to the good health of athletes, officials, and fans.

Fostering and Supporting Player Violence

Television: Violence Is What the Viewers Want

Some of the most respected researchers of television's coverage of sports believe that the mass media highlight and foster violence in a number of ways. Focusing on rough play, replaying spectacular "hits" over and over, and sportscasters praising violent play are three prominent ways violent actions are promoted. Broadcast sports tend to be unrestrained odes to violent action; almost any violent behavior—the more spectacular, the better—is highlighted and given justifications.

In one NFL play-off game, an instant replay showed an offensive lineman clearly and deliberately delivering a viciously illegal elbow into the face of an opponent, virtually twisting off the victim's head. This graphic illegal violence was followed by a comment from one of the sportscasters: "Nobody said this was going to be a tea party!" A similar situation in a televised college football game drew this comment from one of the sportscasters: "Anything that is not called is legal." Camera crews and sportscasters are ever vigilant to the violent collision, the late hit, the shove in the back that can be replayed over and over via instant replay to the horrified fascination of viewers.

As if it weren't enough that people see violent sport actions in person and on television and hear sportscasters praise sport violence, television also

helps sponsor programs whose fundamental ethos is to present gratuitous violence. The highly popular WWE events are, as one commentator put it, "celebrations of violence"—the more outrageous the better—even if not strictly real. But it is a newcomer, mixed martial arts (MMA), the most popular variation of which is UFC, that has captured the golden eighteen-to-thirty-four male demographic. A match ends when one combatant cannot physically continue or gives up. Its show on Spike TV, *The Ultimate Fighter*, has surpassed the TV ratings of the NBA and Major League Baseball (MLB) play-offs. UFC events attract more pay-per-view than any pro wrestling or boxing event. (More about UFC can be found in Chapter 11.)[19]

During NFL seasons 2003–2006, a weekly ESPN segment titled "Jacked Up" highlighted the previous weekend's five most violent legal, noninjury hits. The large voyeuristic audience for shocking, even horrifying, violence was obviously ESPN's target audience for "Jacked Up." However, critics of the program argued that it glorified the violent aspects of football and celebrated cheap shots or injuries, so, despite its popularity, ESPN cancelled the segment. Nevertheless, ESPN, as well as other TV networks, routinely play and replay the most violent actions of sports events.

Sports video games, TV staples for teenage and young adult males, graphically emphasize violent actions. *Madden NFL*, the most popular of these video games, has sold 70 million copies and produced more than $2 billion in sales since it was created in 1989, making the series one of the best-selling in the video game industry's history.

Fans: Violence Reigns

Corporate sports are commercial endeavors, and those who produce the sporting events (professional franchise owners, university athletic departments, etc.) are dependent on fan support. Surveys of fans indicate that spectator enjoyment of games is related to the amount of violence in them. Research findings about viewers' enjoyment of televised sports events clearly indicate that increased player aggressiveness enhances spectators', especially male spectators', enjoyment of watching sports contests. Also, those who perceive high levels of violence in sports events report greater enjoyment than those who perceive low levels of violence.

Related evidence reveals that broadcast commentary stressing roughness of actions facilitates viewers' perceptions of the violence of the event, which, in turn, can lead to greater enjoyment of the sports contest. Finally, play-by-play and color commentary that stresses hostility and animosity between opponents, causing spectators to perceive players' actions as more violent than they really are, can result in greater enjoyment for spectators.[20]

Given the preferences that fans seem to have for violent action, and given that commercial sports must depend on the fans to stay in business, it should not be surprising that the sports industry is quite willing to make sure that violent play is a salient feature of the events. Professional sports executives, coaches, and players frequently exclaim: "We depend on the fans for our existence."

Pressures on Athletes to Be Violent

Pressures exist in sports to use violence, legal and illegal, in the quest for a victory. At all levels of play, incentives exist for athletes to be violent. Coaches teach players the use of intimidating and violent tactics, and peer pressure inspires players to use violence. Athletes are unanimous in saying that the best way to gain coaches' recognition and praise is through aggressive play and, in "contact" sports, to become known for violent hits.

The folklore of the sports world is that aggressive play yields positive results. Youth, high school, and college athletes often either secure a place on the team or are cut from the team, depending on the amount of aggressiveness they display. College athletic scholarships are often awarded by coaches based on the aggressive tendencies shown by recruits. Various financial incentives promote aggressive actions by professional athletes.

Coaches, Owners, Commissioners: Enablers of Violence

Beginning with their first organized sports experience, athletes learn that they must please their coaches if they expect to remain a member of the team. Pleasing the coach often means doing "whatever it takes" to win. Many coaches firmly believe that the most aggressive team wins games; therefore, athletes quickly learn that being aggressive gains the coach's approval. A former NFL player said the message that coaches repeat over and over is that if you're going to make a mistake, make an aggressive one.

Welcoming violent play also applies to dealing with injuries. As one NFL lineman asserted: "If it's not bleeding and it's not completely broken, rub dirt on it and let's go." As we have noted previously in this chapter, concussions are an epidemic in the NFL. Still, one NFL linebacker had this to say about the prospect of incurring a concussion when getting hit: "That's football. It's what makes the game so popular. People love the battle! People love the violence."[21]

Professional team owners refuse to condemn violence because they are convinced it attracts spectators. Among owners and general managers of professional sports franchises there is a tacit agreement that it's hard to justify making changes in the rules to reduce violence because the bottom line is that there are many fans who like it. So it boils down to this: There is no economic incentive to curb violence on the playing field.

Athletes who refuse to participate in violent actions often find themselves demoted on the team roster or even dropped from the team. In professional ice hockey the expectation is that players will participate in fights. One NHL general manager asserted: "Look, we're charged with entertaining you. From the time the puck is dropped, that's what our team will do. That's done with goals, big saves, scoring chances, and a big hit, a fight. I guarantee you—without the requisite level of hitting and fighting, we'd have empty buildings."[22]

Violent Behavior of Athletes in Their Personal Lives

The majority of an athlete's life is lived off the field of play. Even on days in which they practice or play sports, these activities will typically take less than 20 percent of their waking hours. Beyond their role as athletes, athletes do most of the same things that other young people do. They have friends they hang out with, they party, they drink, they develop sexual relationships, they marry and have families, and so forth.

At one time, little was known by the public about what athletes did on their "own" time, nor was it reported by the media. Moreover, if athletes got into trouble of any kind, coaches, owners, administrators, and the media covered it up; "taking care of the athlete" was the explanation given for this action (others have called it a "conspiracy of silence"). In effect, athletes' misbehavior, even unlawful action, was protected from public scrutiny and the criminal justice system.

At the same time that athletes of previous eras were being protected if they ran afoul of the law, they were portrayed as honest, sober, upstanding pillars of the community and role models to be emulated. However, the accumulating literature makes quite clear that in reality many of them engaged in behavior ranging from fun-loving mischief to violent criminal behavior when they were not engaged in playing their sport.[23]

Currently, the private lives and escapades of college and professional athletes in many sports are being spelled out in detail through various mass media. In many cases, it has not been a pretty story because violent criminal behavior, especially sexual assaults and spousal abuse by the athletes, has been a rather persistent theme. The following examples illustrate this point:

- In March 2011 *Sports Illustrated* published a special report about a six-month investigation by *Sports Illustrated* and CBS revealing that an alarming number of players at the twenty-five top college football programs had criminal records. Approximately 7 percent of the players—one out of fourteen—had been in trouble with the law either before or after entering college. Nearly 40 percent of the incidents were serious offenses. Players had been charged with fifty-six violent crimes, such as assault and battery, domestic violence, aggravated assault, robbery, and sex offenses.
- During a sixteen-month period between 2004 and 2005, University of Tennessee football players were involved in some twenty violent incidents involving aggravated assault, gun charges, and disturbing the peace. During the same time period other Southeastern

Conference (SEC) schools had their share of problems off the field: Eleven University of South Carolina players were arrested, and at the University of Georgia three players were suspended for violent off-field incidents and a fourth was kicked off the team.
- NFL player Rae Carruth was found guilty of conspiracy to commit murder, shooting into an occupied vehicle, and using an instrument to destroy an unborn child. He was sentenced to eighteen to twenty-four years in prison.
- In 2007 NFL Atlanta Falcons quarterback Michael Vick admitted that he was involved in an illegal interstate dog-fighting operation. He pleaded guilty to federal felony charges and served twenty-one months in prison, followed by two months in home confinement.
- Pittsburgh Steelers quarterback Ben Roethlisberger has been involved in disreputable incidents that include sexual assault allegations in Lake Tahoe in 2008 and in Milledgeville, Georgia, in 2010. Although neither of the allegations resulted in charges being filed, for the latter allegation the commissioner of the NFL suspended Roethlisberger for six games at the beginning of the 2010 season (reduced to four) under the NFL's personal conduct policy.

There are quite different views about whether athletes as a group, especially athletes in contact sports, commit a greater share of domestic violence and sexual assaults than nonathletes. On one side, largely represented by the sports industry, is the view that the private lives of today's athletes are being scrutinized more closely by the media, and the private-life behaviors of athletes that prevailed for a long time are just now being reported. In this view, big-time college athletes and pro athletes have become celebrities, and, as with other celebrities, there is fierce competition among the media to satisfy the public's appetite for scandal. Finally, it is alleged that many of the reports of athletes' violence against women are inaccurate, charges are dropped, or athletes are not convicted of the charges.

On the other side, there is an acknowledgment that high-profile athletes in the past received special coddling by the media, and their transgressions were ignored or just not reported. But that view doesn't change the empirical evidence in recent years showing that athletes, especially in contact sports, have indeed been overrepresented in domestic violence and sexual assaults. Behavioral and social theories have been employed that suggest that the norms and values of the sport culture socialize athletes into attitudes that valorize male power and control over females, and one outcome is male athletes' propensity toward committing violence against women.[24]

Having said that, we want to emphasize that athletes are not the only assailants and abusers of women. We focus on athletes because this book is about sports. According to the Rape, Abuse & Incest National Network (RAINN), the nation's largest anti–sexual violence organization, one in six women will be sexually assaulted in their lifetime and college women are four times more likely than nonstudents to be sexually assaulted. The U.S. Department of Justice's National Crime Victimization Survey—the country's largest and most reliable crime study—reports nearly 250,000 sexual assaults occur annually. These statistics leave little doubt that male sexual assault against women and spousal abuse are major national social problems and are not unique to the sport world.[25]

Sources for Violence by Male Athletes in Their Private Lives

What accounts for this rather alarming trail of violence by male athletes in their private lives? There is, of course, the fact that they live in a violent culture and that their lives are much more under the media's scrutiny than the average person's. These factors have been previously discussed, but are there other factors? We believe there are at least three other factors that might contribute to this subculture of violence: male bonding rituals, preconditioning to aggressive behavior, and steroid use by many athletes.

Sport Culture and Male Bonding

As part of gender development, both males and females learn culturally prescribed attitudes, rituals, symbols, and behaviors for their sex. Much of this learning, and exhibiting the effects of the learning, take place in sex-segregated activities. Sports teams provide fertile ground especially for male bonding, fostering a spirit of exclusivity, camaraderie, and solidarity among males. Given traditional masculine prescriptions of toughness, dominance, repression of empathy, and competitiveness, athletes may display the effects of this socialization by engaging in reckless and violent behavior as proof of their masculinity. One aspect of this socialization is the attitude that men have a right to dominate women. Sport studies researchers have found that the language of locker room male bonding is a language of power and control over women, of violence against women, and of taking women.

Preconditioning Males for Violence

A number of behavioral and social scientists contend that male socialization tends to be a preconditioning to aggressive behavior as an appropriate response for achieving one's goal, whether it is defending oneself in the streets, making a tackle, or satisfying one's sexual desires against a woman's wishes. Society's concept of masculinity is inextricably woven into aggressive, forceful, physical behavior. Physicality and masculinity have meant the same things for men—male dominance: force, coercion, and the ability to subdue and control the natural world.

The epitome of socially appropriate physical dominance, use of force, and violent action occurs in various sports. Pulitzer Prize–winning journalist H. G. Bissinger spent a year in a Texas community studying its high school football team. His book, *Friday Night Lights: A Town, a Team, and a Dream*, was turned into a movie and then into a popular TV series. All three describe what the players did and what they talked about, much of which was about "hitting" or "sticking" or "popping" someone. These were the things that coaches exhorted players to do. The supreme compliment was to be called a "hitter" or "headhunter." A hitter made bone-crushing tackles that knocked out or hurt his opponents. The book was about something rather small—the culture of high school football in a Texas town—but it and the movie and TV series ended up being about something large—the core values in North America.

Sociologist Derek A. Kreager studied whether participation in contact sports by teenagers also promoted violence off the field and found that involvement in contact sports such as football and wrestling did indeed increase the likelihood of off-field violent behavior.[26] This suggests that a culture of violence can be nurtured on the sporting field. Behavior learned in one context, where it is appropriate, can be transferred to another, where it is not.

Steroid Use and Male Violent Behavior

There is a myriad of evidence that anabolic steroid use is widespread in many sports at the high school, collegiate, and professional levels, especially in sports involving physical contact and feats of strength. There is also convincing anecdotal as well as some empirical evidence showing that the regular use of anabolic steroids can trigger episodes of aggressive behavior in users. Researchers who have studied the effects of steroid abuse agree that athletes who are steroid users seem more inclined to extremely violent behavior than nonuser.[27] The issue of steroid use in sports is taken up again in the section "Substance Abuse and Sport" in this chapter.

Concluding Thoughts on Violence by Male Athletes in Their Private Lives

Undoubtedly, these and other factors can interact in any given situation or incident that ultimately leads to violent, even criminal, behavior by athletes. We want to emphasize, though, that we recognize that the actual percentage of athletes at any level and in any sport who are involved in violence off the field is very small. Nevertheless, there are enough incidents, and they are serious enough, for all of us to be concerned. Concerted efforts need to be made by everyone involved in sport to find ways and means to reduce, even eliminate, the sexual assaultive and domestic violence by athletes that have become all too familiar.

One effort to do something about this problem has been initiated by a woman who was raped by a football player while she was a college student. She has formed the National Coalition Against Violent Athletes (NCAVA). The purpose of the NCAVA is to educate the public on various issues involving athletes and violence, while also providing support to the victims.[28] See Box 7.2 for more information about the NCAVA.

Box 7.2   *Thinking About Sport:* The National Coalition Against Violent Athletes

One of the valuable roles increasingly being played by the Internet is providing a means by which fledgling organizations can quickly communicate with large numbers of people about a social problem, educate them about that social problem, bring those who wish to do something about the problem into contact with one another, and even mobilize people into action to resolve the problem. Those are the purposes behind the founding of the National Coalition Against Violent Athletes. The website of the NCAVA states the following:

The National Coalition Against Violent Athletes was formed in 1997 in response to the growing number of violent crimes committed by athletes in all areas of the sports world. This organization is based solely on the fact that athletes should be held to the same standards and laws as the rest of society.

GAME PLAN

The purpose of the National Coalition Against Violent Athletes is to educate the public on a variety of issues regarding athletes and violent behavior, while also providing support to the victims, including, but not limited to, advocacy, referrals and research. We also strive to promote positive athlete development through education, support and accountability. In doing so, we work to curb the escalation of athlete violence and create an environment in which people are equally respected and equally held accountable. We therefore assail the entitlement given to athletes through a system in which athletes have little fear of reprisal. In doing so, we can help restore the sports world to a former level of respectability while helping its victims restore their sense of value and self-worth.

Source: National Coalition Against Violent Athletes, http://www.ncava.org.

Athletes' Violence Against Teammates: Hazing

Rites of passage are a common feature of many cultures. They are rituals and ceremonies through which people must pass in the transition from one group to another within the culture. Perhaps the most common rites of passage are those that young boys and girls must pass through to become recognized as full-fledged adult men and women of that society. The rites-of-passage principle has also been adopted by many organizations—military, business, social, sport—and specific rituals and ceremonies are established to initiate new members.

Rites of passage, in the form of initiation ceremonies and rituals, became a popular part of belonging to a sports team from the beginning of modern organized sports. But also from the beginning many teams employed a variation called "hazing." Sport hazing involves humiliating, degrading, or endangering the initiate, and it predominately operates as a male-defined, male-dominated practice. Nevertheless, hazing has been a normalized practice (especially in high school and college sports) that resists pressures to change. Many initiates have been seriously harmed physically and/or psychologically.

Administrators periodically attempt to put an end to hazing, but their efforts have been largely unsuccessful. In a survey in three western Canadian cities with amateur and professional teams competing in eight contact sports and three noncontact sports, two sport sociologists found that hazing occurred routinely but in varying degrees across the sports. They concluded that despite increasing social disapproval and closer policing, hazing continues to play a significant role in both men's and women's sports teams. In related research, two University of Northern Iowa investigators obtained corroborating evidence, noting that "athletes reported engaging in risky, hazing behaviors and that both the values of sport as well as the desire to be accepted by teammates encouraged hazing."[29]

In the past few years dozens of high schools and colleges have had hazing incidents in which school officials placed teams on probation, required that team members perform community service, or suspended team members from school or college. To give the reader some understanding of the kinds of hazing incidents that have occurred, several excerpts follow:

- 2006, Molalla High School, Molalla, Oregon: This was a case of alleged sexual hazing and one count of alleged sodomy. Five players were sentenced to short jail terms after they admitted assaulting a younger teammate during hazing incidents on road trips.
- 2007, University of California (UC), Berkeley: Eight Cal baseball players were cited by UC police for participating in hazing six freshman players. According to a police report, UC Police Department officers found the eight veteran baseball players with six freshman players who were wearing only G-string underwear and shoes just after 11 P.M. The six freshmen were standing outside in the 34-degree weather. The hazing activities were just beginning.
- 2007, University of Maine: For violating school policies that prohibit hazing, the university's softball team was placed on probation for three years and the start of the 2008 season was delayed by one week.
- 2010, Springfield, Massachusetts: A hazing incident inside the boy's locker room at Agawam High School in western Massachusetts landed four players and four coaches on suspension from the team and school for ten days.[30]

Similar incidents have occurred in virtually every corner of North America, where initiates have been showered with mixtures of urine and vomit, brutally paddled, or sodomized.

Because hazing has historically been prominent at the high school and college levels, in recent years governing bodies throughout North America have been furiously busy developing no-hazing policies. The NCAA recently published a manual for its member institutions and athletes that includes guidelines on hazing.[31] Their efforts are commendable, but individuals and organizations that develop no-hazing policies face several barriers to eliminating hazing: denial of the problem, arguments that hazing is harmless, silence among victims, fear among victims, and cultural norms that perceive hazing as normal.

SPORTS FANS: VIOLENT AND ABUSIVE ACTIONS

Spectators at a sporting event are not usually passive observers. Typically, they like to "get into it," to become part of the game, as it were. But sometimes their enthusiasm turns into violent and abusive actions. And this is not merely a contemporary phenomenon, nor is it confined to North American sports.

The word *fan* is short for *fanatic* and comes from the Latin word *fanum*. The Romans used the word to describe persons who were overly zealous while attending the chariot races. In one renowned spectator riot at the chariot races in ancient Rome, some 30,000 fans were killed. In 1969 in a World Cup soccer series between El Salvador and Honduras, spectator violence accompanied each of the games. Finally, the riot that followed the third game resulted in the two countries severing political and economic relations and mobilizing their armies against each other; this has been called the "soccer war" between El Salvador and Honduras.

Traditional but typically good-natured heckling of players, coaches, officials, and opponents has taken on a completely new attribute in the past decade. Fans—especially at professional and collegiate sports events—are increasingly resorting to abusive and obscene language. In addition to vocal communication, placards and apparel emblazoned with obscenities are displayed. Student sections at some universities compete to be the most outrageous, vicious, obscene, and offensive, and they believe they have a constitutional (First Amendment free speech) right to engage in such behavior.

Everyone who follows North American sports is quite aware of the many incidents of spectator violence. Several years ago *Sports Illustrated* took what it called an "unscientific poll of fans" and reported that everyone who confirmed having ever been to

a sporting event had witnessed one or more acts of violent behavior by fans. Within the past decade, major fan violence has erupted in all of the professional team sports (NFL, NHL, NBA, and MLB). It has also penetrated into high school and university campuses, where football and basketball games have been marred by riots. Indeed, due to frequent spectator riots at high school sports events, several large city school systems have imposed strict limits on the number of spectators admitted to basketball games in an effort to prevent fights between fans and opposing teams. Several universities have stopped scheduling games against traditional rivals because of fan violence that has accompanied the contests.[32]

Newspaper and magazine articles describing, and usually condemning, a seemingly escalating amount of fan violence are common. "Sports in USA Sick: Violence Out of Hand," "Fans Behaving Badly," and "Uncivil Disobedience" are examples of article titles found in the popular press. The theme of all of these is a contention that an excessively violent equilibrium exists in sports today at almost all levels.

Factors Associated with Fan Violence

Behavioral and social scientists seeking to understand and explain spectator violence and abusive actions tend to center their explanations on fans' social learning and experiences in the wider society. In support of this, there is widespread agreement—and a burgeoning list of recent books to support it—that there is an increasing lack of civility in North American society. This is manifested in growing violence and incivility in all of the major social institutions, including family, schools, business, politics, and media.

Hardly a week passes without some major incidence of violence or interpersonal abuse in these social arenas. Moreover, all of the major sports themselves have become more violent, not only in the games but in the alarming lack of sportsmanship on the field and the widespread trash-talking among the athletes. Given the cultural background pervading fans' general social experiences, it is hardly a coincidence that fan violence and obnoxious actions are escalating.[33]

Although actions during sporting events may play a contributing role in fans' violent and abusive behavior, most behavioral scientists reject cathartic explanations. Instead, they contend that violence viewed in sport contributes to violence in the crowd. A fundamental principle of social learning is that people learn what they observe, and if what they observe goes unpunished, they are likely to consider it appropriate for themselves.

The sequence of witnessing violence-learning-acting might proceed in this manner: Fans watching a violent sporting event are likely to become more aggressively inclined themselves; as they witness violent behavior, they might, under just the right circumstances, act violently themselves. Of course, as we emphasized earlier in this chapter, learning the heritage and culture of violence is the lived experience of everyone in North America, so sports fans have more than their immediate experiences in the stadium or arena mediating a mind-set for violence.

There are other factors as well that can precipitate spectator violence and abusive behavior that go beyond just broad enculturation and witnessing these behaviors in sports. Two forms of "perceived injustice" can trigger fan anger and abuse. The first form occurs when fans believe that officials have applied a rule unfairly or inaccurately; the second occurs when fans believe that a rule itself is unfair, regardless of how accurately employed.[34]

Bad calls by officials, such as calling a batted baseball foul when it was fair or calling a made basket from three-point range two points, are examples of the first. An example of the second might occur when a penalty kick is awarded near the end of a tie game in soccer; since it is such a high-percentage kick, it will almost always result in a victory for the kicking team. The penalty kick in soccer is uniformly condemned as unfair by soccer fans, so a situation as just described may precipitate fan violence.

Social scientists have suggested five social situational factors that can be conducive to spectator violence. They are (1) a large crowd, because of a perceived power inherent in a mass of people, and the anonymity foments irresponsible behavior; (2) a dense crowd, because annoyance and frustration build when one's comfortable space is violated and when one is forced to be near strangers; (3) a noisy crowd, because noise is itself arousing, and arousal is a common precondition to violence; (4) a standing crowd, because standing for long periods is tiring, jostling is common, and the lack of an assigned space is frustrating; and (5) crowd composition, because drinking crowds, young male crowds, and crowds made up of people who are oppressed in the larger society are more predisposed toward violent behavior than more diverse crowds.

Game and Postgame Violence

Recent years have witnessed several violent incidents involving athletes and fans during or immediately after a sports event. There are far too many of these incidents each year to list all of them. But below we summarize a few examples from the past few years.

- During the first half of his first game back following a loan to AC Milan (Italy), LA Galaxy superstar David Beckham was met with obscene chants by fans who were angry that he had expressed a desire to remain with the Italian soccer club. At halftime, Beckham was held back by security from climbing over a barrier to confront an intoxicated fan who had run onto the pitch. The fan was arrested and banned from attending LA Galaxy home games for life, and Beckham was fined $1,000 for the incident.
- After the first home game of the Los Angeles Dodgers 2011 season at Dodger Stadium, two men in Dodgers clothing followed three men in San Francisco Giants gear as they walked to their car after the game. Witnesses said the attackers yelled slurs against the Giants and began kicking and punching the men. One victim suffered a head injury and was hospitalized in critical condition with a severe skull fracture and bad bruising to his brain's frontal lobes. He remained in a coma for weeks.
- At a 2011 *preseason* NFL football game between the Oakland Raiders and San Francisco 49ers at Candlestick Park, mayhem between fans erupted in the stands. Seventy were ejected

from the park, twelve were arrested, two were shot in the parking lot, and one was savagely beaten in a restroom. The president of a sports consulting firm noted, "The viciousness, the escalation of violence is what is so striking. It's escalated, perhaps, as a reflection of society."

Player-fan incidents are not new to sports, but the frequency of these types of violent incidents has been on the upswing for years.[35]

There is a lengthy tradition of sports fans celebrating the winning of a championship, tournament, or contest against a bitter rival. Violence often accompanies these celebrations in stadiums and arenas, as fans storm the playing area. In football, fans tear down the goalposts; in basketball, they clip the basket nets; in hockey, they throw objects onto the ice; and so forth. Frequently these celebrations became violent because security officials attempt to thwart such actions and fans of the losing teams resent the celebrations and taunt and start fights with the celebrants. Sometimes celebratory stampedes move to city streets after an important victory. Revelers set bonfires, destroy property, turn over automobiles, and attack police and security personnel. Conversely, crucial losses by a home team have triggered similar violent street actions.

A unique form of fan celebration that has become widespread in recent years is called court or field storming. Fans pour out of the stands in celebration of an exciting victory, applauding the players, backslapping them, and sometimes lifting them into the air. With the popularity of these stormings, injuries to fans and players have occurred. One of the most shocking and disturbing took place several years ago after a high school basketball game in Tucson, Arizona. A player dunked the ball at the end of a big home win, igniting a frenzied fan celebration. The player was grabbed, tackled, and trampled. He suffered a stroke and paralysis on his right side and has never fully recovered his physical and mental health. Dozens of court/field storming incidents like this one have resulted in injuries to players and fans.

Up to this point in time, North American sport studies scholars have done little research on these forms of sports violence. Most British and European research on sports crowd violence has centered on soccer riots and "hooliganism." Several have explained this behavior in terms of the working-class roots of soccer fans, their team loyalties, and their resentment of and alienation from the larger society. Informal analyses of postgame crowd violence at North American sports events suggest that there is little commonality between the European and British soccer fans and North American college and professional sports fans.[36]

Reducing Fan Violence and Abusive Behavior

Numerous suggestions for reducing spectator violence have been proposed by researchers of violence. Common suggestions include improving the physical facilities and appearances of stadiums and arenas, making them more attractive and less foreboding places; increasing the numbers of security forces at sporting events; limiting the sale of alcohol (already done in some stadiums and arenas); changing the rules of some sports, such as soccer, to make scoring easier; keeping violence under control on the field by preventing fights, excessive displays of anger or aggression by athletes, and arm-waving displays of disapproval of officials' calls by coaches and athletes; and severely punishing offenders.

Sports administrators at all levels have been considering various options to stop court/field stormings. Professional sports and university attorneys have been asked to seek legal opinions over whether they can eject fans from games for abusive actions. University presidents, coaches, and athletic directors have been trying moral suasion, asking for civil behavior among student fans. Several university conferences have considered disbanding student sections.

All of these strategies might indeed reduce fan violence abuse to some extent. However, none of them deals with the larger, structural issue of the heritage and culture of violence and incivility that underlie much of the culture of contemporary North American society beyond the confines of sports but nevertheless affect both athletes and fans alike.[37]

SUBSTANCE ABUSE AND SPORT

Substance abuse is considered such a significant social problem that the U.S. government has pursued a "War on Drugs" for more than forty years. But according to experts who study the importation and use of drugs, drug abuse is still widespread. A recent survey by the federal Substance Abuse and Mental Health Services Administration (SAMHSA) found that nearly one in ten Americans twelve years and older regularly use illicit drugs. Drug use among young adults between eighteen and twenty-five years of age is double that of the general population.

Newspaper and magazine headlines tell of substance abuse in sports: "Steroids Are Just a Click Away," "Drug-Free Sports Might Be Thing of the Past," "Tour de France's Downhill Slide: Doping Scandals Sully World's Biggest Bike Race." The stories that follow these headlines poignantly tell of North America's athletes' involvement with substance abuse. Athletes use a myriad of performance-enhancing drugs, and the laboratories and agencies that test for and regulate athletes' use of these substances find it almost impossible to detect and control all the drugs used, in spite of the advanced technologies they are able to employ. Perhaps the most disturbing feature of this scenario is the indifference of fans to doping by athletes, making it doubtful that sports will ever be drug-free.

Substance Abuse Not New to Sports

The use of substances to enhance performance has been present throughout the history of organized sports. The ancient Greek athletes consumed mushrooms in the belief that they improved performance, and Roman gladiators used a variety of stimulants to hype them up and forestall fatigue. Athletes throughout the nineteenth century experimented with caffeine, alcohol, nitroglycerine, opium, and strychnine. Strychnine, cocaine, alcohol, and caffeine mixtures were used by boxers, cyclists, and British and European soccer players before World War II. Amphetamines and steroids began their rise to the drugs of choice among athletes in the years immediately after World War II.

The Scope of Current Substance Abuse in Sport

As anyone who has followed sports in the past few years knows, any short list of drug-use issues will represent only a speck of dust in the universe of substance abuse in the sports world. Indeed, some knowledgeable authorities believe that substance use by athletes is epidemic in scope, all the way from high school to the professional level (we include Olympic athletes as professionals).

The variety of substances that athletes use in hope of improving their performance has become astounding: Growth-retardant hormones are used by female gymnasts to prolong their careers; archers and shooters use beta-blockers to slow their heart rate for steadier aiming; swimmers use nasal decongestants to enhance airflow through their lungs; weight lifters use amphetamines to release vast amounts of adrenalin into the blood and speed up the systems used for strength activities; endurance athletes use recombinant erythropoietin (EPO) to stimulate the production of red blood cells that transport oxygen throughout the body, thereby improving endurance; wrestlers and boxers use diuretics for weight loss to compete at lower weight classes; and drug-using athletes in many sports use diuretics to minimize detection of other drugs by diluting the urine.[38] Table 7.1 lists the performance-enhancing drugs most commonly used by athletes.

Anabolic Steroids: Promises Big and Strong

Anabolic steroids have been a popular drug of choice for athletes for several decades. (See Box 7.3 for a description of steroids.) For several years the U.S. Department of Health and Human Services has been surveying secondary school students who admit to using steroids. Typically some 40,000 students in more than 400 schools are surveyed each year. Table 7.2 shows the trend for steroid use over the ten-year period from 2000 to 2010. These students might not all be athletes; indeed, if only athletes were surveyed, the percentages would likely be much higher.[39] However, an accurate assessment of steroid use by secondary school athletes is very difficult. Converting the percentages to numbers

Table 7.1   Performance-Enhancing Substances Most Commonly Used by Athletes

Substance	Expected Benefit	Users	Side Effects
Steroids	Promotes muscle growth	Speed, power, endurance athletes	Masculinization of females, feminization of males, liver and heart damage, mood changes
Testosterone	Promotes muscle growth	Speed, power, endurance athletes	Same as steroids
Human growth hormone	Promotes muscle growth	Speed, power athletes	Gigantism, joint and jaw enlargement
Erythropoietin (EPO)	Produces red blood cells	Endurance athletes	Thickened blood leading to stroke or heart problems
Androstenedione (Andro)	Promotes muscle growth	Speed, power, endurance athletes	Similar to steroids
Creatine	Energizes muscle function	Quick, power, speed athletes	Dehydration, muscle cramping, intestinal problems

Box 7.3   *Thinking About Sport: Steroids: What Are They? Effects? Dangers?*

WHAT THEY ARE

Anabolic-androgenic steroids are synthetic forms of testosterone, which is a male hormone that is naturally present in the human body. They are taken either orally or by injection into the muscle.

THEIR EFFECTS

Steroids increase lean body mass, increase strength, increase muscle definition, decrease recovery time from exercise, and increase aggressiveness.

THEIR DANGERS

Steroids cause testicular shrinkage and reduce testosterone production. They also cause benign and malignant liver tumors, bizarre and violent personality changes, and feminized characteristics of males and masculinized characteristics of females.

Table 7.2   Tracking the Trend of Steroid Use Among Secondary School Students (in percentages of total number of students per grade)

Grade Level	2000	2006	2010
Eighth-Graders			
Male	2.2	1.2	0.7
Female	1.2	0.6	0.5
Tenth-Graders			
Male	3.6	1.9	1.3
Female	0.8	0.5	1.0
Twelfth-Graders			
Male	2.5	2.7	2.5
Female	1.1	0.7	1.5

Source: Adapted from *Monitoring the Future: National Results on Adolescent Drug Use: Overview of Key Findings 2010* (Bethesda, MD: National Institutes of Health, National Institute on Drug Abuse, 2010).

of steroid users, eminent expert on sports and steroids Charles Yesalis estimates that well over 1 million young people in the United States have used steroids at one time or another.

Studies of steroid use in intercollegiate athletics vary widely in their results. One study reported that 9.7 percent of college football players acknowledged using the drug. At the other

extreme, in June 2010 the NCAA released a report indicating that positive drug tests for steroids have minimally increased. According to the NCAA, "[T]he year-round testing program from 2008–09 revealed that 72 student-athletes tested positive for anabolic agents (steroids,) compared with 57 in 2007–08 and 27 in 2006–07. Forty-seven of the 72 positive tests have been confirmed, while 25 positives were considered 'inconclusive' and were not sanctioned. While the 72 positives in the most recent cohort are the highest since 2002, it represents just 0.6 percent of the total testing population (11,088 student-athletes)."[40] From these figures, the NCAA claimed that steroid use had only minimally increased, thus displaying complete naïveté about the sophisticated methods athletes use to avoid testing positive. Physicians who have experience with steroid users say that users have found numerous ways to beat the drug-testing systems; drug testing isn't the threat to drug-using athletes that sport organizations often portray it to be.

The situation is similar with professional and Olympic-level athletes. Use is greatest in athletes for whom power, strength, speed, and bulk are important. NFL athletes, coaches, and trainers have claimed that up to 75 percent of NFL players use or have used steroids. It has become clear in the past few years that steroid use is still present in Major League Baseball too, in spite of a stepped-up testing program now employed. It has been estimated that three to eight players per major league team are using or have used steroids.[41] In spite of the increase in testing athletes for steroid use by sport organizations at every level, Yesalis claims that the level of steroid use appears to have increased significantly over the past three decades and is no longer limited to elite athletes or men.

One of the newest trends in sport substance abuse is the use of nutritional supplements. Sales of nutritional supplements reached more than $25 billion in North America in 2011. The sports supplement industry operates, as the director of the Exercise and Biochemical Nutrition Laboratory at Baylor puts it, a "Pandora's Box of false claims, untested products and bogus science."[42] But nutritional supplements are touted by their manufacturers, and hyped by many athletes, as muscle-building aids for increasing muscle size and strength. Many are not banned by most sport governing bodies, nor are they illegal drugs. One in five Ohio high school athletes said that they used supplements to enhance performance. At the national level, between 8 and 12 percent of high school male athletes have said they were using creatine. As many as 60 percent of collegiate male and female athletes report having used nutritional supplements, creatine being one of them.

Up to 50 percent of professional athletes in some sports have used creatine. But the use of this substance seems to have peaked in recent years, primarily because it has become associated with more dangerous performance-enhancing substances, such as anabolic steroids. Supporting this alleged association, professional athletes, such as major league home-run king Barry Bonds, have admitted to using creatine. Bonds is suspected of also using steroids.

Other nutritional supplements that are popular in the athlete culture include cold medications, diet pills, energy pills, and sports drinks, most of which contain ephedra, or synthetic forms of ephedrine. Ephedrine stimulates the central nervous system and thus is an amphetamine-like stimulant.

Human growth hormone (HGH) releasers and gene therapy doping are two other performance enhancers. The first stimulates the pituitary gland into overproducing the natural form of the hormone, which influences the body's growth, cell production, and metabolism. This can boost muscle growth, decrease body fat, and aid in recovery from strenuous sports competition. Gene doping is considered by many experts to be the next frontier for athletes seeking a biologic edge. The experts also agree that it is years away, but the World Anti-Doping Agency, which sets the rules on banned substances, has already outlawed gene doping.

In addition to using performance-enhancing substances, athletes, like the general population, are deeply involved in what are called "recreational" drugs. The main culprit has historically been alcohol—serious enough, to be sure, but not as deadly or debilitating a substance as cocaine, crack, heroin, or speed. Furthermore, the extent of cocaine, crack, heroin, and speed usage is minuscule compared to that of alcohol usage.

Alcoholic beverages have long been one of the most widely used substances by young people. In a 2010 national study of adolescent drug use, 29 percent of high school sophomores and 41 percent of seniors admitted drinking alcohol in the thirty-day period prior to the survey. A survey of almost 800 high school coaches asked them what they considered the greatest threat to athletes on their teams. Their responses: alcohol 88 percent, cocaine/crack 6 percent, marijuana 3 percent, steroids 1 percent.[43]

College students have a well-earned reputation for frequent consumption of alcohol, and several research findings indicate that male college athletes consume more alcohol and more of them binge-drink than male nonathletes. Female athletes consume more alcoholic drinks than female nonathletes.[44] Although the actual incidence of alcohol consumption by professional athletes has not been studied, so many pro athletes have been arrested for drunkenness that eyebrows are hardly raised anymore when such incidents are reported on television or in newspapers. Several high-profile pro athletes have been involved in fatal accidents in which alcohol played a role.

The use of cocaine, crack, heroin, and speed by athletes may be small compared to that of alcohol, but this does not mean it is insignificant. In one study of intercollegiate athletes, 17 percent acknowledged using cocaine in the prior year; two years later, in a study of elite women athletes, 7 percent reported using cocaine, about half of these saying they used it before or during competition. Players representing nearly all of the professional sport leagues have been involved with cocaine use in criminal cases, with some teams having several players arrested.

Sports Anti-Doping Programs in North America

Several organizations have been created to control—even eliminate—the use of performance-enhancing products and practices. We list below those with the most comprehensive anti-doping programs.

- The U.S. Anti-Doping Agency (USADA) is the national anti-doping organization for the Olympic and Paralympic Movement in the United States. It works to preserve the integrity of competition, inspire true sport, and protect the rights of athletes in this movement.
- The Canadian Anti-Doping Program (CADP) integrates several new national and international developments, described below.
- The World Anti-Doping Code (WADC) and mandatory International Standard requirements were formally accepted by the

Canadian Centre for Ethics in Sport (CCES) in March 2003. The code is expected to result in better anti-doping programs for the athletes against whom Canadians compete internationally.
- The Canadian Policy Against Doping in Sport (CPADS) was approved by federal, provincial, and territorial governments. The CPADS is committed to safeguarding the integrity and values of sport by deterring the use of banned substances and providing methods to protect those who commit themselves to sport based on the principles of fair play.
- The Physical Activity and Sport Act was passed in March 2003. It sets out the Canadian government's new approach to physical activity and sport and establishes the Sport Dispute Resolution Centre of Canada.
- The Canadian Strategy for Ethical Conduct in Sport was approved by federal, provincial, and territorial sport ministers. It calls for a comprehensive domestic anti-doping policy that emphasizes prevention and education and establishes clear roles and responsibilities for all stakeholders, especially governments.[45]

Social/Cultural Influences and Substance Abuse Among Athletes

Why do athletes risk their health and their opportunity to compete by using performance-enhancing drugs? There is, of course, no single answer to this question because athletes have different reasons. But athletes are a part of a much larger social community, wherein substance abuse is rampant. Athletes are not immune to the societal influences under which they live. In their world, athletes see drug use all around them: aspirin, tranquilizers, amphetamines, heroin, diet pills, and so forth.

Drug use among athletes must be understood in the context of an increasingly drug-obsessed society. It is not realistic to expect athletes to insulate themselves from a culture in which pharmacists and doctors supply medicines for all symptoms, both physical and psychological. Indeed, some experts on drug abuse refer to the United States as a "Drug

Nation," and that portrayal seems accurate. If the world's countries are divided into those with high-, medium-, and low-level drug problems, the United States is the only developed country that falls into the "high-level" category.

Young athletes are especially susceptible to what they see and hear from high-profile athletes. They often hear TV sportscasters report that a given athlete was given pain suppressants, such as morphine, so that he could play in the game that day. During a Monday Night NFL football game, one of the sportscasters commented approvingly about a quarterback, "Here's a guy who probably had to take a painkiller shot in his lower back so he could play tonight." Many young athletes have seen athletic trainers' rooms, rooms that are filled with all kinds of salves, ointments, and pills, all used to help athletes perform at their best. Is it any wonder that young athletes believe that drugs are widely used in sports? The sports culture itself promotes drug usage.

Another factor that motivates young athletes to turn to chemicals for performance enhancement is that there is enormous social status that goes with being an athlete; as we noted in Chapter 5, being an athlete is admired by both males and females. Most people do not understand how or the extent to which the system of sport and its status-conferring and rewarding properties often lead athletes to a commitment in which they are willing to risk anything, even their life, to achieve their goal. A hypothetical scenario was posed to 198 U.S. Olympians and aspiring Olympians who were sprinters, swimmers, power lifters, and other assorted athletes:

> Suppose you are offered a performance enhancing substance with two guarantees, if you choose to use it: You will win every competition you enter until you win an Olympic Gold Medal. But the substance will cause your death within a year after your achievements. Would you take it? More than 50 percent of the responding athletes said yes![46]

There are other temptations. The best high school athletes are recruited to colleges with "full ride" scholarships—a college education with basic expenses paid. Although there are very few who ultimately become professional athletes or Olympic champions, there are millions of young athletes who devote themselves to years of training and personal sacrifice in attempting to attain this lofty goal. At every level the competition is keen, and athletes know that they must continue to improve if they are to move to the next rung of the ladder.

Many literally devote their lives to the quest to move onward and upward, and they will try anything that will aid them in their quest. Thus, athletes striving to improve often believe that any substance that could give them even the slightest advantage over their opponents is worth trying. Rather than depending upon legitimate training methods and developing a sound approach to their sport, some athletes choose to rely upon drugs to improve their performance.

It is very difficult for young athletes to do their best when they know they might be competing against athletes who are using substances that may be performance enhancing. During the time Dr. Robert Voy was director of drug testing for the U.S. Olympic Committee, he claimed that most of the athletes didn't want to do drugs. They would come to him and say that unless drug abuse in sport was stopped, "we *have* to do drugs." Their argument was that if they didn't use drugs, after years of training to be an Olympian they would be cheated out of a medal by athletes from Europe or Asia who were doing drugs.

Another factor in substance abuse among athletes is that at the high school, college, and professional levels, coaches pressure athletes to improve their performance. Some coaches put demands on athletes to increase their strength and endurance, reduce or increase their weight, and play while injured, knowing such conditions can only be met through the use of substances that are banned. These coaches want world records and bigger-than-life athletes with tremendous physical capacities that yield medals and championships. To meet these demands, some athletes resort to drugs to enhance their performance or to allow them to play when hurt.[47]

Finally, there is the ambiguity (perhaps hypocrisy) in all of the links athletes see every day between sports and substance abuse. They see the cozy financial connection between alcohol and tobacco and big-time sports. Beer and tobacco companies are the number one sponsors and underwriters of sporting events. Beer ads dominate concession stands and scoreboards at sports venues; beer commercials dominate TV and radio advertising during sports events. It is virtually impossible to watch or listen to a sporting event in North America without feeling overwhelmed by beer ads. The St. Louis Cardinals baseball team is owned by Anheuser-Busch, which is the largest beer maker in North America, and this beer company is one of the top five media advertisers during sporting events in North America. The Colorado Rockies baseball team plays in Coors (beer) Field.

As we noted above, alcohol is without question the most abused drug in sport, and a number of college sport officials acknowledge that alcohol is a much more pervasive problem for collegiate athletes than other substances. Still, professional leagues, Canadian and American Olympic sports organizations, and the NCAA happily accept advertising money generated by alcohol companies.

It is little wonder that athletes resort to using performance-enhancing substances. When the rules and customs governing drug use in both the larger society and the sports world itself seem arbitrary and inconsistent, it is easy to understand why athletes may view the use of these substances as acceptable and normative behavior, in spite of the distortions they bring to the ethics of sport competition and their potentially devastating consequences to health and well-being.

Can Substance Abuse in Sports Be Reduced, Even Prevented?

Although the evidence, incomplete as it is, strongly suggests that in terms of percentages only a minority of athletes at any level has a substance abuse problem, there is still the question of what is to be done with the small number who are substance abusers. There are several options, but the one that has received the most attention is the drug-testing programs of the various sports' governing bodies. But these programs have had limited success and many failures at this point. To a large extent this is because they have been implemented without fully resolving at least two important questions: (1) What

are the athletes' individual rights? (2) What are the athletes' responsibilities?

Drug Testing and Athletes' Rights

With respect to athletes' rights, the Fourth Amendment to the U.S. Constitution forbids any unreasonable searches and seizures, or any intrusions on human dignity and privacy, simply on the hunch that incriminating evidence might be found; this protects all U.S. citizens, including athletes. The U.S. Supreme Court has ruled that extracting bodily fluids—such as urine tests—constitutes a search within the meaning of this amendment. The U.S. Constitution, however, protects persons only from intrusion by government, and furthermore, because there can be different interpretations of "reasonableness," this has become a complicated issue involving a balancing of the invasion of personal rights and the need for the search.

Determination of reasonableness requires that the court balance an individual's privacy rights against the government's legitimate interests in deterring drug use. The U.S. Supreme Court has twice made exceptions to students' privacy rights to enable schools to make random drug tests of athletes and other students who participate in extracurricular activities. Still, mandatory, random drug testing is not a fully settled issue in the U.S. court system.[48]

Although some of the major sport organizations, such as the International Olympic Committee, the NCAA, and the National Football League, have taken the lead in mandatory and random drug testing, considering it necessary and appropriate, there are many critics as well. Two Canadian health scientists argue that "the invasion of privacy caused by effective anti-doping measures cannot be justified solely by the good those measures seek to attain. . . . For drug-free sport we need effective enforcement. But the steps required for effective enforcement can be invasive of athletes' rights, particularly the personal right to privacy."[49] They propose an alternative, a way that shares ownership of the rules of sport, and the methods for enforcing those rules, with those most affected by them: the athletes.

Several unresolved issues exist where drug testing has been implemented. The validity and accuracy of the tests have been a continuing controversy, and rightly so, because the test results are not infallible. Drug-testing programs in professional sports have been frequently found to be misleading to the public and unfair to the players. Several sport organizations that now routinely test their athletes do not even have an appellate process in place; thus, an athlete who tests positive does not have a process for appealing the results of the tests.

Another unresolved issue is that sport organizations do not seem to understand or acknowledge that the social conditions of high-pressure sports may actually contribute to drug abuse by athletes. There is a substantial literature documenting the pressures and incredible time demands that go with being a high school, major university, or professional athlete. It does not appear to be stretching the imagination to think that some of these pressures contribute to substance abuse by athletes.

Medical professionals, health educators, and other knowledgeable professionals who have been critical of drug-testing programs acknowledge the social structural factors that cultivate drug abuse by athletes, but they are skeptical about any immediate changes that will discourage athletes from abusing drugs. They are also scornful of random drug testing as a viable tool for behavior change. Instead, many believe that drug education programs can make a better contribution as a key component of drug abuse prevention. Not just any drug education program will do, however; certainly the "one shot" efforts used by many high schools, universities, and professional teams are largely a waste of time. The fundamental strength of any substance abuse prevention program for athletes should be through education, and drug education must include more than just giving information or threatening athletes with punishment for substance abuse. Such programs need to help athletes avoid making decisions about drugs that they may regret for the rest of their lives.[50]

What Are the Responsibilities of Athletes?

Regarding athletes' responsibilities to abstain from substance abuse, various lists have been compiled that range from the personal responsibility that athletes have for keeping their bodies in excellent physical condition to their responsibilities as

society's role models to their responsibilities to spectators who pay money to watch their performances. These appear to be good "common sense" reasons for athletes to abstain from drug abuse, but they ignore a number of related issues. For example, it does not take in-depth investigating into equitable treatment provisions in sports to see how blatantly athletes are victimized by the drug testing system. Although athletes often must undergo mandatory, random drug testing, there is no provision for coaches, athletic directors, sports information directors, athletic trainers, athletic secretaries, and various and sundry others who are part of the big business of sports to undergo the same testing. Instead, the public is encouraged to dwell only on drug use by athletes.

The structure of society, especially at the level of its political and economic institutions, is responsible for many of the problems associated with drug abuse among North Americans. At a more microsocial level, the political economy of sports has contributed to drug abuse among athletes. Thus, solutions to drug abuse among athletes must begin with structural modifications in the larger society as well as in sport culture; when this happens, serious amelioration of drug abuse among athletes will occur.

In the best of all possible worlds—a world for which we should all be striving—there would be no place for drug abuse among athletes. Use of performance-enhancing drugs corrupts the essence of fair sporting competition; it is cheating. As serious as this is within the bounded world of sport, performance-enhancing and recreational drug abuse is improper for a more important reason: It is dangerous to personal health; its use is an unnecessary health risk.

EATING DISORDERS IN SPORT

While steroid use is prevalent among male athletes who are trying to bulk up, eating disorders, mainly anorexia nervosa and bulimia, afflict mostly female athletes who want to slim down. Anorexia nervosa is a psychobiological disorder in which a person is fixated on losing weight and becoming extremely thin, either because they have a distorted perception of their body, or because they feel it is necessary for social or occupational approval. Bulimia nervosa is characterized by bingeing on food and then purging the food by vomiting, laxative abuse, and/or diuretic abuse.

These disorders are not confined to athletes. More than 24 million Americans and Canadians suffer from eating disorders, and the mortality rate for anorexia is twelve times greater than that of any other cause of death among females between the ages of fifteen and twenty-four, according to the National Association of Anorexia Nervosa and Associated Disorders. Eating disorders are widespread among women in the entertainment industry, such as actresses, musicians, and dancers. They are rampant in the fashion business among models. But thousands of adolescent girls, and some boys, are also afflicted. Most experts contend that social norms, media images of females, and advertising portrayals of the "ideal" female body as extremely thin and firmly toned are major contributing factors in the contemporary woman's obsession with thinness.[51]

An accurate assessment of anorexia and bulimia in any group of people is difficult to ascertain because of the secretiveness that surrounds these disorders, but eating disorders are a prominent health and social problem for female athletes. According to studies of college athletes within the past decade, between 20 and 33 percent of female athletes reported disordered eating. In one study 43 percent said they were terrified of being or becoming too heavy, and 55 percent reported experiencing pressure to achieve or maintain a certain weight.[52]

Female athletes are doubly at risk for developing eating disorders. They are subject to the constant social pressure to be thin that influences all females in Western countries. They are constantly bombarded with TV, movie, magazine, Internet, and fashion images of extremely thin women who are portrayed as ideally proportioned. The director of sports nutrition at the University of Pittsburgh Medical Center remarked that female athletes "look at the bodies on the cover of *Glamour* and *Shape* magazines and think those bodies are better than theirs."[53]

Female athletes not only have to contend with these forces, they have to cope with additional ones. In some women's sports, such as gymnastics, figure skating, and diving, a significant part of the judging is on "appearance," and an extremely thin silhouette is a definite advantage. Coaches and athletes know this.

Many female athletes report that their coaches hammer home to them the message of "get thin and stay thin" in a variety of ways, some of which are quite abusive. Many athletes aspire to be the best, to be a national or an Olympic champion, so they are willing to sacrifice to achieve that goal. The combination of these conditions creates the social climate for the development of eating disorders.

Eating disorders also show up in male sports that have rigid weight restrictions, such as boxing, weight lifting, jockeying, and high school and college wrestling. The self-inflicted torture of drastic weight loss to "make weight" before a match has been called wrestling's dirty secret. Indeed, dangerous weight loss has long been the norm in high school and collegiate wrestling, and bulimia, laxatives, and diuretics have been some of the main methods for losing weight.

The deaths of three college wrestlers in 1997 forced the NCAA and high school sports governing organizations to adopt various policies prohibiting unsafe weight loss practices. There are, however, many high school and college wrestlers participating in international-style wrestling events, and dangerous rapid weight loss practices still existed among high school wrestlers participating in international-style wrestling seven years after the deaths of the three NCAA wrestlers. The message: Wrestling's weight loss practices still pose a problem for the athletes in that sport.[54]

GAMBLING AND SPORTS

Gambling is an economic activity with a history that dates back into antiquity. Betting on sports events was popular with the ancient Greeks 500 years before the birth of Christ, and it was very popular in all of their Pan-Hellenic Games—one of which was the Olympic Games. Gambling reached some incredible extremes at the Roman chariot races, with rampant corruption and fixed races. Horse racing was the most popular sport in colonial North America, and one reason for its popularity was the opportunity the races provided to bet on the outcome.

Wherever gambling on sports takes place, the specter of cheating is always a companion. A colonial America historian documented a horse-racing fix scandal in 1674. One of the most stunning professional sports fixing scandals occurred in the 1919 Major League Baseball World Series and involved Chicago White Sox players. Once the fixing was discovered, that team became known as the Black Sox. Pete Rose, the record holder for the most hits in Major League Baseball, was banned from baseball when it was discovered he had bet on MLB games (more on this later in this chapter).

Gambling is a form of entertainment with excitement, risk taking, and challenge that appeals to many people, and in the United States and Canada most moral sanctions against gambling and laws outlawing gambling have largely disappeared. Over 75 percent of North American adults gamble at least once each year. They wager an estimated $500 billion legally, and legal gambling revenue (not counting most sports gambling, Internet gambling, or poker) is approximately $95 billion annually. Moreover, gambling is growing at a phenomenal rate in the United States and Canada, and one reason for this is that there are now more opportunities to gamble than ever before. Some form of gambling is now legal in forty-eight states (gambling is completely illegal in Utah and Hawaii) and in each of the Canadian provinces as well as the Yukon and Northwest Territories.[55]

Approximately 500 Native American gaming facilities dot tribal land in twenty-eight states. Every province and each of the territories of Canada has a government-run lottery. Forty-three states and the District of Columbia have enacted lotteries; more than eighty riverboat or dockside casinos ply the water or sit at berth in several states. The nation wagers more than $45 billion annually in state lotteries.[56]

Internet wagering is the fastest-growing new form of gambling and has become a major force in the gambling industry. Total online gambling revenue generated from U.S. residents is estimated at nearly $6 billion annually. In 2011 there were over 2,500 Internet gambling sites, and a study by the Annenberg Foundation found that 22 percent of young people ages fourteen to twenty-two gambled on the Internet at least once a month.[57]

Sports betting in the U.S. is restricted in the 1992 Professional and Amateur Sports Protection Act. Nevertheless, with the enormous increase of interest in spectator sports over the past thirty years, there has been a corresponding explosion in gambling on sports. Only in Nevada can a person legally bet the line at a sports book, but sports betting is big business. Over $2.5 billion is bet annually in Nevada's 182 licensed sports books. According to one sports analyst, Nevada's $2.5 billion handle is a "drop in the bucket" compared to the sports betting wagered illegally through offshore Internet sites, mob bookies, various casual sports pools, and fantasy sport leagues. He estimated total sports betting of $300 to $380 billion.

In Canada, where it is illegal to bet on single sports events, the most popular form of sports betting is called Pro Line. Here, the gambler must bet on the outcome of a number of different sports events—a process known as a parlay. In order to win, the bettor must win all the games he/she is betting on. The advantage is that the payout can be quite high if the parlay is successful. More often it is not; thus, the gambler loses money.

In the United States the most popular betting action in the Nevada sports books is with professional and college football, professional and college basketball, Major League Baseball, and NHL hockey. Betting is popular for heavyweight boxing championship events, but betting on boxing ranks low overall. The biggest legal sports gambling event is the Super Bowl, on which some $5 to $7 billion in legal and illegal wagers change hands. The most popular sports for betting by Canadians are similar to those in the United States. For ice hockey, many bettors prefer pool betting to team-versus-team betting.[58]

The previously mentioned study by the Annenberg Foundation reported that more than 47 percent of young people ages fourteen to twenty-two bet on sports events at least once per month. Even more troubling, sports gambling is rampant and

Gambling on sports events dates back to the ancient Greeks and Romans. Sports gambling is popular with all adult age groups, and betting takes place on virtually every sport. A major problem with sports gambling is the inevitable issue of compulsive, addictive gambling. (istockphoto)

prospering on campuses throughout the country, and the majority of bookies are students. One writer referred to this phenomenon as "the dirty little secret on college campuses"; another referred to it as a "silent addiction" for many college students. Estimates of sports betting by college students range between 30 and 50 percent of male college students and between 10 and 20 percent of female students.

The NCAA has been a vigorous critic of all forms of legal and illegal sports gambling, but its football and basketball games are favorites of sports bettors. The NCAA prohibits athletics department staff members and student-athletes from engaging in gambling activities as they relate to intercollegiate or professional sporting events. But that policy has not deterred some student-athletes. One study of more than 600 Division I men's football and basketball players found that 72 percent had gambled in some form, 25 percent had gambled money on other college sports events, and 4 percent had bet money on a game in which they had played. Another study assessed gambling on college and professional sports by college students classified as athletes, sports fans, and other students at colleges with students expressing differing levels of "sports interest." All groups—athletes, sports fans, and other students—had higher rates of gambling at colleges with higher sports interest. Athletes and sports fans—both male and female—reported more sports gambling compared to other

students. Figure 7.1 displays the odds of frequent gambling on college sports among athletes, sports fans, and other students by the percentage of students claiming to be sports fans at the college.

Information of this kind prompted the NCAA to convince congressional leaders to introduce legislation in both chambers of Congress banning all gambling on college sporting events. This legislation would remove the "Nevada loophole," which allows Nevada to be the only state to conduct legal gambling on collegiate sports. Proponents of the multibillion-dollar Nevada sports-gambling industry have used their powerful resources to oppose the proposed legislation.

Considering their popularity and the huge sums of money bet on them, professional sports have been relatively free of cheating scandals—Chicago White Sox players conspiring to fix the 1919 World Series and Major League Baseball player Pete Rose being permanently banned from baseball for gambling on MLB games are the two most notorious cases. But two shocking gambling revelations that came to light in the summer of 2007 may ultimately acquire the "most notorious" tag. NBA referee Tim Donaghy admitted that he had been making bets on NBA games—including games that he refereed—for four years and, furthermore, that he had tipped off professional gamblers with inside information.[59]

NFL quarterback Michael Vick became the subject of a gambling scandal. He pleaded guilty to operating a multistate dogfighting and gambling scheme for five years, where mistreatment and killing of dogs by strangulation, drowning, or electrocution were frequent. As noted earlier in this chapter, Vick was sentenced to twenty-three months in prison for his involvement in this operation. The promising careers of Vick and Donaghy are both tarnished, as are the sports in which they were employed. After Vick served his sentence, the NFL gave him another opportunity, and he has since resurrected his football career.[60]

The popularity of intercollegiate football and basketball, and the naïveté and financial desperation of many college athletes, have made these sports attractive for professional gamblers. College football and basketball have gone through a series of fixing and point-shaving scandals during the

Figure 7.1   Percentage of Students Who Are Sports Fans (College-Level)

Prototypical model displaying the odds of frequent gambling on college and professional sports among male athletes, fans, and other students by the percentage of sports fans at the college (N = 10,559). Vertical scale is percentages. The scale on the horizontal axis is the percentage of college students attending colleges classified by percentage as sports fans.

Source: Adapted from Toban F. Nelson et al., "Sports Betting and Other Gambling in Athletes, Fans, and Other College Students," *Research Quarterly for Exercise and Sport* 78, no. 4 (2007): 271–283.

past decade. During the late 1990s thirteen Boston College football players were suspended for betting on college and pro football. Two players bet against their team in a loss to Syracuse University. Between 2003 and 2006 two University of Toledo football and basketball players were charged with attempting to fix games through bribes and shaving points in games. In 2011 a former University of San Diego assistant basketball coach and two former players were among ten people indicted in an alleged conspiracy to affect the outcome of games.[61]

The legalization of gambling and the use of the profits as a source of income to help support sports organizations and state, provincial, and national governments have been proposed in a number of states and provinces in recent years, but Nevada remains the only state permitting some forms of legalized sports gambling. Given the economic crisis in sport and in government, the prospect of the enormous windfall that could be generated from legalized betting is very attractive to some sport organizations and to politicians. But there are vocal critics of legalized sport betting. First, some think that it stimulates excessive betting—betting

more than the person can afford to lose. Second, there is the prospect that athletes and coaches will be corrupted. The point-shaving scandals of collegiate basketball come easily to mind. What of the heightened pressures on athletes resulting from the inevitable dropped pass, strikeout, or missed free throw? A suspicion that perhaps the action was deliberate and charges of dumping the game or shaving points would follow.

With sports gambling, just as with any other form of gambling, there is the inevitable issue of compulsive, addictive gambling. Obtaining an accurate number of compulsive gamblers is extremely difficult, but several agencies and organizations that have conducted surveys of these conditions estimate that 1.0 to 3.5 percent of the U.S. population (3–10.5 million) are pathological gamblers, and this disorder is more common in men than in women. Extensive research at the Center for Compulsive Gambling clearly shows that wherever there is availability and opportunity for gambling, compulsive gambling problems increase accordingly. Thus, current trends and future predictions suggest that a growing social problem for both sport and the larger society will likely be large numbers of tragic compulsive gamblers; many of these will be sports gamblers.[62]

SUMMARY

It is not surprising that violent behavior, substance abuse, eating disorders, and gambling are conspicuous problems in North American sports, given the close connections between sport and society. Three theories of human aggression dominate the scientific literature: the instinct theory, the frustration-aggression (F-A) theory, and the socially grounded theory. Advocates of the instinct and F-A theories have often claimed that participation and observation of aggressive activities have a cathartic effect by allowing one to discharge pent-up aggressive energy, and sporting activities have often been suggested as a means of dispelling aggression in a socially healthy way. Research findings suggest that, contrary to the predictions of the instinct and F-A theories, aggression tends to produce more aggressive predispositions and actions rather than serving as a catharsis.

Another theory about aggressive behavior has come from scholars who advance a perspective that postulates that aggression is learned in the social environment. This perspective places emphasis on learning aggression through the socialization process. Socially based explanations have much more research support than the other aggression models. Directly and indirectly, sports research has overwhelmingly supported this perspective of human aggression.

Violent behavior has been part of sporting practices for as long as we have records of organized sports. The nature of some sports literally demands violent actions. Other sports are not inherently violent, but the tactics employed and the way the rules are interpreted increasingly encourage violent actions.

Violence on the playing field is often mirrored by sports fans in the stadium, arena, or the environs, and it is not merely a contemporary phenomenon, nor is it confined to North American sports. Everyone who follows North American sports is quite aware of the many incidents of spectator violence. Within the past decade, major fan violence has erupted in all levels of competition—high school, collegiate, professional.

The use of substances to enhance performance has been present throughout the history of organized sports. Some behavioral and social scientists believe that drug use by athletes is an epidemic, from the high school to the professional level. The variety of substances athletes use in the hopes of improving their performances is astounding.

There is no single answer to the question of why some athletes risk their health and their opportunity to compete by using drugs, because athletes have different reasons. Athletes are a part of a much larger social community, and substance abuse is rampant in this larger social community. There is enormous social status that goes with being an athlete, and undoubtedly that is one factor that motivates young athletes to turn to chemicals for performance enhancement. There is also the potential of the fulfillment of young athletes' dreams of being a professional athlete or being an Olympic gold medalist.

Only a small minority of athletes at any level have a substance abuse problem. There is still, however, the question of what is to be done with those who are drug abusers. There are several options, but the one that has received the most attention is the drug-testing programs of the various sports governing bodies. Two questions that have been raised about drug testing are What are the athletes' individual rights and What are the athlete's responsibilities? Also, several unresolved issues exist where drug testing has been implemented. The validity and accuracy of the tests have been a continuing controversy.

Eating disorders, especially anorexia nervosa and bulimia, are common among female athletes in sports that emphasize appearance and a lean body. Female athletes are influenced by both the societal pressures that all girls and women contend with to be extremely thin and the pressures in certain sports to be thin in order to win. Although more than 90 percent of athletes with sports-related anorexia and bulimia are female, many males who compete in sports in which there are weight classifications also develop eating disorders.

Sporting events have always been a site for gambling because the events themselves are a source of great interest, the outcomes are uncertain, and sport fans often have a favorite to win. Thus, sports provide an excellent opportunity for wagering on the outcome. Moral restrictions against gambling and laws prohibiting gambling have largely been swept away in North America. Furthermore, mass communications have made sporting events more popular to the general public while also making it easier to place bets. Compulsive, addictive gambling is one of the social problems that are inevitable outcomes of gambling.

The NCAA has been trying to get legislation passed to ban college sports gambling in Nevada, the only state where it is legal. But it has been unsuccessful, largely because the Nevada casino industry has been successful in lobbying Congress against passing the legislation.

WEB RESOURCES

www.ncava.org
This is the website of the National Coalition Against Violent Athletes. The purpose of the NCAVA is to educate the public on athletes' violent behavior and to provide support to the victims, including advocacy, referrals, and research.

www.ncaa.org
The NCAA publishes a periodical titled *The NCAA News*, which carries articles dealing with intercollegiate athletic problems, such as violence, drugs, eating disorders, and gambling. One feature of this website is an "Archives" link. Most university and public libraries computers have access to the news page on this server.

www.ahealthyme.com
Blue Cross and Blue Shield of Massachusetts makes this website available for the sole purpose of providing educational information on articles about drug abuse and eating disorders among teenage athletes.

www.cbc.ca/sports/indepth/drugs/
This website provides ongoing coverage of issues surrounding drug use in sports, including news, drug dictionary, history, and links.

www.anad.org
This is the website of the National Association of Anorexia Nervosa and Associated Disorders (ANAD). One of the specific pages in this website provides an excellent overview of athletes with eating disorders.

www.gamblersanonymous.org
The Gamblers Anonymous website indicates that the organization is a fellowship of men and women who share their experience, strength, and hope with each other so that they can solve their common problem and help others recover from a gambling problem.

NOTES

1. For other historical examples of violence in North America, see John Smolenski and Thomas J. Humphrey, eds., *New World Orders: Violence, Sanction, and Authority in the Colonial Americas* (Philadelphia: University of Pennsylvania Press, 2005); Ned Blackhawk, *Violence Over the Land: Indians and Empires in the Early American West* (Cambridge, MA: Harvard University Press, 2008); and Amy Louise Wood, *Lynching and Spectacle: Witnessing Racial Violence in America, 1890–1940* (Chapel Hill: University of North Carolina Press, 2011).

2. D. Stanley Eitzen, Maxine Baca Zinn, and Kelly Eitzen Smith, *In Conflict and Order: Understanding Society*, 12th ed. (Boston: Allyn & Bacon, 2010), 68.

3. Department of Justice, *Bureau of Justice Statistics: Homicide Trends in the U.S.* (2011), http://www.ojp.usdoj.gov.

4. Maren Strenziok, Frank Krueger, Gopikrishna Deshpande, Rhoshel K. Lenroot, Elke van der Meer, and Jordan Grafman, "Fronto-Parietal Regulation of Media Violence Exposure in Adolescents: A Multi-Method Study," Social Cognitive and Affective Neuroscience, published online 7 October 2010, http://scan.oxford-journals.org/content/early/2010/10/07/scan.nsq079; Jeanne B. Funk, Heidi Bechtoldt Baldacci, Tracie Pasold, and Jennifer Baumgardner, "Violence Exposure in Real Life, Video Games, Television, Movies, and the Internet: Is There Desensitization?" *Journal of Adolescence* 27 (2004): 23–39; and Nicholas L. Carnagey, Craig A. Anderson, and Brad J. Bushman, "The Effect of Video Game Violence on Physiological Desensitization to Real-Life Violence," *Journal of Experimental Social Psychology* 43 (2007): 489–496.

5. John H. Kerr, *Motivation and Emotion in Sport* (Hove, UK: Psychology Press, 1997), 115–116; see also

John H. Kerr, *Rethinking Aggression and Violence in Sport* (New York: Routledge, 2005).

6. David Churchman, *Why We Fight: Theories of Human Aggression and Conflict* (Lanham, MD: University Press of America, 2005); see also Theodore Avtgis and Andrew S. Rancer, eds., *Arguments, Aggression, and Conflict: New Directions in Theory and Research* (New York: Routledge, 2010), especially ch. 14, "Trash Talk and Beyond: Aggressive Communication in the Context to Sport."

7. Ronald L. Akers, *Social Learning and Social Structure: A General Theory of Crime and Deviance* (Piscataway, NJ: Transaction Publishers, 2009); see also Kenneth Gergen, *Social Construction in Context* (Thousand Oaks, CA: Sage, 2001), and Gina Kolata, "A Study Finds More Links Between TV and Violence," *New York Times*, 29 March 2002, p. A25.

8. Konrad Lorenz, *On Aggression* (New York: Harcourt, Brace & World, 1963), 281.

9. Kerr, *Rethinking Aggression and Violence in Sport*; see also Craig A. Anderson and Brad J. Bushman, "Effects of **Violent** Video Games on Aggressive Behavior, Aggressive Cognition, Aggressive Affect, Physiological Arousal, and Prosocial Behavior: A Meta-Analytic Review of the Scientific Literature," *Psychological Science* 12, no. 5 (2001): 353–359.

10. Richard G. Sipes, "Sports as a Control for Aggression," in *Sports in Contemporary Society: An Anthology*, 6th ed., ed. D. Stanley Eitzen (New York: St. Martin's Press, 1996), 154–160.

11. Donald G. Kyle, *Sport and Spectacle in the Ancient World* (Malden, MA: Blackwell, 2007); and Judith Swaddling, *The Ancient Olympic Games*, 3rd rev. ed. (London: British Museum Press, 2004).

12. Fik Meijer, *The Gladiators: History's Most Deadly Sport* (New York: St. Martin's Press, 2007); and Robert Crego, *Sports and Games of the 18th and 19th Centuries* (Westport, CT: Greenwood Press, 2002).

13. Erik Brady and J. Michael Falgoust, "Concussions: New Game Plan," *USA Today*, 13 April 2011, pp. 1C–2C; "Football's High Attrition Rate Is Crippling America's 'Game'" (editorial), *USA Today*, 4 February 2011, p. 11A; Sean Gregory, "The Problem with Football," *Time Magazine*, 8 February 2010, pp. 36–43; and Steve Wieberg, "Amputation Followed by Questions," *USA Today*, 13 October 2010, p. 9C.

14. Tim Layden, "The Big Hit," *Sports Illustrated*, 30 July 2007, p. 54; see also Sigmund Loland, Berit Skirstad, and Ivan Waddington, eds., *Pain and Injury in Sport: Social and Ethical Analysis* (New York: Routledge, 2006).

15. Layden, "The Big Hit," 54; see also Robert Lipsyte, "Only We Can Save the NFL from Itself," *USA Today*, 23 November 2010, p. 9A, and "Football's High Attrition Rate Is Crippling America's 'Game.'"

16. Peter King, "Concussions: The Hits That Are Changing Football," *Sports Illustrated*, 1 November 2010, pp. 34–40; see also David Epstein, "The Damage Done," *Sports Illustrated*, 1 November 2010, pp. 42–47; Nate Jackson, "The NFL's Concussion Culture," *The Nation*, 15/22 August 2011, pp. 22–23; and Kevin Young, *Sport, Violence and Society* (New York: Routledge, 2012).

17. Michael Farber, "Why Good Teams Fight," *Sports Illustrated*, 13 October 2008, pp. 56–62.

18. Ibid.

19. See, for example, *The Ultimate Fighter* website (2011), http://www.ultimatefighter.com; see also L. Jon Wertheim, "The New Main Event," *Sports Illustrated*, 27 May 2007, pp. 50–60.

20. Arthur A. Raney and A. Depalma, "The Effect of Viewing Varying Levels of Aggressive Sports Programming on Enjoyment, Mood, and Perceived Violence," *Mass Communication and Society* 9, no. 3 (2006): 321–338; Arthur A. Raney, "Why We Watch and Enjoy Mediated Sports," in *Handbook of Sports and Media*, ed. Arthur A. Raney and Jennings Bryant (Mahwah, NJ: Erlbaum, 2006), 313–329; and Arthur A. Raney and William Kinnally, "Examining Perceived Violence in and Enjoyment of Televised Rivalry Sports Contests," paper presented at the annual meeting of the International Communication Association, San Francisco, CA, 23 May 2007, http://www.allacademic.com/meta/p172675_index.html.

21. King, "Concussions: The Hits That Are Changing Football," p. 37; see also Kevin Allen and Erik Brady, "NHL Concussions Touch Off Debate," *USA Today*, 8 March 2011, pp. 1C–2C.

22. Farber, "Why Good Teams Fight," 62.

23. The following are some examples: Jane Leavy, *The Last Boy: Mickey Mantle and the End of America's Childhood* (New York: Harper, 2010); Mark Kriegel, *Namath: A Biography* (New York: Penguin, 2004); Mark Fainaru-Wada and Lance Williams, *Game of Shadows: Barry Bonds, BALCO, and the Steroids Scandal That Rocked Professional Sports* (New York: Gotham Books, 2007); and Jose Canseco, *Juiced: Wild Times, Rampant 'Roids, Smash Hits, and How Baseball Got Big* (New York: HarperCollins, 2007).

24. Todd Crosset, "Male Athletes' Violence Against Women: A Critical Assessment of the Athletic Affiliation, Violence Against Women Debate," *Quest* 51 (August 2008): 244–257.

25. Rape, Abuse & Incest National Network (RAINN), http://www.rainn.org/statistics; and U.S. Department of Justice's National Crime Victimization Survey, http://bjs.ojp.usdoj.gov/index.cfm?ty=dcdetail&iid=245.

26. The book by H. G. Bissinger, *Friday Night Lights: A Town, a Team, and a Dream* (Reading, MA: Addison-Wesley, 1990), was made into a movie, *Friday Night Lights*, in 2004; in the fall of 2006, a television serial drama by the same

name began airing on NBC. See also Derek A. Kreager, "Unnecessary Roughness? School Sports, Peer Networks, and Male Adolescent Violence," *American Sociological Review* 72 (October 2007): 705–724.

27. "Steroid Use Causes Long-Term Aggression," *about.com*, 10 June 2006, http://alcoholism.about.com/cs/steroids/a/blnu031120.htm; see also Nathan Jendrick, *Dunks, Doubles, Doping: How Steroids Are Killing American Athletes* (Guilford, CT: Lyons Press, 2006).

28. Home page, National Coalition Against Violent Athletes, http://www.ncava.org.

29. Jay Johnson and Margery Holman, "Gender and Hazing: The Same But Different," *Journal of Physical Education, Recreation and Dance*, 80 (May/June 2009): 6–9; Jennifer J. Waldron and Christopher L. Kowalski, "Crossing the Line: Rites of Passage, Team Aspects, and Ambiguity of Hazing," *Research Quarterly for Exercise and Sport* 80 (June 2009): 291; see also Jay Johnson and Margery Holman, *Making the Team: Inside the World of Sport Initiations and Hazing* (Toronto: Canadian Scholars' Press, 2004).

30. Associated Press, "Hazing Case Ends in Some Jail Time for Ball Players," *KATU.com*, http://www.katu.com/news/local/18905864.html. See also Ryan Gorcey and Julie Strack, "Officials Investigating Baseball 'Initiation,'" *Daily Californian*, 13 April 2007, http://archive.dailycal.org/article/24177/officials_investigating_baseball_initiation_; "Maine Softball Team on Probation for Hazing," *USA Today*, 16 August 2007, p. 11C; and "Agawam Mass. Football Players, Coaches Suspended for Alleged Hazing," *JusticeNewsFlash.com*, 23 November 2010, http://www.justicenewsflash.com/2010/11/27/football-players-coaches-suspended-for-hazing_201011276278.html.

31. NCAA, *Building New Traditions: Hazing Prevention in College Athletics* (Indianapolis: National Collegiate Athletic Association, 2007); see also John Nicoletti, Sally Spencer-Thomas, and Christopher Bollinger, *Violence Goes to College: The Authoritative Guide to Prevention and Intervention* (Springfield, IL: Charles C. Thomas, 2010).

32. Tim Sullivan, "Fan Violence & the Law," *Youth Sports New York*, 3 December 2009, http://www.youthsportsny.org/2009/12/fan-violence-the-law.html; see also Steve Wieberg, "Are Rivalries Getting Out of Hand?" *USA Today*, 26 August 2011, pp. 1D–2D.

33. Jerry M. Lewis, *Sports Fan Violence in North America* (Lanham, MD: Rowman & Littlefield, 2007).

34. Ibid.; see also Kevin G. Quinn, *Sports and Their Fans: The History, Economics and Culture of the Relationship Between Spectator and Sport* (Jefferson, NC: McFarland, 2009).

35. Terry Baddoo, "Beckham Fined $1,000 by MLS for Conduct Toward L.A. Galaxy Fan," *SI.com*, 24 July 2009, http://sportsillustrated.cnn.com/2009/soccer/07/24/

beckham.fine/index.html; see also Lee Jenkins, "The Day That Damned the Dodgers," *Sports Illustrated*, 29 August 2011, pp. 50–58, and Robert Klemko, "Ominous Signs in Stands," *USA Today*, 30 August 2011, pp.1C–2C.

36. Anastassia Tsoukala, *Football Hooliganism in Europe: Security and Civil Liberties in the Balance* (New York: Palgrave McMillan, 2009).

37. Lewis, *Sports Fan Violence in North America*, 121–141; see also Quinn, *Sports and Their Fans*.

38. Norah Piehl, *Performance-Enhancing Drugs* (Farmington Hills, MI: Greenhaven Press, 2010); see also Lydia Bjornlund, *How Dangerous Are Performance-Enhancing Drugs?* (San Diego: Referencepoint Press, 2010).

39. Lloyd D. Johnston, Patrick M. O'Malley, Jerald G. Bachman, and John E. Schulenberg, *Monitoring the Future: National Results on Adolescent Drug Use: Overview of Findings 2010* (Bethesda, MD: National Institute on Drug Abuse, 2010).

40. NCAA, "Latest Testing Shows Minimal Increase in Steroid Use," *NCAA News Archive-2010*, 7 June 2010, http://fs.ncaa.org/Docs/NCAANewsArchive/2010/aWide/latest_testing_shows_minimal_increase_in_steroid_use.html.

41. Teri Thompson, Nathaniel Vinton, Michael O'Keeffe, and Christian Red, *American Icon: The Fall of Roger Clemens and the Rise of Steroids in America's Pastime* (New York: Knopf, 2009); and Selena Roberts and David Epstein, "Confronting A-Rod," *Sports Illustrated*, 16 February 2009, pp. 28–31.

42. Quoted in David Epstein and George Dohrmann, "What You Don't Know Might Kill You," *Sports Illustrated*, 18 May 2009, p. 57.

43. Johnston, O'Malley, Bachman, and Schulenberg, *Monitoring the Future*.

44. The Higher Education Center for Alcohol and Other Drug Abuse and Violence Prevention, "College Athletes and Alcohol and Other Drug Use" (Newton, MA: Education Development Center, 2008), http://www.higheredcenter.org/files/product/fact_sheet3.pdf.

45. United States Anti-Doping Agency, *About USADA, Mission/Vision* (2011), http://www.usada.org/about; and Canadian Centre for Ethics in Sport, *Canadian Anti-Doping Program* (2009), http://www.cces.ca/files/pdfs/CCES-POLICY-CADP-E.pdf.

46. Michael Bamberger and Don Yaeger, "Over the Edge," *Sports Illustrated*, 14 April 1997, pp. 60–70.

47. Kevin Young, ed., *Sporting Bodies, Damaged Selves* (Bingley, UK: Emerald Group Publishing, 2004).

48. Jeff Gray, "Let Legal Games Begin: Drug-Testing v. Charter," *Globe and Mail*, 10 February 2010, p. B1; Nathan T. Martin, "Drug Testing in Interscholastic Athletics," *Journal of Physical Education, Recreation, and Dance* 78 (March 2007): 8–9.

49. Angela J. Schneider and Robert B. Butcher, "An Ethical Analysis of Drug Testing," in *Doping in Elite Sport: The Politics of Drugs in the Olympic Movement*, ed. Wayne Wilson and Edward Derse (Champaign, IL: Human Kinetics, 2001), 129–130; see also Richard W. Pound, *Inside Dope: How Drugs Are the Biggest Threat to Sports, Why You Should Care, and What Can Be Done About Them* (New York: Wiley, 2006), 79–120.

50. Rob Beamish, *Fastest, Highest, Strongest: A Critique of High-Performance Sport* (New York: Routledge, 2006).

51. ANAD, "Eating Disorders Statistics," National Association of Anorexia Nervosa and Associated Disorders (2011), http://www.anad.org/get-information/about-eating-disorders/eating-disorders-statistics.

52. Katherine A. Beals, *Disordered Eating Among Athletes: A Comprehensive Guide for Health Professionals* (Champaign, IL: Human Kinetics, 2004); see also Tiffany C. Sanford-Martins et al., "Clinical and Subclinical Eating Disorders: An Examination of Collegiate Athletes," *Journal of Applied Sport Psychology* 17, no. 1 (2005): 79–86.

53. Quoted in Nanci Hellmich, "Athletes' Hunger to Win Fuels Eating Disorders," *USA Today*, 6 February 2006, pp. 1A, 6A; for an excellent in-depth discussion of eating disorders in sports, see Trent A. Petrie and Christy A. Greenleaf, "Eating Disorders in Sport: From Theory to Research to Intervention," in *Handbook of Sport Psychology*, 3rd ed., ed. Gershon Tenenbaum and Robert C. Eklund (New York: Wiley, 2007), 352–378.

54. Hugh C. McBride, *Eating Disorders*, http://www.eatingdisordershelpguide.com/eating-disorders/dying-to-gain-a-competitive-edge-wrestlers-at-risk-for-disordered-eating-habits.htm (retrieved 12 March 2011).

55. Earl L. Grinols, *Gambling in America: Cost and Benefits* (Cambridge, UK: Cambridge University Press, 2009); see also David Forrest, "Sports Gambling," in *Handbook on the Economics of Sport*, ed. Wladimir Andreff and Stefan Szymanski (Cheltenham, UK: Edward Elgar Publishing Co., 2009), 40–48.

56. *Nations Indian Casinos SuperSite!*, http://500nations.com/Indian_Casinos.asp; see also Rob Jennings, "States Gamble on Web Lottery Sales," *USA Today*, 10 June 2011, p. 3A.

57. Andy Vuong, "Internet Gambling Tempting to States," *Denver Post*, 24 April 2011, pp. 1K, 8K; Dan Romer, *Internet Gambling Grows Among Male Youth Ages 14 to 22; Gambling Also Increases in High School Age Female Youth* (Annenberg Public Policy Center, National Annenberg Survey of Youth), 14 October 2010. See also Andrew F. Cooper, *Internet Gambling Offshore: Caribbean Struggles Over Casino Capitalism* (New York: Palgrave Macmillan, 2011).

58. AGA, "Sports Wagering," American Gaming Association, http://www.americangaming.org/government-affairs/key-issues/past-issues/sports-betting (retrieved 12 March 2011).

59. Michael S. Schmidt, "Former N.B.A. Referee Is Sentenced," *New York Times*, 30 July 2008, D7; see also Tim Donaghy, *Personal Foul: A First-Person Account of the Scandal That Rocked the NBA* (New York: Simon & Schuster, 2008).

60. George Dohrmann, "The Case Against Vick," *Sports Illustrated*, 30 July 2007, pp. 38–39. See also Kathy Strouse, *Badd Newz: The Untold Story of the Michael Vick Dog Fighting Case* (New York: BookSurge Publishing [an Amazon.com company], 2009); and Sean Patrick Griffin, *Gaming the Game: The Story Behind the NBA Betting Scandal and the Gambler Who Made It Happen* (Fort Lee, NJ: Barricade Books, 2011).

61. Pablo S. Torre, Kostya Kennedy, Mark Bechtel, ans Stephen Cannella, "Unholy Toledo!" *Sports Illustrated*, 18 August 2008, p. 28; see also Elliot Spagat, "Ex-USD Star Figures in Sports Bribery Indictment," *USA Today*, 11 April 2011, http://www.usatoday.com/sports/college/mensbasketball/2011-04-11-3764994019_x.htm.

62. Hale Humphrey, *This Must Be Hell: A Look at Pathological Gambling* (Bloomington, IN: iUniverse, 2009); see also Rex M. Rogers, *Gambling: Don't Bet on It* (Grand Rapids, MI: Kregel Publications, 2005).

CHAPTER 8

Sport and Religion

Religion and sport especially are joined at the altar of commercial interest. As sports promoters seek publicity and lively attendances at their events, and as churches seek wholesome activities and a podium for their message, their marriage seems made in heaven.
—William J. Baker*

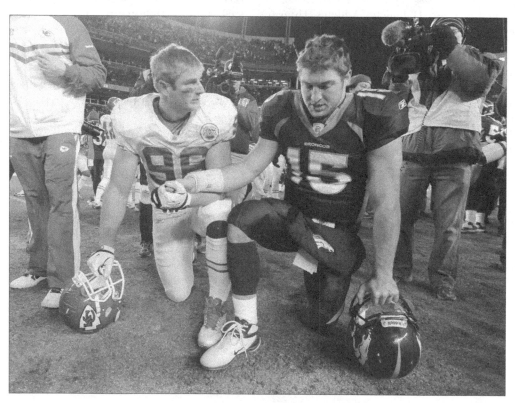

It has become a common practice for athletes to publicly display their religious beliefs through various gestures and actions. Denver Broncos quarterback Tim Tebow (15) and Kansas City Chiefs linebacker Andy Studebaker (96) hold hands to pray following an NFL football game between the Broncos and the Chiefs. (AP Photo/Jack Dempsey)

*William J. Baker, *Playing with God: Religion and Modern Sport* (Cambridge, MA: Harvard University Press, 2007), 4.

On the one hand, there may seem to be little in common between sport and religion; going to religious services, singing hymns, studying scripture, and worshiping God all seem quite unrelated to the activities that we associate with sport. On the other hand, like religion, contemporary sport symbolically evokes fervent commitment from millions of people. Sports fans worship their favorite athletes much as followers of various religions worship their special deities. Also, sports fans, like religious groups, consider themselves to be part of a community. Finally, the rituals and ceremonies common to religion are paralleled by rituals and ceremonies in sport. Former NFL and Major League Baseball player Deion Sanders summed up the connections between sport and religion by declaring that they go together "like peanut butter and jelly."

Religion is a major part of people's lives, and religious practices of some kind are present in every society. There are followers of a broad variety of religions in North America, but the emphasis in this chapter will be on Christian linkages to sport in the U.S. and Canada. There are several reasons for this focus. First, North Americans who self-identify as Christians are the overwhelming majority; indeed, about 76 percent of U.S. citizens identify themselves as Christians. About 4 percent self-identify with other religions, leaving about 15 percent who self-identify with no religion (see Table 8.1). *Statistics Canada* reports very similar religious affiliations for Canadians. Second, the historical traditions of both the United States and Canada are closely tied to the United Kingdom and Western European countries, all of whom have historically been "Christian" countries. Finally, as we pointed out in Chapter 2, the rise of sport in North America was closely linked to Christian leaders and organizations; therefore, Christian attitudes, values, and practices have been a dominating force in North American sport.[1]

As sport and religion have become increasingly intertwined, each has made inroads into the traditional activities and prerogatives of the other. For example, for Christians of previous generations, Sunday was the day reserved for church and worship, but with the increase in opportunities for recreational pursuits—both for participants and for spectators—and the virtual explosion of televised

Table 8.1 Self-Described Religious Identification of Adult Population in the United States, 2008 (in thousands)

Religious Group	Adult Population
Total	228,182
Christian (top eight described)	
Catholic	57,199
Baptist	36,148
Methodist/Wesleyan	11,366
Lutheran	8,674
Pentecostal/Charismatic	5,416
Presbyterian	4,723
Mormon/Latter-Day Saints	3,158
Episcopalian/Anglican	2,405
Jewish	2,680
Muslim	1,349
Buddhist	1,189

Source: U.S. Census Bureau, *Statistical Abstract of the United States: 2010*, 129th ed. (Washington, DC, 2010), table 75.

sports, worship on weekends has been replaced by worship of weekends. As a result, sport has captured Sunday, and churches have had to revise their schedules to oblige sport. At most Roman Catholic churches, convenient Saturday late-afternoon and evening services are now featured in addition to traditional Sunday masses, and other denominations frequently schedule services to accommodate the viewing of professional sports events.

In many respects churches have had to share Sundays with sports, and the idea that the Sabbath should be reserved for worship now seems merely a quaint idea from the past. Former *Sports Illustrated* columnist Rick Reilly noted that "priests and pastors have noticed that God is competing more and more with Sunday sports—and losing."[2]

At the same time that sport appears to be usurping religion's traditional time for worship and services, many churches and religious leaders are attempting to weld a link between the two activities by sponsoring sports events under religious auspices and by proselytizing athletes to religion and then using them as missionaries to spread the Word and to recruit new members. Thus, contemporary religion often uses sport for the promotion of its causes. Sport uses religion as well and in more ways than just seizing the traditional day of worship. People involved in sports—as participants or as spectators—employ numerous activities with religious connotations in connection with the contests. Ceremonies, rituals, taboos, fetishes, and so forth—all originating in religious practice—are standard observances in the world of sport.

In this chapter we examine the multidimensional relationship between religion and sport.

THE RELATIONSHIP BETWEEN RELIGION AND SOCIETY

Religion is the belief that supernatural forces influence human lives. There are many definitions of religion, but one by a founder of the discipline of sociology, French sociologist Émile Durkheim, has perhaps been cited most. Durkheim said that "religion is a unified system of beliefs and practices relative to sacred things, that is to say, things set apart and forbidden—beliefs and practices which unite into one single moral community called a Church, all those who adhere to them."[3] As a social institution, religion is a system that functions to maintain and transmit beliefs about forces considered supernatural and sacred. It provides codified guides for moral conduct and prescribes symbolic practices deemed to be in harmony with beliefs about the supernatural. The world religions, including Christianity, Hinduism, Buddhism, Confucianism, Judaism, and Islam, are cores of elaborate cultural systems that have dominated world societies for centuries. For all practical purposes we may assume that religious behavior among human beings is universal in that ethnologists and anthropologists have not yet discovered a human group without traces of the behavior we call "religious."[4]

Personal and Social Roles of Religion

Religions exist because they perform important roles at several levels of human life, including personal, interpersonal, institutional, and societal. At the personal level, religious experience meets psychic needs by providing individuals with emotional support in this uncertain world. The unpredictable and sometimes dangerous world produces personal fears and general anxiety that revering the powers of nature or seeking cooperation through religious faith and ritual may alleviate. Fears of death, too, are made bearable by beliefs in a supernatural realm into which a believer passes. If one can believe in a God-giving scheme of things, the universal quest for ultimate meaning is validated, and human strivings and sufferings seem to make some sense.

At the interpersonal level, religion contributes to human social bonding. It unites a community of believers by bringing them together to enact various ceremonies and rituals, and it provides them with shared values and beliefs that bind them together. The need to proclaim human abilities and to achieve a sense of transcendence is met and indeed fostered by many religions through ceremonies and rituals that celebrate humans and their activities.

At the social institutional level, one of the paramount functions of religion is the promotion of social integration. This idea has been a tenet of the functionalist theorists since it was advanced by Durkheim over a century ago. The central point here is that religion advances a bonding of both the members of a society and the social obligations that help unite them because it organizes individuals' experiences in terms of ultimate meanings that include but also transcend the individual. When many people share this ordering principle, they can deal with each other in meaningful ways and can transcend themselves and their individual egoisms, sometimes even to the point of self-sacrifice.

Religious ceremonies and rituals also promote integration because they serve to reaffirm some of the basic customs and values of society. Here, the societal customs, folkways, and observances are symbolically elevated to the realm of the sacred. In expressing common beliefs about the supernatural, in engaging in collective worship activities, in recounting the lore and myths of the past, the community is brought closer together and linked with its heritage.

Another functionalist view about the social integrative role of religion is that it tends to legitimize the secular social structures within a society. There is a strong tendency for religious ideology to become united with the norms and values of secular structures, producing, as a consequence, religious support for the values and institutions of society. From its earliest existence, religion has provided rationales that serve the needs and actions of a society's leaders. It has legitimized as "God-given" such disparate ideologies as absolute monarchies and egalitarian democracies.

At the institutional level, too, religion serves as a vehicle for social control; that is, religious tenets constrain the behavior of the community of believers to keep them in line with the norms, values, and beliefs of society. In all the major religions, morals and religion are intertwined, and schemes of otherworldly rewards or punishments for behavior, such as those found in Christianity, become powerful forces for morality. The fear of hellfire and damnation has been a powerful deterrent and control in Christian societies. The virtues of honesty, conformity to sexual codes, and all the details of acceptable, moral behavior in a society become merged with religious beliefs and practices.

Advocates of a conflict/cultural perspective of religion are especially troubled by the notion of religion serving as a mechanism of social control. They recognize functionalist analysts' claim that religion meets the need that many people have for emotional support in dealing with the unknown, the unpredictable, the ultimate questions about life and death, and the inclinations of people to create gods and believe in supernatural phenomena. But conflict/culturists contend that religion for social control has been primarily a tool of the rich and powerful that has been particularly harmful to poor and oppressed people. Furthermore, they argue that religion has been a means of legitimating the interests of the dominant class, justifying existing social injustices and inequalities, and, like a narcotic, lulling people into ready acceptance of the status quo—into a "false consciousness." Indeed, historically religion has often reinforced existing social structures and promoted socially inequitable conditions.[5]

THE RELATIONSHIP BETWEEN RELIGION AND SPORT

Ancient Greece: Creators of Organized Sports Events

Scholars who have studied the origins of sport claim that it began as a religious rite. The ancient Greeks, who worshiped beauty, entwined religious observance with their athletic demonstrations in such a way that to define where one left off and the other began is difficult. The strong anthropomorphic (humanlike) conceptions of gods held by the Greeks led to their belief that the gods took pleasure in the same things that mortals enjoyed, such as music, drama, and displays of physical excellence. The gymnasia located in every city-state for all male adults (females were not allowed in the Greek gymnasia) provided facilities and places for sports training as well as for the discussion of intellectual topics. Furthermore, facilities for religious worship, an altar and a chapel, were located in the center of each gymnasium.

The Olympic Games, the most important athletic meetings of the Greeks, were part of religious festivals. They were sacred contests, staged in a sacred location and as a sacred festival; they were a religious act in honor of Zeus, king of the gods. Athletes who took part in the Olympics did so in order to please Zeus and the prizes they won came from him. Other Pan-Hellenic games were equally religious in nature. Victorious athletes presented their gifts of thanks upon the altar of the god or gods whom they thought to be responsible for their victory. The end of the ancient Olympic Games was a result of the religious conviction of Theodosius, the Roman emperor of A.D. 392–395. He was a Christian and decreed the end of the Games as part of his suppression of paganism in favor of Christianity.[6]

The Early Christian Church and Roman Sport Spectacles

In Western societies, religious support for sport found no counterpart to that of the Greeks until the beginning of the twentieth century. The Christian religion was dominated by the Roman Catholic Church until the Reformation in the sixteenth century. Since then, Roman Catholicism has shared religious power with Protestant groups. At first Christians opposed Roman sport spectacles such as chariot racing and gladiatorial combat because of their paganism and brutality, but later Christians opposed sport because they came to regard the body as an instrument of sin.

The early Christians did not view sports as evil per se, for the Apostle Paul wrote approvingly of the benefits of physical activity. He said, for example, "Do you not know that those who run in a race, all indeed run, but one receives the prize? So run as to obtain it" (1 Cor. 9:24). In another verse, Paul reminded Timothy of the importance of adhering to the rules: "One who enters a contest is not crowned unless he has competed according to the rules" (2 Tim. 2:5).

The paganism prominent in the Roman sports events, however, was abhorrent to the Christians. Moreover, early Christianity gradually built a foundation based on asceticism, which is a belief that evil exists in the body and that therefore the body should be subordinate to the pure spirit. As a result, church dogma and education sought to subordinate all desires and demands of the body in order to exalt the spiritual life. Twelfth-century Catholic abbot, Saint Bernard, argued, "Always in a robust and active body the mind lies soft and more lukewarm; and, on the other hand, the spirit flourishes more strongly and more actively in an infirm and weakly body." Nothing could have been more damning for the promotion of active recreation and sport.[7]

Pre-Columbian Societies: Sport in the Americas

The Mayans and Aztecs are examples of pre-Columbian societies that included physical activities as part of their religious rituals and ceremonies. The purpose of many games of these societies was rooted in a desire to gain victory over foes seen and unseen, to influence the forces of nature, and to promote fertility among crops and cattle. The Zuni Indians of New Mexico played games that they believed would bring rain and thus enable their crops to grow. One Eskimo tribe, at the end of the harvest season, played a cup-and-ball game

to "catch the sun" and thus delay its departure. In his monumental work on the Plains Indians, Stewart Culin wrote, "In general, games appear to be played ceremonially, as pleasing to the gods, with the objective of securing fertility, causing rain, giving and prolonging life, expelling demons, or curing sickness."[8]

Reformation and Protestantism in the North American Colonies

The Reformation of the early sixteenth century signaled the end of the viselike grip that Roman Catholicism had on the minds and habits of the people of Europe and England. But Protestantism had within it the seeds of a new asceticism, and in its Puritan form, became a greater enemy to sport than Roman Catholicism had been.

Puritans were among the earliest English immigrants to America, and they had considerable influence on the social life in the colonies. Perhaps no Christian group exercised a greater opposition to sport than the Puritans. As a means of realizing amusement and unrestrained impulses, sport was suspect for the Puritan; one historian asserted that "Puritans' opposition to sport was grounded on at least seven propositions: sport was frivolous and wasted time; sport did not refresh the body as good recreation should, but tired people instead; much sporting activity was designed deliberately to inflict pain or injury; sporting contests usually led to gambling; more sport took place on Sunday than on any other day, so sport encouraged people to defile the Sabbath; sport was noisy and disrupted others, sometimes entire communities; and many sports had either pagan or 'Popish' origins."[9] The renowned nineteenth-century English historian Thomas B. Macaulay claimed that the Puritans opposed bearbaiting (tying a bear to a stake and urging dogs to attack it) not so much because it was painful for the bear but because it gave pleasure to the spectators.

The Puritans of New England were not the only colonists who had compunctions about sports. Most of the colonies passed laws against play and sport on the Sabbath. Like the Puritans, the most prominent objection to sport by religious leaders in the other colonies was that participation would divert attention from spiritual matters. The practical matter was that survival in the New World required hard work from everyone; thus, time spent in play and games was typically considered time wasted. Finally, the associations formed and the environment in which play and sport occurred conspired to cast these activities in a bad light. The tavern was the center for gambling and table sports, dancing had obvious sexual overtones, and field sports often involved gambling and cruelty to animals.[10]

Religious Objections to Sport Declined in the Nineteenth Century

Church opposition to leisure pursuits was firmly maintained in the first few decades of the nineteenth century, and each effort to liberalize attitudes toward leisure pursuits was met with a new attack on sport as "sinful." Sports were still widely regarded by the powerful Protestant religious groups as snares of the devil himself. However, in the 1830s social problems became prominent concerns of U.S. social reformers, many of whom were clergy and intellectual leaders. There were crusades against slavery, intemperance, and poor industrial working conditions; widespread support for the emancipation of women, for public education, and for industrial reform; and indeed, scrutiny of every facet of American life.

Social conditions had begun to change rapidly under the aegis of industrialization. The physical health of the population became a major issue leading a number of reformers to propose that people would be happier, more productive, and healthier if they engaged in vigorous sports activities. Surprisingly, some of the leading advocates were clerics who began to soften their attitude toward play and sport. Although the development of a more liberal attitude by church leaders toward sport began to appear by the mid-nineteenth century, not all church authorities subscribed to the trend. A staid Congregationalist magazine, the *New Englander*, vigorously attacked sport:

> Let our readers, one and all, remember that we were sent into this world, not for sport and amusement, but for labor; not to enjoy and please ourselves, but

to serve and glorify God, and be useful to our fellow men. That is the great object and end in life. In pursuing this end, God has indeed permitted us all needful diversion and recreation. . . . But the great end of life after all is work. . . . It is a true saying. . . "We come into this world, not for sports." We were sent here for a higher and nobler object.[11]

Although some church leaders fought the encroaching sport and leisure mania throughout the late nineteenth century, many gradually began to reconcile play and religion in response to pressure from medical, educational, and political leaders for games and sport. Increasingly, churches broadened their commitment to play and sport endeavors as a means of drawing people together. The book *Muscular Christianity: Manhood and Sports in Protestant America, 1880–1920* begins with this sentence: "Between 1880 and 1920, American Protestants in many denominations witnessed the flourishing in the pulpits and seminaries of a strain of religiosity known, both admiringly and pejoratively, as 'muscular Christianity.'"[12] The church's prejudice against pleasure through play had broken down almost completely by the beginning of the twentieth century.

Religion and Sport Conciliation

Churches were confronted with ever-increasing changes in the twentieth century; economic pressures, political movements, and social conditions were the chief forces responsible for the drastically changed relationship between religion and sport. Increased industrialization turned the population into a nation of urban dwellers, and higher wages were responsible for an unprecedented affluence. The gospel of work (the Protestant work ethic) became less credible, and increased leisure enhanced the popularity of a new professional sports industry. Sport historian William J. Baker elaborates on these trends, writing, "In the 1920s and 1930s religious links to sport in the United States grew clearer and broader. Protestants and Catholics continued to stake claims on the American soul, frequently endorsing sport for sectarian purposes. At the same time other, smaller groups came to the marriage of religion and sport."[13]

The story of changes in the attitudes of religionists in the later twentieth and early twenty-first centuries was largely one of increasing accommodation. Much of both Catholic and Protestant North America came to view sport as a positive force and even as a useful means of promoting God's work. Sports and leisure activities became an increasingly conspicuous part of the recreation programs of thousands of churches and many church colleges, a trend that one sociologist called the "basketball-ization" of churches. One sports study scholar elaborated, suggesting that sport has "captured the imagination of modern evangelical churches. No forward-looking church will overlook the value of sport as an adjunct to its social programs, and no architect will overlook the opportunity to include at least one gymnasium in first drafts for a new church."[14] Times have changed, and the conciliation between sport and organized religion has approached finality.

SPORT AS RELIGION

Sport has taken on so many of the characteristics of religion that some have argued that sport has emerged as a new religion, supplementing, and in some cases even supplanting, traditional religious expressions. Almost two decades ago, a professor in the religious studies program at Pennsylvania State University made a claim that startled both clergy and laypeople—that "sport is a religion." He asserted: "For me, it is not just a parallel that is emerging between sport and religion, but rather *a complete identity. Sport is religion* for growing numbers of Americans, and this is no product of simply facile reasoning or wishful thinking. Further, for many, sport religion has become a more appropriate expression of personal religiosity than Christianity, Judaism, or any of the traditional religions. . . . It is reasonable to consider sport the newest and fastest growing religion, far outdistancing whatever is in second place."[15]

More recently, a professor of comparative religion at Dalhousie University in Halifax, Nova Scotia, argued that it is not sport in general that is a religion. Instead, for him it is Canadian ice hockey that is a religion. He focuses on ice hockey in Canada, and concludes his analysis by saying, "There is considerable evidence here to support the view that when one becomes a hockey fan or player, one is doing more than 'merely' taking up a game or an entertainment. There is a sense in which one is justified in speaking of hockey as a religion."[16]

And there are still other sport sites where religion is alleged to reside. Eric Bain-Selbo, professor of philosophy and religion at Western Kentucky University, claims that "there is a compelling case to conclude that college football in the South is a form and expression of religious life. . . . I believe that sport is replacing religion. . . . [E]xpressing one's religiosity predominantly in the context of one's college football team in the South is really no different from being a Methodist or Baptist."[17]

Of course, preceding all of the previous declarations was that of Avery Brundage, an American who for twenty years (1952–1972) was president of the International Olympic Committee. Brundage claimed that the Olympic Movement itself was a religion: "The Olympic Movement is a Twentieth Century religion, a religion with universal appeal which incorporates all the basic values of other religions, a modern, exciting, virile, dynamic religion. . . . It is a religion for which Pierre de Coubertin was the prophet, for Coubertin has kindled a torch that will enlighten the world."[18]

Similarities Between Sport and Religion

There is no doubt that organized sport has taken on the trappings of religion. A few examples will illustrate this point:

- Every religion has its god or gods (or saints or high priests) who are venerated by its members. Likewise, sports fans have gods (superstar athletes) they worship.
- Christianity has its saints, and other religions have religious models they admire and worship. Sports fans also have their saints—those who have passed to the great beyond (such as Jim Thorpe, Knute Rockne, Tim Horton, and Babe Didrikson Zaharias).
- Religion has priests and clergy. The high priests of contemporary sport are the

professional, collegiate, and national amateur team coaches who not only direct the destinies of their athletes but also control the emotions of large masses of sports fans.

- Religion has scribes who record the word of God. Sport also has its scribes, the sport journalists and sportscasters who disseminate the "word" of sports deeds and glories.
- Religion has it churches, synagogues, mosques, and temples. Sport has its houses of worship, such as Fenway Park and Soldier Field.
- Religion has its congregations. Sport has its masses of highly vocal "true believers."
- Religion has its proverbs that express the "true" word of God. Numerous proverbs fill the world of sport: "Nice guys finish last," "When the going gets tough, the tough get going," "*Lose* is a four-letter word," and so forth. In sports, these proverbs are frequently written on posters and hung in locker rooms for athletes to memorize.
- Religious shrines are commonplace wherever religion is found. They preserve sacred symbols and memorabilia that followers can admire and honor. The achievements of athletes and teams are celebrated in numerous shrines, called halls of fame, built to commemorate and glorify sporting figures. Halls of fame have been established for virtually every sport played in North America, and some sports have several halls of fame devoted to them.
- Religions demand fidelity from their followers in the form of faithfulness to obligations, duties, and observances. Symbols of fidelity abound in sport. The athletes are expected to give total commitment to the cause, including abstinence from smoking, alcohol, and in some cases even sex.
- Religions require devotion to specific beliefs, traditions, and practices. Devout followers of sports witness and invoke traditional and hallowed chants and show their devotion to the team by adding "spirit" to its cause. In cheering for the Green Bay Packers, New York Yankees, or Montreal Canadians, devoted fans can experience feelings of belonging to a "congregation." It is not unusual for these sports pilgrims to travel hundreds of miles, sometimes braving terrible weather conditions, to witness a sports event, thus displaying their devotion to their team.
- Religions sponsor a variety of holidays and festivals that function to promote communal involvement, thus nurturing a sense of belonging to the religious community. The Super Bowl functions as a major sporting festival for American culture, seeming to unite the entire nation with its pageantry and sporting extravaganza.

Two popular—one can even say iconic—motion pictures, *Field of Dreams* and *Bull Durham*, used numerous religious themes and symbols suggesting baseball-as-religion. They do not claim that baseball is a religion in a traditional theological way, but they do suggest a symbiosis (an intimate association or close union) between the two. *Bull Durham* reveals how baseball exemplifies the qualities of an institutional religion. The movie opens with gospel music in the background and the female lead, Annie (Susan Sarandon), delivering this prologue: "I believe in the church of baseball. I've tried all the major religions and most of the minor ones. . . . I gave Jesus a chance, but it just didn't work out between us. The Lord laid too much guilt on me. . . . There's no guilt in baseball, and it's never boring. . . . The only church that truly feeds the soul, day in and day out, is the church of baseball."

Field of Dreams makes clear its baseball-as-religion point of view. In the basic plot a supernatural voice of revelation tells a young farmer and baseball fanatic (Kevin Costner) to plow up part of his cornfield and build a baseball field. The farmer does this, and soon baseball players from the past are playing on the baseball diamond, like saints from a land beyond the first rows of the cornfield. After the farmer has made a pilgrimage and faced his need for forgiveness, he is miraculously reconciled with his long-dead baseball-player father. At the end of the movie, the farmer's baseball field is a shrine that draws flocks of people seeking "the truth." The movie has many religious themes and symbols: life after death, a seeker who hears a voice and has to go on a spiritual quest, an inner healing, becoming a child in order to enter the kingdom, and losing your life to gain it.

Critical Views About Sport-as-Religion

In spite of the many seeming parallels between sport and religion, sport does not fulfill what are considered by many to be the key functions of "churchly" religion. For example, the question of why humans are created and continue to wrestle with their purpose here on earth and life hereafter is not addressed by sports. In this connection, several social scientists have noted that regardless of the eminence of those who contend that sports are a form of religion in this age of the Super Bowl and World Cup, sports and play are not even a natural religion. Instead they are an entirely different category of human experience, one that is significant in itself. Some scholars contend that the appropriation of traditional religion by advocates of sport-as-religion borders on heresy.

Other critics of sport-as-religion also emphasize that many activities that humans become deeply committed to can be referred to as a religion, when speaking metaphorically, but if we include in religion all meaningful or spiritual activities, we then wind up including practically all activities into which humans pour their will, emotions, and energy. Although sport does have some religious-like symbols, rituals, legends, sacred spaces and time, and heroes, it is organized and played by humans for humans without supernatural sanction. So for James A. Mathisen, North American sport is what he calls a folk religion. He says, "Sports looks like a religion, but it is not one. It is sort of like civil religion, but not quite. The best conceptual response amid this uncertainty is to interpret American sport as a contemporary folk religion." By this he means there "is a combination of shared moral principles and behavioral customs . . . a common set of ideas, rituals, and symbols . . . an overarching sense of unity." Joseph Price disagrees with Mathisen's comment about sport and civil religion. But for Price it is baseball, not sport in general, that is a civil religion. Price argues, "For true believers . . . the word of baseball is the gospel of an American civil religion that finds safety and wholeness— completion and salvation—where the game begins and where it ends: at home."[19] For religious historian Craig A. Forney, a holy trinity of football, baseball, and basketball forms a civil religion in American sports. He claims that "[f]ootball, baseball, and basketball are yearly rituals of civil religion in the United States."[20] Religion from these perspectives is not the universalistic posture of the world's institutional religions.

RELIGION USES SPORT

Churches

From a position of strong opposition to recreation and sport activities, most religions have made a complete reversal within the past century and now heartily support these activities as effective tools to promote "the Lord's work." Social service is a major purpose of the religious leaders who provide play and recreation under the auspices of their churches. Church-sponsored recreation and sport programs offer services to members and sometimes the entire community that are often unavailable in acceptable forms anywhere else. Church playgrounds and recreation centers in urban areas have facilities, equipment, and instruction that municipal governments often cannot provide. The Young Men's Christian Association (YMCA), the Young Women's Christian Association (YWCA), the Catholic Youth Organization (CYO), and other church-related organizations perform a variety of social services for old and young alike, one of which is the sponsorship of sports leagues.

Promoting sport to strengthen and increase fellowship in their congregations has been beneficial to the churches as well as to their members. In a time of increasing secularization, such as that witnessed by the United States and Canada in the past fifty years, it is understandable that churches would seek to promote activities that solidify and integrate church membership.

Religious Leaders Embrace Sport

Not content merely to provide recreational and sports opportunities under the sponsorship of the church, some religious leaders outwardly avow the association between religion and sport in their preaching and use of sport as a metaphor for the social enterprise of the church. Recently deceased

Jerry Falwell, founder of Liberty University and one of the self-styled leaders of fundamental Protestantism in the United States, told an audience: "[Jesus] wants you to be a victor for God's glory. A champion is not an individual star but one of a team who knows how to function with others." Several of the most popular contemporary evangelists enthusiastically support the virtues of sports competition and the sanctity of Christian coaches and athletes. They have made sport a basic metaphor in their ministries. For them, the source of Christianity, the Bible, legitimates sport involvement, and they often claim that the Bible says leisure and lying around are morally dangerous for us. Sports keep us busy.

Church Colleges and Universities

Intercollegiate sports programs were originally organized and administered by the students for their own recreation and amusement. By the early years of the twentieth century, however, the programs gradually changed form and character, and one of the new features that emerged was the use of collegiate sports teams to publicize the school and to bind alumni to their alma mater.

Church-supported colleges and universities began to use their athletic teams to attract students, funds, and public attention to impoverished (and sometimes academically inferior) institutions. The classic, but by no means only example is Notre Dame; many other Roman Catholic colleges and universities also have used football and basketball for publicity. Basketball, especially, has become a popular sport for Catholic colleges; indeed, Catholic university teams have played in the NCAA basketball championship games numerous times.

Protestant institutions have followed the same pattern of using their athletic teams to advertise; Brigham Young University (BYU), Texas Christian University, and Southern Methodist University (SMU) are among the most visible. Of these, BYU has become a renowned athletic powerhouse. It meshes conservative religious tenets with big-time sports and produces some of the more prominent professional athletes in North America. One BYU All-American football player said that he believed the athletes bring more attention to the Mormon church than anything else, and when he enrolled at BYU, the president of the university told him BYU was giving him a chance to be a missionary for the church by playing football for it.

Liberty University has aggressively embraced big-time athletics to publicize the school and use the school as a means of carrying out its mission of preaching the gospel of Christ to the world. Falwell said he wanted to make Liberty University to born-again Christians what Notre Dame is to Catholics and Brigham Young University is to Mormons. To that end, he hired a former NFL coach to lead the football team. Although the Liberty University teams have not achieved the exalted status that Falwell aspired to, the university has gradually climbed to NCAA Division I status.

Ironically, it was a church college, Southern Methodist University, that was hit with the most severe penalty ever meted out by the NCAA, the so-called death penalty—canceling SMU's entire football season schedule for one year. The NCAA took this drastic action after those connected with the SMU football program continually lied, cheated, and generally violated NCAA rules.

RELIGIOUS ORGANIZATIONS AND SPORTS

One of the most notable outgrowths of religion's use of sport has been the rise of nondenominational religious organizations composed of coaches and athletes. According to one estimate, some eighty organizations minister to the needs of athletes throughout the world; but it seems likely that there are many more than this, because there are more than twenty-five organizations of this type just in North America. These organizations provide a variety of programs designed to serve current members and recruit new members to religion. Several major incorporated organizations offer everything from national conferences to services before games. The best known are Fellowship of Christian Athletes (FCA), Sports Ambassadors, Athletes in Action (AIA), Pro Athletes Outreach (PAO), Motor Sports Ministries, Hockey Ministries International, and Baseball Chapel. The movement that these organizations represent has been labeled "Sportianity" or, more derisively, "Jocks for Jesus."[21]

The Fellowship of Christian Athletes

The prototypical organization for using sport as a tool for evangelism is the Fellowship of Christian Athletes, which was founded in 1954 with a focus on high school and college coaches and athletes and currently has about 600 paid employees and a membership of 1.2 million athletes. Its avowed purpose, which appears on most of its publications and on the title page of each issue of the official magazine of the FCA, *Sharing the Victory*, is "to present to athletes and coaches, and all whom they influence, the challenge and adventure of receiving Jesus Christ as Savior and Lord, serving him in their relationship and in the fellowship of the Church." The FCA attempts to combat juvenile delinquency, elevate the moral and spiritual standards of sports in a secular culture, challenge athletes to stand up and be counted for or against God, and appeal to sports enthusiasts and youth through hero worship harnessed.

The FCA uses older athletes and coaches to recruit younger ones to Christianity. It has a mailing list of more than 55,000 persons and a staff of over 650 nationwide. Its most important activity is the sponsorship of annual, weeklong summer camps attended by more than 13,000 participants, where coaches and athletes mix religious and inspirational sessions with sport instruction and competition.

Another important facet of the FCA's work is the "huddle fellowship program," in which junior high, high school, and college athletes in a community or on a campus get together to talk about their faith, engage in Bible study, and pray. They also take part in projects such as becoming "big brothers" for delinquent or needy children, visiting nursing homes, and serving as playground instructors.

There are now some 8,000 high school and college huddles in North America, the bulk of which are found in the South, Southwest, and Midwest. Most of the members of the FCA are white, middle-class males; however, female athletes are admitted to the FCA, and their membership in the organization is growing. In addition to these activities, the FCA sponsors state and regional retreats and provides various informational materials such as films, records, and tapes.[22]

Religion and Professional Sports Organizations

Organizations that focus on specific athletic groups supplement the work of the FCA. The NFL and major baseball leagues sponsor chapels and Bible studies for their athletes. Baseball Chapel, an evangelical Christian ministry, provides Sunday services to teams throughout the major and minor leagues. In conjunction, many pro teams have a "God Squad," a group of teammates who pray together and make public appearances on behalf of the Christian cause.

Professional sport organizations have sponsored religious events. Several NBA teams have sponsored a God and Country Night for their fans, a mixing of basketball, church, and state that attempts to recognize the role faith and patriotism play in the lives of management, players, and fans associated with the NBA. Third Coast Sports Foundation is a nonprofit ministry organization focused on promoting and organizing "Faith Nights" that seek to provide churches with opportunities for outreach and church-wide fellowship through sports and music. Faith Nights began in minor league baseball parks in 2002; by 2006 over seventy Faith Nights were scheduled for minor league teams across the United States. Faith Days and Faith Nights began in MLB ballparks in 2006, and in 2007 they were held in ten MLB cities.

Faith Nights feature bands, giveaways, and revival-style testimonials from players. They have migrated from the Deep South to northern stadiums from Spokane, Washington, to Bridgewater, New Jersey. Third Coast Sports has partnered with over sixty professional sports. A *New York Times* writer described these events: "Churches get discounted tickets to family-friendly evenings of music and sports with a Christian theme. And in return they mobilize their vast infrastructure of e-mail and phone lists, youth programs and chaperones, and of course their bus fleets, to help fill the stands."[23]

While these organizations and events have attracted the participation of many professional team franchises, athletes, coaches, and fans, not everyone is an advocate of this practice, claiming that it signals the Christianization of pro sports. Some believe that making religion part of the spectacle of public sporting events risks trivializing God and alienating nonbelieving teammates and fans. As one *USA Today* writer noted: "It is undoubtedly true that baseball, like the National Football League and National Basketball Association, has allowed itself to become a prime proselytizing vehicle for the evangelical sports ministries. No similar privilege is enjoyed by other religious movements." He continues, "major league sports do not exist for the chief purpose of promoting Christianity."[24]

Sport and Religion Publications

Several of the religious organizations identified in this chapter publish magazines or newsletters; however, one publication with a focus on sport and religion but with no affiliation with any specific religious organization is *Sports Spectrum*. *Sports Spectrum* is not an institutionalized evangelical organization but is, instead, a Christianized version of *Sports Illustrated*. According to its mission statement, it "seeks to highlight Christian athletes of all sports and levels to help motivate, encourage and inspire people in their faith through the exciting and challenging world of sports." Each issue covers a wide variety of sports, interviews with top athletes, and articles about top Christian athletes. Its website home page claims that "*Sports Spectrum* magazine gives you all the sports stuff you need with the values you want. . . . It is indeed the No. 1 Christian magazine for sports."[25]

Missionary Work of Churches and Sport

Religious leaders have increasingly used sport as a drawing card for attracting new members and retaining their followers. An often-used slogan of the clergy nicely sums up their view: "Many a one who comes to play remains to pray." Getting persons into church recreation and sports programs is often viewed as a first step into the church and into religious life. Playgrounds and recreation centers in or near churches, and the supervision of these facilities by clergy or laypersons with a strong religious commitment, provide a convenient setting for converting the non-churchgoing participant. A great deal of informal but successful missionary work is done in these settings. Famous sports figures make effective missionaries because of their prominence and prestige, and virtually every religious group has used coaches and athletes as evangelists to recruit new members.

There are several dozen ministry groups within North America working with international religious groups to mobilize massive recruiting efforts at the site of each Olympic Games. They use the Olympic Games, the most prestigious sporting event in the world—and an event that attracts people from all over the world—as a venue for recruiting people. They sponsor World Congresses on Sport prior to every Olympic Games.

Religious Evangelizing by Athletes and Coaches

Of all the purposes or consequences, or both, of religion's association with sport, certainly one of the most important is the use of athletes, coaches, and the sports environment to recruit new members to the church. Evangelical athletes who have made a personal commitment to religion accept the responsibility of witnessing their faith to others. As a result, the practice of athletes and coaches serving as lay evangelists is so widespread that it has been called a modern crusade.

One of the best known of the sport missionary groups is AIA, a ministry of Campus Crusade for Christ, made up mostly of former collegiate athletes. Its mission is to build "spiritual movements everywhere through the platform of sport. . . . AIA staff reach athletic influencers for Christ and train them to talk about the Lord one-on-one, with the media, and in other public forums to help fulfill the great commission."[26] With a special dispensation from the NCAA, the AIA fields several athletic teams that compete against amateur teams throughout the world each year. As part of each appearance of an AIA team, the AIA athletes make brief evangelical speeches and testimonials to the crowds and distribute free religious materials.

One major advantage of using athletes to evangelize is access. They interact closely and for prolonged periods of time with other athletes, and because they are widely admired, they are warmly welcomed by the general public. The missionary techniques of athletes are fairly straightforward. Those who are already committed to religion convert others. Because athletes are among the most visible and prestigious persons in North America, they may be used for missionary work in spreading their religion not only to their teammates but to anyone with whom they come in contact. Religious witnessing among athletes is tolerated and has become rather common in sports in the past two decades.[27]

Combining their popular appeal as celebrities with the metaphors of the sports world, athletes are able to catch and hold the attention of large groups of people. A high-profile athlete who understands the basics of his/her faith can reach more people, and especially young people, than a typical priest or minister can ever hope to reach. One sports scholar noted that many sports fans who wouldn't think of attending church to hear the eloquent sermons of a member of the clergy will patiently sit and listen to an athlete's inarticulate testimonial to "God, guts, and glory."

The Promise Keepers: Patriarchy, Gender, and Sexuality

In 1990 Bill McCartney, then the University of Colorado football coach, and a dedicated evangelical Christian, started the Promise Keepers as a fundamentalist Christian movement whose main goal is to evangelize men. It became one of the country's fastest-growing religious movements. The first event in Boulder, Colorado, in 1990 attracted 70 people; by 1996 over a dozen conferences were held nationwide, with between 20,000 and 75,000 in attendance at each. In the fall of 1997, an estimated 600,000 people attended a Promise Keepers "Stand in the Gap" rally on the Mall in Washington, D.C. The size, shape, and focus of Promise Keepers conferences have changed over the years.[28] In 2010 thirty-nine organizations were listed as ministry partners, and seven large conferences were held in cities such as Los Angeles, Dallas, Orlando, and Denver.

The central philosophical message of the Promise Keepers is that God commanded that men be dominant, the head of the family, and reclaim their leadership in the family and in the community, thus becoming better men of God. The traditional patriarchal gender role, with men as the family leader, is said to be dictated by God. This statement appears on its website: "Promise Keepers' mission is to ignite and unite men to become warriors who will change their world. . . . Promise Keepers' vision is simply put in three words: 'Men Transformed Worldwide.'"[29]

A focal theme of this male-only movement is that current social problems, especially what Promise Keepers consider the moral depravity and confusion over appropriate female and male social roles in our society, are caused by a lack of appropriate male leadership. The result, they claim, has been a feminization of the American male that has produced a nation of sissified men who abdicate their role as spiritually pure leaders, thus requiring women to fill the vacuum. The Promise Keepers' solution is the promotion of a traditional masculinity, with men taking the leadership roles and women accommodating to supporting roles. Such views have always restricted the popularity of the Promise Keepers. Perhaps to make the organization more palatable to greater numbers, in 2009, for the first time in the history of the nineteen-year-old Promise Keepers, its single-mindedness was broadened to invite women, the poor, and Jewish believers to one of its events.

In line with traditional masculine/feminine role definitions, the Promise Keepers share the position of religious fundamentalist Protestants and the Catholic Church that homosexuality violates God's creative design for males and females. McCartney publicly denounced homosexuality as "an abomination of almighty God." For women and men who have been struggling against traditional patriarchy and gender-specific social roles in contemporary society, groups like Promise Keepers seem to be a threat to the progress that has been made in recent decades. A number of women's organizations have been highly critical of the Promise Keepers, complaining that the organization preaches a subservient role for wives and, more broadly, assigns second-class citizenship to all females, a condition that women have lived with for generations. Gay and lesbian groups have expressed dismay at what they feel is a classic example of old-fashioned homophobic rhetoric.

The connections of the Promise Keepers to sport have been described in this way: "Although this group does not engage in sport or directly promote sport as an important part of its movement, it has used sport symbolically to communicate the ideologies of the organization. Sport venues become religious settings, sport rituals are converted into religious ones, sport heroes are revered as saints and moral exemplars, and sport metaphors are means for communicating key truths and desirable character traits."[30]

The Promise Keepers and sports intersect in a common vision of traditional male dominance and leadership. Sports culture has long been the site of male domination and the main source for defining appropriate masculine attitudes, values, and behaviors. As sport sociologist Becky Beal explains, "The Promise Keepers message is aimed at men for one main reason. The Promise Keepers firmly espouse that the moral depravity in our society is due to the lack of appropriate male leadership."[31]

Sportianity Confronting Social Issues

There is little inclination on the part of religious leaders and the various organizations that make up Sportianity to confront the pressing social issues of sport or of the larger society. Virtually all of the leaders in the Sportianity movement are reluctant to take a stand on moral issues within sports. In reviewing the numerous publications circulated by the organizations involved in Sportianity, one thing stands out rather glaringly, namely that there is little in the way of thoughtful critique of the culture of sport or little direct effort being channeled into improving the morality of sports.

There is no noticeable social reform movement on the part of Sportianity. Tom Krattenmaker, author of *Onward Christian Athletes*, contends that "many evangelical athletes who publicly thank Jesus for victory have nothing to say about other issues such as the pervasive use of steroids in sports or racial discrimination against aspiring minority coaches. It's an incomplete Christianity that's brought to bear on sports. They are blind and silent on the larger moral issues that vex the sports sector."[32]

The various religious organizations and their members have not taken forceful or prominent stands against or been at the forefront against racism, sexism, cheating, violence, the evils of collegiate athletic recruiting, or any of the other well-known unethical practices, excesses, and abuses in the world of sport, with the exception of exhortations about refraining from drugs. Instead, the pervasive theme is "stick with the positive; don't deal with the problems in sports." The impression is "don't stir the waters. Just publicize the good story about the good ole boy who does good things."

In the final analysis, then, sports morality does not appear to have been improved by the Sportianity movement. Instead, Sportianity seems willing to accept sport as is, and seems more devoted to recruiting new members and publicizing the achievements of athletes and coaches who publicly avow their religion than to dealing with sports as a social practice with many of the same problems of the larger society that need attention and resolution.

VALUE ORIENTATIONS OF RELIGION AND SPORT

Value orientations underlying competitive sports in North America may appear only remotely connected with religion, but most values that are central to sports are more or less secularized versions of the core values of Protestantism, which has been a dominant religious belief system throughout American and Canadian history.

The Protestant Ethic and Sports

The classic treatise of the Protestant ethic and its relationship to other spheres of social life is sociologist Max Weber's *The Protestant Ethic and the Spirit of Capitalism*, originally published near the beginning of the twentieth century.[33] The essence of Weber's thesis is that there is a parallel relationship between the Calvinist doctrine of Protestantism as a theological belief system and the growth of capitalism as a mode of economic organization. Weber suggested the relationship between Protestantism and capitalism was one of mutual influence; he used the term *elective affinity* (one of his translators used the word *correlation* in place of *elective affinity*).

The relationship exists in this way: For John Calvin, God could foresee and therefore know the future; thus, the future was predestined. In a world whose future was foreordained, the fate of every person was preestablished. Each person was, then, saved or doomed from birth by a kind of divine decree; nothing the individual did could change what God had done. Although each person's fate was sealed, the individual was plagued by "salvation anxiety" and craved some visible sign of his or her fate; and since Calvin taught that those elected by God acted in a godly manner, the elected could exhibit their salvation by glorifying God, especially by their work in this world.

According to Weber, "the only way of living acceptably to God . . . was through the fulfillment of obligations imposed upon the individual by . . . his calling." Thus, the best available sign of being among the chosen was to do one's job, to follow one's profession, to succeed in one's chosen career. According to Weber, "In practice this means that God helps those who help themselves." Work per se was exalted; indeed, it was sacred. The clearest manifestation of being chosen by God was success in one's work. Whoever enjoyed grace could not fail since success at work was visible evidence of election. Thus, successful persons could think of themselves, and be thought of by others, as the righteous persons. The upshot was that this produced an extreme drive toward individual achievement, resulting in what Weber called "ascetic Protestantism," a life of strict discipline and hard work as the best means of glorifying God.[34]

Although the Protestant ethic gave divine sanction to the drive to excel and encouraged success in business, industry, and science, it condemned the material enjoyment of success. The chosen person merely used success to document salvation. Persons who used success for personal gratification and luxury merely showed that they were doomed by God. To avoid the accumulation of vast personal wealth, Calvinism promoted the reinvestment of profits to produce more goods, which created more profits and, in turn, represented more capital for investment ad infinitum, the essence of entrepreneurial capitalism.

Weber's study of the relationship between religious beliefs and capitalism investigated the religious principles that provided a rationale for the ideology of capitalism and for the authority of the capitalist. The spirit of capitalism, according to Weber, consisted of several principles, each of which was compatible with Protestant principles. Collectively, they constituted a clear, elective affinity (correlation) between Calvinist Protestantism and the spirit of capitalism. Weber made it quite clear that he was not suggesting that one social process was a causal agent for the other. In his final paragraph, he said: "It is . . . not my aim to substitute for a one-sided materialistic an equally one-sided spiritualistic causal interpretation of culture and history."[35]

What does this have to do with sport? It is rather obvious that Weber's notion about the relationship between the Protestant ethic and the spirit of capitalism can be applied to the "spirit" of sport. In a book-length essay titled *The Influence of the Protestant Ethic on Sport and Recreation*, Steven Overman undertook to examine "the forms, values, meanings, and spirit of American sport and recreation within the context of secular Protestant culture." He argues that "American sport reveals the legacy of Protestantism. The Protestant ethic transformed sports into a medium in which individuals proved themselves through hard work and by the applications of scientific training. . . . What I am proposing is that the Protestant ethic has instilled American sport with a spirit, an *ethos*, which provides its distinct character, meaning, and guiding beliefs."[36]

Anyone familiar with contemporary sports and the Protestant ethic cannot overlook the unmistakable link between them (a correspondence also exists between capitalistic ideology and modern sports, but that will not be examined here). The emergence of sport as a pervasive feature of North American life undoubtedly owes its development to various social forces, one of which may be Protestant Christianity, the value orientations of which form the basis of the fundamental doctrine of the North American sport ideology. This ideology suggests that persons involved with sports, especially coaches and athletes, adhere to a particular kind of orthodoxy, the overriding orientation of which is individual achievement through competition. The phrase *ideology of sport* is a generic designation for all ideas espoused by or for those who participate in and exercise authority in sports as they seek to explain and justify their beliefs.

If we place the values inherent in the Protestant ethic and the ideology of sport side by side, it immediately becomes apparent that the two are congruent; that is, they share a significant equivalence. Without attempting to claim a causal link between the two belief systems, it does seem possible to suggest an elective affinity between them. Success, self-discipline, and hard work, the original tenets of the Protestant ethic, are the most highly valued qualities in sport.

Success

The Protestant stress on successful, individual achievement is in keeping with the values of contemporary sport. The characteristics of the good Christian are also those needed by the successful athlete. The social climate of organized sport is competitive, with an overriding sense of wins and losses. The notion that achievement separates the chosen from the doomed is seen in the winning-is-everything ideology in sports. Winners are the good people; personal worth is equated with winning. The loser is obviously not one of God's chosen people; failure in one's occupation stamps the Protestant-ethic believer as doomed to hell.

The Protestant ethic re-created in sport is captured by this assertion: Christians play their games for fun, but more important than fun is the responsibility to play them well and, of course, to win. Self-described "Christian athletes" have told researchers studying values in sports that to be successful in sports you've got to be downright mean sometimes, and sometimes you have to beat your opponent up to do well. Researchers report that most of the Christian athletes they study do not seem to have a conflict between their Christian faith and the values of their sporting behaviors.

The importance of winning is legitimized by implying that Christ himself would do whatever it takes to win. One Major League Baseball player who was a member of Baseball Chapel told a postgame interviewer that if Jesus Christ was sliding into second base, he would knock the second baseman into left field to break up a double play.

Religious groups that use athletes to evangelize and persuade potential converts to religion recognize the importance of selecting athletes who are winners. They know quite well that evangelical appeals by chronic losers or bench sitters are not likely to be effective. Athletes in Action teams play throughout the world, and AIA athletes often comment: "We have to win. That's what the world looks at. The world won't listen to our message if we are losers." This is true. Winning is critical to evangelical work. To the similar values of Protestantism and sports can be added American societal values. Christian athletes from both Canada and the United States who represent their countries in international sports events recurrently note: "It's important for us to win, not because God wants winners, but because our country does."

Although the quest, even the obsession, for victory in sport is congruent with the Calvinistic view as it is manifested in the Protestant ethic, the theology of Christianity contains a worldview that places the unmitigated quest for winning in question. To the question "What would Jesus do?" on the baseball field, Frank Deford, a Hall of Fame member of the National Association of Sportscasters and Sportswriters, described the sports ideal of legendary Hall of Fame Major League Baseball pitcher Christy Mathewson, a practicing "muscular Christian," in this way: "[Y]oung Christian men didn't have to be wimps. They won games, but they won them only in Jesus' image, playing by the rules."[37]

Self-Discipline

The notion that dedication, self-discipline, and sports participation may be an occupational calling is central to the ideology of Sportianity. God is glorified best, so the thinking goes, when athletes give totally of themselves in striving for success and victory. This is manifested in the traditional Christian asceticism that emphasizes sacrifice, control, and self-discipline as relevant means to salvation.

Christian athletes frequently describe their self-discipline and commitment in terms of not wanting to disappoint Jesus by giving anything less than a total effort with the talents they have been given by God. The greatest self-discipline challenge for the Christian athlete is to maintain the desire to win without compromising his or her faith, to maintain competitive enthusiasm with just the right amount of spiritual grace, in order to create the requisite competitive disposition without diminishing their Christian witness. The eternal quest of Christian athletes seems to be to attain spiritual control over their competitive attitudes while being careful not to be overly controlled and thus ineffective as a competitor.

Hard Work

Just as the businessperson is responsible to God to develop his or her talents to the fullest, according to the Protestant ethic, so it is that if God has granted one athletic abilities, then one is obligated to use those abilities to glorify and honor God; anything less than total dedication to the task is insufficient. A major league pitcher echoed this sentiment, saying that he had a responsibility for the talent he had been given, and that on the days when he didn't give his best, God should be upset with him.

Firmly embedded in the North American sport culture is a belief that hard work, training, and unremitting dedication by athletes and coaches not only will lead to success but are ways of using God-given abilities to glorify God, an important Protestant requirement. Sport culture is replete with slogans touting the necessity for hard work: "Workers are winners," "The harder you work, the luckier you get," "Winning is 99 percent perspiration and 1 percent inspiration." A favorite exhortation of coaches during practices is "Work, work, work!" And the highest praise a coach can give an athlete is to say that she or he "has a good work ethic."

Success can be considered as the justly deserved reward of a person's purposeful, self-denying, God-guided hard work. Giving less than 100 percent is regarded by some Christian athletes as a direct violation of God's law. A testimonial often expressed by these athletes is "I have been blessed by God with a lot of ability. My motivation for working hard is to use tools that God gave me for His glory."

Protestantism and Contemporary Sport

Any belief system that can help provide athletes and coaches with a rationale for their deep commitment to sports provides a means of expressing the essence of their striving, and Protestant theology does just that. In short, it is a belief system to which athletes and coaches can hold an elective affinity. Whether they actually do hold such an elective affinity remains a matter of speculation. Moreover, we hasten to add that Protestantism certainly is not responsible for the creation of the sport culture, but it does provide religious reinforcement for it.

Perhaps it is not coincidental that the belief systems of fundamentalist Protestantism and modern sports are so congruent. The two institutions use similar means to respond to their members' needs. Each tries to enforce and maintain, through a strict code of behavior and ritual, a strict belief system that is typically adopted and internalized by most involved. Each performs cohesive, integrative, and social control functions for its members, giving them meaningful ways to organize their world. Both religion and sport, because of the sacredness nurtured by these systems, resist social change and, in this way, support traditional values and practices.

SPORT USES RELIGION

Religious observances and competitive sports constantly impinge on each other, and religious practices of various kinds are found wherever one finds sports. Religion can be viewed from one point of view as an important means of coping with situations of stress. There are several categories of stress situations. One of these comprises situations in which largely uncontrolled and unpredictable forces may imperil the vital personal and social concerns of an individual or group. Sports competition falls into this category of stress because competition involves a great deal of uncertainty about a typically important outcome—winning and losing a sports event.

Coaches and athletes have great respect for the technical knowledge, skills, tactics, and strategy required for successful sports performance, but they are also aware of their limitations. As a supplement to the practical techniques, sports participants often employ religious practices. Coaches and athletes do not believe that these practices make up for their lack of technical knowledge, failure to acquire necessary skills, or employment of inappropriate strategy. However, religious practices help them adjust to stress by providing opportunities for them to dramatize their anxieties, thus reinforcing their self-confidence.

Religion invokes a sense of "doing something about it" in uncertain undertakings where practical knowledge and techniques alone cannot guarantee success. One of the most noted twentieth-century anthropologists, Bronislaw Malinowski, concluded from his research that when the outcome of vital social activities is greatly uncertain, magico-religious or other comparable techniques are inevitably used as a means of allaying tension and promoting adjustment.[38]

The Use of Prayer and Divine Intervention

Prayer is perhaps the most frequently employed use of religion by coaches and athletes; prayer for protection in competition, prayer for good performance, and prayer for victory are three examples. Sometimes the act of prayer is observed in gestures, such as a Roman Catholic basketball player crossing himself or herself before shooting a free throw or an athlete pointing an index finger skyward, or a football team praying in the huddle before or after a game. Several researchers who have studied so-called Born-Again Christian athletes concur that most of them use prayer to influence God to help their team win or to help them perform well.

The first historical example of prayer and the direct intervention of gods in sports competition is described by Homer in the *Iliad*. During the funeral games held in honor of Patroclus, who was killed in battle, one of the events was a footrace in which three men competed. Ajax took the lead from the start, followed closely by Odysseus: "Thus Odysseus ran close behind him and trod in his footsteps before the dust could settle in them, and on the head of Ajax fell the breath of the godlike hero running lightly and relentlessly on." As they neared the finish line, Odysseus prayed for divine assistance, and his prayer was answered by Athena, who not

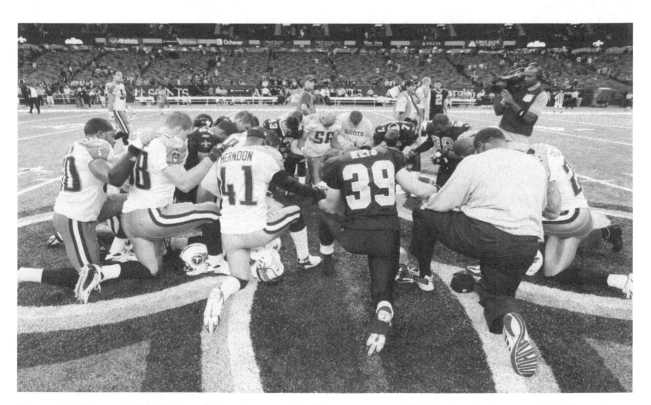

Tennessee Titans and New Orleans Saints players gather for a prayer at midfield after their game. (AP Photo/ Ann Heisenfelt)

only inspired him to make a last-minute dash but caused Ajax to slip and fall in a mass of cow dung, and Odysseus won the race. Ajax received an ox as second prize: "He stood holding the horns of the ox and spitting out dung, and exclaimed: 'Curse it, that goddess tripped me up. She always stands by Odysseus like a mother and helps him.'"[39]

Very little is known about the actual extent to which individual athletes use prayer in conjunction with their participation, but it seems probable that if some athletes are seen praying, others are doing so without outward, observable signs. Coaches often arrange to have religious services on the Sabbath or on game days. At present, almost every professional Major League Baseball and football team—more than fifty of them—hold Sunday chapel services, at home and away, and Sunday services are also held in sports as varied as NASCAR racing and golf. One of the claims for these religious services and prayers is that it strengthens a group's sense of its own identity, provides unity, and accentuates its "we" feeling.

There are probably other reasons why coaches sanction locker-room prayers. Observers who suspect that locker-room prayers are about coaches' only concession to religion imply that one coach does it because the other coaches are doing it, and "you can't let them get the edge." Others have suggested that it may be only a sweaty-palmed response to the anxieties and uncertainties of competition, a way to seek help in those gut-wrenching moments before a big game. In *The Prince of Tides* (also made into a movie), author Pat Conroy relates the events in one high school locker room before a football game. Although the book is a novel and the locker room is therefore fictitious, the situation as Conroy relates it seems very close to the reality many athletes have experienced in real-life locker rooms.

The coach began to speak:

"Tonight I'm gonna learn and the town's gonna learn who my hitters are. All you've proved so far is that you know how to put on pads and get dates to the sock hop after the game, but until I see you in action, I won't know if you're hitters or not. Real hitters. Now a real hitter is a headhunter who puts his head in the chest of his opponent and ain't happy if his opponent is still breathing after the play. A real hitter doesn't know what fear is except when he sees

it in the eyes of a ball carrier he's about to split in half. A real hitter loves pain, loves the screaming and the sweating and the brawling and the hatred of life down in the trenches. He likes to be at the spot where the blood flows and the teeth get kicked out. That's what this sport's all about, men. It's war, pure and simple. Now tonight, you go out there and kick butt all over that field. If something moves, hit it. If something breathes, hit it. . . .

"Now do I have me some hitters?" he screamed, veins throbbing along his temple.

"Yes, sir," we screamed back. . . .

"Do I have me some goddamn headhunters?"

"Yes, sir."

"Am I going to see blood?"

"Yes, sir."

"Am I going to see their guts hanging off your helmets?"

"Yes, sir."

"Am I going to hear their bones breaking all over the field?"

"Yes, sir," we happy hitters cried aloud. "Let us pray," he said.

He led the team in the recitation of the Lord's Prayer.[40]

This seems to epitomize what many coaches have been accused of—treating religion as group bonding that has little, if anything, to do with genuine heartfelt religious faith.

Although there is little empirical work on the use of prayer by athletes and coaches, a review of the research on this topic concluded: "This review has identified that athletes utilized religious prayer in sport for three main reasons: coping with uncertainties and the concomitant anxiety, putting life and sport into perspective, and providing meaning to sports participation and competition."[41]

Many athletes who pray believe that the use of prayer might affect the outcome of the game. So they ask God for a victory. One professional athlete asserted, "The question was posed to us, 'Does [God] control wins and losses?' Yes, He does." Another described the prayer he uses: "I ask for victories: 'God, I want to win so I have an even bigger platform for you.'" A college football player acknowledged that he and his teammates prayed that an opposing placekicker would miss a field goal that, if made, would have defeated his team. After the field goal was missed, the player said: "God came through and answered all our prayers on the sidelines and out there on the field."

Many athletes, coaches, and sport managers strongly believe that God intervenes on their behalf. In an interview after beating Tiger Woods to win the 2007 Master's Golf Tournament, Fellowship of Christian Athletes member Zach Johnson said, "I was not alone out there. Jesus was with me every step of the way." In 2006, Major League Baseball's Colorado Rockies, from the owners down, revealed they have become an organization guided by Christianity, and they believe God has had a hand in the team's improvement. General Manager Dan O'Dowd asserted, "You look at things that have happened to us this year. You look at some of the moves we made and didn't make. You look at some of the games we're winning. Those aren't just a co-incidence. God has definitely had a hand in this."[42]

Perhaps the most public sign that athletes be-lieve that God is aiding their performance is the seemingly ever-present index finger pointed to the sky thanking God. One CNN sport analyst noted, "Baseball players point to the heavens after hitting home runs; NFL players pray in the end zone after scoring. Competitors routinely thank Jesus, along with their sponsors, in post-game interviews."[43] Tim Tebow, shortly after becoming the Denver Broncos starting quarterback, in addition to regularly using the "finger to the sky thank you," introduced the "Tebow pose"—kneeling on one knee, bending forward, lowering his head, bringing a fist up to his forehead—closes his eyes, and recites a "thank you" prayer. The pose has been picked up and used by other prayerful athletes. It has also been used by other athletes to ridicule such public displays of religion.

These expressions have become commonplace at sports venues, even after run-of-the-mill perfor-mances. A few athletes that use them claim they are not religious signs but rather that they use the displays to pay tribute to a relative or friend. Most, however, admit they are a "thank you" to God.

Some religious leaders, athletes, coaches, and even fans renounce asking God for a victory, claiming it is crass and greedy. Furthermore, for many of them the idea that God intervenes in sports—that God roots for one team, but not the other—is offensive, even absurd and blasphemous. As William J. Baker,

author of *Playing with God*, puts it: "Athletes who publicly thank God for victory are often calling more attention to themselves than to their faith. . . . I don't think it's the right place and it's not the right gesture. It's an athlete using a moment to sell a product, like soap."[44] Even executives within the AIA are critical. As one of them said, "What's become so distasteful is this idea that God is only on the side of the winner. Winning players say they've been blessed, that God was in the details when it worked out in their favor. It's become almost a cliché among winners to go there. [But] to be credible you have to go there in both cases—winning *and* losing."[45] The Rev. Patrick Kelly, a faculty member of Seattle University's Center for the Study of Sport, adds another insight to this issue: "We don't want to get into this thing where God is on my side helping me to win all the time. God isn't there to help us achieve. He's there in much more significant ways."[46]

Tom Krattenmaker moves beyond the actions of individual athletes and coaches into a more sociological perspective. He contends: "The ath-letes' gestures and shout-outs to God are fruits of a campaign by well-organized, well-financed evan-gelical sports ministries committed to leveraging sports to reach and change the broader American culture." In another publication Krattenmaker asks, "[S]hould we be pleased that the civic resource known as 'our team—a resource supported by the diverse whole through our ticket-buying, game-watching, and tax-paying—is being leveraged by a one-truth evangelical campaign that has little appreciation for the beliefs of the rest of us?"[47]

Freedom of religious expression is guaranteed to citizens of both Canada and the United States. But less than 40 percent of the people in these countries regularly attend religious services, in spite of there being a greater diversity of religious groups than in any other industrialized countries. More-over, millions of Canadians and Americans do not subscribe to any institutionalized religion. Thus, it probably is not surprising that in North America there is growing resentment and opposition to the use of prayers in the locker room before games, in the huddles before and after games, and as public ceremonies before sports events, especially when they are part of public school events. If we assume journalists somewhat have their finger on the pulse of the public, the titles of recent newspaper articles clearly illustrate the collective mind on this issue of sports' use of religion: "For God's Sake, Leave Religion Out of the Game," "Prayer by Athletes Better Left on Sidelines," "Avoid Mix of Prayer and Points," "Athletes' Moralizing Cheapens Religion," "When Did God Become a Sports Fan?"

Undoubtedly, the most controversial practice is for clergy, athletes, and coaches to use prayer as a part of public school and university sporting events—especially in the United States, where the Constitution requires the separation of religion and state. Controversy over the proper interpretation of church-state relations in public educational institutions has a long history in the United States.

On the one side, Christian individuals and organizations have promoted prayer and other religious activities in the schools; on the other side have been individuals and groups who have claimed that the First Amendment to the Constitution specifically prohibits religious practices of any kind under the jurisdiction of the public schools. Since 1962 the U.S. Supreme Court has handed down several rulings on prayer in the schools, but lawsuits continue to arise against schools that practice religious observances of various kinds.

Two of the most notable incidents to gain widespread media coverage, and the most recent Supreme Court ruling, occurred in Texas and New Jersey. In the first, organized student-led prayers

---

Box 8.1   *Thinking About Sport:* Pregame Prayer at Public School Sports Events: Constitutional or Unconstitutional?

The fusing of sport and religion is readily observable at sporting events: The index finger pointed to the sky after a good performance, a team huddling together to pray just before or immediately after a game, and religious objects worn around the neck are tangible religious symbols that have become a common feature of the sports landscape. Many athletes admit to silently making a brief prayer just before shooting a free throw, stepping into the batter's box, while crouching in the starting blocks, and so forth. These are all acts of individual conscience and do not require anyone's attention or participation. They also meet the First Amendment "freedom of speech" guarantee.

The U.S. Constitution uses the word *religion* only once, stating: "[N]o religious test shall ever be required as a qualification to any office or public trust under the United States" (Article VI, C). The First Amendment to the Constitution states: "Congress shall make no law respecting an establishment of religion, or prohibiting the free exercise thereof." It is clear that the Founders of the Constitution wished to establish a separation of church and state, and once the United States was established, many of them spoke out and wrote adamantly opposing any state-church integration. Indeed, Thomas Jefferson referred to the First Amendment as creating a "wall of separation" between church and state.

Efforts to merge state and religion have been persistent throughout the history of the United States. However, when these efforts have confronted the U.S.

judicial system, the courts have overwhelmingly sided with the separation of church and state doctrine.

Individual acts of religious prayer and ritual, such as those mentioned above, have been interpreted by the courts as protected by the "free exercise thereof" phrase in the First Amendment because the state has no role in their practice. On the other hand, when prayers or religious rituals are conducted under the auspices of a federal, state, or municipal governmental entity during a public event, the courts have interpreted these as falling within the "establishment clause of the First Amendment," meaning the state is favoring a religion and therefore illegal.

From the beginning of public education in the early nineteenth century to the present, some Christian church leaders and their congregations have attempted to use the power of government, through the schools, as an instrument for promoting one favored view of religion—Christianity. Holding official prayers in the classrooms, posting the Ten Commandments in classrooms, distributing Bibles to students, and promoting attendance at specific churches during classes are a few of the techniques used.

With the rise of modern sports organizations during the twentieth century, two pregame rituals gradually became widespread: playing/singing the national anthem and prayers being given by a clergy or a designee. The former was a patriotic observance while the latter was

continues

at the high school in Galveston, Texas, during graduation exercises and football games resulted in a lawsuit filed by a Roman Catholic family and a Mormon family challenging prayers at these school functions (*Santa Fe Independent School District v. Doe*).

In the second, in the fall of 2005 a veteran East Brunswick, New Jersey, high school football coach, Marcus Borden, was told he would have to stop leading or taking part in prayers he initiated at pre-game meals and before the games. School officials explained that the prayers violated the separation between church and state in public schools.

In the Galveston, Texas, lawsuit, the Supreme Court delivered a strong rejection of prayer in public schools (see Box 8.1). A *USA Today* writer

said: "The court provided an unusually direct con-demnation of school-sanctioned prayer. 'School sponsorship of a religious message is impermissible because it [tells] members of the audience who are non-adherents that they are outsiders,' Justice Paul Stevens wrote."[48]

Subsequent to the Court's ruling on this case, advocates of school pregame prayer who contend the government should not limit prayers at high school events have experimented with a variety of ways to defy the Court's ruling. The defiance has been most pronounced in the southern states, the so-called Bible Belt, where public expressions of religious faith are a part of the daily routine, including school life. In a commentary about the

---

Box 8.1   Continued

clearly a religious ceremony. When a public prayer is conducted at a sporting event under the jurisdiction of either a private organization (as in the case of a professional sports event) or a religious organization, the courts have judged the prayer to be legal, since government agencies are not involved.

However, when a pregame prayer is conducted at a sporting event sponsored by a government agency, such as a public high school or college, it clearly raises an issue about violating the "establishment clause" of the First Amendment. In 1999 a Mormon and a Roman Catholic family filed a lawsuit against the Galveston, Texas, Santa Fe Independent School District for per-mitting "student-selected, student-given" prayers being read over the public address system at football games. Such prayers are a long-standing tradition in Texas, and in some other states as well. Nevertheless, the U.S. Court of Appeals for the Fifth Circuit declared the Santa Fe School District practice to be unconstitutional, saying that football games are "hardly the type of event that can be appropriately solemnized with prayer."

Then Governor of Texas George W. Bush in-structed the Texas attorney general to file an appeal, and thirteen Texas members of Congress introduced a resolution in the U.S. House of Representatives to negate the Circuit Court of Appeals decision. Congress passed a nonbinding resolution—which has no legal status in law—that encouraged Christian prayer before public school athletic games. Within two weeks of the congressional resolution, the U.S. Supreme Court

announced that it would hear arguments on this case during 2000.

Consistent with several previous court decisions in similar cases, on June 19, 2000, by a vote of six to three, the U.S. Supreme Court declared that the practice of Santa Fe School District school adminis-trators of allowing students to conduct formal prayers before school games was unconstitutional. The Court found that:

- including prayers before a sports event when school administrators were involved was a state-sponsored religious activity and was therefore unconstitutional.
- formal prayers unconstitutionally coerced at-tendees into participating in a religious activity.
- the state may not endorse overtly religious mes-sages, even if the majority of the people favor it.
- a prayer truly initiated by an individual stu-dent is protected free speech. For example, a player can spontaneously call for a group prayer huddle. A person in the stands can assemble an informal group prayer.
- an individual, truly voluntary prayer by a student is protected speech, both before, during, and after school.

Source: The text of the Supreme Court's decision in *Santa Fe Independent School District v. Doe* can be found at http://supct.law.cornell.edu/supct/html/99-62.ZS.html.

Court's decision in this case, a legal scholar also addressed those who defy the Court's decision, saying, "it is reasonable for concerned citizens to disagree strongly about when student prayer crosses the constitutional line. But, when those who disagree with *Santa Fe* deliberately violate the decision, they are unintentionally undermining respect for all of the laws they want others to uphold."[49]

As for the issue of the New Jersey high school football coach, Coach Borden immediately resigned, saying that coaches across the state lead similar prayers with their teams. He subsequently returned to his job but brought a lawsuit against the East Brunswick school district, claiming the school district's action violated his First and Fourteenth Amendment rights to free speech, free association, and academic freedom. In the lawsuit, Coach Borden contended that he merely bowed his head and "took a knee" during prayers initiated and led by student-athletes. In March 2009, the Supreme Court rejected Coach Borden's appeal to bow his head and kneel during prayers led by his players despite a school district policy prohibiting it. The high court's order forbids him and other staff members from joining in student-led prayer, but declined to weigh in on whether Borden's actions violate the Constitution's prohibition on government endorsement of religion.

Previous Supreme Court decisions have established that public school officials and employees may not offer, initiate, or lead prayers before sporting events. Borden's court did not frame the legal issue as a test of whether a reasonable, objective observer would view "head bowing" or "taking a knee" as government endorsement of religion. But it did support the school officials that Borden's actions violated the separation between church and state in public schools.[50]

Religious services in connection with sporting events are still held at church-sponsored high schools and colleges, as well as at professional sporting events; indeed, to have an important sports event started by a religious invocation is not unusual. Some invocations are brief and to the point, but others are used by clergy to conduct a religious service or to metaphorically dramatize the relationship between sports and religion.

The Use of Magic

The reader may be surprised, even shocked, that a section on magic is included in this chapter, because many people see no relationship between magical practices and religion. In practice, however, religion and magic, as defined by anthropologists, are closely intertwined. Although magic and religion are alike in assuming the existence of supernatural powers, a significant difference exists between the ends that they seek. Religion is oriented to the otherworldly, toward a supreme supernatural god, and religion typically centers on such overarching issues as salvation and the meaning of life and death; this is not true of magic. The practitioner of magic seeks ends that are in the everyday world of events; magic is oriented toward immediate, practical goals.

There are other ways in which religion and magic differ. Religious worshipers possess an attitude of awe and reverence toward the sacred ends they pursue, but the users of magic are in business for practical and arbitrarily chosen ends. The latter are manipulators of the supernatural for their own private advantage rather than worshipers of it; the attitude of magic users is likely to be utilitarian. In this respect, Bronislaw Malinowski, noted that magic has an end in pursuit of which the magical ritual is performed. The religious ritual has no purpose, that is, the ritual is not a means to an end but an end in itself. Malinowski said, "While in the magical act the underlying idea and aim is always clear, straightforward and definite, in religious ceremony there is no purpose directed toward a subsequent event."[51] Furthermore, the content of magic and religion differs. The content of magic has no unified inclusive theory but instead tends to be atomistic, somewhat like a book of recipes. Religion, on the other hand, tends to encompass the whole of life; it often provides a comprehensive theory of both the supernatural and human society.

The Malinowski Thesis

According to Malinowski, magic flourishes in situations of uncertainty and threat; it is most commonly invoked in situations of high anxiety about accomplishing desired ends. The origin of most magical rites can be traced to fears experienced individually or collectively. These rites are associated with human helplessness in the face of danger and unpredictability, which give rise to superstitious beliefs and overt practices to ward off impending danger or failure and to bring good luck. Malinowski reported: "We find magic wherever the elements of chance and accident, and the emotional play between hope and fear have a wide and extensive range. We do not find magic wherever the pursuit is certain, reliable, and well under control of rational methods."[52] In support of this contention, Malinowski compared two forms of fishing among natives of the Trobriand Islands of Melanesia: lagoon and open-sea fishing. "It is most significant that in the lagoon fishing, where man can rely completely upon his knowledge and skill, magic does not exist, while in the open-sea fishing, full of danger and uncertainty, there is extensive magical ritual to secure safety and good results."[53]

Malinowski's thesis about the conditions under which magic appears is applicable to the world of sport. Athletes and coaches are engaged in an activity of uncertain outcome in which they have a great deal of emotional investment. Even dedicated conditioning and practice and the acquisition of high-level skills do not guarantee victory because opponents are often evenly matched and player injury and other dangers are often present. Thus, "getting the breaks" or "lucking out" may be the determining factor in the outcome of a contest. Having a weakly hit baseball fall in for a base hit, a deflected hockey puck go in the net, or a deflected football pass caught by an unintended receiver are examples of luck or "getting the breaks" in sports. Although the cliché "the best team always wins" is part of the folk wisdom of sport, athletes and coaches know that this is not always so and indeed believe that factors leading to a win or a loss are somewhat out of their control.

According to Malinowski's theory, athletes and coaches may use magic to bring them luck and to ensure that they "get the breaks," thus supplying themselves with beliefs that serve to bridge over uncertainty and threat in their pursuit of victories. The magic enables them to carry out their actions with a sense of assurance and confidence and to maintain poise and mental integrity in the face of opponents.

Magic and Its Uses in Sports

It is difficult to assess just how extensive the uses of magic are in sport. Newspaper and magazine stories leave little doubt, however, that magical beliefs and practices play a prominent role in the lives of athletes and coaches. One form of magical belief is superstition, which is a belief that one's fate is in the hands of mysterious external powers, governed by forces over which one has no control. Sports studies scholars who have scrutinized the superstitions of athletes claim that many athletes turn to superstitions for the same reasons that others turn to religion—they provide a mental confidence, a feeling of assurance, that often makes the difference between success and failure at the highest levels of athletic competition.

In a book-length treatment of magic in sports, one of North America's most respected hockey writers, Andrew Podnieks, describes the fascinating and fun world of hockey superstitions: their origins, their quirks, and the mythology around them. In the process, he illustrates that athletes and coaches employ almost anything imaginable that might ensure "getting the breaks," and this often involves some form of superstitious behavior.[54]

Sport superstitions are similar for athletes who compete in teams and for those who compete in individual sports, but team athletes indicate greater use of superstitions related to equipment and its use, to the order of entering the sports arena, and to dressing-room rituals than do individual-sport athletes. Pregame superstitions of basketball players center on warm-up rituals; game superstitions are directed toward free-throw shooting, team cheers, and gum chewing. Endorsement of superstitions increases with involvement in sport; in other words, the higher the competitive level and the greater the involvement in a sport, the greater the prevalence of superstition. The gender of the athlete is less important than the level of involvement. Superstitions are related to the uncertainty and importance of the outcome, as Malinowski indicated.

Beyond superstitions, other forms of magic such rituals, taboos, fetishes, and witchcraft can also become co-mingled in a sport. Applying the Malinowski thesis to baseball, anthropologist George Gmelch, a former professional ball player, published what has now become one of the classic studies of athletes and their uses of magical practices. Gmelch hypothesized that in baseball magical practices would be associated more with hitting and pitching than with fielding; the first two involve a high degree of chance and unpredictability, whereas the average fielding success rate is about 97 percent, reflecting almost complete control over the outcome. From his observations as a participant in professional baseball, Gmelch reported that there was indeed a greater incidence and variety of rituals, taboos, and use of fetishes related to hitting and pitching than in fielding. He concluded—in support of Malinowski's hypothesis about the relationship between magic and uncertainty—that baseball players associate magic with hitting and pitching, but not with fielding. Indeed, despite the wide assortment of magic associated with both hitting and pitching, Gmelch never observed any directly related to fielding.[55]

To illustrate how magical practices are used in sports, we devote a section to each of these forms of magic practice: ritual, taboo, fetishism, and witchcraft.

Ritual

Rituals are standardized routines that impart the sense that cause-and-effect relationships are within an individual's power to control, and sports are infused with ritualistic practices. An almost infinite variety of rituals are practiced in sport, because all athletes are free to ritualize any activity they consider important for successful performance. Whether they are a psychological placebo, a desire to control fate, or merely a way of sustaining a winning method, rituals have been a long-standing staple in sports.

Typically, rituals arise from successful performances. Unable to attribute an exceptional performance to skill alone but hoping to repeat it in future contests, athletes and coaches single out something they did before the performance as being responsible for their success. That "something" might be a certain food they had eaten before the

Youth sports players gather to stack hands before a game, one of the oldest rituals in several sports. (istockphoto)

game, a new pair of socks or sneakers they had put on, or a specific sequence of behaviors preceding the contest. Some examples follow:

- Serena Williams won't change her socks at tournaments she's winning.
- Jason Giambi (the former Oakland, Yankees, and Colorado Rockies first baseman) slips on a pair of "lucky" thong underwear when his batting average falls. The thong's reputation is so potent that slumping teammates reportedly beg to borrow it.
- Brian Urlacher, Chicago Bears linebacker, eats exactly two chocolate chip cookies prior to every game. Not one, not three, two.
- Before every game, LeBron James tosses the scorer's chalk into the air. The motive behind James's chalk ritual is still unknown. Some might say that its purpose is to boost his confidence; others, that this ritual shows his arrogance and disrespect for his opponents.
- Arizona Cardinals safety Matt Ware's pregame ritual always must proceed like this: Cut off six pieces of surgical tape, four long and two short. Get two H-shaped bandages, plus four Blist-O-Ban blister bandages for the toes and feet. Go back to the locker and tape up. Grab a Gatorade and drop a cramp-fighting fizzy electrolyte tablet into it.
- Tiger Woods wears a red shirt on the last day of every tournament he plays.

In addition to individual rituals, there are a number of team rituals. In basketball the ritual of stacking hands is frequently employed just before the team takes the floor at the beginning of the game and after time-outs. The most universal hockey ritual occurs just before the start of a game when players skate in front of their goal and tap their goalie on the pads for good luck. In a story of the rituals of a girls' high school field hockey team, the reporter revealed that before every game the girls would kneel before the coach; he then blessed them with a charitable helping of "Hockey Dust" (which was actually an exclusive blend of ninety-nine-cent sparkle and precious good luck).

Taboo

A taboo is a strong social norm prohibiting certain actions that are punishable by the group or by magical consequences. There are numerous institutional taboos in each sport and, of course, many personal taboos. Athletes and coaches believe breaking a taboo will lead to undesirable outcomes or bad luck. Two of the strongest taboos in baseball prohibit crossing the handles of bats and mentioning that the pitcher has a no-hitter in progress. Crossing bats is believed to bring bad luck and mentioning a no-hitter to the pitcher is believed to break his spell on the batters, ending his chances to complete a no-hit game.

During a winning streak, athletes and coaches in many sports will insist on wearing some or all of the same clothing—uniform, socks, jock, bra, shoes, sweatshirt, warm-up, etc.—that they were wearing when the winning streak started. Washing apparel during a winning streak is one of the most common taboos. Several years ago the uniforms of the entire Purdue University women's rugby team went unwashed, as long as they were winning. The coach explained the taboo this way: "If the luck is in the fabric, why risk washing it out?"

Some athletes develop taboos about not stepping on portions of the playing surface, such as the chalk foul lines (just as children avoid stepping on sidewalk cracks). One of the common game taboos in baseball and softball is to avoid stepping on the foul line when sprinting onto or off the field. Next time you watch a game in one of these sports, notice how often players jump over the lines as they run to and from the dugout.

Fetishism

Fetishes are revered objects believed to have "supernatural" power to attain the desired ends for the person who possesses or uses them. Fetishes are standard equipment for coaches and athletes. They include a bewildering assortment of objects: rabbits' feet, pictures of heroes or loved ones, pins, coins, remnants of old equipment, certain numbered uniforms, and so forth. Typically, these objects obtain their power through association with successful performances. For example, if the athlete or coach happens to be wearing or using the object during a victory, the individual attributes the good fortune to the object; it then becomes a fetish embodied with supernatural power. The extent to which some athletes take fetishes seriously is illustrated by this Colorado State University men's basketball player: In an early season game, the player made two three-pointers in the final seven-tenths of a second in an unexpected comeback victory over Purdue University. Directors at the Basketball Hall of Fame requested the shoes he was wearing at the time of his incredible feat so they could place them in a display case in the Hall of Fame. Believing that his shoes had magical power, the player made the Hall of Fame wait until the end of the season before turning over the shoes. Those shoes had become a fetish to him.

Particular items of athletic apparel and equipment commonly are turned into fetishes, and athletes and coaches believe that not wearing that apparel or not using certain equipment will result in poor performance and cause a loss. Uniform numbers also frequently become fetishes for athletes. For some professional athletes the uniform number attains fetish significance to the point that if they are traded they seek assurances that they will be assigned that number by the new team.

Almost everyone who has been around sports has a story of an athlete, coach, or team that had apparel or equipment fetishes of some kind and went to bizarre extremes to make sure nothing interfered with the use of those items.

Witchcraft

Magical practices that are intended to bring misfortune on others are known as black magic, witchcraft, or sorcery. In sport, those who employ this form of magic believe that supernatural powers are being harnessed to harm or bring misfortune on opponents. In Africa witchcraft dominates some sports. Medicine men who claim that they can make the ball disappear or that they can cast a spell on opposing players are especially active in soccer. In 2002 in the African country of Cameroon, a soccer coach was banned from coaching for a year when he was charged with dropping a charm believed to contain black magic onto the field during a semifinal match at the African Cup of Nations. It is estimated that about 95 percent of Kenyan soccer teams hire witch doctors to help them win, and matches have been marred by witchcraft-inspired riots.

In North America we laugh when reading about African soccer teams traveling with witch doctors, and we are amused by such practices of witchcraft as players painting their bodies with pig fat to ward off evil spirits, reasoning that sports teams in North America are much too sophisticated to travel with witch doctors or to wear pig fat. North American teams, instead, often travel with Catholic priests and Protestant ministers and wear medals around their necks! We may not recognize that some of the social antics of our athletes and coaches aimed at calling for the intervention of the supernatural on their behalf can be viewed as acts of sorcery.

Actually, witchcraft is not confined to African sports. During an American League baseball game several years ago, a Kansas City player hit a two-run homer to beat the New York Yankees. One of the Kansas City coaches claimed that the victory was the result of his enlisting the help of his godfather, a practitioner of voodoo. The coach revealed that he called his godfather to ask what could be done to ensure that the Royals would win the pennant. Although the godfather was a Yankees fan, he felt obligated to help his godson, and so he told him, "Stick the Yankee line-up card in the freezer," an action that he said would "freeze their bats." Before the game, the Kansas City coach dutifully obtained a copy of the New York lineup, went into a back room in Yankee Stadium, and placed the card in a freezer. This is why, the coach said, the Yankees scored only two runs and lost the game.

SUMMARY

In this chapter we have examined the reciprocal relationship between sport and religion. Although sport and religion may appear to have little in common, we have attempted to demonstrate that contemporary sport and contemporary religion are related in a variety of ways. Religions perform several important functions: At the individual level they provide individuals with emotional support; at the interpersonal level they provide a form of human bonding; at the institutional level they serve as a vehicle for social control; and at the societal level they promote social integration. For many centuries Christian church dogma was antithetical to play and sport activities, but over the past century, with the enormous growth of organized sport, churches and religious leaders have welded a link between these two institutions by sponsoring sports events under religious auspices and by proselytizing athletes to religion and then using them as missionaries to convert new members.

Although contemporary religion uses sport for the promotion of its causes, sport uses religion as well. Numerous activities with a religious connotation—ceremonies, rituals, and so forth—are employed in connection with sports contests.

The most common use of religion by athletes, coaches, and fans is prayer. One of the persisting social problems is the use of public prayer ceremonies before sporting events and the practice of some coaches of conducting prayers with their athletes in locker rooms and in sporting venues before a sporting event. Such practices give rise to many personal objections and legal controversies. The practice of magic—through rituals, taboos, fetishism, and witchcraft—is widespread in sport. Such behaviors are most common in sporting situations where there is uncertainty, threat, and high anxiety about accomplishing desired ends.

WEB RESOURCES

www.fca.org
The official site for the Fellowship of Christian Athletes has links to information about huddles, camps, resources, and global FCA.

www.athletesinaction.org
The Athletes in Action site describes the AIA mission and what its members do and has links to ministry sites.

www.sportsambassadors.org
The website for People to People Sports Ambassadors has descriptions of history, programs, tournaments, and coaches.

www.baseballchapel.org
The website of the Baseball Chapel has discussions of its mission, vision, and history and the impact of the Baseball Chapel.

www.promisekeepers.org
The website for the Promise Keepers mainly features news and articles about Promise Keepers and other Christian sport topics.

www.sportsspectrum.com
Sports Spectrum magazine online claims to feature Christians who happen to be some of the world's top athletes.

NOTES

1. For a good source of detailed information about religious affiliation, see the Pew Forum on Religion & Public Life, *U.S. Religious Landscape Survey* (Washington, DC: Pew Research Center, 25 February 2008), http://pewresearch.org/pubs/743/united-states-religion; for a superb comprehensive examination of religion and its relationship with sports, see Shirl L. Hoffman, *Good Game: Christianity and the Culture of Sports* (Waco, TX: Baylor University Press, 2010).

2. Rick Reilly, "Let Us Play," *Sports Illustrated*, 26 April 2004, p. 172.

3. Émile Durkheim, *The Elementary Forms of Religious Life*, trans. Carol Cosman, *Oxford World Classics* (New York: Oxford University Press, 2001), 62.

4. For a good explanation of religion as a social institution, see Inger Furseth and Pal Repstad, *An Introduction to the Sociology of Religion: Classical and Contemporary Perspectives* (Burlington, VT: Ashgate Publishing, 2006); see also James A. Beckford and N. Jay Demerath, eds., *The SAGE Handbook of the Sociology of Religion* (Thousand Oaks, CA: Sage Publications, 2007).

5. Lois Tyson, *Critical Theory Today: A User-Friendly Guide*, 2nd ed. (New York: Routledge, 2006); and Paul D'Amato, *The Meaning of Marxism* (Chicago: Haymarket Books, 2006). Karl Marx argued: "Religion is the sigh of the oppressed creature, the heart of a heartless world, and the soul of soulless conditions. It is the opium of the people."

6. Judith Tyson, *The Ancient Olympic Games*, 2nd ed. (Austin: University of Texas Press, 2008); see also Stephen G. Miller, *Ancient Greek Athletics* (New Haven: Yale University Press, 2006).

7. Robert Mechikoff, *A History and Philosophy of Sport and Physical Education: From Ancient Civilizations to Modern World*, 5th ed. (New York: McGraw-Hill, 2009).

8. Stewart Culin, *Games of the North American Indian* (Washington, DC: U.S. Government Printing Office, 1907), 34; see also Joseph Oxendine, *American Indian Sports Heritage* (Champagne, IL: Human Kinetics, 1998); and Donald M. Fisher, *Lacrosse: A History of the Game* (Baltimore: Johns Hopkins University Press, 2002).

9. Bruce C. Daniels, *Puritans at Play: Leisure and Recreation in Colonial New England* (New York: Palgrave, 2005), 166.

10. Bruce C. Daniels, "Sober Mirth and Pleasant Poisons: Puritan Ambivalence Toward Leisure and Recreation in Colonial New England," in *Sport in America: From Colonial Leisure to Celebrity Figures and Globalization*, Vol. II, ed. David K. Wiggins (Champaign: IL: Human Kinetics, 2010), 5–21.

11. "Amusements," *New Englander* 9 (1851): 358; see also Steven J. Overman, *The Influence of the Protestant Ethic on Sport and Recreation* (Brookfield, VT: Avebury, 1997), 134–157, and Tony Ladd and James A. Mathisen, *Muscular Christianity: Evangelical Protestants and the Development of American Sports* (Grand Rapids, MI: Baker Books, 1999), 22–68.

12. Clifford Putney, *Muscular Christianity: Manhood and Sports in Protestant America, 1880–1920* (Cambridge, MA: Harvard University Press, 2003), 1; see also David K. Wiggins, ed., *Sport in America: From Colonial Leisure to Celebrity Figures and Globalization*, Vol. II (Champaign: IL: Human Kinetics, 2010), Part III, 123–192.

13. William J. Baker, *Playing with God: Religion and Modern Sport* (Cambridge, MA: Harvard University Press, 2007), 171.

14. Shirl Hoffman, "The Decline of Civility and the Rise of Religion in American Sport," *Quest* 51 (February 1999): 80.

15. Charles S. Prebish, comp., *Religion and Sport: The Meeting of Sacred and Profane* (Westport, CT: Greenwood, 1993), 62, 74.

16. Tom Faulkner, "A Puckish Reflection on Religion in Canada," in *From Season to Season: Sports as American Religion*, ed. Joseph L. Price (Macon, GA: Mercer University Press, 2004), 185, 200.

17. Eric Bain-Selbo, *Game Day and God: Football, Faith, and Politics in the American South* (Macon, GA: Mercer University Press, 2009), 213, 235; see also Robert J. Higgs and Michael C. Breaswell, *An Unholy Alliance: The Sacred and Modern Sports* (Macon, GA: Mercer University Press, 2004), ch. 8.

18. *The Speeches of Avery Brundage* (Lausanne, Switzerland: Comité International Olympique, 1968), 80.

19. James A. Mathisen, "American Sport as Folk Religion: Examining a Test of Its Strength," in *From Season to Season: Sports as American Religion*, ed. Price, 142; and Joseph L. Price, *Rounding the Bases: Baseball and Religion in America* (Macon, GA: Mercer University Press, 2006), 175.

20. Craig A. Forney, *The Holy Trinity of American Sports: Civil Religion in Football, Baseball, and Basketball* (Macon, GA: Mercer University Press, 2007), 189.

21. Tom Krattenmaker, *Onward Christian Athletes* (Lanham, MD: Rowman & Littlefield, 2010).

22. Official site for the Fellowship of Christian Athletes, http://www.fca.org; see also Krattenmaker, *Onward Christian Athletes*, 51–67.

23. Warren St. John, "Sports and Salvation on Faith Night at the Stadium," *New York Times*, 2 June 2006, p. 1A.

24. Garth Woolsey, "Christian Theme Riding High on a Pigskin," *ThirdCoastSports.com*, 7 October 2010, http://www.faithnights.com/content.asp?CID=89573; and Murray Chass, "Is a Night Devoted to Faith Really About the Money?" *New York Times*, 14 March 2008, p. D4.

25. Home page, *Sports Spectrum Magazine*, http://www.sportsspectrum.com/daily/.

26. Home page, "About Athletes in Action," *Athletes in Action Online*, http://www.athletesinaction.org.

27. Baker, *Playing with God*, 200–201.

28. John P. Bartkowski, *The Promise Keepers: Servants, Soldiers, and Godly Men* (Piscataway, NJ: Rutgers University Press, 2004).

29. "About Us," *PromiseKeepers.org*, http://www.promisekeepers.org/about/.

30. George D. Randels, Jr., and Becky Beal, "What Makes a Man? Religion, Sport and Negotiating Masculine Identity in the Promise Keepers," in *With God on Their Side: Sport in the Service of Religion*, ed. Tara Magdalinski and Timothy J. L. Chandler (New York: Routledge, 2002), 160.

31. Becky Beal, "The Promise Keepers' Use of Sport in Defining 'Christlike' Masculinity," in *The Promise Keepers: Essays on Masculinity and Christianity*, ed. Dane S. Claussen (Jefferson, NC: McFarland & Co., 2000), 155.

32. Quoted in John Blake, "When Did God Become a Sports Fan?" *CNN.com*, 25 May 2010, http://articles.cnn.com/2010-05-25/living/God.sports_1_god-athletes-faith?_s=PM:LIVING; see also Krattenmaker, *Onward Christian Athletes*.

33. Max Weber, *The Protestant Ethic and the Spirit of Capitalism*, 2nd ed., trans. Talcott Parsons (Los Angeles: Roxbury, 1998). This essay, probably the most famous work on the sociology of religion, has aroused a great deal of controversy among sociologists and historians.

34. Ibid., 80, 115.

35. Ibid., 183.

36. Overman, *The Influence of the Protestant Ethic on Sport and Recreation*, 10, 158, 159.

37. Frank Deford, *The Old Ball Game* (New York: Atlantic Monthly Press, 2005), 36.

38. Bronislaw Malinowski, *Magic, Science, and Religion and Other Essays* (Long Grove, IL: Waveland Press, 1992).

39. Louise R. Loomis, ed., *The Iliad of Homer*, trans. Samuel Butler (Ann Arbor, MI: Borders Classics, 2006), 307.

40. Pat Conroy, *The Prince of Tides* (New York: Bantam Press Trade Paperbacks, 2002), 394–395.

41. Nick J. Watson and Daniel R. Czech, "The Use of Prayer in Sport: Implications for Sport Psychology Consulting," *Athletic Insight* 7, no. 4 (December 2005): 29, http://www.athleticinsight.com/Vol7Iss4/PrayerPDF.pdf.

42. Quoted in Dave Zirin, "The Rockies Pitch Religion," *The Nation*, 2 June 2006, http://www.thenation.com/doc/20060619/zirin; see also Electa Draper, "Split on Tebow: Some Fans Laud the New Bronco's Public Faith, While Others Wish Religion Stayed Off the Field, *Denver Post*, 4 August 2010, p. B1.

43. Blake, "When Did God Become a Sports Fan?"; see also Jorge L. Ortiz, "Pointing: It Isn't Just for Pop-Ups Anymore," *USA Today*, 14 June 2006, p. C3.

44. Quoted in Blake, "When Did God Become a Sports Fan?"

45. Quoted in Krattenmaker, *Onward Christian Athletes*, 81.

46. Quoted in Ortiz, "Pointing: It Isn't Just for Pop-Ups Anymore."

47. Krattenmaker, *Onward Christian Athletes*, 6; Tom Krattenmaker, "And I'd Like to Thank God Almighty," *USA Today*, 12 October 2009, p. 11A.

48. Quoted in Joan Biskupic, "School Prayer Rejected," *USA Today*, 20 June 2000, p. 1A. See also Adam Thompson, "Prayer and Preps," *Denver Post*, 20 June 2000, pp. 1D, 8D.

49. David Schimmel, "Court Outlaws School-Sponsored Student Prayer: An Analysis of *Santa Fe v. Doe*," *West's Education Law Reporter* 150, no. 1 (1 March 2001): 13. See also Julia Duin, "School Prayer Charges Stir Protests," *Washington Times*, 14 August 2009, http://www.washingtontimes.com/news/2009/aug/14/criminal-prayer-case-stirs-protests/?feat=home_headlines, and Bill Mears, "Supreme Court: Justices Refuse Appeal of Coach Banned From Student-Led Prayers," *CNN.com*, 2 March 2009, http://articles.cnn.com/2009-03-02/us/scotus.school.prayer_1_student-led-prayers-pregame-prayers-prayer-activities?_s=PM:US.

50. Associated Press, "U.S. Supreme Court Rejects Appeal by East Brunswick Football Coach in Prayer Case," *nj.com*, 2 March 2009. http://www.nj.com/news/index.ssf/2009/03/us_supreme_court_rejects_appea.html.

51. Malinowski, *Magic, Science, and Religion and Other Essays*, 12–30.

52. Ibid., 116.

53. Ibid., 14.

54. Andrew Podnieks, *Hockey Superstitions: From Playoff Beards to Crossed Sticks and Lucky Socks* (Toronto: McClelland & Stewart, 2010); see also Lysann Damisch, Barbara Stoberock, and Thomas Mussweiler, "Keep Your Fingers Crossed! How Superstition Improves Performance," *Psychological Science* 21 no. 7 (2010): 1014–1020; and Michaéla C. Schippers and Paul A. M. Van Lange, "The Psychological Benefits of Superstitious Rituals in Top Sport: A Study Among Top Sportspersons," *Journal of Applied Social Psychology* 36 (2006): 2532–2553.

55. George Gmelch, *Inside Pitch: Life in Professional Baseball* (Lincoln: University of Nebraska Press, 2006), 133–143.

CHAPTER 9

Sport and Politics

One thing is certain: we can pretend sports aren't political just as well as we can pretend there is no such thing as gravity if we fall out of an airplane.
—Dave Zirin*

A giant American flag is displayed on the field before an NFL football game during the playing of the national anthem. This patriotic pageantry is frequently employed at sports events symbolically uniting citizens in a common bond of patriotism. (AP Photo)

*Dave Zirin, *A People's History of Sports in the United States: 250 Years of Politics, Protest, People, and Play* (New York: The New Press, 2009), 268.

A statement often heard in discussions among friends about issues and problems in sport is "Keep politics out of sport" or the reverse, "Keep sport out of politics." Such a comment is usually followed by expressions of agreement with the speaker. But these assertions do not correspond at all with reality. A more realistic point of view is expressed by journalist and sport administrator Des Wilson, who declared: "To seek to isolate sport as an activity that stands alone in human affairs, untouched by 'politic' or 'moral considerations'. . . is as unrealistic as it is (self-destructively) self-serving."[1] Indeed, examples of the ties between sport and politics are plentiful. A few are described below:

- At the 1972 Munich Summer Olympic Games, Palestinian terrorists attacked Israeli athletes, killing eleven of them. The terrorists demanded the release and safe passage to Egypt of 234 Palestinians and non-Arabs jailed in Israel.
- The United States (and other nations) boycotted the 1980 Summer Olympic Games in Moscow; the Soviet Union (and other nations) boycotted the 1984 Los Angeles Summer Olympics.
- In South Africa, sport was isolated worldwide from international sports events from the 1960s through the 1980s because of the country's apartheid governmental policies.

Each of these examples illustrates the intermingling of sport and politics at international sporting events, but sport-political connections are present at all levels of sport and politics, from the local to the state (or province) to the national. For example:

- A decision by the city council of a town to build (or not to build) a public golf course is a political decision.
- A decision by a city metropolitan district to seek public funds to build a baseball field for the Colorado Rockies Major League Baseball team was a political decision.
- A decision to pay a large percentage of the cost to build the SkyDome (now Rogers Centre), a multipurpose stadium in Toronto, Ontario, Canada, as a home venue for the American League's Toronto Blue Jays was

a political decision by all three levels of Canadian government (metro Toronto, provincial, and federal).

- In 1990 President George H. W. Bush signed the Americans with Disabilities Act (ADA)—a political decision—which turned out to include protecting the rights of athletes with physical or mental disabilities. As a result the United States Olympic Committee provides sport training and competition for athletes with physical disabilities, and U.S. athletes participate in the Paralympics.

POLITICS AS A SOCIAL INSTITUTION

Before exploring the sport and politics connections in depth, we believe it is necessary to develop some basic understandings about the social institution of politics.

There is no single agreed-upon definition of *politics,* but the word brings forth considerations about government, politicians, and public policies. The network of administrative and bureaucratic agencies that make up municipal, state, provincial, and national government is the core political entity. Beyond that, there is an organized power structure comprising a great variety of organizations, including hundreds of elected officeholders, appointed officials, the military, the legal system, and the many public bureaucracies and agencies involved in public policy making, opinion shaping, and ideology formation.

The feminist movement popularized the slogan "The personal is political" during the 1960s and 1970s to rebut critics who accused women of "playing politics" when they sought equal treatment and opportunity in the economic, political, religious, educational, social, and sporting sectors of their lives. Since then, other oppressed groups have adopted this slogan.

In connection with politics, power is a central theme for sociologists because it is present in all social organizations. Max Weber, one of the most prominent pioneer sociologists, defined *power* as the ability to get others to do one's will even in the face of opposition. Power is present in personal relationships, in groups, in formal organizations, and in nation-states. It can be exercised by force and threats of force, meaning actual or threatened use of coercion or violence to impose one's will on others. Power can also be exercised by authority, which is a form of power that is recognized or legitimated by those over whom it is employed. Influence is a third form of exercising power, and it can be exercised through a power holder's persuasion or extraordinary personal qualities ("charisma").[2]

Sociologists tend to study how power is distributed—who has power and who does not and why, who benefits by the power arrangements and who does not, and how power is distributed and changed. The struggle for power and authority can involve entire nations, large organizations, small groups, and even persons in intimate association.

Social Theories and Politics

Functionalists view the political social institution as a system of people occupying specific positions because they are necessary for the orderly accomplishment of the group's, organization's, or nation's objectives. Where it involves the government, the use of power and authority is seen as necessary and beneficial to all because it reflects the laws and customs of citizens—a government of, by, and for the people—and ensures order, stability, and justice. The will of the majority is believed to prevail, there is equality before the law, and decisions are made to maximize the common good.

The conflict/cultural perspective emphasizes that power often becomes concentrated in an economically elite group of people who are motivated largely by their own self-interests. Conflict/cultural theorists view government as habitually existing for the benefit of the ruling, or dominant, class. "The power elite" is what social theorist C. Wright Mills labeled the leaders of the military, corporate, and political elements of society, and he argued that their power is exercised to serve their interests rather than the common good. Furthermore, he maintained that the ordinary citizen is a relatively powerless subject of manipulation by those entities. Several other scholars have advanced the same theme in the years since Mills first articulated it.[3]

INTERTWINING OF POLITICS AND SPORTS

In this section we focus on how politics is manifested in the world of sports. Our main contention is that sport and politics are closely intertwined.[4]

Governmental intervention into sports has never been a central feature of legislation and policy making, but government involvement has played a role in the games and sports of citizens in a variety of ways. For instance, government actions to control or prohibit domestic sporting practices actually have a lengthy history in North America. In the North American colonies, religious influence resulted in laws prohibiting boxing, wrestling, and cockfighting because they were violent and play and games in general because they were often performed on the Sabbath. In the early twentieth century, U.S. President Theodore Roosevelt threatened to abolish intercollegiate football unless changes were made to reduce the brutality of the game.

More recently, gender discrimination in U.S. high school and college sports programs was made illegal when the federal government passed Title IX of the Educational Amendments Act of 1972, which specified: "No person in the United States shall, on the basis of sex, be excluded from participation in, be denied the benefits of, or be subjected to discrimination under any education program or activity receiving Federal financial assistance."[5]

Another example of the sports and politics connection is the allegiance that people have to a particular sports team or organization (e.g., "their" high school, university, company, community, nation), such that they become committed representatives of that sport organization. Many of the rituals accompanying sporting events (such as slogans, chants, music, wearing of special clothing, and so forth) are aimed at symbolically representing or affirming fidelity to a team or sponsoring organization, pitted against opposing teams. Such events are primarily affairs for spectators, who are drawn to them not so much by the spectacle or the rituals, or by an appreciation of the skills involved, but because they identify themselves with "their" team.

Yet another illustration of the close relationship between sport and politics is found in the process of organization itself. As sport has become increasingly organized, numerous teams, leagues, players' associations, and ruling bodies have been created. These groups acquire certain powers that by their very nature are distributed unequally. Thus, power struggles have developed between players and owners (e.g., threats of strikes by the players or lockouts by the owners), within organizations (e.g., the NCAA and university athletic departments moving too slowly on gender equity), between leagues, and between various sanctioning bodies.

As we noted above, the essence of politics is power. In sports, various organizations have power over teams, coaches, and athletes. Television networks, for example, have enormous power over sport. They have insisted on changes in sports, such as converting golf from match play to medal play and interrupting the continuous sports of basketball, soccer, and hockey with mandatory time-outs to broadcast commercial advertising. The Disney Corporation owns ABC Sports and ESPN and through these entities has exerted tremendous power over schedules, moving times and dates to accommodate TV programming schedules rather than the fans or the teams involved. Consider also the power exerted over sports by Time Warner, which owns *Sports Illustrated* as well as the TNT, HBO, and TBS television networks—to name just a few of its media conglomerates.

Behind the scenes, power brokers for television networks have sometimes determined the opponents in football bowl games and invitational basketball tournaments. Other corporations, most notably those selling beer, soda, cars, cable television, and athletic apparel, have enormous power over sport. Some of these corporations actually own teams (e.g., Molson Brewing owns 20 percent of the Montreal Canadiens; Madison Square Garden, Inc., owns Madison Square Garden and manages the assets of the New York Knicks and the New York Rangers).

The linkage between sport and politics is quite obvious when the impact of the government on sports is considered. Several illustrations at the federal level make this point:

- Legislation has been passed exempting professional sports from antitrust laws.
- Tax laws give special concessions to owners of professional teams (see Chapter 10).

- Congress crafts legislation that exempts college sports and their benefactors from taxes. (See Box 9.1 for more information on this subject.)
- For the 2002 Winter Olympics in Salt Lake City, the federal government contributed an estimated $1.5 billion in taxpayers' dollars for road and sport venue construction, the laying of fiber-optic cable, and security.
- The President's Council on Physical Fitness and Sports advises the president through the Secretary of Health and Human Services about physical activity, fitness, and sports; it also recommends programs to promote regular physical activity for the health of all Americans.
- The U.S. Congress chartered the United States Olympic Committee to govern American participation in the Olympic Movement.

The close relationship between sport and politics was on display when the U.S. boycotted the 1980 Olympics and the Soviet Union boycotted the 1984 Olympics in retaliation. The apartheid policies of South Africa resulted in that nation being barred from many international sports competitions, including the Olympic Games. These actions clearly demonstrate that sport has been used as a tool of foreign policy, inasmuch as the refusal by one country to compete in sports against another is a way of applying political pressure on that country.

Within the U.S. and Canada, municipal, state, and provincial governments may encourage sports organizations through various forms of funding. These levels of government are very generous in subsidizing local teams owned by private entrepreneurs (as we will describe in detail in the next chapter). For example, Atlanta and other local governments spent approximately $90 million, and the state of Georgia spent $150 million, on projects related to the 1996 Summer Olympics.

The institutional character of sport is a final source of the strong relationship between sport and politics. Sport, like other social institutions, is conservative; consequently, it has served as a preserver and a legitimator of the existing order

---

Box 9.1   *Thinking About Sport:* Government Decisions Aid Big-Time College Sports

Congress has passed legislation that subsidizes big-time college athletic programs through a variety of tax breaks:

- Boosters are allowed to claim 80 percent of the money they spend on the premiums (fees) they pay to obtain season tickets. These are considered (by Congress) to be charitable contributions.
- Corporations underwrite bowl games and pay millions for the right to connect their corporate names to the bowls and to display their names and logos throughout the stadiums. Congress ruled that this is not advertising but philanthropy, thus exempting the bowl committees from taxation on the income money received from the corporations.
- Athletic departments benefit from taxpayer-subsidized loans to construct stadiums and arenas. Much of the multibillion-dollar building boom in college athletics is underwritten with bonds that, because of the colleges' charitable status, are tax-exempt. This helps the purchasers of the bonds to escape taxes and saves the

schools millions of dollars because the bonds pay interest several points below market level.

- College sports are exempt from the unrelated business income tax, a tax levy on the commercial activities of nonprofit organizations. This means, in effect, that the colleges pay no taxes on the income they receive from individual contributors, booster clubs, television networks, bowl and tournament payouts, corporate gifts, and ticket sales (including the sale of luxury suites).

These subsidies to college sports amount to millions of dollars each year. Congress justifies these subsidies on the grounds that college sport is a vital part of the broader educational mission of universities. (For a contrary argument, see Chapter 6.)

Sources: Lynnley Browning, "The I.R.S. Considers Pressing Schools to Further Reveal Their Business Activities," *New York Times*, 14 January 2009, p. B3; Charles Clotfelter, "Stop the Tax Deduction for Major College Sports Programs," *Washington Post* (op-ed), 10 January 2011, http://www.cambridgeblog.org/2011/01/clotfelter-booster-donations/.

---

on many occasions. The patriotic pageants that accompany sporting events reinforce the political system. Moreover, sport perpetuates many myths, one of which is that anyone with talent, regardless of race or social station, has an equal chance to succeed.

We have seen that the very nature of sport makes politics endemic to it. The remainder of this chapter will demonstrate this relationship further by examining the various political uses of sport, and the politics of the Olympic Games.

THE POLITICAL USES OF SPORT

Sport as a Vehicle for Propaganda

Success in international competition frequently serves as a means by which a nation's ruling elite unites its citizens and attempts to impress the citizens of other countries. Nations have increasingly forged direct propaganda links between

sport triumphs and the viability of their political-economic systems. A classic example of this was Adolf Hitler's use of the 1936 Olympic Games to strengthen his control over the German people and to introduce Nazi culture to the entire world. According to Christopher Hilton in his book *Hitler's Olympics*, the activities planned for these Games was a shrewdly propagandistic and brilliantly conceived charade that reinforced and mobilized the hysterical patriotism of the German masses.[6] The success of the German athletes at those Olympics—they won eighty-nine medals, twenty-three more than U.S. athletes, and more than four times as many as any other country won—was touted as "proof" of German superiority.

Before the breakup of the Eastern European bloc countries, the reunification of the two Germanys, and the demise of the Soviet Union, the Communist nations used sport for promoting their common cause. Between the 1952 Helsinki Olympic Games and the 1988 Seoul Olympics, the Communist countries dominated the Olympics, even

America's Jesse Owens, center, salutes during the presentation of his gold medal for the long jump at what is often called the Nazi Olympic Games in Berlin, Germany in 1936. Adolf Hitler used those Games to strengthen his control over the German people. (AP Photo)

though they were about 10 percent of the athletes at those events. This, the Communists argued, provided convincing evidence of the superiority of the Communist political-economic system.

Of the Communist nations that currently remain, perhaps Cuba takes sport the most seriously. Fidel Castro, president of Cuba from 1976 to 2008, decreed that sport is a right of the people. Most of his policies toward sports remain. No admission is ever charged to a sporting event. The most promising athletes are given the best coaching and training. Cuba devotes 3 percent of its national budget to its sports ministry, which encourages and trains elite athletes. In the Pan-American Games, Cuba tends to win about fifteen times more medals than the United States on a per capita basis, and Cuban Castro proclaimed to the Americas that this is proof of the superiority of the Cuban people and the

Cuban system. (See Table 9.1 for an analysis of how the nations ranked in the 2008 Beijing Summer Olympics, taking population into account.)

The most striking example of success in the modern Olympics before the breakdown of the Communist countries was East Germany (German Democratic Republic). Although it was a nation smaller in population than California (16.6 million compared to 25 million in California at the time), East Germany consistently ranked in the top three nations in total medals and clearly outdistanced the Soviet Union and the United States on a per capita basis. In 1987, East Germany spent about 1 percent of its national budget on its massive sports program. From the age of seven, children were tested, and the most promising athletes were enrolled in sixteen special schools, where they received special training, medical and scientific expertise, and expert coaching in addition to their normal schooling. After their formal education was completed, the star athletes were given special jobs, permanent military deferments, and apartments.

Why did East Germany devote so much money, time, and talent to sport? One reason was the competition between East and West Germany. A second reason was East Germany's goal of international acceptance as a sovereign state. Another reason was the desire to demonstrate the superiority of the Communist way of life. Shortly after the demise of East Germany, *U.S. News and World Report*'s Lynn Rosellini wrote: "For the Communist nations, each victory was proof, as East German party General Secretary Erich Honecker put it, of 'their better socialist system.'"[7] East Germany was not unlike the other Communist countries in using sport for the accomplishment of political goals.

Currently, China is using the Soviet model to develop sports talent and to enhance the stature of the Chinese political and social system worldwide. About 6 million young athletes are trained at sport schools, with those at the highest levels subsidized by the state. The United States estimated that China spent from $400 million to $500 million to train athletes in the four years leading up to the 2008 Olympic Games.[8]

National efforts to use sport for political purposes are not limited to Communist countries. International sports victories are just as important

Table 9.1   Beijing Olympics, 2008: Medal Standings per Country by Population

(1) Rank by Population	(2) Rank by Medals Won	(3) Country	(4) Population (Millions)	(5) Actual Medal Totals
1	13	Jamaica	2.7	11
2	65	Bahamas	0.3	2
3	71	Iceland	0.3	1
4	41	Slovenia	2.0	5
5 * *	21	Norway	4.7	10
9 *	26	New Zealand	4.2	9
11 * *	28	Cuba	11.3	24
17 * *	30	Denmark	5.5	7
22 * *	4	Great Britain	61.0	47
30 *	10	France	61.7	40
32 * *	5	Germany	82.3	41
36 * *	3	Russia	141.6	72
44	2	United States	301.6	110

Column 1 shows rank according to weighted per capita total. Column 2 shows the actual rank according to actual medals.
Source: Bill Mitchell, "Bill Mitchell's Alternative Olympic Games Medal Tally–2008," *BillMitchell.org*, 27 August 2008, http://www.billmitchell.org/sport/medal_tally_2008.html.

to nations such as Canada and the United States. Canada has a federal agency, Sport Canada, and similar organizations at the provincial level that work to promote sports excellence in elite athletes. There is a federal Athlete Assistance Program, which gives living and training grants to outstanding athletes. There is also a network of national training centers, with professionalized coaching, and a calendar of events. These efforts are done to enhance Canadian nationalism and the Canadian state's legitimacy.

After the 1972 Olympics, when the U.S. fared worse than was expected (especially in track and basketball), many editorial writers and politicians advocated plans whereby U.S. athletes would be subsidized and would receive the best coaching and facilities to regain international athletic supremacy

for propaganda purposes. This did not happen, and the cry arose again after the 1976 Olympics. As a result, Congress appropriated funds for the United States Olympic Committee (USOC) and for the establishment of permanent training sites for the Winter and Summer Games.

By 1990 the International Olympic Committee (IOC) had loosened the eligibility rules for participation, and athletes participating in the Olympic Games did not have to be amateurs—professional athletes could compete in the Olympics. Currently, Olympic-level athletes receive money from a variety of sources and, most significant, from the USOC and the sports' national governing bodies, which spent around $225 million from 2004 to 2008 to prepare them for the 2008 Olympic Games. Sport can be an effective propaganda tool only if it is associated with victorious performances.

The U.S. government uses athletes to promote international goodwill and to enhance the American image abroad. The State Department, for example, sponsors tours of athletes to foreign countries for these purposes.

Sport as an instrument of propaganda is not limited to the industrialized nations of the world. The developing countries use sport even more for this purpose, with almost 90 percent having a cabinet-level post related to sport. The probable reason for such keen interest is that sport provides a relatively cheap political tool to accomplish national objectives of prestige abroad and unity at home.[9]

Sport and Nationalism

When athletes and teams of one country compete against those of another, nationalistic sentiments arise. Identification with the athletes and teams representing one's country tends to unite citizens regardless of social class, race, and regional differences. Citizens take pride in "their" athletes' accomplishments, viewing them as collective achievements. For example, even war-ravaged Iraq, with its ethnic and sectarian divides, was united briefly in 2008 when Iraqi athletes were permitted to participate in the 2008 Beijing Olympics. Spontaneous celebrations occurred, with people dancing in the streets and waving Iraqi flags. (See Box 9.2, concerning South Africa.)

The Olympic Games and other international games tend to promote an "us versus them" feeling among athletes, coaches, politicians, the press, and fans. The Olympic Games, in this sense, represent a political contest, a symbolic world war, in which nations win or lose. This interpretation is commonly held; that is why citizens of each nation involved unite behind their flag and their athletes.

Box 9.2   *Thinking About Sport:* Sport Unifies Whites and Blacks in South Africa

South Africa was barred for a time from the Olympic Games and other international competitions, most notably the World Cup of the favorite sport of whites—rugby. With the fall of apartheid and the election of Nelson Mandela, the sports world accepted South Africa, so much so that it was allowed to host the 1995 World Cup in rugby.

President Mandela used the rugby World Cup as an opportunity to bring change in South Africa. He visited the training camp of South Africa's team—the Springboks. While there he put on a Springbok cap.

This was no casual gesture. The nickname *Springbok* is controversial in South Africa, strongly associated with the apartheid white regimes of the past.

Then Mandela pointedly told the rugby players, "The whole nation is behind you."

The Springboks (white except for one black player) took that message to heart. The day before their game against Australia, the players requested a tour of Robben Island, off Cape Town, where Mandela had been imprisoned for eighteen years. They visited his former cell and afterward vowed to dedicate their efforts in the World Cup to their president.

Before one of the matches Mandela gave a speech in front of a primarily black audience. He said, "This cap does honor to our boys. I ask you to stand by them tomorrow because they are our kind."

The Springboks won the World Cup, defeating the world's two rugby powers, Australia and New Zealand, in the process. For the first time in South Africa's troubled history, whites and blacks found themselves unified by a sport.

That was 1995. Now fast-forward to 2006. Whereas the Springboks had only one black player in 1995, eleven years later they had six black or colored players in the starting fifteen. For the first time in the history of South African cricket, the national team was captained by a nonwhite player in 2006, and five of its squad of thirteen were black or colored. Clearly, there has been progress, but whites, who are but 9 percent of the population, remain the majority on the field. The point, though, is that the national teams in rugby and cricket are multiracial, and in this country obsessed by sport, that is an important symbol of progress toward racial integration and national unity.

Sources: John Carlin, *Playing the Enemy: Nelson Mandela and the Game That Made a Nation* (New York: Penguin Press, 2008); John Carlin, *Invictus: Nelson Mandela and the Game That Made a Nation* (New York: Penguin Press, 2009).

Many people will watch the Olympic Games for one reason: There is a competitor or team who, they feel, is representing them. That athlete or team is "their" athlete or team—running, jumping, throwing, or boxing—for their country. For a few minutes at least, their own evaluation of themselves will be bound up with the performance. The athlete or team will be the embodiment of their nation's strength or weakness. A victory will be victory for them; a defeat will be defeat for them.

This last point requires emphasis. Evidence from the Olympic Games and other international competitions shows that for many nations and their citizens, victory is an index of that nation's superiority (in its military might, its political-economic system, and its culture). Clearly, the outcomes of international sports contests are very often interpreted politically, a topic we will return to later in this chapter.

The integral interrelationship of sport and nationalism is easily seen in the blatantly militaristic pageantry that often surrounds sporting events. The playing of the national anthem, the presentation of the colors, the jet aircraft flyovers, and the band forming a flag or a liberty bell are all political acts supportive of the existing political system.

This patriotic pageantry was especially evident at sports events following the terrorist attacks on September 11, 2001. Such a crisis momentarily brought people together, uniting them in a common cause and a common bond of patriotism. Whereas before the terrorist tragedies, sports events began with the traditional singing of the national anthem, after September 11 sports events began with a moment of silent tribute to the fallen, a patriotic display of huge flags and other symbols, cannons firing, presentation of the colors, crowd chants of "U-S-A, U-S-A," and the sports crowds singing the national anthem with enthusiasm. Sport sociologist Samantha King noted that "it becomes increasingly hard within U.S. national culture to discern where the war ends and the games begin."[10] Shortly after the 2002 Super Bowl, one of us reflected on the politically themed pageantry before and during the football game:

The first Super Bowl after the September attack, on February 3, 2002, in New Orleans, outdid itself in nationalistic fervor. For the first gathering of 131 million U.S. households since September 11th, television and the NFL took the opportunity to celebrate all things American. . . . Included in the event was . . . Barry Manilow singing "Let Freedom Ring," and Paul McCartney singing his song "Freedom," with young women dressed as Statues of Liberty, military personnel, firefighters, and police holding flags. . . . At halftime, the NFL presented the band U2, who sang several songs on a stage in front of a huge unfurling scroll listing those whose lives were lost on September 11th. . . . The message was the nexus of politics and sports, football and nationhood.[11]

In such ways, sports can have the important political consequence of helping to "glue" citizens back together after a national tragedy.

The irony is that nationalistic displays typically are not generally interpreted as political because they are perceived as merely reinforcing nonpolitical patriotic feelings. But what would happen if during the Iraq or Afghanistan Wars, a college band formed a peace symbol at halftime? Such a display of what many would view as antiwar spirit would likely be interpreted as blatantly political. But is not a halftime show in support of the government's policies just as "political"?

Athletes who do not show proper respect for the flag or for the national anthem are subject to stiff penalties. Perhaps the most world-renowned example of this was when U.S. Olympic track

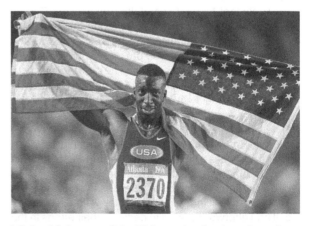

Michael Johnson of the U.S. carries the American flag after winning the gold medal in the men's 200 meters during the 1996 Olympic Games at the Olympic Stadium in Atlanta, Georgia. (Getty Images)

athletes Tommie Smith and John Carlos raised gloved, clenched fists and bowed their heads during the national anthem at the 1968 Olympics as a symbol of support for the anti-racism movement in the U.S. The USOC banned them from further Olympic competition.

In 2003 the captain of the women's basketball team at Manhattanville College in Purchase, New York, turned her back on the U.S. flag during the pregame playing of the national anthem to protest the U.S. invasion of Iraq. This action sparked outrage, with calls for the dismissal of the player, threats by several colleges not to play Manhattanville unless the offending player was dismissed, and debates about the issue throughout the sports and political worlds.

Occasionally there are questions raised about the commonplace patriotic rituals at sports events on the grounds that they do not occur at most other public events (e.g., plays, lectures, concerts, and movies). However, the support for these patriotic rituals is so strong that whenever an occasional administrator decides not to play the national anthem at a sports event, there is, typically, a public outcry.

Sport as an Opiate of the Masses

We have shown that sport success can unite a nation through pride. This pride in and devotion to a nation's success transcends the social classes and has been said to serve as an "opiate of the masses" (a phrase used by Karl Marx about organized religion). In the present context, this means that sport conceals and obscures significant realities of contemporary life, thus distracting peoples' attention from the harshness of social or economic life that many of them daily endure, as well as leading them to disregard endemic social inequalities and injustices all around them.

In 1994, for example, when Haiti was on the verge of a severe crisis, the embattled military ruler, Raoul Cedras, paid for the broadcasting rights to the World Cup soccer matches. The spirits of the Haitians were raised when their adopted team, Brazil, won the World Cup. Rather than massing in the streets to demonstrate against a political regime that oppressed them, citizens danced in the streets because their favorite team had won. Moreover, the

matches were played on the government-owned television station, so the rulers used halftime to inflame anti-American feelings by showing footage of the U.S. invasion of Panama in 1989, focusing on the bombing of residential areas. Thus, sport served as a safety valve for releasing tensions that might otherwise be directed toward challenging the existing social order.

Sport can also act as an opiate by perpetuating the belief that persons from the lowest classes can be upwardly mobile through success in sports. Chapter 12 will deal with this topic in more detail; for now, it is enough to say that for every professional team sport athlete who came up from poverty, tens of thousands did not. The point, however, is that most North Americans believe that sport is a mobility escalator. Poor youths who might otherwise invest their energies in improving their education work instead on a jump shot or catching a football. Thus, for many the potential for social mobility is impeded by sport.[12]

The Exploitation of Sport by Politicians

The reciprocity of politics and sports is made transparent when athletes become politicians. An athlete can use his or her athletic fame as a springboard to getting elected or appointed to office. Some examples are professional basketball players Tom McMillen and Bill Bradley, who served in Congress; world-class runners Ralph Metcalfe, Bob Mathias, and Jim Ryun, who also served in Congress; former NFL quarterback Jack Kemp, who was a member of the House of Representatives from 1971 to 1989 and, in 1988, campaigned for the United States presidency; former NFL players Steve Largent and J. C. Watts, who, during the Republican wave in 1994, were swept into Congress as representatives from Oklahoma; former NFL player Heath Shuler, who was elected to the House in 2007; Jon Runyan, who played in the NFL for fourteen seasons and was elected to that chamber in 2010; Major League Baseball player Wilmer "Vinegar Bend" Mizell, who served in the House; and MLB player Jim Bunning, who served in the Senate.

In Canada, Leonard Patrick "Red" Kelly became so popular among Toronto NHL fans that he was elected to the Canadian Parliament where he served from 1962 to 1965, while playing for the Toronto Maple Leafs. Another Canadian, Ken Dryden, a former goaltending star for the NHL Montreal Canadiens and member of hockey's Hall of Fame, was a member of Parliament from 2004 until he lost his seat in the 2011 elections.

The vast majority of former professional athletes who have been elected to the U.S. Congress are Republicans. The one notable exception is Representative Heath Shuler, a Democrat from North Carolina. And both former Canadian NHL athletes who have been elected to Parliament have been members of the Liberal Party of Canada. Based just on these results, and with so few former professional athletes becoming national politicians, it would be difficult to draw any conclusions between being an elite athlete and having a particular political predication.

Politicians find it beneficial to get the approval and active campaign support of sports stars. Athletes, because they are well known and admired, can secure votes either for themselves or for candidates whom they support. Moreover, politicians find it useful to identify with teams and to attend sports events. For example, on that special evening in 1995 when Cal Ripken, Jr., broke Lou Gehrig's record of 2,130 consecutive games played, President Clinton attended and was highly visible as he congratulated Ripken publicly and spent time in the television booth during the broadcast. Presidents Ronald Reagan, George H. W. Bush, Bill Clinton, George W. Bush, and Barack Obama have thrived on interaction with athletes and sports teams. Routinely, champions from colleges, the professionals, and the Olympics are invited to the White House. The trend is for presidents, governors, members of Congress, mayors, and other political officials to identify more and more with sports and sports stars.

Politicians capitalize on the popularity of athletes by using them to support the system. In the United States, for example, athletes are often sent overseas to maintain the morale of service personnel. Athletes appear in advertisements that urge the viewer or reader to join the military or Reserve Officers' Training Corps (ROTC), to vote, and to avoid drugs. Athletes are also asked to give patriotic speeches on holidays and other occasions.

Use of athletes for the maintenance of the ruling regime is common in other countries as well. Athletes may be asked to visit factories and villages to hold demonstrations and make political speeches. These activities spread the conventional political philosophy of the dominant class in those countries, helping to unify the general population and bolstering the morale of middle- and low-income workers to maintain their patriotic feelings toward existing societal conditions.

Sport as a Vehicle of Change in Society

A recurring theme of this book is that sport reflects the dynamics of the larger society. It is not surprising, therefore, that when social and political turmoil has occurred in North America it has affected the sports world as well. To illustrate our point, we use several examples from the past.

Sport and sporting events were used by activists and reformers to attack racism and U.S. involvement in Vietnam, the two major societal issues of the latter twentieth century. Racism was attacked in a number of ways. Most dramatic was the proposed boycott of the 1968 Olympics by African American athletes. Harry Edwards, an African American sociologist and former athlete, was a leader of this boycott. His rationale for the protest was: "The roots of the revolt of the black athlete spring from the same seed that produced the sit-ins, the freedom rides, and the rebellions in [several cities]. . . . The athletic revolt springs from a disgust and dissatisfaction with the racism prevalent in American society—including the sports world."[13]

Several other boycotts and protests involving racist practices in sport occurred at about the same time as the Olympic boycott. One boycott was directed against the New York Athletic Club's annual indoor track meet to dramatize and to change the club's policy of excluding Jews, African Americans, and other minorities from membership. And in the late 1960s African American athletes at San Jose State and the University of Wyoming participated in a symbolic protest against Brigham Young University, a Mormon-supported university. The athletes wore armbands to symbolize their contempt for the racial policies of the Mormon Church, which at that time excluded African American males from the priesthood. The Wyoming protestors were removed from the team by the coach.

We now cite four examples from the past two decades, two from the early 1990s and two from the twenty-first century, to show another avenue for sport challenging the existing social order. In these cases it was the power structure of sport that was doing the confronting. In 1990 the Professional Golf Association (PGA) was pressured to adopt a new policy mandating that it would no longer hold its championship tournaments at private country clubs that excluded minorities as members. This in turn forced Shoal Creek Country Club in Birmingham, Alabama, the scheduled site of the 1990 championship, to alter its admissions policies and open its membership to nonwhite members. What followed is that many private country clubs opened their memberships (although a few refused and, as a result, were ineligible to host a PGA championship).[14]

The second example of efforts by a sport organization to use its power to confront racism in the 1990s was a political decision by the National Football League. The NFL had awarded the 1993 Super Bowl to Tempe, Arizona, the home of the Arizona Cardinals, but because the Arizona legislature refused to have an official, statewide holiday to celebrate the birthday of Martin Luther King, Jr., the NFL decided to take the 1993 Super Bowl away from Arizona and hold it in Pasadena, California. In effect, the league was saying to the citizens of Arizona, "If you want to play the game of bigotry, we'll take our millions of dollars in tourist trade and scores of hours of television time someplace else."[15] This strategy worked, and Arizona endorsed the King holiday, after which the league awarded Phoenix the 1996 Super Bowl.

Turning now to the twenty-first century we find an example of a sports organization using its power to bring social change. Shortly after the beginning of the new millenium, the NCAA executive committee agreed not to schedule championship events in South Carolina until at least 2004 because the Confederate flag was being displayed on the statehouse grounds. This boycott of South Carolina began in January 2000 with actions by the National Association for the Advancement of Colored People (NAACP), followed by individual university teams canceling games and matches in South Carolina. Several prominent individuals in sport expressed support of the boycott, including Lou Holtz, then head football coach at the University of South Carolina.

As a follow-up to its position against racist symbolism in South Carolina, the NCAA ruled in 2005 that any school with a nickname or logo considered racially or ethnically "hostile" or "abusive" would be prohibited from using it in postseason events. This meant that mascots would not be allowed to perform at NCAA-sponsored tournament events and band members and cheerleaders would be barred from using Native Americans as symbols on their uniforms. In short, the NCAA made a political decision—that it would not permit the use of Native American symbols by athletic teams at their championship events because they often are demeaning caricatures of native peoples.

Internationalization of Social Activism and Sport

At the international level, there has been a campaign against the use of sweatshop labor to produce sporting goods in developing nations. United Students Against Sweatshops organized anti-sweatshop campaigns on hundreds of campuses, mandating that the clothes bearing their collegiate logos be manufactured under fair and ethical conditions. This effort, most notably against Nike's exploitation of Third World workers, has been student-led in the United States. As a consequence of activists pressing Nike and other companies, in 2005 Nike revealed the location of its factories in the Third World and admitted to widespread problems in its Asian factories.

Nike is not the only company that has followed this global economy model. However, because it has had the largest share of the sports footwear market and the accompanying profits, it can most easily afford to lead a change in corporate directions.[16]

These examples of sport serving as a vehicle of social change are interesting for three reasons:

1. The power structure of sports has typically been reluctant to take the lead in social causes, so the actions we have described may actually be anomalies or, perhaps, the beginning of an emerging trend for the sports world.

2. Sports have political potential, ironically, either way: (a) positively, because the powerful sport organizations hold the potential to "blackmail" recalcitrants into line, and (b) negatively, because of a backlash from the public who resents blatant politics—specifically, anti–status quo politics by sports organizations.

3. Each example of social change shows once again how sport and politics are intertwined.

The worldwide popularity of sport and the importance attached to it by fans and politicians alike actually make sport an ideal platform for political protest. However, the use of sport for protest is often unsuccessful in causing meaningful change because of the institutional character of sport, given its built-in bias for preserving and legitimizing the status quo.

GLOBALIZATION AND SPORT

Sports have historically had a narrow geographical base. In this sense, sports were local. We have tended to identify with the local high school, college, or professional team. But this identification with the local is breaking down. Concurrent with trends and events in business, music, the other arts, education, politics, travel, and so forth, college and professional teams have become more global. They now often have foreign players, some of whom do not speak English well and are unfamiliar with U.S. and Canadian cultural habits and customs.[17]

Of course, international exchange is not a recent phenomenon. For thousands of years, people have traveled, traded, and migrated across political boundaries exchanging food, artifacts, and knowledge. But the current global perspective accentuates greater connectedness among the world's people. It is a process whereby goods, information, people, money, communication, sport, and various other forms of culture move across national boundaries and throughout the globe.

For example, for several centuries British colonists brought their sports (soccer, rugby, cricket) to their colonies, where they flourished.

Golf began in Scotland and has become a sport played almost everywhere. The Olympic movement spread around the globe during the twentieth century. While the popularity of baseball began in the United States, it is now extremely popular in Latin America, the Caribbean countries, Japan, and South Korea. So, too, with basketball, which has spread especially to China, Australia, and Western and Central Europe.

Still, the frequency of international competition, the migration of athletes and coaches, and the proliferation of global sport organizations are rather recent. Some sports, golf and tennis, for example, are already global sports with athletes competing regularly in tournaments worldwide. The Ladies Professional Golf Association, primarily a U.S. organization, has been dominated in recent years by South Koreans and Mexicans. And the U.S. Open in tennis—both men's and women's—is routinely won by foreign players—mostly Europeans and Russians. (We will return to this issue of the global migration of athletes in Chapter 13.) Indeed, there is a large presence of U.S. influence around the world as sports events are televised globally and U.S. sports leagues seek global expansion.

The globalization of sport has political consequences. The process blurs national allegiances. Friendships through sport extend across political boundaries. However, nationalism may be exacerbated or diminished by global processes. People in one society may readily adopt new sports forms from other societies or they may reject them as cultural imperialism. Similarly, transnational sports organizations may decide to exclude certain nations from participation because of their political actions, as we will see in the next section.[18]

THE POLITICAL OLYMPIC GAMES

The motto of the Olympic Games is "Citius, Altius, Fortius" (Faster, Higher, Stronger). It implies that athletes should strive for ever better performances. Moreover, the goal of the Olympic Movement is to "contribute to building a peaceful and better world by educating youth through sport practiced in accordance with Olympism and its values."[19] Since the revival of the Olympics in 1896, however, there has been an erosion of the prominence of sports accomplishments and a corresponding ascendance of political considerations. This section addresses the political side of the Olympics and offers suggestions for reducing the corrosive effects of politics on the Olympic movement and its ideals.

Political Problems and the Olympic Movement

Politics surrounding the Olympics is manifested in five major ways:

1. through excessive nationalism within nations concerning the performance of their athletes in the Olympics.
2. through use of the Olympics as a site for political demonstrations and violence by political dissidents in the host country.
3. through decisions by ruling bodies to deny participation by certain nations.
4. through decisions by nations to boycott the Games for political reasons.
5. through the political organization of the Olympics.

Excessive Nationalism Within Nations

Nationalism in the Olympics that goes beyond its appropriate boundaries is expressed in several ways. Foremost, there is the use of athletics to promote political goals. As we described in an earlier section, Adolf Hitler turned the 1936 Games in Berlin into a propaganda show to legitimate Nazi Germany. Similarly, nations tend to use their showing in international athletic events as an indicator of the superiority of their political-economic systems. This was especially true during the Cold War era from 1952 to 1988, when the United States and the Soviet Union were the two powers contending against each other for world supremacy. Some nations have been quite blatant in their efforts to demonstrate their superiority, offering large prizes to their athletes to win medals.

A second manifestation of excessive nationalism is that in the zeal to win, some national Olympic committees have ignored the use of performance-enhancing drugs for their athletes.

This was clearly true for the East Germans before 1990. In each of the Olympics Games over the past thirty years, some athletes have been forced to forfeit medals because they have failed drug tests.[20]

A third indication of national chauvinism has to do with the reporting of international events. Members of the media in reporting the Olympics may let their politics distort their analyses. Television coverage of the Olympics conveys a distorted, nationalized, and commercialized portrayal of the Games. The TV networks that buy the broadcast rights to Olympic events subcontract with TV outlets worldwide, which then add their own narratives to the broadcasts to appeal to audiences in their countries. Thus, the Olympics Games become filtered through individual nations, producing widely varying interpretations of the Games.[21]

Use of the Olympics by Political Dissidents in the Host Country

At virtually every recent Olympics there have been political demonstrations, threats, and violence by disaffected groups. The host country has usually responded with extra security and police violence. The 1992 Olympics in Barcelona faced this problem as Basque separatists threatened to use the Games as a vehicle for worldwide recognition of their struggle for independence. A bomb was exploded at the Atlanta Olympics in 1996 by a domestic terrorist who objected to the legalization of abortion. During the Sydney Olympics in 2000, there were peaceful demonstrations by Aborigines against the discrimination they face in Australia. The Athens Olympics in 2004 was confronted by demonstrators against the Iraq War who marched on the U.S. embassy, protesting a visit of U.S. Secretary of State Colin Powell. Anticipating Chinese protestors and demonstrators at the 2008 Beijing Olympics, organizers of the Games took preemptive action and incarcerated many activists, thereby crushing potential political dissidents.

Use of the Olympics for Political Purposes by Organizations Outside the Host Nation

We will not repeat what we have already said in this chapter about the Tommie Smith and John Carlos clenched-fist protest on the medal stand at the 1968 Mexico City Olympic Games, except that it was related to a boycott campaign organized in the United States as a way to reveal to the world the indignities and discrimination suffered by African Americans. The call to boycott failed (although a few athletes did boycott), but for many African American athletes who participated in the Olympics, their mood was sullen and resentful.

Four years later at the Munich Olympics a group of Palestinian terrorists stormed the living quarters of the Israeli team, capturing them. Their goal was to negotiate a trade whereby the Israeli athletes would be freed if Israel would release 234 Palestinians held in Israeli jails. German commandos tried to free the captive athletes, but a terrorist unpinned a grenade, killing eleven Israeli athletes and five kidnappers.[22]

With the terrorist attacks on the World Trade Center in New York City and the Pentagon in Washington, D.C., on September 11, 2001, the world was on heightened alert for future attacks, whether by planes, bombs, germs, or computer. Although these attacks were not intended to affect the Olympic Games in any way, they did. For example, at the 2004 Athens Olympics, Greece spent an unprecedented 1 billion euros (US$1.33 billion) for the security of the first post–September 11 Summer Games.

Preceding the Beijing Olympics, various groups protested against China's alleged complicity with mass killings in Sudan (because the Sudanese sell the Chinese 400,000 barrels of oil a day and China owns 40 percent of Sudan's largest oil company), calling those Games the "Genocide Olympics." Film director Steven Spielberg publically withdrew from his appointment as artistic advisor to the opening ceremony of the Beijing Olympics, saying that his commitment to overcoming intolerance, bigotry, and the suffering they cause was incompatible with China's support for the Sudanese government. As a lead-up to the 2008 Beijing Olympics, Tibetan activists carried out a four-year campaign to spoil China's hosting of the 2008 Olympics. At the same time, a demonstration was staged in Beijing, aiming to focus attention, in the protestors' words, on Tibetan political prisoners and stating that the Tibetan people live without human rights under Chinese rule.[23]

Political Decisions by National and International Olympic Committees

The international and national Olympic ruling bodies make a number of decisions based on politics. The choice of Olympic sites is made by the members of the IOC. This decision is crucial to the potential host nations and cities because of the possible economic benefits, the legitimacy of that nation's government, and the potential of being the center of world attention. This site-selection decision historically has been based on either bribery or politics (or both).

Let's consider bribery first. Andrew Jennings, an investigative journalist, has cited numerous scandals involving the IOC, including the use of bribery to buy votes for Olympics site selection.[24] His argument was validated by the scandals associated with the awarding of the 2002 Winter Olympics to Salt Lake City. The USOC spent $60,000 on favors for foreign sports officials who, in return, supported Salt Lake City's bid. Another $1.2 million was spent by the Salt Lake City Organizing Committee on scholarships, shopping sprees, cash payments, free housing, jobs, and other gifts to those who would make the decision—IOC members and their family members. Similar bribes were made by the organizers of the Nagano Winter Olympics in 1998, and the Atlanta organizers for the 1996 Summer Games.

During the Cold War the IOC was careful to alternate Olympic sites between countries in the U.S. sphere and Communist nations. In 2001 the IOC selected Beijing for the 2008 Olympics in a highly charged political atmosphere. Opponents argued that China was in violation of human rights. Others argued that giving China the Olympics might promote a greater opening up of the country, promote ties with Taiwan, and ease tensions with the United States and its allies. Friends of China argued that awarding the Games to China would be a sign of that country's emergence as a major power, one befitting its population of 1.4 billion.

Although they do not officially vote in these decisions on Olympic sites, some unofficial players have power, such as corporations that sometimes pay millions of dollars for the designation as an official sponsor. If a number of them threatened to withdraw their support, the IOC would likely give in to their demands. Likewise, when NBC paid the IOC $3.5 billion for the rights to televise the Olympics from 2000 to 2008, the network became a major player in the decision making.

In addition to site selection, the IOC has made a number of other blatantly political decisions. The following are a few examples from the last sixty years of decisions made for political reasons by Olympics ruling bodies.[25]

- 1952: East Germany was denied participation because it was not a "recognized state."
- 1960: The IOC decreed that North and South Korea should compete as one team, using the same flag, emblem, and uniform. Nationalist China was forced to compete under the name of Taiwan.
- 1964: South Africa was banned from the Olympics for its apartheid policies.
- 1968: The IOC was outraged by the Tommie Smith and John Carlos clenched-fist salute during the American national anthem. It ordered the USOC to disallow the two from further competition in Mexico City. The United States refused but capitulated when the IOC threatened that it would disqualify the entire U.S. track-and-field team. The USOC sent Smith and Carlos home and banned them from Olympic competition for life.
- 1972: The IOC ruled that Rhodesia would be allowed to participate. Many African nations were incensed by this action because of the racist policies of the ruling elite in Rhodesia and threatened to boycott of the Games unless Rhodesia was barred. The IOC bowed to this pressure and rescinded its earlier action.
- 1991: The IOC agreed to let South Africa participate in the 1992 Olympics provided that it met certain conditions regarding the dismantling of apartheid.
- 2000: North and South Korea marched as one nation in the opening ceremonies under a single white flag with a blue depiction of an undivided peninsula, though they competed as separate nations.
- 2008: Research by the Centre on Housing Rights and Evictions on Olympic Games from 1988 through 2008 shows that the host nations displaced thousands.[26] (See Box 9.3 for examples.)

Political Decisions by Individual Nations Regarding the Olympics

International incidents that have nothing to do with the Olympic Games have sometimes caused nations to withdraw their teams from Olympic competition. Some examples follow:

- 1952: Taiwan boycotted the Games when Communist China was admitted to the International Olympic Committee.
- 1956: Egypt, Lebanon, and Iraq boycotted the Olympics because of the Anglo-French seizure of the Suez Canal. Spain, Switzerland, and the Netherlands withdrew from the Olympics in protest after the Soviet Union invaded Hungary.
- 1976: Twenty-eight African nations boycotted the Games because New Zealand, whose rugby team had toured South Africa, was allowed to compete.
- 1980: Some fifty-four nations, including the United States, West Germany, Canada, and Japan, boycotted the Games because of the Soviet Union's invasion of Afghanistan.
- 1984: Fourteen nations, most notably the Soviet Union, East Germany, Cuba, Bulgaria, and Poland, boycotted the Games because they were held in the United States.
- 1988: Cuba boycotted the Summer Games because North Korea was not allowed to co-host the Games with South Korea. North Korea joined in the boycott.

Political Organization of the Olympics

In addition to the corruptions of the Olympic ideals that have been outlined, the ways that the Games are organized are political. Nations select which athletes will perform (i.e., no athlete can perform without national sponsorship). The IOC provides ceremonies where athletes march behind their country's flag. After each event, the winner's national anthem is

---

Box 9.3 *Thinking About Sport:* The Olympic Games and the Displacement of People

The Switzerland-based Centre on Housing Rights and Evictions examined each Olympic Games from 1988 to the buildup for the Beijing Games in 2008 and concluded that the host countries, collectively, had displaced more than 2 million people, mostly minorities such as the homeless and the poor. Consider these examples:

- As a result of policies enforced at the 1988 Olympics in Seoul, South Korea, 720,000 people were evicted from their homes to provide space for various venues, street vendors were banned to "clean up" the city for visitors, and homeless people and beggars were rounded up and housed in a prison camp.
- The Barcelona Games in 1992 saw Gypsy communities evicted and dispersed. The streets were "cleansed" by dispersing beggars, prostitutes, and street sellers. Between 1986 and 1992, housing prices rose by 240 percent as the Olympic districts were gentrified and public housing was demolished.
- In preparation for the 1996 Olympics in Atlanta, large housing projects (whose residents mostly were African Americans) were demolished and replaced with middle-class homes. Around 30,000 families were evicted, and 9,000 homeless people were arrested and locked up until the Games were over.

- Because the 2000 Games in Sydney were built on surplus government land no one was directly displaced, but as a result of the city's gentrification, housing prices more than doubled from 1996 to 2003 and rents soared by 40 percent, forcing people to move. In the year before the Olympics, there was a 400 percent increase in tenant evictions.
- In Beijing, a year before the Games were to begin, 1.25 million people had already been displaced and another 250,000 were due to be evicted.

So, while the Olympic Games enhance the prestige of the host city and nation, and many businesses and individuals benefit economically, some pay a huge price for the Games. Not surprisingly, the costs and burdens are borne by those least able to bear them—the powerless.

Sources: Centre on Housing Rights and Evictions, "Fair Play for Housing Rights: Mega-Events, Olympic Games and Housing Rights," 2007, http://www.sheltercentre.org/sites/default/files/COHRE_FairplayForHousingRights.pdf; George Monbiot, "Everywhere They Go, the Olympic Games Become an Excuse for Eviction and Displacement," *The Guardian*, 2 July 2007; and Calum MacLeod and Paul Wiseman, "Whatever It Takes, China Aims for Dazzling Games," *USA Today*, 6 August 2007, pp. 1C, 2C.

---

played and the flags of the three medal winners are raised at the awards ceremony. The IOC also considers political criteria in the selection of the site of the Olympics and in the choice of judges.

To be fair in this appraisal, the Olympic Games do attempt to promote the idea of oneness with the use of the Olympic hymn and the Olympic flag (five interlaced rings representing the five continents) and the meeting of athletes from all over the world at the Olympic Games in a spirit of fair competition. However, nationalism does not merely intrude, it dominates.[27]

A Proposal for Change

Is there a way to organize the Olympics to accomplish the aim of neutralizing the crippling political problems that work to negate the Olympic ideals?

Many scholars, journalists, and other people from various walks of life have suggested ways to improve the Olympic Games. Even members of the IOC, international sport federations, and national Olympic committees have proposed ways of advancing the mission of the Olympics. In this last section of the chapter we offer a series of proposals to achieve the Olympic purpose. Our goal in making these suggestions is to encourage readers to consider them, analyze them, and then construct their own set of proposals for reforming the Olympic Games.

1. *Establish two permanent sites for the Games.* Each permanent site must be neutral; otherwise, the Games will continue to be subject to the influence of power politics. The choices often mentioned in connection with proposals like this are Greece for the Summer Olympics and

Switzerland for the Winter Games. Greece is a natural choice because the ancient Olympian Games were held there every four years for more than one thousand years, ending in 393 A.D. Even better, each of the permanent sites should be in a free zone—land ceded to the International Olympic Committee and therefore land that no nation claims, just as the United Nations is located in a free zone in New York City.

2. *An alternative to two permanent sites is to use multiple sites for each Olympic Games.* For example, track and field might be held in one nation, boxing in another, and so on. A format like that would enable poorer nations to be hosts and to benefit economically. It would also enable spectators watching on television to view and appreciate a variety of geographic and cultural landscapes instead of being restricted to the narrow focus on one city and nation that presently exists.

3. *Athletes must represent only themselves.* Athletes, in actuality and symbolically, should not represent a country, nor should any nation-state be represented by uniforms, flags, national anthems, or political leaders. When an athlete is awarded his or her medal for winning an event, only the Olympic hymn should be played. Athletes should also be randomly assigned to housing and eating arrangements at the Games to reduce national identification and to maximize cross-national interaction.

4. *Revise the opening ceremonies so that athletes enter the arena with other athletes in their events.* This would deemphasize the nation in which athletes are citizens and emphasize the sports events of the Olympic Games, and it would promote fellowship among the athletes.

5. *Make all athletes (amateur and professional) eligible for competition.* The nation-state should not be involved in the selection process because this encourages nationalistic feelings. To ensure that the best athletes of the world are able to compete, a minimum standard for each event should be set by an Olympic governing board. Athletes meeting this standard would compete at a regional event where another and higher standard of excellence would be set for athletes to qualify for the Olympics. Those athletes qualifying for the regional competition and the Olympics would have all expenses for travel and per diem paid by the International Olympic Committee.

6. *Subsidize the cost of the Olympics from revenues generated from spectators' admissions to the regionals, from admissions to the Games, and from television.* Establishing permanent sites would significantly reduce the cost of the Olympics. Revenues from admissions and television (the IOC receives one-third of television revenues) should cover the costs after the Games are established. During the building of the permanent sites, though, the IOC may need a subsidy or loan from the United Nations.

7. *All media coverage and broadcasts should be controlled by the IOC.* Television revenues present a particularly thorny problem because the revenue potential is great and this lends itself to threats of overcommercialization, the intrusion of corporations into the decision-making arena, and jingoism by chauvinistic television commentators. To reduce these potential dangers, all media coverage should be reported by a firm strictly controlled by the IOC. Media coverage of the Olympics should be provided to each country at a cost determined by the existing number of media outlets in that country. No single country would have any control over what would be shown or the commentary emanating from the Games.

8. *Establish an Olympic committee and a secretary-general to prepare for and oversee each Olympic Games.* The composition of this committee would be crucial. Currently the members of the IOC are taken from national committees, with an important criterion being the maintenance of a political balance between opposing factions. The concept of a ruling body is essential, but the committee should be reorganized to reduce political considerations. This is a baffling problem because the selection will inevitably involve politics. One possibility would be to incorporate the selection procedures used in the United Nations to select its secretary-general. These procedures have worked, in spite of national differences.

Now is a propitious time to depoliticize the Olympics. The tensions and paranoia associated with the Cold War have receded. We have seen cooperative efforts between the major superpowers that have not been present since World War II. The Eastern European bloc is no longer a force. East and West Germany are now Germany. The European Economic Community will break down nationalistic barriers further. Although there are international tensions, wars, and acts of terrorism, Olympic and political leadership could take this turning point in history and reorganize the Olympics to eliminate as much of the politics from it as possible. The Olympic movement is important. That is why it must be radically altered from its present form if its lofty goals are to be realized.

SUMMARY

Two themes have dominated this chapter: Sport is political in character, and sport, like all institutions, is conservative. This basic conservatism in sport has two important implications for society. First, the athletic programs of the schools, to which most persons are exposed, support and reinforce a view of the world and of society that perpetuates the status quo. In North America this is accomplished through the promotion of national values and the support of the political-economic system.

A second implication, given the institutional character of sport, is that efforts to change sport will rarely come from those who control sport. Moreover, any attack on sport will be defined as an attack on society itself. Thus, change in sport will be slow and congruent with what is happening in society.

WEB RESOURCES

www.olympic.org
The official site of the International Olympic Committee.

www.usoc.org
The official site for the United States Olympic Committee.

www.cohre.org/topics/mega-events/
This is a report by the Centre on Housing Rights and Evictions that shows how the staging of mega-events, most notably the Olympic Games, creates the forced eviction of thousands of people from their homes, causing severe hardship and misery.

http://usas.org
The site of the Sweat-Free Campus campaign, which has been successful in achieving better wages and humane working conditions for workers making athletic apparel.

NOTES

1. Des Wilson, "Cricket's Shame: The Inside Story," *New Statesman* 133, no. 4717 6 (December 2004): 28.

2. Max Weber, *Economy and Society*, trans. Guenther Roth and G. Wittick (New York: Bedminster Press, 1968), first published in 1922; see also Adrian Leftwich, *What Is Politics: The Activity and Its Study* (Malden, MA: Polity Press, 2004).

3. C. Wright Mills, *The Power Elite* (New York: Oxford University Press, 2000), first published in 1956; see also G. William Domhoff, Who *Rules America? Challenges to Corporate and Class Dominance*, 6th ed. (New York: McGraw-Hill, 2009).

4. Good discussions of this topic can be found in the following books: Dave Zirin, *A People's History of Sports in the United States: 250 Years of Politics, Protest, People, and Play* (New York: The New Press, 2009); George H. Sage, *Globalizing Sport: How Organizations, Corporations, Media, and Politics Are Changing Sport* (Boulder, CO: Paradigm Publishers, 2010); and Alan Bairner, *Sport and Politics* (New York: Routledge, 2011).

5. Gerald Gems, Linda Borish, and Gertrud Pfister, *Sports in American History: From Colonization to Globalization* (Champaign, IL: Human Kinetics, 2008); see also Zirin, *A People's History of Sports in the United States.*

6. Christopher Hilton, *Hitler's Olympics: The 1936 Berlin Olympic Games* (Charleston, SC: The History Press, 2008).

7. Lynn Rosellini, "The Sports Factories," *U.S. News and World Report*, 17 February 1992, p. 51.

8. Calum MacLeod, "Chinese Sports Schools Feel an Urgency to Find Gold," *USA Today*, 14 June 2007, pp. 1A, 6A, 8.

9. Sage, *Globalizing Sport: How Organizations, Corporations, Media, and Politics Are Changing Sport*, especially ch. 6.

10. Samantha King, "Offensive Lines: Sport-State Synergy in an Era of Perpetual War," *Cultural Studies—Critical Methodologies*, 8 (November 2008): 538.

11. D. Stanley Eitzen, *Fair and Foul: Beyond the Myths and Paradoxes of Sport*, 4th ed. (Lanham, MD: Rowman & Littlefield, 2009), 20.

12. Clint Newlin, "Estimated Probability of Competing in Athletics Beyond the High School Interscholastic Level," *National Collegiate Athletic Association*, last updated 5 November 2010, http://www.ncaa.org/wps/portal/ncaahome?WCM_GLOBAL_CONTEXT=/ncaa/NCAA/Academics+and+Athletes/Education+and+Research/Probability+of+Competing/Methodology+-+Prob+of+Competing.

13. Quoted in Art Spander, "A Moment in Time: Remembering the Olympic Protest," *CSTV.com*, 24 February 2006, http://www.cstv.com/sports/c-track/stories/022406aas.html; see also Sue Curry Jansen and Don Sabo, "The Sport/War Metaphor: Hegemonic Masculinity, the Persian Gulf War, and the New World Order," *Sociology of Sport Journal* 11 (March 1994): 1–17.

14. Michael Bamberger, "The Changing Face of Shoal Creek," *GOLF.com*, 27 July 2010, http://www.golf.com/golf/tours_news/article/0,28136,2002845-0,00.html.

15. Teri Thompson, "Ban the Klan," *Westword*, 13 November 1993, p. 28.

16. George H. Sage, "Justice Do It! The Nike Transnational Advocacy Network: Organization, Collective Actions, and Outcomes," *Sociology of Sport Journal* 16 (1999): 206–233; see also George H. Sage, "Corporate Globalization and Sporting Goods Manufacturing: The Case of Nike," in *Sport in Contemporary Society: An Anthology*, 8th ed., ed. D. Stanley Eitzen (Boulder, CO: Paradigm Publishers, 2009), 391–410.

17. Sage, *Globalizing Sport: How Organizations, Corporations, Media, and Politics Are Changing Sport*; see also Eitzen, *Fair and Foul*, ch. 12, and Grant Wahl, "They Pledge Allegiance," *Sports Illustrated*, 13 June 2011, pp. 55–57.

18. Sage, *Globalizing Sport: How Organizations, Corporations, Media, and Politics Are Changing Sports*.

19. International Olympic Committee, *Olympic Charter* (8 July 2011), p. 13, http://www.olympic.org/Documents/olympic_charter_en.pdf.

20. For an excellent account of East Germany's use of banned drugs, see Steven Ungerleider, *Faust's Gold: Inside The East German Doping Machine* (New York: Thomas Dunne Books, 2001); see also Molly Johnson, *Training Socialist Citizens: Sports and the State in East Germany* (Boston: Brill Academic Publishers, 2008).

21. Dusty Saunders, "Olympic Games on TV: Bigger, Better," *Denver Post*, 12 February 2010, http://www.denverpost.com/dustysaunders/ci_14378803.

22. For an excellent account of Palestinian terrorist attack at the 1972 Olympic Games, see Simon Reeve, *One Day in September: The Full Story of the 1972 Munich Olympics Massacre and the Israeli Revenge Operation "Wrath of God"* (New York: Arcade Books, 2011).

23. Dave Skretta, "Steven Spielberg Withdraws from Role with Beijing Olympics over Human Rights Issues," *Orange County Register*, 12 February 2008, http://www.ocregister.com/entertainment/china-156355-darfur-olympics.html; see also Heather Timmons, "Corporate Sponsors Nervous as Tibet Protest Groups Shadow Olympic Torch's Run," *New York Times*, 29 March 2008, p. C4.

24. Andrew Jennings, *The New Lord of the Rings* (London: Pocket Books, 1996); Andrew Jennings and Clare Sambrook, *The Great Olympic Swindle: When the World Wanted the Games Back* (New York: Simon & Schuster, 2000).

25. For a sample of the sources dealing with the political aspects of the Olympics, see Robert K. Barney, Stephen R. Wenn, and Scott G. Martyn, *Selling the Five Rings: The IOC and the Rise of Olympic Commercialism* (Salt Lake City: University of Utah Press, 2002); Allen Guttmann, *The Olympics: A History of the Modern Games*, 2nd ed. (Champaign: University of Illinois Press, 2002); and Christopher A. Shaw, *Five Ring Circus: Myths and Realities of the Olympic Games* (Gabriola Island, British Columbia, Canada: New Society Publishers, 2008).

26. Centre on Housing Rights and Evictions, "Fair Play for Housing Rights: Mega-Events, Olympic Games and Housing Rights," Geneva, Switzerland, 2007, http://www.sheltercentre.org/sites/default/files/COHRE_FairplayForHousingRights.pdf.

27. Shaw, *Five Ring Circus: Myths and Realities of the Olympic Games*.

CHAPTER 10

Sport and the Economy

Although many consider professional sports to be mere entertainment, the business aspects of the industry—including escalating salaries, frequent labor conflicts and strikes, and public investment in stadiums and arenas—can captivate and infuriate fans and nonfans alike.

—Nathaniel Sampson and Gerard C. S. Mildner*

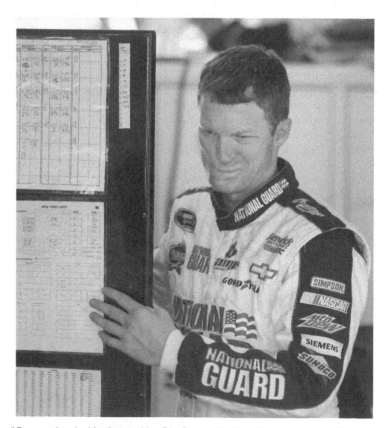

Driver Dale Earnhardt, Jr., stands in the garage during practice for the NASCAR Sprint Cup Series auto race at Kansas Speedway in Kansas City, Kansas, 2011. (AP Photo/Ed Zurga)

*Nathaniel Sampson and Gerard C. S. Mildner, "Cooperation Amidst Competition," in *Sport and Public Policy*, ed. Charles A. Santo and Gerard C. S. Mildner (Champaign, IL: Human Kinetics, 2010), 3.

Sociology and economics are distinctly separate academic fields of study, but in the real world of people the social and the economic are closely intertwined. Our social lives are closely connected with our economic status in terms of lifestyle, education, occupation, health, and so forth. Sports are one of the most significant social/cultural practices in North America, and they are associated with the economy in multiple ways. The major purpose of this chapter is to describe and illustrate the ways in which the social practices of sport are linked to the economic social institution. We will examine the intimate relationship between money and sports and the various consequences involved.

In Chapter 1 we characterized three levels of sport: informal sport, organized sport, and corporate sport, the latter referring to levels of sporting activity dominated by economic and political factors extrinsic to sport itself. Corporate sport, in which the relatively spontaneous, pristine nature of informal sport has been corrupted, is characteristic of sport in contemporary North America. Money is the foundation of corporate sport, even at the so-called amateur level. The profit motive shapes the decisions of owners, school administrators, and the corporations that use sport. Fans are left with the gnawing sense that they are the victims of the greed of professional sports franchise owners and players alike.

Scholars and journalists have criticized this trend, claiming that sport has been transformed into economic snake oil—indeed, that sport has been transformed by commerce from something wonderful to something grotesque. Going further, they argue that sport has been distorted and polluted by money, and the never-ending quest for more. Contemporary sport is certainly big business. Some relevant examples demonstrate this:

- The estimated size of the entire sports industry in 2011 in the United States was $414 billion.
- The North American sporting goods and equipment manufacturing sector is currently a $113 billion industry. Nike, the world's leading manufacturer of athletic shoes and

Phil Mickelson watches his tee shot on the second hole during the third round of the Tour Championship golf tournament at East Lake Golf Club in Atlanta on September 24, 2011. He was recently elected to the World Golf Hall of Fame. (AP Photo/Dave Martin)

apparel and a major manufacturer of sports equipment, generated revenue in excess of $20.6 billion in its 2011 fiscal year. Thus, the manufacturing of sporting goods and equipment is a key economic component in North American sport.
- In the 1960s the prize money for the entire Professional Golf Association tour was about $8 million. In 2011 it was nearly $280 million, with the winner of the FedExCup earning an additional $10 million.
- The National Football League has had total revenues of about $9.3 billion in recent years.
- The Manny Pacquiao–Shane Mosley boxing match in 2011 generated $270 million in pay-per-view revenue.
- More than $100 billion is bet illegally on the annual Super Bowl. Another $100 million was bet legally in Nevada in 2011 on this game.
- Sports video games represent a $1 billion industry, accounting for more than 30 percent of all video game sales.[1]

There is no longer any question that corporate sport is a business, although sports franchise owners and certainly big-time sport universities would like to perpetuate the myth that it is not.

PROFESSIONAL SPORT AS A BUSINESS

Contrary to what some owners would have the public believe, professional sport is a business—a big business structured to maximize profit. Business enterprises are part of North America's economic systems, and the social theoretical perspectives we previously identified are applicable to the economy. So we briefly explain how functionalism and conflict/cultural perspectives apply. We then describe the ways and means by which professional sports are made profitable by monopoly organization and the public subsidization of professional teams. We also consider the changes in the owner-player relationship in professional team sports brought about by players' agitation to increase their power and monetary rewards.

Social Theories and the Economy

Functionalism views the economy as a central social institution because it is the means by which vital goods and services are produced and distributed. Social stability requires a smoothly functioning economic system, which leads to confidence in the society's future. An industrious workforce with a committed work ethic is the essential functional component of a society because dedicated productive work is the model value of society and integrates citizens within the social order.

A conflict/cultural position on the economic system considers it an instrument of powerful and wealthy social class domination, deriving its power from its ownership and control of the forces of production. The dominant class exploits and oppresses other classes, thereby reproducing and perpetuating the economic class structure. The exploitative economic arrangements of capitalism are viewed by conflict/cultural theorists as the foundation upon which the superstructure of social, political, and intellectual consciousness is built. As a result there is a basic conflict of interest between the two classes.

Professional Sport as a Monopoly

A monopoly exists when a single business firm controls a market. Professional team sport leagues have been allowed to become monopolies over the

years by the public and by the government—and they are not only monopolies but unregulated ones. Unlike the broadcasting industry, for example, whose monopolistic practices are regulated by the Federal Communications Commission, the sport industry is left to regulate itself. Each professional league operates as a cartel, whereby competitors join together as a self-regulating monopoly. This means that the teams make agreements on matters of mutual interest (e.g., rules, schedules, promotions, expansion, and media contracts).

A recent effort by the NFL to be legally considered a single entity, and thus not a cartel and thus immune from antitrust laws, was struck down by the U.S. Supreme Court (*American Needle, Inc., v. NFL et al.*). The Court ruled that the NFL is a "cartel" subject to antitrust law.[2]

Monopolistic agreements are illegal in most businesses because they lead to collusion, price-fixing, and restraint of trade, all of which are socially detrimental. Economists James Quirk and Rodney Fort have argued that professional sports teams create various social and economic problems from the monopoly power of the sports leagues. As they put it:

> Eliminate the monopoly power of leagues and you eliminate the blackmailing of cities to subsidize teams. Eliminate the monopoly power of leagues and you eliminate the sources of revenue that provide the wherewithal for high player salaries. Eliminate the monopoly power of leagues and you eliminate the problem of lack of competitive balance in a league due to disparity in drawing potential among league teams. Eliminate the monopoly power of leagues and you transfer power from the insiders, owners and players alike, to the outsiders, fans and taxpayers.[3]

The enormous advantages to the league cartel are several. Foremost, each sports franchise is protected from competition. The owner of the Kansas City Royals, for instance, is guaranteed that no other Major League Baseball team will be allowed to locate in his or her territory. There are some metropolitan areas with two Major League Baseball teams, but these exceptions occurred before baseball had agreed to territorial exclusivity. Even in these cases, the teams are in different leagues, ensuring that, for example, Chicago baseball fans who want to see American League games can see them only by attending White Sox games.

This protection from competition eliminates price wars. The owners of a franchise can continue to charge the public a maximum without fear of price cutting by competitors.

The cartel also controls the number of franchises allowed. Each cartel is generally reluctant to add new teams because scarcity permits higher ticket prices, more beneficial media arrangements, and continued territorial purity. In short, the value of each franchise is increased by the restriction on the number of teams. When new teams are added, such as the addition of the Denver and Miami franchises in 1993 to baseball's National League, they are selected with economic criteria paramount, especially concerning new television markets. (Neither the Rocky Mountain time zone nor Florida had a major league team at that time, making them attractive additions to the league.)

This monopolistic situation enables a league to negotiate television contracts for the benefit of all members of the cartel. The 1961 Sports Broadcast Act allowed sports leagues to sell their national television rights as a group without being subject to the antitrust laws. As a result, the national networks and cable systems may bid for the right to televise, for example, NFL football.

The final advantage of the monopoly is that the athletes are drastically limited in their choices and bargaining power. In football, players are drafted out of college. If they want to play in the NFL, they must negotiate with the team that drafted them. Their other choices are to play in the much less prestigious Arena League, to play in Canada (but the Canadian Football League limits the number of non-Canadian players per team, and the average pay is about one-third that of the NFL), or not to play that year. We will return to the owner-player relationship later in this chapter.

Public Subsidization of Professional Team Franchises

Subsidies to franchise owners take two forms—tax breaks and the availability of arenas at very low cost. We examine these in turn.

The bleak financial picture typically painted by some owners of professional teams is misleading because it refers only to accounting losses. The tax benefits available to sports promoters have been largely unpublicized. Even in those cases in which owners have not profited directly from their investments, owning a professional team is by no means the liability that publicly stated accounting losses would indicate. In short, for many wealthy individuals, owning a sports franchise has lucrative tax advantages.

Investment in professional franchises enables a wealthy owner to offset the team's gate losses or to minimize taxable profits of the team or of other investments by large depreciation allowances. The purchase of a professional sports franchise includes (1) the legal right to the franchise; (2) player contracts; and (3) assets such as equipment, buildings, cars, and so forth. However, since the most valuable assets of a pro sports team are its players, most of the purchase cost will be attributed to player contracts, which, in turn, can be depreciated in the same way a steel company depreciates the investment costs of a new blast furnace.

Similarly, acquisition of a player from another team will enable the new owner to depreciate the player's value over a period of years, usually five. Thus, the player's status as property is readily apparent, for no other business in the United States depreciates the value of human beings as part of the cost of its operation. There is an inconsistency here—the team is allowed to depreciate its players, but players are not permitted to depreciate themselves for tax purposes. This anomaly indicates the bias in the tax code favoring owners over players and that players are considered as property.

Ownership of professional sports franchises provides this kind of tax shelter even if the team shows accounting losses. That is why it has become an attractive investment for many wealthy persons, who can use losses and player depreciation as a means of offsetting other taxes on individual income.

These factors contribute to a relatively high turnover of professional team ownership. Since a team can depreciate the value of its players over a relatively short period (five years or less), expansion teams or newly franchised teams composed of players purchased from other owners can depreci-ate, but old leagues and established teams cannot, except with players purchased from previously established clubs. Thus, buying and selling teams is more profitable than retaining them for extended periods of time.

Consider the example of the tax shelter ben-efits of the NFL Houston Texans franchise owned by Robert McNair, whose net worth in 2010 was $1.4 *billion*. Economist Andrew Zimbalist reported:

> Assuming McNair holds the team as a partnership or subchapter S corporation, the IRS will allow him to presume that up to 50 percent of the team's purchase price ($350 million) is attributable to the player contracts he will eventually sign. This amount is generally amortizable over five years, allowing McNair to add $70 million annually to the team's costs before calculating its tax liability. (Of course, McNair will also be allowed to expense players' sala-ries.) Then McNair can transfer any reported losses from the team to reduce his personal income-tax liability, potentially saving him some $28 million a year for five years. . . . On top of this, McNair will benefit from the pleasures, perquisites, and power that accrue to the elite owners of NFL teams.[4]

The second type of public subsidy to profession-al sport is the provision of sports facilities to most franchises at very low cost. Adequate facilities are of great concern to sports promoters because they are essential to the financial success and spectator appeal of professional and big-time amateur sports. Conventional wisdom holds that the presence of major league sports teams enhances a city's prestige and generates considerable economic activity.

Regarding the former, image is important, especially to civic boosters, and having a major league team conveys the impression of being a first-class city. Concerning the latter, the myth is that the presence of a major league team brings substantial economic growth. This is a myth for at least three reasons. First, subsidizing a team drains government resources—the cost of building and maintaining arenas and of providing access roads, and the loss of revenues because of "sweetheart deals" with team owners. Second, the deflection of government money toward a sports team often

means that services to the poor may be reduced or dropped altogether. Third, the economic benefits are not spread equally throughout the community. The wealthy benefit (team owners, owners of hotels and restaurants) while the costs are disproportion-ately paid by the middle and lower classes.[5]

The empirical facts that never quite get com-municated to the public about the claims touting the economic benefits of public subsidies to sports franchise owners are that no hard evidence exists to support the notion that public financing of these venues makes economic good sense for a community. The opposite is closer to the truth. In a comprehensive review of the empirical literature assessing the effects of subsidies for professional sports franchises and facilities, economists Dennis Coates and Brad Humphreys assert: "The evidence reveals a great deal of consistency among econo-mists doing research in this area. That evidence is that sports subsidies cannot be justified on the grounds of local economic development, income growth or job creation, those arguments most frequently used by subsidy advocates." Economist Allen Sanderson eloquently summarized what em-pirical research suggests about the economic effects of building sports venues in cities: "If you want to inject money into the local economy, it would be better to drop it from a helicopter than invest it in a new ballpark."[6]

As the boom in sports in North America has increased, so also has the demand for facilities to accommodate the demands of fans for entertain-ment and of promoters for profits. During the past two decades, team owners in the "big four" pro sports leagues—NFL, MLB, NBA, NHL—have reaped some $20 *billion* in taxpayer subsidies for new sports venues.[7] Generally, these subsidies are from revenue bonds that allegedly are to be paid off with the revenue from the project. However, whenever a bond-financed public project cannot pay for itself, the obligation becomes a general public one. Other subsidies are indirect, such as providing light rail to the stadiums or access roads to interstate highways.

New sports venues, most of them publicly financed, are being built at the same time that human needs have reached crisis proportions, especially in North American cities. The same public funds would have much broader economic benefit if spent on improving public education, low-cost housing, mass transit, public parks, and small-business development in dilapidated areas. Two examples make the point:

- First, in 2008 Lucas Oil Stadium in Indianapolis opened at an estimated cost of $720 million. It was financed with funds raised jointly by the State of Indiana and the City of Indianapolis, with the Indianapolis Colts providing $100 million. To supply funding for the stadium, Marion County (where Indianapolis is located) raised taxes for food and beverage sales, auto rental taxes, innkeepers' taxes, and admission taxes for its share of the costs. Meanwhile, an increase in food and beverage taxes in six surrounding counties and the sale of Colts license plates completed the total. Such taxes are regressive taxes, meaning that the burden of these taxes falls disproportionately on low-income citizens; moreover, none of the taxes contribute to the human needs of those who are paying most of them.
- Second, in 2010 the Minnesota Twins celebrated the opening of their $517 million stadium, Target Field—$350 million of which is to be paid by a 0.15 percent county sales tax. Meanwhile, the state of Minnesota was facing a $5 billion budget crisis, and the legislature was considering massive cuts to health and human services programs to help erase the state's budget deficit.

Stadium funding with public money to support wealthy owners has not been without public criticism, although it is significant that bond elections for stadium construction have often succeeded when other proposed expenditures (e.g., for education and for municipal facilities) have been defeated. Numerous critics have scorned the priorities demonstrated and have argued that these facilities represent a direct subsidy to the sports industry by the public, many of whom are not even sports fans and few of whom are able to use or to benefit from the facilities their money supports.

Another subsidy to the owners involves the 50 percent tax deduction for business entertainment expenses. Professional teams rely on corporations to buy blocks of season tickets and to rent expensive skyboxes. A significant feature of recently built stadiums is the fact that revenue from skyboxes, private suites, and club seats is not shared with visiting teams—a huge benefit to the resident owner. So powerful is the urge by municipal officials and local chambers of commerce to have big-league teams in their cities that they will go to extreme lengths to placate present or future owners.

The recent move of an NBA team illustrates the kind of thing that happens when a franchise owner does not get what he or she wants from a city. The members of the Seattle Supersonics ownership group were unhappy with their former home, KeyArena, and petitioned the city of Seattle to build a new arena. Their plea was refused so the owners explored moving, which would entail breaking their lease with the City of Seattle for KeyArena. An out-of-court lawsuit was settled, and the team moved to Oklahoma City as the Oklahoma Thunder for the 2008–2009 season, while the owners wound up paying Seattle a measly $45 million to break the lease.

Oklahoma City attracted the team by promising to spend $100 million renovating its existing arena to bring it up to current NBA standards and an additional $20 million to construct a practice facility. Economists Dennis Coates and Brad Humphreys contend that the Seattle–Oklahoma City case suggests relevant lessons: "Professional sports leagues are able to restrict entry and play one city off against another to extract the best subsidy deal. In doing so, there is a significant positional element—one city's fan-base loses, another gains. And teams exploit the cities where politics most effectively taps the taxpayers."[8]

Other moves by NBA franchises since 2001: The Vancouver Grizzlies moved to Memphis, and the Charlotte Hornets moved to New Orleans only to have another expansion franchise, the Charlotte Bobcats, replace them.

For the NFL the decade of the 1990s was an active one with respect to the creation of new franchises and the relocation of others. We describe two of those relocations because they illustrate how franchise owners and local politicians manipulate cities for their own benefit.

- In 1995 St. Louis enticed the Los Angeles Rams to leave Los Angeles with a package that included a new $300 million stadium, all proceeds from concessions, parking, club seats and luxury suites, and a $15 million practice facility. To finance this largesse, Missouri taxpayers paid $24 million a year, St. Louis taxpayers paid another $12.5 million, and visitors to the county paid a 7.25 percent room tax to raise another $6 million annually.
- Art Modell, owner of the Cleveland Browns (which averaged 70,000 tickets sold per game), moved the team (now the Ravens) to Baltimore in the mid-1990s because he was given a $220 million stadium with 108 luxury boxes and 7,500 club seats, $75 million for moving expenses, $50 million for doing the deal, and all revenues from ticket sales, concessions, parking, and stadium advertising. The taxpayers guaranteed sellout crowds for ten years. Moreover, when the stadium is used for other events, Modell collects a 10 percent management fee plus half the profits. Use of the stadium is rent-free for thirty years, although Modell will pay back $24 million in construction costs.

It is clear that franchise owners are greatly subsidized. To what extent do the communities that pay these subsidies benefit? Sociologists and economists argue that the benefits are not widespread, for the following reasons: First, the wealthy benefit disproportionately when public municipalities use general taxes to build a sports venue. Although more jobs may be created while the venue is being constructed, the long-term profits accrue to the owners, not the general public. Team owners profit from fan attendance with little investment in the land or construction. They cannot lose financially because the burden is on the taxpayers. This is clearly a case of the wealthy receiving a public subsidy.[9]

The obvious beneficiaries of subsidized public sports venues are the owners of sports teams, plus the owners of hotels, media, commercial modes of transportation, restaurants, construction firms, and property affected by the location of the new arena site. There is a strong relationship between professional team owners and the decision makers at the highest political, corporate, financial, and media levels. These strong ties may explain the commonly found affirmative consensus among the political and economic elite for the building of public sports venues.

Second, the prices of individual and season tickets are usually too high for lower-income citizens. Ironically, bringing a major league team to an area (a primary reason for building a new stadium or arena) usually means that lower-income people see fewer games than before, primarily because building a new venue or refurbishing an old one invariably results in higher ticket prices.

Third, new stadiums are often built in downtown locations rather than in suburban or residential areas. The old stadiums, typically in rundown neighborhoods, are abandoned upon completion of the new. One consequence is that the poor living near the old venues are deprived of incomes previously derived from the games (e.g., jobs as parking attendants, salespersons, janitors, cooks, and so forth). When venues are built in downtown locations, they often displace old warehouses and cheap hotels with upscale restaurants, apartments, and boutiques. This gentrification increases rents and other costs, forcing the poor to live elsewhere.

Fourth, publicly financed venues tend to be built for those professional sports that appeal more to the affluent—baseball, football, basketball, and hockey. "Prole" sports—in other words, sports for the working classes—tend to occur in privately owned facilities (see Chapter 12).

Ownership for Profit

The first thing to understand about ownership of sports franchises is that it requires enormous wealth. Many of the owners of professional team sports franchises are *billionaires*. To illustrate, Table 10.1 identifies the ten richest owners in sports. They bought sports franchise for various reasons. For those teams owned by individuals, psychic gratifications are inherent in owning a professional team. Many owners derive great personal satisfaction from knowing athletes personally. In addition, a great

Table 10.1 Richest Owners in Sport

Name	Worth ($)	Team
1. Mikhail Prokhorov	18 billion	New Jersey Nets
2. Paul Allen	13 billion	Portland Trail Blazers Seattle Seahawks
3. Philip Anschutz	7.5 billion	Los Angeles Kings
4. Micky Arison	5.9 billion	Miami Heat
5. Richard DeVos	4.2 billion	Orlando Magic
6. Charles Dolan	3.3 billion	New York Knicks New York Rangers
7. Stephen Ross	3.1 billion	Miami Dolphins
8. Stan Kroenke	2.7 billion	St. Louis Rams
9. Malcolm Glazer	2.6 billion	Tampa Bay Buccaneers
10. Mark Cuban	2.5 billion	Dallas Mavericks

Source: Zack Pumerantz, "The Most Absurdly Rich Owners in Sports," *Bleacher Report*, 11 October 2011, http://bleacherreport.com/articles/887527-the-most-absurdly-rich-owners-in-sports#/articles/887527-the-most-absurdly-rich-owners-in-sports/page/22.

Table 10.2 North America's Most Valuable Teams, 2011 (in $US billions)

Name	Worth
Dallas Cowboys	1.81
New York Yankees	1.70
Washington Redskins	1.55
New England Patriots	1.37
New York Giants	1.18
Houston Texans	1.17
New York Jets	1.14
Philadelphia Eagles	1.12
Baltimore Ravens	1.07
Chicago Bears	1.07

Source: "The World's 50 Most Valuable Sports Teams," *Forbes*, 12 July 2011, http://www.forbes.com/sites/kurtbadenhausen/2011/07/12/the-worlds-50-most-valuable-sports-teams.

deal of social status comes with ownership of a sports franchise. Owners are feted by the community as service leaders and achieve a degree of celebrity status, social prestige, and publicity that can enhance other facets of their business ventures. Apart from the "psychic income" of team ownership, there are very substantial economic motives. Indeed, for most investors the primary motivation would seem to be a rationally economic one: Ownership of a sports franchise is a profitable long-range investment.

The value of sports franchises has consistently increased. Several examples make this point: The Philadelphia Eagles entered the NFL at a cost of $2,500 in 1933. In 1949 the franchise was sold for $250,000. The value of the Eagles franchise in 2011 was estimated by *Forbes* magazine at $1.12 *billion*. In 1960 Clint Murchison purchased the Dallas Cowboys franchise for $50,000 plus another $550,000 for the players. In 1989 the Cowboys were purchased by Jerry Jones for an unprecedented $140 million. By 2011 that franchise had increased in value to $1.81 *billion*. Similar increases have occurred in the three other major professional team sports, with the increases correlating closely with new stadium and arena construction at taxpayers' expense. Table 10.2 lists North America's ten most valuable teams. As

we have seen, the main reasons for the great appreciation in franchise value are the advantages of monopoly, television revenues, tax breaks, and subsidized venues.

That the structure of professional team sports tends to be lucrative is established, but the wealthy owners often downplay the business profit potential and highlight the notion that sports franchise are providing a service to their respective communities. This raises an important dilemma: If a franchise's status is seriously considered that of a privately owned capitalist business enterprise, then special commerce concessions and subsidies for venue construction are inappropriate. If, on the other hand, professional team owners deserve these advantages because they are providing sport as a community service, then their profits should be scaled down and the major benefits should accrue to the players and the fans.

Perhaps the best test of the owners' primary motivation involves their policies regarding ticket prices. The test is simple. If the owner is basically civic-minded, then the better the attendance during the season, the lower the prices should be. But the data on ticket prices consistently show that the greater the demand for tickets, the higher the prices tend to be.

Consider, for example, the cost for attending a Washington Nationals game in their new Nationals Park venue in the spring of 2008. Fans in the 1,800 most desirable seats paid at least $150 per game, with the most expensive seat at $400 (the most expensive seat in the old stadium was $140 in 2007). These prices, by the way, do not include prices for the new venue's sixty-six luxury suites, which start at $150,000 for the season. The new stadium was built with $611 million in public funds. As Thomas Heath observes, "The opening of a new stadium typically gives professional teams an increase in ticket demand and a corresponding opportunity to increase prices to match that demand."[10]

The rationale usually offered to explain ticket price increases is that costs are skyrocketing, especially because of the high salaries of superstars. As a result, fans typically vent their anger on the athletes rather than on the owners. The anger seems misplaced; apparently the fans do not recognize that greed motivates the owners as well as the players. Profit is, of course, the basic rule of capitalism. Still, the owners should not have it both ways. If they are capitalists, then subsidies are inappropriate. Their monopolies should not be supported by Congress and the courts. Their tax breaks should be eliminated. If public arenas are provided for professional teams, then the rent should be fair for both the owners of the teams and the citizens of the city.

A Radical Question: Are Owners Necessary?

Professional sport franchise owners receive anywhere from 50 to 75 percent of the profits from professional teams. What have they provided to receive such generous compensation? They did buy the teams from other owners, but what else? The stadiums and arenas, except on rare occasions, have been provided by taxpayers. So, too, the practice facilities. Sports analyst Dave Zirin argues: "Owners are uniquely charged with being the stewards of the game. It's a task that they have failed to perform in spectacular fashion. . . . Cities and city councils that allow their funds to be used by private franchises should, in turn, have some say in the relationship between team and fan."[11]

This leads to the question, Why don't the municipalities own these teams? They could hire competent general managers to sign players, make schedules, hire coaches and support staff, and negotiate for television and radio contracts. Indeed,

that is exactly the way the Green Bay Packers professional football team has functioned since it began; it is the only major professional sports team owned by the public. As such, it provides a model for what could be. Following are some of its features:

- The Green Bay Packers football club was organized back in 1923 as a community-owned, nonprofit company. Today, some 111,921 of the locals, including truckers, barkeeps, merchants, and bus drivers can lay claim to part of the franchise ownership in the Pack. The stockholders draw no profit, and the locally elected board of directors that operates the team is unpaid, but all concerned draw great pleasure from knowing that the Packers are theirs.
- Home-game ticket prices are some of the lowest in the NFL.
- Parking is permitted on some lawns for home games. No, really. Residents will snow-plow their lawns and driveways and charge anywhere from $5 to $20 to park there depending on walking distance.
- Nonprofit groups, which include service organizations and school groups, commit to working concessions at each game of the season.
- Off-duty police provide stadium security and are paid overtime by the team.
- Green Bay fans and citizens do not have to worry that some pirate of an owner is going to commandeer the Pack and haul their team to Los Angeles or some other big city, because Green Bay is their team. It stands as a shining model for how fans in other cities could control their sports franchises and stop corporate rip-offs.

WHO BENEFITS ECONOMICALLY FROM SPORTS?

Only a small percentage of people participating in sporting activities derive direct economic benefits from them. As we will document more fully in Chapter 12, the number of professional athletes in elite sport competitions is extremely small. For instance, the total number of full-time players in the four top North American team sports—baseball, basketball, football, and hockey—is slightly more than 3,000 annually. Add to this the very few professional golfers who earn their living on the PGA and LPGA tours and the handful of tennis players on the WTA and ATP tours, race-car drivers, boxers, and jockeys, and it is apparent that the business of professional sport is based on the performances of a very small group of talented individuals.

Professional Athletes' Earnings

For those who do attain the elite status of professional athlete, the financial benefits can be substantial, but the well-publicized salaries of a handful of superstars have given the public a distorted and inflated idea of professional athletes' incomes. Moreover, professional athletes' salaries should be balanced against their generally brief, often tenuous, careers. For instance, the median length of an NFL player's career is 3.6 years, which does not even qualify the typical player for a retirement pension.

In addition to their salary, successful professional athletes often receive benefits gained through product endorsements, speeches and other public appearances, and jobs as actors, entertainers, and sports announcers. They are also well positioned to take advantage of opportunities for investments in business ventures as diverse as sports camps, real estate developments, quick-order franchises, motels, and restaurants.

Forbes magazine ranked the top fifty North American athletes in terms of income in 2011. Two years after Tiger Woods' image was forever tarnished, he still led the way, earning $75 million—$22 million more than the number-two athlete, NBA star Kobe Bryant. Four of the top ten earners were NBA players. There was not a single U.S. or Canadian woman in the top twenty-five athlete income earners. For most whose livelihoods are dependent on their sports abilities, the financial rewards are not nearly as great as they are for the publicized athletes.[12]

The examples below indicate players' salaries and income in several professional sports:

- In professional basketball a lucrative sports career awaits the successful athlete but only about 276 players, and approximately

40 rookies, are hired each year. And while the average annual salary of NBA players in 2011 was estimated to be $3.5 million, those just one rung below in the developmental league make between $12,000 and $24,000 a season.[13]

- In professional golf some 350 men and 270 women pursue the multimillion-dollar prize money, but only about 200 make a living at it. The rest have trouble meeting expenses.

- More than 7,000 individuals play minor league baseball, and fewer than 7 percent of them will make it to the major leagues. None of these minor league players is covered by the minimum-salary scales of Major League Baseball.

- In auto racing, winnings are split among owners, drivers, and their crew. Annual sponsorship revenue and the licensing market are other sources of income for racers, who need over $1 million a year for expenses to be competitive on the auto racing circuit. Meanwhile, unknowns, people of color, and women have great difficulty obtaining racing contracts, sponsorships, and licensing deals.

- The scholarship athlete in college is paid a paltry stipend for his or her services. Calculated on the basis of the room, books, meals, and tuition allowed by the NCAA, a college athlete's salary does not greatly exceed the federal government's stated poverty level and approximates the federally established minimum hourly pay scale.

Professional athletes' salaries in the four major team sports have increased dramatically in the past two decades (see Table 10.3). As a result, the gap between the salary of the average professional athlete and that of the average worker has increased even more dramatically.

In Major League Baseball, for example, the average baseball player in 1950 earned $13,300 a year, a little more than four times the median family income. By 2011, the average baseball player was earning $3.1 million, about fifty-five times as much as the median family income. These higher average salaries reflect the very high salaries paid to superstars and do not reflect the salaries for most players. In baseball, for example, the New York Yankees had

Table 10.3	Average Salaries in Major Professional Leagues for Selected Years (in U.S. dollars)			
Year	National Basketball Association	Major League Baseball	National Football League	National Hockey League
1976	110,000	51,500	63,200	90,000
1984	246,000	325,900	162,000	130,000
1991	990,000	850,000	355,000	370,000
2001	3,170,000	2,290,000	1,169,000	1,430,000
2007	5,200,000	2,920,000	1,400,000	1,600,000
2010	5,360,000	3,300,000	1,800,000	1,800,000

a total player payroll of $206.3 million in 2011. The average Yankee player salary was $8.25 million, because four players exceeded $20 million in salary. A better measure is the use of the median salary (the midpoint, with half above and half below), which in 2010 was $5.5 million for the Yankees.[14]

Athletes of superstar status in individual sports sometimes receive even higher incomes than those in team sports. The most popular heavyweight boxers can make as much as $20 million for a single fight. The elite tennis players make more than $5 million annually. A few golfers approach $10 million a year in winnings, as do a few auto racers and jockeys.

These huge incomes, which are supplemented by endorsements and personal appearances, raise two important questions: (1) Are athletes paid too much? and (2) How do such enormous salaries for athletes affect the fans?

To the fans, their once-noble sports heroes are now businesspeople. Athletes demand huge salaries to perform in games. They threaten not to play. Their grandstand convictions are often regarded this way: "Players no longer have loyalty to their team or city," "Players have gotten too greedy," "They're all paid too much." We have all heard these complaints, and others, from disenchanted, angry people both inside and outside of the sports world.

The high salaries are resented because many people view athletes as "merely" employees who are "playing" while others work. Fans see these athlete-employees as behaving like workers who

are trying to acquire the most money, the most favorable working conditions, and the most favorable retirement benefits—even forming unions to collectively bargain to strengthen their demands, which is what the laboring workforce has done for over 150 years. While the labor union movement has been publicly supported for over a century in its struggles, professional athletes and their player unions—using the same model for advancing their cause as trade and labor unions have employed to improve their incomes and working conditions—are criticized and resented for what they have accomplished. This is a perplexing reaction.

It is rather ironic that sports fans and the public have tended to take the side of the team owners in salary disputes, strikes, and other disruptions, even though the owners over the years have had the monopoly, have taken economic advantage of the athletes, and have had the temerity to move franchises to more lucrative communities. Furthermore, fans resent the high salaries of athletes but take in stride the huge earnings of other entertainers. In 2010, for example, one entertainer—Oprah Winfrey—received an annual compensation of $315 million, more than three times that of the highest-paid athlete—Tiger Woods, who was the only athlete among the top twenty in entertainers' income.[15] For some reason the huge monies collected by nonathlete entertainers are accepted by the public, but the lesser monies received by athletes tend to foster resentment.

In addition to the entertainment analogy, four other arguments justify the amounts paid to superstars for playing games. The first is that their salaries are paid on the basis of scarcity. There are some 400 NBA basketball players in a nation of 310 million people, which makes NBA players about one in a million, and the capitalist principle of supply and demand—the economic foundation of North American countries—suggests that they should be paid accordingly.

The second argument is that a typical pro sports career is brief, so players should be paid well (out of all the players in the NBA, only thirty or so are thirty years of age or older). Third, the owners are paying the athletes what they are worth, because the superstars bring out the fans. Finally, related to the last point, salaries have escalated but so have owners' and league office revenues from television, ticket sales, royalties from the sale of merchandise, and the like. In 2010, the NFL received $4.3 billion from television contracts, the NBA $900 million, Major League Baseball $479 million, and the National Hockey League some $160 million.

Auxiliary Professions and Occupations in Sport

In the sports industry numerous auxiliary professions and occupations are made up of persons who have knowledge and skills that facilitate the development and progress of athletes and teams. Unquestionably, the most noted of these are coaches. Coaches are a universal component at all levels of organized sport, yet they are frequently overlooked in calculating the economic effects of sport in North America. It is estimated that about 3,200,000 coaches are employed in secondary schools, and some 25,000 men and 4,500 women are engaged in coaching at the college level.

Umpires and referees constitute another sports occupational category. MLB umpires are the best paid, with salaries ranging from $104,704 to $324,545. The NHL and NBA also require full-time officials, but the pay is lower. The NFL pays its officials on a part-time, game-by-game basis.

Thousands more officiate at the other levels of sport for relatively low fees (e.g., in Class A minor league baseball, umpires receive less than $20,000 a season). At a lower level still, there are many thousands who officiate high school sports. In Colorado, for example, there are almost 5,000 registered officials for thirteen different sports. The per-game pay per official in Colorado is $56 for varsity football, basketball, baseball, and ice hockey, and it is slightly less for other sports.

Another occupational category dependent on sport is the specialist in sports medicine. The treatment of sports injuries requires specialized education and training in treatment techniques, and sports medicine professionals are present at most sports events at all levels of organized sports.

Sports medicine clinics are becoming relatively commonplace in metropolitan centers.

A relatively new sports job is that of the player agent. With the advent of free agency in professional team sports and accelerated player incomes, agents for the players are performing an ever greater function in professional and college sports. They provide a service to the players because they know the tax laws and the market value of the athletes. Their goal is to maximize monetary benefits for the athlete by extracting the most beneficial contract from management. For their services the agents receive a percentage of the agreement (from 5 to 10 percent), which can be a considerable amount in this era of multimillion-dollar contracts. Agents sometimes violate NCAA amateur rules by signing college athletes and giving them bonuses.

This profession is so unregulated (and lucrative) that some agents have been able to take advantage of their naive clients by, for example, having them sign huge contracts with payments deferred over as many as forty years; in such instances the agent takes a percentage of the total up front, while the player receives no interest on the deferred money, which is further devalued by inflation.

Sport-Related Businesses

In addition to those directly involved in producing the sport product, many businesses benefit from the sports industry—hotels, taxis, restaurants, parking, and other business establishments—and can thereby increase their volume of business. The presence of a major league team generates millions of dollars for a city's economy, and this is why cities are so generous to sports teams (in stadium rentals, concession revenues, and various tax subsidies). Huge sports spectaculars such as the Kentucky Derby, the Indianapolis 500, the World Series, and the Super Bowl are major tourist attractions bringing an economic bonanza to numerous ancillary businesses (hotels, restaurants, stores, casinos, caterers, florists). The 2011 Super Bowl, for example, poured an estimated $300 million into the Arlington/Dallas area economy. (See Box 10.1 for the numbers generated from the 2011 Super Bowl.)

Box 10.1   *Thinking About Sport:* 2011 Super Bowl in Arlington, Texas: Economic Contradictions

The Super Bowl is much more than a football game. It is business—big business, the magnitude of which is seen in these numbers for the 2011 game at Cowboy Stadium in Arlington, Texas:

- At the newly built $1.1 billion Cowboy Stadium, 103,219 Super Bowl fans attended and visitors spent about $180 million. The total economic impact was $300 million.
- The face value of tickets was $800–$900, but many sold for over $2,700. A Packers fan from Austin, Texas, was willing to pay $2,500 apiece for four tickets. A couple of hours before kickoff, he could not find takers. Several people scalping tickets said that the going rate was closer to $4,000 a ticket.
- U.S viewership was estimated at 111 million, with an estimated 162.9 million total, making it the most-watched Super Bowl and the single most-watched program of any kind in U.S. television history.
- The cost of a thirty-second commercial was $3 million.
- The estimated amount of money bet legally and illegally on the game was $10.1 billion.
- Each member of the winning team received $83,000, and each member of the losing team received $42,000. (For the personnel of the two competing clubs, the total was more than $6 million.)

- Eighty percent of those attending the game were executives, managers, sales representatives, or professionals.

The Super Bowl is a celebration of concentrated wealth—wealthy players and very wealthy owners, corporate executives and their affluent clients, lobbyists and legislators, and high-rollers of various stripes with money to spend on lavish parties, food, and lodging at very inflated prices. As one sports columnist described the situation just before each Super Bowl: An armada of Lear jets touch down, delivering dozens of America's corporate tycoons. Local streets are jammed with stretch limos; bars are stocked with $500 bottles of champagne to go with the epicurean dinners. Hotel suites are swarming with the rich, the celebrated, and the fortunate—an unadulterated symbol of class inequality.

Sources: Revenue and Tax Estimates Regarding the National Football League's Super Bowl XLV in 2011, prepared for North Texas Super Bowl XLV Host Committee, Inc., Dallas Texas (La Mesa, CA: Marketing Information Masters, Inc.), 3 February 2010; Mitchell Schnurman, "Super Bowl's Economic Impact Hard to Tackle," *star-telegram.com*, 12 January 2011, http://www.star-telegram.com/2011/01/11/2762224/schnurman-super-bowls-economic.html; Jessica Rao, "The Super Bowl as Economic Game Changer," *cnbc.com*, 31 January 2011, http://www.cnbc.com/id/41044141/The_Super_Bowl as Economic Game Changer.

The concessions business provides sports spectators with food, drink, and merchandise. A concessionaire is typically given a monopoly by a team management, league, or city; in return the grantor receives a percentage of the proceeds. The beer and hot dogs consumed by thousands of fans generate a lot of revenue for every team.

As sports mania has pervaded the U.S. and Canada, public pressure to legalize sports betting has intensified and pressure has been exerted both by the financial distress of many state and prudential governments and by bet-eager constituents. In Chapter 7 we discussed sports gambling and the enormous sums of money involved in that industry.

Sporting goods corporations are some of the greatest beneficiaries of sport, both directly, through the sale of sports-related products, and indirectly, through the use of sports to generate interest in their products. Wilson, Spaulding, Mizuno, Nike, Adidas, and Reebok are all global sporting goods firms selling dozens of sports products.[16] (See Box 10.2, on Nike, for a look at the leading sports corporation.)

Corporate Advertising in Sport

Commercial sports enhance big business in a variety of industries. Sports themes and prominent athletes are used in advertisements to sell products.

Box 10.2   *Thinking About Sport:* Nike, the Sports Corporate Behemoth

In 1964 legendary University of Oregon track coach Bill Bowerman and one of his former distance runners, Phil Knight, formed a company called Blue Ribbon Sports to manufacture and sell running shoes. This company later became Nike, Inc., and today it is a huge global corporation with more than five hundred factories and offices located in forty-five countries and sales of $20.9 billion in fiscal 2011. Nike's products have expanded to all types of athletic shoes, apparel, sports equipment, and accessories.

Nike has signed many of the world's major athletes to focus attention on its products—for example, Michael Jordan, LeBron James, and Kobe Bryant in basketball; cyclist Lance Armstrong; skateboarder Paul Rodriguez, Jr.; golfer Tiger Woods; tennis players Roger Federer, Rafael Nadal, and Maria Sharapova; motorsport racer Michael Schumacher; and several Chinese athletes in basketball, track, and swimming. In fact, Nike sponsors more than twenty of the twenty-eight Chinese athletic federations.

In the United States Nike provides free equipment to professional, college, and some high school teams. Multimillion-dollar deals have been made with many major collegiate teams to supply equipment and supplements for coaches' salaries. Nike also sponsors elite U.S. track-and-field athletes, allowing them to train without having to work at a job. Nike also sponsors high school tournaments and track meets and over five hundred sports camps in fifteen different sports.

There is a dark side to the Nike story. Most of its products are manufactured in low-wage countries in Asia, where not only is labor cheap but regulations are scarce. There have been charges of exploitation of young women and children working under oppressive conditions for pennies an hour, making goods that sell for a huge profit in the United States. A Nike transnational advocacy network was formed to publicize these labor abuses and to mobilize efforts to pressure Nike (and other sports manufacturing firms) to stop these human rights abuses. Slowly, Nike has responded with some policy changes but has seemed less committed to reform than to damage control and public relations.

Labor relations within the United States have also been a negative for Nike. For example, a class-action race discrimination lawsuit against Nike was filed on behalf of four hundred African American employees of the company's Niketown Chicago store. Although Nike denied the allegations, it reached a $7.6 million settlement.

Nike has also been accused of having an undue influence on college sports. By giving equipment and money worth millions to big-time college programs, Nike has increased the gap between the college "haves" and the "have-nots." There is also a Nike network, which means that when there is a coaching vacancy, a "Nike school" may be limited to selecting a "Nike coach"—that is, a coach who has a contractual agreement with Nike. Similarly, Nike's sponsorship of certain prominent high schools, Amateur Athletic Union (AAU) teams, tournaments, and sports camps may have an influence on recruiting for colleges. In other words, "Nike high school coaches" or "Nike AAU coaches" may steer their athletes to "Nike colleges."

Sources: George H. Sage, "Corporate Globalization and Sporting Goods Manufacturing: The Case of Nike," in *Sport in Contemporary Society*, 7th ed., ed. D. Stanley Eitzen (Boulder, CO: Paradigm Publishers, 2005), 362–382; George H. Sage, *Globalizing Sports: How Organizations, Corporations, Media, and Politics Are Changing Sports* (Boulder, CO: Paradigm Publishers, 2010), 118–126.

Companies are convinced that through the proper selection of sports and sports personalities, they can reach particular pre-identified consumer categories or strengthen the general visibility of their products.

The commercialization of sport is also readily seen in the advertising at the ballparks, stadiums, and arenas of professional, college, and even high school sports. Many of these arenas have corporate names, purchased at significant cost. In 2011 there were over sixty professional league North American sports facilities with corporate names with a sponsorship value of more than $5 billion. In 2009 the New York Mets began play in their new stadium, called Citi Field, which costs Citibank $20 million a year for twenty years for the naming rights. In 2011 Mercedes-Benz USA announced that it had signed a ten-year agreement for naming rights for the newly renovated Superdome in New Orleans.

Corporate naming rights contracts are not limited to sports venues. Even game time is for sale—7-Eleven pays the Chicago White Sox $500,000 a year to start their home games at 7:11 P.M.[17] Nor is the naming game limited to professional sports. Corporate names are widespread on college sports venues. Some examples:

- Papa John's Stadium—University of Louisville
- Jones AT&T Stadium—Texas Tech
- Bright House Networks—Central Florida University
- Wells Fargo Arena—Arizona State University
- BB&T Field at Groves Stadium—Wake Forest
- Chevy Chase Bank Field at Bryd Stadium—University of Maryland
- Movie Gallery Stadium—Troy University[18]

Corporations have also paid to have their names associated with various college bowl games. A few examples of the thirty-six bowl games (yes, really) that were held in December 2011 and January 2012 are:

- Tostitos Fiesta Bowl
- Little Caesars Pizza Bowl
- Chick-fil-A Bowl
- Allstate Sugar Bowl
- Capital One Bowl

The use of sport to promote business interests takes a number of other forms as well, some reciprocal. Corporations sponsor such sports as running, bowling, golf, rodeo, tractor pulls, tennis, and skiing. For example, becoming a "title sponsor" on a PGA tour costs as much as $6 million. Sponsorship has been especially crucial to the advances in women's professional sports: General Mills' MultiGrain Cheerios, Crowne Plaza Hotels and Resorts, Gillette's *Golf* magazine, J. M. Smucker Co., WorldTek Travel, Usana Health Sciences, and Oriflame have all underwritten women's professional golf and tennis tournaments and have thus significantly raised both the prize money and the visibility of women's sports.

The most blatant expression of the commercial presence in sports occurs in automobile racing, because the races themselves are unabashedly organized to hype a variety of corporations. For example:

- Bank of America—Official Bank
- Canadian Tire—Official Automotive Retailer of NASCAR in Canada
- Chevrolet—An Official Passenger Car
- Coors Light—Official Beer
- DuPont—Official Finish
- Exide—Official Auto Batteries

Beyond that, drivers as well as owners of race cars receive a fee for using corporate logos on their racing vehicles and on the clothing of the drivers. These logos usually represent corporations involved in products for automobiles (e.g., tires, oil, auto parts, mufflers, shock absorbers), but they also include corporations selling chewing tobacco, cigarettes, clothing, soft drinks, and the like. The ubiquitous jumpsuits that drivers wear are the extreme in unabashed corporate advertising. Corporate logos adorn virtually every salable space of drivers' jumpsuits, making drivers appear to be walking sandwich boards.

A special relationship seems to exist between beer companies and sport. Beer is largely consumed by men, and men are overrepresented among the spectators at sporting events and among the avid followers of sport. The result is that the beer companies have partially subsidized sport. Some have owned teams: Coors Beer is part owner of the Colorado Rockies, and the venue is named Coors Field; Molson Breweries of Canada owns the Montreal Canadiens. Most sports teams have several sponsors for their local radio and television broadcasts, but a beer company is almost always one of them.

The major corporations of the United States have been active in the sponsorship of the U.S. Olympic team for the presumed benefits of public relations, advertising, and a generous allotment of tickets. For the rights to televise the Olympics from the 2000 Sydney Games through the 2008 Beijing Games, NBC paid $3.5 billion, which they made up in the sales of thirty-second advertising spots to various advertisers. Various corporations pay the IOC for the right to be the official soft drink (or whatever) of the Olympics.

THE RELATIONSHIP BETWEEN OWNERS AND ATHLETES

One of the reason ownership of a professional sports team has tended to be profitable is that the courts have allowed sport to be an exemption from U.S. antitrust laws. Early in the twentieth century Supreme Court Justice Oliver Wendell Holmes ruled that MLB was a game that did not involve interstate commerce and was therefore exempt from federal antitrust laws. This enabled MLB sport team owners to function as a monopoly. As other professional team sports leagues developed, their franchise owners operated under the special legal status conferred on MLB until the mid-1970s. The major consequence of professional team sports functioning as monopolies was the right of owners to own and control their players.

The Draft and the Reserve Clause

The 1970s were characterized by a concerted attack by athletes on the employment practices of professional team sports owners. Unlike employees of other businesses, athletes were not free to sell their services to whomever they pleased. Players' salaries were determined solely by each team's owner. In MLB, before the landmark cases of the mid-1970s (to be discussed below), once a player signed a contract with a club, that team had exclusive rights over him, and he was no longer free to negotiate with any other team. In succeeding years, the player had to sell his services solely to the club that owned his contract unless it released, sold, or traded him, or he chose to retire. The reserve clause specified that the owner had the exclusive right to renew the player's contract annually, and thus the player was bound perpetually to negotiate with only one club; he became its property and could be sold to another club without his own consent.

The NFL was more restrictive in one respect and more open (at least on paper) in another. Unlike MLB, the NFL had a draft of college players, and the selected athletes had no choice as to the team for which they would play. The player would play for the team that drafted him and at the salary offered or else join a team in the Canadian League (the number of foreign players allowed to play in Canada was limited, however, so that option was a real one only for the most sought-after football athletes). As in MLB, after signing with a team, the NFL player was bound to that team. He could, however, play out his option, in other words, play a year at 90 percent of his previous salary without signing a contract, whereupon he would be free to negotiate with another team. This apparent freedom of movement for the players was severely limited, however, by what was called the "Rozelle Rule." This rule allowed the NFL commissioner at that time, Pete Rozelle, to require the team signing any such "free agent" to compensate (with other athletes or with money of equal value) the club the player had left. This rule made signing free agents rarely in a club's interest; therefore, the free agent did not in reality have full economic freedom.

These provisions in the NFL and MLB (and similar ones in the NBA and NHL) were clearly one-sided, giving all the power to the owners, binding the employees (athletes) without binding the employers. The owner was free to decide whether to continue the relationship; the player was not. It was sarcastically observed that after the Civil War settled the slavery issue, owning a professional teams sport franchise was the closest one could come to owning a plantation.

Professional Team Sport Athletes Fight for Free Agency

In the late 1960s, various downtrodden groups (racial minorities, women, gays) became militant in attempts to overcome social injustices and change existing power arrangements. By the early 1970s professional athletes, too, began to recognize their common plight and organized to change it. Most fundamentally, professional athletes felt that because the owners had all the power, players did not receive their true value in the marketplace. The result was that athletes, singly and together in player associations, began to assert themselves against what they considered to be an unfair system. MLB is where the battle by athletes was waged most vociferously and over a period of decades. Their struggle is outlined in Box 10.3. Even a cursory

Box 10.3 *Thinking About Sport:* The Business of Baseball: Shifting Power and Increased Salaries

1879—Reserve rules instituted.

1922—The Supreme Court decided that baseball was not a trade in interstate commerce and therefore not subject to federal antitrust laws.

1953—A minor league player, George Toolson, wanted to change teams but was denied. The Supreme Court agreed with the owners that the players were bound to a club for life, citing the 1922 decision.

1966—Marvin Miller was elected executive director of the Players' Association. At this time the average player salary was $19,000, and the minimum for a major league player was $6,000 (a rise of only $1,000 since 1947).

1968—Players agreed not to sign 1969 contracts until a benefits plan (pensions and health insurance) agreement could be reached. This was the first mass holdout in baseball history. The minimum salary was increased to $10,000.

1970—The Players' Association negotiated a grievance and arbitration procedure with the owners.

1970—Curt Flood refused to leave the St. Louis Cardinals for Philadelphia.

1972—The Supreme Court ruled five to three against Flood.

1972—The first strike in the history of professional sports, lasting thirteen days. (Overall, there were four strikes in the preseason and nine during the season.) As a result the owners added $500,000 to the health care insurance and agreed to a cost-of-living increase in retirement benefits. The average salary was $22,000, and the minimum salary was $13,500.

1974—Jim "Catfish" Hunter became a free agent. As a result he left his $100,000 salary with Oakland for $750,000 with the Yankees.

1975—Andy Messersmith and Dave McNally became free agents.

1976—Free agency rights were created in the contracts of baseball. The average salary at this time was $51,500.

1979—The average salary was $113,558.

1980—A new pension agreement increased all benefits. The owners' contribution to the pension plan was one-third of the national television and radio package.

1981—A strike occurred for fifty days because the owners demanded restricted free agency (compensation for the loss of a free agent), which would have lost what the players had won in 1976. The players lost $34 million (an average of $52,000 each) in the strike, but they won by retaining free agency. The average salary at this time was $186,000.

1985—The average salary was $371,000.

1989—The average salary was $489,000.

1990—The average salary was $597,000, with the minimum salary at $100,000. The combined salaries for major leaguers was $388 million, and the owners' combined revenues were $1.5 billion (players thus received 26 percent of the revenues they generated).

1992—The average salary was $1 million.

1994 to 1995—A 232-day shutdown of MLB with no World Series in 1994. After a delay of the 1995 season and still no labor agreement, attendance for the season was down around 18 percent and television audiences were off by 11 percent.

1998—Congress passed the Curt Flood Act, a compromise that amended the special exemptions from antitrust for major league players but excluded minor league players and baseball owners from dealing with communities over franchise location.

2001—The owners voted to eliminate two teams.

2001—The average player salary was $2.29 million.

2006—The average player salary was $2.69 million.

2011—The average player salary was $3.1 million.

Sources: Marvin Miller, *A Whole Different Ball Game: The Inside Story of the Baseball Revolution* (Lanham, MD: Ivan R. Dee, 2004); Brad Snyder, *A Well-Paid Slave: Curt Flood's Fight for Free Agency in Professional Sports* (New York: Plum, 2007).

study of this box should demonstrate the impressive persistence that was shown by MLB players to obtain their goals of free agency and fair salaries.

Victories for the MLB players were not won easily. Owners fought them at every instance. There were strikes by the players and lockouts by the owners. Most significant, the owners were found guilty of *collusion* by the courts—that is, they conspired not to sign free agents from 1985 to 1987. This was an attempt to stop the salary spiral in baseball by taking away the players' power. The arbitrator, George Nicolau, in his opinion found that "there was no vestige of a free market [during these years]. It was replaced by a patent pattern of deliberate contravention of baseball's collective bargaining agreement." As a result, the owners had to pay $280 million in damages to the players adversely affected by the owners' collusion. In 2000 a federal appeals court commented on this collusion in a case involving an ex-MLB player. The court wrote in a unanimous opinion: "The owners' mendacity in the 1980s collusive effort to depress the ballplayers' income was in many ways as damaging to baseball as the Black Sox scandal of 1919 [referring to the Chicago White Sox throwing the World Series against Cincinnati]. The scope of the owners' deceit and fabrications in their 1980s effort to cheat their employees out of their rightful wages was wholly unprecedented, as was the financial injury suffered by the players."[19]

The NFL did not have as far to go as MLB did because players were already allowed to play out their option. The obstacle, as we noted earlier, was the Rozelle Rule, which was voided after two court cases. The first occurred when an NFL quarterback signed a nonstandard contract with the New England Patriots and it was voided by Commissioner Rozelle. The player gave up his career and sued the league. A district court judge ruled in the athlete's favor, saying that the standard player contract violated federal antitrust laws and that the Rozelle Rule was illegal.

That case involved an individual player rather than the entire NFL system and was subject to a prolonged appeal process, so the NFL Players Association brought suit to change the system for all players. A federal court judge decided that the Rozelle Rule was illegal. He directed the NFL and all of its teams to cease enforcing the rule. The result was that twenty-four new free agents began searching for the best offers.

In 1982 the NFL Players Association conducted a fifty-seven-day strike that cost the owners $210 million in lost revenues. The eventual settlement allowed the modified Rozelle Rule to continue but gave considerable overall monetary benefits to the players ($1.6 billion over five years, designating 46 percent of the NFL owners' gross to the players). In 1987 the union again went on strike—missing forty-two games—demanding free agency and $18 million for the pension fund. The strike failed as the owners hired replacement players, the networks televised the games, and public opinion sided with the owners. The strike cost the players $79 million in lost salaries and the owners $42 million in fewer ticket sales and $60 million in rebates to the television networks.

Although the players lost this battle, the war was not over. A groundbreaking 1993 agreement instituted a salary cap and unrestricted free agency (eliminating the Rozelle Rule). Then in 2001 the owners and the players' union agreed to a three-year extension of the collective bargaining agreement that ensured labor peace until 2006. A war of words and actions over a new labor agreement began in earnest months before the 2006 contract expired. The owners threatened to lock out the players, and the union decertified and filed an antitrust suit against the owners. The owners claimed that they needed to receive additional cost benefits if they were to have a fair return on investment and continue to grow the game. For their part, the players' said the owners wanted an additional $1 billion in relief, but the players wanted to maintain the status quo on the division of revenue and suggested that the sport's popularity pointed to an operation that was not in need of repair. Despite their differences, the NFL commissioner and NFL Players Association negotiated a five-year contract that expired in 2011. Under that agreement players received 63 percent of the NFL's designated gross revenue and had a rich benefits package. This revenue sharing was especially lucrative given the multibillion-dollar television package that was in force.[20]

Another contentious round of negotiations took place in 2011 between NFL owners and the NFL Players Association over a new contract for future years. Once again, the owners imposed a lockout and the NFL Players Association decertified, as both groups struggled for the upper hand. This is not the place for a detailed account of the various strategies the two sides used in the negotiations that took place over several months; suffice it to say that the players and owners finally came to an agreement with a last-minute deal between owners and players to save the 2011–2012 NFL season.

Historically, negotiations within the NBA, unlike those in the NFL and MLB, have been characterized by considerable cooperation between owners and athletes. Agreements have also been much more progressive. This spirit of cooperation on the part of the owners, however, has been prompted by the clear messages of the court decisions in the other sports: Owners may no longer treat their players as highly paid slaves.

In 1995, after the NBA Players Association negotiated a deal with the league, a number of high-profile athletes (e.g., Michael Jordan, Patrick Ewing) led an attempt by the players to decertify the union. The union members voted against this effort, followed by the owners' ratification of the collective bargaining agreement. This new plan allowed a dramatic increase in the salary cap, taking the average player salary to nearly $3 million by the conclusion of the contract; decreased the amount of rookie contracts; and guaranteed all first-round choices three-year deals, after which they become free agents. A collective bargaining agreement made in 2005 expired following completion of the 2010–2011 season. After prolonged negotiations, a new ten-year NBA contract, due to expire in 2022, was made.

AMATEUR SPORT AS A BUSINESS

The trend toward greater bureaucratization, commercialization, and institutionalism—the trend toward corporate sport—is not restricted to professional sports; it is also true of much of organized amateur sport. Analysis of the sports industry must therefore deal with both amateur and professional categories of sports, although in reality they are often virtually indistinguishable.

The amateur concept was a product of the late-eighteenth-century leisure class in Britain, the U.S., and Canada, where the ideal of an aristocratic sportsman was part of the pursuit of conspicuous consumption. Consequently, to be a pure amateur required independent wealth, because the true amateur derived no income from his sports participation. Explicit in the amateur ideal was the belief that one's sports endeavor must be unrelated to one's work or livelihood and that sport itself is somehow sullied, tarnished, or demeaned if one is paid for performing it.

Actually, the distinction between professional and amateur sport has always been largely artificial. Over the past century this has gradually been recognized throughout the sports world, and the archaic idea that amateurs and professionals cannot compete against each other has largely been laid to rest. Even the Olympic Movement, through the various international sport organizations, has eliminated the requirement that competing athletes must be amateurs and not professionals. In a few other sport organizations, though, the distinction is still made, but it is usually applied inconsistently.

The Ambiguous Case: Intercollegiate Sports and Amateurism

In Chapters 2 and 6 we described the rise of intercollegiate sports from a thoroughly amateur student-centered and student-controlled activity to the massive commercial industry that now exists. As college sports became more popular and more commercial, it became impossible to deny that they had become a very big business enterprise. Its member institutions are dependent upon attracting outstanding high school athletes for its sports teams, and this is done by subsidizing them with what is called an "athletic scholarship." Ignoring for the moment the long-range value of a college degree, the typical U.S. athletic scholarship (a legal maximum of room, books, board, tuition, and fees, as specified by the NCAA) has an annual value of

$25,000 at a state-supported school with low tuition and $50,000 at a private school with high tuition. These sums do not include the widespread illicit payments frequently discovered through NCAA investigations.[21]

College athletic scholarships do not constitute incomes comparable to professional contracts; nevertheless, college athletes are being compensated financially for their sports exploits. Thus, the distinction between amateur and professional sport is primarily one of degree. However, subsidization in the way of an athletic scholarship has not kept up with the colossal sums of money that currently characterize NCAA big-time college sports. For example, the NCAA's annual television rights alone generate more than $771 million, and eleven of the sixty-eight coaches whose teams played in the 2011 NCAA Division I men's basketball tournament have salaries exceeding $2 million (one salary was $6.1 million). Salaries ranging from $3 million to $5 million are common among NCAA subdivision football coaches. Major university athletic departments currently manage yearly budgets in excess of $100,000.[22]

But the NCAA athletic scholarship has remained essentially the same for over thirty years. Even a former NCAA executive director acknowledged that it is astonishing "when you see the money and the kind of salaries you see now and the only group in the system that hasn't received any additional funding is at the student-athlete level."[23] What seems clear is that the decisions made by the NCAA and its various universities have resulted in considerable hypocrisy.

The Economics of Collegiate Sport

The intercollegiate sports system, initially student-organized and student-run, came under the control of school administrators early in the twentieth century. It has since become a major business industry, generating, as noted above and in Chapter 6, as much as $100 million in individual university budgets, millions of dollars for football bowl appearances, and lucrative television contracts for men's basketball.

Operating a big-time collegiate athletic program as a business proposition has not been profitable for most universities. Various responses to financial crises have been made by universities and the NCAA. The NCAA has responded by permitting first-year students to compete at the varsity level, reducing the maximum number of scholarships that each institution may annually award, and eliminating the "laundry" allowance once given to scholarship athletes each month. Some universities have even reduced their commitment to intercollegiate athletics, either by deemphasizing the level of competition in their athletic programs or by dropping support for specific (typically nonrevenue) sports, such as golf, tennis, swimming, wrestling, soccer, rugby, and lacrosse. This was explained in Chapter 6.

In universities where sports have been dropped by university athletic administrations as financially prohibitive, some have been reinstituted as student-initiated "club sports," which are student-run without any real institutional assistance, thus moving them back to their original level: organized sport.

When financial losses have occurred or have been impending, many athletic departments have redoubled their efforts to remain competitive and thus approach fiscal solvency. One common strategy has been to fire the incumbent coach, typically of football or basketball, and to replace him or her—often with a public statement that "we are moving in a different direction"—with another coach who promises to reverse the institution's athletic fortunes. The new coach inevitably negotiates an agreement that the institution intends to make a commitment of greater financial outlays to support the new and invigorated program. The characteristic consequences of this strategy of escalating financial costs is that it further intensifies the pressures on coaches to recruit athletes legally and illegally while the administrators at the institution often ignore what is happening.

The lure of money affects even athletic programs below the big-time level. A common practice is for institutions that devote fewer resources to intercollegiate sports to schedule major university football or basketball teams, so-called big-time teams, just for a guaranteed fee. Both institutions benefit from such an arrangement. The smaller universities make relatively big money, and the

Oregon State University's Jared Cunningham in action against University of Texas player Sterling Gibbs (13) at the Izod Center (East Rutherford, New Jersey) on November 19, 2011. (Sports Illustrated/Getty Images, Porter Binks)

"big-time" university teams add to their winning records and pocket most of the gate receipts.

The extensive financial involvement of American colleges and universities in sports makes it difficult to distinguish their operations from openly professional sports enterprises. In fact, the average game attendance of many universities in football and basketball exceeds that of professional teams. As mentioned earlier, the money paid college athletes in the form of athletic scholarships raises the question of how they are to be distinguished from professionals. In other words, the money an admitted professional athlete receives is merely greater than that paid the typical college player—although the professional player is not confronted with the necessity of diverting energies to studies or to the hassle of remaining academically eligible, and the professional is free to devote himself or herself solely to developing sports skills.

Not surprisingly, collusive practices have infiltrated college athletics because the professional-amateur distinction is difficult to make realistically. A free market does not exist for college athletes; they are subject to severe restrictions by the NCAA, which functions as a cartel. NCAA regulations regarding recruiting, scholarships, and eligibility are collusive, and as with the reserve clause in professional sports, their effect is to prevent one team from raiding another for players. Although colleges have not yet fully rationalized procedures to the point of instituting a draft of eligible high school and community college players, fierce competition exists. The national and conference letters of intent that all recruited athletes must sign require an athlete to declare his or her intention of enrolling in and competing for a specific university. This has the effect of insulating a given university from competition for an athlete by other universities in its conference.[24]

The effect of such practices is, of course, advantageous for competing universities; it enables them to restrict their feverish recruiting of high school talent to a few months of the year. NCAA rules also preclude "tampering" with athletes who have already committed to attend and play at a university. A university cannot recruit an athlete already attending another university unless the athlete is willing to be penalized by being declared ineligible for a year. In other words, only if the athlete is willing to forgo competing for a year can he or she transfer to another university's athletic program. Such control and restrictions apply only to the athletes; they do not apply to the coaches of intercollegiate teams. Indeed, coaches are even able to break their employment contracts at the university where they are coaching in order to accept better coaching offers at another university.

In Chapter 6 we explained how NCAA regulations also seriously limit the freedom of college athletes. The effect of these NCAA regulations is to allow American colleges to conduct their sports programs in a monopolistic manner by regulating and limiting the freedom of athletes. They also create a ceiling on players' income, regulate the length of and criteria for participation, and restrict player mobility.

For the very few who have the ability and skill, collegiate sports participation has historically been the prelude to professional competition in basketball and football, whereas this has been infrequently (although increasingly) the case in baseball and ice hockey. Although the minor league systems of Major League Baseball and the National Hockey League have diminished considerably from their heydays after World War II, they are still much more extensive than those of any other major professional team sports. For a professional baseball or hockey player not to have served at least a minimal apprenticeship in the minor leagues is highly atypical; for a professional basketball or football player to have done so is highly atypical.

Awareness of the commercialism that now exists in collegiate sports, and of their function as minor leagues, or training grounds, for a future professional sports career, has led to the suggestion that the professionalism of collegiate athletics be explicitly recognized. This would be accomplished by having a college athlete's letter of intent be considered a legal contract with the university in the same way that a professional athlete's contract is owned by his or her team. Professional sports league owners desiring the services of a college athlete would have to purchase the contract, thereby reimbursing that university for the cost of player development and training and simultaneously improving the financial position of the university team supplying the pro team with its raw material.

Recognizing this natural source of player development, professional basketball and football leagues have entered into informal agreements with colleges and universities. The NBA has established an age limit and a "one year out of high school" rule that prohibit teams from drafting players. Top high school players who qualify academically can enroll in college, play one year of college basketball, and then bolt to the NBA. For a football athlete to be eligible for the NFL draft, at least three years must have passed since he graduated from high school. The NCAA allows college players to "test the waters" of the NFL draft once while they are in college. However, if a player makes any kind of agreement to be represented by a player agent or accepts anything from an agent or anyone working for an agent, the NCAA will void all his remaining college eligibility.

The NCAA has always vigorously opposed college athletes leaving early for professional careers. It reluctantly allows this practice only because its legal advisors have cautioned that attempts to prohibit it would not stand up in court.

SUMMARY

We have shown the economic side of North American sport in this chapter. The message is clear: Corporate sport is a multimillion-dollar enterprise selling sporting events and a variety of ancillary products. Indeed, it is big business. The owners of professional teams are in a constant search for better markets and higher profits. The possibility that a franchise will move increases the probability that municipalities will provide facilities or other inducements at taxpayers' expense to entice teams to their city or to encourage them to remain there.

Professional sports have sold out to the demands of television. In return for large TV rights contracts, the leagues allow the television networks to dictate schedules, time-outs, and the like. But without those contracts, professional sports would be a small struggling industry.

Professional sports owners squeeze as much money as they can from fans and taxpayers. The principle of supply and demand operates in setting admission charges for athletic events. If sport were truly a public service, as the sports industry often claims, rather than a business, the most successful teams would charge the lowest ticket prices, but this is not the case.

Professional athletes demand high salaries and other monetary inducements (bonuses, retirement benefits, insurance policies, interest-free loans, and so forth). The frequent result is pugnacious negotiations between owners and athletes. An ongoing struggle exists between athletes (through union-like organizations) and entrepreneurs for the power to regulate sports and to apportion profits. This is manifested in court battles, player strikes, owner lockouts, and press agencies by both sides attempting to sway public opinion.

College sports have evolved from mostly a student recreation to a major business industry. Big-time intercollegiate sports are merely another form of professional sports. Intercollegiate sports serve not only as a minor league farm system for many professional sports but also as a public relations avenue for future pro stars.

In short, the economics of professional sport has become similar to that of the world of work. As such, it reveals, in microcosm, the values of the larger society. The result is the ultimate loss of sport as a meaningful, joyous activity in itself.

WEB RESOURCES

www.sportsbusinessdaily.com/Journal.aspx
SportsBusiness Journal provides coverage of the deals, trades, contracts, and power plays that shape the changing sports landscape. Regular columns cover every aspect of the sports industry, from media and marketing to finance, facilities, and labor.

www.bus.ucf.edu/sportbusiness/
This is the website of the DeVos Sport Business Management program at the University of Central Florida. It not only provides a comprehensive business curriculum approach and a global sports network in a hands-on environment but also offers a master's degree in sports business management and a master's degree in business administration.

www.askmen.com/sports/business/
This website for the men's magazine *Askmen* often includes essays on the business aspects of sports, including the Olympics, and the accounting practices of professional teams.

www.fieldofschemes.com
This site provides information critical of public subsidies for building stadiums and arenas for private profit.

www.forbes.com
The website for *Forbes* magazine, which from time to time provides data on wealthy Americans (including owners of professional teams and pro athletes) and financial information on professional teams.

www.sportslinkscentral.com
Sports Links Central is a comprehensive Internet directory with links to sports industry websites, including official sports leagues, teams, businesses, education, and media links.

NOTES

1. Jack W. Plunkett, *Plunkett's Sports Industry Almanac 2011* (Houston, TX: Plunkett Research, 2010), 30.

2. *American Needle, Inc., v. National Football League et al.*, No. 08-661. U.S. (2010) (May 24, 2010).

3. James Quirk and Rodney Fort, *Hard Ball: The Abuse of Power in Pro Team Sports* (Princeton: Princeton University Press, 2009), 9.

4. Andrew Zimbalist, *The Bottom Line: Observations and Arguments on the Sports Business* (Philadelphia: Temple University Press, 2006), 29–30; see also Kevin J. Delaney and Rick Eckstein, *Public Dollars, Private Stadiums: The Battle over Building Sports Stadiums* (New Brunswick, NJ: Rutgers University Press, 2003); and J. G. Long, "Full Court: The Real Cost of Public Funding for Major League Sports Facilities," *Journal of Sports Economics* 6, no. 2 (2005): 119–143.

5. Zimbalist, *The Bottom Line*, 130–170; see also Neil deMause and Joanna Cagan, *Field of Schemes: How the Great Stadium Swindle Turns Public Money into Private Profit*, revised and expanded ed. (Lincoln: University of Nebraska Press, 2008).

6. Dennis Coates and Brad R. Humphreys, *Do Economists Reach a Conclusion on Subsidies for Sports?*, American Association of Sports Economists, Working Paper Series, Paper 08-18, August 2008, 1, http://college.holycross. edu/RePEc/spe/CoatesHumphreys_LitReview.pdf; David B. Sullivan quoted in Brian Tuohy, *The Fix Is In: The Showbiz Manipulations of the NFL, MLB, NBA, NHL, and NASCAR* (Port Townsend, WA: Feral House, 2010), 21.

7. Neil deMause, "Why Do Mayors Love Sports Stadiums?" *The Nation*, 15–22 August 2011, pp. 14–17.

8. Coates and Humphreys, *Do Economists Reach a Conclusion on Subsidies for Sports?*, 4.

9. deMause and Cagan, *Field of Schemes*.

10. Thomas Heath, "That's Not Peanuts," *Washington Post National Weekly Edition*, 18 June 2007, p. 56; see also Michael T. Friedman, "'The Transparency of Democracy': The Production of Washington's Nationals Park as a Late Capitalist Space," *Sociology of Sport Journal* 27 (2010): 327–350.

11. Dave Zirin, "What Owners Owe Us," *The Progressive Populist*, 1 September 2010, p. 21; see also Tim Dahlber, "Impossible to Believe Owners Who Cry Poverty," *journalgazette.net*, 20 July 2010, http://www.journalgazette. net/article/20100720/SPORTS02/307209996/-1/ SPORTS12.

12. "Full List: The World's 50 Highest-Paid Athletes," *Forbes.com*, http://www.forbes.com/2011/05/31/highest-paid-athletes_slide.html.

13. Kurt Badenhausen, "The NBA's Highest-Paid Players," *Forbes.com*, 4 November 2010, http://www. forbes.com/2010/11/04/nba-best-paid-players-business-sportsmoney-nba-top-paid-players.html.

14. Peter Barzilai, Scott Boeck, Gabe Lacques, and Bob Nightengale, "Baseball Salaries," *USA Today*, 1 April 2011, p. 12C.

15. Lacey Rose, "Hollywood's 10 Highest-Earning Women," *Forbes.com*, 8 November 2010, http://www. forbes.com/2010/11/08/hollywood-top-earning-women-business-entertainment-top-earning-women.html.

16. George H. Sage, *Globalizing Sport: How Organizations, Corporations, Media, and Politics Are Changing Sports* (Boulder, CO: Paradigm Publishers, 2010).

17. Ben Klayman, "Citigroup Naming Rights Deal Still in Place—Mets," *Reuters*, 21 November 2008, http:// www.reuters.com/article/2008/11/21/citigroup-mets-idUSN2149039220081121; see also Richard Sandomir, "White Sox Have New Start Time: 7-Eleven," *New York Times*, 11 October 2006, p. D3.

18. Barnet D. Wolf, "The Name Game: Company Banners Flying on More College Stadiums, Arenas," *The Columbus Dispatch*, 29 April 2007.

19. Quoted in "Court Says '80s Collusion as Bad as Scandal in '19," *Arizona Republic*, 15 February 2000, p. 6C; for an interesting account of one MLB player's fight for free agency and its widespread impact, see also Brad Snyder, *A Well-Paid Slave: Curt Flood's Fight for Free Agency in Professional Sports* (New York: Penguin, 2006).

20. Michael Oriard, *Brand NFL: Making and Selling America's Favorite Sport* (Chapel Hill: University of North Carolina Press, 2010).

21. Brett McMurphy, "Ex-Players Tell of Receiving Illicit Payments at Auburn and Elsewhere," *New York Times*, 31 March 2011, p. B17.

22. Jodi Upton, "NCAA Tourney Coaches Cash In," *USA Today*, 31 March 2011, pp. 1A, 4C; see also "Football Bowl Subdivision Coaches Salaries for 2010," *USAToday.com*, http://www.usatoday.com/sports/college/ football/2010-coaches-contracts-table.htm.

23. Quoted in Steve Wieberg, "This Shot Was Worth $1.4 Million to Arizona and the Pac-10: Should Players Get Some of It?" *USA Today*, 30 March 2011, p. 2A.

24. Mark Yost, *Varsity Green: A Behind the Scenes Look at Culture and Corruption in College Athletics* (Stanford, CA: Stanford University Press, 2010); and William C. Dowling, *Confessions of a Spoil Sport: My Life and Hard Times Fighting Sports Corruption at an Old Eastern University* (University Park: Pennsylvania State University Press, 2007).

CHAPTER 11

Sport and the Mass Media

The relationship between sport and the media is not predicated on benevolence or generosity. The media does not report on sport as a function of public service, nor does sport provide the media with access merely to increase public awareness. Rather, the sport media nexus is driven by commercial forces.
—Matthew Nicholson*

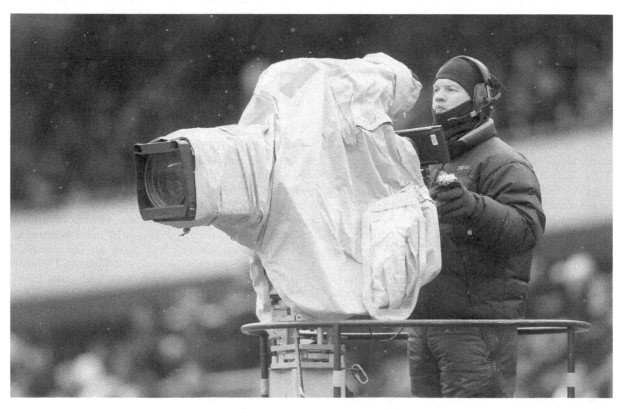

Fox cameraman Dan Gibbons operates an HD camera from an elevated platform during the Chicago Bears NFC divisional football play-off game against the Seattle Seahawks at Soldier Field in Chicago. (AP Photo/David Stluka)

*Matthew Nicholson, *Sport and the Media: Managing the Nexus* (Boston: Elsevier, 2007), 13.

Social institutions that appear to be independent of one another frequently are found, on closer examination, to be very interdependent. Such is the case of sport and the mass media, even though the former is concerned with physical action, skill in a highly problematic task, and the outcome of a competitive event, while the latter communicates information and entertains. Both commercial sports and the printed and electronic media are preeminently commercial industries that constitute two of the most successful businesses in North America. Thus, the goal (and logic) of both is mainly economic profit. As one sport studies noted: "We live in a world that is saturated by sport media, the result of a . . . cultural and commercial relationship between these two massive industries."[1]

SOCIAL ROLES OF THE MASS MEDIA

The term *mass media* refers to all of the print (newspapers, magazines, and books) and electronic (radio, satellite radio, television, movies, and the Internet) means of communication that carry information to widespread audiences. Advertising falls into both categories, and it is also a component of mass media.

Over the past decade, new technologies have changed the viewing and listening habits of people. For example, media consumers have shifted toward digital images on their computers and portable devices and away from radio and television. Social media—Facebook, YouTube, Twitter, texting—and Internet browsing have become the preferred media sources, especially for people under the age of forty.

Prominent and Subtle Roles of the Media

One of the prominent roles of the mass media is the communication of information. Culture depends upon communication; indeed, culture cannot exist without an effective system of transmitting and disseminating information. In small primitive societies information is transmitted by direct one-to-one, face-to-face contact, but this form of information transmission is efficient only in a society of limited geographical size with a sparse population. Modern societies require complex networks of printed and electronic media to keep people informed about other people and events. Information binds people to their friends, neighbors, cities, states, and other nations of the world.

Another prominent role of the mass media is to provide entertainment for people from all walks of life. Newspapers carry special features and the comics. Magazines and books offer stories of adventure, humor, and mystery. Radio and television provide a wide variety of entertainment, from music to sporting events. The Internet, the newest form of mass communication, offers everything that the other media offer, but it offers such a stunning variety of everything that it is impossible to try to enumerate all of its entertainment forms.

In performing these two fundamental roles, the mass media fulfill two more subtle roles: providing collective experiences for the members of society and promoting social change. Shared information and entertainment via the media contribute to the socialization of citizens in a particular culture and thus serve to socially integrate persons into that culture. In effect, the messages and images that the media create help shape the national and international cultural environment. As for social change, this is one of the major features of modernization, and the media are on the forefront of reporting social change, while also contributing to it.

Mass Media and Social Theories

As we have emphasized in previous chapters, social functionalism views society as a vast network of interconnected parts, each helping to maintain the system as a whole. Each component of the system is expected to contribute to stability, social integration, and the promotion of value consensus within the society. To the extent that the mass media provide a collective experience for members of a society, they promote shared values and norms and secure a common consensus among citizens. Thus, they may be said to contribute to society's stability and integration. In short, the mass media are a powerful ideological institution because the messages and images that they create help shape and mold the national and international cultural atmosphere.

In North America the media present a more or less standardized version of culture by broadcasting important events and ceremonies, such as press conferences, political campaign debates, inaugurations, parades, Super Bowls, and Stanley Cups, and by covering local, national, and international happenings. Collectively, these promote social cohesion by providing a collective experience for all citizens.

Print and electronic advertising in the media functions to sustain the economy, provide information about services and products, and finance the cost of the media. In this role the media contribute to a socially integrated consumer culture that constructs needs and beliefs about what is necessary to be content and satisfied, in accordance with functionalists' expectations.[2]

Conflict/cultural advocates recognize that the media are a powerful source for forming values and beliefs and for organizing consensus within North America; indeed, the media are often labeled "the consciousness industry." But ownership of contemporary mass media is in the hands of huge corporations, which in turn are owned by wealthy stockholders and run by managers. Profits are paramount, and publishing and broadcasting decisions about what actually reaches the public are made by a small number of decision makers who are overwhelmingly white, male, and wealthy. Those decisions largely ignore and disrespect subordinate groups and reinforce many of the established attitudes, inequalities, and injustices found in North America centered on race, gender, ethnicity, age, sexual orientation, disability, and social class.

Conflict/cultural theorists are in agreement with functionalists that the media tend to promote the established social order and reigning consensus, not necessarily out of cynical self-interest or subservience to particular group interests, but certainly as an instrument for the promotion of economically and politically powerful stakeholders. While functionalists consider this arrangement as appropriate for social stability, conflict/cultural advocates contend that it tends to promote and sustain the unequal distribution of power and wealth, as well as legitimize existing unequal social relations related to class, gender, and race.

Both functionalist and conflict/cultural theorists agree the mass media nevertheless promote social change as well. The media present information about cutting-edge research, new social practices and values, and critiques of contemporary attitudes and behaviors; in doing this they are supporting social change. The mere reporting of new ideas and events stimulates reinterpretations of the world and promotes changes in many spheres of life.[3]

THE SYMBIOSIS OF MASS MEDIA AND SPORT

All of the roles of the mass media are represented in their association with sports. First, the media supply information about sports—for example, game results and statistics about individual players and teams. Second, they provide exciting entertainment. Reading about, listening to, or watching sporting events allows individuals opportunities to escape temporarily the burdens and frustrations that bind them to reality. Media sport has the perfect combination for entertainment, including controlled violence, excitement, and lots of audio and visual power.

One of the media's subtle roles—providing collective experiences—is often played out through conversations about sport. One can ask almost any stranger about sports or well-known sporting events and the stranger will likely know the relevant information because he or she has read about it, heard about it, or seen it in the media; consequently, the conversation can be sustained and sometimes transformed into a more enduring social relationship. Media sport, then, provides a communal focus whereby large segments of the population can share common norms, rituals, ceremonies, and values.

Finally, the media have played a significant role in social change as it relates to sports through the creation of new sports, the popularity of others, and the rule changes of still others (more about this later in the chapter). Attitudinal and value changes in the sport culture about competition, winning, losing, cheating, and so on, have been adopted in the general culture.

Enduring Linkages Between the Mass Media and Sport

Little did the inventors of our technical means of communication realize how their inventions would become associated with sport. Johannes Gutenberg invented movable type in the mid-fifteenth century. As his invention was refined during the following centuries, the ability of the printing press to produce reading material quickly and cheaply increased and made possible the growth of the publishing industry. Wireless telegraphy, invented at the end of the nineteenth century, served as the technological foundation for the various electronic media of today's world.

Newspapers

In the mid-nineteenth century North American newspapers began periodic coverage of sports events, but it was not until the 1890s that the first sports section became a regular feature of a newspaper. In 1895, William Randolph Hearst, publisher of the *New York Journal*, developed the first modern sports section.

Over the past hundred years the symbiosis between the newspaper and sport has become so well established that in many of North America's most popular newspapers, sports coverage constitutes almost 50 percent of the space devoted to local, national, and international stories, and the sports pages have about five times as many readers as any other section of the newspaper. So the newspaper sports section has not been curtailed by the growth of radio, television, or the Internet; instead, other forms of communication have strengthened rather than replaced the sports section of newspapers.[4]

Magazines

Today, magazines represent a large component of the media industry. Around 19,000 different titles exist in the United States.[5] Historically, magazines and books chronicled the activities of athletes and teams before the newspaper sports sections existed. In the years between the American Revolution and the 1830s, there arose a widespread interest in journals of all kinds, and magazines cropped up everywhere to exploit the popular interest in horse racing, hunting, fishing, and athletic sports.

The momentum of sports literature accelerated in the 1830s, and the first prominent sports journal in the United States, *Spirit of the Times*, began publication in 1831. This journal featured horse racing in particular but also reported on other sports and indirectly helped to establish what was to become "the national pastime"—baseball. Another popular nineteenth-century sports magazine, *The Sporting News*, began publication in 1886 and continues to be one of the most successful sport magazines. In 2008 it launched a daily online newspaper, *Sporting News Today*.

Magazines specializing in sports have been standard fare in the publishing business for the past one hundred years, with almost every sport having its own publication. Indeed, one indication that a new sport is rising in popularity is the appearance of a magazine describing its techniques and strategies, profiling its best players, and advertising equipment and accessories for playing or watching the sport. *Sports Illustrated*, founded in 1954, is currently the best-selling sports magazine. It has over 3.5 million subscribers and is read by more than 25 million readers each week.[6]

Books

The first massive book wave in the United States began in the two decades before the Civil War as dime novels began to appear in large quantities. Numerous books on field sports, horse racing, boxing, and the increasingly popular team sports poured from the publishing houses throughout the late nineteenth century, but the youth literature contributed most significantly to arousing interest in sports among the youngsters of this era. Undoubtedly the most prolific of the youth literature authors was Burt L. Standish (whose real name was Gilbert Patten), who in 1896 began turning out a story every week about a fictitious schoolboy athlete, Frank Merriwell. In the early 1900s the Merriwell stories sold about 135,000 copies weekly. Youth athletic stories also streamed from the pens of many other authors.

Serious novelists tended not to focus on sport to any extent, although some of the most powerful passages in Ernest Hemingway's novels dealt with blood sports (e.g., bullfighting). A trend has now developed toward serious writing about sport, and North American novelists have increasingly employed sports themes in their works. A coalition of university professors and friends founded the Sport Literature Association in the early 1980s; it publishes *Aethlon: The Journal of Sport Literature*, which issues works about sport literature, including original fiction and poetry.

Perhaps the greatest impact of sport on the literary field has been made by former athletes and sports journalists. The United States and Canada have been virtually deluged with books by professional athletes (most of these are actually ghostwritten) who describe their experiences in sports. A number of former athletes have written "kiss-and-tell" books either mocking or criticizing their sports experiences. Sports journalists have also shared in the publishing windfall; several have written what might be called exposé, or muckraking, types of books. The consequence: Most bookstores have an entire section of sports books.

Radio

While sports sections of newspapers, sport magazines, and books about sports continue to have significant linkages to sport, the electronic media—radio, motion pictures, television, and the Internet—have made dramatic inroads into the traditional information and entertainment functions of the printed media. Only a few years separated the invention of wireless broadcasting and the advent of radio sportscasts. The first permanent commercial radio station, KDKA in Pittsburgh, went on the air in 1920. Less than a year later, in July 1921, the first heavyweight championship boxing bout was broadcast. From the mid-1920s to the early 1950s, radio reigned supreme in broadcasting sports news and live sports events.

Radio's popularity as a medium for sport information and entertainment declined with the beginning of network television in the 1950s. Nevertheless, there are some 11,000 radio stations in North America that broadcast more than 700,000 hours of sport annually. Sports call-in shows and interviews with sports celebrities as well as play-by-play game reporting have sustained the role of radio in sports, and the twenty-four-hour-per-day, all-sports radio stations appear to have created excitement in this industry. There are now more than 435 all-sports radio stations in the United States and 7 in Canada, devoted almost solely to discussion, debate, and analysis of athletes and teams by both hosts and callers.[7]

Motion Pictures

Thomas Edison's rudimentary motion-picture camera, the kinetoscope, which he patented in 1891, marked the birth of the movie industry. Movies quickly became a favorite popular culture phenomenon. As popular as the movies were, though, sports stories were relatively rare before 1970, although *Knute Rockne All-American*, the story of the legendary Notre Dame coach, and *The Pride of the Yankees*, the story of the famous New York Yankees first baseman Lou Gehrig, among a few others, had gained some popularity. In recent decades several sports films have received critical acclaim; *Rocky* and *Chariots of Fire* were awarded Oscars for best picture.

In 2010, the *New York Daily News* sports staff ranked what it considered the top twenty-five sports movies of all time. The top ten were:

1. *Raging Bull* (1980)
2. *Hoosiers* (1986)
3. *Rocky* (1976)
4. *Slap Shot* (1977)
5. *Bull Durham* (1988)
6. *The Natural* (1984)
7. *Caddyshack* (1980)
8. *Breaking Away* (1979)
9. *Major League* (1989)
10. *Field of Dreams* (1989)[8]

Of course, these *New York Daily News* selections are arbitrary. Increasingly, though, sports films tend to transcend mere entertainment and attempt to explore broader social issues of power, race, masculinity, and gender relations.

Television

Currently the predominant mass media presenter of sport is television. The technology to produce telecasts was developed during the 1930s, but World War II delayed the large-scale growth of commercial television for nearly a decade. When television began to grow, however, its rate of growth was staggering. In 1950 fewer than 10 percent of households had television; in 2010, 98 percent of North American homes had at least one set, 40 percent had two sets, and 42 percent had three or more sets.

The average television viewer received only 4 or 5 channels in 1970, 3 of which were broadcast networks; the average viewer in 2010 received around 65 channels (broadcast and cable), and some received more than 100. There are currently about 11,000 cable TV systems offering more than 150 channels of programming. To watch this plethora of TV choices, North Americans own more than 250 million television sets, representing more than one-third of the world's total. According to the Nielsen "Three Screen Report," on average, Americans spend 35.5 hours a week watching television while Canadians watch for 24.5 hours weekly. Older viewers watch more than younger viewers.[9]

Other Electronic Media

Other media viewership and multimedia viewership have increased rapidly. Americans spend 3.8 hours per week using the Internet. With digital video recorders (DVRs) in more than 36 percent of U.S. homes, timeshifting—that is, recording programs to a storage medium to be viewed at a more convenient time—DVRs and video on demand are surging in popularity, with the average user now timeshifting 2.4 hours per week. Moreover, the number of mobile subscribers watching video on mobile phones increased by over 50 percent between 2009 and 2010.

The newest type of mass media takes the form of social interaction and is called *social media*. Social media are primarily Internet- and mobile-based instruments for sharing and discussing information. According to the CTIA Advocacy, 93 percent of Americans now use cellphones or wireless devices; one-third of those are smartphones that allow users to browse the Web and check email, among other things. These media most often involve activities that integrate technology, telecommunications, and social interaction through the construction of words, pictures, videos, and audio. Among the various types of social media are forums, message boards, blogs, wikis, and podcasts. Social media applications include Google Plus, Facebook, YouTube, Twitter, Flickr, and LinkedIn, each of which allows end users to engage in multidirectional conversations in or around the content on the website.[10]

As smartphone penetration continues to proliferate, consumers will be increasingly using these devices (as opposed to PCs) to access the Internet. The emergence of other connected devices, including tablet computers like Apple's popular iPad, will create additional options for media consumption anytime, anywhere.

TELEVISION: THE MONSTER OF THE SPORTS WORLD

Even with the growth of high technology and new forms of media, television still remains a dominant choice for consumers. TV viewing per week has continued to increase during the past decade, with time spent simultaneously watching the Internet and watching TV increasing as well. Television has come to have a dominating grasp on sport, but the influence has been reciprocal; television programming is greatly influenced by sport as well.

Sport made a union with television while the tube was still in its infancy. The first televised sports event was a college baseball game between Columbia and Princeton in 1939. The announcer was located in the stands with the spectators; there was only one camera, and its range was so limited that it could not show the batter and the pitcher at the same time. Other technical difficulties made it almost impossible for viewers to know what was happening during the game. In describing the TV coverage, the *New York Times* reported: "The players were best described by observers as appearing like white flies running across the screen. . . . When the ball flashed across the grass, it appeared as a comet-like white pinpoint. . . . The commentator saved the day, otherwise there would be no way to follow the play or tell where the ball went except to see the players run in its direction."[11]

Despite the many problems encountered by the infant television industry, it grew enormously in a short time, and television is now by far the most popular and most time-consuming leisure activity in the United States.

Increasing TV Sports Coverage

The most dramatic programming trend in television has been the enormous increase in sports coverage. Spectators consume sport to a far greater extent through television than through personal attendance at events. Table 11.1 lists examples of the variety of sports television that now exists.

In the United States, more than 60,000 hours of sport are televised annually by four major free-to-air networks as well as pay-TV platforms such as cable, pay-per-view (PPV), and satellite television, along with various digital channels and local sports cable networks. Cable TV networks, such as ESPN and ESPN2, which reach over 80 percent of American homes with cable TV, broadcast more than 9,000 hours of live sports each year.[12]

Regional sports cable networks and direct satellite broadcasts are growing rapidly, and they broadcast countless thousands of hours of sport each year. The trend that is perhaps the most remarkable is the sport organizations that are becoming their own media companies—such as the NFL (NFL Network reaches about 57 million households), NBA (NBATV), MLB (MLB Network), NHL (NHL Network), the Big Ten Network, and the Longhorn Network—thus are bypassing the traditional TV and cable networks. The Longhorn Network, which premiered in the fall of 2011, broadcasts round-the-clock coverage of University of Texas sports and is the first TV sports channel devoted to a single university. It has created considerable controversy, especially over its potential to give the University of Texas an unfair recruiting advantage over other universities.[13]

The Super Bowl has dominated network TV ratings during the past two decades, ranking as the top TV program nine of the past twenty years. Super Bowl telecasts usually attract 40–45 percent of the households watching TV. The 2012 Super Bowl between the New York Giants and the New England Patriots became the most-watched American television program in history, drawing an audience of 111.3 million viewers. In recent

Table 11.1   Examples of the Expanding Sports Television Menu

Original major networks	ABC—*Wide World of Sports* (1961), NBC—Olympic Games (1980), CBS—Sunday afternoon football
New major networks	FOX—FOX Sports, formed in 1994
Cable television sports networks	ESPN, Versus (previously called OLN)
Superstations that broadcast sports	TBA, WGN
Regional cable sports networks	MSG Network, Comcast Sports Net Chicago, FOX Sports Net Pittsburgh
Sports specialty channels	NFL Network, MLB Network, NHL Network, NBATV, Golf Channel, Tennis Channel, Fox Soccer Channel
College sports networks	Big Ten Network, BYUtv, PAC-12 Network, Longhorn Network
Satellite TV	NFL Sunday Ticket (by DirectTV; subscriptions give viewers access to NFL games)

years, over 200 countries and territories have had TV coverage of the Super Bowl.[14]

But the Super Bowl is not the only mega-TV sport. The Associated Press reported that 4.7 billion viewers—more than two out of three people worldwide—tuned in to the Beijing Olympics for at least some of its seventeen days of TV coverage. In the years when the World Cup is played, the month-long tournament draws a total worldwide audience of up to 33 billion viewers.

Pay-per-view television has been a growing reality throughout North America since the mid-1990s. Some TV analysts believe PPV will become the norm for broadcasting major sporting events. In a way, it already has. In 2011 Comcast listed thirty-one PPV sports channels.

NFL Sunday Ticket, available on satellite or cable, costs approximately $300 per season; subscribers get every out-of-market, non-nationally televised NFL game. As we noted above, professional baseball, basketball, ice hockey, and intercollegiate athletics have similar PPV networks. ESPN GamePlan is the ultimate college football PPV package. Available on cable, satellite, and the Internet, it provides access to a handful of games per week and provides an alternative to the local game of the week. Even high school sports have a PPV network. HighSchoolSports.net is the nation's number-one Internet site devoted to high school sports. Over 7,000 schools subscribe to the Schedule Star athletic management system that feeds HighSchoolSports.net.

All-sports news channels are a unique innovation in sports television. ESPNews and CNN/SI began this form of twenty-four-hour sports coverage in the fall of 1996. They do not carry live sports events. Instead, they telecast only sports news.

Economic Aspects of Televised Sports

Money is the fuel propelling the TV sports machine, and sport and television are mutual beneficiaries in one of the most lucrative business associations. In return for the rights to telecast sports events, professional and collegiate sports receive free publicity as well as broadcast rights fees. At the same time, television companies profit from the use of their products (the telecasts) by sport consumers.

The system works this way: Television networks pay money for the "broadcast rights" to televise a professional (or college) league's (e.g., NFL) games. The networks hope to get that money back, plus a profit, by selling advertising time to corporations, like General Motors, for the games. Administrators of the sports leagues take the money received from the television network and distribute it according to the sports leagues' policies.

In essence, then, the television industry is basically a broker, bringing together the sellers (sports leagues), the buyers (advertisers), and the consumers (fans). The relationship between media and sport is one of planned, calculated business rationality.

The extent to which the fees for telecasting rights have escalated can be seen in Table 11.2.

The economics of television are changing because of these escalating broadcast rights fees, and the reign of the television networks as the exclusive carrier of the Olympics ended after the 1988 Summer Games in Seoul. Cable television has gotten a larger and larger piece of the Olympic pie. Satellite is also making its mark in the industry.

Professional sports are able to operate the way they do primarily through the television contracts

Table 11.2 Television Network Rights Fees to Olympic Games (in U.S. dollars)

Summer Olympic Games	Television Rights Fees
1960	394,000
1972	7,500,000
1984	225,000,000
1996	456,000,000
2008	894,000,000
2012	1,180,000,000
2016	1,226,000,000
2020	1,418,000,000

Winter Olympic Games	Television Rights Fees
1960	50,000
1972	15,500,000
1984	243,000,000
1996	545,000,000
2010	820,000,000
2014	775,000,000
2018	963,000,000

they have been able to negotiate. Realizing the popularity of broadcast sports, the sports industry has successfully negotiated large contracts with media organizations for the rights to broadcast events. This in turn helps make commercial sports profitable. Following are a few examples of recent contracts:

- Three American over-the-air television networks—CBS, NBC, and FOX—as well as cable television's ESPN are paying a combined total of $24.4 billion to broadcast NFL games through the 2011 season for CBS, FOX, and NBC and through 2013 for ESPN. The current NFL agreement with DirecTV continues through the 2014 season. That does not include the "value" of the games the NFL Network televises. About 65 percent of all NFL team revenues comes from the sale of television rights.
- The national TV and radio rights to Major League Baseball were sold to FOX and Turner Broadcasting for $3 billion over seven years (2006–2013); MLB shares 24 percent of its revenues with its thirty teams. About half the teams

can pay their entire annual player payrolls just from their national broadcast revenues.

- The NBA has an eight-year TV contract (2008–2016) with ESPN/ABC and TNT for $7.4 billion, a huge increase over the previous TV rights contract.
- In 2010, the NCAA signed a fourteen-year television, Internet, and wireless rights agreement with CBS Sports and Turner Broadcasting to present the Division I Men's Basketball Championship beginning in 2011 through 2024 for more than $10.8 billion.
- U.S. broadcaster NBC paid $2.2 billion for the rights to the 2010 Winter Olympics and the 2012 London Games, and $4.38 billion for the four Olympic Games from 2014 until 2020.

It can be seen that the networks, the superstations, the cable sports stations, and local TV stations have bankrolled commercialized team sports with a veritable bonanza of dollars. Contracts like these have made the commercial sports industry very profitable, resulting in expanded franchises, higher salaries, and all-around plush lifestyles for many in the industry. Indeed, so many pro sports organizations have built their budgets around TV income that if television ever did withdraw its money, the entire pro sports structure in its present form would collapse. Sports executives often remark, "There is no way we could survive without television" or "If sports lost television revenues, we'd all be out of business."[15]

One might ask, Why is television so eager to spend such lavish sums for the rights to telecast sporting events? It's simple. Corporations spend lavishly on advertising during sports events in order to create a demand for their products. Broadcast sporting events are immensely popular and attract large audiences; many people are interested in the beauty and drama of sports events, and find them more exciting and suspenseful than most other broadcast programming. Audiences who hear and see the broadcast commercials become consumers of the products, bringing profits to the advertisers. So sports are a natural setting for corporate advertising.

The escalating rates of advertising time can be seen from the following examples of Super Bowl rates for a thirty-second commercial (see Table 11.3).

Table 11.3 Super Bowl Rates for a Thirty-Second Commercial (in U.S. dollars)

Year	Advertising Rate
1970	75,000
1985	500,000
1996	1,200,000
2002	1,900,000
2005	2,400,000
2008	2,700,000
2010	2,800,000
2011	3,000,000
2012	3,500,000

TELEVISION'S INFLUENCE ON SPORT

Each medium has made an impact on sport in its own way. Newspapers of the late nineteenth century and early twentieth century contributed to the rise of professional and collegiate sports by creating an interest in these activities. Magazines and books helped create and sustain the hero worship of the athlete in succeeding generations. Radio brought live sports action into the home for the first time. It was television, though, that had the most profound impact. Several interpreters of the impact of television on sport have argued that TV has produced more revolutionary and irrevocable changes in sport than anything since modern sport began in the mid-nineteenth century.

Increases in Sport Revenue

Before the advent of television, professional sport was only a skeleton of what it has become, and the professional franchises that did exist were struggling financially. There were only sixteen Major League Baseball teams in the 1950s, and no new teams had come into the leagues in more than fifty years; now there are thirty teams. This expansion, and baseball's prosperity, has been due to television. Similar patterns can be seen in professional football, basketball, and hockey. All of these sports entered the 1950s as struggling enterprises with fewer than ten franchises each, and neither the owners nor the players were making much money. These sports now have thirty or more franchises each, and all have expansion plans. Television contributes a substantial portion of every league's revenues. Professional golf, tennis, soccer, and other professional sports either did not exist or were inconsequential prior to the infusion of large sums of television money.

Professional sports owners have not been the only beneficiaries of this windfall. Television money has increased athletes' incomes as well. Pro athletes' salaries have tripled or even quadrupled; television money has largely made it possible for them to command their enormous salaries and endorsements. Table 11.4 lists the highest-earning North American athletes in 2011, according to *Forbes.com*.

Table 11.4   Highest-Paid Athletes in North America in 2011 (in U.S. dollars)

Name	Sport	Earnings
Tiger Woods	Golf	75 million
Kobe Bryant	Basketball	53 million
LeBron James	Basketball	48 million
Phil Mickelson	Golf	46.5 million
Alex Rodriguez	Baseball	35 million
Tom Brady	Football	31 million
Derek Jeter	Baseball	29 million
Dale Earnhardt, Jr.	Auto Racing	28.5 million
Dwight Howard	Basketball	27.6 million
Dwayne Wade	Basketball	26.2 million

Source: "Full List: The World's 50 Highest-Paid Athletes," *Forbes.com*, http://www.forbes.com/2011/05/31/highest-paid-athletes_slide.html.

These spectacular incomes of contemporary professional athletes have a very high correlation with the increases in broadcast television rights. Television supports sports. TV networks move in with their money and support sports in a style that would have been unbelievable just a generation ago.

The extent to which sports has been influenced by its increasingly economic dependence on the mass media is illustrated by the number of professional sports teams that are owned wholly or partly by media companies (see Table 11.5). As an example, in 2010 three Major League Baseball teams were owned by media corporations: the Atlanta Braves by Liberty Media, the Seattle Mariners by Nintendo, and the Toronto Blue Jays by Rogers Communications. Rupert Murdoch, the media mogul with arguably the largest global media sports empire, once called sports the "cornerstone of our worldwide efforts."

Television Drives Shifts in Popularity of Sports

Television's dominating role is demonstrated most clearly in the changing popularity of the various sports. Telecasts have greatly increased the popularity of some sports and decreased interest in others. Football and baseball with their series of crises, tennis with its evolving drama, basketball

Table 11.5   Examples of Media/Communications Corporations with Whole or Part Ownership in Professional Sports, 2000–2010

Owner/Corporation	Teams
Arturo "Arte" Moreno (radio/news/talk sports)	MLB's Los Angeles Angels of Anaheim
Liberty Media Group	MLB's Atlanta Braves
Rogers Communications	MLB's Toronto Blue Jays
Comcast/Spectacor	NBA's Philadelphia 76ers, NHL's Philadelphia Flyers
Madison Square Garden LP	NBA's New York Knicks, NHL's New York Rangers
Ackerley Group	NBA's Seattle SuperSonics
Anschutz Entertainment	Major League Soccer's Los Angeles Galaxy, Houston Dynamo (50 percent), Los Angeles Kings, Colorado Rapids; American Hockey League's Manchester Monarchs; Germany's Eisbären Berlin and Hamburg Freezers (ice hockey); New Los Angeles Lakers (minority interest), WNBA's Los Angeles Sparks (49 percent); Sweden's Hammarby IF (soccer)
Nintendo (Japan)	Seattle Mariners
AOL Time Warner	NBA's Atlanta Hawks
Cablevision Systems Corporation	NBA's New York Knicks
Walt Disney	NHL's Anaheim Ducks
Paul Allen Telecommunications	NFL's Seattle Seahawks, NBA's Portland Trailblazers, MLS's Seattle Sounders

with its fast action, and boxing with its violence in a confined space are ideal sports for television. Natural breaks in the action permit viewers to contemplate the next moves; more importantly, they provide the opportunity for periodic commercial breaks without seriously disturbing the flow of the sporting event. Other sports, such as soccer, have been less successful because they lack predictable crises, natural breaks, or action in a manageable space.

If television viewing is the criterion of national pastime status, football has replaced baseball as America's national pastime. It has also eroded the TV popularity of ice hockey in Canada. There is little doubt that football is ideally suited for television, with its fast, violent action confined to a rather restricted area, its periods of inaction between plays, and its rigidly controlled time orientation.

Professional Sports Franchise Locations and the Media

Not only has television influenced the popularity and the fortunes of entire sports, it has more selectively come to play a direct role in decisions about the number and locations of professional franchises. The promise of lucrative television contracts explains why the number of professional football, basketball, baseball, and hockey franchises has more than doubled in the past three decades. Moreover, when the NFL, NBA, MLB, and NHL have awarded new franchises, the size of the potential television market in a region has been a major consideration.

Prior to television, professional sports franchises were considered to be permanent fixtures in a city, but the practice of jumping from city to city has become common. There have been seven moves of NFL teams since 1983 (two in 1997 alone—the Cleveland Browns to Baltimore, where they became the Ravens, and the Houston Oilers to Tennessee, where they became the Titans) and more than a dozen city changes for NBA teams, the most recent being the Seattle SuperSonics, who moved to Oklahoma City in 2008. A major factor for moving in almost every case has been the promise of additional television revenues. Given the economic structure of professional sports, it is not surprising

that professional leagues and their franchise owners gravitate toward television money.[16]

Although television revenues have been responsible for the health and expansion of some professional sports enterprises, the lack of network television contracts has been responsible for the demise of others. In the early 1980s the United States Football League failed to secure network sponsorship and folded. Professional track died for similar reasons, and professional volleyball and several women's professional sports have had an off-and-on existence for lack of television contracts. On the other hand, the NFL European League (NFLEL) was created by the NFL in 1991 primarily to provide American football to European audiences to capitalize on the popularity of televised American football. In the summer of 2007, it was shut down by the NFL, mostly for media reasons.

Television: The Financial Foundation for Big-Time Intercollegiate Sport

At the same time that television was enhancing the expansion and financial status of the openly professional sports, it was also furthering the professionalization of a self-proclaimed amateur sport enterprise, intercollegiate sport, which has actually been a professional enterprise for many years. When collegiate football became one of the most popular viewer events on early TV, the NCAA, the controlling organization of intercollegiate athletics, quickly stepped in to regulate television coverage of collegiate football games. Under that system of regulation, the NCAA always limited the number of football games that could be televised each week and the number of times a particular team could appear on television each season. Nevertheless, a few of the football "powers" were seen frequently, while most collegiate football teams never appeared on television. Teams that were televised received large payments per appearance, so the television package increased the gap between the "haves" and the "have-nots" in college football.[17]

A challenge to the NCAA's right to negotiate TV contracts on behalf of all of its member institutions was settled by a U.S. Supreme Court decision in which the Court invalidated the NCAA's exclusive college football TV contract. The effect was to free

Notre Dame's Kayla McBride, left, and Ariel Braker along with Indiana State's Deja Mattox, second from left, and Andrea Rademacher look for a rebound during an NCAA college basketball game in South Bend, Indiana. (AP Photo/South Bend Tribune, Mike Hartman)

individual colleges and conferences to negotiate their own television contracts with the networks, cable companies, and local stations. College football broadcasts on national cable and syndication channels have skyrocketed since that decision.

A book with the lengthy title *The Fifty-Year Seduction: How Television Manipulated College Football, from the Birth of the Modern NCAA to the Creation of the BCS* explains how television helped shape college football and how it became the common denominator in the sport's rise as a big business. In summary, the author declares: "Over the last half-century, televised college football has manufactured money, greed, dependence, and envy; altered the recruiting process, eventually forcing the colleges to compete with the irresistible force of National Football League riches; . . . fomented

the realignment of conferences; and seized control of the postseason bowl games, including the formation of the lucrative and controversial Bowl Championship Series."[18]

The Supreme Court decision regarding college football did not affect the NCAA's control over its men's basketball tournament. The growth of the NCAA men's basketball tournament provides a vivid demonstration of television's influence on collegiate sports. The more teams in the NCAA basketball tournament, the greater the television revenue and the greater the amount of money paid to the NCAA. Therefore, the NCAA continued to increase the number of teams participating in the tournament until it became a 68-team tournament.

In 1990 CBS signed a seven-year $1 billion (yes, billion) contract with the NCAA for the rights to televise the men's basketball tournament. In December 1994 that contract was replaced with a new seven-year *$1.725 billion* deal. As we noted above, in 2010 the NCAA negotiated the current *$10.8 billion* fourteen-year television rights fee with CBS and Turner Sports to televise the Division I men's basketball tournament. In mid-2001, the NCAA signed an eleven-year, $200 million television rights contract with ESPN, giving the network broadcasting control of the women's basketball tournament and twenty other national championships.[19]

What is the financial impact of these television contracts on intercollegiate sports? As we explained in Chapter 6, the majority of universities with big-time intercollegiate sports programs run a deficit in their annual budgets; the deficits would be huge were it not for television money, and for those that do not run a deficit it is largely because of the television money they receive. Television money is the financial foundation for the administrative agency of college sports—the NCAA. The men's basketball TV contract provides around 80 percent of the NCAA's total revenue!

With a view toward receiving television money and public exposure, universities throughout the country throw enormous human and financial resources into their football and basketball programs while they have been dropping other sports from their offerings. Some universities have dropped as many as six sports in the past decade; we noted this, too, in Chapter 6. Universities have frequently blamed the abolishment of sports on Title IX, which requires gender equity in the expenditures of resources. But in most cases the dropping of sports has been precipitated by the desire to pour more money into football and men's basketball in the hopes of attracting more media money to the athletic program.[20]

Television Taps High School Sports

The television industry has reached down to tap a different source of revenue: high school sports. In the fall of 1989, SportsChannel America, a cable network, signed a multiyear agreement with the National Federation of State High School Associations, the administrative organization for high school sports. At the time the negotiations were under way, an executive for SportsChannel said: "We think high school sports are going to be the TV sport of the 90s." Although this prediction was a little too optimistic, televised high school sports, especially football and basketball, have become a regular feature of local television stations throughout the United States and Canada during the first decade of the twenty-first century.

Several state high school activity associations have begun coverage of regular season games. Television coverage of state championships and tournaments has become an annual event in many states. In fact, there have been several proposals in recent years for national championships in high school sports. This trend is exactly what many educators feared. Can pressures for national high school championships be far behind if television becomes the financial support for high school sports? The answer is "no." Educational leaders fear that if that happens, educational priorities will be sacrificed in the interests of keeping the television industry happy.

ESPN has been in the business of televising high school football and basketball games since 2005. ESPN networks select the nationally top-ranked teams and televise about twenty football and fifteen basketball games as part of the ESPNU Old Spice High School Showcase. ESPN's coverage of high school football culminates with an annual All-America High School Football Game on ESPN. In an interview with the *Miami Herald*, one of the co-authors of this book warned that ESPN's incursion into "high school sport is moving in the wrong direction, away from its place in education and toward the big-time college model."[21]

Television has even become a factor in recruitment of high school athletes. Many high school athletes are choosing to attend a university because of the TV coverage that university gets. The football games of some universities are carried on national TV much more frequently than those of others. In the case of big-time collegiate basketball, some high school athletes are selecting eastern universities because the viewing audiences of the games are much larger than in midwestern or western states due to the time the games are played. Football and basketball athletes believe that greater television exposure helps their chances of being drafted by the pros.

Modifying Sports to Accommodate TV

To enhance spectator appeal and to accommodate programming needs, the television industry has increasingly manipulated the structure and the processes of televised sports. Because TV networks charge corporations advertising fees based on the anticipated number of viewers—the more viewers, the larger the advertising fee—the networks want the sports events to which they have bought broadcast rights to attract huge audiences. In their pursuit of viewers, media networks have been able to persuade pro sport leagues and franchise owners (who want larger broadcast rights fees) to modify rules and schedules in the hopes of attracting larger numbers of viewers. Because broadcasting rights fees are based on anticipated audience size, pro sport owners and leagues have been willing to make these changes to the game. Thus, to enhance viewer appeal and accommodate programming needs, both the media sports industry and the commercial sports industry have manipulated the structures and processes of sport. Here are some examples:

- In NFL football, rule changes (such as moving the sideline hash marks and the kickoff spot, reducing defensive backs' contact with receivers, and liberalizing offensive holding) have been adopted to open up the games and make them more attractive to television viewers. To permit more commercials, time-outs are called at the discretion of television officials, and the automatic two-minute warning near game's end is merely a time-out to show another set of commercials.
- To enhance spectator and viewer interest, NBA basketball led in the adoption of the shot clock, the slam dunk, and the three-point shot. The NBA has acceded to a more physical, rougher style of play because television decision makers believe that fans prefer this style and are more likely to watch games of this kind.
- In televised golf, match play (where the golfers compete hole by hole, and the golfer who wins the most holes is the winner) has largely been replaced by medal play (the golfer with the lowest score over the entire course wins). The skins game—another variation of professional golf, where large sums of money ride on the outcome of each hole—has become a popular form of televised professional golf. These new forms of golf competition are more compatible with television coverage.
- In professional tennis, to accommodate television scheduling, tennis executives established the tiebreaker system for sets tied at six games all; tiebreakers tend to play out quickly, making it easier to complete matches within a designated time period.
- Major League Baseball introduced the designated hitter and lowered the strike zone, and there is strong suspicion that the baseball itself has been modified to make it livelier. These changes have been motivated by an interest in increasing what spectators like to see: more extra-base hits and home runs. Time-honored afternoon World Series and All-Star games were switched to evenings to serve the interests of television.
- The sudden-death tiebreaking rule in professional football, ice hockey, and soccer, and the extended play-off system in all of the pro sports leagues, are additional examples of modifying rules to increase TV viewer interest, and make the sporting events more profitable for both TV networks and professional sports.
- For recent Winter and Summer Olympic Games, the International Olympic Committee agreed to reschedule championship events so they take place during North America's prime time, to accommodate television networks. However, much of the Olympic Games TV coverage is broadcast after the events are completed, but frequently the events are presented to television viewers without informing them of this fact, leading them to believe they are seeing events live.

Most of the changes identified here, and others, are tied directly to television's interest in enhancing the action for television viewers and keeping them in their chairs to watch the commercials. After all, this is the means by which the television industry makes its profits. As the television industry's investment in sports continues to grow, so does TV's resolution to get the most for its investment by orchestrating the sporting events for maximum viewer appeal.

Television's Own Sports

As we have noted, sports have been an important part of television programming since the early years of network TV. Because sports are so popular with television viewers, television executives sought ways to broadcast other events involving sport-like characteristics—such as competition requiring physical strength, endurance, agility, tenacity, speed, and skill. This resulted in TV networks creating made-for-television sports events.

Made-for-television sports, with names like "Challenge of the Sexes" and "Battle of the Network Stars," began with outstanding elite athletes or TV actors and actresses competing in physically competitive events contrived by TV executives. The idea of these programs was promoted as a way to find out who the "best" athletes were and which sports had the "best" athletes (or at least the best athletes among TV personalities). Winners of these events were awarded titles like "world's best athlete." The point was to exploit the celebrity status of athletes and TV stars, whose status as celebrities had been constructed by the media, in order to attract viewers to the contrived sports program—and to the commercials shown on the program. Actually, though, the TV networks' motive was economic. Competitions of this sort were often called "trash sports."

Most of the original made-for-television sports events have disappeared. But with the popularity of almost any kind of competitive event, and with the all-sports TV channels needing to fill numerous hours of programming time, various made-for-television and alternative sporting events now appear. In 2009 ABC revived *The Superstars*, pairing athletes and celebrities competing against each other as a teams.

Some of these are legitimate sports, but few have a large number of participating athletes or a large spectator following. However, when they are telecast, nearly all aspects of the events are aimed at making the events appealing to viewers, and thus to corporate advertisers and sponsors.

ESPN's X Games (originally called eXtreme Games) fit into this genre of TV sports. Some of the X Games activities, such as skateboarding, in-line skating, freestyle biking, and snowboarding, were originally popular among teenagers who were looking for alternatives to the traditional individual and team sports. In 1995 ESPN created the X Games as a made-for-TV alternative multisports festival. The X Games appeal to a very large, young, TV-watching audience because many of them are involved in these action activities.

ESPN's marketing director said the network aims to "reach anybody between 12 and 24 who is interested" in alternative sports. Currently, these games are divided into two seasons: The Winter X Games, held in January or February, and X Games, usually held in August. X Games Asia debuted in 1998 and has been held annually in an Asian country.

Because the X Games were created by and are owned by ESPN, the network does not have to pay broadcast rights fees to air them. Thus, the network keeps all revenue from advertisers. Reruns and qualifying events fill many hours on the ESPN broadcast schedule. Advertising revenues pour in to ESPN from all of these.

There is widespread criticism of the X Games among alternative sports enthusiasts, claiming that ESPN's X Games have turned informal, alternative physical activities into mainstream sports with the codification of rules, equipment, categories of participants, and so forth. There is also the complaint that these annual events are fundamentally an advertising medium, targeting specific age, gender, and racial groups. Indeed, the X Games seem to illustrate social analysts' claim that capitalism—in this case in the form of television networks—is so enterprising that it will find a way to turn everything into a marketable commodity.

In the spring of 2001, the World Wrestling Federation (WWF) and NBC co-created a made-for-television football league called the XFL. With teams nicknamed the Enforcers, the Hitmen, and the Maniacs, the XFL was hyped as a violent, trash-talking, sexualized form of football. XFL games started with TV ratings well above expectations, but interest declined drastically, and the league was cancelled after the first season.

One of the newest contributions to the merging of sports to create a fanatical TV audience is called Ultimate Fighting Championship (UFC), which is a combat sport combining the striking techniques of boxing and kickboxing with floor techniques of jujitsu and wrestling. The action takes place in an octagon cage. As with the X Games, many of the young men attracted to combat sports disliked the mainstream combat sports and experimented with alternatives, one of which became Ultimate Fighting Championship. It quickly became popular with the eighteen-to-thirty-four male demographic.

Once TV executives saw how popular UFC was becoming, TV contracts followed. By 2010 PPV and Spike UFC programs often had higher television ratings than the NBA and baseball play-off games in the eighteen-to-thirty-four age audience. UFC events had bigger pay-per-view numbers than any pro wrestling event or boxing event. In 2010 UFC's president, Dana White, revealed that plans are under way for UFC's expansion into global markets.[22]

Televised Sport as a Mediated Event

Television has not only revised the way sport is played and the way it is watched, it has redefined the meaning of sport in many ways. Contemporary sport has become part of media culture, meaning that its form and content have been altered to suit the interests of the media. A common assumption among the public is that a broadcast sport event is an objective mirror of the reality of the contest, and that TV's framing, camera angles, use of scan and zoom, and sportscaster commentary are neutral conduits for presenting "the facts" of the event. In reality, however, a broadcast game is an entertainment spectacle sold in the marketplace, a tool for attracting and keeping listeners and viewers so the media can broadcast the commercials they have sold to advertisers.

Superficially, sportscasters simply keep listeners and viewers apprised of essential information as the contest unfolds. But they do much more: They mediate the event and thus create the listeners' and viewers' experiences of the event through their intervention. Because of sportscasters' mediation, a sporting event becomes a collage of happenings—and thus "reality" is socially constructed by the sportscasters, who decide what to reveal to listeners

and viewers and how. What they reveal and what they conceal become, in effect, the "event," and the way listeners and viewers experience it becomes their reference point for its very existence—but it is a mediated version of reality.

In a televised sports event, cameras, camera angles, producers' choices of focus, and sportscasters' interpretations—all of which are the invisible apparatus of a televised presentation—stand between the viewers and the event. Viewers do not see the entire event; instead, they see only those parts that are sifted and filtered through the broadcasting process. This is very different from attending the event itself. Spectators in a stadium or arena perceive the event as is (at least, what can be seen and heard of it from the seats). But broadcast listeners and viewers experience an event that is socially constructed by a team of broadcast professional gatekeepers and dramatic embellishers.

The public has many options as to what to listen to and watch, so a variety of techniques are used to attract listeners and viewers. Some of the most important decisions media executives must make are about selection, such as decisions about which sports events to broadcast and which sports events not to broadcast, decisions to accentuate certain aspects of the sporting event for listeners and viewers and not others. Thus, televised sports are the result of a carefully crafted selection process that takes into account listener and viewer interests, attitudes, and beliefs about sports.

Two examples of broadcast selection can illustrate the selection and exclusion in media sports coverage. First, coverage of male sporting events dominates broadcast sports and helps reinforce cultural attitudes about gender specificity in sport and gender appropriateness of sports. Second, team sports have dominated sports broadcasts. Indeed, male team sports are TV's "authorized sports"; in many ways the media have advanced the popularity of male team sports at the expense of other forms of sport. Thus, social values are conveyed through particular choices made by the media's selective coverage.[23]

The selection process is at work within a particular sporting event. Production executives foreground particular aspects of the event for the viewers. In baseball, home runs are highlighted over "routine" singles; in football the quarterback gets the focus, rather than any of the ten other positions; in multiple events, such as track and field, some events get more attention than others—for example, in track and field the sprints get more coverage than most other events.

Beyond mere selecting, viewers are provided with descriptions of what has been selected through narrative themes and interpretations of preferred meaning about the action or the event itself. Televised sporting events do not merely consist of pictures, they also involve commentary on the pictures—a commentary that shapes what viewers are seeing and believing.

This selective highlighting is not "natural." It is based on media assumptions about what is good television and what keeps viewers watching. Such decisions involve an active process of representation; what viewers see, then, is not the actual event but a mediated event—in other words, a media event.

Once particular sports events are chosen for broadcasting, the next task is to "hook" listeners and viewers to the broadcasts. This begins with pregame programs that are mostly a contrived mix of interviews, network promos, and hoopla (e.g., theme building). The main purpose of these programs is to frame and contextualize the game by artificially building dramatic tension and solidifying allegiances, thus convincing listeners and viewers to stay tuned to the event, while preparing them for how they should hear, see, and understand it. The rhetoric concentrates listeners' and viewers' attention on the overall importance of this particular contest, individual athletes' (and coaches') personalities, "matchups," statistics, records, and team styles of play.

The selecting, screening, and filtering of sports events that are carried out by television through images and verbal commentary result in the presentation of a whole new game, a game created from an entertainment perspective, because in essence entertainment is what televised sport is all about. In consequence, the basis for interest in sport has changed from an appreciation of the beauty, style, skill, and technical accomplishments of the performers to a primary concern for titillating excitement and productive action, usually meaning scoring and winning.

The overarching value in media sport is winning. Broadcast sports tend to be single-minded odes to winning, so much so that almost any action in the pursuit of victory is considered justified; indeed, sportscasters frequently admiringly declare that an athlete will do "whatever it takes to win." No sacrifice is too great in the interest of winning; athletes who surmount injury, endure pain, and continue to play are valorized.

During one NFL football game, the camera zoomed in on the heavily taped right arm of a defensive lineman. One of the sportscasters then explained that the player had incurred a compound fracture of one of his fingers—meaning the bone was sticking out of the skin. The player had gone to the bench, shoved the bone back in, taped up the finger, and returned to the game. The sportscaster then said, in a thoroughly admiring manner, "It just goes to show how badly these guys want to win." Another example: During another NFL game, one of the sportscasters applauded a quarterback by saying, "Here's a guy that probably had to take a painkiller shot in his lower back so he could play tonight." Because the definitions, values, and practices of media sport commentary are privileged, they become the "commonsense" constructions about sport that grow out of the production of broadcast sport.

The intrinsic, process-oriented participation motive to engage in sport has been redefined by media sport, as it has increasingly become the national definer of meaning in sport and how to "do" sport. Media sport valorizes the obsession with victory above all else. Television executives, camera personnel, sportscasters, and even the vast majority of viewers are not attuned to the aesthetic nuances of a well-executed play; instead the overriding ethos is a win by whatever means it takes. Indeed, the mantra expressed over and over by sportscasters is "Whatever it takes."

THE IMPACT OF SPORT ON THE MASS MEDIA

Increased Sport in the Media

The relationship between the mass media and sport is one of financial interdependence. As noted in an earlier section of this chapter, the sports section helps sell newspapers; indeed, in many of these, sports occupy a special, separate section. Print media managers like to say they publish what the public wants, and it's obvious that newspaper editors believe that the public wants vast amounts of sports news and that sports information will sell more and more papers.

Sport has also invaded other sections of newspapers. Not too many years ago a sports story or photo on the front page of papers like the *New York Times* would have been unheard of. Now it is a regular occurrence. *USA Today*, the self-proclaimed "Nation's Newspaper," regularly features stories about sports in its "Newsline" section and often has a special section about sports leagues (e.g., the NFL) and about major sporting events (e.g., the Masters, the Indy 500). Editorial cartoonists routinely use sport themes to illustrate political, economic, and social issues.

Over the past fifty years, there were many peaks and valleys, as TV networks competed against each other for sports events, struggled with advertisers for revenue, and sought viewers for televised sports events. During that time, viewers became increasingly addicted to watching sports of all kinds on TV. Even the prime-time evening slots were invaded by Monday Night Football, All-Star games, the World Series, and the Super Bowl. The enormous popularity of all kinds of sports programs led to the creation of entire television networks, such as ESPN. But ESPN has moved well beyond televising sports events. Table 11.6 illustrates how ESPN communicates with its fans through numerous distribution channels.

Table 11.6   A Partial List of ESPN's Pipeline of Sports Media*

Television	ESPN, ESPN2, ESPN3, ESPNEWS, ESPN Classic, ESPN Deportes, ESPNU, ESPN Plus
Radio	ESPN Radio
Magazine	*ESPN the Magazine*
Mobile phone	ESPN Mobile
Restaurant	ESPN Zone

*We say "partial" because there are over fifty ESPN sports business ventures.

During the first decade of the twenty-first century, network television sold advertisers $1 billion worth of time for sports programs, which greatly contributed to the $30–$50 million profit that the networks reported each year.

Sport's Privileged Treatment by the Media

The mass media are fiercely independent (or claim to be), and reporters staunchly defend their right to freedom of the press. But commercial sport receives an enormous amount of free publicity via the media. Media coverage of sports itself tends to promote sports—the leagues, teams, athletes, and coaches—but typical sports coverage is blatant boosterism designed to hype interest in the athletes and teams. Stories are withheld or distorted, and sports news is edited to ensure a favorable image of the home team.

Newspaper sport sections are basically advertising sections for commercial sports. Radio and television segments dealing with sports news are essentially advertising for commercial sports. Indeed, many sports news announcers act like cheerleaders for the local professional sports teams, often referring to them as "our team." No other privately owned, profit-making industry—which is what the commercial sport industry is—receives as much free publicity for its product. Of course, the reciprocal business aspects of this are quite clear: The more interest generated in commercial sports, the greater the profits for the mass media.

The motives of the media are quite clear as well: The media ethos is rooted in profit maximization, and it is driven by the competition to be number one to reap the power and prestige that accompanies this. The more interest generated in local sports, the more people will buy local newspapers, listen to radio, and watch local television to follow the teams. The result is greater profits for the local mass media.

Sports Consumers and the Mass Media

The home has become the major site of leisure in postindustrial society. The main force for this has been the mass production of cheap home entertainment systems in the form of radio, television, audio and video equipment, and the computer.

Surveys of adult viewing habits conducted by several opinion research agencies have consistently found that professional football and baseball were the most favorite sports to watch on TV and on handheld devices. (istockphoto)

Exact figures on the amount of time people spend with the mass media are not readily available, but the best estimates for both the United States and Canada indicate that newspaper reading accounts for about two and one-half hours per person per week and television viewing for some thirty-five hours per person per week.

Televised sports have produced a dramatic shift in the mode of the fans' consumption of sport. It has become the most important source of sports spectating for the sports consumer, and television provides this at a very low cost to the fan (even assuming the price of the television set and the advertising costs that are passed on to the public). The opportunity to see sports events on television at low cost has also had the effect of creating fans among segments of the population that have traditionally had little interest in sport, especially women and the elderly.

Surveys of adults in the United States conducted by various opinion research agencies have consistently found that professional football and baseball are the most favorite sports to watch. NFL game broadcasts are averaging 10.8 percent of U.S. TV households. For perspective, note that this 10.8 percent average more than doubles the average rating for broadcast network prime-time programs.[24] Next most popular are college football, college basketball, and pro basketball.

People from all walks of life find enjoyment in watching televised sports events. The specific factors that contribute to viewers' enjoyment are not well understood at present, but research into this topic has led to some tentative answers. Mass-communications researchers have found that viewers' enjoyment is related to broadcast commentary, the presence of a crowd, the skill displayed by the athletes, and the viewers' disposition toward the players and the teams in competition.

The enjoyment of televised sports closely corresponds to the perception of roughness, enthusiasm, and even violence, and the perceptions of all of these aspects of play are strongly influenced by the commentary of the telecasters. The larger the crowd and the more enthusiastic its responses to play on the field, the more television viewers enjoy a game. Seeing teams battle down to the wire enhances suspense and increases the viewers' enjoyment. Finally, the highest level of fan enjoyment results when a well-liked team defeats an intensely disliked team.[25]

THE INTERNET: THE NEWEST FORM OF MASS COMMUNICATIONS FOR SPORTS

The current cutting edge in communications is the Internet. It is a quantum leap beyond previous forms of communication because it makes possible the inexpensive transmission of messages and images throughout the world in seconds. Consequently, the Internet has profoundly altered many people's relationship to work and leisure, transforming both business and private life. By 2011, the total number of Internet users passed the 2 billion mark; about 80 percent of the North American population had access to the Internet from their homes.[26]

Sport is a central part of the Internet; indeed, it has become one of its most important thematic areas. The implications for the Internet as a source of sports information of all kinds for sports consumers are seemingly limitless. It has the potential to someday surpass all other forms of mass communication as a source of sport information and entertainment. Literally millions of websites currently provide sports information to consumers.[27] In December 2010, a Google search using the keywords *sports AND websites* produced a list of 206 million websites. In the history of the Internet, sports sites have consistently ranked among the leaders in terms of traffic and commercial activity.

Once the technology was developed to make the Internet respect geographical borders, sports organizations began offering their TV rights holders the option to show sports events video on their websites. Online live sports coverage hit the big time in 2007 when TBS, for mlb.com, produced live online coverage of first-round MLB play-off games and the National League Championship series. During the 2008 Beijing Summer Olympics, several broadcasters, including NBC, BBC, and the European Broadcasting Union, posted thousands of hours of free live-video coverage of events on the Internet. In addition, broadcasters worldwide streamed on the Web 2,200 hours of free online Beijing Olympic action that grew exponentially with highlights and replays. ESPN360.com, ESPN's signature 24/7 broadband sports network, is an online website for live sports programming that streams over 3,500 hours of live sports coverage from a broad selection of global sports events each year.

Integration of the Internet, Television, Computers, and Video Games

Video games are one of the by-products of the integration of television, the Internet, and computer technologies, which were introduced commercially in the early 1970s. The video game industry, like other by-products of these technologies, has had a rapid and sustained growth and is now a $60 billion global industry—16 percent of which constitutes sports games such as Madden NFL and NBA2K—rivaling the motion picture industry as the most profitable entertainment medium in the world. According to the Pew Internet Project, fully 97 percent of twelve- to seventeen-year-olds play computer, Web, portable, or console video games. More than half—53 percent—of all American adults play video games of some kind.[28]

Over the past fifty years, nearly 100,000 video games have been released, and virtually every sport played in the world has had its own video game. Like the auto industry, the sports video game industry brings out a new version annually to prime the pump for profits. The processing power of the new generation of video game equipment—Microsoft's Xbox 360, Sony's PlayStation 3, and Nintendo's Wii—has brought the real world, like real-time weather conditions, into game play. Since *John Madden Football* (renamed *Madden NFL* in 1994) was first released in 1989, over 85 million copies of the sports video game have been sold, earning more than $3 billion. It is the top-selling sports video game, second overall only to Nintendo's *Mario* games. *FIFA Soccer 11* sold 2.6 million copies during it release week in 2010, the biggest opening ever for a sports video game—undoubtedly stimulated by the popularity of the World Cup in South Africa that year.[29]

In 2006, Nintendo introduced the Wii, a wireless motion-sensitive remote, transforming people of all ages into video gamers. By 2011, 86 million Wiis had been sold worldwide. The Wii Sports game allows players to make the physical body movements involved in playing a sport. Originally bundled with bowling and tennis, more recent versions enable players to engage in over a dozen activities. Microsoft and Sony have entered the market with their own gesture-based devices—Microsoft Kinect and Sony Move—for controlling the companies' respective video game consoles, the Xbox 360 and PlayStation 3.[30]

As with other forms of entertainment, especially television, sociological questions have arisen about the effects of video game playing on the habits, behaviors, and social development of players. For example, how does playing sports video games affect the play habits of children and youth who play these games? Do the games influence attitudes and behaviors toward values, such as sportsmanship, nonviolence, and morality? Does prolonged sports video game playing affect physical fitness, weight management, and social interaction with peers of participants? There is little research at this time that provides answers to these questions and many others as well, but undoubtedly this will be a rich area for psychological and sociological scholarship in the coming years.[31]

Social Media: Facebook, YouTube, and Twitter

The most recent manifestation of the integration of computer and Internet technologies is found in the various social media tools. In 2011 CTIA, the Wireless Association trade group, reported that 96 percent of North Americans use cellphones or wireless devices, one-third of which are smartphones that allow users to browse the Web.[32]

Sport organizations throughout the world are employing direct communications with customers—mostly fans—through social media tools, especially Facebook, YouTube, and Twitter. These popular communications technologies have helped professional sports teams to quickly and inexpensively respond to customers and to tailor services for fans. Facebook and YouTube are fostering sport fan services through online communities to exchange comments, ideas, and questions. Through their respective services they can offer massive bulletin boards for consumers to weigh in on major issues about athletes and teams.

Twitter is a social-networking application that has taken "immediacy" to new heights; it is rapidly becoming a staple in businesses customer service, and that includes sport organizations. Because it is organized as a private corporation, accurate numbers of Twitter users are hard to find, but at the beginning of 2011 it was predicted that Twitter was on track for 200 million users, and there were 25 billion tweets on Twitter in 2010, according to Twitter's corporate communications office.

Twitter has quickly become an indispensible part of global sports. To illustrate: In 2010 Twitter listed the World Cup as the number-one global sports trend, with LeBron James as the number-one non–World Cup sports trend. Spain's 1–0 victory against the Netherlands for the World Cup title attracted users from 172 nations in 27 languages. Entering 2011 the NBA Twitter feed had more than 2 million fans, the most of any sports league. In MLB's 2009 First-Year Player Draft, MLB.com launched the first online "social community" integration of the draft by integrating Twitter into its expanding live interactive media experience, the Draft Caster, and its searchable draft database, the Draft Tracker.[33]

MEDIA SPORT: GENDER AND RACE ISSUES

Reproduction of Hegemonic Masculinity in Media Sport

Linkages between sport and masculinity are long-standing. The British slogan "The Battle of Waterloo was won on the fields of Eton" suggests that participation in sport formed the manly qualities of a military leader. Parents urge their sons to play sports because "sports make men out of boys." Ideals of masculinity are constructed through competitive sport.

Communications scholars who have analyzed how male athletes and the male body are portrayed in the media make clear that media sport is a prominent site for sustaining and displaying traditional Western cultural ideals of masculinity. Verbal and visual media representations of the male athletic body are interpreted as a key source in cultivating, legitimating, and reinforcing the dominant definitions of masculinity as well as general masculine dominance. Although this is accomplished to some extent in all media sports, the sports that are especially physically violent—such as rugby, American football, ice hockey, and boxing—present the most frequent and most vivid examples of hegemonic masculinity.

As for ice hockey, sports scholars have noted that this sport has come to occupy the place it holds in Canadian culture in part because it provides a public platform for celebrating a traditional masculine ideal. NFL football telecasts are exemplars for reproducing traditional images of masculinity that highlight three aspects of the male body—as instrument, weapon, and object of gaze—in their telecasts.[34]

Masculinity propagated throughout media sport has serious consequences for both women and men: It not only marginalizes subordinates and symbolically annihilates women but also marginalizes nontraditional images of masculinity for men, especially nonwhite and nonheterosexual images.

Media Sport and Gender Inequities

Chapter 14 is devoted to a comprehensive examination of females in sport. In this section the focus is on the specific topic of females and media sport.

Prior to the women's movement in the 1970s, sport was considered an exclusively male domain, and women in media sport were not deemed worthy of coverage. So sportswomen were rarely seen in either print or broadcast media. With widespread women's sport participation, media sport coverage began, but women's achievements were denigrated, and female athletes were framed in terms of women's traditional private roles, such as girlfriends, wives, or mothers; they were objectified in ways similar to soft-core pornography; and their sports records were often compared with men's to deliberately belittle women's achievements.

By the first decade of the twenty-first century, considerable progress has been made in how media sport represent females, but women's sports have not achieved parity with men's sports in any of the media forms. Studies of the contents of newspapers and magazines in the United States and Canada, as well as several other countries, have consistently found that stories and photos of women's sports constituted a minority of the coverage; stories and photos of men's sports dominated the print media. Furthermore, much of the coverage still reveals a conventional and restricted view of female sport participation, often framing female athletes in terms of sexual appeal, homosexuality, and sports achievements that do not measure up to those of males.

The most recent study about gender and televised sport focused on three local network affiliates in Los Angeles and, in the evening, on ESPN's *SportsCenter*. The first-time data for this study were collected in 1989, and the researchers have repeated data collection every five years since then. In 1989 and 1993, coverage of women's sports on the evening news programs was about 5 percent. The researchers thought the percentage would continue to go up over time, as the media responded to the upsurge of girls' and women's sports throughout the country. In 1999 their beliefs were supported inasmuch as media coverage increased to 8.7 percent of all sports coverage. But in 2004 it fell back to 6.3 percent, and the data collected in 2009 surprisingly revealed that the coverage on the evening news programs had almost evaporated—down to 1.6 percent, the lowest amount ever. ESPN was down, too, with only 1.4 percent of its *SportsCenter* program. The researchers admitted that they were stunned by the drop-off.[35]

One of the most promising trends toward increasing women's sports coverage is the emergence of magazines and websites devoted exclusively (or almost exclusively) to women's sport and fitness. *Women's Sports and Fitness* is highly acclaimed for its variety of articles. LadySports Online (www.ladysports.com), Women's Sports Wire (www.womenssportwire.com), and Women's Sports Network (www.wspn.net) are three examples of websites devoted exclusively to women's sports. These print and Internet outlets provide comprehensive coverage of women's sport activities, focusing on individual female athletes, women's teams, and women's sport organizations; they also examine issues and problems in women's sports.

Until 1996, no women's professional team sport league had ever secured a major national TV network contract. No doubt there were several reasons for this, but certainly a major one was that advertisers were not convinced that women would watch women's sport. Advertisers buy sports programming to reach a targeted audience, so they did not buy women's sports events.

This pattern was broken in the fall of 1996 when the new American Basketball League (ABL) secured a national cable network contract; in 1997 when the Women's National Basketball Association (WNBA) began play, a national network television contract was in place. The ABL went out of business, but the WNBA network coverage remained in place, and several WNBA teams negotiated local TV contracts with regional sports networks. Currently, ESPN has an eight-year broadcast rights contract with the WNBA through the 2016 season. Network radio and TV contracts for other women's sports organizations are gradually increasing.

In the past thirty years there has been a significant social transformation in opportunities for females to be involved in sports. Accompanying this trend, significant strides have been made to include females in media sport coverage. Ironically, as female athletes and coaches strive for parity with men in media sport, they are being co-opted by the forces of commercialism in subtle ways that make them just another commodity to be sold to media sports audiences.

Media Sport and Racial and Ethnic Inequities

In Chapters 2 and 13 we discuss the historical and contemporary struggles of racial and ethnic minority North Americans for involvement in sport; here we focus specifically on ethnic and racial issues in media sport.

African Americans were largely segregated from commercial sports in the United States until about forty years ago. Over the past four decades most barriers to African American participation in organized sports have been swept away. Consequently, African American male athletes have played an increasingly prominent role in North American sports; indeed, they dominate some of them, in terms of percentage of players at the elite levels.

The recent history of outstanding African American and minority male athletes playing on the same teams with, and competing against, white male athletes has made it essential for the media to recognize and report their performances and achievements. Still, several studies over the past 20 years have documented underrepresentation of African American and minority male athlete coverage by both print and electronic media.

African American sportswomen have suffered more from the lack of coverage in media sport than African American males. One example will suffice to illustrate this point: There was a 30-year gap between the first and second *Sports Illustrated* cover featuring an African American female athlete. Over a 35-year period, African American female athletes appeared on only 5 of 1,835 covers of *Sports Illustrated*.

Wherever African American, Native American, Asian American, and Latino American athletes have had a presence in sport, subtle racial stereotyping

has been present in all the media forms. The most blatant examples are the frequent attributions of black athletes' achievements to their "natural" abilities to run fast and jump high and their "instincts" to react fast; at the same time, white athletes' achievements are typically attributed to their "intelligence" and superior "thinking ability." Historical stereotypes of black athletes are coded into characterizations of this kind.[36]

Male African American athletes have also been stereotyped in media sport commentaries as innately violent, thuggish, sexually uncontrolled, selfish, and arrogant. The social transgressions of high-profile black athletes and media accounts of professional black athletes as out-of-wedlock fathers and as drug addicts often are highlighted in print and broadcast news. For example, on 10 April 2007, the front page of the sports section of *USA Today* was virtually filled with what looked like police mugshots of 41 NFL football players. Accompanying the photos was a statement saying that "since 2006 more than 50 arrests have been made of NFL football players." Of the 41 photos, all but 2 were African Americans. The title of the article was "NFL Confronts Discipline Issue."

Assuming the article that accompanied the photos is true, it was a legitimate news story, but the impression that set of photos made was unmistakable. Clearly, it reinforced stereotypical prejudiced representations of African American males, even though the percentage of black athletes involved in such actions is small. *USA Today* editors knew very well how the set of photos would be interpreted by millions with racist beliefs.[37]

The U.S. government's reservation system has been a major structural barrier to sport opportunities for Native American youth. Typically, the sports facilities at reservation schools are inadequate for Native Americans to develop sports skills and experience sports competition against a variety of skilled athletes. The media have generally portrayed stereotypical representations of the few Native American athletes who have achieved elite-level status by using nicknames like "the Chief," "Redskin," and "Wahoo" in media stories about them. Native Americans' images as team mascots are approvingly portrayed in the media as TV cameras pan the spectators in arenas and stadiums when fans do the tomahawk chop and show close-up camera shots of costumed "Indians" dancing around venues after touchdowns and three-point baskets.[38]

Asian American and Latino American athletes have been either neglected in the media or, when covered, given stereotyped representations and nicknames. In light of the limited personal contact between most whites and people of color in North America, media portrayals, rather than personal experiences, become the primary source of information that shapes whites' perceptions of other groups. Unfortunately, the depictions in media sports help institutionalize the social and information gap between people of color and whites.

SPORTS JOURNALISM AND THE MASS MEDIA

Sports journalism, including sportscasting, is a peculiar occupation. On the one hand, a certain amount of prestige and power is associated with the occupation. Sports journalists' names are seen and heard by the public daily, they control access to the sports information that the public wants, and their stories and commentaries can influence the destinies of franchises and athletes. On the other hand, in a book titled *Sports Journalism: Context and Issues*, the author (a sportswriter) claims: "In the hierarchy of professional journalism, [sports journalism] has been traditionally viewed disparagingly as the 'toy department,' a bastion of easy living, sloppy journalism and 'soft' news." Another sportswriter remarked: "Sports writing is categorized alongside beer-tasting and aphrodisiac-evaluation. People say 'More of a hobby than a job, isn't it.'"[39]

Ostensibly, sports journalists are expected to report information about the results of sports events; provide inside information on particular players, teams, and sports organizations; and give opinions that help the public interpret sports news. While accuracy and objectivity in reporting are valued norms in journalism, the image of the sports journalist is one of obsequious appeasement. More than one critic of sportswriters has observed that their work all too often reflects jock worship, press-agentry, and awe rather than solid, in-depth reporting.[40]

Several practices of sports journalists contribute to their disparagement as objective reporters. Some sportswriters, through their columns and reports about the local teams, convey the impression that *they* are extensions of the teams; they are frequently called "housemen" or "housewomen" because their stories often read like publicity on behalf of the local team or teams. In return the local teams are expected to treat these reporters favorably in providing access to coaches and players and obtaining exclusive stories about the team or teams. This practice has declined because of the criticism within the journalism occupation itself, but it is easy to see how such an approach can create a cozy interdependence between journalists and sports teams.

Also contributing to the low status of sport journalism is the practice whereby TV sports news reporters share time with weather forecasters and with anchors reporting on local, national, and international events. Sports news is relegated to a very few minutes that are filled mostly with reporting scores and hyping upcoming events. In cities where pro teams reside, or big-time collegiate sports (or both) are nearby, the TV sports reporters are frequently outright cheerleaders for these local teams, referring to them as "our team." In some cases they virtually become public relations agents for them.

In general, there is no place in the sports news broadcasts for investigative journalism. The major reason for the lack of investigative sports reporting is that media corporations, such as CBS, NBC, ABC, and ESPN, are sponsoring sports events and generating profits, so critical reporting can create conflicts and problems. Media corporations have major business relationships with sports organizations that are worth billions of dollars, so journalists working for, say, CBS Sports cannot readily critique the morals of the sports organizations that CBS does business with.

In other words, because of the friendly business relations between the media industry and sports, broadcast news does not operate in a serious journalistic manner; its concern is more with promoting the teams and leagues in which it has invested than with operating in a serious journalistic manner.

Sportscasters: Narrators of Mediated Sport

Because radio and TV sportscasters "tutor" listeners and viewers in what they should hear, see, and believe about the sports events being broadcast, they are extremely important in such broadcasts. Consequently, they are carefully selected for their ability to command credibility, because they play a big role in attracting and holding listeners' and viewers' attention. The usual selections are former professional and elite amateur athletes and coaches with high name recognition. The rise of celebrity sportscasters can be directly attributed to television. As sporting celebrities and "certified experts," these former athletes and coaches have immediate recognition and credibility with the listeners and viewers, and audiences of sporting event broadcasts will accept their interpretations and opinions as objective and true.

Employing former athletes and coaches to describe the technical skills, strategy, and tactics used during a broadcast sports event may seem reasonable enough, but it is important to realize that they also act to articulate moral values and to comment prescriptively on social relationships. Former sport stars are uniquely qualified for this task because

Sport and television are mutual beneficiaries in a lucrative business association. Sport spectators consume sport to a greater extent through television than through personal attendance at sports events. (istockphoto)

they are survivors—even models—of the competitive sport meritocracy. Largely their attitudes and values are congruent with commercialized sports perspectives because they are fully integrated into the dominant values and beliefs of that system.

Preventing viewer boredom is one of the main concerns of broadcast producers, so one basic job of sportscasters is to keep listeners and viewers tuned in to the broadcast. To do this, they provide a commentary that heightens the drama of the event, using methods like the following:

- Constructing themes, such as "these teams hate each other" or "this is a grudge game." The message in both cases: The audience can expect a hard-fought contest with lots of fierce action.
- Highlighting "matchups" between players on opposite teams. This sets up a kind of one-on-one competition on which the audience can focus. Similarly, elaborate discussions of "keys to winning" are calculated to get viewers absorbed in the contest.
- Framing the game as an extremely crucial game for both teams (even if they are both hopelessly out of championship contention); heightening the significance of the game enhances audience interest (or so it is believed).
- Other sportscaster techniques include personal interest stories, recitation of statistics and records, anticipation of what to expect, dramatic embellishments of the action, and second-guessing.

All of these narratives are designed to keep audiences tuned in to the broadcast.

Another important job of sportscasters is selling the sport organization, league, and network for which they are broadcasting. Game commentary is frequently commercial hype for those organizations. For example, sportscasters tend to effusively praise the athletes, teams, and leagues throughout the broadcasts. Another favorite "sales" practice of sportscasters is creating attention-attracting monikers to develop team name recognition and get fans to identify with teams or athletes; for instance, the Dallas Cowboys of the NFL have become known as "America's Team" through sportscaster commentary.

Sportscasters who broadcast live events on radio or television typically have no background in journalism, and indeed the journalism profession has disavowed any connection with their work. They are usually selected by radio and television executives for their ability to narrate sports events as much as for their knowledge of the game. Many are former athletes and coaches who are articulate in explaining the intricacies of the game or are charismatic.

They must satisfy not only the media corporation that employs them but also the league commissioners and team owners whose games are being broadcast. The latter routinely screen the announcers and instruct the media executives as to how the announcers can improve their performances, letting it be known that all comments should cast the league, teams, and players in a favorable light. Consequently, objective reporting takes a backseat to the creation and maintenance of a favorable image of both sport and the media. A sportswriter for the *New York Times* once noted that "televised sport is not journalism; it is entertainment, shaped to keep people in front of the beer advertisements as long as possible." And other media analysts have suggested that a more appropriate portrayal of sportscasters would be sport public relations agents, whose main function is to elevate the banal.

In studies of the impact of commentary on audience perception and appreciation, researchers have exposed subjects to two segments of prerecorded, televised games that have been pretested for perception of roughness. Viewers were exposed to one of two presentation modes: with or without sportscasters' commentary. The results showed that the viewers' perceptions of the play were dramatically influenced by the nature of the accompanying commentary. Thus, through the commentary by sportscasters, viewers can be influenced to "see" fierce competition and roughness where it really does not exist. The researchers concluded that viewers seem to become "caught up" in the commentary and the sportscasters' interpretation of the game, and they allow themselves to be persuaded by the narration of "drama" in the event. There is, then, overwhelming evidence that sports telecasts can be presented and manipulated to create different levels of enjoyment for viewers.[41]

It is one thing for television networks to employ up to three sportscasters to cover a game; it is quite another to believe that these persons are giving viewers an accurate or inside view of the game. They are, in fact, doing just the opposite. They report actions where they do not exist; they protect owners, coaches, and athletes from serious scrutiny; and they constantly hype the sport and its participants. All of these actions are predicated on obtaining high ratings for the network. Of course, the bottom line is that both professional sport and television are big businesses, each dependent upon the fiscal health of the other. By reporting an exciting game, the sportscasters promote both sport and television.

What a person sees and reads about sports via the mass media has been deliberately filtered to show the best side of sports. Although a certain amount of criticism may be reported, sports journalists in the main are supportive of the system. Very few report anything that might cause discomfort. By omission and commission, complicity and docility, the media reports seldom stray from the promotion of sport. Despite an occasional exposé, and for all the talk about muckraking, sports journalists have very little to say about the seamier aspects of sports.

The reason for sports journalists' cooperation with the sports establishment may be more fundamental than selling newspapers or obtaining high radio and TV ratings. Those few sports journalists who do not report sport in the traditional way often incur the outrage of committed sports fans. They are often targets of hate letters and ugly phone calls in the middle of the night. In one way, this is understandable because it is almost heretical to attack sport. To attack sport is to impugn the North American value system. To challenge the sanctity of sport is to criticize what for many people is their main anchor for understanding how the real world works.[42]

Minority Sport Journalists and Broadcasters

Sportswriting and broadcasting have been largely white male professions in the United States and Canada, closely mirroring the hierarchical racial division of labor so evident in the broader mass communications occupational structure. Examples are: In 2010, according to the American Society of Newspaper Editors (ASNE), minorities, who constitute about 32 percent of the American population, accounted for just 12.8 percent of newspaper journalists, and this had not changed a single percentage point since 2003; only 18.7 percent of full-time journalists working on their newspapers' websites were minorities; and 441 newspapers responding to the ASNE survey had no minorities on their full-time staff.[43]

Many fans have formed the impression that African Americans represent a substantial portion of sports journalism because they see African American professional athletes and coaches so often in sports. The reality is something quite different in sports journalism. According to the *2010–11 Associated Press Sports Editors Racial and Gender Report Card* published by Richard Lapchick, the vast majority of people holding key positions on the major newspapers and media websites in the United States and Canada are white and male. The findings show that

- 97 percent of the sports editors were white.
- 85 percent of the assistant sports editors were white.
- 86 percent of the columnists were white.
- 86 percent of the reporters were white.
- 90 percent of the copy editors/designers were white.
- 94 percent of the sports editors were men.
- 90 percent of the assistant sports editors were men.
- 90 percent of the columnists were men.
- 89 percent of the reporters were men.
- 84 percent of the copy editors/designers were men.[44]

These are bleak figures when one considers the fact that in the world of sports, a disproportionate number of athletes in basketball, football, and baseball are African American, and between 30 and 45 percent of high school, college, and professional athletes are female.

The Radio Television Digital News Association (RTDNA) reports annually on minorities in that industry. The general pattern has been a slow, but gradual, increase of minorities working in radio and television, but the percentage of minorities on television news staffs is still less than 22 percent, while the minority workforce in radio remains below 6 percent. The percentage of minority TV news directors is less than 15 percent; in radio, minority news directors comprise less than 8 percent.[45] Of course, diversity is not just about numbers; it is about making journalism and broadcasting better. Diverse staffs lead to better journalism and broadcasting.

Many barriers have fallen by the wayside, as ethnic minorities and blacks have gained increasing respect for their sports reporting and broadcasting skills, but one fact is clear: There are still very few minority sportswriters and sportscasters in this profession. The percentages of those working in sports journalism and broadcasting are a poor reflection of the proportion of black and minority athletes playing sports in North America. The subordination of minorities in media sports continues, and each new breakthrough requires concerted struggle against the persistent white-dominated division of labor in media sport.

Women Sport Journalists and Broadcasters

Women who have wished to have careers in journalism and broadcasting have had an arduous struggle. Media organizations currently do not provide a level playing field for women. Women make up more than 50 percent of the adult population, but in 2011 Lapchick and his colleagues found that women made up only 11.4 percent of the total staffs of Associated Press Sports Editors (APSE) member newspapers and websites. The percentage of APSE women serving as sports editors was 6.3 and the percentage of women columnists was 8.8. Not a pretty picture for the principle of gender equity in media organizations (although conditions are better in radio and television broadcasting). Lapchick and his colleagues gave the APSE newspapers and websites a grade of "F" for gender hiring practices in the key positions covered.[46]

Despite the indignities and the discrimination that female sportswriters and sportscasters have experienced, and the relatively few women in the field, gains have been made. Women now hold important positions in both print and broadcast media sports in the United States and Canada. They have acquired access to press boxes, locker rooms, and other facilities important to their work. A few sportscasters, such as Robin Roberts, have moved into prestigious network positions.

Notwithstanding the increased number of women in sports journalism and broadcasting, Lapchick's report conveys a sobering account of the barriers that still exist. At a time when white males hold 90 percent of the AP sports editor positions whereas women of all races and ethnicities hold only 6.3 percent of such positions, it is clear that there are substantial obstructions to gender equity for women in sports journalism.

SUMMARY

A symbiotic relationship exists between sport and the mass media; each is a commercial industry whose success has been greatly influenced by the other. The print media contributed to the rise of sport during the nineteenth century. At the same time, the interest in sports information assisted in the growth of newspapers, magazines, and books. The electronic media—radio and television—have been instrumental in the promotion of big-time intercollegiate sports and professional sports. Indeed, without these media, collegiate and professional sports could not function as they presently do.

The dominating role that the mass media play in the economic aspects of sport has a number of effects. Televised sport has produced a dramatic shift in the mode of fans' consumption of sport; the popularity of several sports has been greatly influenced by television; and television has furthered the professionalization of amateur sport enterprises, such as intercollegiate athletics and the Olympic Games. Television has also manipulated the structure, meaning, and process of sports.

Studies estimate that television viewing accounts for some eight hours per household per day. Televised sports programs are some of the most popular on TV. The three major commercial networks no longer are the main sports events providers. Beginning with ESPN as the first all-sports, all-the-time network and continuing with regional sports networks, single sport networks, satellite networks, and so on, countless hours of live sports are a significant feature of contemporary entertainment and news. Internet sports have become a huge player in the mediated sports industry, and some media analysts contend that its potential is overwhelming.

Ethnic minorities and blacks have gradually gained respect for their sports reporting and broadcasting skills, but there are still very few minority sportswriters and sportscasters in the sports journalism profession. Those working in sports journalism and broadcasting are a poor reflection of the proportion of black and minority athletes playing sports in North America. So the subordination of minorities in media sport continues, and concerted struggle is necessary against the persistent, white-dominated division of labor in media sport.

Media sport is a site where verbal and visual representations of the male athletic body are interpreted as a key source in cultivating, legitimating, and reinforcing the dominant definitions of masculinity as well as general masculine dominance. The sports that are especially physically violent— such as rugby, American football, ice hockey, and boxing—present the most frequent and most vivid images of hegemonic masculinity.

Sports journalists have increased in number, but they have a rather low status among other journalists. The sports department of a newspaper, a radio station, or a television newsroom is commonly referred to as the "toy department."

One reason for news reporters' low regard for sports journalists (especially sportscasters) is that they are not actually professionally trained reporters; they are, instead, employees of professional teams or of television networks, and their jobs are basically promotional. They do not merely report the events; instead, they manage the accounts of the events to make them more interesting, more dramatic, and more important than they really are. Their role, rather than to provide information, is to translate games into mass entertainment aimed at high ratings. In doing so, they promote the media and the sports in which they are employed.

Discrimination, both gender and racial, has been present in the ways in which the mass media report sports and in the hiring practices of media corporations. There are, however, encouraging signs that conditions are improving for women and minorities.

WEB RESOURCES

www.usatoday.com/sports/
This website is the home of the sports section of *USA Today*. It has the daily sports stories and an archives link from which the user can secure copies of previous *USA Today* sports articles.

www.sportsillustrated.cnn.com
This is the website for *Sports Illustrated*, which has the largest circulation of any sports magazine. It reports on a variety of sports news items and has links to a variety of news sources and specific sports. The website provides the most comprehensive media coverage of sports of all kinds that currently exists.

www.awsmonline.org
The official website of the Association for Women in Sports Media. This is an organization of women who work in the sports media and of women and men who support them in their work. It has online features and news.

NOTES

1. Matthew Nicholson, *Sport and the Media: Managing the Nexus* (Boston: Elsevier, 2007), 16.
2. David Buckingham, "Selling Childhood? Children and Consumer Culture," *Journal of Children and Media* 1, no. 1 (2007): 15–24; see also Stanley J. Baran and Dennis K. Davis, *Mass Communication Theory: Foundations, Ferment, and Future*, 6th ed. (Belmont, CA: Wadsworth, 2011).
3. For more detailed discussions of mass media and social theories, see ibid. as well as Nick Stevenson, *Understanding Media Cultures: Social Theory and Mass Communication*, 2nd ed. (Thousand Oaks, CA: Sage, 2009).
4. Scott Reinardy and Wayne Wanta, *The Essentials of Sports Reporting and Writing* (New York: Routledge, 2009).
5. Tim Holmes, "Mapping the Magazine: An Introduction," *Journalism Studies* 8, no. 4 (2007): 510–521.
6. Rob Fleder, *Sports Illustrated 50: The Anniversary Book* (New York: Time Inc., 2005).
7. Alan Eisenstock, *Sports Talk: A Journey Inside the World of Sports Talk Radio* (New York: Atria Publishing, 2007); see also Tim Holland, *Sports Talk Radio Is a Waste of Time (and So Is This Book): A Common Sense Look at the Sports World Past and Present* (iUniverse.com, 2010).
8. Matt Marrone, Andy Clayton, and Kristie Ackert, "The 25 Greatest Sports Movies Ever," *NYDailyNews.com*, 29 May 2010, http://www.nydailynews.com/sports/galleries/the_25_greatest_sports_movies_ever/the_25_greatest_sports_movies_ever.html.
9. Nielsen, "Television, Internet and Mobile Usage in the US: Three Screen Report" (1st Quarter 2010).
10. CTIA Advocacy, "U.S. Wireless Quick Facts," 2010, http://www.ctia.org/advocacy/research/index.cfm/aid/10323; see also Richard H. R. Harper, *Texture: Human Expression in the Age of Communications Overload* (Boston: MIT Press, 2010).
11. "First Television of Baseball Scene," *New York Times*, 18 May 1939, p. 29.
12. Claude Jeanrenaud and Stefan Késenne, "Sport and the Media: An Overview," in *The Economics of Sport and the Media*, ed. Claude Jeanrenaud and Stefan Késenne (Northampton, MA: Edward Elgar, 2006), 1–25.
13. Michael Hiestand, "How Texas Is Steering College TV Sports," *USA Today*, 12–14 August 2011, pp. 1A–2A; see also Michael Hiestand, "In TV Sports, More Is More," *USA Today*, 31 December 2009, p. 3C; and Michael Hiestand, "Viewers Tune In to NFL, Turn Off College Football," *USA Today*, 17 December 2010, p. 3C.
14. Richard Sandomir, "Super Bowl Nets Record Viewership," *New York Times*, 6 February 2012, http://fifthdown.blogs.nytimes.com/2012/02/06/super-bowl-nets-near-record-ratings.
15. Rodney D. Fort, *Sports Economics*, 3rd ed. (Upper Saddle River, NJ: Prentice Hall, 2010); and Jerry Gorman and Kirk Calhoun, *The Name of the Game: The Business of Sports* (New York: Wiley, 2004); and Michael Leeds and Peter von Allmen, *Economics of Sports*, 4th ed. (Upper Saddle River, NJ: Prentice Hall, 2010).
16. Dave Zirin, *Bad Sports: How Owners Are Ruining the Games We Love* (New York: Scribner, 2010).
17. John S. Watterson, *College Football: History, Spectacle, Controversy* (Baltimore: Johns Hopkins University Press, 2000).
18. Keith Dunnavant, *The Fifty-Year Seduction: How Television Manipulated College Football, from the Birth of the Modern NCAA to the Creation of the BCS* (New York:

St. Martin's Press, 2004), xvi; see also Randy R. Grant, John Leadly, and Zenon Zygmont, *The Economics of Intercollegiate Sports* (Hackensack, NJ: World Scientific Publishing, 2008).

19. Richard Sandomir and Pete Thamel, "TV Deal Pushes N.C.A.A. Closer to 68-Team Tournament," *New York Times*, 23 April 2010, p. B9.

20. Michael Oriard, *Bowled Over: Big-Time College Football from the Sixties to the BCS Era* (Chapel Hill: University of North Carolina Press, 2009); and Mark Yost, *Varsity Green: A Behind the Scenes Look at Culture and Corruption in College Athletics* (Stanford, CA: Stanford University Press, 2010).

21. Quoted in Fred Grimm, "Exploiting Sports Prodigies Now Is ESPN," *Miami Herald*, 1 October 2009, p. B1.

22. Kevin Lole, "UFC Eyes Cards in Afghanistan and China," *Yahoo.com*, 8 April 2010, http://sports.yahoo.com/mma/news?slug=ki-ufcafghanistan040810.

23. Michael A. Messner, Michele Dunbar, and Darnell Hunt, "The Televised Sports Manhood Formula," in *Sport in Contemporary Society: An Anthology*, 8th ed., ed. D. Stanley Eitzen (Boulder, CO: Paradigm Publishers, 2009), 71–84; see also Garry Whannel, "Mediating Masculinities: The Production of Media Representations in Sport," in *Sport and Gender Identities: Masculinities, Femininities, and Sexualities*, ed. Cara Carmichael Aitchison (New York: Routledge, 2007), 7–21.

24. Hiestand, "Viewers Tune In to NFL, Turn Off College Football."

25. Arthur A. Raney, "Why We Watch and Enjoy Mediated Sports," in *Handbook of Sports and Media*, ed. Arthur A. Raney and Jennings Bryant (Hillsdale, NJ: Lawrence Erlbaum, 2006), 313–329.

26. Internet World Stats, *Internet Usage Statistics for the Americas*, 30 June 2010, http://www.internetworldstats.com/stats2.htm.

27. Eileen Kennedy and Laura Hills, *Sport, Media and Society* (New York: Berg, 2009), especially ch. 8.

28. Kathryn Zickuhr, *Generations Online in 2010*, Pew Research Center Publications, 16 December 2010, http://pewresearch.org/pubs/1831/generations-online-2010; see also Mike Snider, "Game Consoles Under Attack," *USA Today*, 6 June 2011, pp. 1B–2B.

29. Mike Snider, "BOOM! Madden Still Calls the Plays," *USA Today*, 10–12 December 2010, pp. 1C–2C.

30. Mike Snider and Brett Molina, "Nintendo Plans Successor to Wii as Sales Slump," *USA Today*, 26 April 2011, p. 3B.

31. Garry Crawford and Victoria K. Gosling, "More Than a Game: Sports-Themed Video Games and Player Narratives," *Sociology of Sport Journal* 26 (2009): 50–66; see also Mark Wolf, *The Video Game Explosion: A History from PONG to PlayStation and Beyond* (Westport, CT: Greenwood, 2007).

32. "Wireless Quick Facts," *CTIA Media*, http://www.ctia.org/media/industry_info/index.cfm/AID/10323.

33. David Murphy, "Twitter: On Track for 200 Million Users by Year's End," *PC Magazine*, 31 October 2010, http://www.pcmag.com/article2/0,2817,2371826,00.asp; and "New Media on Tap," *USA Today*, 2 August 2010, p. 3C.

34. Kristi A. Allain, "'Real Fast and Tough': The Construction of Canadian Hockey Masculinity," *Sociology of Sport Journal* 25 (2008): 462–481; and Michael A. Messner and Raewyn Connell, *Out of Play: Critical Essays on Gender and Sport* (Albany, NY: SUNY, 2007).

35. Michael A. Messner and Cheryl Cooky, *Gender in Televised Sports: News and Highlight Shows, 1989–2009*, Center for Feminist Research, University of Southern California, June 2010.

36. Dana D. Brooks and Ronald C. Althouse, eds., *Diversity and Social Justice in College Sports: Sport Management and the Student Athlete* (Morgantown, WV: Fitness Information Technology, 2007), especially sec. 4, "Media, Media Images, and Stereotyping."

37. Jarrett Bell, "NFL Confronts Discipline Issue," *USA Today*, 10 April 2007, pp. 1C–2C.

38. Richard King, *Native Americans and Sport in North America: Other People's Games* (New York: Routledge, 2007); and C. Richard King, *The Native American Mascot Controversy: A Handbook* (Lanham, MD: Scarecrow Press, 2010).

39. These two quotes are from Raymond Boyle, *Sports Journalism: Context and Issues* (Thousand Oaks, CA: Sage Publications, 2006), 1; see also Andrew Baker, *Where Am I and Who's Winning? Travelling the World of Sport* (London: Yellow Jersey Press, 2004), ix.

40. Kathryn T. Stofer, *Sports Journalism: An Introduction to Reporting and Writing* (Lanham, MD: Rowman & Littlefield, 2009).

41. Raney, "Why We Watch and Enjoy Mediated Sports," 313–329; see also Arthur A. Raney and Anthony J. Depalma, "The Effect of Viewing Varying Levels and Contexts of Violent Sports Programming on Enjoyment, Mood, and Perceived Violence," *Mass Communication and Society* 9, no. 3 (2006): 321–338.

42. Several excellent articles about sports fans can be found in Lawrence W. Hungerberg, Paul M. Haridakis, and Adam C. Earnheardt, eds., *Sports Mania: Essays on Fandom and the Media in the 21st Century* (Jefferson, NC: McFarland, 2008).

43. "Newsroom Employment Up Slightly, Minority Numbers Plunge for Third Year," *ASNE*, 7 April 2011, http://asne.org/article_view/articleid/1788/

newsroom-employment-up-slightly-minority-numbers-plunge-for-third-year.aspx.

44. Richard Lapchick with Austin Moss II, Christina Russell, and Rodney Scearce, *The 2010–11 Associated Press Sports Editors Racial and Gender Report Card* (Orlando: The Institute for Diversity and Ethics in Sport [TIDES] at the University of Central Florida, 27 April 2011).

45. Bob Papper, "Number of Minority Journalists Down . . . Story Mixed for Female Journalists," *Radio Television Digital News Association*, 22 September 2010, http://www.rtnda.org/pages/posts/rtdnahofstra-survey-number-of-minority-journalists-down-in-2009-story-mixed-for-female-journalists1083.php.

46. Lapchick with Moss, Russell, and Scearce, *The 2010–11 Associated Press Sports Editors Racial and Gender Report Card.*

CHAPTER 12

Sport, Social Stratification, and Social Mobility

The meritocratic ideal of a "level playing field" is illusory and conceals the fact that a person's origins (family circumstances, social class, etc.) continue to have a major impact on his/her ability to become socially mobile.
—Ramón Spaaij*

Sport is generally assumed to be an egalitarian institution that promotes interaction across social class lines and racial lines. But sport, like the larger society, is highly stratified, and like all social institutions, sport accommodates and reinforces the existing structure of social inequality. Many sports activities, such at yachting, are too expensive for the less well-to-do. (istockphoto)

*Ramón Spaaij, "Sport as a Vehicle for Social Mobility and Regulation of Disadvantaged Urban Youth," *International Review for the Sociology of Sport* 44, nos. 2–3 (2009): 262.

Sport is generally assumed to be an egalitarian and a meritocratic institution. It is accepted as egalitarian because it promotes interaction across social class and racial lines and because interest in sport transcends class and social boundaries. Sport is also believed to be meritocratic because within it persons who have talent, regardless of social background, can be upwardly mobile. The argument is that when athletes compete together, socioeconomic status disappears. Black or white, Christian or Jew, rich or poor, socioeconomic locations are irrelevant; all that matters is that everyone is giving their all, and high-fives are exchanged by all when a victory is achieved.[1]

Similar assertions reinforce conventional wisdom about how sport transcends social class in North America. However, empirical examinations of the sports world clearly demonstrate that sport, like the larger society, is highly stratified. Like all institutions, sport is a powerful contributor to the existing structure of social stratification and social inequality. There are exceptions, as we will note, but as exceptions they prove the rule.

TERMINOLOGY AND THEORY IN SOCIAL STRATIFICATION AND MOBILITY

Basic Terminology in Social Stratification

If members of a social grouping have differing amounts of wealth, power, or prestige, a condition of social inequality is said to exist. When these attributes are ranked hierarchically in that grouping—from lower to higher—sociologists call the situation *social stratification*; by this they mean that inequality is present in the system of social relationships that determines who gets which of the rewards and power in a society, and why. Even though social inequality benefits some members of a society while oppressing others, it is acknowledged as the way things are.[2]

When a group of people occupy the same relative economic rank in a stratified social system, they form what is called a *social class*. Members of a

society are socially located in a class position on the basis of income, occupation, and education, either alone or in combination. One's placement in the class hierarchy determines access to the rewards and resources of society, such as wealth, power, and privilege. And, crucially, differential access to these societal resources and rewards produces different life experiences, lifestyles, and different life chances.

The chances one has to live and experience good things or bad things in life are called *life chances*. The affluent members of society and their children will have a good education, good medical care, comfortable homes, safe neighborhoods, expert services of all kinds, the best in leisure activities, and, likely, a long life span—all of which could be called favorable life chances. The converse, of course, is that the poor and the near-poor members of society will have inadequate health care, shelter, and diets. Their lives will be more miserable, and they will have shorter life expectancies—unfavorable life chances, to be sure.

In addition to class, race, gender, and ableness are structured systems of inequality that organize society as a whole and create varied environments for individuals and families through their unequal distribution of social opportunities. They are also structured systems of exploitation and discrimination in which the affluent dominate the poor, men dominate women, whites dominate people of color, and the disabled are dominated by the general public.

Functional Theory and Social Stratification

Functional theorists insist that a differentiated system of rewards and privileges is essential for the efficient processes of society, so functionalism is replete with explanations for the existence and necessity of social inequality and stratification. Without incentives for achievements, functionalists argue, people would not seek to discover, develop new and better products, strive for medical advances, and work for better livelihoods. Rewards and the power and prestige that go with these achievements function to make for a better society.

Advocates of a functionalist viewpoint argue that without this inequality, division of labor would be difficult (not everyone can be owner, boss, team captain). They also maintain that attracting people to important social roles and positions requires variation in rewards that motivate individuals to make the effort needed to gain these top positions.

Conflict/Cultural Theories and Social Stratification

On the other hand, conflict/cultural theorists contend that in a competitive capitalist system—which exists in both Canada and the United States—capitalist interests dominate both the economy and the social culture. Capitalism enables business owners and corporations to employ and, often, to exploit workers and employees, who must sell their labor—that is, their ability to work—in return for wages. The consequence is that social inequality and exploitation become inherent in capitalism.

According to this theoretical perspective, exploitation of the working class has resulted in members of each social class possessing large differences in income, power, and social prestige, resulting in distinctive social classes and cultures. The current manifestation of that in North America is the huge gap between the wealthy and the poor, and the enormous differences in lifestyles and therefore life chances. Moreover, because they are the beneficiaries of the status quo, those with wealth, power, and prestige have a clear interest in resisting social change.

DIMENSIONS OF INEQUALITY

North Americans rank differently from one another on a number of socioeconomic dimensions, such as wealth, income, education, and occupation. Wealth and income, the bases of social class, are concentrated among individuals and families. The following facts illustrate the range on each of these dimensions:

- In 2010 the 400 richest Americans had a total net worth of $1.37 trillion. At the other extreme, 43.6 million Americans (15.4 percent) were living below the poverty line.[3]

- One in four African Americans and one in four Hispanic Americans are now living below the federal poverty line.

- In 2010 the top 1 percent of wealth holders controlled 43 percent of total net worth and the top 20 percent owned 84 percent of the nation's wealth; the bottom 20 percent accounted for just 1 percent of the wealth. In Canada 70 percent of the wealth is held by the wealthiest 20 percent of Canadians, while 3.7 million (10.9 percent) live in poverty.[4]

- The share of U.S. national income of the richest 20 percent of households was 50.3 percent in 2009, while the bottom 20 percent received only 3.4 percent of the nation's income. According to *Statistics Canada*, the income of full-time, full-year earners rose for those at the top of the earnings distribution, stagnated for those in the middle, and declined for those at the bottom over the past thirty years.[5]

- The mean income of American households headed by persons identifying as African American or black is 61 percent of that of households headed by persons identifying as white.

- In 2011, some 3 percent of the North American population aged twenty-five and older had a doctorate or professional degree; about 6 percent had an eighth-grade education or less.

- Occupational prestige is correlated with income level, but the gender of the worker makes a tremendous difference: In the U.S., women make about 80 percent, on average, of what men earn. Women also find it more difficult than men to reach the highest levels of management (to move above the "glass ceiling"). In Canada women earn 85 percent of what men do, with little change since 2000.

These facts make clear that the United States and Canada are certainly not classless societies. There are wide disparities in economic resources and what those resources can yield. The remainder of this chapter deals with two issues involving inequality and sport: (1) the influence of stratification on sports participation and spectatorship and (2) the possibility that sport can help individuals move up (increase their upward social mobility) in the stratification hierarchy.

SOCIAL CLASS AND SPORT

North Americans enjoy playing and watching sports. Is what they do or prefer to do with respect to sports related to their socioeconomic status? Looking first at participation, we find that the data from empirical research provide consistent support for the generalization that the higher the socioeconomic status of the individual, the more likely that individual will be to participate actively in leisure activities.

Adult Participation Preferences for Sports by Socioeconomic Status

The evidence is clear that high-income, high-education, and high-status occupational groups have the highest rates of active sport participation and attendance at sports events. Consider first the data in Table 12.1, which show a consistent and strong pattern in the relationship between social class and involvement in sports. That is, the higher a person's level of educational attainment and income, the more likely a person is to attend a sports event and to participate in sports.

Similarly, Table 12.2 illustrates that for all types of individual and team sports activities, the higher the income, the greater the rate of participation. This trend can be seen by scanning left to right across Table 12.2.

There are several bases for this tendency. The most obvious is that many activities (e.g., skiing and golf) are too expensive for the less well-to-do. The affluent also have access to private clubs and resorts where golf, tennis, skiing, and swimming are available. Communities rarely provide inexpensive access to these activities, other than tennis and swimming.

An interesting speculation as to why the affluent are disposed toward certain sports was presented in *The Theory of the Leisure Class* by sociologist/economist Thorstein Veblen near the beginning

Table 12.1 Attendance at Sports Events and Participation in Sports by Education and Income (in percentages)

Variable	Attendance at Sports Events	Participation in Sports
Education (highest level attained)		
Grade school	6.6	6.7
Some high school	17.8	19.0
High school graduate	22.8	17.4
Some college	33.7	29.1
College graduate	44.9	38.9
Graduate school	44.2	40.0
Income ($)		
Less than 10,000	14.9	15.9
10,000–19,999	13.4	14.5
20,000–29,999	21.1	14.9
30,000–39,999	22.3	23.3
40,000–49,999	28.7	26.5
50,000–74,999	33.3	26.0
75,000–99,999	42.2	37.0
100,000–149,000	46.8	39.1
150,000 and over	53.1	46.0

Source: U.S. Census Bureau, *Statistical Abstract of the United States: 2011*, 130th ed. (Washington, DC, 2011), table 1238.

of the twentieth century, at a time when organized sports were becoming widely popular. Veblen argued that the affluent engaged in leisure activities in order to impress upon observers that they can afford expensive and time-consuming activities. In other words, sport is used by these persons as a form of *conspicuous consumption*, to prove that they can spend great amounts of money and time away from work.[6]

This rationale explains why the upper class has held amateur sport as an ideal and why Olympic competition was traditionally limited to the more well-to-do. Another explanation for the greater likelihood of the affluent to engage in sports is that their occupations, unlike lower-income jobs, offer more flexible schedules. This allows them more freedom to go to the gym, club, or golf course whenever they wish.

The affluent and educated are more prone than lower socioeconomic groups to engage in health and physical fitness activities such as

Table 12.2 Participation in Selected Sports Activities by Household Income (in percentages)

Activity	Under $25,000	$25,000–$74,000	$75,000+
Team Sports			
Basketball	8.3	11.3	12.2
Baseball	4.4	5.6	6.4
Volleyball	2.0	4.4	6.0
Soccer	4.0	5.3	7.3
Softball	3.7	4.8	5.3
Football	3.4	4.2	3.8
Individual Sports/Leisure			
Aerobic exercise	9.4	12.2	17.3
Exercise: with equip.	14.6	22.3	29.8
Exercise: walking	32.5	35.3	39.0
Running/Jogging	7.2	12.8	17.5
Golf	2.9	8.1	15.0
Tennis	1.7	3.9	7.4
Swimming	14.8	23.0	29.5
Weight lifting	7.8	13.1	18.4

Source: U.S. Census Bureau, *Statistical Abstract of the United States: 2011*, 130th ed. (Washington, DC: 2011), table 1248. (Percentages calculated from data in table.)

running, aerobics, swimming, and bicycling. An interesting difference between white-collar and blue-collar workers involves participation in workplace-centered fitness programs. Many corporations provide sports equipment and facilities for their workers and encourage them to participate. The typical reaction is enthusiastic support from the salaried professionals and relative nonsupport from the hourly workers.[7]

There are several reasons for this. First, the lower the social status, the less likely the individual will be to exercise regularly, to participate in wellness programs, to maintain a proper weight, and to stop smoking. Second, the activities provided (e.g., running, swimming, and racquetball) are of more interest to higher-status workers. Third, blue-collar workers may mistrust such programs because they suspect that management provides exercise programs to serve the interests of management, not the workers. Finally, many blue-collar workers may resent the money spent on exercise equipment and the like because it does not address their real needs (e.g., the monotony of repetitive work, the exposure to toxic chemicals or other dangers, and the negative effects of shift work). Health promotion is viewed as a luxury, not as a relief from the physical harshness of much blue-collar work. In other words, when blue-collar workers are encouraged to become more self-reliant and to take charge of their health, they see this as "blaming the victim" because it refocuses the need for changes in the job environment to the individual worker.

At the lowest end of the stratification hierarchy—the working poor or the unemployed poor—participation in organized team sports is practically nonexistent. Their access to organized sports is severely limited by their lack of resources and the unavailability of teams, equipment, or facilities.

Youth Sport Participation by Socioeconomic Status

There are several tendencies concerning sports participation by the children in low-income households. First, they are more likely than the children of the affluent to engage in physical contact sports (wrestling, boxing, football). This is a social arena where they can be somebody, where they can achieve the respect they otherwise do not get.[8] Evidence from the United States, Canada, and Germany confirms the generalization that athletes from lower social origins are much more likely to compete in contact sports, and to gravitate to sports that emphasize physical strength (e.g., weight lifting or arm wrestling) and physical toughness (e.g., boxing or wrestling).

A second tendency for children of low-income families is to engage in sports that require little equipment or that are publicly funded, such as community youth programs and schools. Basketball, both the playground variety and school teams, is the sport at which urban children of the poor tend to excel. Prowess in basketball begins for these youngsters not in organized leagues or teams, but as individuals joining with individuals to challenge another loosely organized group of individuals. Pete Axthelm sensitively characterized it in this way:

> Basketball is the city game. Its battlegrounds are strips of asphalt between tattered wire fences or crumbling buildings; its rhythms grow from the uneven thump of a ball against hard surfaces. It demands no open spaces or lush backyards or elaborate equipment. It doesn't even require specified numbers of players; a one-on-one confrontation in a playground can be as memorable as a full-scale organized game.
>
> Basketball is the game for young athletes without cars or allowances—the game whose drama and action are intensified by its confined spaces and chaotic surroundings. . . .
>
> The game is simple, an act of one man challenging another, twisting, feinting, then perhaps breaking free to leap upward, directing a ball toward a target, a metal hoop ten feet above the ground. But its simple motions swirl into intricate patterns, its variations become almost endless, its brief soaring moments merge into a fascinating dance. To the uninitiated, the patterns may seem fleeting, elusive, even confusing; but on a city playground, a classic play is frozen in the minds of those who see it—a moment of order and achievement in a turbulent, frustrating existence. And a one-on-one challenge takes on wider meaning, defining identity and manhood in an urban society that breeds invisibility.[9]

The prolonged fiscal crisis at all levels of government (federal, state, and local) has had a negative impact on sports programs for the children of the poor. Municipal governments often cannot fund recreational programs at an appropriate level. City schools are especially hard hit as their funds, which come mostly from property taxes, diminish and federal and state assistance programs are reduced or eliminated.

The children of the affluent, on the other hand, either go to private schools or attend public schools in wealthier districts. Wealthy districts provide more sports opportunities, more coaches, and better facilities and equipment than do the poorer districts. When sports in the more affluent areas are threatened by cuts, the shortfall can usually be saved by "participation fees"—an arrangement that increases the gap between sports participation possibilities for the children of the poor and the affluent.

For youngsters growing up in a country club milieu, interest in the sports provided there is natural, and they tend to develop the skills, enhanced by coaches at the clubs, important to successful sports performance. Children of the poor, on the other hand, do not have access to golf courses, tennis courts, swimming pools, and traveling sports club teams. Nor do they receive coaching in these sports. The only sports in which they tend to receive coaching outside of schools are track and field (through community track clubs) and boxing, because gyms are located in the poorest and racially segregated urban areas.

Spectator Preferences for Sports by Socioeconomic Status

The mass media have been instrumental in generating an interest in professional football, basketball, baseball, and hockey that transcends social class. Although lacking precise data, we may reasonably assume that since over 98 percent of all North American homes have at least one television set, those tuning in to the Super Bowl, the Stanley Cup Championship, or the World Series will not be disproportionately from one social class.

There are two kinds of spectators—those who attend in person and those who watch or listen on television or radio.[10] Examining first the attendance at a live sporting event, we find that the data show a consistently strong relationship between sports attendance and social class. For example, as shown in Table 12.1, only 17.8 percent of the survey participants with only some high school education attended sporting events, whereas 44.9 percent of the surveyed college graduates did so. Clearly, the higher the income, the educational attainment, or both, the more likely it is that individuals will attend and participate in sports.

During the past twenty years, overall participation in and attendance of sporting events in general have shifted toward more educated and affluent people. This is not surprising, given the relatively high costs of travel, tickets, parking, and concessions. The average price of a ticket for a National Football League game in 2011, for example, was $76, with New England the highest at $117.84. This is ironic because many of the stadiums were built with public funds, yet only the affluent can afford to attend.

Statistics on sports watching on television reveal these patterns: (1) The affluent are much more likely than the poor to watch golf and tennis; (2) the college-educated are more likely to watch college sports than those who did not attend college; and (3) high school graduates or those who have less education are overrepresented among those watching auto racing, demolition derbies, tractor pulls, bowling, and professional wrestling.

An excellent indicator of what type of audience watches a sporting event on television is the sponsors who have purchased advertising for them. Advertisers for golf events include corporations such as IBM, Xerox, Prudential, and United Airlines; professional wrestling is typically sponsored by used-car dealers, beer distributors, and country-music record companies. Clearly, advertisers have researched sports audiences and have discerned that for some sports activities, the audiences are disproportionately from certain social classes.

Prole Sports

Why are lower-income adults especially attracted to particular kinds of sport activities—such as boxing, strongest-man competitions, demolition derbies, Ultimate Fighting Championship, kickboxing, and drag racing? While simple logic suggests why college graduates appreciate college sports, there is no ready explanation for why working-class fans gravitate toward "prole" sports, a name derived from Karl Marx's term for the working class, *proletariat*. On the surface, it would appear that these

sports have several common attributes: speed, machines, daring, physical strength, and violence. Let us examine such activities more closely to see why these and other characteristics make them so appealing to this socioeconomic category. However, the possible reasons are speculative because no systematic research has yet been undertaken to assess the actual motivations of blue-collar fans.

The various forms of automobile and motorcycle racing appeal to working-class fans for several reasons. First, the artifacts (the machines, the necessary tools, and the equipment) are part of lower-income experience. Less educated, low-income people easily identify with these sports because they have access to the machines and the skills to drive them. A second reason is that these vehicles and their drivers represent speed, excitement, and daring to persons whose work is often dull and repetitive. Another possible symbolic reason is that automobiles and motorcycles are symbols of liberation to the working-class person who otherwise feels trapped by his or her situation. The image is one of human and machine united in rebellion against a hostile environment.

Pseudosports

Professional wrestling, which we have characterized as a pseudosport because its competition is contrived, depends in very large measure on the interest and attendance of blue-collar workers and their families. These types of shows have several common characteristics that may offer some clues as to why low-income citizens are especially attracted to them. First, they emphasize strength, power, and violence, thus emphasizing physical prowess and manhood (machismo). Example: NHRA Drag Racing fans are 77 percent male and 23 percent female. Recently the sport of Ultimate Fighting Championship has emerged, where the combatants hit, kick, and pummel each other with few if any limitations. The goal is to defeat the opponent without the normal rules of combat sports.

Second, the actors are easy to identify with. There is strong identification with heroes who are like the spectators in ethnicity, language, racial background, or behavior. Some heroes are wrapped in outer-space symbols; some are villains—often representing the nation's enemies. Female athletes are featured, in contrast to other sports, giving working-class women someone with whom they can identify.

Third, there is a strong propensity for spectators to become physically and emotionally involved in the events because of the drama ("good" vs. "evil"). They shout encouragement to their heroes, boo the villains, and occasionally throw things when they get upset with the officiating or with the outcome of the event. Symbolically, wrestling matches are morality plays. They often feature a "hero" who attempts to defeat the "villain" within the moral framework of the rules of the game. It is the classic scenario of law versus outlaw, cops versus robbers, "good guys" versus "bad guys."

Fans tend to identify with the virtuous hero. When justice prevails and the hero triumphs, the fans' belief in law and order is reinforced. When the villain wins (rarely), the victory is attributed to foul play; when the rematch occurs, justice will finally reign. If it does not, then an alternate view of the world is reinforced. In this view—a major working-class belief—the world operates such that some persons take advantage of others and get away with it.[11]

The intensity of fans' feelings is also occasionally manifested in arguments or fights among themselves. The crowd behavior at these events is exactly the opposite of behavior found at country club events such as golf or tennis. Unlike the passive spectators at those sports, the fans at wrestling matches are intensely involved.

Segregation in Sports by Social Class

We have previously noted that the different social strata have some unique preferences in sport. Although they enjoy some of the same sports (especially the mass media presentations of professional football, basketball, and baseball), the self-selection process in sports tends to segregate by social class. Let us look beyond this process to ascertain whether there are any other barriers that separate the social classes.

At the participatory level, some barriers serve to segregate the social classes. As we noted earlier in this chapter, in sports such as swimming, golf, and tennis, the affluent compete in private clubs or at facilities limited to residents in an exclusive neighborhood or condominium complex (at some of these, access is controlled by fences, walls, and even armed guards). The middle and lower classes may participate in these sports only at public facilities. In a given city, then, a dual system of competition often exists—tournaments or competitions for the wealthy and a separate set of events for the general public. The quality of play at these two levels varies, with the wealthy usually rated better because of their access to better facilities, equipment, and private tutors. This difference in skill also serves to segregate affluent from less affluent players.

Spectators, too, are often segregated by social class at general-interest sporting events. This is accomplished in several ways. First, ticket prices often exclude the poor, especially when season tickets are considered. The common practice of different prices according to seating location also tends to segregate persons by socioeconomic status. The affluent rarely sit in the relatively low-cost bleacher seats, and the poor rarely purchase reserved seats or box seats and do not have access to seats in the skyboxes.

The ultimate in differentially priced seating locations, and thus segregation by social class, is the purchase of skyboxes. These exclusive luxury suites are typically outfitted with expensive furniture, a bar, and other luxuries. They are purchased by individuals or corporations for very high prices, as noted in Chapter 10. For example, the season price for the top luxury suite at New York Yankees Stadium in 2011 was $850,000.

This ostentatious display of wealth is an example of *conspicuous consumption*, the purchase and display of expensive items to flaunt one's high status. It is a phenomenon found among the wealthy, the near-wealthy, and those who fake wealth. There is an often-repeated observation that polo's reputation as snobbish is a given—after all, Ralph Lauren never considered naming his pricey line *Bowling* or *Softball*.

Although several sports offer the opportunity for conspicuous consumption spectating, it is most commonly found at the premier events—for example, at the Super Bowl, the Stanley Cup Championship, the World Series, the Kentucky Derby, and heavyweight boxing championship matches. Many status-conscious persons use these highly visible events to impress others. They buy the expensive seats, wear costly jewelry and furs, and are driven in limousines to the venue.

At the other end of the stratification hierarchy are the poor and near-poor, who cannot afford to attend sports. The high costs likely keep the poorest away from the sports arenas except as workers (vendors, janitors, parking attendants). Even if the poor could afford seats for regular events, they would be completely priced out of premier events. Since these events are sold out (with corporate sponsors holding huge blocks of seats), scalpers sell the precious few remaining seats at premium prices. The high cost of going to sports events has prevented the poor and the working poor from attending them. The poor have, instead, become that huge mass of television fans. More on this in Chapter 11.

SOCIAL MOBILITY AND SPORT

Social mobility is the term used to describe the movement of individuals from one social location in a society's stratification system to another. Income mobility is the most common measure of social mobility. *Intra*-generational mobility refers to people who move from one social class to another during their life. Those whose income and financial resources increase within their lifetime are said to be upwardly mobile, while those whose income and resources decrease are said to be downwardly mobile. A second commonly measured form of social mobility is *inter*-generational mobility, which refers to sons and daughters whose lifetime income and financial standing is upward or downward relative to that of their parents.

Typically, North Americans believe that the United States and Canada have fluid, socially mobile class systems—in other words, that positions of high pay and prestige are open to those with the requisite talents and aptitudes, regardless of their social origin. Indeed, a central creed of the so-called American Dream is a vision of a society in which one becomes upwardly mobile by working hard and competing to become wealthy, and this article of faith is reinforced by rags-to-riches successes that do, rarely, occur.

While there are certainly opportunities to be upwardly mobile in the United States and Canada, citizens of Denmark, Austria, Norway, Finland, Australia, and Spain actually have higher rates of socioeconomic mobility than U.S. citizens. Moreover, social mobility in the U.S. has actually been declining in the past three decades. The data in Figure 12.1 illustrate this trend; they show that in 2000 about 58 percent of children whose parents were in the bottom fifth of the wealth distribution ended up in that same bottom fifth themselves as adults. Canada has a higher level of social mobility than the United States, but it is not as open as the four European countries we have listed above.[12]

More than almost any other cultural practice, the sports world has been one of the most influential contributors to shaping the belief about widespread social mobility in North America through sport. This belief has been reinforced by the stories of a few youth from poor rural and urban areas, whether white or black, skyrocketing to fame and fortune through success in professional sports. The

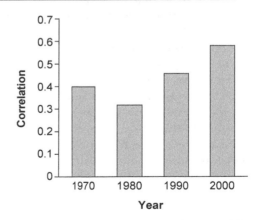

Figure 12.1   Intergenerational Social Mobility in the U.S., 1970–2000

The correlations between the earnings of sons and the income of their families, showing a trend toward diminished mobility. Higher correlations mean greater income persistence across generations, and thus less mobility.

Source: Lawrence Mishel, Jared Bernstein, and Sylvia Allegretto, *The State of Working America 2006–2007*, an Economic Policy Institute Book (Ithaca, NY: ILR Press, an imprint of Cornell Press, 2007), 97.

next section investigates the extent to which social mobility actually operates in the sports world—and if so, to what extent. Let us first examine the arguments and evidence supporting this belief.

Sport as a Mobility Escalator

The most obvious examples of sports participation facilitating upward social mobility are persons from low socioeconomic backgrounds who become wealthy and famous because of their sports achievements. This happens in almost all sports except those largely restricted to the upper class, such as polo, skiing, golfing, and yachting. Most typically, it occurs in boxing, where young athletes are recruited almost exclusively from the lower socioeconomic levels, and a few will earn many millions of dollars during their careers—very few. Loïc Wacquant, a sociologist who spent three years in a boxing gym, quotes a veteran boxing trainer as having told him: "If you want to know who's at d'bottom of society, all you gotta do is look at who's boxin'."[13]

Successful professional athletes in some sports (football in particular) must attend both high school and college. In this way, sports participation has the effect of encouraging or (in some cases) forcing young athletes to attain more education than they might otherwise achieve. This, in turn, increases their opportunities for success outside the sports world.

At the high school level, athletic participation appears to have positive consequences for mobility. Research shows consistently that, compared to their nonathlete peers, high school athletes as a category have better grades, more positive attitudes toward school, and more interest in continuing their education after high school.[14] But there are three confounding problems with the findings in this research. First, researchers have found it difficult to determine whether sports participation makes the difference or whether there are qualities that successful athletes have that give them an edge in academic achievement, such as willingness to work hard and follow orders as well as a strong goal-orientation. There is also a powerful selection factor at work here, inasmuch as coaches have been know to weed out certain types of problematic students. These are more likely to be low academically

performing students. Thus, where this happens, the grade point average for the sports team tends to rise.

Second, perhaps the differences are effects of family background and social class. Third, there is a problem with comparing athletes with nonathletes on grades, delinquency, and the like, given that athletes must maintain a minimum grade point average to remain athletes. Similarly, students can lose their athlete status if they get into serious trouble in school or in the community. Again, removing problem students from the athlete category "loads the dice" in favor of finding positive results when comparing athletes with nonathletes.

For these reasons we should be wary of research comparing athletes with nonathletes. That said, the research shows that there are positive consequences for participation in high school sports. Sports success translates into high status in the school, which has positive benefits for self-concept and for identifying positively with the school. Athletes are less likely than nonathletes to drop out of school. And athletes who believe that they will get a scholarship to college will be motivated to prepare for post–high school education.

Turning now to college athletes, we find that those who come from a family of low social status will almost automatically surpass their parents' socioeconomic status because of their superior educational attainments. Although the job prestige of former college athletes is fairly stable regardless of the sport played, the occupational prestige of fathers varies a good deal. Apparently, a college education makes the attainment of upper-middle-class jobs possible, regardless of student-athletes' social origin. College athletes surpass their fathers in occupational prestige regardless of the college sport they play. Research data indicate upward social mobility achieved by college athletes when they are compared with their fathers.

This seemingly upward mobility by college athletes compared to their fathers may be spurious, however. First, the comparison guarantees that the sons will have exceeded the fathers. Not all of the fathers have graduated from college, but athlete samples are composed of sons who have. Second, a gap between fathers and sons will always exist because of the general trend to higher educational levels. The best method to determine whether athletes have more potential for social mobility, therefore, is to compare them with nonathletes.

Cases where success in high school sports enhances the possibility of attending college suggest an increased probability of attaining high-paying, high-status jobs—and that is what several studies seem to have demonstrated. We summarize three of them here.

One of the first studies of intra-generational mobility of athletes compared football players with nonathletes who had graduated from Notre Dame University. The researchers found that (1) although the Notre Dame football players had come from poorer backgrounds, they had achieved equivalent incomes with the nonathletes; (2) nonathletes were more likely to have higher-status jobs and to have obtained advanced degrees; and (3) first-string players had much higher incomes than nonstarters and were overrepresented among top-ranking executives in their companies. This study provided strong evidence that athletic participation in college plus graduation does enhance upward social mobility.[15]

Another study compared male athletes and nonathletes six years after their class graduation from college. The researchers found that former athletes working in business, military, or manual labor occupations were better off financially than former nonathletes. The exception was that former athletes who had become high school teachers lagged behind nonathletes in income.[16]

As a final example, a study of high school seniors compared the educational and labor market outcomes for athletes and nonathletes eight years after their scheduled high school graduation. The findings were that high school athletes, compared to nonathletes, were more likely to (1) have attended college and earned a bachelor's degree, (2) be employed full-time, and (3) be earning a higher income.[17]

Each study suggests that athletes possess achievement indicators for more upward social mobility than nonathletes. These studies lead to the tentative conclusion that male athletes are upwardly mobile.

There are at least three possible reasons for this. First, athletic participation may lead to various forms of "occupational sponsorship." The male college athlete is a popular hero; therefore, a greater likelihood exists that he will date and marry a woman who comes from a higher socioeconomic background than if he were a nonathlete. If this occurs, then the chances are that the college athlete's father-in-law will provide him with benefits in the business world much greater than those available to the average nonathlete. Another form of sponsorship may come from well-placed alumni who offer former athletes positions in their businesses after graduation. This may be done to help the firm's public relations, or it may be part of a payoff in the recruiting wars that some alumni are willing to underwrite.

A second reason athletes may fare better is that the selection process for many jobs requires the applicant to be "well-rounded," that is, to have had a number of successful experiences outside the classroom. An extreme example of this is in the selection of Rhodes Scholars, which requires, in addition to superior grades, participation in extracurricular activities and demonstrated athletic ability.

Finally, there is the possibility that participation in highly competitive sports situations will lead to the development of attitudes and behavior patterns highly valued in the larger occupational world. If attributes such as leadership, human relations skills, teamwork, good work habits, and a well-developed competitive drive are acquired in sports, they may ensure that athletes will succeed in other endeavors. (See Chapter 5.)

Considerable debate surrounds the issue of whether sports build character or whether only certain kinds of personalities survive the sport experience. There may be a self-fulfilling prophecy at work here, however: If employers assume that athletes possess these valued character traits, they will make their hiring and promotion decisions accordingly, giving athletes the advantage.

Demythologizing the Social Mobility-Through-Sport Hypothesis

While there is evidence suggesting that involvement in high school and college sport may facilitate upward social mobility, that notion needs to be balanced with the reality that much of the upward social mobility acquired through sport is constructed on a succession of *myths*. These myths are: (1) Sport provides a free college education. (2) Sport leads to a college degree. (3) A professional sports career is possible. (4) Sport is a way out of poverty, especially for racial minorities. (5) Because of Title IX, women now have many opportunities for upward mobility through sport. (6) A professional sports career provides security for life.

Myth: Sport Provides a Free College Education

One assumption of the "social mobility through sports participation" position is that involvement in high school sport leads to college scholarships, which is especially helpful to poor youth who could not afford college otherwise. The problem with this assumption is that very few high school athletes receive athletic scholarships. Consider the following facts:

- NCAA Division I and II universities offer athletic scholarships. Division III schools do not offer athletic scholarships; they offer academic scholarships only. According to the NCAA, only about 2 percent of high school athletes are awarded athletic scholarships to compete in college.
- Fewer than 1 in 35 or 2.9 percent of male high school basketball players will go on to play at an NCAA member institution. Three in 100 or 3 percent of female high school basketball players will go on to play women's basketball at an NCAA member institution.
- Six percent or fewer than 1 in 16 of all high school football players will go on to play football at an NCAA member institution. Three in 50 or about 6 percent of high school soccer players will go on to play men's soccer at an NCAA member institution. Three in 50 or about 6 percent of high school baseball players will go on to play men's baseball at an NCAA member institution.[18]

As these figures clearly show, the notion that if one is a good high school athlete an athletic scholarship to a reputable university will likely follow—a belief held by many high school athletes and their parents—does not correspond to reality.

Myth: Participation in Sports Leads to a College Degree

A problem with the assumption that sports participation leads to a college degree is that fewer than half of college athletes graduate with college degrees (see Chapter 6). This is especially true for those athletes who believe that they will become professional athletes. Data show that, among the small percentage of college athletes who do become professional athletes, many have not graduated from college. For example, only about 53 percent of NFL players have college degrees, and only 20 percent of NBA players are college graduates; the rate is even lower for professional baseball, where over 90 percent have not graduated, and in hockey, where over 90 percent of NHL players have not graduated.[19]

There are a number of barriers to graduation for athletes. One obvious problem is the inordinate demand on their time and energy for practices, meetings, travel, and other sport-related activities. Many college athletes, because of these pressures, are counseled to take easy courses that maintain eligibility but that may not meet graduation requirements. The result is either to delay graduation or to make graduation an unrealistic goal.

Another barrier to graduation for many college athletes is that they are recruited for athletic prowess rather than for academic achievement. Athletes from low-income families who have typically attended inferior high schools, for example, are generally not prepared for the intellectual demands of college. As noted in Chapter 6, after six years, only about four out of ten black football players and three out of ten black basketball players in big-time programs graduate. Put another way, *whereas about one-half of white players do not graduate, two-thirds of black players do not graduate.*

A third barrier to graduation for college athletes is their own behavior, as many of them do not take advantage of their scholarships to work toward graduation. This is the case for those who perceive their college experience merely as preparation for their professional careers in sport. Study for them is necessary only to maintain their eligibility. An NBA rule change in 2006 mandates that players be at least one year removed from high school and at least nineteen years old to be drafted. For many basketball players, that has meant attending at least one year of college and then entering the NBA draft. In basketball circles this rule change is known as the "one and done rule."[20]

These attitudes and practices by college athletes are shortsighted because even a successful professional athletic career is limited to a few years, and not many professional athletes are able to translate their success in the pros to success in their post-athletic careers. Such a problem is especially true for African Americans, who often face employment discrimination in the wider society.

Myth: A Professional Sports Career Is Probable for Successful High School and College Athletes

When queried about their aspirations as athletes, many youth sport and high school athletes say that they believe they can become a professional in their sport. A survey by the Center for the Study of Sport in Society found that two-thirds of African American males between the ages of thirteen and eighteen believed that they could earn a living playing professional sports. Slightly less optimistic were the more than 30 percent of young white males who held such a belief. Moreover, African American parents were four times more likely than white parents to believe that their children were destined for careers as professional athletes. Obviously, for both young athletes and their parents, the higher echelons of sport are readily available and thus will lead to upward social mobility.[21] The reality is quite different:

- Three in 10,000 or 0.0003 percent of boys playing high school basketball will be drafted by a National Basketball Association an NBA team. One in 5,000 or approximately 0.0002 percent of high school girls playing interscholastic basketball will eventually be drafted by a WNBA team.
- About 1 in 75 or approximately 1.3 percent of NCAA male basketball players will get

drafted by an NBA team. Fewer than 1 in 100 or 0.9 percent of NCAA female basketball players will get drafted by a WNBA team.

- Eight in 10,000 or 0.0008 percent of high school football players will eventually be drafted by an NFL team. Approximately 1 in 50 or 2 percent of NCAA football players will get drafted by an NFL team.
- Approximately 1 in 1,250 or about 0.0008 percent of male high school soccer players will eventually be drafted by a Major League Soccer (MLS) team. Fewer than 1 in 50 or about 1.6 percent of NCAA male soccer players will be drafted by an MLS team.
- Approximately 1 in 200 or 0.005 percent of high school boys playing baseball will eventually be drafted by an MLB team. About 9 in 100 or about 9 percent of NCAA male baseball players will get drafted by an MLB team.[22]

If these young athletes do play as professionals, the economic rewards are excellent, as shown in Chapter 10. The dream of financial success through a professional sports career is, however, just a dream for all but an infinitesimal number. Not only are the odds long of making it to the professional level, if one is good enough and lucky enough to make it, the career will be short, averaging three to seven years in team sports and three to twelve years in individual sports. So, in light of what is obviously a false ideology of guaranteed upward mobility for poor youth who excel at sport, the vast majority of youth would stand a better chance of achieving social mobility by focusing their time and energy on their education rather than on sport.

Myth: Sport Is a Way Out of Poverty, Especially for Racial Minorities

Sport appears to be an important avenue out of poverty for African Americans. Several professional sports are dominated numerically by blacks. Although they comprise only 13.5 percent of the U.S. population, African Americans constitute around 82 percent of the players in professional basketball

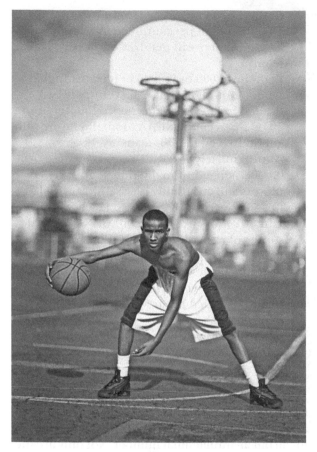

Many people consider sport to be a major way for poor white and African American youth to escape their social conditions. Because several of the popular professional sports are dominated numerically by African Americans, young black youth buy into the myth that with dedication and the development of superior skills in a sport, they can become pro athletes. But less than 1 in 7,000 African Americans become professional athletes. (istockphoto)

and about 70 percent of the players in professional football. Moreover, blacks are high on the list of the highest moneymakers in sport (salaries, commercial sponsorships). At first, these facts seem impressive, but they are illusory. Consider the following:

- There are fewer than 2,500 African American athletes playing in the most popular North American professional team sports leagues—NFL, NBA, WNBA, MLB, NHL, and MLS.

There are approximately 14.3 million African Americans aged eighteen to forty years old, the age range of pro athletes; thus, only 0.0002 percent of African Americans in that age range (2 in 10,000) are professional athletes in those sports.

- African Americans are rarely found in certain sports (automobile racing, tennis, golf, bowling, hockey).
- African Americans are rarely found in positions of authority in sport (head coaches, athletic directors, general managers, owners).

These figures clearly show that only a very small percentage of African Americans make it to the professional level as athletes. Several African American scholars have noted that, statistically, young African American athletes have a better chance of being hit by a meteorite than getting work as an athlete, and the prospects for African American women are much worse than for men.

Nevertheless, this myth is pervasive in the African American community. Despite the low odds of making it as a professional athlete, many poor African American boys see sport as their only hope to escape from a life of crime, poverty, and despair. They latch onto the dream of sport success partly because they have limited opportunities for middle-class success. That is why many African American youth spend countless hours, year in and year out, developing their speed, strength, or "moves" to the virtual exclusion of developing capabilities that have a greater likelihood of paying off in upward mobility—mathematical competence, communication skills, computer literacy, and so on.

It is true that some gifted athletes make out all right, but what happens to the thousands of young unathletic African Americans and poor children whose only heroes are sports stars? How many brilliant doctors, lawyers, teachers, poets, and artists have been lost because intelligent but uncoordinated youth were led to believe that their only chance for getting ahead was to develop a thirty-foot jump shot, throw a 90-mile-per-hour fastball, or run the hundred meter in 9.3?

This largely futile pursuit of sports stardom is of serious consequence, especially in the African

American community. Foremost, they spend their time learning skills that are worthless in the job market. Thus, their belief in the "sports as a way up" myth causes them to spend their energies and talents on athletic skills rather than on pursuing occupations that would help them meet their political and material needs. In short, because of belief in the sports myth, they remain dependent on whites and white institutions.[23]

The conventional rhetoric that sports are an avenue of upward social mobility is accompanied with assertions about how sport plays a progressive role for African Americans. The success of African Americans in the highly visible sports gives white America a false sense of black progress and interracial harmony. But the social progress of African Americans in general has little relationship to their achievements on North America's playing fields. As sports studies scholar John Hoberman notes:

> The illusory sense of racial harmony on countless playing fields across America masks the true depth of the racial conflict that survives in one and the same society. In this sense, the material gains of a Michael Jordan or a Tiger Woods impede the process of social change. For every black Superstar, there are thousands of blacks behind bars.[24]

Hoberman also contends that the numerical superiority of African Americans in several of the most popular sports, coupled with their disproportionate underrepresentation in other professions, reinforces the racist ideology that African Americans are physically superior to whites but are inferior to them intellectually. In short, sport harms African Americans by serving up imagery and metaphors that reinforce racism and the racial divisions that continue to plague North American society.

We are not suggesting that talented African American athletes shouldn't seek a career in professional sport. Professional sport is a legitimate career with the potential for exceptional monetary rewards. What is harmful, to reiterate, is that the odds of success are so slim—rendering extraordinary, sustained effort futile and misguided for the vast majority. If this effort were directed at areas having better odds of success, then upward mobility would occur for many more.

Myth: Women Now Have Sport as a Vehicle for Upward Mobility Because of New Opportunities

Since the passage of Title IX in 1972 (see Chapter 14), sports participation by women in high school and college has increased dramatically. In 1971, for example, there were 294,000 high school girls' sport participants; in 2011 there were some 3.2 million. The number of NCAA women's teams has increased each year since 1984, and women now receive about 45 percent of the money allotted to athletic scholarship (still less than half, but a considerable improvement). This has allowed many women to attend college who otherwise could not have afforded it. That is positive because of the indirect educational benefits accruing from athletic ability.

Upward mobility through sport is another matter for women. Women have fewer opportunities than men in professional team sports. But a few women in individual professional sports do well financially—Serena and Venus Williams in tennis, Paula Creamer in golf, Danica Patrick in automobile racing, and a relative handful of women in other sports. Ironically, the sports with the greatest monetary rewards for women are those associated with the middle and upper classes. These sports are expensive, and they require considerable individual coaching as well as access to private facilities. In short, sport offers poor women very limited opportunities for upward mobility.

Opportunities in sport apart from the athlete role (trainers, scouts, referees, sports journalists, and coaches) are more limited for women than for men. Ironically, with the passage of Title IX, which increased the participation of girls and women so dramatically, there has been a decline in the proportion of women as coaches and athletic administrators. We will have more to say about women in sport in Chapter 14.

Myth: A Professional Sports Career Provides Lifelong Security

Even when a professional sport career is attained, the probabilities of fame and fortune are limited. The average length of a career in professional sport is short—three to five years in the popular teams sports. The pay for professional athletes may be relatively high, but their employment does not last very long. Professional athletes leave sport, on average, when they are in their late twenties or early thirties, at a time when their nonathlete peers have begun to establish themselves in occupations leading toward retirement in thirty years or so. Of course, some pro athletes make an income from salaries and endorsements that, if invested wisely, provides financial security for life. But many have not planned for the future beyond sports, or do not invest wisely, and wind up in financial trouble.

Some professional athletes do plan ahead, preparing themselves for other careers in sport (coaching, scouting, reporting, administering) or for a nonsport occupation. Others do not prepare themselves for this abrupt change. Exiting the athlete role is difficult for many because they *lose* (1) what they have focused on for most of their lives, (2) the primary source of their personal identity, (3) their physical prowess, (4) adulation bordering on worship from others, (5) the money and perquisite fame, (6) the camaraderie with teammates, (7) the intense "highs" of competition, and (8) status (most ex-athletes are downwardly mobile upon retirement from sport).[25]

Ex-professional athletes frequently do not know what to do with their remaining working years. Consequently, many of them have serious personal, social, and economic troubles. Most of us can think of media accounts of ex-professional athletes in trouble over drug addiction, domestic violence, criminal activity, and so forth. Studies of former pro athletes have found that emotional difficulties, divorce, and financial strain were common problems for retired professional athletes.[26]

For most former pro athletes, entry into the "real world" is a step down. Big-time pro athletes are pampered like royalty. They fly first class while hired hands pay the bills and tote the luggage. High-powered executives and heads of state fawn over them. "You begin to feel like Louis XIV," said a former pro athlete. He continued, "Step off the pedestal and everything changes. It's like being dipped into hell."

There is some potential for a sports-related career after one's playing days are over: coaching,

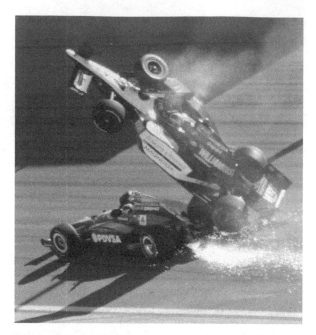

Dan Wheldon goes airborne during a wreck that involved fifteen cars in the IndyCar Series' Las Vegas Indy 300 auto race at Las Vegas Motor Speedway in 2011. Wheldon died following the crash. (AP Photo/ Las Vegas Review-Journal, Jessica Ebelhar)

managing, scouting, sportscasting, public relations, and administration are all possibilities for the former athlete, but the opportunities are severely limited, especially if the athlete is a minority group member (see Chapter 13) or a woman.

A major theme of this chapter is that sport contributes to the ideology that legitimizes social inequalities and promotes the myth that all it takes to succeed is extraordinary effort. In another publication one of us has made this point forcefully. We think it bears repeating here:

> The overall effect of the few athletes who do become professional athletes reproduces the belief system among the general public that the American social class system is more open to social mobility than it really is. Because the few rags-to-riches athletes are made so visible, the social mobility theme is maintained. This reflects the opportunity structure of society in general—the success of a few reproduces the belief in social mobility among the many.[27]

SUMMARY

Two themes dominate this chapter. The first theme is that sport, like the larger society, is stratified. Socioeconomic status is related to the types of sports one participates in and watches. The lower one's status, the more one is inclined toward contact sports and such pseudosports as professional wrestling. The socioeconomic strata are segregated in sport not only by preferences but also by such barriers as entrance requirements and prohibitive costs.

The second theme is that sports participation has limited potential as a social mobility escalator. There is evidence that being a successful athlete enhances self-confidence and the probability of attending college. Thus, social mobility is accomplished through sport indirectly because of the increased employment potential from educational attainment. Social mobility through sport is limited, however, by failure to graduate and the very low number of positions in professional sport. It is limited, even almost nonexistent, for women. Even for those who attain major league status, the probabilities of fame and fortune are small because of the relatively short careers and injuries.

The myth that sport is a mobility escalator is especially perilous for minority youth. Youngsters from poor or near-poor family backgrounds who devote their lives to the pursuit of athletic stardom are, except for the fortunate few, doomed to failure in the real world, where sports skills are essentially irrelevant to occupational placement and advancement.

Another negative consequence is more subtle but is very important. Sport contributes to the ideology that legitimizes social inequalities and promotes the myth that all it takes to succeed is extraordinary effort.

WEB RESOURCES

www.forbes.com
Forbes magazine provides lists each year of the richest entertainers (including athletes), the richest Americans, and the richest people worldwide.

www.census.gov/hhes/www/poverty/poverty.html
The Census Bureau reports poverty data from several major household surveys and programs. This website is a good place to start if one is interested in poverty in the U.S.

www.inequality.org
This website provides general information on various dimensions of inequality in the United States.

www.bus.ucf.edu/sportbusiness/
This website is for the Institute for Diversity and Ethics in Sport at the University of Central Florida. Annually it produces a Racial and Gender Report Card that provides the most recent data on the placement of racial/ethnic minorities and women in various sports occupations (coach, administrator, sports information director, etc.).

NOTES

1. For an in-depth discussion of this topic, see Howard L. Nixon II, *Sport in a Changing World* (Boulder, CO: Paradigm Publishers, 2008), ch. 3, "Stratification and Social Class in Sport."
2. Good discussions of this topic can be found in Martin N. Marger, *Social Inequality*, 2nd ed. (New York: McGraw-Hill, 2002), and Harold Kerbo, *Social Stratification and Inequality*, 7th ed. (New York: McGraw-Hill, 2008).
3. Matt Krantz, "'Forbes' Top 400 Richest Americans Look Familiar," *USA Today*, 23 September 2010, p. B3.
4. Drake Bennett. "Commentary: The Inequality Delusion," *Bloomberg.com*, 21 October 2010, http://www.businessweek.com/magazine/content/10_44/b4201008238184.htm.
5. Robert J. Stonebraker, "What's Fair Is Fair," *The Joy of Economics: Making Sense Out of Life* (Rock Hill, SC: Winthrop University, 2009); see also Eric Beauchesne, "Gap Between Rich and Poor Growing: StatsCan," *NationalPost.com*, 1 May 2008, http://www.nationalpost.com/nationalpost/story.html?id=485124.
6. Thorstein Veblen, *The Theory of the Leisure Class* (New York: Cosimo, 2007) (originally published in 1899).
7. Ilona Bray, *Healthy Employees, Healthy Business: Easy, Affordable Ways to Promote Workplace Wellness*, Pap/Cdr edition (Berkeley, CA: NOLO, 2009).
8. Several articles in this book are relevant to the topic of youth sport participation by socioeconomic

status: Michael S. Kimmel and Michael A. Messner, eds., *Men's Lives*, 8th ed. (Boston: Allyn & Bacon, 2009).

9.   Pete Axthelm, *The City Game: Basketball from the Garden to the Playgrounds* (Lincoln, NE: Bison Books, 1999); see also Darcy Frey, *The Last Shot: City Streets, Basketball Dreams* (New York: Mariner Books, 2004).

10.   For two interesting publications about sports fans, see Kevin G. Quinn, *Sports and Their Fans* (Jefferson, NC: McFarland Publishers, 2009), and Irving Rein, Philip Kotler, and Ben Shields, *The Elusive Fan: Reinventing Sports in a Crowded Marketplace* (New York: McGraw-Hill, 2006).

11.   For a fascinating account of professional wrestling, the gaudiest pop-culture spectacle, see Thomas Hackett, *Slaphappy: Pride, Prejudice, and Professional Wrestling* (New York: HarperCollins, 2006).

12.   Catherine Rampell, "Are You Better Off Than Your Parents Were?" *New York Times*, 10 February 2010, http://economix.blogs.nytimes.com/2010/02/10/are-you-better-off-than-your-parents-were; see also Lawrence Mishel, Jared Bernstein, and Sylvia Allegretto, *The State of Working America 2006–2007*, an Economic Policy Institute Book (Ithaca, NY: ILR Press, an imprint of Cornell Press, 2007).

13.   Loïc Wacquant, *Body & Soul: Notebooks of an Apprentice Boxer* (New York: Oxford University Press, 2006), 42.

14.   See, for example, C. Roger Rees and Andrew W. Miracle, "Sport and Education," in *Handbook of Sport Studies*, ed. Jay Coakley and Eric Dunning (London: Sage, 2000), 277–290; see also James P. McHale, Penelope G. Vendon, Loren Bush, Derek Richer, David Shaw, and Brienne Smith, "Patterns of Personal and Social Adjustment Among Sport-Involved and Noninvolved Urban Middle-School Children," *Sociology of Sport Journal* 22, no. 2 (2005): 119–136.

15.   Allen L. Sack and Robert Thiel, "College Football and Social Mobility: A Case Study of Notre Dame Football Players," *Sociology of Education* 52 (January 1979): 60–66.

16.   Daniel J. Henderson, Alexandre Olbrecht, and Solomon W. Polachek, "Do Former Athletes Earn More at Work?," *Journal of Human Resources* 41 (Summer 2006): 558–577.

17.   Devon Carlson and Leslie Scott, "What Is the Status of High School Athletes Eight Years After Their Senior Year?," NCES 2005-303, National Center for Education Statistics, "Statistics in Brief," September 2005.

18.   Clint Newlin, "Estimated Probability of Competing in Athletics Beyond the High School Interscholastic Level," *National Collegiate Athletic Association*, last updated 5 November 2010, http://www.ncaa.org/wps/portal/ncaahome?WCM_GLOBAL_CONTEXT=/ncaa/NCAA/Academics+and+Athletes/Education+and+Research/Probability+of+Competing/Methodology+-+Prob+of+Competing.

19.   Jonathan Abrams, "Student-Athletes Once Again," *New York Times*, 6 October 2009, p. B12; see also Jason Turbow, "Who Has the Brainiest Team in Baseball?" *Wall Street Journal*, 16 June 2009, p. D16.

20.   Ken Davis, "'One-And-Done' Rule About to Hit Colleges Hard," *NBCSports.com*, 23 March 2010, http://nbcsports.msnbc.com/id/36007533/ns/sports-college_basketball.

21.   Stanley Eitzen, *Fair and Foul: Beyond the Myths and Paradoxes of Sport*, 4th ed. (Lanham, MD: Rowman & Littlefield, 2009), ch. 10.

22.   Newlin, "Estimated Probability of Competing in Athletics Beyond the High School Interscholastic Level."

23.   For detailed discussions of these issues, see William C. Rhoden, *Forty Million Dollar Slaves: The Rise, Fall, and Redemption of the Black Athlete* (New York: Three Rivers Press, 2007), and Shaul Powell, *Souled Out? How Blacks Are Winning and Losing in Sports* (Champaign, IL: Human Kinetics, 2008).

24.   John Hoberman, *Darwin's Athletes: How Sport Has Damaged Black America and Preserved the Myth of Race* (Boston: Houghton Mifflin, 1997); also see John Hoberman, "The Price of 'Black Dominance,'" *Society* 37 (March/April 2000): 49–56.

25.   Peter-Danton de Rouffignac, "Life After Sport? Counseling Professional Athletes Facing Retirement," *iStadia.com*, 5 June 2008, http://www.istadia.com/article/peterdanton/110; see also Thomas L. Schwenk, Daniel W. Gorenflo, Richard R. Dopp, and Eric Hipple, "Depression and Pain in Retired Professional Football Players," *Medicine & Science in Sports & Exercise* 39 (April 2007): 599–605.

26.   Ibid.

27.   George H. Sage, *Power and Ideology in American Sport*, 2nd ed. (Champaign, IL: Human Kinetics, 1998), 53.

CHAPTER 13

Racial-Ethnic Minorities and Sport

Nowadays, except for members of white supremacist organizations, few whites in the United States claim to be "racist." Most whites assert they "don't see any color, just people" . . . Most whites believe that if blacks and other minorities would just stop thinking about the past, work hard, and complain less (particularly about racial discrimination), then Americans of all hues could "all get along." But regardless of whites' "sincere fictions," racial considerations shade almost everything in America.
—Eduardo Bonilla-Siva*

Marty Cutler and Jack Johnson in the ring, circa 1914. In 1908 Johnson became the first African American world heavyweight champion. (Library of Congress)

*Eduardo Bonilla-Siva, *Racism Without Racists*, 4th ed. (Lanham, MD: Rowman & Littlefield, 2010), 1.

Racial minorities in the United States continue to face systematic and pervasive discrimination against them. Although most Americans agree with this sociological fact, they also tend to believe that sport is an oasis free of racial problems and tensions. After all, the argument goes, sports are competitive; fans, coaches, and players want to win; clearly, the color of the players involved is not a factor, only their performance. A further argument is that the proportion of African Americans in the major team sports, which far exceeds their proportion in the U.S. population, indicates an absence of racism. The facts, however, lead to a very different conclusion. Rather than being free from racism, sport as a microcosm of the larger society reflects many of the same racial problems as society.

In this chapter we will document through various forms of evidence that prejudice and discrimination based on race and ethnicity are prevalent in sport. In doing so, we hope to alert readers to this continuing societal problem and to challenge the popular belief that sport is a meritocracy in which skin color is disregarded.

RACIAL-ETHNIC MINORITIES: SOCIAL THEORIES AND RELEVANT CONCEPTS

Social Theories and Race and Minorities

The topics of prejudice and discrimination in connection with race and minorities are found in the social theories we have described in this volume. The functionalist perspective emphasizes that personal and social practices and values must contribute to social order and harmonious societal stability, so the role of racial and ethnic minorities, like other constituents of a society, is to assimilate and integrate socially, economically, and culturally into the general social system. Starting in schools, workplaces, churches, and political activities, the minority racial and ethnic factions must acquire the language, customs, and aspirations for success in the dominant social order and lose, or give up, much of their own culture, mannerisms, customs, rituals, values, and so on.

Critical race theory (CRT) was identified in Chapter 1 as one of the conflict/cultural social theories. It is a theoretical perspective whose premise is that racism is thoroughly rooted in the social fabric of North American society (as well as in other societies) and that it "privileges whiteness as it disadvantages others because of their 'blackness.'"[1] CRT theorists emphasize the socially constructed nature of race and consider it to be based on inherently racist social assumptions. Therefore, they contend that society-wide actions are needed to change these endemic cultural attitudes and values. Analyses of racial inequity as the social construction of race and discrimination are present in the scholarship of CRT theorists.

A variation, called the intersection perspective, claims that the effects of race and gender are interlinked unto themselves as well as interlinked with the effects of social class. Thus, class conflict is an integral part of race and gender differences in society.

Relevant Concepts About Race

Race is a social category regarded as distinct because the members supposedly share some genetically transmitted traits.[2] The races, however, are socially constructed categories. People have arbitrarily placed others into racial categories based on their physical attributes (most notably skin color). But these differences are really minor attributes and can vary greatly within each category. Moreover, the categories used to divide people into races are not fixed; they vary from society to society.

Historically, in the United States the laws defining who is black, for example, have varied from state to state. Tennessee law once defined as black anyone who had at least one great-grandparent who was black. Other southern states defined as black any person who had black ancestry (the "one drop of black blood" rule). By either of these laws Tiger Woods would be black, because he is one-fourth African American, one-fourth Thai, one-fourth Chinese, one-eighth Native American, and one-eighth white European. In Brazil he would be considered white; in the U.S. media he is described as black.

Social scientists reject race as a valid way to define human groups. The accepted view in the scientific community is that races are a social invention. They do not exist biologically. Scientific examination of the human genome finds no genetic differences among the so-called races. Fossil and deoxyribonucleic acid (DNA) evidence show that humans are all one race, evolved in the last 100,000 years from the same small number of tribes that migrated out of Africa and colonized the world. Although there is no such thing as biological race, races are real insofar as they are *socially defined*. In other words, races are real because people believe they are real. Worldwide, and certainly within the United States, race divides people between "us" and "them."[3]

Ethnicity, unlike race, refers to the cultural heritage of a group rather than biology. An ethnic group is a category of people who share a common culture (language or dialect, religion, customs, and history). Examples of ethnic groups in the United States are Italian Americans, Arab Americans, Greek Americans, Irish Americans, and Mexican Americans.

In North America, race and ethnicity both serve to mark groups as different and typically as "others." Groups labeled "races" by the larger society are bound together by their common social and economic conditions. As a result, they develop distinctive cultural (ethnic) characteristics. Thus, we often refer to them as *racial-ethnic groups* (or racially defined ethnic groups). The term *racial-ethnic group* refers to groups that are socially subordinated and culturally distinct in society. It is meant to include (1) the systematic discrimination of socially constructed racial groups and (2) their distinctive cultural arrangements. The categories *African American*, *Latino*, *Asian American*, *Native American*, *First Nations*, and *Indigenous Peoples of America* have been constructed as both racially and culturally distinct.

Different racial and ethnic groups are unequal in power, resources, and prestige. Why are some groups dominant and others subordinate? The basic reason is power—power derived from technology, weapons, property, or economic resources. Those holding superior power in a society—the *majority group*—establish a system of inequality by dominating less powerful groups. A *minority group* is any distinct group in society that shares common group characteristics and is forced to occupy low status in society because of discrimination. A group may be a minority on some characteristics such as race, ethnicity, sexual preference, disability, or age. Crucially, the distinction between a majority and a minority is not numerical superiority but power—with the minority having less power, and therefore low status, relative to other groups in society.

The key to understanding the personal and social issues and problems arising about race and other minorities is that they have structural foundations, which, in turn, debunk conventional misperceptions about race and minority relations. Many North Americans believe that discrimination has disappeared and that African Americans are no longer disadvantaged. But as Eduardo Bonilla-Silva, a prominent scholar of race and ethnicity, contends: "[R]egardless of whites' 'sincere fictions' [meaning unconsciously misrecognizing the reality of the situation or condition—in this case, brutal race relations], racial considerations shade almost everything in America. African Americans and dark-skinned racial minorities lag well behind whites in virtually every area of social life."[4] For example:

- The median family income for African American families was only 59 percent of the median white family income in 2011. The ratio for Latinos was 50 percent.
- The poverty rate in 2011 for whites was 12.3 percent, Latinos 25.3 percent, and African Americans 25.8 percent.
- In 2011, 15.8 percent of whites were not covered by health insurance; the percentages for African Americans and Latinos were 21 and 32.4, respectively. Furthermore, the gap between whites and nonwhites in health insurance coverage is increasing.[5]
- With each step up the ladder of academic achievement, the gap in lifetime income between African Americans and whites increases. Over a work life, African American high school graduates earn $300,000 less, African American college graduates earn $500,000 less, and African Americans with advanced degrees earn $600,000 less than comparably educated whites.[6]
- At every level of educational achievement, African Americans and Latinos have higher rates of unemployment than whites.[7]
- In 2009, there were 5,082 African American men and women in prison for every 100,000 African American residents in the United States, and there were 1,964 Latino prisoners for every 100,000 Latino residents. In sharp contrast, only 799 whites per 100,000 were in prison during that year.[8]

Bonilla-Silva concludes: "Whites have developed powerful explanations—which have ultimately become justifications—for contemporary racial inequality that exculpates them from any responsibility for the status of people of color. These explanations emanate from a new racial ideology that I label *color-blind racism*."[9]

These differences between the races/ethnic groups are not the result of deliberate decisions by racial/ethnic minorities. Instead, the problems lie in social institutions—the common way things are done, such as the way schools are financed by local taxes, using class-based testing to place children in tracks, bank lending practices, "racial profiling" by the police, bias in the criminal justice system, the eligibility requirements for jobs, the informal requirements for job promotion, and the seemingly fair practice of "last hired, first fired"—all of which prevent racial and ethnic "others" from achieving economic and social parity with the dominant whites. This pattern of negative treatment and oppression by society's institutions is called *institutional racism*. This form of discrimination can occur without prejudice or malice toward minorities.

In their well-known text about diversity in society, sociologists Margaret Anderson and Howard Taylor put it this way:

Consider this: Even if every White person in the country lost all of his or her prejudices, and even if he or she stopped engaging in individual acts of discrimination, institutional racism would still persist for some time. Over the years, it has become so much a part of [fundamental social] institutions (hence, the term *institutional racism*) that discrimination can occur even when no single person is causing it. Existing at the level of social structure rather than at the level of individual attitude or behavior, it is "external" to the individual personality.[10]

This chapter focuses on institutional racism in sport and is divided into several parts: (1) sports participation by the various racial-ethnic groups, (2) explanations for the dominance of African Americans in many sports, and (3) discrimination against minority group members in sport. Although the discussion refers to a variety of minorities, a disproportionate amount focuses on African Americans because they are the most prominent racial minority in North American sport.

As useful background for these topics, we refer the reader to Figure 13.1, which contains demographic data about the population for 1990 and 2000 and projected for 2025 and 2050. Note that (1) in 2025, Latinos will have surpassed African

Figure 13.1   Percentage of the Population by Race and Hispanic Origin: 1990, 2000, 2025, and 2050 (middle-series projections)

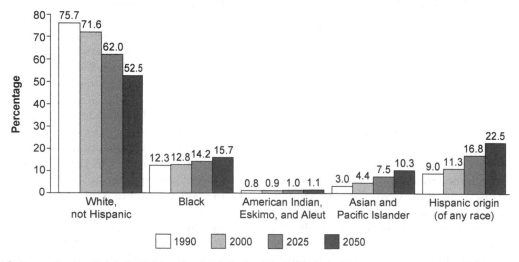

Source: U.S. Census Bureau, Population Division, Population Profile of the United States, http://www.census.gov/population/www/pop-profile/natproj.html.

Americans as the largest racial-ethnic category (in 2003 Latinos actually became the largest racial minority); (2) Latinos will be about one-fourth of the U.S. population in 2050; and (3) minorities will be about one-half of the U.S. population in 2050. These trends have important implications for sports participation and the popularity of particular sports.

SPORTS PARTICIPATION AMONG RACIAL-ETHNIC MINORITIES

Until the last decade, African Americans were the largest minority group throughout the history of the United States. Although they were involved in sports in every era of American history, it has only been in the past sixty years that they, or any ethnic minorities, have become a major part of America's organized sports. However, African Americans continue to be marginalized in some sports and underrepresented in leadership positions.

The History of African American Involvement in U.S. Sport

Africans were brought to North America as slaves throughout the colonial period and into the

Discrimination in sport against African Americans has been pervasive, just as it has been in other social institutions and cultural practices; indeed, in some sports there was complete segregation. Nevertheless, African Americans have played a significant role in the development of modern sport and currently have a dominant presence in several of the most popular sports in North America. (istockphoto)

first half of the nineteenth century. They were concentrated in the southern states because of the plantation system. Despite systematic and pervasive discrimination against African Americans throughout their history in North America, they have played a continuing and significant role in the rise and development of modern sport. The history of African American involvement in sport can be divided roughly into four stages: (1) exclusion before the Civil War, (2) breakthroughs following the Emancipation Proclamation, (3) racial segregation between the two world wars, and (4) racial integration after World War II. This last period is especially interesting and significant from a sociological standpoint, and we will focus on it during this chapter.

Plantation owners often used black slaves to stage boxing matches, and they also used them as jockeys in horse races. Occasionally in boxing, when a slave boxer won an important bout and won his owner a lot of money, he might be set free. Tom Molineaux, a black slave, was a beneficiary of such an arrangement. In the early nineteenth century, after gaining his freedom, he attained a respected reputation in boxing circles in the northern states and in England.

After the Civil War, African Americans made contributions to the rise of spectator sport as boxers, jockeys, and team players, but they were clearly exceptions. Society and sport remained racially segregated by custom and in some places by law (e.g., Jim Crow laws in the South). Between the first Kentucky Derby in 1875 and about 1910, African American jockeys dominated the sport of horse racing. Of the fifteen jockeys in the first Kentucky Derby, fourteen were African Americans, including the winner. By the first decade of the twentieth century, however, horse owners and trainers had succumbed to the segregationist doctrine and no longer employed African American jockeys. African Americans did remain in much lower-status positions around racing, exercising the horses, grooming the horses, and cleaning out their stalls.

When African Americans were barred from professional baseball, football, and basketball in the late nineteenth and early twentieth centuries, they formed all-black teams and leagues.[11] The Harlem Globetrotters and the famous players of the African

American baseball leagues such as Satchel Paige and Josh Gibson emerged from this segregated situation. When Jackie Robinson broke the color barrier, first in 1946 in the minor leagues (the first African American in the International League in fifty-seven years) and then in 1947 in the majors, he received much verbal and physical abuse from players and fans who resented an African American playing on an equal level with whites. The great Major League Baseball player Rogers Hornsby uttered the common attitude of the time: "They've been getting along all right playing together and they should stay where they belong in their league."[12]

Although some champions would not fight them, African Americans made early gains in boxing and increased their numbers over the years, even when they were excluded from other professional sports. Perhaps boxing was the exception because it has typically recruited from the most oppressed social groups. Though African Americans were allowed by the boxing establishment to participate continuously during the early 1900s, they were still the objects of discrimination. In 1909, when Jack Johnson won the world heavyweight championship and became the first African American to win this title, it was clear that racism could not prevent African Americans from becoming the best in a sport.

Largely because of Jack Johnson, boxing achieved a major symbolic role in the sporting lives of African Americans. That was sustained during the 1930s, largely due to the popularity of Joe Louis, who in 1937 became the second African American to win the world heavyweight championship. Nevertheless, even Louis was the target of the same kinds of racist verbal abuse that other African American athletes encountered. Consider, for example, the following comment from Paul Gallico, a noted sportswriter of that era, writing about the world champion boxer Joe Louis: "Louis, the magnificent animal. . . . He eats. He sleeps. He fights. . . . He is as tawny as an animal. . . . He lives like an animal, fights like an animal, has all the cruelty and ferocity of a wild thing."[13]

Throughout the twentieth century African Americans steadily increased their numbers in boxing. But white boxers almost always received more money than African Americans. The white promoters, because of the great-white-hope myth, liked to match whites against blacks in the ring, and African Americans often consented to lose just to obtain a match.

It was not just in boxing that sportswriters referred to African American athletes in racist terms. Consider, for example, the prediction of Jimmy Powers, sports editor of the *New York Daily News*, about Jackie Robinson, the first African American to play Major League Baseball, and who became a Hall-of-Fame major leaguer: "[Jackie] Robinson will not make the grade in major league baseball. He is a thousand-to-one shot at best. The Negro players simply don't have the brains or skills."[14]

African Americans were absent, with a few exceptions, from intercollegiate sports for the first half of the twentieth century. A few Ivy League and other eastern colleges had African American athletes at an early time, but they were exceptions. For the most part, though, prior to World War II African American athletes played at so-called black colleges in black conferences. Although the system was segregated, it did provide many African Americans with the opportunity to play intercollegiate sports.

College sports remained segregated, except for isolated instances, until after World War II. In 1948, for example, only 10 percent of college basketball teams had one or more African Americans on their rosters. The last major conference to integrate was the Southeastern Conference (SEC). The University of Tennessee broke the barrier by signing an African American football player to an athletic scholarship in 1966, and Vanderbilt signed an African American basketball player in that same year. By 1975, African American athletes were common in the SEC and in all the other conferences. The transition from a segregated program to an integrated one is perhaps best illustrated by the University of Alabama: In 1968 there were no African Americans on any of its teams, but its 1975 basketball team had an all–African American starting lineup.

As more and more colleges searched for talented African Americans to bolster their athletic programs, black colleges lost their monopoly on African American athletic talent. The best African American athletes found it advantageous to play at predominantly white schools because of greater visibility, especially on television. This visibility meant, for the best athletes, a better chance to become professional athletes. The result of this trend was a depleted athletic program at black colleges, forcing some to drop their athletic programs and some previously black college conferences to disband.

Since World War II, African Americans have made tremendous strides in professional team sports (except for hockey). From 1940 to 2011 the percentages of African Americans in professional football went from 0 to 68 percent, in professional basketball from 0 to 82 percent, and in baseball from 0 to 9 percent (with another 27 percent Latino in baseball). (See Box 13.1.) Black head coaches in professional football, basketball, and baseball are now common, but still underrepresented. African Americans now officiate games; they are now part of the media reporting the games in newspapers, magazines, and television. Discrimination remains, however, as we will document in the final part of this chapter. Moreover, African American women face dual barriers: racism and sexism.

Latino Involvement in North American Sport

We use the term *Latino* to include men and women whose heritage is traced to Spanish-speaking countries (we use *Latino* even though this usage is sexist because the term is "masculine"; women Latinos are Latinas). This is an inclusive category that shares the Spanish language and Catholicism, but the category is actually quite heterogeneous. For example, among Latinos there are Mexicans, Puerto Ricans, Dominicans, Nicaraguans, Venezuelans, and Cubans, each group with its own cultural heritage. But even within these subdivisions, there are often crucial differences. For instance, Cubans who left Cuba for the United States when Batista ruled Cuba are quite different in social class, occupations, and political behaviors from those who left Cuba later, fleeing Castro.

Latinos in American sport are found most notably in baseball, soccer, and boxing; they are also prominent as fans of these sports. Let's begin with baseball. Latinos have been in the major leagues since 1902, with at least forty-five Latinos, mostly Cubans, playing before Jackie Robinson's

breakthrough for African Americans in 1947. Darker-skinned Latinos whose African ancestry was evident—such as the legendary player Josh Gibson—were barred from major league baseball.

Latinos in major league baseball today constitute 27 percent of all the players (up from 13 percent in 1990), exceeding the 9 percent of African Americans. If the minor leagues are included, Latinos account for 43 percent of all players in organized professional baseball. Almost three out of ten major league players are Latin American; the Dominican Republic leads the way, with roughly one out of seven of all players. (Venezuela has half as many players, followed in order by Puerto Rico, Mexico, Cuba, Colombia, and Nicaragua.)[15]

Many Latino major leaguers were born outside the United States and were discovered by major league scouts as teenagers; they faced language barriers, social isolation, and culture shock when they moved into the Anglo world of U.S. baseball. Although most came to the United States through normal immigration patterns, the players from Cuba have arrived by defecting (they left Cuba illegally but were welcomed in the United States because they provide evidence of the "evils" of the Castro regime).

There are two reasons for the overrepresentation of foreign-born Latinos in MLB. First, baseball is an extremely popular sport in many Latin American countries, where young boys play year-round developing their skills. Many of the poor youth believe that the way out of the barrio is to play baseball in the United States. They are motivated by the success of previous Latino players such as Sammy Sosa, who grew up in poverty and shined shoes and later become a huge star in the major leagues. In 2011 Latinos such as Alex Rodriguez, Albert Pujols, and Carlos Beltran were among the highest-paid athletes in MLB. After the 2011 MLB season, Albert Pujols signed a $254 million ten-year contract with the Los Angeles Angels, which was only the third to break the $200 million barrier, following Alex Rodriguez's two $200-million-plus contracts with the Texas Rangers and the New York Yankees.

The second reason for the expanding Latino presence in baseball is that MLB teams have found a lot of raw but talented athletes whom they can

Box 13.1   *Thinking About Sport:* An Anomaly: The Declining Proportion of African Americans in Baseball

Baseball was rigidly segregated before World War II. Talented African Americans were limited to playing in the Negro Leagues. But in 1947, Branch Rickey, owner of the Brooklyn Dodgers, integrated the major leagues when he played Jackie Robinson against the vehement opposition of his fellow owners. Beginning with Robinson's playing excellence, African Americans soon achieved prominence in baseball and ultimately were accepted by white players and fans.

By 1975, 27.5 percent of all baseball players were African American. Since then, the numbers—in sharp contrast to what has happened in professional basketball and football—have dwindled at a stunning rate. According to Richard Lapchick, in 2011 African Americans were only 9 percent of major league rosters and only 3 percent of players on NCAA Division I baseball teams.

Moreover, it is estimated that African American turnout at major league games is only 8 percent of total attendance. That is below what one might expect, considering that African Americans are about 13 percent of the population and constitute almost half of the population of central cities where more than a third of major league teams are located. For example, only 4.5 percent of those attending games of the Chicago White Sox are African American, in a city with an African American population of 37 percent. The high price of tickets might be a factor, but the cost for Major League Baseball is considerably less than for professional basketball, which African Americans attend in much greater numbers.

Something is going on to suppress the number of African American players. It is *not* discrimination against players of color, as was the case until Jackie Robinson's breakthrough. In 2011, 38.3 percent of the players in MLB were people of color. What has occurred, of course, is the major influx into baseball of Latino players, who have replaced African Americans as the dominating force in baseball. Teams are devoting much more in resources to find and recruit Latino players because those from Latin American countries are much cheaper to sign. Also, baseball teams have established baseball academies in Latin America to locate talent and hone baseball skills. They have not established similar academies in inner cities where African Americans are located.

Another possible reason for the decline of African Americans in Major League Baseball is that the inner cities do not have the space for baseball fields, a luxury found in abundance in the white suburbs. While this does not explain the large proportion of African Americans playing football, it does explain the African American interest in basketball. Clearly basketball is more accessible than baseball to urban youth.

continues

---

sign much more cheaply than U.S.-born athletes. All thirty major league teams scout talent in Latin America (referred to by owners as "the Republic of Baseball"), and many teams have elaborate multimillion-dollar baseball academies there.[16]

Over 90–95 percent of Latino baseball players who sign professional baseball contracts never reach the major leagues. The ones who make it to the United States but fail to make a team tend to stay in the country as undocumented immigrants, working for low wages rather than returning home as "failures." These castoffs represent the other side of the Latino professional baseball hopeful, the rule rather than the exception in the high-stakes recruitment of ballplayers from Latin America and the Caribbean.

There are two major sports in Latin America— baseball and soccer. Major League Soccer (MLS) teams include a number of foreign players, most from Latin America. Unlike other professional team sports, in soccer the players sign a contract with the league, which then assigns players to a franchise. Not surprisingly, the Latino players are assigned to franchises in cities with large Latino populations. As a result, 80 percent of the fans in heavily Latino Los Angeles are Latinos. MLS games are televised on Univision, the nation's largest Spanish-language television company. With the Latino population expected to triple to around 100 million by 2050, the popularity of MLS should grow just as rapidly. See Box 13.2, which describes the ethnic differences between the two professional soccer (futbol) teams in Los Angeles.

Boxers have always typically come from poor or near-poor family backgrounds. Poor racial minorities with little hope for upward mobility other than

Box 13.1 Continued

Football and especially basketball are indeed more appealing to African American youth. When baseball was becoming integrated, there were great African American players for African American youth to emulate, such as Jackie Robinson, John Roseboro, Bob Gibson, Willie Mays, and Hank Aaron. Two of the best young MLB African American players—Tony Gwynn, Jr., and Eric Young, Jr.—are sons of excellent MLB players from an earlier era. Young African American athletes today are looking elsewhere for sports to follow. About the time African American participation began to decline, basketball players became the sports idols of youth—most notably Michael Jordan and LeBron James.

According to some baseball analysts, young African Americans began abandoning baseball in large numbers in the 1980s precisely when flashier African American athletes were rising to mega-stardom in football and basketball. Michael Jordan, with his high-flying dunks and widely popular line of shoes, epitomized the intoxicating blend of money, talent, power, and fame that kids wanted to copy.

Finally, the route to athletic stardom is longer for baseball than for either football or basketball. For aspiring baseball players there are two routes to the major leagues. One is to play in college. But baseball is a minor sport in most schools, so there are fewer scholarships (many are partial) than are available for football and basketball players. The other route is to play in the minor leagues for several years. In either case, the rewards are few. In football and basketball, in contrast, there are full scholarships. The truly gifted can become superstars in the professional ranks at age twenty or so, an extremely rare feat in baseball.

So, it appears that discrimination does not explain the relative paucity of African Americans in Major League Baseball. While there are some structural barriers to African American participation, young African American athletes seem to be choosing basketball and football over baseball. To change this, MLB has established its Reviving Baseball in Inner Cities program and urban youth academies. But many years will likely pass before it is known whether those efforts are paying off.

Sources: Richard E. Lapchick, *2011 Racial and Gender Report Card: Major League Baseball* (Orlando: DeVos Management Program, University of Central Florida, 2011); Whitney Snyder, "African American MLB Players Drop to Nine Percent of Total," *The Huffington Post*, 29 April 2010, http://www.huffingtonpost.com/2010/04/29/black-mlb-players-drop-to_n_556899.html; and Alden Gonzalez, "MLB Wants African-American Presence to Grow," *MLB.com.* 21 December 2010, http://mlb.mlb.com/news/article.jsp?ymd=20101221&content_id=16355704&vkey=civilrights2011.

through sport are likely candidates to become boxers. Thus, African Americans and Latinos are heavily overrepresented among boxers and spectators of boxing. A few boxers (e.g., Oscar DeLaHoya) do extraordinarily well financially. Most, however, do not. Many are exploited by unscrupulous promoters. For example, promising U.S. boxers need to build a history of wins to become known and command higher purses. Many promoters bring overmatched boxers from Mexico (the most important supplier of boxing opponents to the United States) to lose to their boxers. The unknown Mexican boxers are paid $100 for each three-minute round. This is more than they can make in Mexico as boxers or laborers, so they risk injury for the money and the hope of making it.

Domestically, young male Latinos tend to participate most frequently in soccer, football, and wrestling. This has consequences in areas where the population is shifting from predominantly Anglo to Latino. For example, the 2007 population in Seward County, Kansas, was 51 percent Latino (up from 42 percent in 2000). The largest school district in that county is 67 percent Latino. As a result, "the high school soccer team is as popular as—sometimes more than—its football team."[17]

High school–age Latinas are underrepresented in sports. Nationally, about 36 percent of Latina sophomores play interscholastic sports, compared to 42 percent of non-Latinas. Many Latinas in the United States are first- or second-generation immigrants, bringing with them the traditional cultural expectations that girls are to do household tasks (tasks their brothers are not expected to do). Latinas who do participate in interscholastic sports (most commonly third-generation) participate mainly in soccer, track, and softball.

Box 13.2 *Thinking About Sport:* In L.A., It's Soccer vs. Futbol

The arrival of David Beckham to the Los Angeles Galaxy Major League Soccer team in 2007, along with the team's budding rivalry with Chivas (Club Deportivo Chivas USA), made the sport less foreign to Los Angeles fans by accentuating the Galaxy's Anglo appeal. Seemingly Beckham's mission was to raise the profile of American soccer, but another aim of those who brought him to Los Angeles may have been to "de-ethnicize" the sport in Los Angeles. The Galaxy had positioned themselves as the non-Latino team in town, whose game days are considered "mainstream."

This has not always been the case. The Galaxy's early days, when the crowds were less dominated by soccer moms and kids, were solidly Latino. The Galaxy imported some of Mexico's most famous veterans to pack the stands—players such as Jorge Campos, Carlow Hermosillo, and Luis Hernandez, who were far bigger attractions for Mexican immigrants than Beckham will ever be.

However, the Galaxy's Latino flavor began to change when Mexico's famous Chivas de Guadalajara club established its own Chivas franchise in Los Angeles in 2004. This was the equivalent of the Los Angeles Dodgers creating a franchise in Mexico.

Chivas marketed itself as "the" Mexican soccer team in town, with its first-season slogan "*Adios Soccer, El Futbol Esta Aqui*" (Goodbye, Soccer, Futbol Is Here). Chivas Mexican team owner Jorge Vergara told the *Los Angeles Times*: "It's the Latinos versus the gringos, and we're going to win."

Chivas's home games have a far more foreign feel to them than the Galaxy's games. Spanish is the preferred language, and many fans wear jerseys that blend the red-and-white stripes of Chivas with the solid green of Mexico's national team. The Galaxy's roster of twenty-six players has fewer than five Latino players, compared with about a dozen who play for Chivas. The boisterous Chivas fan section is called "Legion 1908," like its counterpart in Guadalajara; the name commemorates the year the Mexican team won its first amateur title.

The teams, of course, dispute that they are engaged in ethnic typecasting, and Chivas officials, for their part, have been less jingoistic in their marketing since their first season. But the ethnic overlay to Los Angeles's soccer rivalry remains indisputable. In 2010, Chivas president Shawn Hunter claimed: "We were natural rivals from day one, and it's only intensified over the years. I think this is American soccer's only true rivalry."

One thing is for sure: Each of America's competing soccer cultures—suburban Anglos and urban Latinos—now has a team in Los Angeles, providing MLS with much-needed rivalry.

Source: Scott French, "Major Talking Points," *ESPNLosAngeles.com*, 1 April 2010, http://sports.espn.go.com/losangeles/news/story?id=5046371; see also Andrés Martinez, "In L.A., It's Soccer *vs.* Futbol," *Los Angeles Times*, 1 September 2007, http://www.latimes.com/news/opinion/la-oe-martinez1sep01,0,4152143,print.story?coll=la-opinion-center.

Asian American Involvement in North American Sport

A few Asians have become stars in North American sports: figure skaters Kristi Yamaguchi and Michelle Kwan, speed skater Apolo Ohno, basketball player Yao Ming, Major League Baseball players Ichiro Suzuki and Daisuke Matsuzaka, and golfer Tiger Woods (whose mother is Thai). More recently, Asians have been making remarkable inroads in women's golf. For example, in 1998 Se Ri Pak was the only South Korean on the Ladies Professional Golf Association (LPGA) tour; by 2001 there were ten South Koreans on the tour, and in 2007 there were forty-five. In the 2010 season, six of the top ten money winners among LPGA golfers were Asian, most typically of Korean heritage.[18]

All of the sports mentioned here are individual sports. This relationship is strengthened when other individual sports are added where Asian Americans excel, such as diving, gymnastics, and the various martial arts (karate, tae kwon do, and judo, sports with Asian origins).

A recent trend is for athletes born in Japan, where baseball is popular, to make it in U.S. Major League Baseball. For example, Daisuke Matsuzaka (his American nickname is "Dice-K") was a superstar in Japan. His rights, owned by the Seibu Lions, were sold at auction to the Boston Red Sox for $51 million. He then signed a six-year, $52 million contract, beginning in 2007. He follows the Japanese superstar Ichiro Suzuki of the Seattle Mariners, who in 2001 won both the American League's "Rookie of the Year" and "Most Valuable Player" awards. Suzuki's location on the West Coast, where there is a significant Asian population (including in nearby Vancouver, British Columbia, where the population is 25 percent Asian), has been important because it has changed the racial-ethnic composition of spectators at Mariners games (at home and away) and has even affected the media (there are Japanese-language broadcasts of Mariners games in Japan).

When considering sports participation of Asian Americans at the high school level, there are differences depending on two diversity dimensions. First, there is immigration history—that is, the length of time that the immigrant group has been in this country. Generally, Chinese, Filipino, and Japanese families have been in the United States for many generations and therefore have been assimilated into the culture of the United States. This is in sharp contrast to many South Asian immigrants (Thai, Vietnamese, Cambodian), who are typically first- or second-generation and are tugged in different directions by their culture of origin and the new culture in which they are immersed.

A second dimension is the social class of recent Asian immigrants. Some were successful in their country and arrived with resources and skills that gave them advantages over other migrants. Others were peasants destined, at least initially, to work at demeaning and low-paying jobs. Clearly, the greater the economic resources of the family, the greater the likelihood that the children will receive sports lessons, attend sports camps, and purchase the requisite equipment. The poorer the family, the greater the probability that the children will have to forgo sports participation and instead work to support the family.[19]

Native North American Involvement in Sport

In 2010 there were about 2.7 million Native Americans (in the continental U.S.) and Native Alaskans (approximately 1 percent of the U.S. population). Aboriginal peoples in Canada comprise the First Nations, Inuit, and Métis (the terms *Indian* and *Eskimo* have fallen out of use in Canada), totaling about 1.2 million aboriginal peoples—less than 4 percent of the national population. The tribes located in North America were and are heterogeneous, with major differences in physical characteristics,

Native American athlete Jim Thorpe, two-time All-American in college football and Olympic gold medal winner in the pentathlon and decathlon, played Major League Baseball and professional football. He is considered by many sport historians to be the greatest athlete of the 20th century. (AP Photos/NFL Photos)

language, and social organization. When Europeans arrived in North America, there were as many as 7 million indigenous people, but disease, warfare, and in some cases genocide reduced the Native American population to less than 250,000 by 1890.

In the first half of the nineteenth century the U.S. government forced Native Americans to leave their homelands and move to areas with marginal land and other resources. The government also developed a reservation system that subordinated Native Americans. By the end of the twentieth century, Native Americans, although better off than they were in the early 1900s, ranked at the bottom on most indicators of well-being (life expectancy, per-capita income, employment, and education).

A few Native Americans have been recognized nationally for their sports prowess. Most notably, a century ago Jim Thorpe was an Olympic hero and a football and baseball star. Then in the 1964 Summer Olympic Games, the relatively unknown Billy Mills won the 10,000 meters. More recently, Notah Begay III, a Navajo, played on the PGA golf tour. But only six Native Americans have ever played in the National Basketball Association. And in 2010 only 0.4 percent of athletic scholarship students in Division I were Native Americans.

There are athletically talented Native American high school athletes, as evidenced by many state basketball championships and cross-country and track titles, but many choose not to attend college, or, if they do, many return home rather than play at the college level. Some of the reasons for this are the racism they experience away from home (see Box 13.3), their lack of economic resources, and not fitting into another social world. Most important, there tends to be a tension between white American and Native American cultures. The first

values the individual above all else; the other, the tribe. For the latter, going away to college means largely forgoing what is good about reservation life: the land, the hunting and fishing, the ceremony, the ties to family, community and history. It also means giving up, at least temporarily, much of what one has learned is the very essence of Native American life.[20] As gold medal Oympian Billy Mills says, "If you go too far into society, there's a fear of losing your Indianness. There's a spiritual factor that comes into play. To become part of white society you give up half your soul."[21]

The Effects of Globalization on Ethnic Diversity in North American Sport

Political boundaries across the globe are becoming increasingly blurred by the ease of communication and transportation and the easing of trade

---

Box 13.3   *Thinking About Sport:* The Negative Images of Native Americans in Certain Sport Names, Logos, and Mascots

Sports teams use symbols (team names, logos, colors, and mascots) to evoke strong emotions of solidarity among the team members and their followers. Most teams use symbols of aggression and ferocity for their athletic teams (birds such as hawks, animals such as tigers, human categories such as pirates, and even otherworldly beings such as devils).

There is a potential dark side to the use of these symbols: The names, mascots, and logos selected for some teams might be derogatory to some groups. Such symbols might dismiss, demean, and trivialize marginalized groups such as African Americans, Native Americans, and women. These symbols then serve to maintain the dominance of the majority and the subordination of groups categorized as "others." That may not be the intent of those using negative symbols, but the symbols diminish these "others" nonetheless and help maintain the racial and gender inequities found in the larger society.

Native Americans are the racial-ethnic group most commonly demeaned by team names. Many professional sports teams have Native American names—for instance, the Atlanta Braves, Cleveland Indians, Washington Redskins, Kansas City Chiefs, Golden State Warriors, and Chicago Blackhawks. And there are high school, college, and university teams known

as Redmen, Seminoles, Hurons, Choctaws, Utes, Fighting Illini, Fighting Sioux, and Savages.

Defenders of Native American names for sports teams argue that their use is a tribute to the indigenous people. In such instances, the argument goes, Native Americans are portrayed as brave, resourceful, and strong. Native American names were chosen for sports teams precisely because they represent these positive traits. Defenders also claim that the use of Native American names and mascots is no different from the use of names and mascots that represent other ethnic groups, such as the Irish or the Vikings, and that people from those heritages accept the use of their names.

But many Native Americans do object to the use of their symbols by athletic teams. Although some names such as Indians, Braves, Warriors, and Chiefs are not manifestly offensive, other names, logos, and mascots project a violent caricature of Native Americans (as scalpers, warriors, savages, and so on).

Teams that use Native American names commonly employ the tomahawk chop, war paint, and mascots who dress as Native Americans and perform replicas of ceremonial dances—all of which trivialize the meaning of Native American rituals.

continues

restrictions among nations. One consequence of this trend toward globalization is the movement of athletes from nation to nation. Some of these migration patterns are seasonal, as athletes move from one climate area to another. North American skiers, for example, might train in the southern hemisphere in places such as South America or New Zealand during its winter (and the northern hemisphere's summer). Many world-class runners go to Colorado, locating in Boulder or Alamosa, so that they can train at high altitude. U.S. universities are eager to give scholarships to foreign-born athletes who can help their programs. This is true for both male and female athletes, most notably in sports such as track and field, basketball, soccer, and volleyball.

Some foreign-born athletes become Canadian or U.S. citizens and compete for the national teams in the Olympics and in the World Cup. The 2011

U.S. men's soccer team had four players eligible to play for the U.S. despite being born or raised outside the country. Professional sports, with the exception of American football, are becoming increasingly stocked with foreign-born athletes. Approximately 25 percent of Major League Soccer's players were born outside the United States. And Major League Baseball has had an enormous influx of players from the Dominican Republic, Cuba, Venezuela, Colombia, Japan, and Korea. About 30 percent of major leaguers are foreign-born, as are almost half of minor league players.

In the National Hockey League, U.S.-based teams are dominated by Canadians, and players from nations such as Sweden, Finland, the Czech Republic, Hungary, and the various countries that once were part of the Soviet Union play on Canadian-based as well as U.S.-based teams. Similarly, the National Basketball Association has players

Box 13.3 Continued

Clyde Bellecourt, national director of the American Indian Movement (AIM), summarizes the complaints:

If you look up the word "redskin" in both the Webster's and Random House dictionaries, you'll find the word is defined as being offensive. Can you imagine if they called the Washington team "Jews" and the team mascot was a rabbi leading them in [the song] *Hava Nagila*, [with] fans in the stands wearing yarmulkes and waving sponge torahs? The word "Indian" isn't offensive. "Brave" isn't offensive, but it's the behavior that accompanies all of this that's offensive. The rubber tomahawks; the chicken-feather headdresses; people wearing war paint and making these ridiculous war whoops with a tomahawk in one hand and a beer in the other. All of these things have significant meaning for us. And the psychological impact it has, especially on our youth, is devastating. (Quoted in *Fair and Foul*, p. 47; see Sources.)

After numerous such protests, many high school and college teams have dropped their racially insulting Native American nicknames (e.g., Stanford, Syracuse, Dartmouth, Marquette, St. John's, Siena, Miami of Ohio, and the University of North Dakota), but no professional sports team has taken a similar step.

A number of prestigious organizations have publicly opposed the negative use of Native American symbols, including the National Congress of American Indians,

the National Education Association, the U.S. Commission on Civil Rights, the American Sociological Association, and the North American Society for the Sociology of Sport. Most significantly, the NCAA ruled in 2005 that it will not conduct championships on the campuses of member institutions where the use of nicknames and mascots representing Native Americans is considered hostile and abusive. Several institutions with Native American symbols have appealed this decision. To date, Illinois, North Dakota, and Indiana University of Pennsylvania have lost their appeals. As a consequence, the University of Illinois announced that Chief Illiniwek will no longer perform at athletic events on the Urbana-Champaign campus, and the university is now eligible to host postseason NCAA championship events.

Sources: C. Richard King, ed., *The Native American Mascot Controversy: A Handbook* (Lanham, MD: Scarecrow Press, 2010); Judy Keen, "Controversial Mascot Ejected," *USA Today*, 7 October 2010, p. 3A; S. L. Price, "Pride of a Nation," *Sports Illustrated*, 19 July 2010, pp. 60–71; D. Stanley Eitzen, *Fair and Foul: Beyond the Myths and Paradoxes of Sport*, 4th ed. (Lanham, MD: Rowman & Littlefield, 2009), 41–58; Laurel R. Davis, "The Problems with Native American Mascots," in *Sport in Contemporary Society*, 8th ed., ed. D. Stanley Eitzen (Boulder, CO: Paradigm Publishers, 2009), 118–125; and D. Stanley Eitzen and Maxine Baca Zinn, "The Dark Side of Sports Symbols," *USA Today: The Magazine of the American Scene* 129 (January 2001): 48–51.

from many other countries, including Germany, the Czech Republic, Russia, Australia, and Serbia. Professional golf and tennis are also truly global sports. The top five golfers on the Ladies Professional Golf Association tour in 2010 included one American, two South Koreans, a Taiwanese, and a Norwegian.[22]

These athletes are a form of global migrant workforce. Many come to North American countries for an education and the opportunities for economic rewards. Both are possible, but so, too, are the sorts of exploitation experienced by foreign-born boxers and baseball players. At a personal level, many of these "migrant workers" find it difficult to adjust to living in a new society, with its language barriers, cultural differences, social isolation, and various forms of racial and ethnic bigotry. Some teams expect their foreign-born athletes to adjust on their own; others provide support to help them learn English and understand the norms and values of their new cultural setting.

AFRICAN AMERICAN DOMINANCE IN SPORT

Since World War II, the number of African Americans in major team sports has increased dramatically. The watershed year in professional sports (when the proportion of African Americans approximated their proportion in the national population) was, for baseball, 1957; for basketball, 1958; and for football, 1960. Since then, however, the rate, except for baseball, has virtually exploded, compared to whites and other races and ethnic groups. As already noted, in 2011 African Americans constituted only 12.5 percent of the general population but they were 82 percent of all NBA players, 69 percent of all WNBA players, 67 percent of all professional football players, and 9 percent of Major League Baseball players.[23]

Over the past half-century an enormous literature has accumulated regarding the proportion of African Americans at the highest levels of North American sports—intercollegiate, professional, and international. During the past five decades African American athletes have achieved a prominence in some sports that, in terms of numbers, far exceeds their percentage of the general population. In other sports they are rarely seen at the upper levels.

This situation has fascinated people in all walks of life, from curious sports fans to social, physical, and biological scientists. Consequently, a variety of speculations and educated (and uneducated) hypotheses, but very little empirical research, have accumulated to explain African American overrepresentation in certain sports and underrepresentation in others. In trying to sort out and provide some organization to this issue, we have come to the conclusion that there are three hypotheses (genetic, cultural, and social) that best explain the disproportionate presence of African Americans in North American team sports. We examine the genetic hypothesis first.

Race-Linked Physical Differences

One explanation for the overrepresentation of African Americans in certain sports is that they are naturally better athletes than whites and that their predominance in sports is therefore attributable to innate physical supremacy. There are some problems with this biological determinism argument. First, there is the issue of who is black. Racial categories in any society, but particularly in the United States, where the amalgamation of Africans, Caucasians, and Native Americans continues, are ill-defined, and of course, socially defined. The point is that racial categories are not fixed, unambiguous, and dichotomous.

Because African Americans, like whites, exhibit a wide range of physical builds and other physiological features, sampling becomes a problem. Does the scientist compare randomly selected whites with randomly selected blacks? More logically, to answer the question of athletic superiority, does the researcher compare a random selection of superior white athletes with superior African American athletes? But how useful would that be? We noted above that African Americans are not a homogeneous physical category. In fact, the recent Human Genome study found that, genetically speaking, there are greater ranges of differences within races than between races.

The word *black* provides little information about anyone or any group. Of the 100,000 genes that determine human makeup, only one to six regulate skin color, so we should assume almost nothing about anyone based on skin color alone. West Africans and East Africans are both black, but in many physical ways they are *more unlike each other* than they are *different from most whites*. When it comes to assumptions about Africans, we should make just one: That the peoples of Africa, short and tall, thick and thin, fast and slow, white and black, represent the fullest and most spectacular variations of humankind to be found anywhere.

Another problem in comparing races on some behavioral pattern is the impossibility of eliminating social variables (social, cultural, and political factors) from consideration. Why, for example, do blacks from Kenya tend to excel in distance running while blacks from Nigeria do not? Is this major difference explained by differences in diet, cultural emphasis, geography, or what? Whatever the explanation, it is not racial difference.

Some scholars argue that although genes are important, they do not work independently of the environment. Genes are influenced by environmental factors that trigger chemical changes. In general they conclude that biology alone cannot explain human differences.[24] Hence, perhaps the issue is not nature versus nurture, but how nature interacts with nurture.

The biological determinist explanation for black athletic superiority also has racist implications. First, the assumption that biological differences exist by race (i.e., blacks are "physically superior" and whites are "mentally superior") reinforces stereotypes of blacks as "naturally" suited for physical activities and, by implication, not suited for activities requiring discipline, intelligence, and judgment. Second, such beliefs reinforce an ideology that seeks to explain and justify the political status quo where blacks are second to whites in power, authority, and resources. Third, this explanation implies that African American athletes do not have to work hard to be successful in sport and that white athletes achieve success due to hard work and intelligence.

The problems with existing empirical studies on racial differences lead us to conclude that they are meaningless on the one hand, that is, they make assumptions that obscure the realities of race as a social rather than biological category, and dangerous, that is, racist, on the other. Moreover, whatever differences are found to exist among the races are explained not by genetic advantages of one social category over another but by cultural and social reasons.

Race-Linked Cultural Differences

Variations in the prominence of black athletes in some sports and not in others have often been explained through cultural differences. The Kalenjin tribe of the Great Rift Valley, in Kenya, represents 2,000 of the earth's population of more than 6 billion, yet they win 40 percent of the top international distance-running honors. With all of their physical advantages for endurance sports, why are Kenyans missing from such endurance events as the Tour de France bicycle competition and other endurance bicycle races, which are dominated by whites? Similarly, if blacks are so good at jumping, as evidenced by their basketball prowess, why don't they dominate the high jump and the pole vault in track? If blacks are superior in physical strength, why don't they excel in the shot put, discus, and weight-lifting events? Why do Russians dominate chess? Why in the music world are there so many superstar Italian tenors? The answer to each of these questions is that categories of people with a similar culture place a greater emphasis on some activities while ignoring others.

African Americans may be overrepresented in some sports because of the uniqueness of the African American subculture in the United States. Some social analysts argue that African American subculture places a positive emphasis on the importance of physical (and verbal) skill and dexterity. Athletic prowess in men is highly valued by both African American women and African American men. The athletically superior male is comparable to the successful hustler or rap singer; he is something of a folk hero. He achieves a level of status and recognition among his peers, whether he is a publicly applauded sports hero or not. There is ample evidence of just such adulation accorded African American basketball players, regardless of age, in the urban playgrounds of the United States.

Cultural differences probably do account for the differences in sport performance between black Africans and African Americans. Here, where physical differences are more or less controlled (although African Americans are more racially mixed), there are great variances. At elite-level track events, for instance, black Africans excel in distance running but not in the sprints and jumping events. African Americans, on the other hand, have dominated the sprints, hurdles, and the long and triple jumps but have had negligible success in the distance events. Clearly, something other than the physiology of race must explain this variance. Cultural differences, along with differences in history and geography, account for much of the sharp contrast.

Unique forms of dance, music, art, and humor have emerged from the African American subculture. Perhaps that subculture also accounts for the interest and ability of African Americans in basketball, where moves, speed, and aggression predominate. The interest of other groups in particular sports is easily explained that way. For example, Japanese Americans, who constitute less than 0.3 percent of the total population, are greatly overrepresented among the top Amateur Athletic Union (AAU) judo competitors. Although African American culture might similarly contribute to black excellence in athletics, especially in certain sports, there is little systematic empirical evidence at present to substantiate the claim.

Social Structure Constraints

Many analysts contend that the most plausible reasons for African American dominance in some sports are found in the structural constraints on African Americans in American society. These constraints can be divided into two types: (1) occupational structure and (2) sports opportunity structure.

African Americans may perceive sport to be one of the few means by which they can succeed in the highly competitive American society because their opportunities for upward mobility in the economic system are limited. A young African American male's primary role models are much more likely to be sports heroes than are a young white male's role models. The determination and motivation devoted by young African American adolescents in the pursuit of a sports career may, therefore, be more intense than those of white adolescents, whose potential career options are broader.

In every society, people are taught to strive for that which is considered the most desirable among potentially achievable goals. With highly rewarding sports opportunities and all the apparent influence, glamour, and so forth that accompany being a successful African American athlete, the talents of African American males are likely disproportionately concentrated toward achievement in this one social domain.

In high-prestige occupational positions outside of sports, African American role models are rare (although Barak Obama may have changed that), and they seldom have high appeal to large numbers of young African Americans. Thus, given the competition among sport organizations for the best athletes, it is reasonable that a high proportion of the extremely gifted African American athletes would be in sports. On the other hand, whites have visible alternative role models and greater access to alternative high-prestige positions, so they can aspire to a broader range of occupational alternatives. Thus, the concentration of highly gifted white athletes in sports is proportionately less than the number of highly gifted African American athletes. Under these conditions, African American athletes dominate sports in terms of excellence of performance, where both groups participate in large numbers.

Occupational limitations for African Americans do not fully explain why they tend to gravitate toward some sports, such as boxing, basketball, football, and track, and why they are underrepresented in others, such as swimming, golf, skiing, tennis, and polo. It has been argued that the reason African Americans tend to be attracted to certain sports lies in what is called the "opportunity structure" of sports. That is, African Americans tend to excel in those sports in which facilities, coaching, and competition are available to them—namely, sports in school and community recreation programs.

African Americans are not prominent in those sports that require the facilities, coaching, and competition usually available only in private clubs. There have been a few excellent African American golfers, for example, but they had to overcome the disadvantages of being self-taught and limited to playing at municipal courses—perhaps with the exception of Tiger Woods. Few African American are competitive skiers for the obvious reasons that most African Americans live far from snow and mountains and that skiing is very expensive.

Social structural reasons help to explain why African Americans outperform whites in certain sports. Basketball provides an excellent example because the style of African American basketball players differs so significantly from that of white players. African American college and professional players learn the game under substantially different conditions than white players. The inner-city basketball courts frequented by African Americans are generally crowded with large numbers competing for valuable playing time on the limited facilities. The norms that prevail under these conditions shape the skills and behaviors of the inner-city players in predictable ways. The games are intensely competitive, with winning teams staying on the court to meet the next challengers. Players must learn to dribble, pass, and shoot in close quarters against a tight person-to-person defense. Players in these circumstances learn to fake and to alter shots in midair. Players are expected to score without much help from teammates. They accept contact as routine. The spectators present at inner-city games often encourage flair and flamboyance.

In contrast, most white college and professional players developed their basketball talents in rural, small-town, and suburban community traveling clubs. Basketball in these settings is characterized by player scarcity rather than by a crowding of players on outdoor courts. White players tend to develop excellent passing and shooting skills mostly in team play rather than in aggressive one-on-one play. The paucity of players leads to a playing environment that encourages the participation of marginal players, makes use of skills developed in team practice, and keeps the pace relatively controlled. Thus, whites develop pure shooting skills and the ability to score when wide open. In sum, the differences in play between whites and blacks

are not found in racial differences but in the social structural conditions under which they develop their basketball skills.

Another social basis for racial differences in participation is that, for economic and social reasons, African Americans have been denied membership in private clubs—and thus, they have been denied access to the best facilities and coaching in sports such as swimming, golf, and tennis. The economic barrier to membership is the result of the discriminatory practices (in types of jobs, salaries, and chances for promotion) that deny most African Americans affluence. The social barriers have occurred because of the discriminatory practices of many private clubs that exclude various racial and ethnic groups. Sports that are often learned and played in private clubs where social interaction is common, and typically includes social relationships between males and females—namely, sports such as golf, tennis, and swimming—exclude or discourage racial and ethnic diversity.

There is still another type of discrimination implied in the sports opportunity structure: The powerful in some sports have denied access to African Americans, even to African Americans with the requisite skills and financial support. Certain golf tournaments (the Masters, for instance) have only begrudgingly admitted African Americans.

Just as golf once allowed African American caddies but not African American golfers, horse racing allowed African Americans as exercise boys but not as jockeys. Automobile racing is another sport in which African Americans have had great difficulty participating. The Indianapolis 500 waited until 1991 for its first African American driver. The explanation for this delay surely lies not in the limitations of African Americans in driving fast or having inferior skills but in the reluctance of corporate sponsors to give financial support to African American drivers.

RACIAL DISCRIMINATION IN SPORT

North American sport—even in the twenty-first century—is not free of racial discrimination. However, the dominant presence of African Americans in the three major team sports appears to belie the existence of racism in sport. Moreover, the prominence and huge salaries of minority superstars such as LeBron James, Alex Rodriguez, and Carmelo Anthony have led many North Americans, black and white, to believe that collegiate and professional sports now provide a broad avenue of upward social mobility for racial-ethnic minorities, thus illustrating, it is often argued, that racial discrimination is a thing of the past.

Not true, according to many commentators—social scientists, journalists, and the athletes themselves. They contend that African American visibility in collegiate and professional sports merely serves to mask the racism that pervades the entire sport establishment. While there is broad acknowledgment that North America's two societies have transformed greatly over the last four decades and that much of the societal discrimination that existed in the 1970s is no longer present, there is a research tradition in the sociology of sport that clearly shows a pattern of racial discrimination in sport that has been persistent. We review this research tradition because it demonstrates the myth perpetrated by promoters and commentators on sports who have made sport sacred by projecting its image as the single institution that is relatively immune from racism.

The following sections focus on two aspects of the research tradition that illustrates a pattern of racial bias in sports: the assignment of playing positions and the rewards and authority structures. The analysis is limited to the major professional team sports (baseball, basketball, and football) in which minorities are found most prominently. In addition to describing and explaining this research tradition, we assess whether any substantial changes have occurred or can be anticipated in the future.

Stacking

One of the best-documented forms of discrimination in both college and professional ranks is popularly known as *stacking*. The term refers to situations in which minority group members are disproportionately found in specific team positions and underrepresented in others. Racial stacking was first empirically verified about forty years ago.

Stacking is not present in college and professional baseball and football the way it once was, but we describe and discuss this phenomenon to illustrate how racism in the general society becomes incorporated into sport—becomes, as it were, an example of the slogan "sport is a mirror of society." Although there has been a revolution in opportunities for African Americans in collegiate and professional sports, as recently as 2005 some form of stacking seemed to exist in Major League Baseball. For example, African Americans were 9 percent of the MLB players that year, but were underrepresented with only 3 percent being pitchers and overrepresented among outfielders with 26 percent.

Research on Stacking

Analysis of the stacking phenomenon was first undertaken by John W. Loy, Jr., and Joseph F. McElvogue, who argued that racial segregation in sports is a function of centrality, that is, spatial location in a team sport unit.[25] To explain positional racial segregation in sport, they combined organizational principles advanced by two social scientists, one of whom argued that (1) the lower the degree of purely social interaction on the job, the lower will be the degree of (racial) discrimination, and (2) to the extent that performance level is relatively independent of skill in interpersonal relations, the degree of (racial) discrimination is lower. The second argument was similar but centered on the formal structure of organizations; it reasoned that, all else being equal, the more central one's spatial location, (1) the greater the likelihood dependent or coordinative tasks will be performed, and (2) the greater the rate of interaction with the occupants of other positions. Also, the performance of dependent tasks is positively related to frequency of interactions.[26]

Combining these propositions, Loy and McElvogue hypothesized that "racial segregation in professional team sports is positively related to centrality."[27] Their analysis of football (in which the central positions are quarterback, center, offensive guard, and linebacker) and baseball (in which the central positions are catcher, pitcher, shortstop, second base, and third base) demonstrated that the central positions were indeed overwhelmingly held by whites and that blacks were overrepresented in the peripheral (noncentral) positions.

Subsequent empirical research over the 1970s and 1980s corroborated this relationship in other sports. For example:

- In women's intercollegiate volleyball, African Americans were overrepresented at the hitter position and whites at setter (the central position) and bumper.[28]
- In Canadian hockey, French Canadians are overrepresented at goalie (the central position), and English Canadians are disproportionately represented in defensive positions.[29]

The situation for the NFL and MLB is found in Table 13.1. Examination of this table reveals that (1) stacking continues over forty years after the Loy and McElvogue research; (2) in football,

Table 13.1 Positional Breakdown by Race/Ethnicity, 2011 (in percentages)

National Football League	White	Black	Other[a]
Offensive positions			
Quarterback	83	16	3
Running back	12	86	2
Wide receiver	15	84	2
Tight end	54	43	2
Offensive tackle	51	48	1
Offensive guard	51	43	7
Center	87	19	7
Defensive positions			
Cornerback	2	98	0
Safety	15	84	3
Linebacker	26	71	4
Defensive end	21	76	3
Defensive tackle	11	82	5

Major League Baseball	White	Black	Latino	Asian
Pitcher	64	5	29	2
Catcher	63	1	36	1
Infielder	54	11	33	2
Outfielder	51	29	18	2

a. Pacific Islander, Latino, or Asian

Source: Richard E. Lapchick, *2011 Racial and Gender Report Card* (Orlando: Institute for Diversity and Ethics in Sport, University of Central Florida, 29 September 2011).

African Americans are found more commonly on defense (where the requisite requirement is "reacting" to the offense) than on offense (which is control-oriented); and (3) whites are found disproportionately at the thinking, leadership, and most central positions, while African Americans are found at those peripheral positions requiring physical attributes (speed, quickness, strength).

Even within the past decade the NFL and MLB exhibited the stacking phenomena, but basketball, which once did, is no longer characterized by racial segregation by position—at either the college or professional level. This appears to be related to the proportion of a minority in a sport. When college and professional basketball were dominated numerically by whites, stacking occurred (with whites disproportionately at the point guard and African Americans overrepresented at the strong forward position). This trend is no longer the case in college men's basketball, where African Americans are now a majority. In professional basketball, where more than 80 percent of the players are African American, stacking has ceased to exist. These patterns substantiate the social-psychological hypothesis that the greater the numerical proportion of a minority in a social organization, the more likely genuine integration will occur.

Explanations for Stacking

The discovery of a social condition, such as stacking, raises the question of why. In the case of stacking, asserting that it is merely a case of racism is inadequate. Several of the social scientists who have reported stacking in their research findings have advanced their interpretations for the stacking phenomenon. Loy and McElvogue, the first investigators to articulate stacking, interpreted it as resting primarily on a position's spatial location in a team unit. However, other scholars have argued that the actual spatial location of a playing position is an incidental factor; for them the crucial variable involved in positional segregation is the degree of *outcome control* or *leadership responsibility* found in each position. In football, for example, quarterbacks have greater team authority and ability to affect the outcome of the game than players who occupy noncentral positions. Thus, it is the leadership and the degree of responsibility for the game's outcome built into the position that account for the paucity of African Americans in central positions.

Insiders in the world of professional football believe that various football positions require specific types of physically—and intellectually—endowed athletes. When these beliefs are combined with the stereotypes of African Americans and whites, African Americans are excluded from certain positions. Normal organizational processes when interlaced with racist conceptions of the world spell out an important consequence—namely, the racial basis of the division of labor in professional football.

This view, then, posits that it is the racial stereotypes of African Americans' natural abilities that lead to the belief that they are more ideally suited to those positions labeled "noncentral." For example, in an early study of stacking in football, a researcher compared the requirements for the central and noncentral positions in football and found that the former require leadership, thinking ability, highly refined techniques, stability under pressure, and responsibility for the outcome of the game. Noncentral positions, on the other hand, require athletes with speed, aggressiveness, "good hands," and "instinct."

Using those positional requirements, the researcher collected data on NFL teams and found evidence for the racial-stereotype explanation for stacking in the small number of African Americans at the most important positions of outcome control in football: quarterback, kicker, and placekick holder. Of course, it is inconceivable that African Americans would lack the ability to play these positions at the professional level. Placekick holders (mostly white backup quarterbacks) must, for example, have good hands, an important quality for pass receivers (who are mostly African Americans). Nine out of ten of the pass receivers in the study were African American, but not one was a placekick holder. Kicking requires a strong leg and the development of accuracy. Are African Americans unable to develop strong legs or to master the necessary techniques?

The conclusion seems inescapable: African Americans are relegated to noncentral positions

that require speed, strength, and quick reactions and are precluded from occupying leadership positions (such as the quarterback and the center, who calls out the blocking assignments) because subtle but widely held stereotypes of African American intellectual and leadership abilities still persist in the sports world.

Another explanation for stacking is that African American youths may segregate themselves into specific sport roles because they wish to emulate African American stars. Contrary to the belief that stacking can be attributed to discriminatory acts by members of the majority group, this interpretation holds that the playing roles to which African American youths aspire are those in which African Americans have previously attained high levels of achievement. The first positions to be occupied by African Americans in professional football were in the offensive and defensive backfield and in the defensive line; therefore, subsequent imitation of their techniques by African American youths has resulted in African Americans being overrepresented in these positions. This explanation may be relevant in explaining the high proportion of Latino baseball players in the positions of second base, third base, and shortstop (see Table 13.2).

Although there is no empirical research confirming that socialization variables contribute to the racial stacking patterns in baseball and football, it seems reasonable to suggest that socialization processes are involved, but in a negative sense. That is, given discrimination in the allocation of playing positions (or at least the belief in its existence), young African American males may consciously avoid those positions for which opportunities are (or are believed to be) low (e.g., catcher, pitcher, quarterback) and will select instead those positions where they are most likely to succeed (e.g., outfielder, running or defensive back).

Consequences of Stacking

Regardless of the reasons for stacking, its effects are far-reaching. First, the stacking of whites in "thinking/leadership" positions and African Americans in "physical" positions reinforces negative stereotypes about African Americans and the ideology of white supremacy. Second, professional football

Table 13.2 Players, Ownership, and Coaching Positions in Professional Sports by Race/Ethnicity, 2011 (in percentages; not 100% in all cases)

League	White	Black	Latino	Asian
National Football League				
Players	30	67	1	2
Ownership	100	0	0	0
Head coaches	75	22	3	0
Asst. coaches	68	31	0	1
National Basketball Association				
Players	17	78	4	1
Ownership	98	2	0	0
Head coaches	67	30	0	3
Asst. coaches	56	42	1	1
Major League Baseball				
Players	61.5	8.5	27	2.1
Ownership	97.5	0	2.5	0
Managers	80	6.7	13.3	0
Coaches	71	12	17	0

Source: Richard E. Lapchick, *2011 Racial and Gender Report Card* (Orlando: Institute for Diversity and Ethics in Sport, University of Central Florida, 2011).

players in those positions requiring speed, quickness, and agility have shorter careers than those in highly skilled positions requiring technique and thinking. The shortened careers that result for African Americans mean lower lifetime earnings and more limited benefits from the players' pension fund, where the amount of payment is based on longevity. Also, as we will see shortly, playing at noncentral positions reduces significantly the chances of a career as a coach or manager.

Leadership, Administration, and Authority

In spite of the spectacular achievements that minority athletes, especially African American athletes, have made in sports during the past twenty-five years, the paucity of minorities in positions of leadership in professional and college sports continues to be a

reality. The reasons proposed for this underrepresentation of racial minorities in leadership positions have centered on two forms of access discrimination. The first is overt discrimination. This is proposed to occur when franchise owners and team executives ignore competent African Americans for coaching and management because of their prejudices or because they fear the negative reaction of fans to African Americans in leadership positions.

The second form of access discrimination is more subtle and applies especially to coaching. Here it is proposed that African Americans are not considered for coaching positions because they did not, during their playing days, play at high interactive positions requiring leadership and decision making. We know that MLB managers, for example, tend to have played as catchers or infielders. African Americans, because of stacking, have tended to play in the outfield and therefore do not possess the requisite infield experience that traditionally has provided access to the position of manager.

The situation is similar in football. Research has shown that the majority of coaches played at the central positions of quarterback, offensive center, guard, or linebacker. African Americans are underrepresented at these positions and are thus almost automatically excluded from head coaching responsibilities. And the same pattern has been found for basketball, in which two-thirds of professional and college head coaches played at guard (the most central position). Once again, since African American athletes in the past were underrepresented at guard, they have been less likely than whites to be selected as coaches when vacancies occur.

Although the percentage of minority players in the NFL and NBA greatly exceeds their percentage of the total population, few opportunities are available to them in coaching and managerial roles. For example, in 2011, only seven of the head coaches in the NFL were African Americans, only ten of the head coaches in the NBA were racial minorities (African American and Asian), and in Major League Baseball, only six of the managers were people of color (two African Americans and four Latinos). All of these leagues have more than thirty teams.

In the same year, there were no racial minorities in head coaching positions in the NHL, and Major League Soccer had two Latino head coaches (12.5 percent of the total). (For a race/ethnicity breakdown of owners, head coaches, and assistant coaches in professional sports, refer again to Table 13.2.) In the women's professional basketball league (the WNBA), there were five African American head coaches (42 percent of the total) and seven African American assistant coaches (38 percent).[30]

During the past decade a number of sports franchise owners and their executives have vowed that hiring of African American coaches and managers was a top priority. Moreover, the National Football League adopted the Rooney Rule in 2002 (named after the owner of the Pittsburgh Steelers, Dan Rooney), which mandated that any team with a head coach opening must interview at least one minority for the job unless it was promoting one of its own assistants. That rule initially made a difference, but it has stalled in the past three years: Whereas the league had only two African American head coaches in 2002, by 2007 there were six, and two of those coached the competing teams in the 2007 Super Bowl. But in 2011 there were still only seven NFL head coaches.

Officiating is another area that is disproportionately white, if the number of players is taken as the reference. For example, in 2011, in the NBA, where 78 percent of the players were African Americans or other minorities, 45 percent of the referee positions were held by African Americans or other minorities. This percentage of African American officials is the highest of any other professional sport league. The NFL, MLB, and NHL employ mostly white game officials. It is important to note that the NBA is the most progressive of the professional sport leagues on various forms of diversity.

Leadership in college sports is also predominantly a white male domain. Intercollegiate football remains behind the NFL in hiring black head coaches. In 2010, of the 582 head coaches of college football teams, only 5.5 percent were racial minorities, yet 41 percent of college football players were racial minorities. College basketball is the most progressive in hiring head coaches, but even there only 15.2 percent of the head coaches

of men's teams and 12.2 percent of women's teams were racial minorities.[31]

While some progress in racial minority hiring has been made in other intercollegiate sports, vacancies still tend to be filled by whites. The *2010 Racial and Gender Report Card: College Sport* reported data on all divisions of NCAA sports. These can be summarized as follows:

- Whites dominated the head coaching ranks on men's teams, holding 89.2 percent, 88.7 percent, and 92.5 percent of all head coaching positions in Divisions I, II, and III, respectively.
- African Americans held 7.2 percent, 5.3 percent, and 4.0 percent of the men's head coaching positions in the three NCAA divisions, respectively.
- Likewise, on the women's teams, whites held 87.7 percent, 88.9 percent, and 91.9 percent of all head coaching positions in Divisions I, II, and III, respectively.
- African Americans held 7.0 percent, 5.1 percent, and 4.4 percent of the women's head coaching positions in the three NCAA divisions, respectively.[32]

African American women who aspire to coaching and management positions are victims of double jeopardy—their race and their gender. These barriers are especially difficult to overcome because African American women have had so few opportunities to participate in high levels of sports and because few persons in the position to hire are willing to take what they consider to be high risks. Here are two examples from Division I college athletics:

- In all Division I women's sports programs, African American women held only 7 percent of the head coaching positions.
- There were no African American women serving as conference commissioners, and fewer than 1 percent of the Division I athletic directors were African American women.[33]

Nearly as dramatic is the dearth of minorities in ownership and administrative roles. Although athletes of color have made significant advances in the past quarter-century, they have not gained comparable access to ownership and decision-making positions. With the exception of professional basketball, the corporate and decision-making structure of professional sports is still about as white as it was before Jackie Robinson entered Major League Baseball in 1947.

The distribution of minorities in the sports world is therefore not unlike that in the larger society. Minorities are admitted to lower-level occupations but virtually excluded from positions of authority and power. Despite some indications of change, discrimination against minorities continues in American team sports.

SUMMARY

Minorities' participation in sports continues to increase. This has led many observers to conclude incorrectly that sports participation is free of racial discrimination. As our analysis has demonstrated, stacking in football and baseball, while occurring less than twenty-five years ago, remains pronounced. African Americans have been disproportionately found in those positions requiring physical rather than cognitive or leadership abilities. Moreover, the data indicate that although the patterns have been substantially altered in collegiate and professional basketball, racial-minority athletes in the two other major team sports have been and continue to be found disproportionately in peripheral positions and relatively absent from central positions.

Sport is not a meritocratic realm where race and ethnicity are ignored. Equality of opportunity is not the rule if race is a variable. Even where there have been significant positive changes, discrimination continues.

WEB RESOURCES

www.ibcsports.com
The website for Inside Black College Sports, providing comprehensive coverage of African Americans participating in intercollegiate sports.

www.bus.ucf.edu/sportbusiness/
The website for the Institute for Diversity and Ethics in Sport, University of Central Florida. This site provides the annual *Racial and Gender Report Card* with current data on race and gender in sport.

www.umich.edu/~ac213/student_projects05/ls/
Information and resources on Latinos in sports.

www.asianamericansports.com/AsianAmerican Sports/Home.html
A website devoted to Asian Americans in sports.

NOTES

1. Kevin Hylton, *"Race" and Sport: Critical Race Theory* (New York: Routledge, 2009), 22.
2. This section on definitions draws on D. Stanley Eitzen and Maxine Baca Zinn, *In Conflict and Order: Understanding Society*, 12th ed. (Boston: Allyn & Bacon, 2009), ch. 11, and Margaret L. Andersen and Howard F. Taylor, *Sociology: Understanding a Diverse Society*, 4th ed. (Belmont, CA: Wadsworth, 2008), ch. 11.
3. Carol C. Mukhopadhyay and Rosemary C. Henze, *How Real Is Race?: A Sourcebook on Race, Culture, and Biology* (Lanham, MD: Rowman & Littlefield Education, 2007).
4. Eduardo Bonilla-Silva, *Racism Without Racists: Color-Blind Racism and the Persistence of Racial Inequality in the United States*, 3rd ed. (Lanham, MD: Rowman & Littlefield, 2010), 1–2.
5. This statistic and the ones cited in the two statements above are from Carmen DeNavas-Walt, Bernadette D. Proctor, and Jessica Smith, U.S. Census Bureau, Current Population Reports, P60-238, *Income, Poverty, and Health Insurance Coverage in the United States: 2009* (Washington, DC: U.S. Government Printing Office, 2010).
6. Marlin Foxworth and Ralph Gordon, *The Black White Divide in America . . . Still: The Inherent Contradiction in Partial Equality* (Berkeley, CA: Regent Press, 2008).
7. Jonathan Teller-Elsberg, Nancy Folbre, and James Heinz, with the Center for Popular Economics, *Field Guide to the U.S. Economy* (New York: The New Press, 2006), 62.
8. "Prison Inmates at Midyear 2009—Statistical Tables," Bureau of Justice Statistics (Washington, DC: U.S. Department of Justice, June 2010).
9. Bonilla-Silva, *Racism Without Racists*, 1–2.

10. Andersen and Taylor, *Sociology*, 280.

11. See Russell T. Wigginton, *The Strange Career of the Black Athlete: African Americans and Sports* (Westport, CT: Praeger Publishers, 2006), and Neil Lanctot, *Negro League Baseball: The Rise and Ruin of a Black Institution* (Philadelphia: University of Pennsylvania Press, 2008).

12. Quoted in Ocania Chalk, *Pioneers of Black Sport* (New York: Dodd, Mead, 1975), 78; see also Richard Lapchick, *100 Pioneers: African-Americans Who Broke Color Barriers in Sport* (Morgantown,WV: Fitness Information Technology, 2008), and Jules Tygiel, *Baseball's Great Experiment: Jackie Robinson and His Legacy*, 25th anniversary ed. (New York: Oxford University Press, 2008).

13. Quoted in Richard Bok, *Joe Louis: The Great Black Hope* (Cambridge, MA: Da Capo Press, 1998), 99; see also Richard Hoffer, "The Great Black Mark," *Sports Illustrated*, 5 July 2010, pp. 14–15.

14. Quoted in Phillip M. Hoose, *Necessities: Racial Barriers in American Sports* (New York: Random House, 1989), xviii; see also Earl Smith, *Race, Sport and the American Dream* (Durham, NC: Carolina Academic Press, 2007).

15. George H. Sage, *Globalizing Sport: How Organizations, Corporations, Media, and Politics Are Changing Sports* (Boulder, CO: Paradigm Publishers, 2010), ch. 3; see also Alan M. Klein, *Growing the Game: The Globalization of Major League Baseball* (New Haven: Yale University Press, 2008).

16. Tony Menendez, "Highest Paid Latinos in MLB," *BleacherReport.com*, 11 March 2010, http://bleacherreport.com/articles/361025-highest-paid-latinos-in-mlb; see also Klein, *Growing the Game*.

17. Brent D. Wisdom, "Hispanic Influx Gives Liberal a New Face," *Wichita Eagle*, 2 September 2007, p. 4A.

18. Official Money List—2010, *LPGA.com*, 9 December 2010, http://www.lpga.com/player_stats.aspx?y=2010&o=1&mid=4&pid=10; see also C. Richard King, *Asian Americans in Sport and Society* (New York: Routledge, 2011).

19. For a discussion of Asian American girls and sports participation, see Sandra L. Hanson, "Hidden Dragons: Asian American Women and Sports," *Journal of Sport and Social Issues* 29 (August 2005): 259–265.

20. Greg Boeck, "The Native American Barrier: Group Culture and Individualism," *USA Today*, 22 February 2007, pp. 1C–2C; see also S. L. Price, "Pride of a Nation," *Sports Illustrated*, 19 July 2010, pp. 60–71.

21. Quoted in Kevin Simpson, "Sporting Dreams Die on the 'Rez,'" in *Sport in Contemporary Society*, 8th ed.,

ed. D. Stanley Eitzen (Boulder, CO: Paradigm Publishers, 2009), 291.

22. See Sage, *Globalizing Sport*, ch. 3; see also Joseph D'Hippolito, "USA Men's Team Tapping into Talent with Foreign Roots," *USA Today*, 19 January 2011, p. 8C.

23. Richard E. Lapchick, *2011 Racial and Gender Report Card* (Orlando: Institute for Diversity and Ethics in Sport, University of Central Florida, 2011).

24. For an argument that gives more primacy to genetics, see Jon Entine, *Taboo: Why Black Athletes Dominate Sports and Why We're Afraid to Talk About It* (New York: Public Affairs, 2000); for contrary views, see Ildus I. Ahmetov and Viktor A. Rogozkin, "Genes, Athlete Status and Training—An Overview," *Medicine and Sport Science* 54 (2009): 43–71, and Ian B. Kerr, "The Myth of Racial Superiority in Sports," *The Hilltop Review* (Spring 2010): 19–29.

25. John W. Loy, Jr., and Joseph F. McElvogue, "Racial Segregation in American Sport," *International Review of Sport Sociology* 5 (1970): 5–24.

26. Hubert M. Blalock, Jr., "Occupational Discrimination: Some Theoretical Propositions," *Social Problems* 9 (Winter 1962): 246; and Oscar Grusky, "The Effects of Formal Structure on Managerial Recruitment: A Study of Baseball Organization," *Sociometry* 26 (September 1963): 345–353.

27. Loy and McElvogue, "Racial Segregation in American Sport."

28. Stanley Eitzen and David Furst, "Racial Bias in Women's Intercollegiate Sports," *Journal of Sport and Social Issues* 13 (Spring 1989): 46–51.

29. Mare Lavoie, "Stacking, Performance Differentials, and Salary Discrimination in Professional Ice Hockey," *Sociology of Sport Journal* 6 (1989): 17–35.

30. Lapchick, *2011 Racial and Gender Report Card*.

31. NCAA Member Institutions' Personnel Report, *Race and Gender Demographics, 2009–10* (Indianapolis, IN: NCAA Publications, February 2011), http://www.ncaapublications.com/productdownloads/2010RaceGenderMember.pdf

32. Richard E. Lapchick, *2010 Racial and Gender Report Card* (Orlando: Institute for Diversity and Ethics in Sport, University of Central Florida, 2010); see also John N. Singer, C. Keith Harrison, and Scott J. Bukstein, "A Critical Race Analysis of the Hiring Process for Head Coaches in NCAA College Football," *Journal of Intercollegiate Sport* 3 (2010): 270–296.

33. NCAA Member Institutions' Personnel Report.

CHAPTER 14

Gender in North American Sport
Continuity and Change

A generation of females has grown up in a post–Title IX era and has benefitted themselves from participating, and they expect the benefits of sport participation to be available for their daughters as well.

—R. Vivian Acosta and Linda Jean Carpenter*

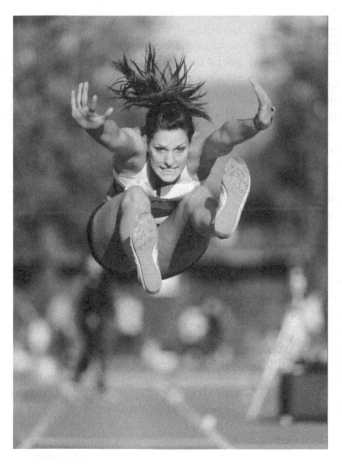

Historically, sport has been a major cultural practice of gender inequality against females. Females have struggled against this prejudice and discrimination and are now admired athletes in many sports. (istockphoto)

*R. Vivian Acosta and Linda Jean Carpenter, "Women in Intercollegiate Sport: A Longitudinal, National Study—Thirty-Three Year Update, 1977–2010" (West Brookfield, MA: Acosta/Carpenter, 2010), 11.

One may question the need for a separate chapter dealing with gender and sport, particularly because we have included gender topics and issues in chapters throughout this book. We believe that in spite of the tremendous social changes that have taken place over the past twenty-five years, sport still promotes and preserves traditional gender differences in many ways. As a consequence, a focused and in-depth consideration needs to be given to gender in a way that has not been possible in the other chapters. In this chapter, the primary focus will be on injustices and inequities females have faced in sports. We realize, however, that gender problems in sports do not just involve females, so we also discuss gender issues related to males in this chapter.

CONSTRUCTING AND REPRODUCING GENDER RELATIONS THROUGH SPORT

American and Canadian societies pride themselves on their concern for the fullest development of each person's human potential, but they have historically been quite insensitive to the social injustices and inequality toward females. A fundamental feature of both societies is the pervasiveness of male privilege. Male/female disparities in wealth, power, and prestige are ubiquitous social phenomena. Men are privileged throughout the occupational structure; they experience greater material rewards, a higher level of deference and esteem, and a more dominant position in the control of both their personal lives and their social activities.[1]

That is only one of the issues that require attention. Another involves the processes of the social construction of gender relations and understanding how meanings about masculinity and femininity serve to promote and sustain gender inequities and injustices, thus creating problems for both men and women. One North American cultural practice that is most influential in the construction of meanings about masculinity and femininity is sport. Historically, it has been a significant cultural practice in constructing and reproducing gender relations.

Social Theories and Gender Relations

According to functionalism, because only females give birth and nurse infants, there is a natural division of labor in which women are more involved in child raising and domestic activities of the home. Natural male-role inclinations are as economic breadwinners and protectors of the family. Thus division of labor in families in preindustrial societies was based on gender. Industrialization made preindustrial gender differentiation less functional, but remnants of that traditional system can still be found today and are viewed by functionalism as contributing to social order, integration, and stability.

Conflict/cultural theorists argue that gender inequality rooted in the male-female power relationship from preindustrial societies is unsuitable for contemporary societies. Domination by males over females has been reproduced and continues because of males' greater control over the major social institutions, especially the family and educational, economic, political, religious, and social resources. Thus, women's subjugation and inequality are prevalent in the social structures and processes of most of human societies today.

Feminist theories began as critiques of patriarchy, stereotyping, discrimination, and oppression of females, and as a commitment to change those conditions. Feminism is grounded in a belief in the social necessity of gender equality and challenges the patriarchal gender ideas that prevail in other social theories.

The Heritage of Gender Inequality in Sport

During childhood, adolescence, and early adulthood, there is a tendency to believe that current social conditions have always existed. There is typically a lack of understanding that current social conditions are historically rooted and have emerged out of quite different conditions in the past. This is certainly the case with gender relations and sport. Young people today see girls playing a variety of youth sports, girls on high school teams winning state championships, women in intercollegiate athletics capturing NCAA national championships, and professional women athletes earning incomes of more than a million dollars a year. Little do they realize that such opportunities and achievements were unheard of only forty years ago. Here is a tip for college-age readers of this book: Ask your grandmothers to tell you what conditions were like for females in sport when they were growing up. We think you will be amazed at what you will hear.

In order to develop an understanding about contemporary gender relations, it is helpful to place social relations between the sexes in historical perspective. For the past 3,000 years Western cultural ideology has been firmly grounded in patriarchy, which is a set of personal, social, and economic relations that enable men to have power over women and the services they provide. Patriarchal ideology defines females as inferior to and dependent on men, and their primary gender-role prescriptions are seen as child-bearers, child-rearers, homemakers, and sex objects.

The traditions of Western civilization have been perpetuated in North America with respect to the status of women. The overemphasis on the historical socialization pattern of preparing women for their adult role as passive helpmates of men—standing on the sidelines of history and cheering men on to their achievements and successes—was persistent. When the framers of the U.S. Declaration of Independence wrote that "all men are created equal" (excluding black and Native American men, of course), that is literally what they meant, and it was not until 144 years later—in 1920, with the passage of the 19th Amendment to the U.S. Constitution—that women were even considered worthy of the right to vote. In the previous year the right to vote was extended to all women in Canada by the Act to Confer the Electoral Franchise upon Women (except in Quebec, which denied women that right until 1940).

As modern sport began to develop in the latter nineteenth century, it served as one of the most powerful cultural forces for reinforcing the ideology of male superiority and dominance. Organized sport created symbols, rituals, and values that preserved patriarchy and women's subordinate status in society. By celebrating the achievements of males through their sporting achievements and marginalizing females into the roles of spectators and cheerleaders, sport reproduced the male claim to privileged status. The overriding societal attitude with respect to sport was that it was for males and not for females.[2]

The combined role of woman and athlete was virtually unthinkable in North America in the nineteenth century. Women who wished to participate in competitive sports and remain "feminine" faced almost certain social isolation and censure. By choosing the physically active life, a woman was repudiating traditional female gender-role expectations. It seemed, therefore, that females would have little role to play in the burgeoning expansion of sport. Notwithstanding the cultural obstacles women had to overcome, their increasing presence and persistent involvement in sport in the late nineteenth and early twentieth centuries actually made a significant contribution to the rise of modern sport.

Social changes were numerous during the latter nineteenth century, as industrialization brought new wealth and more leisure to North Americans. Middle- and upper-class women experienced more freedom than they had ever known. Their interests expanded to activities outside the home, and as organized sport grew, women were often some of the most ardent participants. Croquet, roller-skating, ice-skating, bowling, archery, lawn tennis, golf, and bicycling were a few of the sports that captured the interest and enthusiasm of women during the latter part of the nineteenth century.[3]

One important trend in sport in the latter nineteenth century took place at women's colleges. Several of the best-known women's colleges began including sports as part of their physical education programs. Boating, skating, bowling, horseback riding, swimming, tennis, and golf were all popular on campuses, and they were respectable because participants were protected from public view while they played. When basketball was created as a sport in the 1890s, it quickly became popular at women's colleges. The British game of field hockey was introduced into the United States in the early twentieth century, and it too became immediately popular in the eastern women's colleges.

Throughout the twentieth century, females faced a continuing struggle for equality and justice in sports. This is obvious from the following statement made by two *Sports Illustrated* writers in 1973—just four decades ago—about females still encountering oppression and inequality in the world of sport: "There may be worse (more socially serious) forms of prejudice in the United States, but there is no sharper example of discrimination today than that which operates against girls and women who take part in competitive sports, wish to take part, or might wish to if society did not scorn such endeavors."[4]

This statement makes it quite clear that the sport culture was pretty much the exclusive domain of males. Men typically engaged more often in sports and manifested greater interest in sporting achievements. Sports heroes and superstars were mostly males, and male dominance was notable in the administrative and leadership branches of sports, where men clearly overshadowed women in power and numbers. Female athletes did not suit the ideal of femininity, and those who persisted in sport suffered for it. These same *Sports Illustrated* writers characterized the prevailing view in the 1970s: "Sports may be good for people, but they are considered a lot gooder for male people than for female people."[5]

SOCIAL SOURCES OF GENDER INEQUALITY IN SPORT

The ultimate basis of gender inequality in North American sport is embedded in the sociocultural milieu of society and in the traditions of Western societies that are foundational to the United States and Canada. The historical foundations of the North American gender system and how it has specified behaviors, activities, and values of the sexes were described previously. We showed how the gender system has operated as a mechanism of inequality by ranking women as inferior and unable and by conferring privilege and status to males. In addition to the historical sociocultural influences, more specific socialization agents and agencies tend to reproduce the gender system with

each new generation. We now turn to an examination of some of these influences, emphasizing the role of several social institutions in gender socialization.

Parental Child-Rearing Practices and Gender Construction

Sex is a biological characteristic while gender refers to an ongoing cultural process that socially constructs differences between men and women. Each culture *constructs and teaches its young* the social role expectations for males and females, about what is considered masculine and what is considered feminine. Thus, humans are immersed in a complex network of sex and gender norms throughout life. Almost everything is gendered, and all societies have attitudes, values, beliefs, and expectations based on sex.[6]

The teaching of gender-role ideology comes from a range of social sources, including peers, teachers, ministers, mass media, and so forth, but the earliest and most persistent instruction takes place in the family. Parents are major contributors to the shaping of gender-role ideology by acting differently toward sons and daughters as early as their first exposure to them and throughout the remaining years of their rearing. From infancy there are both marked and subtle differences in the way parents speak to sons and daughters, the way children are dressed, the toys they are given, and the activities in which they are encouraged and permitted to engage. A certain amount of aggression is not only permitted but is encouraged in boys; much less is tolerated in girls. Techniques of control tend to differ also: Praise and withdrawal of love are used more often with girls, physical punishment relatively more often with boys.

Children rapidly learn the difference in parental expectations concerning gender-appropriate behavior. The traditional parental message has been that desirable qualities for males are aggressiveness, independence, and individual achievement striving and that desirable qualities for females are passivity, affiliation, nurturance, and dependence. Studies of the childhood experiences of female and male athletes have found that in a variety of ways, parents, especially fathers, encouraged the sport involvement of their sons more than that of their daughters.[7]

The School and Gender Construction

The school serves to reinforce and extend the gender-role stereotyping that begins in the home. Teachers are in close contact with students throughout the day, day after day, year after year; therefore they are a major influence on children and youth. Teachers mold the traditional gender-role differences both directly and indirectly.

An indirect means by which the school reinforces traditional gender roles is through its own authority structure. While some 82 percent of all elementary school teachers are women, over 44 percent of elementary school principals are men, and about 75 percent of secondary school principals are men, even though some 60 percent of the teachers at this educational level are women. Less than 5 percent of all superintendents are women. Thus, schoolchildren learn the differential status of men and women simply by attending school.

Another mechanism of gender-role reinforcement is sex-segregated, or at least single-sex-dominated, classes. Subjects such as math and science are often viewed as male subjects, and English and fine arts are regarded as female subjects. We realize that educators have made a concerted effort to "de-gender" these courses during the past two decades.

Some textbooks, one of the basic sources of learning in schools, perpetuate gender-role ideology. The kind of history they purvey and the kinds of suggestions they present for adult occupational choices and leisure-time pursuits suggest a negative image of women as unimportant and unable. In studies of the treatment of gender roles in textbooks, investigators have found that women tend to be marginalized in the world of politics, science, and sports, with their future presented as consisting primarily of homemaking, glamour, and service.[8]

Hours of every school day are lived outside the classrooms in hallways, on the playgrounds, and going to and from school. It is during these times that a great deal of interaction takes place between same-sex classmates and between opposite-sex classmates. Much of this time is spent in conversations, informal fun and games, and just plain "horsing around." These interactions between boys and girls turn out to be what some researchers call "power play." By that they mean that through these school-related ritualized interactions gender is socially constructed.[9]

A lot has changed in high school sports in the past thirty years, and we will discuss those changes in more detail later in this chapter. In spite of the greater opportunities for females in interschool sports, these programs are still testimony to the importance of boys and the secondary status of girls. Thus, extracurricular activities, like school athletics, play an important role in the production and reproduction of gender differences. Having said that, this gender differentiation in school sports is not nearly as conspicuous as it once was.

The Mass Media and Gender Construction

As we emphasized in Chapter 11, social contexts and descriptions of women in the mass media—including newspapers, magazines, radio, television, and motion pictures—generally reinforce the gender-role stereotypes. Coverage of women in sport historically tended to reinforce the stereotypes firmly embedded in the cultural heritage regarding women. However, considerable change has taken place in media coverage of women's sports in the past decade.

Despite this significant conversion in media treatment of women in sport, there are still major differences in women's and men's sports coverage. Male sports still dominate sports sections in newspapers, and the content of the vast majority of sport magazines focuses on males. In the leading sports magazine, *Sports Illustrated*, 60–80 percent of the articles in each issue are about male athletes and teams. Between 1997 and 2004 only 29 out of 416 *Sports Illustrated* covers—7 percent—were devoted to women. Even worse, of the 80 issues of *Sports Illustrated* published in 2010, only 3 covers featured females: one showed Serena Williams; another showed four U.S. Vancouver Olympics medal winners, only two of whom were women; and the third showed a female model. This last was the cover of the annual swimsuit issue, which is entirely devoted to women wearing the skimpiest of swimsuits and positioned in soft-porn poses.

Four Minnesota State University researchers examined the covers of *ESPN the Magazine* for gender representation by making a content analysis of the photographic images contained on the covers of 369 issues from 1998 to 2010. Their results revealed that men outnumbered women 14 to 1 on the covers of the issues. When women were featured on the covers, they were more often sexualized through poses and clothing than men.[10]

Television, because of its omnipresence, plays a powerful role in depicting gender relations. Studies extending over twenty years convincingly show the unequal treatment of women's sports on TV. Gender stereotyping and sexist commentary, once rampant on TV sports programs, has become less frequent. However, commentary during a women's sports event will still occasionally focus on the physical attractiveness of the performers, their fashionable attire, their grooming, or their "cute" personality characteristics; commentary on such subjects is rarely part of a men's event. See the "Media Sport and Gender Inequities" section in Chapter 11 for a more detailed account of this topic.

Motion pictures also play a powerful role in keeping women in their place. Movie producers have tended to project two identities for women, as a sex object and wife/mother figure, but seldom as a physically active athlete. An analysis of the 100 top-grossing movies of 2008 by the Annenberg School for Communication and Journalism showed that men had 67 percent of the speaking roles whereas women had about 33 percent. The finding also revealed an overemphasis on beauty, thinness, and sexualization of women at younger and younger ages.

Movies about women in sports have been very rare. But in the past twenty years two films on this subject were not only memorable but commercially successful. The first, *A League of Their Own*, opened in 1992 and is an American comedy-drama that gives a fictionalized account of the real-life All-American Girls Professional Baseball League. The second, a 2004 film titled *Million Dollar Baby*, is about a woman boxer and stars Hilary Swank; it won an Academy Award for Best Picture, and Swank took the Oscar for Best Actress in a Leading Role.

Nicknames, Mascots, and Heroines

One vestige of the past that is gradually disappearing is the trivialization of female sports teams through the nicknames and mascots that are used for high school girls' and college women's teams. Although the nicknames and mascots are chosen by the institutions, it is through the mass media that they are largely communicated to the public. Tigerettes, Rambelles, Teddy Bears, and other "cutesy" mascot names may seem harmless but they have the effect of defining female athletes and females' athletic programs as frivolous and insignificant, even trivial.[11]

Through media accounts of their achievements, athletes become widely known to the public and become role models. Media portrayals of them tend to link their personal lives with their sports achievements; if a socially positive character is created, they become heroes and heroines, especially to children and adolescents. Historically, there have been few feminine counterparts to sport superstars Michael Jordan, Wayne Gretsky, Payton Manning, Pete Sampras, and Derek Jeter. Boys are bombarded with daily accounts of high school, college, and professional athletes, but until the past decade girls rarely read, heard, or saw reports about the feats of outstanding female athletes.

FEMALES SURMOUNT SOCIAL BARRIERS TO PARTICIPATION IN SPORT

Gender inequality directed against females, like prejudice and discrimination of any kind, is insidious and denigrating. For females, it has taken many forms: the perpetuation of myths about the biological and psychological weaknesses of females, unequal opportunity for participation in many activities, and unequal access to the authority and power structure. Each of these forms of gender inequality has been used to discourage women and girls from participating in sports and to deny them equal access to the rewards that sport has to offer.

Negative Myths

A variety of folklore, myths, and slogans traditionally prevalent in North American society supported sport as an exclusively masculine activity and served as barriers to female participation in sport until recently.

Myth: Athletic Participation Masculinizes Females

One of the oldest and most persistent notions about female participation in sport, and a main deterrent, was the idea that vigorous physical activity tended to "masculinize" the physique and behavior of girls and women. For years, women of physical competence were stigmatized as "masculine" by claims that women who engaged in physical activities were not "feminine." This was like a doomsday weapon to discourage female interest and involvement in sport.

From the beginning of modern sport, sport was a male preserve, and images of ideal masculinity for males were culturally constructed through sports. The cultural script was that males validated their masculinity through athletic endeavors. Females had no place there; it could only make them masculine, as it does males. The founder of the modern Olympic Games and an influential leader in sport, Pierre de Coubertin, opposed what he called the "indecency, ugliness and impropriety of women in . . . sports [because] women engaging in strenuous activities were destroying their feminine charm and leading to the downfall and degradation of . . . sport."[12] At another time, de Coubertin drove home the same point: "Would . . . sports practiced by women constitute an edifying sight before crowds assembled for an Olympiad? Such is not [the International Olympic Committee's] idea of the Olympic Games in which we have tried . . . to achieve the solemn and periodic exaltation of male athleticism with internationalism as a base, loyalty as a means, art for its setting, and female applause as its reward."[13]

The impression that physical activity produces masculine body types is undoubtedly due to the fact that some females who become serious athletes do indeed develop muscular and movement characteristics appropriate for performing the skills of a sport. Such muscle development and movement patterns have nothing to do with maleness or femaleness but are merely the most efficient use of the body to accomplish movement tasks.

Nevertheless, the threat of masculinization was sufficiently terrifying to discourage many females from becoming physically active, and those who did become athletes often lived with the fear of becoming "masculine."

Even in the twenty-first century, many female athletes attempt to maintain a "ladylike" appearance in deference to the ideology that sport masculinizes females. They often compensate for the perceived threat to their femininity by wearing feminine artifacts with their athletic attire. By wearing ruffles, pastel colors, or lacy designs and styles, they seem to be saying, "Even though I'm a highly skilled athlete, I'm still feminine." See Box 14.1 for a discussion of this issue.

There is, of course, no evidence to support the notion that vigorous physical activity alters the basic biological constitution of a female, making her more "male." This is not to suggest that no physical or psychological differences exist between female athletes and female nonathletes. Prolonged physical training in a sport alters the female physique, physiological support systems, and psychosocial characteristics just as it does in the male. Actually, these traits may have attracted them to sport in the first place. Sociologist Nancy Theberge studied the sources of pleasure and satisfaction in women ice hockey players and found that many of them were attracted to ice hockey because of the physicality involved in playing it. One of the players told Theberge, "I like the fight for the puck; it's who's going to fight for the puck. . . . That's where the competitiveness comes in, that's where my aggressiveness comes from: this [the puck] is mine and I'm not giving it to you kind of thing. . . . I like a physical game."[14]

There is another social sanction used against active females that is closely linked to the "sport masculinizes females" argument, and that is a charge about female athletes and their sexuality. Two interrelated arguments fuel the supposed connections between sports and lesbianism. One is that there is a profusion of women athletes who are lesbians. The second is that sports participation converts females to lesbianism. Although there is no scientific evidence for the perpetuation of this myth, it has had the effect of producing homophobic (meaning dislike and intolerance of

---

Box 14.1   *Thinking About Sport:* Anyone for Rugby?! Challenging Discourses of Feminine Bodies in American Culture

Women's participation in rugby both challenges and reinforces dominant discourses of sport and sporting bodies. The sport of rugby presents a cultural site, where the shape and size of the female sporting body often contradict dominant ideas of feminine bodies in American culture.

TACKLING NORMATIVE FEMININITY

Rugby provided the women in this study with the opportunity to participate in an aggressive, physically demanding collision sport. For many of them it was the first time they had participated in an organized collision sport. A few of them had tried or considered playing high school football because of the tackling and physicality required in football. But the majority of these women described actively searching for an outlet for their physicality.

Many women in the study discussed how their participation in rugby had changed how they thought and felt about their bodies and their performance. Andrea, one of the smaller players, addressed rugby's impact on the way she feels about her body:

> Definitely I want to be stronger. Since I started playing rugby and lifting weights I want big shoulders. There is some gene in me that says you're not going to have big shoulders because I've been trying for a long time and I haven't gotten them yet. But I want to be stronger and fitter. I don't want to be, you know I used to want to be thin, everybody wants to be skinny, now I don't want to be that, I want to look, I want to be muscular. I want to look like I have muscles. I want to be able to see definition in my arms or my legs. I want that. I don't care if I have a six-pack but I want muscle there. If you can't see it I at least want it to be there anyway. I just want to be strong.

Another player, Natalie, also revealed that playing rugby had changed the poor relationship she had with her body. She wanted to look like a muscular, professional female athlete instead of an emaciated supermodel. This suggests that Natalie had become aware that idealizing a supermodel body was problematic and that desiring an ultra-thin body was not healthy.

Her involvement in rugby significantly changed how she felt about her body.

RESISTING DOMINANT FEMALE BODY IDEALS

While women's rugby bodies are normalized into the disciplinary, docile sporting bodies that they quite unquestionably celebrate, they also enjoy the disciplinary process because it disrupts the gaze supervising the construction of ideal female bodies. Many of these women recognized that by playing rugby they were challenging images of the ideal female body and using their bodies in ways that disturb the boundaries of what is appropriate for women. Shelby very effectively described the pleasure some of the women took in resisting these boundaries:

> I mean that's body on body, women pushing, determination, everything they've ever been told that they can't ever do, they are doing right then. I mean everything, I mean you're not supposed to be tough, you're not supposed to get dirty, you're not supposed to bleed, you're not supposed to whatever, you know don't perspire, what is that? You don't sweat, you glisten, my ass, you know you've got women over there with their ears taped down, and their hair flopping out of their ponytails. I'm sure not everybody thinks about it when they are out there playing but like everything we've been told we can't do, it's like you know what, fuck you, I'm doing it, and it's like, I'm going to kick mud in your face, and I'm going to breathe and I'm going to be dirty and I'm going to love it, and it is the best, to have your body hurt like that, to push it all the way past the end, I mean beyond the end.

This research contributes to answering the call for the recognition of the importance of the body and physicality in women's sport. . . . The women in this study actively worked to construct athletic and powerful bodies that challenge ideals of normative feminine bodies, and they displayed a critical awareness of how their bodies challenge these ideals.

Source: Adapted from Laura Frances Chase, "(Un)Disciplined Bodies: A Foucauldian Analysis of Women's Rugby," *Sociology of Sport Journal* 23 (2006): 229–247.

---

homosexuals) claims about rampant lesbianism among female athletes. Given the widespread homophobic public attitudes that prevail in North American societies, this charge has had ominous consequences for females who might wish to become involved in sports and for those who are involved in sports. It has certainly had a profoundly stigmatizing effect on them.

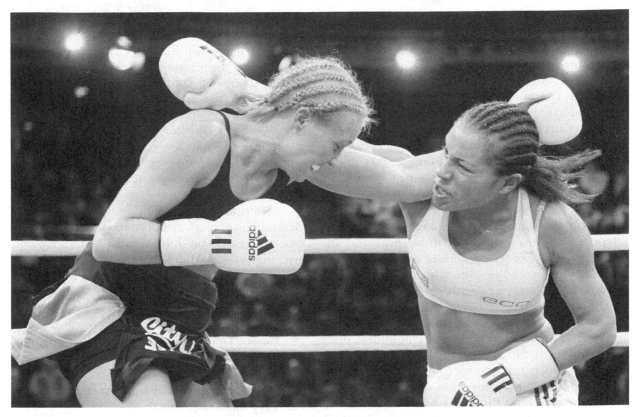

Women boxers during a WBA/WBC female welterweight title fight. Women refuse to be limited to any category of sports. Women's boxing has been added to the 2012 London Olympic Games. (AP Photo/Axel Heimken)

The claims about sport's presumed "masculinizing" and "lesbianizing" of females have been vigorously attacked by a broad spectrum of scholars and scientists who have exposed the ideological foundations of these arguments. They have emphasized that definitions of feminine and masculine behavior are culturally constructed—that they are not natural, biological characteristics at all. Moreover, they emphasize that sexual orientation is irrelevant with regard to sport participation, and there are heterosexual as well as homosexual males and females in sport just as there are in every other sector of social life.

Martina Navratilova, one of the greatest tennis players of all time, was the first well-known female athlete to openly acknowledge she was a lesbian. Since then, a number of other top women athletes have done likewise. In the fall of 2005, WNBA star Sheryl Swoopes publicly announced that she was gay. In a *Sports Illustrated* interview with Swoopes, she

was asked whether the public's reaction was what she expected. Swoopes replied that the support she had gotten had been phenomenal and that on the first five road trips after her announcement there were standing ovations when she was introduced, and not just from gay women or gay men. Swoopes and other women athletes maintain that contemporary women are no longer willing to have traditional definitions of masculine/feminine and sexuality imposed on them, especially when such definitions prevent females from experiencing highly valued social activities.[15]

It is now quite clear that the presumptions that women become masculinized and their sexual orientation is influenced by sports participation have served as social weapons to reinforce cultural traditions of male privilege and female subordination, but they are now being widely rejected. Indeed, some women have completely repudiated the traditional definitions that identify muscles with masculinity and homosexuality, and such sports as bodybuilding, weight lifting, and boxing are growing rapidly among sportswomen. Like male bodybuilders and weight lifters, women bodybuilders and weight lifters are judged pretty much just like men. Furthermore, their sexuality is no more important than is men's.[16]

Of course there are females in sports who are lesbians, just as there are lesbians in every other walk of life. They suffer many of the social troubles that all lesbians live with. These include a sense of isolation, feelings of loneliness, fear of being outed, and, if they do come out, prejudice and discrimination among friends and family. In spite of pervasive homophobia within sport and the wider society, gay females in increasing numbers are deciding to come out and live their sexual orientation openly and with pride in the honesty of their decision.[17]

Gender-role reconceptualization is taking several forms, but in all its variations a prominent place is reserved for the active woman. In the evolving trends in sports and gender roles, girls and women are struggling for identity, and sport has become a significant medium through which females realize meaning in their lives. Sport is one way in which feminist cultural politics are being employed as a form of organized opposition to the domination of men in sport through empowering the bodies of women from diverse backgrounds.

It may be seen, then, that contemporary women refuse to be locked into outmoded role prescriptions and baseless assertions, especially those that limit their physical potential.

Myth: Sports Participation Is Harmful to the Health of Females

From the beginnings of modern sport forms in the mid-nineteenth century, women were cautioned about participation in sport. It was widely claimed that sport was harmful to female health. Principally concerned with physical injury to the reproductive organs and the breasts and with possible effects on the menstrual cycle, pregnancy, and the psychological well-being of females, the literature of the past one hundred years is laden with such opinions. Early in the twentieth century,

a Harvard physical educator discouraged women from engaging in competitive sports because of "the peculiar constitution of [a female's] nervous system and the greater emotional disturbances to which she is subjected." Women themselves reinforced the view that female health was harmed by competitive sports. For example, a member of the Women's Division of the National Amateur Athletic Federation asserted: "Girls are not suited for the same athletic programs as boys. . . . Under prolonged intense physical strain a girl goes to pieces nervously."[18]

There are individual and sex-specific physiological and psychological differences and responses to sport participation, but female athletes have convincingly demonstrated that this is no reason not to provide equal access and opportunity for sporting experiences to females. Furthermore, for the vast majority of females the physiological, psychological, and social benefits gained through physical activity and sports competition are pretty much the same as they are for males.

Myth: Women Are Not Interested in, or Very Good at, Sports

Until about two decades ago, male domination of sport culture was so complete that females could be denied opportunities in sport by those asserting that women were not really interested in or very good at sports. Those who made this point typically referred to the paucity of women in sports, and claimed that the best performances of those who did participate in sport were inferior to men's performances. Such arguments, like all cultural norm explanations of social regularities, tended to ignore social structure. Women in the past chose to pursue certain roles and not others not just because that was the cultural norm, but because males and females were related to each other in a relatively stable social structure of power and differential status. This was a structure in which males appropriated the roles they preferred because they had the power to do so and could thus promote more status for themselves. Females were simply socialized out of sport by a variety of powerful social agents and agencies. Without interest and encouragement, few indeed did play or play very well.

Female achievements in sport during the 1990s and the first decade of the twenty-first century are too numerous and too remarkable to list. In ultra-distance running, swimming, and cycling, as well as equestrian events, dogsled racing, and horse and auto racing, women and men now compete together, even at the highest levels of competition. Women win their share of those events, too. World and Olympic records once set by male athletes in swimming, distance running, cycling, and other sports as well have been broken by female athletes. Clearly, the argument that females are not interested in sports and that they do not play them well enough to be taken seriously has been put to rest for even the most hardened skeptics of women's potential.

The remarkable achievements of female professional, collegiate, and elite amateur athletes in recent years have provided a foundation for role modeling by young female athletes. Women athletes such as Serena and Venus Williams, Annika Sorenstam, Lisa Leslie, and Mia Hamm have achieved celebrity status comparable to that of many male athletes, and many women's teams—such as the America's World Cup women's soccer team and the women's basketball teams at the University of Connecticut and the University of Tennessee—are world-renowned. Thus, "name" female athletes do exist in several sports, and girls of the present generation now have sport heroines to admire.

WOMEN'S STRUGGLE FOR OPPORTUNITY AND EQUALITY IN SPORT

The progress that females have made in gender equality during the last three decades did not come without a struggle. Their targets for change varied from the kinds of legal and extralegal restrictions that prevented females from having equal access to sport opportunities to attempts to elevate the social and political consciousness of women as a group. However, prejudices are not altered by courts and legislation, and culturally conditioned responses to gender ideology are ubiquitous and resistant to sudden changes. Therefore, despite laws that have forced compliance in equality of opportunity for females in the world of sport, inequities in sport continue, albeit in more subtle and insidious forms, as has been the case with racism.

In this section we will describe some of the continuing legal and extralegal struggles females have encountered as opportunities have opened up for women to experience the access and rewards of sports participation at all levels.

From Boys-Only Youth Sports to Opportunities for Both Sexes

As we noted in Chapter 4, youth sports programs introduce most children to the experience of organized sports. The Little League, Babe Ruth, and Connie Mack baseball leagues are three of the most popular baseball programs. Pop Warner football, Junior Hockey, and Biddie basketball initiate youngsters to tackling, blocking, ice-skating, and jump shooting. Age-group programs in swimming, track and field, and gymnastics are only a few of the more than twenty-five youth sports programs that involve millions of youth annually.

Until the mid-1970s, Little League baseball had an all-male policy that prevented girls from playing on its teams as part of its federal charter. This policy was challenged by several girls or their representatives, and it was reluctantly rescinded by Little League officers. But it was not just Little League that opened up for girls. A 2010 national survey of organized youth sports participation sponsored by the Sporting Goods Manufacturers Association (SGMA) found that some 12 million girls ages six to seventeen—48 percent of all girls in that age range—were members of an organized team. The flood of girls into team sports is one of the major sports trends of the present generation.[19] To a large extent this is because the young parents of these children were the first generation of parents since the women's movement began. They were the first generation to renounce the traditional cultural edicts of strict gender differentiation in social life. They tend to have a more favorable attitude toward gender equity, including equity in sport.

Title IX: Federal Government Support for Gender Equity

When the Educational Amendments Act of 1972 was passed, Title IX, a key provision in that law, required schools that receive federal funds to provide equal opportunities for males and females. It constituted a considerable weapon against sex discrimination in the American public school and collegiate sports programs, because some 16,000 public school districts and more than 2,600 colleges and universities benefit from federal funds.[20]

In Canada nothing comparable to Title IX has existed, but sex equality issues have been dealt with in several ways. The Canadian Charter of Rights and Freedoms Constitution Act of 1982 provides legal and constitutional rights of gender equity. The Fitness and Amateur Sports Women's Program was established in 1980, and it provides government programs, training, and policy standards for females. The Canadian Association for the Advancement of Women and Sport (CAAWS) was formed in 1981 "to advance the position of women by defining, promoting, and supporting a feminist perspective on sport and to improve the status of women in sport,"[21] and in 1986 the publication *Women in Sport: A Sport Canada Policy* defined a national policy for women in sport. Specifically, it established goals of equality of opportunity for women in sport and called for specific action-based programs to achieve those goals.

Toward Gender Equity in High School Sports

A little more than thirty-five years ago, a high school with ten or twelve teams for boys might have had no teams, or only a few teams, for girls. Boys' sports seasons might have run three months with fifteen or twenty-five scheduled contests; the season for a girls' sport would typically have extended a mere three to four weeks, with two or three contests. But Title IX was proving to be the beginning of a sports revolution for girls and women. Table 14.1 illustrates the staggering increases that have occurred in girls' high school athletic participation. In the past thirty years the number of girls participating in high school

Table 14.1   High School Sports Participation Survey Totals

Year	Boy Participants	Girl Participants
1971–1972	3,665,367	294,015
1975–1976	3,205,410	1,690,865
1989–1990	3,398,134	1,858,273
2000–2001	3,790,000	2,802,540
2006–2007	4,321,103	3,021,807
2010–2011	4,495,406	3,173,549

Source: National Federation of State High School Associations, "Participation Statistics" (2011), http://www.nfhs.org/Participation/SportSearch.aspx.

athletic programs throughout the nation has increased by more than 900 percent.

In spite of a federal law requiring schools to treat the sexes equally, the transition from a predominantly male athletic program to a two-sex program did not occur without controversy and litigation. Title IX was silent or vague on some issues; therefore, high school girls had to challenge the discrimination in their school sports programs through legal and legislative action. A number of lawsuits were brought by girls against school districts or state high school athletic regulatory bodies. In general, the cases fell into two categories: (1) A girl desired to participate on the boys' team when a girls' team was not provided at her school, or (2) a girl wished to be on the boys' team even though her school provided a girls' team. In the first type of case, the courts generally ruled in favor of the girl, though some of these suits required appeals. In the second type of case, the girl was usually not successful because the court reasoned that equal opportunity had not been denied her.

High school wrestling illustrates the trend that has been taking place with regard to girls' participation. When high school girls first came out for wrestling, they found various legal and policy barriers. They also found less formal objections. In the case of one girl who was a member of a high school wrestling team in Arizona, a fundamentalist religious group protested, saying it was immoral for a boy to wrestle a girl. One coach protested because a girl did not weigh in with the rest of the boys, stripped of all clothing. At the 2011 Iowa State High School Wrestling Tournament a high school female wrestler won by default because her opponent, a male wrestler, refused to wrestle her, saying: "[W]restling is a combat sport. . . . As a matter of conscience and my faith, I do not believe that it is appropriate for a boy to engage a girl in the manner."[22] Despite such objections, more than 6,000 girls now participate on high school wrestling teams across the country annually.

A development that has shown increasing strength involves requests by boys to be allowed to participate on girls' high school teams. In almost every case, the boys have wanted to take part on the girls' team because the school did not have a boys' team in that sport. Volleyball, soccer, gymnastics, field hockey, and swimming have been the sports that have most commonly drawn requests.

In several instances boys have won the right to play on the girls' team. During the fall of 2001, seven of the twenty-one girls' field hockey teams in western Massachusetts had at least one boy on their rosters. Boys were starters on Division I state field hockey championship teams for two of the previous three seasons. Massachusetts has an equal rights amendment in its constitution, and the state's superior court has ruled that the amendment applies to sports. Because the state's high schools do not provide field hockey teams for boys, boys are eligible to join girls' field hockey teams. According to the National Federation of State High School Associations (NFHS) participation survey, about 200 boys were playing high school field hockey in 2011. Throughout the nation, it is clear that boys do not wish to play on girls' teams in large numbers, but the situation does illustrate the unintended consequences of efforts to address gender equity against one sex. Each fall a few girls go out for high school football teams. Some states have ruled that they may not become members of the team. Others have ruled that if they can make the team, they may remain.

Although many positive strides have been made, issues about participation persist. To illustrate: In 2010 the National Women's Law Center (NWLC) filed administrative complaints against twelve school districts across the country to challenge sex discrimination in high school athletics. According to the president of NWLC, these districts are "the tip of the iceberg" in terms of the problem of sex discrimination in sports.[23]

In 2011, about 42 percent of all high school sport participants were female, and the number of sports available to them was more than twice the number available in 1980.[24] Girls' high school sports have become so popular that they rival boys' high school sports for attention in many communities. Indeed, in some communities the girls' teams have a larger following of fans because of their winning records. These conditions for girls' high school sport are quite recent.

Gender Equity in Intercollegiate Sports

For readers to comprehend the current status of gender equity in North American intercollegiate sports for women, we must describe some of the specific struggles that have been intricately bound to Title IX in the U.S. for the past forty years. So, before we turn to an examination of gender equity in intercollegiate sport, we explain the legislative and legal incidents surrounding Title IX.

Legislative and Legal Incidents Involving Title IX

Title IX specifies: "No person in the United States shall, on the basis of sex, be excluded from participation in, be denied the benefits of, or be subjected to discrimination under any education program or activity receiving Federal financial assistance." Although the clear intent of this legislation is to provide equal educational opportunities to females and males where federal funds are being used, Title IX has not brought about the goal of gender equality. A variety of legal challenges to it have been mounted by various groups, including the federal government, the NCAA, and individual universities, many of which still resist, or at least resent, complying with the intent of the legislation.[25]

The Office for Civil Rights (OCR) in the U.S. Department of Education (DOE) issued what became known as the "three-part test" policy, which provides that a university sponsoring an athletic program must provide equal athletic opportunities for members of both sexes. Among other factors, the regulation requires that an institution must effectively accommodate the athletic interests and abilities of students of both sexes to the extent necessary to provide equal athletic opportunity. The OCR indicated that it will apply the three-part test to assess whether an institution is providing nondiscriminatory participation opportunities for individuals of both sexes. An institution only has to pass one of the three parts of the test:

1. *Substantial Proportionality:* Are participation opportunities substantially proportionate to enrollment?
    — This part is satisfied when participation opportunities for men and women are substantially proportionate to their respective undergraduate enrollments.
    — Thus, if 51 percent of the students are female, at least 46 percent and no more than 56 percent of the student-athletes should be female. A few percentage points' deviation from perfect equality is allowed.
2. *History and Continuing Practice:* Is there a history and continuing practice of program expansion for the underrepresented sex?
    — This part is satisfied when an institution demonstrates a continuing history of improving gender equity in its sports program.
3. *Effectively Accommodating Interests and Abilities:* Is the institution fully and effectively accommodating the interests and abilities of the underrepresented sex?
    — This part is satisfied when an institution is meeting the abilities and interests of its female (or male) students even when there are disproportionately fewer female (or male) student-athletes.
    — Here, if there are disproportionately fewer female (or male) student-athletes, the institution must prove that the women (or men) do not have enough ability or interest to provide additional sports opportunities, or that new teams would not be able to compete against other teams.[26]

Although the three-part test for compliance with Title IX has been in place for more than thirty years, resistance to full compliance and the achievement of gender equity in college sport persists into the twenty-first century. Resistance to gender equity in intercollegiate athletics has been met by complaints filed with the DOE's Office for Civil Rights and by legal action through the courts. More than a thousand complaints have been filed with the OCR involving sports. Dozens of lawsuits have been filed on behalf of gender equity in college sports, and in most cases the party or parties claiming discrimination have won.

To give readers a "feeling" for what has taken place, we present two examples. First, during the mid-1990s, Brown University lost a sex discrimination suit brought by women athletes seeking reinstatement of women's gymnastics and volleyball teams that Brown had dropped from varsity status to cut athletic costs. After nearly five years of litigation, including an appeal by Brown to the U.S. Supreme Court (which was denied), the federal courts ruled in favor of the female athletes, basing their ruling on Brown's failure to satisfy any part of the Office for Civil Rights' three-part test for compliance with Title IX.

The second example was a challenge to Title IX in 2002 by the National Wrestling Coaches Association (NWCA) and several other wrestling organizations. They brought a lawsuit against the DOE claiming that the DOE's interpretation of Title IX and its policies had a discriminatory impact on male athletes, especially in wrestling programs. The DOE asked for a dismissal of the lawsuit on the grounds that the alleged injuries to the wrestling programs could not be traced to Title IX. A federal appeals court upheld the dismissal of the suit, saying that the wrestling organizations failed to show how Title IX directly caused a reduction in men's sports. The wrestling organizations appealed to the U.S. Supreme Court; in 2005 the Supreme Court rejected without comment the appeal of the suit by the wrestling organizations.

The basic argument of the wrestling organizations—that Title IX was reducing participation opportunities for male athletes by eliminating men's athletic teams or limiting the number of participants on the teams—turned out to be false.

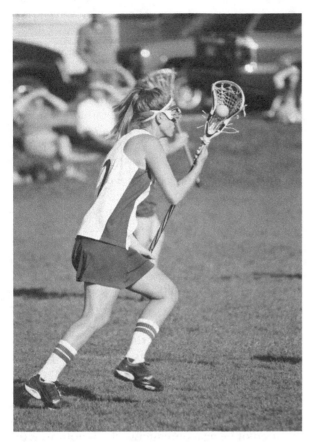

Females are now involved in many sports that their grandmothers would have considered unsuitable for girls and women. (istockphoto)

From 1988 to 2005 NCAA institutions actually had a net gain of seventy sports for men. From 1981 to 2005, annual male sports participation increased by 146,962 athletes.

In addition to those two cases, over the past fifteen years, the OCR has issued several clarifications about the three-part test for compliance with Title IX. The most recent clarification was published in 2010 and is titled "Intercollegiate Athletics Policy Clarification: The Three-Part Test—Part Three." It goes to great lengths to clarify the meaning and implementation of the Title IX three-part test, but concludes with this statement: "The three-part test gives institutions flexibility and affords control over their athletics programs. This flexibility, however, must be used consistent with Title IX's nondiscrimination requirements."[27]

The NCAA makes periodic gender equity reports. The most recent report at the time this chapter was written found:

- Females comprise 57 percent of the college student population, but only 43 percent of NCAA participants are women.
- The number of women's teams has increased over the last twenty-eight years. Men's teams, while having decreased in two of the last ten years, were nonetheless at an all-time high in 2009–2010.
- In 2008–2009, just as in the past two years, the average NCAA member institution sponsored approximately seventeen teams: eight for men and nine for women.
- Male college athletes receive 55 percent of college athletic scholarship dollars; female college athletes receive 45 percent.[28]

It is clear from this report that, although women have been making gains toward gender equity in American intercollegiate athletics, progress is being made much too slowly and there are still inequities that need to be abolished.

Governance and Control in Intercollegiate Sports: Post–Title IX

Conditions in college sport improved for women with the founding of the Association for Intercollegiate Athletics for Women (AIAW), a counterpart to the NCAA. By 1981 the AIAW had more than 950 members. Thirty-nine championships were contested in 1980–1981 under AIAW's aegis. But the NCAA voted to begin sponsoring women's championships. This was an action clearly designed to destroy the AIAW and to integrate women into the NCAA. The strategy was successful and, in 1982, the AIAW ceased to offer programs and services.

Since then, governance of women's sport in colleges has been male dominated. Leadership opportunities for women have lagged far behind those for men. Even into the second decade of the twenty-first century, only 19 percent of intercollegiate athletic director positions are held by women. The executive director position, the highest position in the NCAA, has never been occupied by a woman; opportunities for women to serve on the elite Executive Committee have been virtually unavailable. In 2010 only two of the twenty committee members were women. Each NCAA institution has a faculty athletics representative (FAR) to the NCAA. FARs represent their university on issues regarding athletics. Women from Division I universities held only 27 percent of these posts; there were 23 percent from Division II and 33 percent from Division III institutions.[29]

During the past two decades, concern has arisen that an elite, professionalized approach similar to that of the men's athletic programs was emerging. It has now become clear that despite some protests by women's coaches and athletic directors, many of them actually embrace the NCAA commercial model of college sports and see the NCAA as providing the best avenue for getting on with the "business" of women's collegiate athletics. Indeed, this is exactly the direction that most major university athletic programs have taken. At the University of Tennessee, average attendance at women's basketball games is more than 14,500; at the University of Connecticut it is more than 10,000. Several other universities report an average basketball attendance of more than 8,000. Other women's sports, especially volleyball, soccer, and softball, have experienced escalating spectator appeal.

With the professionalization of women's intercollegiate athletics, involving money, prestige, and popularity, has come falling graduation rates and violations of NCAA rules similar to the kind prevalent in men's programs. In the spring of 2011, fifty NCAA women's sports teams were on probation. Several others have received reprimands for NCAA rule violations—and not just in one or two sports. The teams involved include basketball, softball, tennis, golf, track and field, volleyball, and swimming.

Some sportswomen are distressed about what has happened to women's collegiate sports. They see the control of women's programs being absorbed into male-dominated sporting structures and losing their chance to advance a different ethic and form for intercollegiate sport. It appears such a structure is already well advanced, and there is no discernible sign that women's athletic leaders have any plan for creating a different model of college sports.

Consequences of Title IX for Men's Intercollegiate Sports

Not all gender equity complaints and lawsuits have come on behalf of women. University officials, principally presidents and athletic directors, have refused to rein in the extravagant expenditures of football and men's basketball; therefore, athletic budgets have been under pressure as women's sports teams have been added to meet gender equity provisions of Title IX. Consequently, universities throughout the country have dropped some men's "minor" sports (e.g., swimming, gymnastics, golf, wrestling).

In a previous section of this chapter we described the lawsuit that the NWCA and several other wrestling organizations brought against the DOE. But the cuts in men's sports have led to wide-ranging claims that compliance with Title IX will be the death knell of men's intercollegiate sports and that women's sports leaders are just greedy and out to abolish men's sports.[30]

The NWCA charged that Title IX has been hijacked, diverted from its original purpose of eliminating gender-based discrimination, and fashioned into a handy weapon to enforce a de facto quota system. The assistant secretary of civil rights responsible for dealing with Title IX cases has been accused of being a bureaucrat who is notorious for indifference to the imminent extinction of male sports programs. Many critics assert that Title IX is being misinterpreted, arguing that Title IX was not designed to require that a high school or college sports program reflect the male-female ratio of its student body because males are more interested in sports than are females. Thus, males should have more sport opportunities than females, but institutions are dropping male sports to add female sports just to meet Title IX standards. While NCAA institutions have certainly dropped many sports teams over the past twenty years, research by the NCAA shows quite clearly that male athletes have not lost *opportunities* as a result of Title IX.

- From 1988–1989 to 2009–2010, NCAA universities added 2,947 teams for men while dropping 2,605 men's sports teams, for a net gain of 342 men's sports teams.
- From 1988–1989 to 2009–2010, NCAA male sports participation increased 32 percent.

Furthermore, it appears that NCAA Division I universities have dropped men's sports teams in order to divert more resources into men's football and basketball teams rather than to meet Title IX requirements, as they often claim. But from 1988–1989 to 2009–2010, the NCAA had a net gain of 1,833 men's sports teams, Division I-A universities had a net gain of 163 men's teams, Division II universities had a net gain of 635 men's teams, and Division III universities had a net gain of 1,035 men's teams.[31]

Over the same period cited above, 3,960 NCAA women's sports teams were added. However, increases in women's sports programs have not been accompanied by the downsizing of men's sports teams, as is often claimed by intercollegiate athletic directors and coaches of men's teams; indeed, this is also a perception held by the general public.

The controversy over the effects of Title IX on men's intercollegiate athletics continues to be perhaps the most contentious issue in intercollegiate sports. In the summer of 2007, the College Sports Council (CSC), an advocacy group for men's sports, filed a petition asking the DOE for additional clarification of Title IX because the CSC believes the first test of the three-part test—proportionality—that the DOE uses for compliance with Title IX has led to fewer athletic opportunities for men in college and that the same thing could happen to boys in high schools.

Within the year, the DOE denied the CSC petition. While there is no disputing that hundreds of men's teams have been abolished throughout the nation in the past thirty years, there is also no disputing that 57 percent of NCAA student-athletes remain men while only 43 percent are women and that the average NCAA member institution currently sponsors approximately seventeen teams, eight for men and nine for women—in colleges and universities where 57 percent of the students are women.

Most of those who defend the progress toward gender equity in women's intercollegiate sports do not advocate eliminating men's sports teams to achieve that end. They contend that universities and their athletic departments make decisions to drop men's sports or reduce the squad sizes for a number of reasons, not always just to increase the number of women's teams. So to blame Title IX for universities' decisions to drop some men's sports is misleading and untrue. Moreover, they argue that universities have other options to achieve gender equity.

For example, they argue that men's sports are eliminated largely due to fiscal mismanagement: Schools spend enormous sums of money for revenue-generating, but overwhelmingly non-profit-making, football and basketball programs. Indeed, fewer than 10 percent of intercollegiate football and basketball teams generate a profit; most are by far the biggest financial drain on athletic department budgets, when revenue and expenditures are both considered.

Several sport studies scholars have questioned why Division I-A football teams need ten assistant coaches, why football and basketball coaches must be paid more than $2 million annually, and why Division I-A football teams need eighty-five scholarship players when NFL teams have only fifty-man rosters. They argue that ways and means could be found to reduce spending in areas such as these and divert the savings into preserving men's sports teams.

For their part, most male administrators, coaches, and athletes agree with the spirit behind Title IX. For them, it is the strict gender-based quota they object to. Although one can empathize with the male athletes and coaches who feel that their sports programs face restrictions, and who in some cases see gender equity as the cause of those restrictions, the good news is that recent trends in intercollegiate sports show that the gap between men's and women's intercollegiate sports—in terms of participation, teams, operating expenses, and so forth—is narrowing, without the elimination of men's teams, and that is the intent of Title IX: to end gender-based discrimination.

According to a 2011 investigation of gender equity in Canadian Interuniversity Sport, the results provided "both good news and bad news with regard to gender equity: The good news is that there are almost as many Varsity teams for women (425) as there are for men (431) at Canadian universities. The bad news is that there are disturbingly few women in leadership positions in Canadian university sport, with women occupying only 19% of the head coach positions, and only 17% of the athletic director positions."[32]

MEN RULE IN THE COACHING AND ADMINISTRATION OF WOMEN'S SPORTS

First, it is important to recognize that men dominate the professional/occupational structure in North American society. Overwhelmingly, they hold the most prestigious positions, occupy the powerful leadership roles, and command the highest salaries. A report by the Joint Economic Commission of Congress found that women accounted for only about 40 percent of managers in the United States workforce. So throughout the professional/occupational structure there are differentiated opportunities and rewards for men and women, and management careers in sports follow the same patterns found elsewhere. *The White House Project Report: Benchmarking Women's Leadership* of 2009 asserts, "As this systematic review documents, women's representation in leadership positions within the world of sports remains small."[33]

High School and College Women's Coaching Positions

Title IX does not apply to coaches and administrators, so gender equity is not required with respect to the employment or salaries of high school and college women coaches and administrators. One ironic consequence is that as opportunities for female athletes opened up and high school and college sports programs expanded, positions in coaching and athletic administration formerly held by women were sought and filled by men. In high school, for example, at the time Title IX became law, 80–90 percent of high school girls' sports were coached by women; within fifteen years, only 35–42 percent were coached by women.

This trend has slowly reversed itself and a majority of girls' high school sports are now being coached by women. There were even several dozen women among the more than 60,000 or so coaches of boys' high school sports teams across the United States during the 2010–2011 school year.[34]

The coaching pattern that has just been described for high school girls' sports has been duplicated at the collegiate level. In the early 1970s almost all coaches of women's intercollegiate teams

were women, but the situation changed rapidly and by 1990 only 48 percent of coaches of women's intercollegiate teams at four-year institutions were women. By 2010 this figure had declined to 43 percent (see Figure 14.1).

Even more disturbing, the percentage of African American women head coaches of women's basketball teams in the three divisions of the NCAA was less than 7 percent, which starkly contrasts with the 50 percent of student-athletes playing women's basketball who were African American.

Assistant coaching positions are often seen as a stepping-stone to the position of head coach. There is a marginally higher percentage of college women assistant coaches than head coaches—about 53 percent across the three divisions of the NCAA—hardly an impressive figure when one considers that females have been involved in high-level college sports for more than thirty-five years.[35]

It is still an open question as to the long-term trend in hiring practices, but every year there are more women who are experienced and successful

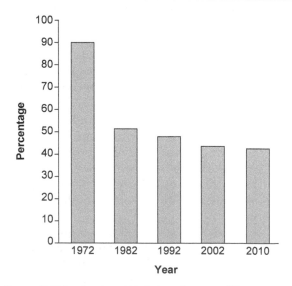

Figure 14.1   Percentage of College Women's Teams Coached by Women

Source: R. Vivian Acosta and Linda Jean Carpenter, "Women in Intercollegiate Sport: A Longitudinal, National Study—Thirty-Three Year Update, 1977–2010" (West Brookfield, MA: Acosta/Carpenter, 2010).

coaches, and it will be increasingly difficult for higher education officials to hire men for positions for which women are as qualified as (or better qualified than) male applicants. Indeed, there are some women coaching men's teams, but they are less than 3 percent. However, there is a growing belief that in the not-too-distant future one of the highly successful women basketball coaches will be hired to coach a men's college basketball team.[36]

Another issue for women college coaches involves payment for services rendered. In a 1992 NCAA survey, the average salary for male coaches was almost twice as much as that of women coaches. That shocking finding caused universities throughout the country to reassess their salary structures because gender equity can never be achieved as long as there are such wide differences in salary for men and women doing essentially the same tasks. Nevertheless, even in the second decade of the twenty-first century, Division I head coaches of women's basketball teams earn only about 47 percent of the salaries of head coaches of men's teams. There is a wide range of salaries for both men and women basketball coaches, but at the upper extremes in 2011, four Division I men's basketball coaches had annual salaries between $3 million and $4 million and the annual salaries of the two eminent coaches of women's basketball teams at Tennessee and Connecticut were $1.9 million (Pat Summitt) and $1.6 million (Geno Auriemma), respectively.[37]

Those defending the difference in salaries for men and women coaches contend that many men's programs generate more money than women's programs, so differential salaries are justified. That argument is countered with claims that because women's programs receive far less for their operating budgets, women are not given equal opportunity to promote and market their programs, factors that are essential to generating equal revenue in return.

High School and College Administrative/Management Positions

Administrative/Management positions in high school sports have remained overwhelmingly held by men. The National Federation of State High School Associations was founded in 1920 and has led the development of education-based interscholastic sports. Throughout its over ninety years it has never had a women executive director, its chief operating officer.

High school athletic directors (sometimes called athletic coordinators) are typically men, with a woman as the assistant, when there is such a position. As of 2010 only three of the fifty-one directors of state high school associations were women, and only three women served on the NFHS's twelve-member board of directors.

Female athletic administrators have lost out too during the past forty years. Women's intercollegiate sports programs in the mid-1970s were administered almost exclusively by women with the title of athletic director. Then, as women's programs grew, many colleges combined their men's and women's athletic departments into one. Most such mergers followed a pattern: After the merger, there emerged a male athletic director and several assistant directors, one of whom was often a woman in charge of women's athletics or the less visible sports.

According to R. Vivian Acosta and Linda Jean Carpenter, two researchers who as of 2010 had been conducting a longitudinal study of colleges and universities for thirty-three years, in 1972 more than 90 percent of women's intercollegiate programs were headed by a female administrator; in 2010 only 19 percent of college and university athletic directors were women. For 13 percent of all intercollegiate programs, no female was involved in the administrative structure. Thus, the practice of institutions hiring men as athletic administrators is continuing into the twenty-first century.[38]

There are signs that the trends in the employment of women in intercollegiate sports are improving. In 2010 more than 12,000 females were employed in intercollegiate sports in positions such as athletic directors, assistant/associate ADs, head coaches of men's or women's teams, paid assistant coaches, head athletic trainers, and sports information directors. Their demonstrated competence and accomplishments show quite convincingly that in this industry, just as in many others that have opened up to women, they are quite capable of performing just as well as men. Nevertheless, it seems likely that men will hold the vast majority of the key athletic positions for the foreseeable future.

Leadership opportunities for women in other types of collegiate governance have been negligible. In 2011, only two of the twenty NCAA Executive Committee members were women, and women held only 35 percent of all administrative jobs within all divisions of the NCAA, at a time when 43 percent of the student-athletes were women.

Canadian high schools and colleges have experienced a similar pattern of declining percentages of female coaches and athletic administrators. Moreover, the percentage of women coaches decreases in proportion to men as the level of competition increases. However, that has begun to turn around in the past few years.

OWNERSHIP, MANAGEMENT, AND COACHING IN PROFESSIONAL AND OLYMPIC SPORTS

The pattern of men dominating the leadership of women's sport prevails at the professional level, just as it does at the other levels of sport. Women are scarcely found in leadership positions in professional team sports. Of all of the women's professional team sports, the WNBA has perhaps the highest profile. It operates under the auspices of the NBA—although seven of the WNBA franchises were independently owned in 2011—and is the beneficiary of the NBA's marketing and promotional resources. The players are some of the most recognizable and popular athletes—women or men.

During the 2011 season, six of the total twelve head WNBA coaches were men, and eleven of the nineteen assistant coaches were women. The ownership and management are overwhelmingly male, but four teams in the WNBA are owned by women, a full third of the league. Sheila C. Johnson is the first African American woman to be an owner of a professional sports franchise; she is an owner,or partner in three professional sports franchises: the Washington Capitals (NHL), the Washington Wizards (NBA), and the Washington Mystics (WNBA).[39] Table 14.2 identifies women's ownership in other professional team sports.

Table 14.2 Women's Ownership in Professional Team Sports
NBA: In 2010, there were six women who had at least part ownership of NBA franchises. Colleen J. Maloof and Adrienne Maloof-Nassif were part of the Maloof family ownership of the NBA's Sacramento Kings. Karen Davidson, wife of the late William Davidson, is the majority owner of the Detroit Pistons. Gail Miller, wife of the late Larry H. Miller, is owner of the Larry H. Miller Group of Companies and chairman of the board over the Utah Jazz. Irene Pollin was co-owner of the NBA's Washington Wizards with her late husband Abe (the team was sold in April to Ted Leonsis' group). Cheri Vander Weide, daughter of owner Rich DeVos, served as the executive vice chairman of the ownership group at the Orlando Magic.
MLB: There are no women who hold a majority ownership.
NFL: Denise DeBartolo York, of the San Francisco 49ers, was the one woman who held ownership of an NFL team.
NHL: Henry and Susan Samueli own the Ducks; Mike and Marian Ilitch own the Red Wings.
Women's Professional Soccer: One team, California-based FC Gold Pride, has a female majority owner, Nancy NeSmith. Her husband is a co-owner. Another WPS team, the Washington Freedom, has a woman as its chairperson: Maureen Hendricks, wife of team founder John Hendricks.

Beyond coaching and ownership, men have a commanding presence from top to bottom in most women's professional sports, and women's involvement in professional men's sports is extremely rare. Of the professional sport leagues, the NBA and WNBA have been the most responsive to advancing diversity. A good example was the selection of Laurel Richie in 2011 to be the president of the WNBA, making her the first African American woman named president of a U.S. professional sports league.

As we pointed out in Chapter 11, women are greatly underrepresented as sportswriters. Despite the addition of a few women sports reporters to the staffs of television networks and a few newspapers, there are still relatively few women in the field. Women are also underrepresented as sports officials, judges, commissioners, athletic trainers, racehorse trainers, and most other sports-related occupations.

There have been eight women umpires in professional baseball history, and none has ever reached

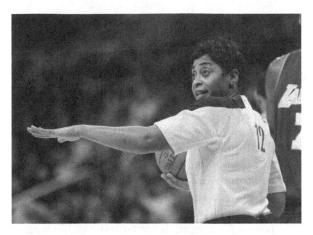

NBA official Violet Palmer during an NBA basketball game between the Los Angeles Lakers and the Phoenix Suns in Phoenix. (Rick Scuteri/AP Images)

the major leagues. Pam Postema came the closest, spending thirteen years in the minor leagues, including seven in Triple-A. She almost broke into the majors—calling two years of spring training games at her peak—but she was dropped in 1989, and Major League Baseball still awaits its first woman umpire.

In 1997 the NBA gave two women, Dee Kantner and Violet Palmer, officiating assignments in the league, but as of the 2010–2011 season Palmer remained the sole woman among the NBA's fifty-nine-member officiating staff and the lone female official at the top level in any of the four major professional sports.

In the fall of 2007 Sarah Thomas became the first woman to officiate a game involving NCAA Division I-A football teams. She worked as a line judge in a game between Memphis University and Jacksonville State.

Fortunately, many barriers to women's involvement in sport leadership careers are falling, and it is becoming more difficult each year to keep women from fulfilling their sport career goals.

Coaching and Administration/ Management in U.S. and Canadian Olympic Organizations

The Olympic organizations continue to be bastions of male dominance. There are hundreds of coaches with Canadian and U.S. Olympic teams, and the fluid movement into and out of those positions makes it difficult to determine the percentage of men and women with any accuracy. One generalization is possible, however: The overwhelming majority of coaches are men. Men coach all of the men's Canadian and U.S. Olympic teams, and men coach many of the women's teams as well. Where the head coach of a women's team is a woman, there are often men holding positions as assistant, or special position, coaches.

Positions with the Canadian Olympic Committee (COC) and the United States Olympic Committee (USOC) are predominantly male, too. In 2010, six (31.5 percent) of the nineteen members of the COC were women. In 2009, 44 percent of the USOC board of directors was female, as was 36 percent of the executive team. Of the 108 active members of the International Olympic Committee (IOC), only sixteen are women, and there is only one woman on the fifteen-member IOC Executive Board.

Reasons for the Persistence of Men in Coaching and Administering Women's Sports

Considerable speculation has centered on why girls' and women's sports coaching and administration have become dominated by men. Some have suggested that higher salaries are attracting men into coaching and administration careers; others have suggested that men have greater access to the hiring system through an "old boys" network, and others contend that when men and women apply for sports jobs, men are perceived to be better qualified because sport has traditionally been a male domain.

On the other hand, there are those who maintain that the changing social and occupational conditions for women in the past twenty years have enabled women to have a much greater menu from which to choose a career. They argue that women who have the drive, determination, self-confidence, and intelligence to make good coaches and sports administrators also now have the option to become physicians, lawyers, and business leaders. These positions often pay better than coaching or administering sports programs, especially when women's salaries for coaching and sports administration lag behind men's in those positions.

For these and other reasons, more job opportunities in women's sport are left open to male applicants. In a recent study, to ascertain why more than 120 female former college coaches had withdrawn from coaching, the investigator found that in addition to gender discrimination, homophobia, and the centrality of male coaches, "conflict between working as a coach and motherhood, or women with children as being 'distracted' by motherhood . . . revealed that women have multiple, complex, and overlapping reasons for leaving collegiate coaching."[40]

Women Athletes' Careers at the Professional and Olympic Levels of Sport

As one might expect, opportunities for women to engage in sports at the highest levels have been severely restricted historically, and differential rewards have been the norm. However, progress has been made toward expanding opportunities for females in top levels of sport during the past two decades. The most popular professional sports for women have traditionally been individual sports, especially golf and tennis, because they have traditionally been "socially approved" sports for women, particularly by the affluent social classes.

Professional women's team sports have been less successful in their struggle for acceptance. Some examples are listed below. As you read the list below, use the sociological perspective we introduced in Chapter 1 to try to understand why some efforts to form stable women's professional sport organizations have succeeded while others failed.

- *Tennis:* Currently, there are some 2,400 women representing more than ninety nations on the Sony Ericsson Woman's Tennis Tour. They are competing for more than $90 million in prize money at the tour's fifty-one events and four grand slams. The top five to ten women on the pro tennis circuit typically win about half as much prize money as the men on its Association of Tennis Professionals (ATP) World Tour. However, men's and women's championship prize monies are the same at the U.S. Open, the

French Open, and Australian tennis tournaments and almost the same at Wimbledon.

- *Golf:* Founded in 1950, the Ladies Professional Golf Association currently has more than 260 players on the LPGA tour. The top five money leaders earn only about 25 percent of what the top five men's PGA tour money leaders win. (In 2010, the top five female money leaders earned an average of $1.8 million compared to $4.6 million for the top five male money leaders.)

- *Baseball:* As far back as World War II, there was a women's professional baseball—yes, baseball—league. It remained a viable league until 1954. Several efforts have been made to establish professional baseball for women, but all have been short-lived.

- *Softball:* The Women's Professional Softball League was formed in the mid-1970s but was disbanded after four years. As in baseball, several unsuccessful attempts have been made to establish a stable women's professional softball league. In 1997 the Women's Pro Softball League (WPSL) was formed, but it folded in 2001. In 2004 the WPSL was revived under the name National Pro Fastpitch (NPF) League and was still operating in 2011, featuring four teams.

- *Volleyball:* Women's professional volleyball has had a number of leagues and several formats during the past twenty-five years. Some of the leagues were mixed-gender, some have been indoor, and some have been outdoor. But there has been very little stability in any of them. The Association of Volleyball Professionals (AVP) Crocs beach volleyball tour is the nation's most prominent professional volleyball tour. It features more than 150 of the top beach volleyball players in the world. In August 2010 the AVP Tour canceled the remainder of its season.

- *Basketball:* Between the mid-1970s and mid-1990s several attempts were made to make a go of women's professional basketball in the United States. All of those efforts ultimately failed. Then in the mid-1990s, two professional leagues began play: the ABL and the WNBA. The former lasted a little less than three years before going out of business. Meanwhile, the WNBA has flourished, having grown to a thirteen-team league by 2011. In spite of its seeming success, its financial viability is heavily dependent upon the financial backing, marketing, and promotions of the NBA. The structure of WNBA players' salaries is paltry—in 2010 the maximum salary was $101,500—compared to NBA salaries—in the same year the average NBA salary was $5.3 million, with thirty teams in the NBA, more than twice the number of WNBA teams. Another notable feature of the WNBA is the diversity of its players. During the 2011 season, 21 percent of players were white and 69 percent were African American; there were four Latinas, and 6 percent were foreign-born. In 2011, five of the twelve head coaches were African American and six of the head coaches were women.[41]

- *Soccer:* When American women won the Women's World Cup in 1999, interest in women's soccer skyrocketed. Women's soccer organizations immediately began talking about forming a women's professional soccer league. But the reality of having to raise a minimum of $30 to $50 million to get even a modest league off the ground stalled the formation of a league. It was not until the spring of 2001 that the Women's United Soccer Association (WUSA) launched its inaugural season of play. Averaging 8,104 admissions per game, the WUSA exceeded expectations at the gate, but within a year it failed. A new league, Women's Professional Soccer, began playing in the spring of 2009. The WPS was composed of six teams during the 2011 season, based solely on the East Coast, but it had plans for future expansion. About 25 percent of WPS players are from outside the U.S., and virtually the entire world is represented among these players. The average WPS salary is about $32,000, but that average includes minimum salaries of $40,000 for national team players and a

few international players—significantly less than the typical Major League Soccer salary, which is about $140,000.[42] The stunning play of the U.S. women's national soccer team at the Women's World Cup in 2011—when the U.S. team upset the seemingly unbeatable Brazilian team in the quarterfinals and advanced to the World Cup championship game, where they lost to Japan on penalty kicks—has triggered a renewed enthusiasm for women's soccer in North America. According to the Sporting Goods Manufacturers Association (SGMA), there are more than 5 million females playing organized soccer in the United States, nearly 70 percent of whom are under the age of seventeen.

- *Football:* There have been several unsuccessful efforts to develop a viable women's football league. The most recent attempt, the Women's Professional Football League (WPFL), "kicked off" in the fall of 2000 with eleven teams; fifteen teams competed in the league during the 2006 season. Within the past few years the United Women's Football League, the Woman's American Football League, and the National Women's Football Association have all attempted to form stable organizations, with little success. Money problems forced the earlier leagues to fold, and the newest leagues seem saddled with the same problems. None of the athletes earn enough money to make a living, so the leagues are more like "semi-pro" operations than full-blown professional ones.

- *Foreign Professional Sports:* Opportunities to play on foreign teams in Europe and Asia have opened up for women in several team sports, and more than three hundred North American female athletes currently participate in foreign leagues. Top players can earn very good salaries. For example, two-thirds of the WNBA's 132 players spend the off-season playing in basketball leagues in foreign countries, where salaries range from $250,000 to $1 million.[43]

- *Other Professional Sports:* Professional opportunities in sports are continuing to diversify for women. Professional ice-skating has provided a chance for a few skaters to make very high salaries, and more than a hundred women are doing well as jockeys in thoroughbred horse racing. A few female track and field athletes, distance runners, triathletes, and race car drivers are making six-figure salaries.

The reality is that except for a few hundred female professional athletes, very few women make a living in pro sports (see Table 14.3), and with the current social and economic conditions for female professional athletes, the day is far away when more than a handful of women can make sports a full-time job.

Female Olympic Athletes

Gender inequality has prevailed in the Olympic Games since the modern Games began in 1896. The quotes by the founder of the modern Olympics, Pierre de Coubertin, in an earlier section of this chapter make quite clear his belief that females did not belong. However, in spite of de Coubertin's belief, which was shared by many of his cohorts, sports events for females have gradually been added to both the Summer and Winter Olympic Games over the past eighty years.[44] Yet substantial gender inequities remain. For example, in the 1992 Barcelona Summer Olympics, 286 events were held

but only 86—30 percent—were open to women. The situation was not much better at the 1994 Winter Games in Lillehammer, Norway. That year, 1,302 men competed, compared to 542 women—42 percent of the total number of athletes.

By the 2004 Athens Summer Olympic Games, among the more than 120 women's events and more than 170 men's events (about a dozen were mixed), 41 percent of the total participants were women and 59 percent were men. Thus, although there were more women's events than ever before, the gap between the number of men's and women's events narrowed to an all-time low. At the 2008 Beijing Olympics, the all-time highest proportion of females participated—43 percent—and yet men still outnumbered women as Olympic athletes.

Along with the increase in female competitors, new opportunities are opening up for women in the Olympics. Women's ice hockey was added for the 1994 Winter Games in Lillehammer, and women's softball and soccer were new to the 1996 Summer Games in Atlanta (although softball was surprisingly dropped from the 2012 Summer Olympics).

In 2000 and 2004, several new sports and more than twenty new events for women were added to the Summer Olympic Games. In 2008, in Beijing, women competed in the same number of sports as in 2004 (26) but in two more events (137). For the 2012 London Summer Olympics, the IOC voted to include women's boxing. Of the sports contested at the 2008 Summer Olympics in Beijing, boxing was the only one that did not include women. New women's sports events have been added to recent Winter Olympic Games, such that the percentage of female athletes participating rose from 27 percent at the 1992 Winter Olympics in Albertville to 40.5 percent at the 2010 Vancouver Winter Olympics[45] (see Figure 14.2).

But even as the percentage of women has been increasing in every Olympiad for the past fifty years, there are, of course, wide variations in the percentage of women representing each country at every Olympic Games. For the Athens Summer Olympics, more than twenty countries sent no women; indeed, even by 2010 three countries—Saudi Arabia, Qatar, and Brunei—had never sent any female athletes to the Olympic Games. On the other hand, at the

Table 14.3 2010 Professional Athletes' Average Salaries or Event Purses (in U.S. dollars)

Sport	Salary		
	Men		Women
NBA	5.85 million	WNBA	51,000
MSL	140,000	WSA	32,000
MLB (baseball)	3.3 million	NPF	Not available
U.S. Open Golf	1.35 million		585,000
British Open Golf	1.2 million		217,000
NYC Marathon	130,000		130,000
Boston Marathon	150,000		150,000

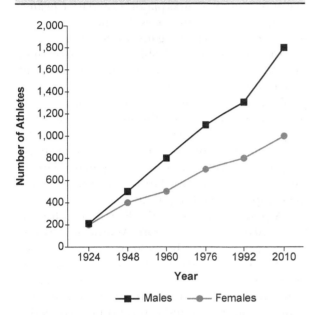

Figure 14.2   Number of Athletes Competing in Winter Olympic Games

injustice, and sexuality involving females. In this section we shift the focus to the role of sports in the social construction of masculinity and its consequences for males. Traditional gender role prescriptions have perpetuated problems for males as well as for females.

At the same time that various social barriers discouraged females from sport involvement to preserve their feminine identity, males have been socialized into attitudes, values, and behaviors in which sport plays a dominant role in actually shaping their masculine identities. Sport has been the cultural activity that makes it seem natural to equate masculinity with competition, physicality, aggressiveness, movement skills, and physical achievements. Two of the best-known slogans that reinforce this are "Sports make men out of boys" and "Sport builds character."

The competitive structures of the sports world socialize young boys into the exciting world of physical skills, tactics, and strategy in the pursuit of victory, but they also introduce them into the structured world of autocratic leadership, hierarchical organization, and bureaucratic relations. That is how the institution of sport is organized at every level.

Sports teams are commanded by strong, forceful male coaches, whose word is taken as incontestable. Sports rules and coaches' orders are understood to be followed without question. Athletes are expected to sacrifice their individual interests, skills, and goals for the benefit of the team. Personal relations are structured around competition against teammates for positions on the team as well as, of course, competition against opponents. While friendships and feelings of connection often develop among teammates, these are not deliberately structured in sport organizations. Instead, what develops from an interpersonal connectedness standpoint is a conditional self-worth, meaning masculine identity and personal value are dependent upon one's individual achievements.[46]

Along with other attitudes and values boys acquire through their sport experiences, they also learn about masculine sexuality. One of the most profound things they learn about masculine sexuality through the sport culture is that

1996 Atlanta Olympics, Canada and China had more women than men on their teams. At the 2000 Sydney Olympics, of the 309 Canadian athletes, 158 were female and 151 were male.

The U.S. and Canadian Olympic Committees and their many sport federations provide various kinds of subsidies to Olympic athletes—from training expenses to grants of money. Some members of U.S. women's teams, as well as female athletes in individual sports, have been paid more than $50,000 annually while they were preparing for the next Olympic Games. This practice was first adopted for male Olympians, but widespread objections to male-only subsidies resulted in opening them up to women.

SPORT AND GENDER IDENTITY FOR MALES

Although this chapter has primarily focused on inequities females have faced in the sports world, gender issues are not just about inequality, to be homosexual, or even be suspected of it, is detestable. Males who have been uninterested in sport or unwilling to allow dominant gender definitions of masculinity force them into sport or into "appropriate" masculine attitudes, values, and behaviors have often faced gender bigotry from both males and females. They have been the butt of jokes about their "effeminacy," and they have been labeled "fags," "queers," and "fairies." Many times they have been physically abused in various ways.[47]

Thus, gender inequality and injustice have been directed at males who for one reason or another do not conform to dominant cultural definitions of masculinity. In a collection of personal stories by gay athletes, one athlete remarked: "Starting with Little League or Pop Warner [football], there's this concept that to be a man is to be an athlete, to be an athlete is to be strong, and to be strong you have to have a certain attitude" about sexuality: Athletes are not gay.[48]

Although there is growing evidence that gay athletes have competed, and continue to compete, at all levels of sport, mostly closeted, the sports world has remained steadfastly homophobic. In 1995, when Olympic diving champion Greg Louganis revealed he was gay, a flood of testimonials came from other gay athletes in other sports, illustrating that sport is no different from other sectors of life, notwithstanding the stigma about homosexuality in sport culture.

Only a handful of male professional athletes have come out, and all of them were retired when they made their sexuality public. The most recent announcement came in early 2007 on ESPN's *Outside the Lines* by former NBA player John Amaechi. Amaechi has followed up the announcement with a memoir titled *Man in the Middle*. NBA superstar LeBron James, reacting to Amaechi's announcement, stated that an openly gay person could not survive in the NBA. James went on to say: "With teammates you have to be trustworthy, and if you're gay and you're not admitting that you are then you are not trustworthy."[49]

All of these former professional athletes have received homophobic remarks from former teammates. A former Seattle Seahawks teammate of Esera Tuaolo, who came out after he retired from the NFL, said that Tuaolo was wise to have concealed his homosexuality while he was an active player because Seahawks players would have beaten him up so badly in practices that he would never have been able to play a game on Sunday.[50]

In spite of homophobic remarks like that, the 2010 version of Gallup's annual Values and Beliefs survey documented a gradual increase in public acceptance of gay relations, finding that Americans' support for the moral acceptability of gay and lesbian relations crossed the symbolic 50 percent threshold in that year. At the same time, the proportion of Americans calling these relations "morally wrong" dropped to 43 percent, the lowest in Gallup's decade-long trend.[51]

A poll conducted by the Pew Research Center in 2010 found that more Americans favored allowing gays and lesbians to marry legally than did in previous years. Forty-two percent favored same-sex marriage. In 2012 there were eight states that recognized or were about to recognize same-sex marriages and several others (plus the District of Columbia) that recognized some form of same-sex civil unions or domestic partnerships. While the broader issue of gay and lesbian rights has been a source of controversy, there is increasing support for giving gays and lesbians the same legal rights as other citizens enjoy. Homophobia has not disappeared, but a growing sense of social humanitarianism has weakened it.[52]

One of the outcomes of the gay/lesbian liberation movement has been the founding of sport organizations by and for gays and lesbians. Gay sports clubs are now found in most major cities of North America; also, a wide variety of gay sports, fitness, and recreational organizations—camping groups, bicycling tours, skiing, hiking, canoeing, and so forth—are popular in urban areas. Gay-governed organizations have developed in a variety of sports; they include the International Gay and Lesbian Aquatics Association, the Gay and Lesbian Hockey Association, and the International Gay Bowling Association. The most prestigious gay sport organization, and event, is the Federation of Gay Games, which governs the Gay Games. The first Gay Games were founded by a former Olympic decathlete, Tom Waddell, and held in 1982 in San Francisco. The Gay Games are held every four years as a celebration of the international gay community. Athletes and teams compete in a variety of sports, and many of the routines and ceremonies are patterned after the International Olympic Games.[53]

SUMMARY

In this chapter we have examined the social bases for the gender inequality and injustice that have traditionally confronted females in sport, the consequences of the processes, and the developments in this topic. Gender inequality and injustice against females in sport have taken many forms. First, a number of myths about the biological and psychological effects on women of competitive sports effectively discouraged their participation. Second, unequal opportunity for participation in sports existed for a long time. Finally, women had unequal access to the authority and power structure of sport. Patriarchal ideology has been employed to socialize females out of sports and to deny them equal access to its rewards.

Legislation and court decisions have made it more difficult for discrimination to be imposed on women and girls in sports. Greater opportunities are now available for those who wish to compete.

Making discrimination illegal does not eliminate it, however, as previous experiences with civil rights legislation so clearly illustrate. Socially conditioned attitudes are slow to change. In some individual cases, they cannot be changed. Stereotypes are persistent and feed on the examples that confirm them. Nevertheless, attitudes and behaviors have changed in remarkably significant ways in response to challenges and demands as well as to federal legislation.

Gender inequality and injustice involve males as well as females. Traditional masculine identity is closely bound with sport culture, and males who do not conform to the social prescriptions face a variety of negative social sanctions.

WEB RESOURCES

www.womenssportsfoundation.org
The website of the Women's Sports Foundation. This is arguably the leading women's sport organization. It is very active in promoting and advancing the cause of women in sport.

www.education.umn.edu/tuckercenter/
Directed by sport sociologist Mary Jo Kane, the Tucker Center for Research on Girls and Women in Sport is an interdisciplinary research center leading a pioneering effort to examine how sport and physical activity affect the lives of girls and women, their families, and their communities.

www.caaws.ca
The website of the Canadian Association for the Advancement of Women and Sport and Physical Activity. CAAWS works to encourage girls and women to get out of the bleachers, off the sidelines, and onto the fields and rinks, into the pools, locker rooms, and boardrooms of Canada. It has good links to other websites.

www.feminist.org
The website of the Feminist Majority Foundation, an organization dedicated to women's equality, reproductive health, and nonviolence. It utilizes research and action to empower women economically, socially, and politically. Many of the actions and activities of this organization involve women in sport.

www.womensportswire.com
The Women Sports Wire website advertises itself as the number-one resource for women's sports news and information. It has lots of useful links.

NOTES

1. For a more detailed discussion of this issue, see Maxine Baca Zinn, Pierrette Hondagneu-Sotelo, and Michael A. Messner, eds., *Gender Through the Prism of Difference*, 4th ed. (New York: Oxford University Press, 2010); Julie McMullin, *Understanding Social Inequality: Intersections of Class, Age, Gender, Ethnicity, and Race in Canada*, 2nd ed.

(New York: Oxford University Press, 2009); and Barbara J. Berg, *Sexism in America: Alive, Well, and Ruining Our Future* (Chicago: Lawrence Hill Books, 2009).

2. Jean O'Reilly and Susan K. Cahn, eds., *Women and Sports in the United States: A Documentary Reader* (Boston: Northeastern University Press, 2007), pt. 1; see also M. Ann Hall, *The Girl and the Game: A History of Women's Sport in Canada* (Peterborough, Ontario: Broadview Press, 2002).

3. Jon Sterngass, "Cheating, Gender Roles, and the Nineteenth-Century Croquet Craze," in *Sport in America, Volume II: From Colonial Leisure to Celebrity Figures and Globalization*, 2nd ed., ed. David K. Wiggins (Champaign, IL: Human Kinetics, 2010), 85–104.

4. Bil Gilbert and Nancy Williamson, "Sport Is Unfair to Women," *Sports Illustrated*, 28 May 1973, p. 90.

5. Ibid. see also Betsy Ross, *Play Ball with the Boys: The Rise of Women in the World of Men's Sports* (Cincinnati, OH: Clerisy Press, 2010).

6. Zinn, Hondagneu-Sotelo, and Messner, *Gender Through the Prism of Difference;* see also Linda L. Lindsey, *Gender Roles: A Sociological Perspective*, 5th ed. (Upper Saddle River, NJ: Prentice Hall, 2010).

7. Sohaila Shakib and Michele D. Dunbar, "How High School Athletes Talk About Maternal and Paternal Sporting Experiences," *International Review for the Sociology of Sport* 39, no. 3 (2004): 275–300; see also Sarah Schmidt, "Dads Coddle Little Girls: Study: Overprotective Actions Can Influence Girls' Lack of Risk-Taking," *The Gazette* (Montreal), 19 December 2006, p. A17.

8. Linda Brannon, *Gender: Psychological Perspectives*, 5th ed. (Boston: Allyn & Bacon, 2007); see also Jessica Valenti, "For Women in America, Equality Is Still an Illusion," *Washington Post*, 21 February 2010, p. B2.

9. Gerald Handel, Spencer Cahill, and Frederick Elkin, *Children and Society: The Sociology of Children and Childhood Socialization* (New York: Oxford University Press, 2006); see also D. Stanley Eitzen, *Fair and Foul: Beyond the Myths and Paradoxes of Sport*, 4th ed. (Lanham, MD: Rowman & Littlefield, 2009), 101–124.

10. Mary Jo Kane, "Sex Sells Sex, Not Women's Sports," *The Nation*, 15/22 August 2011, pp. 28–29; see also Cindra S. Kamphoff, Suzannah M. Armentrout, Inge E. Milius, and Kelly Fallon, "Gender Representation on the Cover of *ESPN the Magazine*, 1998–Present," *Research Quarterly for Exercise and Sport* 82 (March supplement, 2011): A-68.

11. Stanley Eitzen and Maxine Baca Zinn, "The De-athleticization of Women: The Naming and Gender Marking of Collegiate Sport Teams," in *Sport in Contemporary Society: An Anthology*, 8th ed., ed. D. Stanley Eitzen (Boulder, CO: Paradigm Publishers, 2009), 126–135; see also Eitzen, *Fair and Foul*, 41–58.

12. Pierre de Coubertin, quoted in Sheila Mitchell, "Women's Participation in the Olympic Games, 1900–1926," *Journal of Sport History* 4 (Summer 1977): 211.

13. Quoted in Ellen Gerber, Jan Felshin, and Waneen Wyrick, *The American Woman in Sport* (Reading, MA: Addison-Wesley, 1974), 137–138.

14. Nancy Theberge, *Higher Goals: Women's Ice Hockey and the Politics of Gender* (Albany: State University of New York Press, 2000), 113; see also Scott Rawdon and N. Stanley Nahman, Jr., *Women's Rugby: Coaching and Playing the Collegiate Game* (Terre Haute, IN: Wish Publishing, 2005); and Lisa Taggart, *Women Who Win: Female Athletes on Being the Best* (Emeryville, CA: Seal Press, 2007).

15. Lori Selke, "11 Powerful Lesbians in Sports," *Curve Magazine*, 2 February 2011, http://www.curvemag.com/Curve-Magazine/Web-Articles-2010/The-11-Most-Powerful-Lesbians-in-Sports; see also Mark Harris, "Women, Gays, and Basketball," *Z Magazine*, January 2006, pp. 49–50; and Jayne Caudwell, ed., *Sport, Sexualities and Queer/Theory* (New York: Routledge, 2006).

16. Kristin Kaye, *Iron Maidens: The Celebration of the Most Awesome Female Muscle in the World* (New York: Thunder's Mouth Press, 2005); see also Sarah Fields, *Female Gladiators: Gender, Law, and Contact Sport in America* (Champaign: University of Illinois Press, 2008).

17. Jill Lieber, "Harris Stands Tall in Painful Battle; Talks on Monday Could Change Course of Bias Suit Against Penn State, Coach," *USA Today*, 11 May 2006, p. 3C; see also Jodi Mailander Farrell, "Sexism, Softball and the Supreme Court," *Miami Herald*, 30 May 2010, p. L1; and Sherry Wolf, "America's Deepest Closet," *The Nation*, 15/22 August 2011, p. 29–31.

18. Dudley A. Sargent, "Are Athletics Making Girls Masculine?" *Ladies Home Journal* 29 (1912): 72; and Ethel Perrin, "A Crisis in Girls Athletics," *Sportsmanship* 1 (December 1928): 10–12.

19. Sporting Goods Manufacturers Association, *2010 Sports and Fitness Report* (Washington, DC: Sporting Goods Manufacturers Association, 2010).

20. Linda Jean Carpenter and R. Vivian Acosta, *Title IX* (Champaign, IL: Human Kinetics, 2005).

21. Quoted in M. Ann Hall, *The Girl and the Game*, 173; also see pp. 163–187 for a detailed description of the struggle for gender equity in sport in Canada during the 1970s and 1980s.

22. Jim Halley, "By Default, Girl Wins in State Wrestling Meet," *USA Today*, 18 February 2011, p. 11C. See also National Federation of State High School Associations, "2011 Athletics Participation Totals" (2011), http://www.nfhs.org/Participation/SportSearch.aspx; Laura Strecker, "Women in Men's Sports," *UPDATEPLUS*, July/

August 2010, pp. 29, 31; and Katie Hnida, *Still Kicking: My Journey as the First Woman to Play Division I College Football* (New York: Scribner, 2006).

23. Quoted in Katie Thomas, "Women's Group Cites 12 Districts in Title IX Complaint," *New York Times*, 11 November 2010, p. B18.

24. National Federation of State High School Associations, "2011 Athletics Participation Totals."

25. Pamela Grundy and Susan Shackelford, "The Fight for Title IX," in *Sport in America, Volume II: From Colonial Leisure to Celebrity Figures and Globalization*, ed. David K. Wiggins (Champaign, IL: Human Kinetics, 2010), 359–375; Welch Suggs, *A Place on the Team: The Triumph and Tragedy of Title IX* (Princeton: Princeton University Press, 2005); Nancy Hogshead-Makar and Andrew Zimbalist, eds., *Equal Play: Title IX and Social Change* (Philadelphia: Temple University Press, 2007); and Katherine Hanson, *More Than Title IX: How Equity in Education Has Shaped the Nation* (Lanham, MD: Rowman & Littlefield, 2009).

26. Department of Education, Office for Civil Rights, the Assistant Secretary, "Clarification of Intercollegiate Athletics Policy Guidance: The Three-Part Test," 16 January 1996, www.ed.gov/offices/OCR!docs/clarific.html; for a more detailed discussion of the three-part test, see Suggs, *A Place on the Team*, 232–239.

27. Office for Civil Rights, "Dear Colleague Letter," in *Intercollegiate Athletics Policy Clarification: The Three-Part Test—Part Three* (Washington, DC: U.S. Department of Education, 20 April 2010), http://www2.ed.gov/about/offices/list/ocr/letters/colleague-20100420.html; for an example of one of the many court rulings about the three-part test, see Claire Darnell and Jeffrey Peterson, "Eliminating Sports for Title IX Compliance," *Journal of Physical Education, Recreation and Dance* 82 (February 2011): 9–10.

28. NCAA, *Student-Athlete Participation, 1981-1982–2009-2010* (Indianapolis, IN: National Collegiate Athletic Association, November 2010), http://www.ncaapublications.com/productdownloads/PR2011.pdf; see also Jennifer L. VanSickle, "Staving Off Complacency Concerning Title IX," *Journal of Physical Education, Recreation and Dance* 82, no. 4 (2011): 5–6, 56; and Michael Sanserino, "Despite Title IX, Female Athletes Trail in Aid," *post-gazette.com*, 15 August 2010, http://www.post-gazette.com/pg/10227/1080157-449.stm.

29. Richard Lapchick, *The 2009 Racial and Gender Report Card: College Sport*, The Institute for Diversity and Ethics in Sport (Orlando: University of Central Florida, 2009); see also Gary Brown, *NCAA Study Shows Slow Progress with Women and Minority Hiring* (Indianapolis, IN: National Collegiate Athletic Association), 19 May 2010.

30. Erik Brady, "School Locked in Gender War," *USA Today*, 22 July 2010, pp. 1C–2C; and Bradley David Ridpath, Athena Yiamouyiannis, and Heather Lawrence, "Changing Sides: The Failure of the Wrestling Community's Challenges to Title IX and New Strategies for Saving NCAA Sport Teams," *Journal of Intercollegiate Sports* 1 (2009): 255–283.

31. NCAA, "Participation Climbs to 430,000 Student-Athletes" (Indianapolis, IN: The National Collegiate Athletic Association), 8 December 2010, http://www.ncaa.org/wps/wcm/connect/public/NCAA/Resources/Latest+News/2010+news+stories/December/Participation+rate+climbs+to+430,000+student-athletes.

32. Peter Donnelly, Bruce Kidd, and Mark Norman, *Gender Equity in Canadian Sport: A Biannual Report* (Centre for Sport Policy Studies, University of Toronto, October 2011), 4.

33. The White House Project, *The White House Project Report: Benchmarking Women's Leadership* (New York: The White House Project, November 2009), 102; for an article about the Joint Economic Commission of Congress, see Catherine Rampell, "Slow Climb for Female Managers," *New York Times*, 28 September 2010, p. B1.

34. Jim Halley, "Woman Successfully Coaching Boys Hoops Evokes Jealousy, Kudos," *USA Today*, 25 March 2011, p. 8C.

35. Vivian Acosta and Linda Jean Carpenter, "Women in Intercollegiate Sport: A Longitudinal, National Study—Thirty-Three Year Update, 1977–2010" (West Brookfield, MA: Acosta/Carpenter, 2010); see also Lapchick, *The 2009 Racial and Gender Report Card: College Sport*.

36. Cindra S. Kamphoff, Suzannah M. Armentrout, and Andrew Driska, "The Token Female: Women's Experiences as Division I Collegiate Head Coaches of Men's Teams," *Journal of Intercollegiate Sport* 3 (2010), 297–315.

37. Tom Van Riper, "The Highest-Paid College Basketball Coaches," *Forbes.com*, 3 March 2011, http://www.forbes.com/2011/03/03/highest-paid-college-basketball-coaches-business-sports.html; and Steve Berkfowitz and Jodi Upton, "Elite Women's Coaches See Rise in Salaries," *USA Today*, 5 April 2011, p. 3C.

38. Acosta and Carpenter, "Women in Intercollegiate Sport."

39. WNBA, "Coaches," *WNBA.com*, http://www.wnba.com/coaches/coaches.html; see also Vicki Michaelis, "Women Buy into Owner Opportunities," *USA Today*, 7 September 2010, pp. 1C–2C.

40. Cindra S. Kamphoff, "Bargaining with Patriarchy: Former Female Coaches' Experiences and Their Decision to Leave Collegiate Coaching," *Research Quarterly for Exercise and Sport* 81, no. 3 (2010): 360.

41. WNBA, "Coaches"; Richard Lapchick, *The 2011 Racial and Gender Report Card: Women's National Basketball Association*, The Institute for Diversity and Ethics in Sport (Orlando: University of Central Florida, 2011).

42. Karen Rosen, "Survival Is Goal as 3rd Year Dawns," *USA Today*, 13 April 2011, p. 2C; see also Grant Wahl, "In Need of a Save," *Sports Illustrated*, 5 September 2011, p. 38.

43. Kelli Anderson, "Endless Season," *Sports Illustrated*, 26 July 2010, p. 29.

44. For an interesting account of U.S. women and their struggles with the Olympic leadership during the 1920s, see Mark Dyreson, "Icons of Liberty or Objects of Desire? American Women Olympians and the Politics of Consumption," *Journal of Contemporary History* 38, no. 3 (2003): 435–460.

45. International Olympic Committee, "Women Make Their Way in Vancouver." *Olympic.org*, 13 February 2010, www.olympic.org/en/content/Olympic-Games/All-Future-Olympic-Games/Winter/Vancouver-2010/?articleNewsGroup=-1&currentArticlesPageIPP=10&currentArticlesPage=7&articleId=77001; see also Christopher Clarey, "Women's Boxing Added for 2012 Olympics," *New York Times*, 14 August 2009, p. B8.

46. For an excellent selection of readings about gender, see Peter F. Murphy, ed., *Feminism and Masculinities* (New York: Oxford University Press, 2004). For an examination of how men "do" masculinity in a sporting environment (in this case, the extreme sport of rock climbing), see Victoria Robinson, *Everyday Masculinities and Extreme Sport: Male Identity and Rock Climbing* (London: Berg Publishers, 2008); see also Caudwell, *Sport, Sexualities and Queer/Theory*.

47. Douglas Victor Janoff, *Pink Blood: Homophobic Violence in Canada* (Toronto: University of Toronto Press, 2005); and Sam Dolnick, "Openly Gay in the Bronx, but Constantly on Guard," *New York Times*, 16 October 2010, p. A13.

48. Quoted in Dan Woog, *Jocks: True Stories of America's Gay Male Athletes* (Los Angeles: Alyson Books, 1998), 43–44.

49. John Amaechi, *Man in the Middle* (New York: ESPN Books, 2007); LeBron James quoted in Gene Farris, "Amaechi Takes Bold Step," *USA Today*, 8 February 2007, p. 11C.

50. Esera Tuaolo and John Rosengren, *Alone in the Trenches: My Life as a Gay Man in the NFL* (Naperville, IL: Sourcebooks, 2006); for interesting accounts about athletes who have come out of the closet and about the impact their revelation has had on their particular sport, see Cyd Zeigler and Jim Buzinski, *The Outsports Revolution: Truth and Myth in the World of Gay Sports* (New York: Alyson Publications, 2007).

51. Lydia Saad, "Americans' Acceptance of Gay Relations Crosses 50% Threshold," *Gallup.com*, 25 May 2010, http://www.gallup.com/poll/135764/americans-acceptance-gay-relations-crosses-threshold.aspx.

52. Pew Research Center, "Support for Same-Sex Marriage Edges Upward" (Washington, DC: The Pew Forum on Religion & Public Life, 6 October 2010); see also "Homosexuality Issues Find Online Ally in Sports," *USA Today*, 19 May 2011, p. 3C.

53. Caroline Symons, *The Gay Games: A History* (New York: Routledge, 2010).

CHAPTER 15

Contemporary Trends and the Future of Sport in North America

My interest is in the future because I am going to spend the rest of my life there.
—Charles F. Kettering (American inventor, engineer, businessman, and the holder of 140 patents)

In the past decade the number of North Americans participating in ecosports activities has grown dramatically. (istockphoto)

"We live in a changing society" is an often-heard cliché. It is voguish to depict contemporary social life as dynamic and progressive, the pace of living as fast, growth and change as the only constants, and an accelerating rate of change as likely to inflict "future shock" on many of us. These ideas are buttressed by an apparent obsession with the future. Business leaders look for predictions about population trends and shifts in consumer preferences; young adults seek information about trends in occupations in hopes that the career for which they prepare will be a gateway to opportunity rather than a dead-end street; and even video games have a definite futuristic orientation, as much of the simulated action takes place in outer space. Several of the most popular books of the past few years have been futuristic: *The Future of Everything: The Science of Prediction*; *Future Files: A Brief History of the NEXT 50 Years*; and *Future Minds: How the Digital Age Is Changing Our Minds, Why This Matters and What We Can Do About It*.[1]

Meanwhile groups of social forecasters, societal scientists who are actively involved in forecasting societal activity, have also been busy with futuristic studies under the auspices of private foundations and government agencies. Some of the most well known are the International Institute of Forecasters, the Trends Research Institute, and the National Research Council of Canada Study of 2010. The World Future Society is a thriving organization of 25,000 members in more than eighty countries who are interested in how social and technological developments are shaping the future. Finally, the publication of at least five periodicals on futurism (e.g., *The Futurist*) indicates that people like to read speculation about what this twenty-first century is going to be like.

Notwithstanding the cliché, change in North America is a ubiquitous fact. Today's social and physical environments are vastly different from those of only a generation ago, to say nothing of those of three or four generations ago. The changes over the past three decades have been in direction as well as in rate, and the total amount of change has been so vast and thorough that it can only be conceptualized as a social and cultural revolution. Therefore, we conclude this volume with a chapter that examines the trends and the future of sport in North America, for as we have frequently argued, sport reflects society, and as the society changes, sport will also undoubtedly undergo transformation.

DEMOGRAPHIC TRENDS IN NORTH AMERICA

One of the divisions of sociological study is called demography; it focuses on population size, characteristics, trends of groups, neighborhoods, communities, patterns of migration, and analyses of change. In describing the assumptions of the sociological perspective in Chapter 1, we noted that humans are naturally social beings who are greatly affected by their social and natural environments, but they are also capable of changing those social and natural formations within their lives. We have emphasized at various places in this volume that changes in population characteristics have played an important role in the rise of modern sport forms, the popularity and demise of some sports, and who plays and does not play sports. We now turn to trends in North American population and the potential impact they may have on sport. Trends in population growth, composition, and location are sociologically significant because they impact the social lives of people, including their lives as participants and consumers of sports.

One of the most significant trends in North America is the changing nature of its population—total numbers, composition, and location. Futurists are much concerned about population trends. Although improved birth control measures and a vague social commitment to zero population growth have partially controlled the numbers of newborns, a continued increase has occurred as the "baby boom" generation reached adulthood and began producing families of its own. Indeed, during the 1990s, the U.S. population grew by 32.7 million, an increase of 10 percent. Estimates are that the population of the United States will increase from 310 million in 2010 to around 325 million by 2020. The Canadian population, presently 34 million, is expected to increase to 35 million by 2020.[2] Thus, the populations of both the United

States and Canada will continue to grow in the next generation. In all likelihood, sports will continue expanding as well.

Population Composition

During most of the twentieth century North America had a young population because the birthrate remained high for an increasing number of people of childbearing age. This condition is now changing rapidly because the long-term trends for birthrates and death rates are expected to decline. Thus, the proportion of young people will diminish, and the proportion of older people will increase, markedly affecting population composition. The average age in the United States will rise dramatically, from thirty-seven in 2010 to about forty in 2040. The U.S. Census Bureau projects that the over-sixty-five population will more than double between 2010 and 2050, when one in five Americans will be over sixty-five years old (see Figure 15.1). The trend is similar for Canada. Even more dramatic will be the average life expectancy, which will climb from the current 78.1 to an estimated 82.6 years by 2050.

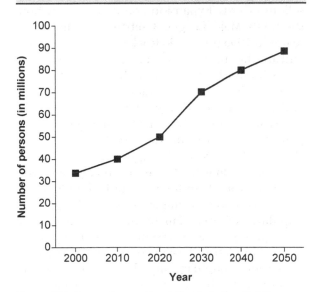

Figure 15.1   Projections of U.S. Seniors Sixty-Five and Older

Year

Number of persons (in millions)

Source: U.S. Census Bureau, *Population Projections* (2010).

Persons aged sixty-five and older currently make up 12 percent of Canada's population; that will rise to between 20 and 25 percent in 2025. Not only will there be many more older persons, but they will be healthier and more active than ever before.[3]

Both the United States and Canada have long been havens for immigrants, but the nationalities of those who have come to these two countries have changed with the political and economic winds. Political oppression or economic hardship was the incentive for millions of people to migrate, legally or illegally. Due to both immigration and high birthrates, the Hispanic population in the United States grew from 14.6 million in 1980 to 50 million in 2010, over 100 percent in thirty years. Hispanics became the largest ethnic minority in 2003, surpassing African Americans. Even more remarkably, while the United States as a whole grew 19.8 percent, growth in the Asian American population from 1980 to 2010 was 200 percent, mostly due to immigration. It is projected that the U.S. population will continue to become more diverse in the coming decades and that, by 2050, 54 percent of the population will be minorities.

In an effort to preserve its essentially loyal British character, Canada severely curtailed immigration from countries outside Europe right up until the reforms of the Trudeau administration in the 1960s. Consequently, prior to the 1960s, 80 percent of all immigrants came from Europe. In the past three decades, 70 percent of immigrants to Canada have been Asian or "nontraditional" (mostly Africans and Latin Americans). This rapidly changing ethnic and racial complexion in North America will alter everything in society, from politics and education to industry, values, and sports and leisure activities.

Location of Population

North Americans continue to gravitate toward large metropolitan areas, with about 85 percent of Americans living in central cities and their surrounding suburbs, and the majority of Canadians living within one hundred miles of the U.S.-Canadian border are urbanites. Over the next quarter century Americans will probably continue to congregate in megacities, or megalopolises, that futurists have labeled

"Boswash," "Chipitts," and "Sansan." Boswash will extend between Boston and Washington, D.C.; Chicago and Pittsburgh will be the centers for Chipitts; and Sansan will stretch from San Francisco to San Diego. These megalopolises appear likely to contain about one-half of the total U.S. population, including the majority of the most technologically and scientifically advanced, prosperous, intellectual, and creative elements.

In the United States the migration from the Northeast and Midwest into states in the South and West has been the most pronounced demographic shift in the past two decades. The surge of newcomers helped the population of the South jump by 25 percent and of the West by 30 percent between 1980 and 2000; indeed, the Sun Belt has absorbed virtually all the U.S. population growth since 1975, and the trend is expected to continue. The West and South are projected to be the fastest-growing regions in the United States, and the two regions combined are projected to account for 82 percent of the 68 million persons added to the nation's population between the mid-1990s and 2020. In Canada, population in the Atlantic provinces is slipping significantly, and the big gains have been in Alberta and British Columbia. Ontario and Quebec have substantially more than half the country's population and they will still have a majority in the year 2015, but the winds from the west are rising.[4]

Population Trends and Sport

The giant metropolitan areas, stretching out over hundreds of miles and engulfing many small communities as well as large cities, may very well require the reorganization of professional sports organizations on some feature other than a city name. Indeed, professional sport managements are already preparing for a future in which state and regional considerations will take precedence over city loyalties. The names of professional team sport franchises demonstrate that the leagues and owners are aware of the outmoded practice of single-city affiliation. Several of the franchises have adopted state or regionalistic team names (see Table 15.1).

Professional sport has been one of the most financially successful and growing industries during the past twenty years, riding the crest of a huge

Table 15.1 Professional Team Sport Franchises with State or Regional Names

Major League Baseball
  Minnesota Twins
  Texas Rangers
  Florida Marlins
  Colorado Rockies
  Arizona Diamondbacks
National Football League
  New England Patriots
  Arizona Cardinals
  Minnesota Vikings
  Carolina Panthers
  Tennessee Titans
National Basketball Association
  Golden State Warriors
  New Jersey Nets
  Indiana Pacers
  Minnesota Timberwolves
  Utah Jazz
National Hockey League
  New Jersey Devils
  Florida Panthers
  Colorado Avalanche
  Carolina Hurricanes
  Minnesota Wild

population of young people. Consumer-spectator interest appears to have no limit. New franchises spring up all over North America to be greeted by sellout crowds. Expansion continued throughout the 1990s. Major League Baseball expanded by two teams in 1993 (Colorado Rockies, Florida Marlins) and another two teams in 1998 (Arizona Diamondbacks, Tampa Bay Devil Rays); the National Hockey League added nine new franchises between 1991 and 2000; and the NFL and NBA expanded by two teams in 1995 (NFL: Carolina Panthers, Jacksonville Jaguars; NBA: Toronto Raptors, Vancouver Grizzlies), with the NFL adding two more franchises since then (Houston Texans, Cleveland Browns).

The World Cup held in the United States in 1994 served as a strong stimulus to the growing popularity of soccer. Furthermore, the increase in immigrant populations from Mexico, Central and South America, and Asian countries, where soccer is extremely popular, helped create a subculture of support for the creation of the ten-team Major League Soccer (MLS) league in 1996. Although still not as popular as the traditional professional sports leagues, professional soccer is gradually acquiring a devoted following of fans; indeed, MLS had increased to nineteen teams by the 2012 season.

As we noted in Chapter 14, Title IX and the expansion of high school and college sports for females, in conjunction with trends in population characteristics, created opportunities for women's professional sports to grow. Perhaps the most notable example of this was the launching of two women's professional basketball leagues in the mid-1990s, the American Basketball League and the WNBA. Although only the WNBA remains, with twelve teams in the 2011 season, it appears to have become a permanent part of professional sports.

Professional men's and women's golf and tennis have extended their tour seasons, and both tennis and golf now have seniors' tours. In addition, a number of other professional sports (such as NASCAR, cycling, distance running, and lacrosse) are gaining a following in live attendance and television coverage. The future trajectory seems quite clear: Professional sports will become another global industry in the next decade. They are already well on the way, with team franchises, tournaments, and championship events held around the globe.

Over the past two decades a wide variety of sports have acquired professional status—including cycling, triathlon, racquetball, distance running, beach volleyball, and lacrosse—and with the changing interests of the younger generations, some will challenge the more established sports for fans. Within twenty years the total number of professional sports could double. We will have more to say about some of these sports in later sections of this chapter.

A growing population, especially an older population, forms an infrastructure for the continued financial success of professional sports. However, ticket prices have skyrocketed at a rate four to five times the rise in the cost of living, and at a time when real income has increased very little. Figures compiled by various sources have begun to show that, for the average fan, these prices will take their toll on live attendance over the next decade. Actually, low- and average-income fans have already been priced out of attending. A survey conducted by the NHL revealed that the household income of fans

attending its games averaged in the top 15 percent of North American family incomes.

A larger proportion of the population is now forty years old and older, a fact that is manifested in sport in a number of ways. Some of the biggest sports stories of the past few years have been about older athletes: Randy Johnson continuing to pitch in Major League Baseball well into his forties, Cal Ripken breaking Lou Gehrig's consecutive-games record, and golf pro Annika Sorenstam captivating the hearts of North American sports fans by continuing to play excellent golf way past her prime years. The senior tours of the Professional Golfers Association and the Professional Tennis Association illustrate quite well that older athletes can perform at high levels, and that sports fans will pay to see them compete in their sport.

There is little doubt that people are remaining physically active later in their lives, and more and more sports programs are being created to allow the aging population to participate. Recent surveys have found that about 48 percent of seniors between the ages of fifty-five and seventy-four participate in exercise programs and 15 percent of the same age group report playing a sport. Women over sixty-five grew up and passed through their early adulthood at a time when women had few opportunities to be involved in sport activities, but many senior women have now embraced the physically active life they see girls and younger women enjoying. Many senior women are as involved in physical activities as their male counterparts.[5]

The Masters Sports Tournaments and Senior Olympics have become major forces in organizing competitive sports for senior men and women. These are only the most visible programs. Retirement communities are typically built to encourage the sport interests of their citizens. Many community recreation departments have expanded their programs to include senior leagues in several sports; indeed, in some communities these leagues are the fastest growing. In all likelihood, participant sports will be a major growth industry wherever large groups of older persons settle.

The changing racial and ethnic composition of the North American population has provided greater opportunity for minority groups in sports. It is one of the most salient trends at the present and will, if futurists' predictions are correct, continue in the coming years. One of the main reasons to expect that minorities will secure increasing access and opportunities is, as we described previously, that their percentage of the population is increasing dramatically. There is no question that organized sports, from youth programs to the professional level, have made great strides toward equalizing opportunities in the past decade, but the goal has not yet been achieved.

In Chapters 13 and 14 we demonstrated that overt discrimination against African Americans and females, such as denying them access to sports, has been gradually eliminated, but that inequalities and injustices continue in subtler forms. Even these are giving way, as more and more racial, ethnic, and gender diversity is achieved in positions of prestige, power, and leadership within sport.

In general, minorities are underrepresented in many of the most popular high school, college, and professional sports, but each year new inroads are made into more and more sports. Minorities are taking their rightful place among teammates, and they hold coaching and management positions in a number of sports programs. The future for racial, ethnic, and gender diversity in North American sports appears to be quite promising.

DOMINATING FORCES IN OUR LIVES: WORK, TECHNOLOGY, AND SPORTING ACTIVITIES

For the vast majority of adults, involvement in sport is related to their work. Whether they are participating in sport themselves or watching others perform, the extent to which they can do either depends upon the nonwork time (so-called free time) available to them. In brief, the less time they must work, the more free time they have available for sporting activities; thus, trends in the work life of people will be instrumental in trends that take place in sport.

Industrialization and technology changed not only the way that goods are produced but also the conditions under which they are produced. At first, factories brought workers into sweatshops to toil, literally, from sunrise to sunset. Later, as steel and other large industries grew, workers were attracted to the plants by the prospect of steady work and a livable wage. Hours were long, but until the emergence of labor unions, workers could do little about that if they wished to remain employed. However, in the early twentieth century, a gradual reduction in the average workweek began for nonagricultural workers, from about sixty-five hours to just under forty hours.

The trend toward a shorter workweek, which started in the early twentieth century, began to reverse itself in the past two decades (more on that below). Accompanying and supporting working trends over the past century have been remarkable technological innovations, and technology is increasingly dominating the economy. The previous state of the art in production and services is being quickly replaced by new high-tech developments. Large transnational corporations have come to dominate economies around the world. Indeed, economically they exceed the size of many nation-states. Combined, these forces form the most salient feature of North American life, and their effects are manifested in the contours of labor and leisure.[6]

An Information/Service North American Society

The ways in which the economy is being transformed and the occupational system reworked by new technology confirm that North Americans have entered an "information-based" society, or an information-producing service economy, rather than a goods-producing manufacturing economy. Futurists predict that computers and other technological innovations will change the nature of work and the balance between jobs and personal lives. In the next ten years, four out of five people will be doing jobs differently from the way they have been done in the last thirty years. Computer networking and social media will be one reason for this trend. We will, in essence, become an electronically connected society, as these technologies enable work to be done anywhere, at any time, at any distance from the office or factory.

Robotics and computer-integrated manufacturing are creating entirely new industries, employing millions of people in jobs that did not exist a decade ago. According to the Robotics Industries Association (RIA), there are nearly 1 million industrial robots employed in the world, with about 196,000 in the U.S. (second only to Japan). With the inclusion of nonindustrial robots, the number ramps up to about 8 million. According to the RIA, "robots have a significant impact on the global economy by increasing production levels and decreasing (over the long term) production costs while requiring less human labor. As impressive as these numbers are now, there's little doubt that they'll see big growth in the years ahead."[7]

Careers in information services are well under way. Some 65 percent of North American workers are currently in information industries. Indeed, more people are involved in information and communication occupations than in mining, agriculture, manufacturing, and personal services combined; by the year 2020, over three-fourths of the workforce will be information workers.

Technological developments that have brought about, on an ever-increasing scale, giant organizations have spawned a depersonalization of social relationships and the eclipse of personalized community. About a decade ago the author of a book titled *Bowling Alone: The Collapse and Revival of American Community* amassed impressive data on the decline of social capital and civic engagement in American society. He claimed that Americans have lost much of the social glue that once held our society together, that we have become a nation of strangers to one another, lacking mutual social bonds. In the intervening years, several other social analysts have taken up the same theme, and most claim that the trend is continuing.[8]

Although most North Americans would not wish to give up many of the products of technological creations—television, central heating, air conditioning, automobiles, and so forth—there are, nevertheless, many people who find that the technocratic-bureaucratic society is dehumanizing. There has been a growing hostility to many forms of technological innovation and transnational corporate organization, and a wide range of spontaneous, activist, and democratic actions have tried to recapture some sense of control over daily lives.[9]

The Information/Service Workplace and Sporting Activities

One promise made by industry and technology, at least covertly if not overtly, has been that modernization and technological advances will ultimately free the ties that bind workers to their jobs. Accompanying this promise has been the prediction that there will be a "great flowering of leisure-time" activities for the common person. Despite the promises about the diminishing workweek, the flowering of leisure time has not yet materialized, and some people question whether it will occur in the near future.

To a great extent, the prediction of a "leisure society" was based on a misperception of the amount of leisure time that would be made available by technological advances. The work-nonwork cycle created by modernizing the workplace has been altered over the past century, so that there now appears to be more time away from work. But recent studies have found that, on average, U.S. workers work more hours annually than workers in any other industrialized country. In addition, the average commuting time for American workers is twenty-six minutes. The consequence of longer commutes is that workers are spending as much as an additional working week traveling to and from work every year (see Table 15.2). In studies carried out at the Families and Work Institute in New York, 44 percent of the respondents said they were overworked often or very often, and many wished they could reduce their work hours. Researchers report that one-third of the U.S. workforce can be viewed as being chronically overworked.[10]

Table 15.2   American Workers' Average Annual Hours of Work (in Nonagricultural Industries)

	1969	2010	Change 1969–2010
All participants	1,786	2,110	+324
Men	2,054	2,165	+111
Women	1,406	2,035	+629

Source: Extrapolated from U.S. Department of Labor, *Labor Force Statistics from the Current Population Survey, 2010,* Bureau of Labor Statistics, 2010.

The male "breadwinner" household is now the exception. Some 68 percent of households are now two-income households, and the proportion is expected to increase to 80 percent by 2020. Although this markedly increases the hours worked per week in households, the increased income has expanded the market for consumer goods and services and leisure activities.

Four-Day and Flextime Workweeks and Free Time

Many private and public organizations have experimented with four-day and flextime workweek schedules. The number of firms using flexible work hours has more than doubled in the past twenty years. These flexible arrangements take different forms, such as satellite work centers, customized work schedules, staggered shifts, and telecommuting with personal computers to the place of work. Projections suggest that by 2020 over half the workforce could be on some form of flextime.

These work schemes have been hailed as important steps toward creating a leisure society. However, in all four-day and flextime schemes tried so far the workweek remains near forty hours, so this trend has little to do with a reduction in working time; it is merely a rescheduling of the workload. It fails to even touch upon the more important issue of the desirability of a reduction in the overall length of the workweek.

Although the hours of the workweek remain about the same under the various nontraditional plans, several potential benefits accrue with respect to leisure time. The extra-long weekends make travel and other extended leisure activities possible, and commuting time may be reduced, some of which might be used for leisure activities. On the other hand, the extra time afforded by the four-day workweek may be a mixed blessing. For example, many people use the time working at a second job because continuing inflation tends to require more money to maintain the current living standard. Increases in free time, then, are often used primarily as an opportunity to perform extra work of some kind. It appears that the emergence of a true leisure society will require a respiritualization of our society and the rise of a fundamentally different valuation of work and leisure.

Ignoring for the moment that the greater amount of free time that technology was supposed to have provided has not materialized, how then can we account for participation rates in leisure activities and expenditure on leisure pursuits being at an all-time high? Leisure accounts for about one in every eight dollars spent by North American consumers. Explanations for the leisure pursuits of North Americans tend to converge on the idea that people are just cramming more activities into each twenty-four hours. The commonly heard "24/7" isn't just an expression; it's a cultural earthquake that is changing the way people live. The main argument is that the nation's business day is now twenty-four hours long because many businesses stay open all night, and cell phones, iPads, iPhones, and BlackBerry devices enable business communication and transactions to be conducted "24/7."

The traditional schedule of being awake during the day and asleep at night has become obsolete; millions of people are awake at any given time throughout the twenty-four-hour day. Those who are awake do not just shop at supermarkets and department stores. They engage in around-the-clock leisure activities, including sports. Many golf ranges, batting cages, tennis courts, swimming pools, and so forth are now open around the clock. Televised sports can be found on cable and satellite at every hour of the day. Sports consumers have many choices "24/7" to fulfill their sporting interests.

The tendency to do several things simultaneously and many things in a short period of time—including using the ever-present digital devices—has been called "time deepening." It has also been called "the more, the more"—meaning that under the pressure of expanding interests and motivations, the more people do, the more they wish to do, and vice versa. The consequence is that many people suffer from "leisure-time stress." Despite feeling "free" during their free time, many people worry about leisure and hurry from one activity to another, leaving little time to stop and think. Moreover, obsessive consumer attitudes about leisure time do not allow personal initiative and doing one's own thing.

A FUTURE SOCIETY AND SPORT

The twenty-first-century society is expected to become increasingly more of a "learning society." In part, this will be a function of the "information explosion"; thus, information (its acquisition and use) will become extremely important. A major problem will be the lack of an adequate supply of educated persons with professional and technical competence; therefore, futurists expect education, especially college and graduate education, to be acquired by a much greater proportion of the population than at present.[11]

What are the implications for sport for a highly educated population? Two opposing predictions have been proposed. The first suggests that there will be a trend away from violent forms of sport with a greater emphasis upon "cerebral" sports; the other suggests that violent sports will increase.

Cerebral Sports of the Future

Some futurists propose that as we become more cerebral, our choices will trend away from such violent sports as football, hockey, boxing, and auto racing. In addition, greater attention may be paid to the technical competence of the performers rather than just the outcome of the contest.

Perhaps one indication that intellectual or cerebral activities are gaining in popularity is that the latest forms of indoor recreation for young people are "smart" board games and computer and video games in which the players are expected to outwit or to outthink each other, or, in the case of the latter, beat the game program. PlayStation 3, Nintendo Wii, and Xbox 360 games pose daunting intellectual challenges requiring detailed strategy, role-playing, and simulations. According to the Entertainment Software Association, 227 million console games were sold worldwide in 2011 and video games are played in 72 percent of U.S. households. The average game player is thirty-seven years old.

The best of the video games are called "simulations" because of their capability to re-create the strategic requirements and sensuous experiences of the real sports. Entertainment Arts' *Madden Football*, *FIFA Soccer*, and *MVP Baseball* are among the most popular in the market. About one-fourth of the products sold by computer game companies are simulated sports games. Players of simulation games say that your muscles tighten, your pulse quickens, and you feel you're actually in the game. Even more realistic simulation sports games will be developed in the future. The goal in this industry is true-to-life experience.[12]

Fantasy sport leagues have emerged as an extremely popular form of "intellectual" sport, especially among young men—but women are becoming attracted as well. Football is the most popular of the growing fantasy sports games; it is estimated that there are more than 15 million fantasy football players. This form of sport involvement enables a "player" to get involved in selecting a team of athletes from a league, such as the NFL, to compete in a fantasy league. After each of the games played by the "real" players, the members of the fantasy league compile the statistics for each of the athletes the members of the fantasy league have drafted. Those statistics determine how each of the fantasy league "players" have "performed."

The first generation of fantasy sports involved face-to-face interaction between participants, usually friends. Belonging to a fantasy sports club was a particularly satisfying social experience because members were able to engage in a social activity in which everyone in the group had an interest—professional sports. All of this involved accumulating an extensive knowledge of athletes, teams, and strategy in "real" leagues, creatively thinking about their use, and outsmarting the others in the fantasy league. So participating was intensely cerebral for each member.

With the growth and popularity of the Internet, the popularity of Internet sports fantasy leagues—where all interactions take place online—has skyrocketed during the past decade. A search on Google.com for "Internet sports fantasy leagues" turned up 2,570,000 websites. Subscribers to an Internet sports fantasy league pay a fee to become a member, or "team owner." According to the Fantasy Sports Trade Association, nearly one in five males twelve and older in North America play fantasy sports—a rate of participation that helps to generate $1.9 *billion* in revenue annually in league entry fees. The Web's ability to deliver immediate sports statistics takes interaction in the fantasy league to a completely new level, increasing the enjoyment of fantasy games by providing a more exciting experience for participants. Subscribing to a sports fantasy league is the closest thing you can find to owning your own team franchise and becoming the team's manager and president all in one. You make all the decisions. You are supplied with everything you need to build a team in the best manner possible. Armed with all these resources, you are free to create the team of your dreams. To be a winner, you have to be astute because all the other owners are equally determined to win.[13] Winners of Internet-based fantasy sport leagues typically win prize money. The game known as *Sports Fantasy Leagues* has awarded $210,000 in guaranteed weekly prize money.

Many of the technosports and ecosports, both to be discussed in a later section of this chapter, can also be considered cerebral sports.

Violent Sports of the Future

Violence continues as a prominent part of both our real world and our sports world. High homicide rates plague our cities and even small towns; indeed, it is dangerous to be on the streets in some urban areas after dark. Some of the most popular television programs and movies feature gratuitous violence, and the high-tech violence of TV and movies may foretell future violent societies.

Given the broad societal violence, the possibility of continued or even increased violence in sports certainly exists. As we noted in Chapter 7, there are those who believe that sport provides a cathartic discharge of aggressive urges, and, therefore, violence done under the auspices of sports keeps the cap on social violence. Still others propose that the meaning of sport may be in the "quest for excitement in an unexciting society," and vigorous and violent sport may serve to restore tension and excitement.[14]

The popularity of football, hockey, boxing, professional wrestling, ultimate fighting, and auto racing validates the public interest in violent sports. The public image of these sports projected through radio and television commercials promotes the idea of violence. For example, the National

Hockey League has consistently marketed its games through television commercials as violent, almost promising fans that they can expect to see lots of fighting. For many years, the opening commercial for Monday Night Football showed a helmet of each of the competing teams for that night; the helmets turned to face each other and smashed together, with fragments of each flying away. The message of the imagery was clear: The viewer could expect to see some violent collisions.

World Wrestling Entertainment debuted on the USA Network in 1983, and it has maintained a fanatical following into the second decade of the twenty-first century. The staged violence of the World Wrestling Federation, its interlacing narratives, music, pyrotechnic stagecraft, and good-versus-evil plots are timeless theater, and some forecasters of future sports believe that it will be a powerful influence in the sports world of the future.

In the previous section of this chapter we described the widespread popularity of computer-driven games, especially sport simulation games. These are extreme caricatures of professional baseball and basketball where gratuitous violence and questionable morality are rampant. One of these, MLB SlugFest—advertised as "the most aggressive arcade-style baseball games EVER"—takes Major League Baseball to the extreme, with hard tags, home plate collisions, breaking up double plays with spikes high, pitchers throwing at batters, and fights breaking out after nearly every play.

From their beginning, video games and computer-driven games have overwhelmingly had violent themes—warfare, enemies from outer space, urban crime, etc. It seems that games such as MLB SlugFest have merely transferred the violence from nonsport settings to a sport setting. Computer-based games have embedded themselves into North American culture. The role of violence in future computer-based games will depend on consumer demand and, possibly, legislation regulating them.

Technology and Future Sport

The world of sports has made tremendous use of technology, and much in current sport is the product of technological innovation. The type of sport that emerges from technological advances has sometimes been called technosport.

Technosport and the Future

Technology has always altered the way sports are played and observed. Scientific advances in materials have revolutionized sporting goods and equipment and transformed training and coaching methods. The high-tech synthetic materials now used in athletes' apparel and equipment have been major contributors to the improvement of athletes' performances in almost every sport. Technological innovations are transforming many sports—from NASCAR (aerodynamic cars) to the NFL (helmet radio)—modifying strategy, playing styles, and even game rules.[15]

As for training, conditioning, and coaching, to a great extent the emergence of superior athletic performance is a consequence of a pool of specialized experts who are knowledgeable about the newest biotechnologies. These are sport scientists—biomechanists, exercise physiologists, biochemists, nutritionists, and orthopedists—whose expertise is being widely used by trainers and coaches. One of the areas in which sports scientists have been involved is attempting to select potentially superior athletes more deliberately and rationally. In recent years, biochemical, biomechanical, and behavioral sciences have been used with young children in an effort to sort out the potential future champions from the average athlete.

We may expect that scientific selection of future athletes during their early childhood on the basis of their physical and psychological attributes will become commonplace in the future. Once potential athletes have been identified, they will receive special training in preparation for their ultimate careers in sport. There are already programs of this type under way in North America in the form of elite sports academies and youth clubs, and the successes in the Olympic Games of some of the athletes from these programs are publicly attributed to the early selection procedures.[16]

Many of the record-breaking feats of the past few years can be attributed to advanced training techniques and better equipment and facilities, but a growing trend among athletes and their coaches is to resort to various chemical substances

in order to enhance sports performance, as we noted in Chapter 7. As performance standards increase in every sport, substance abuse will probably escalate. It is likely that new biotechnology will enable biochemists to perfect substances that will increase athletes' chances of winning and will be undetectable in the fluids of the body. In spite of increased sophistication in drug-testing procedures, some new drugs are undetectable before or after competition. Futurists expect that the development of new substances might enable a runner, for example, to shave seven- or eight-tenths of a second off his or her 100-meter dash or a javelin thrower to gain an extra seven or eight feet on his or her throw.

At perhaps the most futuristic extreme, sport technologists might turn to "genetic engineering." Indeed, the World Anti-Doping Agency (WADA) has already asked scientists to help find ways to prevent gene therapy from becoming the newest means of doping. But eventually, preventing athletes from gaining access to gene therapy may become impossible.[17]

Technosport will be evident in the playing arenas of the future. The domed stadiums built during the past twenty years are miniature prototypes of the giant arenas on the drawing boards. Specialists in stadium design believe that in the future most stadiums and ballparks will be built with fully retractable roofs. The entire natural grass field of the recently completed stadium of the Phoenix Cardinals NFL team is retractable. The grass field remains outside the stadium in the sun until game day, getting the maximum amount of sunshine and nourishment. While the field is outside the stadium, this provides unrestricted access to the stadium floor for events and staging of various kinds.

Future edifices will be equipped with many spectacular accoutrements, including push-button vending machines and individual video screens mounted on each seat. As the new millennium began, New York's Madison Square Garden outfitted four sections of club seating and all luxury suites with interactive seats. Through a complex system of computers and touch-screen monitors, those seating areas can access live, isolated camera angles, multiperspective replays with slow motion, sports highlights and statistics, and stored video and outside network feeds. Undoubtedly, entire venues will be wired like this in the future, with additional features. Seats will be equipped with earphones so that spectators can listen to press-box scouts giving advice to the bench, conversations at the pitching mounds, quarterbacks' calls in the huddle, and even locker-room pep talks.

Architects and developers of future sports venues see them as more than purveyors of sporting events. They believe that in the synergistic bliss of the globalized economy, stadiums and arenas will simply turn into malls and food courts. The live sporting events themselves will become, at best, a point-of-purchase display. Although at first one might find this statement merely cynical, a close study of the business establishments within current sports venues clearly shows that they have moved beyond being just food and drink outlets and have indeed begun to become social settings like shopping malls.

Computers and mobile devices will be the central objects because future society will be an information-based society. Computers, smartphones, and other mobile instruments will be staples for technosport, just as they will be for technoindustry. Coaches and athletes will be able to receive instant information about their own teams and their opponents. Coaches at all levels have used computer technologies for several years for the selection of athletes and as an aid in scouting opponents, and the use of such "tech toys" will proliferate. In football, college and professional teams often use computers to print out tables about opponents' tendencies and to help coaches and athletes make decisions during the game. This trend will undoubtedly accelerate during the next decade, perhaps to the point where each play in football will be called on the basis of printouts, and baseball coaches will use computers to call each pitch and each infield shift.

The fascination with enhanced sports performances and the obsession with winning have meant that technological innovations have been eagerly sought and employed in sports. However, thoughtful people within and outside the sports world are raising important social questions such as: Just because science and technology makes it possible for athletes and teams to set new speed, distance, and weight records, should they? Are the higher risks to the life and limb of athletes worth using whatever is scientifically and technologically possible?[18]

Many times people simply accept the idea that if it can be done, it should be done; the question of whether something should be done is seldom asked. There are compelling social and psychological reasons why that question, and others like it, will be increasingly asked, and with good reason. For example, there is no doubt that one of the consequences of employing the latest technological innovations is that various injuries and illnesses are increasing for athletes. Their incidence and seriousness are rising in many sports at the elite levels.

Scientific and technical terminology, when used in sport, often conceives of athletes as objects, little different from inanimate machines. Indeed, the terms "human machine" and "mortal engine" have been favorite metaphors for athletes' bodies among sport technicians. However, the human-as-machine notion has inherent dangers. Humans are not machines, and acting as if they are can be a source of major problems. After all, when a machine ceases to function properly, or quits working altogether, it can be discarded or scrapped. Humans are their body, and they have only one body, and it must last a lifetime; if it is damaged or parts of it destroyed, the quality of life is irreparably damaged.

There is another dimension to questioning the unqualified acceptance of scientific and technical developments in the interest of enhanced performances and sporting victories. The scientific-technical ethos gives priority to the product—the outcome; but the aspect of sport that has always been its prevailing essence is its process—its fun, its spontaneity, its creativeness, its expressiveness. Scientizing and technocizing sport subverts what have always been sport's most endearing features.[19]

It is likely that over the next twenty years a major debate will center on the social-ethical questions that have been raised here about the scientific-technical directions of sport. The dominant view that prevails in the sports world is not guaranteed. Resistance, opposition, even rejection of that dominant view have already begun, and will probably continue in some form for the foreseeable future.

A Counterpoint to Technosports: Ecosports

At the same time that technosports trends are altering sports at an incredible pace, another trend is moving forward with an extraordinary momentum of its own. For lack of a better name for it, many of its participants refer to it as "ecosports." Ecosports involve natural play and unstructured games; many of them are done out-of-doors, without boundaries, and with few or no codified rules. Ecosports also include a variety of what have been called "nontraditional" or "alternative" physical activities. Some of the various forms of ecosports tend to emphasize cooperation rather than competition, the struggle rather than the triumph; the main point of many of them is to play, to enjoy, and to exist.

Ecosports and the Future

Early twenty-first-century society confronts us with a congested urban lifestyle. Houses are jammed tightly against each other, apartments are stacked story on story, offices and factories are made up of steel and concrete, and our jobs are forcing us to work among multitudes of our fellow human beings. Thus, many North Americans yearn for the out-of-doors, to be away from the crush of people. The mountains, oceans, lakes, rivers, and sky all beckon.

The outdoor form of the ecosport movement is well under way, manifested in activities such as hiking, rock climbing, kayaking, scuba diving,

Many North Americans yearn for high-risk, high-adventure, extreme sports. These sports have become a new category of sports. (istockphoto)

canoeing, sailing, waterskiing, skydiving, snow-boarding, and so forth. Attendance at national parks, recreational facilities, and local parks has skyrocketed. In the past decade the number of North Americans participating in outdoor ecosport activities has grown dramatically: Cross-country skiers increased from a few thousand in 1980 to more than 3 million in 2011. There are an estimated 44 million runners, including a group of more than 8 million "hard-core" runners (they prefer *not* to be called joggers) who run at least 120 days a year. The number of hikers has more than doubled in the past ten years to about 40 million. At the national parks, backpacking increased by more than 100 percent between 1985 and 2011. The number of mountaineers has been doubling about every five years. The trend is clear: The public mindset is moving toward outdoor physical activities as an alternative to traditional organized sports.

There are even new categories of ecosports. One of these is called "action sports" by the sporting goods industry. In-line skating, with 29 million skaters, is one of the largest contributors to the explosive growth in action sports in North America. Other rapidly growing sports in this category are skateboarding, snowboarding, windsurfing, BMX, triathlon, kayaking, and downhill mountain biking.

Another new category of sports is called "adventure sports." Although it is rather new as a distinct category, there is already an astonishing variety of these sports, including adventure racing (biking, running, climbing, hiking, and canoeing over courses of 80 miles or more), long-distance cycling (the Race Across America race is 2,983 miles), and extreme trail hiking—the Pacific Crest Trail is 2,655 miles long, the Continental Divide Trail is 2,600 miles long, and the Appalachian Trail is 2,168 miles long. The Primal Quest Adventure Race and others like it are five- to ten-day competitions of trekking, mountain biking, and whitewater rafting.

Some of the action sports and adventure sports overlap into a rather ill-defined category called "extreme sports." We discussed extreme sports in Chapter 11 in connection with the X Games competitions, broadcast on ESPN. For many people, what ESPN covers in its telecasts of extreme sports competitions defines extreme sports. But for those who participate in the plethora of nontraditional sports, there is a much broader variety of sports that are considered "extreme." Perhaps the most extreme of these is BASE (an acronym for building, antenna, span [bridge], and earth [cliffs] jumping). Between 1985 and 2005, more than fifty participants were killed in this extreme sport. BASE is an example of a new approach to sports that coincides with a larger sensation-seeking cultural shift toward collecting experiences. Experiences are a large status symbol for people of all ages. They feel satisfaction in saying, "I jumped off this . . ." or "I climbed that. . . ."[20]

Nontraditional or "alternative" indoor ecosports include several of the Oriental martial arts, such as aikido, karate, judo, and tae kwon do, as well as various forms of yoga. Most do not require elaborate equipment and organization; also competition is not important to their mastery (indeed, in aikido, competition is forbidden). Skilled movements in these activities are frequently like dances, and the performers achieve a transcendent beauty in the whirling, throwing, kicking, and jumping common to these activities.

Most ecosports do not attract the publicity of the technosports, and most of them certainly do not attract masses of spectators. For many participants in ecosports, the essence is participation, so the fanfare and hoopla associated with technosport are not missed. That is precisely what is attractive about these sports for many of the participants.

Will the ecosport momentum carry through the first decades of the twenty-first century? Many social dynamics influence the popularity of sports, but most forecasters of sport in the twenty-first century agree that this form of sport will increase in popularity.

Some view these forms of sport as a reaction not only against the technocorporate form of organization characteristic of North American social institutions but also against the organized and corporate levels of sport described in Chapter 1, where the outcome supersedes the process. This certainly may be why many of the participants of these sports took them up and popularized them, but ecosports are increasingly being seized on by commercial interests as new markets for products and services.

The commercial sport industry seeks to organize sports activities on strict market principles—the pursuit of profits, rather than the satisfaction of personal and social needs. The play elements of the activities are squeezed out as corporate profit motives increase. Over thirty-five years ago social analyst Harry Braverman eloquently described this trend toward the commercialization of all sporting activities: "So enterprising is [capitalism] that even where the effort is made by one or another section of the population to find a way to nurture sports . . . through personal activity . . . these activities are rapidly incorporated into the market so far as is possible."[21]

There is compelling evidence that this phenomenon is occurring in ecosports. Jogging and running began as a way to increase health and fitness, but within a few years a massive commercial "running industry" had emerged with multinational firms selling high-tech running shoes and a variety of other apparel and accessories. "Fun runs" were largely replaced with 10-K and marathon races, then triathlons, and finally Ironman competitions with corporate sponsors and prize money winners. On Ironmanlive.com at one point there was a sidebar titled "The Anatomy of an Ironman Product," followed by this statement:

> The process of identifying, developing, manufacturing and selling an Ironman-Triathon-branded product can be just as challenging as the long and obstacle-ridden path an athlete follows to become an Ironman. Just like every elite triathlete who crosses an Ironman finish line anywhere, these products can only bear the Ironman label if they can meet the Ironman standards. Simply put, Ironman-licensed products must deliver the benefits implied by the Ironman label.[22]

This makes clear that Ironman sports is a brand name that is for sale.

Aerobic exercise began as a movement to improve cardiovascular conditioning in people who were in poor physical condition. Before long, several related commercial industries appeared: aerobic centers, aerobic shoes, and aerobic apparel. Local, state, and national championships are now part of the aerobics industry, all sponsored by commercial firms that market and sell their products and services to aerobics participants. But they also use aerobics practitioners as models

to sell a wide variety of products and services that consumers associate with the lean, hard-body look of the models.

In Chapter 11 we described how nontraditional, youth-oriented sports had been captured by ESPN and turned into the X Games TV programming, which is an advertising bonanza for corporations selling products to a teenage following. Consequently, X Games have gone from antiestablishment to mainstream and commercial—becoming extremely organized, with special training camps and elite coaches. Famed X Games skateboarder Tony Hawk, whose name is on dozens of products, was voted "coolest big-time athlete," ahead of megasport superstars such as Alex Rodriguez, LeBron James, and Serena Williams, in a poll conducted by a marketing firm.[23] Similar trends can be seen with all of the action and adventure sports. Unfortunately for those who seek physical activities that are not dominated by codified rules, professional event organizers, and corporate sponsorships, or hyped by paid endorsers, the tendencies of the past suggest the trends of the future will be in the direction of commercial takeover rather than blissful carefree independence.

TRENDS IN THE ECONOMY AND FUTURE SPORTS

The North American economic systems are complex mixtures of capitalism and socialism, and the free trade agreements between the United States, Canada, and Mexico tend to integrate the individual economies. Throughout the world during the twentieth century there was steady movement away from laissez-faire (virtually unregulated) capitalism and toward managerial capitalism, with the adoption of many socialistic features, which has caused some observers to predict that capitalism will die in North America. This view is not shared by most futurists, however. Capitalism has proved extremely adaptable, and despite the growth in social entitlement programs and the growth in government over the past twenty years, there has been no fundamental challenge to the capitalist economy in North America.

Given the enormous influence of the corporate rich and the tendency for most North Americans to accept the present economic structure as proper, capitalism will undoubtedly remain a pillar of society in the United States and Canada.

The future economy, barring nuclear holocaust, unforeseen energy problems, or other catastrophic events, will probably continue to go through its cycles of prosperity and recession. The terrorist attacks on September 11, 2001, were a severe shock to the social climate and economic systems of North America. Everyone has heard "The world will never be the same" repeated over and over. But in spite of these events, and the security measures that we all live with in their aftermath, our lives do go on. According to economic forecasters, North America will face increasing international economic competition and will be challenged to find better ways to accommodate the emerging global economy rather than trying to dominate international economic competitors.[24]

The Future of Professional Sports

The professional sports industry in North America has grown at an unprecedented rate in the past twenty years. It is now a sprawling, multibillion-dollar-a-year industry that is clearly big business, and in which winning and losing count far less than making a profit. Professional sport franchise owners once generally had a deep emotional commitment to the sport and believed that the administration and financial operations were merely necessary adjuncts to owning a team.

Current owners are increasingly corporate conglomerates of one kind or another, and they think primarily of maximizing profit through rational business procedures. Providing sports entertainment for loyal hometown fans is only a secondary consideration. The most visible example of this is found in the numerous threats by ownership to move franchises if demands for new stadiums, better lease deals, and so forth are not met. They are not idle threats, as can be seen in the number of franchise moves.[25]

As we indicated in an earlier section in this chapter, the trend appears to be toward an expansion of professional sports in the foreseeable future.

However, most sports forecasters predict that there will be little expansion in the four major North American team sports (MLB, NFL, NHL, NBA) in the next twenty years. Instead, expansion will take place in other sports, such as soccer, lacrosse, auto racing, and women's basketball. One way professional sports might expand is by becoming more international. The four major North American team sports are played worldwide, and with air travel speeds increasing, there seems little reason not to expand into other continents. Soccer is already a sport played worldwide, and it seems imminent that North American soccer teams will be incorporated into European and/or Asian soccer leagues.

Fan support depends on adequate disposable income. Within the past decade, serious economic downturns have occurred in North America. Should a prolonged economic downturn occur, people will have less disposable income, and this could adversely affect professional sports. Moreover, as noted earlier, if ticket prices outstrip the cost of living, professional sports may price themselves out of the market.

The Future of Televised Sports

Television Coverage

Before television rescued the professional sports industry, professional sports owners were beset with decreasing attendance and the prospect of failure. The importance of television and radio markets has been a prominent factor in the growth and expansion of all professional sports. Professional sport and television enjoy a reciprocal relationship. Both pro sport and television executives realize that if any of the professional sports lost television revenues, their industry would be devastated. Therefore, for professional sports to maintain their entertainment status and continue to expand, they will have to depend on the benevolence of television. As long as the television networks consider pro sports a moneymaker, pro sports will prosper.

In the future, sports leagues and teams will develop pipelines directly targeted at their fans. Sports leagues are becoming their own media companies and are interacting directly with their consumers without the mediation of traditional media. For example, despite the NFL's television rights monopoly, the NFL has built its own television channel, the NFL Network, which broadcasts games throughout the season. It also builds the legends of the league with its popular NFL Films. Furthermore, the National Basketball Association's NBATV, the Baseball Network, and other team-only channels are revolutionizing sports television and transforming the sports rights infrastructure. As for the future, according to some media analysts, "the only certainty about the sports media marketplace is that it is adapting, and for stakeholders, this means constant monitoring of change and a commitment to innovation."[26]

Television Technology and Sports Viewing

Mediated sports spectating at first meant people sitting in their living rooms listening to accounts of the events on their radios. Today many people sit in their home entertainment centers and watch sports events on their huge high-definition TV screens. But that will change too. Anticipated technological advances with computer enhancement in the next decade or two will enable TV viewers to interact with the coverage and the game and to customize the content of the broadcast sports coverage they receive. Viewers will have control over what aspects of events they will watch. They will be able to direct camera angles and request regular and slow-motion replays of viewer-defined action. They will be able to call up certain cameras to focus on a single player, coach, or part of the field or court, and they will be able to ask for statistics and personal background on the players and coaches. Sports TV networks will also proliferate. The prospect of the thousand-channel universe has excited many sports fans. It seems likely that all of the most popular sports will have their own networks, so viewers will be able to watch their favorite sport 24/7.

As we noted in Chapter 11, PPV television is going to become a major factor in the next decade. There appears to be little doubt that within ten years sports fans will have to pay for many events they now see on free TV or basic cable. Some forecasters predict that as costs to attend sports events escalate and as television increasingly makes viewing of all important sports events available at low cost, attendance at sports facilities will dwindle.

Regardless of the trends in viewing options and interactivity, high-definition television gives sports viewers a much sharper view of the action than was once possible. Those who have high-definition equipment confirm that the images are so incredibly clear and lifelike that regular TV pictures look blurred and out of focus.

Internet Technology and Sports Viewing

We discussed the Internet in a previous section in connection with cerebral sports. But it is pertinent to mention it here as well. The Internet is one of the most sophisticated and useful outcomes of innovations in modern technology. Those who work on the cutting edge of this technology claim that we are still in the early stages of achieving what the future holds for the Internet. Within a short time the complete integration of Internet technology, computer technology, telecommunications, and the World Wide Web will make it possible for users to use computers, the Internet, and television interchangeably. They will not only have incredible choices of sporting events at their command but will also have virtually unlimited control over what they will watch and how they will view the events. (See Box 15.1.)

Video Technology and Sports Video Games

Another form of mediated sports "participation" is video games. Video games, which provide simulations of various kinds, are extremely popular with a broad spectrum of age groups, but especially with teenagers. Sports games, in particular, are plentiful. Some of the most popular are exhilarating simulations of professional and college football and basketball games, but racing games are also popular, as are extreme sports videos.

With the increase in technological sophistication over the past decade, the best sport video games feature outstanding graphics and put players squarely in the middle of the action. In football video games, players have play-calling options that mirror actual coaches' playbooks, making for a seamlessly realistic experience. Incredibly photo-realistic graphics make the virtual sports games mesmerizing.

Box 15.1   *Thinking About Sport:* Mediated Sports and Fans of the Future

The emergence of professional and intercollegiate sports in the latter half of the nineteenth century gave rise to sports fandom and became one of the prime reasons for groups to gather to be entertained. Moreover, people formed alliances toward specific teams. On-site spectatorship was a way to know about the game—who won and who lost—but also to witness the performances of the players and coaches.

But on-site spectatorship had a major limitation: Only those people with the location, time, and means to actually view the game knew what happened in the contest. The print media—newspapers and magazines—quickly realized there was a market for pregame as well as postgame information about sports events. A mediated—meaning acting or brought about through an intervening agency—sports industry was born. Print media was the only mediated sport until the 1920s, when radio broadcasts of sports events brought families, drinking friends, and workers together to listen to sports events.

With the technological innovations of the 1940s and 1950s, television quickly became a dominating force around which families and bar buddies gathered to watch televised sports events. For fifty years television was the preferred way for social groupings to participate in mediated sports.

The explosive development of the World Wide Web in the last decade of the twentieth century created an ideal mediated sports medium as well as a useful resource for dedicated sports fans. The accessibility, interactivity, speed, and multimedia content triggered a major change in the delivery of mediated sports, a change that no one could have predicted.

Social scientists are concerned about the effects a computer-based, Internet-connected lifestyle will have on social relations. Although television tended to turn social life indoors and to socially isolate entertainment, it did bring families together to watch the programs, especially sports, and sports bars became a popular social site for watching sports events. By contrast, as ownership of computers, cell phones, iPhones, iPads, and BlackBerry devices becomes universal and as free live online coverage of sports events becomes mainstream, mediated sports may become an individual rather than a social activity.

Indeed, the way some futurists see it, with everyone in a home owning a computer, and with so many live online sports to view, each member of the family will retreat to his or her corner of the house to view preferred sports events. Future mobile handheld instruments will contribute to individual, independent, nonsocial viewing of mediated sports as well. One sports media analyst who claims that the next great frontier for mediated sports is probably in your pocket right now believes that it will provide a personal rather than a social form of spectating.

Sources: Pierre D. Bognon, *The Anatomy of Sports Fans: Reflections on Fans & Fanatics* (Charleston, SC: BookSurge Publishing, 2009); see also Lawrence W. Hugenberg, Paul M. Haridakis, and Adam C. Earnheardt, eds., *Sports Mania: Essays on Fandom and the Media in the 21st Century* (Jefferson, NC: McFarland Publishers, 2008).

Sony, Microsoft, and Nintendo, the major makers of video game systems, are working diligently to make the audio and video of these games more and more realistic, and the control equipment more precise. Given the growth of all forms of mediated sports over the past decade, there is every reason to expect that the introduction of remarkable new video game systems will be an annual event in the foreseeable future.

A number of futurists have expressed concern that TV, Internet, and video technology will become so exciting, so mesmerizing, that it will have an isolating effect. They fear that masses of sports fans may choose to remain in the comfort of their homes with their TV sets, computers, and video game systems rather than actually attending sports events. A number of social scientists have been warning that the privatization of leisure, through the retreat into the home for entertainment, has the danger of bringing about a collapse of a civic ethic within society, the sense of belonging to a society.[27]

Intercollegiate Athletics and the Future

As we have noted at several places in this volume, professional sport is not limited to privately owned sport franchises. Big-time collegiate sports constitute a professional industry in every sense of the word. They are every bit as dependent on economic considerations as other professional sports, and one can confidently predict that as television goes, with respect to buying rights to broadcast intercollegiate sports events, so will go the big-time collegiate programs.

Even with the bonanza of television money, intercollegiate athletic programs have had increasing financial problems. The major problem is money—or the lack of it. Growth in attendance has slowed as competition, from both professional sports and other attractions, has increased. Meanwhile, increased costs have taken a brutal toll on the athletic budgets of many colleges. Adding additional games to the traditional ten-game football schedule, permitting first-year students to play on varsity teams, expanding play-off schedules in basketball and bowl games in football, limiting the size of coaching staffs, and de-emphasizing or dropping so-called nonrevenue sports are all economic measures that have been adopted to add revenue or to reduce expenses in intercollegiate athletics.

All is still not well on the campuses. For example, many state-supported universities receive substantial support for collegiate athletics from tax funds, and public opposition to this is growing. Legislatures are weighing the athletic appropriations against, for example, faculty salaries and state aid for disadvantaged students. Other educational considerations include more spending for community colleges and expansion of vocational education. Needs are also being considered in other fields, such as mental health, welfare, law enforcement, and the general administration of government.

What does the future hold for intercollegiate athletics? Finally, slowly, gradually, and reluctantly, major universities with big-time football and basketball programs are moving toward paying college athletes a salary for their hard work on behalf of the university. The charade that universities have advanced—that college sports are amateur athletics and therefore the athletes must not accept financial remuneration for playing—has become so ludicrous that even leaders in the NCAA have begun to acknowledge that athletes should be given some form of direct payment. As we described in Chapter 6, football and basketball coaches at major universities are making annual salaries of more than $2 million; major university budgets range from

$40 million to over $120 million. Assistant coaches, athletic trainers, sports information directors, even equipment managers receive livable incomes. Only the athletes are without a salary. Prognosticators for intercollegiate sports expect that within the next five to ten years the NCAA and its member universities will develop a system for direct payment to student-athletes at major universities. It is a disservice to intercollegiate athletes to remain committed to an outdated code of amateurism for economic controls.[28]

Growing criticism of the practice of colleges admitting a large number of academically unqualified athletes and possibly diminishing the academic environment of their campuses prompted a number of small liberal arts colleges in the northeastern states to change their admission policies. Beginning in 2002, these colleges admitted fewer applicants whose prowess as athletes is the difference between being admitted and being rejected by the college considering them. The new policy has stimulated supportive talk throughout higher education. It is too soon to know whether this recent action will create a new trend in higher education, but the widespread dissatisfaction with admitting academically unqualified athletes suggests that the new directions taken by a few small colleges might gain support and emulation.

Sports club programs are growing on college campuses. These are student-oriented sports teams coached by older students or interested persons with a love for the sport (they typically receive no pay) and are funded by the participants or by small sums from the institution's student activity funds. Some higher education administrators have even predicted that over the next twenty years most of the athletic teams on a college campus will be of the sports club type, with the university having only one or two sports of the high-visibility, commercial type.

Secondary School Sports and the Future

Over the past two decades high school sports have been faced with two major challenges: bringing the sports programs into compliance with Title IX and coping with the increasing costs of conducting the expanding sports programs. In the latter case, in 2011 the National Federation of State High School Associations reported that for the twenty-second consecutive year the number of student participants in high school athletics increased. But the increasing reluctance of taxpayers to support education and the hesitancy of many state legislatures to raise taxes combined to force many school systems to consider reducing extracurricular activities, including sports programs. Even though the cost of a high school athletic program is only 1 to 3 percent of a high school's overall budget, the general public seems increasingly indifferent to supporting these programs.[29]

If financial difficulties continue to plague secondary schools, modifications in the funding of the programs will probably occur. Indeed, one trend of the past decade is the "pay-for-play" plans that require athletes to assume some of the costs of equipment and other expenses associated with their participation. This trend is likely to grow, as it has been successful in many communities. Other means may be tried in the next decade to salvage high school sports programs. More active booster clubs, corporate sponsorship, and television contracts have all been tried, but further development is likely. As an alternative to high school athletics, some communities may consider phasing sports out of the schools entirely and having the municipal recreation departments administer sports programs for all age groups.

TRENDS IN SOCIAL VALUES AND FUTURE SPORT

In Chapter 3 we identified the dominant values in Canadian and American societies. These mainstream values include an entire constellation of beliefs involving the importance of personal effort and accomplishment in defining one's status and worth, both economic and social, and one's relation to social institutions. These values, like other aspects of North American life, have been undergoing significant change; indeed, some social scientists claim we are on the verge of a cultural crisis that will ultimately revolutionize our values

and institutions. The roots of this crisis reside in a strong disillusionment with traditional values.

The Quest for Democracy and Equality

During the past twenty years a continuing debate has taken place in North America, as well as in countries throughout the world, over the issue of democracy and equality. We have witnessed the downfall of autocratic governments on every continent. Leaders of almost every political revolution or of countries with substantial chronic social unrest have vowed to provide greater democracy and equality; indeed, there is said to be a worldwide yearning for a "democratic revolution." This is a theme with great appeal to people throughout North America who have been disadvantaged by their ascribed statuses and are demanding to be considered full members of society.[30]

North Americans have actually been in the forefront of those seeking a democracy and equality revolution, and futurists expect that there will continue to be demands for more autonomy, more democracy, and greater participation in places of work and in government. All of these demands add up to a quest for more control over one's life and for the reduction of economic, political, and social inequalities that now restrict people from improving their quality of life.

The essence of the quest for social change is related to new ideas about humanity and methods of interpersonal relations. A more optimistic, democratic, humanistic conception of human nature is emerging. These new values have already had an impact on such social institutions as education, politics, and religion, and they are making their presence felt in the business world.

There is no longer only one acceptable lifestyle; nor is there one set of social values. Because of this, we find many changes in economic and political organization and a variety of sports activities and leisure patterns. The result has been a shift in consciousness, a shift in personal goals and priorities and in the ways of perceiving and ordering the world outside the individual. According to scholars who track social change and trends, more North Americans are beginning to resist the frantic pace of the business world and are feeling the urge to return life to a time of greater simplicity and ease. People are turning to relaxing hobbies like gardening and fishing, and some are seeking balance through job sharing or telecommuting. Many younger citizens are protesting traditional rules, policies, and social practices through various social movements.[31]

Several years ago, economic historian and Nobel laureate Robert Fogel demonstrated through his research that eras of great affluence, such as the 1990s, typically are followed by what he refers to as "Great Awakenings," and we may be due for one in the next decade. As a consequence, futurists expect the next twenty years to be characterized by more humane, expressive, and creative approaches to life. Futurists predict that many young people will discover satisfaction in the opportunity to become involved with activities that test their talents, give them more responsibility for their behavior, and let them stretch their minds and bodies.

Trends in Sports Values

Social practices are based on traditional norms and values and are therefore vulnerable to the effects of value changes among significant segments of the society. Many traditional values have come under attack in the past decade, and since sport is a social practice, it too has been challenged by emerging values.

Democracy and Equality in Sport

Traditional athletic priorities and practices have begun to be challenged by a new set of standards premised on the notion that democratic processes have relevance in sport as well as other sectors of life. Consequently, athletes are demanding changes in sports at all levels; they are especially pressing for greater participation in the decisions that affect their athletic lives and for a greater responsiveness on the part of coaches and athletic administrators. They have also pressed for more autonomy, for the freedom to be what they want to be and to choose how they will live.

Although some athletes have called for a change toward greater freedom and personal responsibility within the structure and functioning of sport, they have been a minority, and it is unlikely that athletes will be in the vanguard of social change

in the future. The world of sports generates a fundamental acceptance of the established norms and values. Even if athletes as a group do not catalyze much change, they are nevertheless members of their own youth culture, a culture that is pressing for change. In previous eras, athletes tended to confront authorities infrequently; today's athletes are more likely to challenge the management establishment. This attitude is demonstrated by the strikes in pro baseball, hockey, and football. In the past decade, collegiate and Olympic athletes have demanded, and have won, representation on important decision-making committees of the NCAA and the U.S. and Canadian Olympic committees. Directions in sport, then, suggest increased egalitarianism, democracy, and humanism, but these are trends that will occur only gradually and only as they become a part of society.

Opportunity and Equality for Special Groups in Sport

Historical inequalities and injustices for females and racial-ethnic minorities were described in Chapters 13 and 14. As part of each chapter, we also highlighted the remarkable changes that have taken place in the sports world in the past generation that have given greater access and opportunity to African Americans, women, and ethnic minorities in sport. Other groups as well have experienced historical discrimination in sport, but here too conditions are changing for the better and will likely continue to do so.

People with Disabilities and Sport. One of those groups is people with disabilities, who make up about 20 percent of the population. People with disabilities historically have been subject to systematic prejudice and injustice, and only in the past few decades have national laws and enlightened public attitudes reversed the practices that treated people with disabilities as outcasts.

One of the oldest and most effective organizations supporting and promoting sports for people with disabilities is the nonprofit National Sports Center for the Disabled (NSCD), which began in 1970 with children with amputations from Children's Hospital in Denver, Colorado. Presently, participants come to the NSCD from all fifty states and from countries all over the world. They can choose among twenty different winter and summer sports, from skiing and snowshoeing to river rafting and rock climbing. More than 23,000 lessons are provided annually. The NSCD Competition Program is the largest of its kind in North America. The program has been very successful at attracting and training some of the best ski racers with disabilities and placing them on the U.S. Disabled Ski Team.[32]

Another national organization serving the needs of the disabled is Disabled Sports USA (DS/USA), which was founded in 1967 by disabled Vietnam veterans. It was then called the National Amputee Skiers Association. After going through a series of names, it settled on its present name. Its website states that it offers nationwide sports rehabilitation programs to anyone with a permanent disability. Activities include winter skiing, water sports, summer and winter competitions, and fitness and special sports events. Participants include those with visual impairments, amputations, spinal cord injury, dwarfism, multiple sclerosis, head injury, cerebral palsy, and other neuromuscular and orthopedic conditions. As a member of the United States Olympic Committee, DS/USA sanctions and conducts competitions and training camps to prepare and select athletes to represent the United States at the Summer and Winter Paralympic Games.[33]

As one of the many horrible legacies of the Iraq and Afghanistan Wars, more than 1,286 (as of November 2011) young American men and women are now amputees. Sports are helping some of them recover and reclaim a somewhat normal life. Several special sports events have been established to help military amputees in the rehabilitation and return to healthy, active lives.[34]

The Paralympic Games are the Olympic-equivalent competitions for individuals with disabilities and are recognized by the International Olympic Committee. In 1960, in parallel with the Summer Olympic Games in Rome, a Games for wheelchair users was organized. Four hundred athletes from twenty-three countries competed, and these Games are considered the first Paralympic Games. The 2008 Beijing Paralympics had 148 nations participating and some 4,200 disabled athletes competing in 20 sports. The 2010 Winter Paralympics were

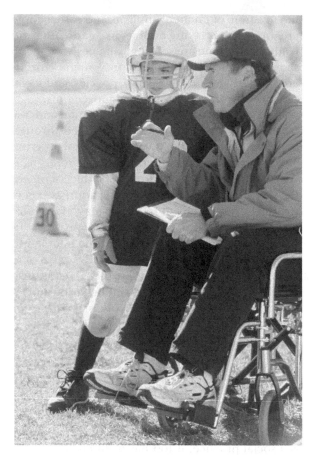

People with disabilities make up about 20 percent of the population. Historically, they have been virtually excluded from even trying sporting activities. But today, with enlightened public attitudes, the disabled are now a part of every category of sports participant—even coaching. (istockphoto)

held in Vancouver, British Columbia, with 506 athletes representing 44 countries.[35]

Our discussion has focused on the dramatic changes that have occurred in the past two decades for disabled athletes. It is clear that athletes with disabilities now have access and opportunities not only to participate in sport, but also to become elite athletes competing for gold medals and large sums of money. The future for disabled athletes looks very encouraging because widespread support is now in place for opportunities to increase.

Another world-renowned program for people with special needs is the Special Olympics—an international program of year-round sports training and athletic competition for developmentally disabled children and adults. The Special Olympics began in 1968 when Eunice Kennedy Shriver organized the First International Special Olympics Games at Soldier Field in Chicago. Since then, it has grown to include nearly 3.5 million athletes in 226 programs in 170 countries, providing year-round sports training and athletic competition for developmentally disabled children and adults. The mission is to provide a variety of Olympic-type sports for developmentally disabled individuals, thereby giving them opportunities to develop physical fitness, experience joy, and participate in a sharing of skills and friendship with their families and other Special Olympics athletes.

In the United States, there are Special Olympics chapters in all fifty states, the District of Columbia, Guam, the Virgin Islands, and American Samoa. About 25,000 communities in the United States have Special Olympics programs. In Canada more than 16,400 volunteers, including over 13,000 trained coaches, currently support Special Olympics programs every day in virtually every community nationwide. There seems little doubt that these programs will continue to grow in the coming years and provide sporting opportunities to a broader spectrum of individuals with disabilities.[36]

Senior Populations and Sport. In an earlier section of this chapter, we noted that the over-65 population will more than double between 2010 and 2050, when one in five North Americans will be over 65 years old. The trend toward a greater proportion of the population being over 50 years of age has been under way for some time now, and older adults are remaining physically active.

The organizations they choose to join to continue to play sports vary from local community recreation programs to the National Senior Games Association (NSGA). The NSGA is a nonprofit organization dedicated to motivating senior men and women to lead a healthy lifestyle through the senior games movement. The organization governs the Summer National Senior Games (Senior Olympics) and the Winter National Senior Games. About 250,000 senior athletes participate in these senior games competitions each year.

Participating athletes must be fifty years old or older and must qualify in an NSGA-sanctioned state senior game in order to compete. The Senior Olympics has grown to be one of the largest multisports athletic competitions in the world. Participation in the Summer National Senior Games has grown rapidly. In 2011, 15,000 athletes participated in this event. The Winter National Senior Games provide an opportunity for a new and different population of senior athletes to compete in a national sports event.[37]

Demographic trends that point to increasing life expectancy and a growing population of seniors who are healthy and active clearly indicate that sports of all kinds will grow in popularity and in participation among seniors. Indeed, sport planners claim that new sport organizations for seniors are where the action will be in the coming years.

Gays and Lesbians in Sport. Another group that has faced pervasive injustice is homosexuals. Historically, there has been little tolerance of homosexuality in North America. Despite substantially improved attitudes over the past decade, gays and lesbians still suffer various forms of social stigma and injustice. As we noted in Chapter 14, sport has been a bastion of homophobia; indeed, sport has been a cultural practice where homophobic attitudes have actually been socially constructed and reproduced.

As with other sectors of society, attitudes and values about human sexuality are gradually changing, and there is a greater acceptance of individuality in sexual orientation. In sport, as well, gays and lesbians have been "coming out," acknowledging their homosexuality. While there is still a deep division in attitudes toward homosexuality among North Americans, the taboo about homosexuality that once prevailed in sport is beginning to diminish. Gay and lesbian athletes compete at all levels of sport, from novices to Olympic champions. In addition to competing with and against heterosexual athletes in sports at all age and proficiency levels, many gays and lesbians participate in privately sponsored and community-sponsored leagues and events.

To provide a special sporting event for homosexual athletes and improve public attitudes about homosexuality, leaders of the homosexual community organized the first Gay Games in 1982 (the name changed to Federation of Gay Games in 1989), which are patterned after the Olympic Games and held every four years. The number of participants in the Federation of Gay Games has grown phenomenally—from 1,200 in the first Games to more than 12,000 from 70 countries in the 2010 Games in Cologne, Germany. The number of spectators has grown from a few thousand to more than a million. The Federation of Gay Games believes the growth potential for the future of these Games looks excellent.[38]

Gays and lesbians are also dedicated and loyal sports fans, and their attendance and support for some sports events and leagues are well known. One of the notable aspects of the new open visibility of gays and lesbians as sports fans is that they are beginning to be viewed as a "niche market" by commercial interests.

The San Francisco Giants are often credited with being the first professional team to market to gay fans. Beginning in 1994 the team designated one game per season as a fundraiser for acquired immunodeficiency syndrome (AIDS) research. By 2010 the event had generated nearly $1.4 million to support Bay Area HIV/AIDS education, service providers, and international AIDS research. The Giants say technically the game is not a "gay game day," but it does draw twice as many fans as a "normal" day game, and it is clear that gay fans make that difference.

It is obvious that the WNBA understands that lesbians have been its fan base since the league started. The league needs the money, so their marketing efforts are targeting lesbians. Some WNBA teams claim they have always sought the support of lesbian fans. Several promotions directors for WNBA teams say they have been doing it from day one and that members of the lesbian community are indicating their support.

The kinds of value changes that are taking place in North America and the adoption of new values in sport point clearly to a future where stereotyped and marginalized groups—people with disabilities, seniors, gays, lesbians, and others—are going to have more opportunities to play an integral role in sports of the future.

New Emphasis on Participation and Cooperation

Traditional youth and high school sports programs were practically built on a foundation in which a few athletes played on a few "varsity" teams, while the vast majority of people became "substitutes" or spectators. A new, active, participative orientation is gaining adherents. One visible trend in youth sports programs is the structuring of play to foster participation, cooperation, and sportsmanship. For example, rules decreeing that every child who registers should be assigned to a team and that every child on a team should play in every game are becoming more common. Some leagues feature no-win games, that is, no points are awarded for a win or loss and no records are kept of league standings or of leading scorers. Those who conduct such programs report that the youngsters appear to have a lot more fun than under the traditional format.

Earlier in this chapter we discussed various forms of alternative sports—action, adventure, extreme—that are rapidly gaining adherents and are flourishing. There seems to be little doubt that sports of these kinds will be the wave of the future. It is also reasonable to expect that new sports will be created. The traditional sports model has been shattered by the alternative sports, and there is now an atmosphere of creative experimentation with new sport forms. One manifestation of that is what is called junkyard sports. These offer an alternative to the traditional sports model because they stress personal involvement, active participation in rules and decisions, creativity, and most of all inclusiveness so all share the fun.[39]

New Forms of Intramural Sports

The intramural sports program has been the place where more student-athletes participate than anyplace else on a college campus. It is likely that this will continue as student enrollments get larger and larger. College students are increasingly rejecting the traditional offerings of campus intramural programs and demanding more innovative programs with greater potential to satisfy their immediate and long-term needs. As a consequence, intramural programs have had to devise new and different activities that de-emphasize championships, eliminate trophies, sponsor sports clubs, include equal sports opportunities for women, and provide greater use of facilities for open recreation.

Several colleges have experimented with the abolishment of all extrinsic rewards; no point systems or awards of any kind are employed. The importance of victory is de-emphasized by doing away with championships and limiting protests to on-the-spot, right-or-wrong, final decisions by activity supervisors. Any combination of undergraduate and graduate students and faculty is allowed to form teams. Women participate on teams that compete in the men's division. Here too the social climate is favorable for continuing to create new forms of sports practices. So the trend toward change and innovation to meet student interests will probably endure.

A Troubling Trend: Sports Incivility

Our emphasis throughout this chapter has been on the future and how changes in demography, social relationships, and technology will likely bring about a future of sport forms that will provide greater access, variety, opportunity, and inclusion to participants and fans. The trends that we have identified and discussed point to a generally optimistic future for sport and those involved in sport. However, one current trend is, in our view, detrimental to the advancement and enrichment of sport and everyone associated with it. We are going to identify that trend and suggest why we think it is counterproductive to enriching both the sport and the larger culture. We hope our discussion will stimulate thinking about ways to solve this problem.

Research and everyday experience tell us all that there is a growing social incivility in North American culture. Behavioral and social scientists have been studying this trend for the past decade, and the literature on this issue is enormous. The evidence is clear that civility is increasingly disappearing from our society. In its place is a disrespect, indifference, and uncaring attitude toward other people and toward social institutions and practices. Whether it's on the job or in the marketplace or on the highway, the I-don't-care-about-other-people attitude appears to be worsening.

Multiple factors have contributed to this trend. Some social analysts point to rural-to-urban demographic changes, others to the contingent nature and lack of security in the workplace, others to the individualistic nature of our value system, and still others to the decline of social capital in community life. Although no consensus has formed around the cause, there is uniform agreement that the general mood of incivility is pervasive.[40]

Throughout this text we have emphasized the close connections between the larger North American culture and sporting practices. The issue of growing incivility applies to trends in sport. The weakening social bonds of mutual respect, courtesy, and compassion have carried over into sports. Incidents like the following are becoming more commonplace:

- Vulgarities from fans directed at athletes and coaches during games
- Projectiles, such as beer bottles, batteries, and snowballs, thrown at athletes from the stands
- Fans fighting in the stands
- Fires being set by fans in stadiums
- Player violence and illegal actions that intentionally injure opponents
- Athletes (at all levels now) talking trash, belittling, and seeking to intimidate opponents
- Athletes preening, taunting, and spitting in the faces of opponents
- Street rioting and looting of businesses in cities after the winning or losing of a championship game

As with the decline in civility in society in general, social analysts point to a variety of potential precipitating factors for the growing incivility in sports. There is the obvious explanation that attitudes and behaviors found in the larger society will be manifested in sport. Fan behavior is often explained as an alienation formed by the huge salaries of professional athletes at the same time as free agency has led to a widespread player movement for even better salaries. This has been accompanied by a perceived athlete arrogance toward fans. Simultaneously, owners are perceived as gouging fans with higher and higher ticket prices and threats of moving to another city, unless fans, and other local taxpayers, build the millionaire owner a new arena or stadium. Some analysts see fans believing that the purchase of a ticket or the support of a team allows them to become rowdy, coarse, and lawbreaking. There are even cases where team management encourages fan misbehavior.[41]

While there are additional explanations that we could cite for the spreading uncivil, rude, and unsportsmanlike behavior of sports fans, athletes, and coaches, we think it is important to say that these practices are unfortunate and inappropriate, and they show disrespect for the sports themselves, for the athletes and coaches, and for one's fellow human beings. Longtime consumer activist Ralph Nader recently announced that he is working toward the establishment of a National Sports Commission. According to him, the Commission would develop a national sports policy and code of ethics that would protect and represent *all* sports stakeholders—players, fans, taxpayers, and other sports participants at all levels—and would be a positive step forward.[42]

The future is not something out there waiting to happen. Sports are practices that are socially constructed within the culture in which they exist, and any adequate account of them must be grounded in an understanding that they can be changed and shaped by the people who are involved with them. Sports play an important role in many lives; it is too significant to be despoiled by a future dominated by rude, disrespectful, and uncivil behaviors.

minorities in the population is increasing rapidly, and the different cultural traditions of minority groups will influence the trends and patterns of sport involvement. Women, minorities, the oppressed, and stereotyped groups have gained greater opportunities in the world of sport, and the egalitarian trend suggests that sport opportunities will increase in the years ahead for all persons.

Industrialization and technology reduced the average workweek until two decades ago, but other conditions have arisen to increase work time and nullify the actual leisure time of adults. The leisure time available in the future may be used in sports of either a more "cerebral" nature or a more violent nature; moreover, technological developments will probably result in new and more techno sport forms, and human reactions against technology will result in many more ecosports.

Professional and big-time intercollegiate sports have become successful business enterprises, mainly because of television involvement. Their future rests heavily upon the directions dictated by television.

Changes in value orientations over the past decade have emphasized equality and pluralism, and the world of sport has experienced protest and even violent revolt as athletes have rebelled against traditional authoritarian leadership. There is a troubling trend in sports that needs serious attention and reform—rude, disrespectful, uncivil behavior.

SUMMARY

This is an era of rapid change in North America, and sport, like other social institutions, is undergoing changes in form and content—changes related to those of the larger society. We have identified a number of the more salient social changes and speculated about how current and future trends may affect sport.

Trends in population suggest that the rapid expansion of professional sports is continuing and that pro franchises are organizing along regional rather than single-city lines. As the average age of the population increases, men and women are going to continue to stay active longer, even in high-level competitive sport. The proportion of

WEB RESOURCES

www.dol.gov
The U.S. Department of Labor website. Excellent for the reports on future work—trends and challenges in the twenty-first century.

www.census.gov/compendia/statab/
The website for the *Statistical Abstract of the United States*, as well as summary items.

www.statcan.gc.ca
The home page for Statistics Canada. It contains projections for a variety of topics for 2006, 2011, 2016, 2021, and 2026.

www.extreme.com
The home page for extreme sports, with numerous links to specific sports and future competitive extreme sporting events.

www.dsusa.org
This is the home page for Disabled Sports USA. The site features much information, especially up-to-date information on events and programs.

www.specialolympics.org
This is the home page for the Special Olympics. It has separate pages for each event, tips for coaches and athletes, and a good list of links to other sites.

www.sportinsociety.org
Sport in Society at Northeastern University is the world's leading social justice organization that uses sport to create social change.

NOTES

1. Richard Watson, *Future Files: A Brief History of the NEXT 50 Years*, rev. ed. (Boston: Nicholas Brealey Publishing, 2010); Richard Watson, *Future Minds: How the Digital Age Is Changing Our Minds, Why This Matters and What We Can Do About It* (Boston: Nicholas Brealey Publishing, 2010); and David Orrell, *The Future of Everything: The Science of Prediction* (New York: Basic Books, 2008).

2. U.S. Census Bureau, *Statistical Abstract of the United States: 2011*, 130th ed. (Washington, DC: U.S. Government Printing Office, 2011); and "Population Projections for Canada, Provinces, and Territories 2009–2036," *Statistics Canada* (Ottawa, Ontario: Statistics Canada, 2010).

3. U.S. Census Bureau, *Statistical Abstract of the United States: 2011*; and "Population Projections for Canada, Provinces, and Territories 2009–2036."

4. "Population and Dwelling Count Highlight Tables, 2006 Census," *Statistics Canada*; and U.S. Census Bureau, *Statistical Abstract of the United States: 2011*.

5. U.S. Census Bureau, *Statistical Abstract of the United States: 2011*, p. 763; Kay Van Norman, *Exercise and Wellness for Older Adults: Practical Programming Strategies*, 2nd ed. (Champaign, IL: Human Kinetics, 2010).

6. Stanley Eitzen and Maxine Baca Zinn, *Globalization: The Transformation of Social Worlds*, 2nd ed. (Belmont, CA: Wadsworth Cengage Learning, 2009).

7. Aaron Saenz, "Robotics Industries: We're Creating Jobs, Helping the Economy," *Singularity Hub.com*, 19 June 2010, http://singularityhub.com/2010/06/19/robotics-industries-association-were-creating-jobs-helping-the-economy.

8. Robert D. Putnam, *Bowling Alone: The Collapse and Revival of American Community* (New York: Simon & Schuster, 2000); see also John F. Wasik, *The Cul-de-Sac Syndrome: Turning Around the Unsustainable American Dream* (Hoboken, NJ: John Wiley, 2011).

9. George Ritzer, *The McDonaldization of Society 6*, 6th ed. (Thousand Oaks, CA: Pine Forge Press, 2011).

10. David Kusnet, *Love the Work, Hate the Job: Why America's Best Workers Are Unhappier Than Ever* (Hoboken, NJ: John Wiley, 2008); and Lawrence Mishel, Jared Bernstein, and Heidi Shierholz, *The State of Working America, 2008–2009* (Ithaca, NY: ILR Press, 2009), ch. 8.

11. Lynne M. Schrum and Barbara B. Levin, *Leading 21st-Century Schools: Harnessing Technology for Engagement and Achievement* (Thousand Oaks, CA: Corwin, 2009); Allan Collins and Richard Halverson, *Rethinking Education in the Age of Technology: The Digital Revolution and Schooling in America* (New York: Teachers College Press, 2009).

12. Mike Snider, "Game Consoles Under Attack," *USA Today*, 6 June 2011, pp. 1B–2B.

13. Fredreka Schouten, "Fantasy Sports Enter Political Arena," *USA Today*, 19 October 2011, p. 6A; Sam Hendricks, *Fantasy Baseball for Beginners: The Ultimate "How-to" Guide* (Austin, TX: Extra Point Press, 2010); and Richard G. Lomax, "Fantasy Sports: History, Game Types, and Research," in *Handbook of Sports Media*, ed. Arthur A. Raney and Jennings Bryant (Mahwah, NJ: Lawrence Erlbaum, 2006), 383–392.

14. Norbert Elias and Eric Dunning, *The Quest for Excitement: Sport and Leisure in the Civilizing Process* (Cambridge, MA: Blackwell, 1993).

15. Stewart Ross, *Sports Technology* (London: Evans Brothers, 2011).

16. One example: Elite Sports Analysis, a world leader in the field of performance analysis consultancy, http://www.elitesportsanalysis.com. See also Claude Bouchard and Eric P. Hoffman, eds., *Genetic and Molecular Aspects of Sports Performance* (Hoboken, NJ: Wiley/Blackwell, 2011).

17. Angela J. Schneider and Theodore Friedmann, eds., *Gene Doping in Sports, Volume 51: The Science and Ethics of Genetically Modified Athletes* (New York: Academic Press, 2006); and Angela J. Schneider, *Gene Doping in Sports: The Science and Ethics of Genetically Modified Athletes* (Boston: Elsevier Press, 2006).

18. Schneider, *Gene Doping in Sports*.

19. Robert L. Simon, *Fair Play: The Ethics of Sport*, 3rd ed. (Boulder, CO: Westview Press, 2010); see also William Morgan, *Ethics in Sport*, 2nd ed. (Champaign, IL: Human Kinetics, 2007).

20. Matt Gerdes, *The Great Book of BASE* (Delafield, WI: Bird Brain Press, 2010); see also Eric Brymer, "Extreme Sports as a Facilitator of Ecocentricity and Positive Life Changes," *World Leisure Journal* 51, no. 1 (2009): 47–53.

21. Harry Braverman, *Labor and Monopoly Capital* (New York: Monthly Review Press, 1974), 279.

22. Ironmanlive.com, Sponsors and Licensees, http://www.ironmanlive.com/corporate/licensees/sandl.

23. John Branch, "From Violin to Skateboard," *New York Times*, 21 November 2010, p. SP-11; see also James Sullivan, "X Games Plan Bigger Footprint Outside USA," *USA Today*, 19 May 2011, p. 3C.

24. Robert B. Reich, *Aftershock: The Next Economy and America's Future* (New York: Vintage, 2011); see also Andrew Liveris, *Make It in America: The Case for Re-Inventing the Economy* (Hoboken, NJ: John Wiley, 2011).

25. Frank P. Jozsa, Jr., *Football Fortunes: The Business, Organization and Strategy of the NFL* (Jefferson, NC: McFarland Publishers, 2010); see also David George Surdam, *The Ball Game Biz: An Introduction to the Economics of Professional Team Sports* (Jefferson, NC: McFarland Publishers, 2010).

26. Irving Rein, Philip Kotler, and Ben Shields, "The Future of Sports Media," *The Futurist*, January–February 2007, pp. 42–43.

27. Amina Zafar, "Video Game Addiction: Does It Exist?" *CBC.ca*, 16 September 2010, http://www.cbc.ca/news/health/story/2010/09/13/f-videogames-addiction-health.html.

28. Greg Auman, "NCAA President Favors Supplement for Athletes," *St. Petersburg Times* (Florida), 1 June 2011, p. 1C; and Eric Olsen, "Proposal to Pay Players Is Debatable," *Denver Post*, 5 June 2011, p. 3C.

29. National Federation of State High School Associations, *2009–2010 High School Athletics Participation Survey* (Indianapolis: National Federation of State High School Associations, 2010).

30. William E. Hudson, *American Democracy in Peril: Eight Challenges to America's Future* (Washington, DC: CQ Press, 2010); see also Yuval Levin, *Imagining the Future: Science and American Democracy* (New York: Encounter Books, 2008).

31. Nicole A. Lipkin and April J. Perrymore, *Y in the Workplace: Managing the "Me First" Generation* (Franklin Lakes, NJ: Career Press, 2009); see also Eric H. Greenberg and Karl Weber, *Generation We: How Millennial Youth Are Taking Over America and Changing Our World Forever* (Emeryville, CA: Pachatusan, 2008).

32. For a thorough description of the programs of the NSCD, go to its website at http://www.nscd.org; see also Nigel Thomas and Andy Smith, *Disability, Sport and Society: An Introduction* (New York: Routledge, 2009).

33. For a complete description of the programs of the DS/USA, go to its website at http://dsusa.org/index.html.

34. See, for example, Wounded Warrior Disabled Sports Project at http://dsusa.org/programs-wwdsp-about.html.

35. For more information about the Paralympics, see http://www.paralympic.org/index.html; see also Ian Brittain, *The Paralympic Games Explained* (New York: Routledge, 2010).

36. For more information about the Special Olympics in the U.S., see http://www.specialolympics.org; for more information about the Special Olympics in Canada, see http://www.specialolympics.ca.

37. For more information about the National Senior Games Association, see http://www.nsga.com.

38. Caroline Symons, *The Gay Games: A History* (New York: Routledge, 2010).

39. Terry Orlick, *Cooperative Games and Sports: Joyful Activities for Everyone* (Champaign, IL: Human Kinetics, 2006); Josette Luvmour and Sambhava Luvmour, *Everyone Wins: Cooperative Games and Activities*, updated ed. (Gabriola Island, BC, Canada: New Society Publishers, 2007); and Bernie DeKoven, *Junkyard Sports* (Champaign, IL: Human Kinetics, 2005).

40. Susan Herbst, *Rude Democracy: Civility and Incivility in American Politics* (Philadelphia: Temple University Press, 2010).

41. Pierre D. Bognon, *The Anatomy of Sports Fans: Reflections on Fans & Fanatics* (Charleston, SC: BookSurge Publishing, 2009); see also Lawrence W. Hugenberg, Paul M. Haridakis, and Adam C. Earnheardt, eds., *Sports Mania: Essays on Fandom and the Media in the 21st Century* (Jefferson, NC: McFarland Publishers, 2008).

42. Ken Reed, *League of Fans SPORTS MANIFESTO: It's Time to Establish a National Sports Commission*, League of Fans Sports Reform Project, 26 October 2011, http://leagueoffans.org/pdf/Manifesto9.pdf.

Index

Ninth Edition

Sociology of North American Sport

George H. Sage
D. Stanley Eitzen

New York   Oxford
OXFORD UNIVERSITY PRESS

Oxford University Press is a department of the University of Oxford. It furthers the University's objective of excellence in research, scholarship, and education by publishing worldwide.

Oxford New York
Auckland Cape Town Dar es Salaam Hong Kong Karachi
Kuala Lumpur Madrid Melbourne Mexico City Nairobi
New Delhi Shanghai Taipei Toronto

With offices in
Argentina Austria Brazil Chile Czech Republic France Greece
Guatemala Hungary Italy Japan Poland Portugal Singapore
South Korea Switzerland Thailand Turkey Ukraine Vietnam

Oxford is a registered trade mark of Oxford University Press in the UK and certain other countries.

Published in the United States of America by
Oxford University Press
198 Madison Avenue, New York, NY 10016

Library of Congress Cataloging-in-Publication Data
Sage, George H.
   Sociology of North American sport / George H. Sage and D. Stanley Eitzen.—9th ed.
      p. cm.
   Includes bibliographical references and index.
   ISBN   978-0-19-995083-6 (pbk. : alk. paper)
   1. Sports—Social aspects—United States. 2. Sports—Social aspects—Canada. 3. Sports—United
States—Sociological aspects. 4. Sports—Canada—Sociological aspects. I. Eitzen, D. Stanley. II. Title.
GV706.5.E57 2012
306.4'83—dc23
2011043100

Printing number: 9 8 7 6 5 4 3

Printed in the United States of America on acid-free paper.